THIRD EDITION

1,001

DELICIOUS

SOUPS &

STEWS

EDITED BY

SUE SPITLER, WITH
LINDA YOAKAM R.D., M.S.

**SURREY
BOOKS**

CHICAGO

Surrey Books is an imprint of Agate Publishing, Inc.
Art direction, book design, and typesetting: Joan Sommers Design, Chicago
Nutritional analyses: Linda R. Yoakam, R.D., M.S.

Printed in Canada.

Library of Congress Cataloging-in-Publication Data
   1,001 delicious soups & stews : from elegant classics to hearty one-pot meals / edited by Sue Spitler With Linda R. Yoakam. -- 3rd ed.
   p. cm.
   Earlier ed.: 1,001 low-fat soups & stews, 2000.
   Summary: "Over 1,000 soup recipes"—Provided by publisher.
   Includes index.
   ISBN-13: 978-1-57284-091-1 (pbk.)
   ISBN-10: 1-57284-091-9 (pbk.)
   1. Soups. 2. Stews. I. Spitler, Sue. II. Yoakam, Linda R. III. 1,001 low-fat soups & stews.
IV. Title: One thousand one, soups & stews. V. Title: One thousand and one, soups & stews.

   TX757.A1601 2007
   641.5'13—dc22

                                                                        2007025701

12 11 10 09 08 07

10 9 8 7 6 5 4 3 2 1

Agate and Surrey books are available in bulk at discount prices. For more information, go to agatepublishing.com.

CONTENTS

ACKNOWLEDGMENTS

A huge thank you to editor Perrin Davis and editorial assistants Caroline Olson and Caitlin Garibaldi for their amazing editing, computer, and indexing skills and dedication in producing this book. Another thank you to Linda Yoakam, R.D., M.S. for the nutritional calculations, which are so helpful. Joan Sommers' art direction and new cover design are to be applauded. Doug Seibold, your support in producing this book is greatly appreciated.

INTRODUCTION

F EW FOODS ARE AS SATISFYING and flavorful as delicious homemade soups and stews. They're wholesome and comforting. They're the heart and soul of the kitchen; they restore our spirit. The glorious aroma of a simmering soup or sumptuous stew is guaranteed to whet appetites and bring folks into the kitchen to check on what's cooking for dinner.

The varieties of soups and stews are nearly endless, as you'll find with the more than 1,001 creative and healthful recipes in *1,001 Delicious Soups and Stews*. Fourteen delectable chapters are filled with stocks, chowders, chilis, supper soups, vegetarian soups and stews, meat, poultry and seafood stews, and more. There are recipes for comfort foods, old-fashioned favorites, recipes with a foreign flair, vegetarian recipes, and recipes that highlight new food trends. You'll find hearty full-flavored soups and stews, perfect for crisp fall and frosty winter seasons, and light, lovely soups and stews for the fresh days of spring and the sultry summer season. There's a soup or stew recipe for every occasion, whether a family meal, a festive celebration, or a casual evening with friends.

Included in Chapter 1 are 18 recipes for homemade stocks to use for best flavor in soups and stews. Stocks are very easy to make, as they simmer untended to flavorful goodness. They can be made ahead in large quantities and frozen for convenient use later. Of course, canned or packaged broths can be substituted in any recipe.

Chapter 13, Breads and Accompaniments, has many new recipes and offers a bounty of recipes for breads, biscuits, muffins, and pestos to enhance your soup and stew dining experiences.

You'll enjoy Chapter 14, Menu Magic, which presents menus for 10 complete meals for family dinners or casual entertaining. Each menu includes preparation tips, plus nutritional data for the entire menu as well as for individual recipes. We hope this chapter will be a helpful guide in planning balanced and delicious repasts.

Recipes have been carefully created for fabulous flavors, using high-quality, healthy ingredients that are readily available in your local super-market—no special shopping excursions needed! Recipes are designed for cooking ease, requiring no special cooking skills or gourmet kitchen equipment. We've taken advantage of the fast/slow convenience that microwave ovens and slow cookers offer, with dishes that cook in minutes and others that simmer all day. Preparation and cooking times are stream-lined in every recipe, complementing today's busy lifestyles. More than 490 recipes can be prepared and cooked in no more than 45 minutes, and often in much less time. And, as soups and stews are perfect candidates for advance preparation, you can make them ahead to refrigerate or freeze—a great do-ahead bonus!

NEW IN THIS EDITION

The soup and stew recipes that can be prepared in 45 minutes or less have a special designation. We know busy lifestyles allow precious little cooking time for many of us, so these recipes are designed to get you in and out of the kitchen as quickly and effortlessly as possible.

For easy identification, these recipes will have this symbol **45**. If the recipe requires baking, refrigeration, or freezing in addition to the actual preparation time, the symbols **◐**, for baking, and **❄**, for refrigeration/ freezing, will also appear.

The recipes in the Vegetarian Soups and Stews chapters are coded as follows so you can quickly tell if they are vegan, lacto-ovo vegetarian, lacto-vegetarian, or ovo-vegetarian.

V (vegan)—Recipes contain only plant-based food, with no dairy products or eggs.

LO (lacto-ovo vegetarian)—Recipes contain dairy products and eggs.

L (lacto vegetarian)—Recipes contain dairy products, but no eggs.

O (ovo vegetarian)—Recipes contain eggs, but no dairy products.

NUTRITIONAL INFORMATION

The recipes in this book have been developed to be healthy as well as delicious. Hundreds of the recipes are low in carbohydrates, not exceeding 30 to 35 grams per serving, which is recommended for a healthy maintenance carbohydrate diet. All of the recipes are also low in fat and calories. In accordance with American Heart Association guidelines, very few recipes in this book exceed 30 percent of calories from fat, and almost all adhere to the following nutritional criteria.

Type of Recipe Maximum Amounts per Serving

	Calories	*Cholesterol (mg)*	*Sodium (mg)*
Soups, First Courses	200	50	600
Main-Dish Soups, Entrées, Salads, Sandwiches	400	100	800
Main-Dish Meals (including pasta, rice, grains)	500	125	800
Main-Dish Eggs, Cheese 400	450	800	
Side-Dish Salads, Pasta, 200 Grains, Vegetables	50	600	
Sauces, Condiments	200	25	600
Breads	200	50	600
Desserts	350	90	600

Specific nutritional information is provided for each recipe (not including variations). The nutritional analyses are derived by using computer software highly regarded by nutritionists and dietitians, but they are meant to be used only as guidelines. Results may vary slightly depending upon the brand or manufacturer of an ingredient used.

Ingredients noted as "optional" or "to taste" or "as garnish" are not included in the nutritional analyses. When alternate choices or amounts of ingredients are given, the ingredient or amount listed first is used for analysis.

Other factors that can affect the accuracy of nutritional data include variability in sizes, weights, and measures of fruits, vegetables, and other foods. There is also a possible 20 percent error factor in the nutritional labeling of prepared foods.

If you have any health problems that impose strict dietary requirements, it is important to consult a physician, dietitian, or nutritionist before using recipes in this or any other cookbook.

INGREDIENT INFORMATION

T HE INGREDIENTS IN THIS BOOK are readily available in supermarkets and health food stores. Following is helpful information on some of the ingredients we've used, with explanations of those you may not be very familiar with.

Butter — Butter is suggested as an alternate for margarine as it has no trans-fat and provides improved flavor, except in Vegan recipes in the Vegetarian Soups and Stews chapters.

Cream Cheese — The block-type of reduced-fat and fat-free cream cheese is usually specified in the recipes in this book; the tub-type is much softer in texture and does not always work the same in recipes. If substituting fat-free cream cheese in your favorite recipes for dips, use the block type and add any liquid ingredients gradually, as the cream cheese thins much more quickly than full-fat or reduced-fat cream cheese. Fat-free cream cheese can be used to make cake glaze but not frosting, as it thins with the addition of powdered sugar and cannot be thickened.

Cooking sprays — Vegetable and olive oil cooking sprays are used to greatly reduce the amounts of oil or fat needed in recipes. When a recipe calls for "sautéing in a lightly greased skillet", spray the skillet lightly with cooking spray or wipe the pan with a lightly oiled paper towel.

Herbs and Spices — In most recipes, dried herbs are called for, but where fresh are used, an amount for dried is also given. As a general rule, fresh herbs may be substituted for dried by using two to three times as much as indicated for the dried version.

Margarine — Use an all-vegetable product. Use regular rather than diet margarine, and be sure to shop for one of the new trans-fat free varieties.

Olive Oil — As we have kept the use of oil to a minimum, we prefer using virgin olive oil to take advantage of its more intense flavor. Canola oil can be substituted, if desired.

it is most commonly packaged in liquid in plastic tubs. Once opened, tofu has a several-day limited storage time in the refrigerator; it should be stored covered in water, and the water should be changed daily. Tofu can also be frozen; it changes to an amber color in the freezer and when thawed is firmer in texture and somewhat crumbly.

Vegetarian Protein Products — A number of interesting and flavorful vegetarian protein products are available in the freezer section of the supermarket. Many are seasoned to resemble the flavor of beef sausage, and chicken. They come in various forms, such as patties, links, strips, and crumbles. Usually soy-based, these products may also contain grains, vegetables, nuts, and cheese.

Check your local grocery periodically for new food items. Literally hundreds of fresh, frozen, canned, and packaged new food products find their way to grocery shelves each year. An occasional visit to a gourmet store may garner specialty items to keep in your pantry or freezer for interesting menu additions.

Pasta, Grains, and Beans — When a dried and uncooked ingredient is called for, the ingredient will read: "8 ounces spaghetti, cooked." When a cooked ingredient is called for, the ingredient will read: "12 ounces cooked spaghetti." When dry pasta or rice noodles are called for, they are always egg-free and can be used in vegan dishes. Fresh pasta or refrigerated pasta such as ravioli, tortellini, wontons, and some flat noodles do contain eggs and can be used in lacto-ovo- and ovo-vegetarian recipes.

Sesame Oil — We have specified Asian sesame oil in recipes, as this dark oil has an intense sesame flavor; it can be purchased in ethnic sections of supermarkets. There is also a light-colored sesame oil that can be found in the vegetable oil section of the supermarket; it can be substituted, but the sesame flavor is extremely subtle. Store at room temperature.

Shortening — The manufacturing process of shortening usually creates trans-fats; shop carefully for one of the new trans-fat free brands.

Tamari Soy Sauce — This highly flavored soy sauce is naturally brewed and is made without sugar. It is available in regular or low-sodium brands in Asian sections of supermarkets. Other soy sauce products can be substituted. Store in the refrigerator.

Tempeh — A nutritious cultured product made from cooked soybeans, tempeh has its origins in Indonesia. The soybean mixture is pressed into cakes, sometimes being combined with grains and/or other ingredients, and has a texture that is firmer, or "meatier," than tofu. Like tofu, it readily absorbs flavors from soy sauce or marinades. Because of its firm texture, tempeh is great for grilling. Purchased in the produce section of super-markets, tempeh can be stored in the refrigerator or freezer.

Tofu, or **Bean Curd** — Originating in China, tofu is made by coagulating soy milk, which is the liquid remaining from cooked ground soy beans. Pressed into cakes, tofu is made in a variety of textures—soft or silken, firm, and extra-firm. It is also available seasoned and in baked and smoked forms. Soft tofu has a very fine, delicate texture and is perfect for dips, sauces, soups, and dressings; the firmer textures are better for cooking, stir-frying, broiling, and baking. As tofu is extremely mild in flavor, it is generally marinated in soy sauce or other marinades before cooking. Tofu is extremely nutritious, but it is not low in fat, ranging between 40 and 45 percent calories from fat. We call for lower fat light tofu in most recipes. Purchase tofu in the produce section of supermarkets;

ONE

Stocks

QUICK SAGE CHICKEN STOCK

45   *Canned broth makes this stock very quick to make!!*

Makes about 2 cups

1 can (14 ounces) reduced-sodium fat-free
   chicken broth
1 medium onion, quartered
½ rib celery, thickly sliced
½ teaspoon dried sage leaves
2 teaspoons dry sherry (optional)
Salt and pepper, to taste

Per Cup:
Calories: 35
% calories from fat: 1
Protein (g): 5.1
Carbohydrate (g): 1.1
Fat (g): 0
Saturated fat (g): 0
Cholesterol (mg): 0
Sodium (mg): 142

Exchanges:
Milk: 0.0
Vegetable: 0.0
Fruit: 0.0
Bread: 0.0
Meat: 0.0
Fat: 0.0

1. Heat all ingredients, except salt and pepper, to boiling in large saucepan; reduce heat and simmer, covered, 10 minutes. Strain stock, discarding vegetables and sage; season to taste with salt and pepper.

CHICKEN STOCK

A subtly flavored, low-sodium stock that's easy to make.

Makes about 2 quarts

1 pound boneless, skinless chicken breast, cubed
2½ quarts water
2 ribs celery, thickly sliced
4 each: thickly sliced large onions, medium carrots
1 small turnip, quartered
2 bay leaves
6 each: cloves garlic, whole peppercorns
2 teaspoons dried sage leaves
Salt and pepper, to taste

Per Cup:
Calories: 9
% calories from fat: 7
Protein (g): 1.1
Carbohydrate (g): 1.1
Fat (g): 0.1
Saturated fat (g): 0.0
Cholesterol (mg): 2.5
Sodium (mg): 7

Exchanges:
Milk: 0.0
Vegetable: 0.0
Fruit: 0.0
Bread: 0.0
Meat: 0.0
Fat: 0.0

1. Sauté chicken in lightly greased large saucepan until browned, about 10 minutes. Add remaining ingredients, except salt and pepper, and heat to boiling; reduce heat and simmer, covered, 1 hour, skimming any foam from surface. Strain stock through double layer of cheesecloth, discarding meat, vegetables, and seasonings; season to taste with salt and pepper. Refrigerate until chilled; remove congealed fat from surface of stock.

LOW-SALT CHICKEN STOCK

Save chicken bones in a plastic bag in the freezer for making chicken stock.

Makes about 2 quarts

2½ quarts water

1 pound skinless chicken breast

2 each: thickly sliced medium onions, ribs celery, carrots

l large red potato, quartered

½ cup packed parsley sprigs

Salt and pepper, to taste

Per Cup:
Calories: 8
% calories from fat: 0
Protein (g): 1.6
Carbohydrate (g): 1.2
Fat (g): 0
Saturated fat (g): 0
Cholesterol (mg): 0
Sodium (mg): 4

Exchanges:
Milk: 0.0
Vegetable: 0.0
Fruit: 0.0
Bread: 0.0
Meat: 0.0
Fat: 0.0

1. Heat all ingredients, except salt and pepper, to boiling in large saucepan; reduce heat and simmer, covered, 1½ hours, skimming any foam from surface. Strain stock through double layer of cheesecloth, discarding chicken, vegetables, and parsley; season to taste with salt and pepper. Refrigerate until chilled; remove congealed fat from surface of stock.

RICH CHICKEN STOCK

Veal knuckle adds richness to this stock.

Makes about 4 quarts

5 quarts water
1 cup dry white wine or water
1 chicken (about 4 pounds), cut up, fat trimmed
2½ pounds chicken necks and wings
1 veal knuckle, cracked (optional)
2 each: thickly sliced medium onions, leeks
    (white parts only)
4 each: thickly sliced medium carrots, ribs celery
1 clove garlic, peeled
½ teaspoon each: dried basil, thyme, and
    tarragon leaves
10 black peppercorns
4 whole cloves
Salt and pepper, to taste

Per Cup:
Calories: 39
% calories from fat: 18
Protein (g): 4.9
Carbohydrate (g): 0.8
Fat (g): 0.8
Saturated fat (g): 0.2
Cholesterol (mg): 1
Sodium (mg): 36

Exchanges:
Milk: 0.0
Vegetable: 0.0
Fruit: 0.0
Bread: 0.0
Meat: 0.5
Fat: 0.0

1. Heat all ingredients, except salt and pepper, to boiling in large
Dutch oven; reduce heat and simmer, covered, 3 to 4 hours,
skimming any foam from surface. Strain stock through double
layer of cheesecloth, discarding bones, meat, vegetables, and
seasoning; season to taste with salt and pepper. Refrigerate until
chilled; remove congealed fat from surface of stock.

TURKEY STOCK

The perfect ending for the Thanksgiving turkey, this stock can be used for
Turkey-Noodle Soup (see p. 202) or as a substitute in recipes calling for
chicken stock.

Makes about 4 quarts

5 quarts water
1 cup dry white wine or water
1 meaty turkey carcass, cut up
2 each: thickly sliced medium onions, leeks (white parts only)

4 each: thickly sliced medium carrots, ribs celery

1 teaspoon dried thyme leaves

10 black peppercorns

6 sprigs parsley

Salt and pepper, to taste

Per Cup:
Calories: 29
% calories from fat: 28
Protein (g): 2
Carbohydrate (g): 0.9
Fat (g): 0.9
Saturated fat (g): 0.2
Cholesterol (mg): 5.6
Sodium (mg): 7

1. Heat all ingredients, except salt and pepper, in large Dutch oven to boiling; reduce heat and simmer, covered, 3 to 4 hours, skimming any foam from surface. Strain stock through double layer of cheesecloth, discarding bones, vegetables, and seasonings; season to taste with salt and pepper. Refrigerate until chilled; remove congealed fat from surface of stock.

Exchanges:
Milk: 0.0
Vegetable: 0.0
Fruit: 0.0
Bread: 0.0
Meat: 0.0
Fat: 0.0

BEEF STOCK

A flavorful stock that's easy to prepare.

Makes about 2 quarts

2½ quarts water

2 each: ribs from cooked beef rib roast, fat trimmed

4 each: thickly sliced large onions, medium carrots, small ribs celery

1 parsnip, halved

2 bay leaves

8 black peppercorns

5 sage leaves

Salt and pepper, to taste

Per Cup:
Calories: 8
% calories from fat: 31
Protein (g): 0.2
Carbohydrate (g): 1.3
Fat (g): 0.3
Saturated fat (g): 0
Cholesterol (mg): 0.3
Sodium (mg): 4

Exchanges:
Milk: 0.0
Vegetable: 0.0
Fruit: 0.0
Bread: 0.0
Meat: 0.0
Fat: 0.0

1. Heat all ingredients, except salt and pepper, to boiling in large saucepan; reduce heat; simmer, covered, 2 hours, skimming any foam from surface. Strain stock through double layer of cheese-cloth, discarding bones, vegetables, and seasonings; season to taste with salt and pepper. Refrigerate until chilled; remove congealed fat from surface of stock.

FRAGRANT BEEF STOCK

Dried mushrooms, red wine, and herbs give a rich flavor to this stock.

Makes about 3½ quarts

4 quarts water

1 cup dry red wine or water

2 pounds each: short ribs of beef, fat trimmed,
   beef marrow bones

1 pound cubed beef chuck, fat trimmed

1 large onion, chopped

3 each: thickly sliced medium carrots, ribs celery

½ cup dried mushrooms

1 clove garlic, halved

10 black peppercorns

1 bay leaf

1 teaspoon each: dried basil and thyme leaves

1 tablespoon soy sauce

Salt and pepper, to taste

Per Cup:
Calories: 16
% calories from fat: 28
Protein (g): 2.7
Carbohydrate (g): 0.6
Fat (g): 0.5
Saturated fat (g): 0.3
Cholesterol (mg): 3
Sodium (mg): 42

Exchanges:
Milk: 0.0
Vegetable: 0.0
Fruit: 0.0
Bread: 0.0
Meat: 0.0
Fat: 0.0

1. Heat all ingredients, except salt and pepper, to boiling in large
Dutch oven; reduce heat and simmer, covered, 3 to 4 hours,
skimming any foam from surface. Strain stock through double
layer of cheesecloth, discarding bones, meat, vegetables, and
seasonings; season to taste with salt and pepper. Refrigerate
until chilled; remove congealed fat from surface of stock.

QUICK-SPICED BEEF STOCK

45

When you want a spicy stock, give this easy version a try.

Makes about 2 cups

1 can (14 ounces) reduced-sodium fat-free beef broth

1 medium onion, quartered

1 clove garlic

1 tablespoon dry red wine or water

1 teaspoon pickling spice

Salt and pepper, to taste

1. Heat all ingredients, except salt and pepper, to boiling in large saucepan; reduce heat and simmer, covered, 10 minutes. Strain; discard vegetables and seasonings. Season to taste with salt and pepper.

Per Cup:
Calories: 25
% calories from fat: 0
Protein (g): 4.3
Carbohydrate (g): 0.9
Fat (g): 0
Saturated fat (g): 0
Cholesterol (mg): 0
Sodium (mg): 133

Exchanges:
Milk: 0.0
Vegetable: 0.0
Fruit: 0.0
Bread: 0.0
Meat: 0.0
Fat: 0.0

VEAL STOCK

Veal bones and stew meat can be hard to find, so make this delicately flavored stock when you can find the ingredients and freeze it.

Makes about 2 quarts

1½ pounds veal stew meat
½ cup each: chopped onion, carrot, celery
2 quarts water
1 veal knuckle or veal bones (about 1¾ pounds)
2 bay leaves
6 black peppercorns
3 whole cloves
Salt and pepper, to taste

Per Cup:
Calories: 17
% calories from fat: 36
Protein (g): 2.4
Carbohydrate (g): 0.2
Fat (g): 0.6
Saturated fat (g): 0.1
Cholesterol (mg): 8.9
Sodium (mg): 6

Exchanges:
Milk: 0.0
Vegetable: 0.0
Fruit: 0.0
Bread: 0.0
Meat: 0.0
Fat: 0.0

1. Cook veal stew meat in lightly greased large Dutch oven until browned, 8 to 10 minutes; remove and reserve. Add vegetables and sauté until browned, about 5 minutes. Return veal to Dutch oven; add remaining ingredients, except salt and pepper, and heat to boiling. Reduce heat and simmer, covered, 4 hours, skimming any foam from surface. Strain through double layer of cheesecloth, discarding meat, bones, vegetables, and seasonings; season to taste with salt and pepper. Refrigerate until chilled; remove congealed fat from stock.

FISH STOCK

Make arrangements with the fish department of your supermarket to save fish bones for you.

Makes about 1½ quarts

2 quarts water
2–3 pounds fish bones (from a non-oily fish, such as haddock)
1 each: chopped large onion, rib celery
2 bay leaves
7–8 black peppercorns
½ teaspoon each: kosher or sea salt, white pepper

1. Heat all ingredients to boiling in large saucepan; reduce heat and simmer 30 minutes, skimming foam from surface. Strain through double layer of cheesecloth, discarding bones, vegetables, and seasonings.

Per Cup:
Calories: 17
% calories from fat: 0
Protein (g): 2.8
Carbohydrate (g): 0.3
Fat (g): 0.1
Saturated fat (g): 0
Cholesterol (mg): 0
Sodium (mg): 191

Exchanges:
Milk: 0.0
Vegetable: 0.0
Fruit: 0.0
Bread: 0.0
Meat: 0.0
Fat: 0.0

EASY FISH STOCK

Any kind of mild-flavored fish will make a delicious stock; avoid strongly flavored fish such as salmon or tuna. Stock will keep in refrigerator for 2 days, or up to 2 months in the freezer.

Makes about 1 quart

3½ cups water
¾ cup dry white wine or water
1½ pounds fresh or frozen fish steaks, cubed (1-inch)
1 each: finely chopped medium onion, carrot
3 ribs celery with leaves, halved
3 sprigs parsley
3 slices lemon
8 black peppercorns
Salt and pepper, to taste

Per Cup:
Calories: 10
% calories from fat: 3
Protein (g): 0.7
Carbohydrate (g): 0.2
Fat (g): 0
Saturated fat (g): 0
Cholesterol (mg): 2
Sodium (mg): 3

Exchanges:
Milk: 0.0
Vegetable: 0.0
Fruit: 0.0
Bread: 0.0
Meat: 0.0
Fat: 0.0

1. Heat all ingredients to boiling in large saucepan; reduce heat and simmer 30 minutes, skimming any foam from surface. Strain stock through double layer of cheesecloth, discarding fish, vegetables, and seasoning; season to taste with salt and pepper.

BASIC VEGETABLE STOCK

As vegetables used in stocks are later discarded, they should be scrubbed but do not need to be peeled.

Makes about 2 quarts

1 each: thickly sliced large onion, leek (white part only), carrot, rib celery

8 cups water

1 cup dry white wine or water

4 cups mixed chopped vegetables (broccoli, green beans, cabbage, potatoes, tomatoes, summer or winter squash, bell peppers, mushrooms, etc.)

6–8 parsley sprigs

1 bay leaf

4 whole allspice

1 tablespoon black peppercorns

2 teaspoons dried bouquet garni

Salt and pepper, to taste

Per Cup:
Calories: 4
% calories from fat: 3
Protein (g): 0.1
Carbohydrate (g): 1
Fat (g): 0.0
Saturated fat (g): 0.0
Cholesterol (mg): 0.0
Sodium (mg): 3

Exchanges:
Milk: 0.0
Vegetable: 0.0
Fruit: 0.0
Bread: 0.0
Meat: 0.0
Fat: 0.0

1. Sauté onion, leek, carrot, and celery in lightly greased large saucepan 5 minutes; add remaining ingredients, except salt and pepper, and heat to boiling. Reduce heat and simmer, covered, 1½ to 2 hours. Strain stock, discarding vegetables and seasonings; season to taste with salt and pepper.

NO-SALT VEGETABLE STOCK

45

This no-salt-added vegetable stock with its light onion flavor makes a perfect base for many of the soups and stews in this book.

Makes about 2 quarts

2½ quarts water
3 each: quartered medium onions,
   halved carrots, ribs celery
2 bay leaves
¼ cup packed fresh basil
10 whole white peppercorns
1 teaspoon dried thyme leaves

Per Cup:
Calories: 5
% calories from fat: 0
Protein (g): 0.1
Carbohydrate (g): 1.1
Fat (g): 0
Saturated fat (g): 0
Cholesterol (mg): 0
Sodium (mg): 2

Exchanges:
Milk: 0.0
Vegetable: 0.0
Fruit: 0.0
Bread: 0.0
Meat: 0.0
Fat: 0.0

1. Heat all ingredients to boiling in large saucepan; reduce heat and simmer, covered, 30 minutes. Strain stock through double layer of cheesecloth, discarding vegetables and seasoning.

CANNED VEGETABLE STOCK

45

A quick and easy solution for stock when you haven't the time or inclination to start from scratch.

Makes about 1½ quarts

1 each: coarsely chopped medium onion, tomato,
   carrot, rib celery
4 teaspoons minced garlic
1 teaspoon olive oil
2 cans (14½ ounces each) reduced-sodium
   vegetable broth
2 cups water
1 cup dry white wine or water
4 sprigs parsley
2 bay leaves
Salt and pepper, to taste

Per Cup:
Calories: 62
% calories from fat: 11
Protein (g): 0.8
Carbohydrate (g): 6.7
Fat (g): 0.8
Saturated fat (g): 0.1
Cholesterol (mg): 0
Sodium (mg): 55

Exchanges:
Milk: 0.0
Vegetable: 1.0
Fruit: 0.0
Bread: 0.0
Meat: 0.0
Fat: 0.0

1. Sauté onion, tomato, carrot, celery, and garlic in oil in Dutch oven 5 minutes; add remaining ingredients, except salt and pepper, and heat to boiling. Reduce heat and simmer, covered, 30 minutes. Strain, discarding vegetables and seasonings; season to taste with salt and pepper.

ROASTED VEGETABLE STOCK

Roasting vegetables intensifies their flavors, adding richness to the stock. The beet adds a subtle sweetness to the stock, but use only if you don't object to the pink color it creates!

Makes about 2 quarts

1 each: coarsely chopped medium onion, leek (white part only), carrot, zucchini, turnip, beet, tomato

½ small butternut or acorn squash, sliced (2-inch)

1 bulb garlic, cut crosswise in half

8 cups water

1 cup dry white wine or water

3 cups coarsely chopped kale

6 sprigs parsley

1 bay leaf

1–2 teaspoons dried bouquet garni

1 teaspoon black peppercorns

4 whole allspice

Salt and pepper, to taste

Per Cup:
Calories: 25
% calories from fat: 1
Protein (g): 0.2
Carbohydrate (g): 1.5
Fat (g): 0
Saturated fat (g): 0
Cholesterol (mg): 0
Sodium (mg): 12

Exchanges:
Milk: 0.0
Vegetable: 0.0
Fruit: 0.0
Bread: 0.0
Meat: 0.0
Fat: 0.0

1. Arrange vegetables, except kale, in single layer on greased, foil-lined jelly-roll pan; bake at 425 degrees until tender and browned, 35 to 40 minutes. Transfer vegetables to Dutch oven; add remaining ingredients, except salt and pepper, and heat to boiling. Reduce heat and simmer, covered, 1½ to 2 hours. Strain, discarding vegetables and seasonings; season to taste with salt and pepper.

MEDITERRANEAN STOCK

A lovely stock scented with orange, fennel, and saffron.

Makes about 2 quarts

1 each: thickly sliced large onion, leek (white part
only), carrot, sweet potato, zucchini, rib celery
½ each: sliced small fennel bulb, red bell pepper
2 teaspoons olive oil
8 cups water
Juice of 1 orange
1 cup dry white wine or water
2 medium tomatoes, quartered
1 medium bulb garlic, cut crosswise in half
3 cups coarsely chopped spinach or romaine lettuce
6 sprigs parsley
1 each: strip orange zest (3 x 1-inch), bay leaf
1–2 teaspoons bouquet garni
1 teaspoon black peppercorns
4 whole allspice
Salt and pepper, to taste

Per Cup:
Calories: 43
% calories from fat: 24
Protein (g): 0.5
Carbohydrate (g): 3.3
Fat (g): 1.2
Saturated fat (g): 0.2
Cholesterol (mg): 0
Sodium (mg): 15

Exchanges:
Milk: 0.0
Vegetable: 0.5
Fruit: 0.0
Bread: 0.0
Meat: 0.0
Fat: 0.5

1. Sauté onion, leek, carrot, sweet potato, zucchini, celery, fennel,
and bell pepper in oil in Dutch oven 8 to 10 minutes; add remaining
ingredients, except salt and pepper, and heat to boiling. Reduce
heat and simmer, covered, 1½ to 2 hours. Strain, discarding
vegetables and seasonings; season to taste with salt and pepper.

ORIENTAL STOCK

A light, fragrant stock that can be used in Asian soups and entrées.

Makes about 2 quarts

8 cups water
6 cups shredded bok choy or Chinese cabbage
1¼ cups loosely packed cilantro, coarsely chopped
1 each: sliced large onion, carrot, small red bell pepper
⅓ cup sliced gingerroot

1 tablespoon minced garlic

3 dried shiitake mushrooms

4 teaspoons reduced-sodium tamari soy sauce

2 star anise

2 teaspoons five-spice powder

1½ teaspoons toasted Szechuan peppercorns

Salt and pepper, to taste

Per Cup:
Calories: 8
% calories from fat: 11
Protein (g): 0.6
Carbohydrate (g): 1.1
Fat (g): 0.1
Saturated fat (g): 0
Cholesterol (mg): 0
Sodium (mg): 110

Exchanges:
Milk: 0.0
Vegetable: 0.0
Fruit: 0.0
Bread: 0.0
Meat: 0.0
Fat: 0.0

1. Heat all ingredients, except salt and pepper, to boiling in Dutch oven; reduce heat and simmer, covered, 1 hour. Strain, discarding vegetables and seasonings; season to taste with salt and pepper.

RICH MUSHROOM STOCK

Dried shiitake mushrooms, also known as Chinese black mushrooms, add richness and depth of flavor to this stock.

Makes about 2 quarts

1 each: sliced large onion, leek (white part only), rib celery

12 ounces cremini or white mushrooms

1 tablespoon minced garlic

1 teaspoon olive oil

7 cups water

¾ cup dry white wine or water

1½–2 ounces dried shiitake mushrooms

6 sprigs parsley

¾ teaspoon each: dried sage and thyme leaves

1½ teaspoons black peppercorns

Salt and pepper, to taste

Per Cup:
Calories: 27
% calories from fat: 22
Protein (g): 0.4
Carbohydrate (g): 1.6
Fat (g): 0.7
Saturated fat (g): 0.1
Cholesterol (mg): 0
Sodium (mg): 9

Exchanges:
Milk: 0.0
Vegetable: 0.0
Fruit: 0.0
Bread: 0.0
Meat: 0.0
Fat: 0.0

1. Sauté onion, leek, celery, cremini mushrooms, and garlic in oil in Dutch oven 5 minutes; add remaining ingredients, except salt and pepper, and heat to boiling. Reduce heat and simmer, covered, 1½ hours. Strain, discarding vegetables and seasonings; season to taste with salt and pepper.

TWO

First-Course Soups

ICED VEGETABLE GAZPACHO

45

This refreshing soup is the easiest gazpacho ever.

4 first-course servings

1 each: medium zucchini, large peeled, seeded cucumber, clove garlic

½ green bell pepper

¼ jalapeño chili, seeded

2 tablespoons chopped chives

1½ cups reduced-sodium tomato juice

¼ cup reduced-sodium fat-free beef broth

1 tablespoon sugar

Salt and pepper, to taste

Per Serving:
Calories: 48
% calories from fat: 4
Protein (g): 2 1
Carbohydrate (g): 11
Fat (g): 0.2
Saturated fat (g) 0
Cholesterol (mg): 0
Sodium (mg): 22

Exchanges:
Milk: 0.0
Vegetable: 2.0
Fruit: 0.0
Bread: 0.0
Meat: 0.0
Fat: 0.0

1. Cut vegetables into 1-inch pieces. Process all ingredients, except salt and pepper, in food processor or blender until finely chopped, adding additional beef broth if needed for desired consistency. Season to taste with salt and pepper; refrigerate until chilled.

CITRUS-TOMATO SOUP

45

Orange and lemon juices add a refreshing tang to this easy tomato soup.

4 first-course servings

2 tablespoons finely chopped onion

1 cup each: reduced-sodium fat-free chicken broth, frozen orange juice concentrate

1 quart reduced-sodium tomato juice

2 tablespoons each: light brown sugar, lemon juice

1–2 drops hot pepper sauce

Salt, to taste

Thin orange slices, as garnish

Per Serving:
Calories: 92
% calories from fat: 1
Protein (g): 2.9
Carbohydrate (g): 21.9
Fat (g): 0.2
Saturated fat (g): 0
Cholesterol (mg): 0
Sodium (mg): 90

Exchanges:
Milk: 0.0
Vegetable: 2.0
Fruit: 0.5
Bread: 0.0
Meat: 0.0
Fat: 0.0

1. Heat onion and broth to boiling in small saucepan; reduce heat and simmer, covered, until tender, about 5 minutes; transfer to bowl and add remaining ingredients, except salt and orange slices. Season to taste with salt; refrigerate until chilled. Garnish each bowl of soup with an orange slice.

ASPARAGUS LEMON SOUP

This perfect spring luncheon soup is similar to the classic Greek egg lemon soup, with the addition of asparagus and pasta.

6 first-course servings

1 quart Chicken Stock (see p. 2)
½ cup orzo or other small soup pasta
12 ounces asparagus, sliced
2 eggs, lightly beaten
¼ cup each: lemon juice, sliced green onions
Salt and pepper, to taste

Per Serving:
Calories: 105
% calories from fat: 22
Protein (g): 12.3
Carbohydrate (g): 6.2
Fat (g): 2.6
Saturated fat (g): 0.6
Cholesterol (mg): 73
Sodium (mg): 32

Exchanges:
Milk: 0.0
Vegetable: 3.0
Fruit: 0.0
Bread: 0.0
Meat: 1.0
Fat: 0.5

1. Heat stock to boiling in large saucepan. Add orzo; reduce heat and simmer 5 minutes. Stir in asparagus and heat to boiling. Reduce heat and simmer until asparagus and orzo are tender, about 7 minutes. Whisk in eggs gradually; cook 1 minute. Add lemon juice and green onions; season to taste with salt and pepper.

CREAM OF TOMATO SOUP

45 *A soup similar to the favorite-brand canned tomato soup we all remember eating as kids! Canned tomatoes are necessary for the flavor, so don't substitute fresh.*

4 first-course servings

2 cans (14½ ounces each) reduced-sodium whole
   tomatoes, undrained
1–3 teaspoons beef bouillon crystals
2 cups fat-free milk
3 tablespoons cornstarch
⅛ teaspoon baking soda
2 teaspoons sugar
1–2 tablespoons margarine or butter
Salt and pepper, to taste

Per Serving:
Calories: 142
% calories from fat: 22
Protein (g): 6.3
Carbohydrate (g): 22.6
Fat (g): 3.7
Saturated fat (g): 0.8
Cholesterol (mg): 2
Sodium (mg): 395

Exchanges:
Milk: 0.5
Vegetable: 2.0
Fruit: 0.0
Bread: 0.5
Meat: 0.0
Fat: 0.5

1. Process tomatoes with liquid in food processor or blender until smooth; heat tomatoes and bouillon crystals to boiling in large saucepan. Stir in combined milk and cornstarch, stirring until thickened, about 1 minute. Add baking soda, sugar, and margarine, stirring until margarine is melted. Season to taste with salt and pepper.

CELERY-TOMATO SOUP

45 *This quick and easy recipe showcases the delicate flavor and crisp texture of celery, which is usually assigned a supporting rather than primary role in cooking.*

8 first-course servings

4 cups thinly sliced celery
2 medium onions, finely chopped
1 tablespoon olive oil
3 cups fat-free chicken broth
½ cup dry white wine
¼ cup finely chopped parsley
1 teaspoon dried marjoram leaves

¼ teaspoon each: dried thyme and tarragon leaves

2 cans (14½ ounces each) whole tomatoes, undrained, puréed

1 teaspoon sugar

Salt and pepper, to taste

Per Serving:
Calories: 76
% calories from fat: 20
Protein (g): 3.6
Carbohydrate (g): 10.5
Fat (g): 1.8
Saturated fat (g): 0.3
Cholesterol (mg): 0
Sodium (mg): 365

1. Sauté celery and onion in oil in large saucepan until onion is tender, about 8 minutes. Add remaining ingredients, except tomatoes, sugar, salt, and pepper and heat to boiling. Reduce heat and simmer, covered, about 10 minutes or until celery is tender. Add tomatoes and sugar and simmer 5 minutes; season to taste with salt and pepper.

Exchanges:
Milk: 0.0
Vegetable: 2.0
Fruit: 0.0
Bread: 0.0
Meat: 0.0
Fat: 0.5

ZUCCHINI SOUP

45

Make this soup when your garden is overflowing with zucchini!

4 first-course servings

2 cups each: reduced-sodium fat-free chicken broth, sliced zucchini

1 cup chopped onion

3 cloves garlic, minced

1 tablespoon tarragon vinegar

1 teaspoon curry powder

½ teaspoon dried marjoram leaves

⅛ teaspoon celery seeds

1 cup fat-free plain yogurt

Salt and cayenne pepper, to taste

Paprika, as garnish

Per Serving:
Calories: 84
% calories from fat: 4
Protein (g): 8.5
Carbohydrate (g): 11.9
Fat (g): 0.4
Saturated fat (g): 0.1
Cholesterol (mg): 1.4
Sodium (mg): 144

Exchanges:
Milk: 0.5
Vegetable: 2.0
Fruit: 0.0
Bread: 0.0
Meat: 0.0
Fat: 0.0

1. Heat all ingredients, except yogurt, salt, cayenne pepper, and paprika, to boiling in medium saucepan; reduce heat and simmer, covered, until vegetables are tender, about 8 minutes. Process soup and yogurt in food processor or blender until smooth; season to taste with salt and cayenne pepper. Refrigerate until chilled; sprinkle each bowl of soup with paprika.

HOT-AND-SOUR CABBAGE SOUP

45 *Reminiscent of classic Chinese hot-and-sour soup, this version cooks in under 15 minutes.*

4 first-course servings

1 large carrot, coarsely shredded

¼ cup finely chopped red bell pepper

1½ teaspoons canola oil

3 cups shredded green cabbage

1 large garlic clove, minced

1 tablespoon minced gingerroot

4 green onions, thinly sliced, divided

2 quarts reduced-sodium fat-free chicken broth

1½ tablespoons apple cider vinegar

1 tablespoon plus 1 teaspoon light brown sugar

3 tablespoons reduced-sodium soy sauce

½ teaspoon Oriental hot chili oil

2 tablespoons cornstarch

Per Serving:
Calories: 81
% calories from fat: 21
Protein (g): 6.2
Carbohydrate (g); 10.8
Fat (g): 2
Saturated fat (g): 0 3
Cholesterol (mg): 0
Sodium (mg): 635

Exchanges:
Milk: 0.0
Vegetable: 2.0
Fruit: 0.0
Bread: 0.0
Meat: 0.0
Fat: 0.0

1. Sauté carrot and bell pepper in oil in large saucepan 2 minutes. Add cabbage, garlic, gingerroot, and half the green onions; sauté until cabbage is tender, about 8 minutes. Add broth and heat to boiling; reduce heat and simmer, covered, 5 minutes. Stir in combined remaining ingredients, stirring until thickened, about 1 minute. Garnish each bowl of soup with remaining green onions.

GREEN ONION-POTATO SOUP WITH DILL

45 *Very simple, and very good. Use fresh dill for best flavor.*

6 first-course servings

2½ cups chopped green onions
1 tablespoon margarine or butter
2 tablespoons flour
1½ quarts fat-free chicken broth, divided
1¾ cups cubed, peeled potatoes
2 tablespoons finely chopped fresh or 1 tablespoon
  dried dill weed
¼ cup low-fat plain yogurt
Salt and white pepper, to taste

Per Serving:
Calories: 105
% calories from fat: 16
Protein (g): 6.2
Carbohydrate (g): 16.6
Fat (g): 1.9
Saturated fat (g): 0.4
Cholesterol (mg): 0.5
Sodium (mg): 316

Exchanges:
Milk: 0.0
Vegetable: 0.0
Fruit: 0.0
Bread: 1.0
Meat: 0.0
Fat: 0.5

1. Sauté onions in margarine in large saucepan until tender, about
5 minutes. Stir in flour and cook 1 minute. Stir in 3 cups broth,
potatoes, and dill; heat to boiling; reduce heat and simmer, covered,
until potatoes are tender, about 10 minutes. Process 1 cup soup in
food processor or blender until smooth; add 1 cup broth and yogurt
and process until smooth. Return soup to saucepan; add enough
remaining 2 cups broth to make desired consistency. Heat to
simmering; simmer, uncovered until hot, 3 to 4 minutes. Season
to taste with salt and white pepper.

CRUNCHY VEGETABLE SOUP

45 *Any combination of vegetables may be used for this soup—broccoli, cauli-flower, cucumbers, radishes—just as long as they're crunchy!*

4 first-course servings

1½ cups cut asparagus (1-inch)
¼ cup each: coarsely chopped carrot, celery, onion,
  mushrooms
1 cup each: reduced-sodium fat-free chicken broth,
  fat-free plain yogurt
Pinch dried tarragon leaves
Salt and pepper, to taste
Chopped parsley, as garnish

Per Serving:
Calories: 63
% calories from fat: 4
Protein (g): 6.3
Carbohydrate (g): 9.3
Fat (g): 0.3
Saturated fat (g): 0.1
Cholesterol (mg): 1
Sodium (mg): 102

Exchanges:
Milk: 0.0
Vegetable: 2.0
Fruit: 0.0
Bread: 0.0
Meat: 0.0
Fat: 0.0

1. Process vegetables and chicken broth in food processor or blender until finely chopped; pour into medium saucepan and heat to boiling. Reduce heat and simmer, covered, until vegetables are crisp-tender, 5 to 8 minutes. Stir in yogurt and tarragon; season to taste with salt and pepper. Garnish each bowl of soup with parsley.

CONFETTI SOUP

45 *A no-time-to-cook soup that can be made in minutes, using frozen broccoli and cauliflower.*

8 first-course servings

2 carrots, sliced

1 cup sliced green onions

1 package (10 ounces) each: frozen chopped broccoli, cauliflower

1½ cups reduced-sodium fat-free chicken broth

3 cups fat-free milk, divided

1 tablespoon cornstarch

Salt and pepper, to taste

Per Serving:
Calories: 75
% calories from fat: 4
Protein (g): 6.3
Carbohydrate (g): 12.6
Fat (g): 0.4
Saturated fat (g): 0.1
Cholesterol (mg): 1.7
Sodium (mg): 104

Exchanges:
Milk: 0.0
Vegetable: 3.0
Fruit: 0.0
Bread: 0.0
Meat: 0.0
Fat: 0.0

1. Sauté carrots and green onions in lightly greased large saucepan until lightly browned, about 8 minutes. Add broccoli, cauliflower, and chicken broth; heat to boiling. Reduce heat and simmer, covered, until vegetables are tender, about 5 minutes. Process half the vegetable mixture in food processor or blender until smooth; return to saucepan and heat to boiling. Stir in combined ½ cup milk and cornstarch, stirring until thickened, about 1 minute. Stir in remaining 2½ cups milk; cook, covered, over medium heat until hot, about 5 minutes. Season to taste with salt and pepper.

SPEEDY SQUASH SOUP

45 *For quickest preparation, cook halved squash in microwave on high power 10 to 12 minutes or until tender.*

6 first-course servings

2 acorn squash, halved, seeded, cooked

½ cup chopped onion

2 cups reduced-sodium fat-free chicken broth

½ teaspoon ground cinnamon

¼ teaspoon each: ground coriander and cumin

⅛ teaspoon ground turmeric

1 cup buttermilk

1 tablespoon each: apple cider vinegar, light soy sauce

Salt and pepper, to taste

Chopped parsley, as garnish

Per Serving:
Calories: 90
% calories from fat: 5
Protein (g): 4.0
Carbohydrate (g): 19.2
Fat (g): 0.6
Saturated fat (g): 0.3
Cholesterol (mg): 1.6
Sodium (mg): 317

Exchanges:
Milk: 0.0
Vegetable: 0.0
Fruit: 0.0
Bread: 1.5
Meat: 0.0
Fat: 0.0

1. Scrape cooked squash from shells; process with onion and chicken broth in food processor or blender until smooth. Transfer to medium saucepan and add remaining ingredients, except salt, pepper, and parsley. Cook over medium heat until soup is hot, 5 to 8 minutes. Season to taste with salt and pepper; sprinkle each bowl of soup with parsley.

GARLIC AND SWEET PEPPER SOUP

45 *A heart-healthy soup you're sure to enjoy!*

6 first-course servings

½ cup chopped onion

6 cloves garlic, chopped

2 teaspoons olive oil

1 cup each: cubed peeled uncooked potato, chopped red bell pepper

3½ cups reduced-sodium fat-free chicken broth

Salt and pepper, to taste

6 tablespoons reduced-fat sour cream

Chopped parsley, as garnish

Per Serving:
Calories: 107
% calories from fat: 25
Protein (g): 6
Carbohydrate (g): 14.1
Fat (g): 2.9
Saturated fat (g): 1.2
Cholesterol (mg): 5
Sodium (mg): 113

Exchanges:
Milk: 0.0
Vegetable: 0.0
Fruit: 0.0
Bread: 1.0
Meat: 0.0
Fat: 0.5

1. Sauté onion and garlic in oil in medium saucepan until tender, about 3 minutes. Add potato, bell pepper, and broth. Heat to boiling; reduce heat and simmer, covered, until potato is tender, about 15 minutes. Process soup in food processor or blender until smooth; season to taste with salt and pepper. Refrigerate until cold; top each serving with a dollop of sour cream and sprinkle with parsley.

GARDEN GREEN SOUP

45 *Use the freshest greens your garden, or grocer, can provide. This soup can be served hot or cold.*

4 first-course servings

4 shallots, sliced

3 cloves garlic, minced

1 teaspoon canola oil

4 cups mixed greens, torn (romaine, red leaf or
   Boston lettuce, spinach, escarole, or sorrel)

2 cups fat-free milk

1 cup reduced-sodium fat-free chicken broth

¼ cup chopped fresh or 1 tablespoon dried
   basil leaves

Grated zest of ½ lemon

Salt and pepper, to taste

Per Serving:
Calories: 81
% calories from fat: 17
Protein (g): 7.3
Carbohydrate (g): 10.4
Fat (g): 1.7
Saturated fat (g): 0.3
Cholesterol (mg): 2.2
Sodium (mg): 123

Exchanges:
Milk: 0.5
Vegetable: 1.0
Fruit: 0.0
Bread: 0.0
Meat: 0.0
Fat: 0.5

1. Sauté shallots and garlic in oil in large saucepan until tender, about 3 minutes. Add remaining ingredients, except salt, and pepper, and heat to boiling; reduce heat and simmer until greens are wilted, about 5 minutes. Process soup in food processor or blender until smooth; season to taste with salt and pepper.

FRAGRANT MUSHROOM SOUP

You'll love this delicately flavored mushroom soup.

4 first-course servings

1 pound mushrooms

2 teaspoons margarine or butter

1½ tablespoons flour

1 quart Fragrant Beef Stock (see p. 6) or
   reduced-sodium beef broth

1 tablespoon light soy sauce

2 tablespoons dry sherry (optional)

½ teaspoon lemon juice

Salt and pepper, to taste

Per Serving:
Calories: 86
% calories from fat: 28
Protein (g): 6
Carbohydrate (g): 9.2
Fat (g): 2.9
Saturated fat (g): 0.7
Cholesterol (mg): 3
Sodium (mg): 245

Exchanges:
Milk: 0.0
Vegetable: 2.0
Fruit: 0.0
Bread: 0.0
Meat: 0.0
Fat: 0.5

1. Slice 4 large mushroom caps and reserve. Chop remaining mushrooms and stems. Sauté chopped mushrooms in margarine in large saucepan until mushrooms are tender and juices are almost evaporated, about 8 minutes. Sprinkle with flour and cook 1 minute; add stock and soy sauce and heat to boiling. Reduce heat and simmer 5 minutes. Process soup in food processor or blender until smooth; return to saucepan and heat to simmering. Add sliced mushrooms and simmer, covered, 5 minutes; stir in sherry and lemon juice. Season to taste with salt and pepper.

DILLED BEET SOUP

It's not necessary to peel beets, as the skins slip off easily after cooking.

8 first-course servings

12 medium beets

3 cups water

2–3 chicken bouillon cubes

Water

½–¾ cup dry red wine or water

2 teaspoons dried dill weed

2–3 tablespoons red wine vinegar

Salt and pepper, to taste

Thin lemon slices, as garnish

Per Serving:
Calories: 63
% calories from fat: 3
Protein (g): 1.8
Carbohydrate (g): 10.6
Fat (g): 0.3
Saturated fat (g): 0
Cholesterol (mg): 0
Sodium (mg): 318

Exchanges:
Milk: 0.0
Vegetable: 2.0
Fruit: 0.0
Bread: 0.0
Meat: 0.0
Fat: 0.0

1. Heat beets, 3 cups water, and bouillon cubes to boiling in large saucepan; reduce heat and simmer, covered, until beets are tender, 30 to 40 minutes. Drain, reserving cooking liquid. Slip skins off beets and cut into quarters. Add enough water to reserved cooking liquid to make 6 cups. Process reserved liquid, beets, wine, and dill weed in food processor or blender until smooth. Season to taste with vinegar, salt, and pepper. Serve warm or chilled; garnish each bowl of soup with a lemon slice.

CREAM OF BROCCOLI SOUP

45   *Eat broccoli often—it's high in antioxidants and packed with nutrients.*

6 first-course servings

1 cup chopped onion
3 cloves garlic, minced
2 pounds broccoli, cut into pieces (2-inch)
½ teaspoon dried thyme leaves
⅛ teaspoon ground nutmeg
3½ cups reduced-sodium fat-free chicken broth
½ cup fat-free half-and-half or fat-free milk
Salt and white pepper, to taste
6 tablespoons fat-free sour cream
1½ cups Croutons (½ recipe) (see p. 636)

Per Serving:
Calories: 99
% calories from fat: 9
Protein (g): 6.8
Carbohydrate (g): 17.6
Fat (g): 1.1
Saturated fat (g): 0.2
Cholesterol (mg): 0
Sodium (mg): 110

Exchanges:
Milk: 0.0
Vegetable: 2.0
Fruit: 0.0
Bread: 0.5
Meat: 0.0
Fat: 0.0

1. Sauté onion and garlic in lightly greased large saucepan until tender, 3 to 5 minutes. Stir in broccoli, thyme, and nutmeg; cook 2 minutes. Add broth to saucepan and heat to boiling; reduce heat and simmer, covered, until broccoli is tender, about 10 minutes. Stir in half-and-half. Process soup in food processor or blender until smooth; season to taste with salt and white pepper. Serve warm or chilled; stir 1 tablespoon sour cream into each bowl of soup and sprinkle with Croutons.

VARIATIONS

Dilled Broccoli Soup — Make recipe as above, deleting thyme, nutmeg, and Croutons. Add ⅔ cup loosely packed fresh dill weed to soup when puréeing.

Broccoli-Kale Soup — Make recipe as above, increasing broth to 5 cups and deleting the half-and-half, Croutons, and nutmeg. Stir 2 cups lightly packed kale into the soup during the last 5 minutes of cooking time. Add more broth if needed for desired consistency.

Cream of Asparagus Soup — Make soup as above, substituting 2 pounds asparagus for the broccoli, and reserving 18 small asparagus tips for garnish. Omit thyme leaves. Add 1 teaspoon dried marjoram leaves and 1 teaspoon grated lemon zest. Steam reserved asparagus tips until crisp-tender, and use to garnish soup.

CREAMY BROCCOLI-POTATO SOUP

This soup can also be served cold. Stir 1 tablespoon lemon juice and ¼ cup additional Chicken Stock into soup; refrigerate until chilled. Garnish each bowl of soup with a lemon slice.

6 first-course servings

4 medium leeks (white parts only), sliced
2 teaspoons margarine or butter
3 cups Chicken Stock (see p. 2)
3½ cups diced peeled potatoes
1 quart thickly sliced broccoli
1¼ cups whole milk
Salt and white pepper, to taste

Per Serving:
Calories: 148
% calories from fat: 15
Protein (g): 6.3
Carbohydrate (g): 26.9
Fat (g): 2.5
Saturated fat (g): 1
Cholesterol (mg): 5.2
Sodium (mg): 175

Exchanges:
Milk: 0.0
Vegetable: 0.0
Fruit: 0.0
Bread: 1.5
Meat: 0.0
Fat: 0.5

1. Sauté leeks in margarine in large saucepan until leeks are tender, but not browned, about 10 minutes. Add stock, potatoes, and broccoli; heat to boiling. Reduce heat and simmer, covered, until vegetables are tender, about 10 minutes. Process soup in food processor or blender until smooth; return to saucepan. Stir in milk and heat to boiling; reduce heat and simmer, covered, 5 minutes. Season to taste with salt and white pepper.

HERBED BROCCOLI-CAULIFLOWER BISQUE

This healthful soup is so delicious, you'll want to make enough for the freezer!

6 first-course servings

2 medium stalks broccoli

½ small head cauliflower

1 cup thinly sliced green onions

2 teaspoons margarine or butter

1 tablespoon flour

3 cups Chicken Stock (see p. 2)

1½ cups coarsely chopped peeled potatoes

1 tablespoon dried basil leaves

1½ cups 2% reduced-fat milk

Salt and pepper, to taste

Per Serving:
Calories: 121
% calories from fat: 19
Protein (g): 7
Carbohydrate (g): 18.6
Fat (g): 2.7
Saturated fat (g): 1
Cholesterol (mg): 4.5
Sodium (mg): 230

Exchanges:
Milk: 0.0
Vegetable: 1.0
Fruit: 0.0
Bread: 1.0
Meat: 0.0
Fat: 0.5

1. Cut enough broccoli and cauliflower into florets to make ¾ cup each; reserve. Coarsely chop remaining broccoli and cauliflower. Sauté green onions in margarine in large saucepan until tender, about 4 minutes. Stir in flour; cook 1 minute. Stir in stock, chopped vegetables, and basil; heat to boiling. Reduce heat and simmer, uncovered, until vegetables are tender, about 10 minutes. Process soup in food processor or blender until smooth; return to saucepan. Add milk and reserved vegetable florets. Heat to boiling; reduce heat and simmer until florets are crisp-tender, about 5 minutes. Season to taste with salt and pepper.

GOLDEN CARROT SOUP

Orange juice adds a subtle sweetness to this carrot soup.

6 first-course servings

8 medium carrots, sliced

1 cup coarsely chopped onion

1 tablespoon margarine or butter

3 cups Chicken Stock (see p. 2)

½ cup fresh orange juice

1 strip orange zest

¼ cup dry sherry or orange juice

1 tablespoon sugar

Salt and white pepper, to taste

6 thin slices orange

Per Serving:
Calories: 109
% calories from fat: 20
Protein (g): 2.3
Carbohydrate (g): 18
Fat (g): 2.5
Saturated fat (g): 0.5
Cholesterol (mg): 1.7
Sodium (mg): 60

1. Sauté carrots and onion in margarine in large saucepan 10 minutes. Add stock, orange juice, and orange zest and heat to boiling. Reduce heat and simmer, covered, until carrots are tender, about 20 minutes. Process soup in food processor or blender until smooth; add sherry and sugar. Season to taste with salt and white pepper; garnish each bowl of soup with orange slices.

Exchanges:
Milk: 0.0
Vegetable: 2.0
Fruit: 0.5
Bread: 0.0
Meat: 0.0
Fat: 0.5

VARIATION

Orange Sweet Potato Soup — Make soup as above, substituting 2 peeled, cubed medium sweet potatoes for the carrots. Omit sherry and add ½ teaspoon ground cinnamon and a pinch each ground nutmeg and mace.

DILLED CARROT SOUP

45 *Carrots team with dill for a fresh, clean flavor.*

6 first-course servings

1½ cups chopped onions

2 cloves garlic, minced

1½ quarts reduced-sodium fat-free chicken broth

1 can (14½ ounces) reduced-sodium diced tomatoes, undrained

2 pounds carrots, thickly sliced

1 medium Idaho potato, peeled, cubed

1–1½ teaspoons dried dill weed

2–3 tablespoons lemon juice

Salt and white pepper, to taste

6 tablespoons fat-free plain yogurt

Per Serving:
Calories: 139
% calories from fat: 6
Protein (g): 4.4
Carbohydrate (g): 30.5
Fat (g): 1
Saturated fat (g): 0.1
Cholesterol (mg): 0.3
Sodium (mg): 88

Exchanges:
Milk: 0.0
Vegetable: 6.0
Fruit: 0.0
Bread: 0.0
Meat: 0.0
Fat: 0.0

1. Sauté onions and garlic in lightly greased large saucepan until tender, about 5 minutes. Add broth, tomatoes with liquid, carrots, potato and dill weed; heat to boiling. Reduce heat and simmer, covered, until vegetables are tender, about 15 minutes. Process soup in food processor or blender until smooth; season to taste with lemon juice, salt, and white pepper. Serve soup warm or chilled. Garnish each bowl of soup with a dollop of yogurt.

CREAM OF CAULIFLOWER SOUP WITH CHEESE

45 *Fat-free half-and-half adds a rich creaminess to the soup.*

6 first-course servings

½ cup chopped onion

2 cloves garlic, minced

2 tablespoons flour

3½ cups reduced-sodium fat-free chicken broth

12 ounces cauliflower, cut into florets

1 large Idaho potato, peeled, cubed

¼–½ cup fat-free half-and-half or fat-free milk

¾ cup (3 ounces) reduced-fat Cheddar cheese

Salt and white pepper, to taste

Ground mace or nutmeg, as garnish

Per Serving:
Calories: 98
% calories from fat: 22
Protein (g): 5.5
Carbohydrate (g): 13.6
Fat (g): 2.4
Saturated fat (g): 1.1
Cholesterol (mg): 7.6
Sodium (mg): 214

Exchanges:
Milk: 0.0
Vegetable: 1.0
Fruit: 0.0
Bread: 0.5
Meat: 0.5
Fat: 0.0

1. Sauté onion and garlic in lightly greased large saucepan until tender, about 10 minutes; stir in flour and cook 1 minute. Add broth, cauliflower, and potato and heat to boiling; reduce heat and simmer, covered, until vegetables are tender, 10 to 15 minutes. Remove about half the vegetables from the soup with a slotted spoon and reserve. Purée remaining soup in food processor or blender until smooth; return to saucepan. Add reserved vegetables, half-and-half, and cheese; cook over low heat, stirring, until cheese is melted, 3 to 4 minutes. Season to taste with salt and white pepper; sprinkle each bowl of soup with mace.

VARIATIONS

Chilled Cauliflower Soup — Make soup as above, omitting Cheddar cheese and mace. Add 1 tablespoon dried dill weed to simmering soup; process all the soup in food processor, without reserving any vegetables. Refrigerate until chilled; garnish each bowl of soup with chopped dill or parsley.

Fennel Bisque with Walnuts — Make soup as above, substituting 1 large leek, sliced, for the onion, and 2 large fennel bulbs, sliced, for the cauliflower. Complete soup as above, omitting Cheddar cheese. Ladle soup into bowls; sprinkle with 3 ounces crumbled blue cheese, and ¼ cup chopped toasted walnuts.

Cream of Turnip Soup — Make soup as above, substituting chopped turnips for the cauliflower and reduced-fat Swiss, Gouda, or Havarti cheese for the Cheddar; add ½ teaspoon dried thyme leaves.

CELERY AND FENNEL SOUP

Summer living is easy, with this flavorful cold soup ready in the refrigerator.

6 first-course servings

3 cups coarsely chopped celery
8 green onions, sliced
1 small garlic clove, minced
1 teaspoon olive oil
1 quart Chicken Stock (see p. 2)
2½ tablespoons uncooked rice
1 teaspoon fennel seeds
Salt and white pepper, to taste
Fat-free plain yogurt, as garnish

Per Serving:
Calories: 53
% calories from fat: 15
Protein (g): 4.1
Carbohydrate (g): 7.7
Fat (g): 1.0
Saturated fat (g): 0.1
Cholesterol (mg): 0
Sodium (mg): 277

Exchanges:
Milk: 0.0
Vegetable: 0.0
Fruit: 0.0
Bread: 0.5
Meat: 0.0
Fat: 0.0

1. Sauté celery, onions, and garlic in oil in large saucepan until onions are tender, about 5 minutes. Add stock, rice, and fennel seeds tied in a cheesecloth bag; heat to boiling. Reduce heat and simmer, covered, until rice is tender, about 20 minutes; discard cheesecloth bag and contents. Process soup in food processor or blender until smooth; season to taste with salt and white pepper. Refrigerate until chilled; garnish each bowl of soup with a dollop of yogurt.

CUCUMBER AND SORREL SOUP

45

Spinach, kale, or any favorite leafy green can be substituted for the sorrel.

6 first-course servings

¼ cup sliced green onions

1 clove garlic, minced

3 cups peeled, seeded, chopped cucumbers

1 cup coarsely chopped sorrel

2 cups each: fat-free milk, reduced-sodium
  fat-free chicken broth

1 tablespoon cornstarch

2 tablespoons water

Salt and white pepper, to taste

1½ cups Herb Croutons (½ recipe) (see p. 636)

Per Serving:
Calories: 70
% calories from fat: 10
Protein (g): 4.5
Carbohydrate (g): 11.7
Fat (g): 0.8
Saturated fat (g): 0.2
Cholesterol (mg): 1.3
Sodium (mg): 94

Exchanges:
Milk: 0.0
Vegetable: 2.5
Fruit: 0.0
Bread: 0.0
Meat: 0.0
Fat: 0.0

1. Sauté onions and garlic in lightly greased large saucepan until tender, 3 to 4 minutes. Add cucumbers and sorrel, and cook over medium heat 5 minutes. Add milk and broth; heat to boiling. Reduce heat and simmer, covered, until cucumbers are tender, 5 to 10 minutes. Process soup in food processor or blender until smooth; return to saucepan and heat to boiling. Whisk in combined cornstarch and water, whisking until thickened, about 1 minute. Season to taste with salt and white pepper. Refrigerate until chilled; top each bowl of soup with Herb Croutons.

45-MINUTE PREPARATION TIP: Make Herb Croutons and bake while preparing soup.

DILLED CUCUMBER BUTTERMILK SOUP

A refreshing soup for the dog days of summer!

6 first-course servings

⅔ cup chopped onion

⅓ cup sliced green onions

½ teaspoon minced garlic

1 tablespoon margarine or butter

1 medium russet potato, peeled, cubed

2½ cups Rich Chicken Stock (see p. 4)

2 medium cucumbers, peeled, seeded, chopped
¼ cup chopped fresh or 1 tablespoon dried dill weed
1 cup reduced-fat buttermilk
Lemon juice, to taste
Salt and white pepper, to taste
Dill Sour Cream (recipe follows)

Per Serving:
Calories: 116
% calories from fat: 22
Protein (g): 6.2
Carbohydrate (g): 15.5
Fat (g): 2.8
Saturated fat (g): 0.7
Cholesterol (mg): 1.8
Sodium (mg): 103

Exchanges:
Milk: 0.0
Vegetable: 0.0
Fruit: 0.0
Bread: 1.0
Meat: 0.0
Fat: 1.0

1. Sauté onion, green onions, and garlic in margarine in large saucepan until tender, about 4 minutes. Add potato and stock and heat to boiling; reduce heat and simmer, covered, until tender, about 15 minutes. Process soup, cucumbers, and dill in food processor or blender until smooth; stir in buttermilk and season to taste with lemon juice, salt, and white pepper. Refrigerate, covered, until chilled; tops each bowl of soup with dollop of Sour Cream with Dill.

Sour Cream with Dill

Makes about ½ cup

½ cup fat-free sour cream
2 tablespoons chopped fresh or 1½ teaspoons dried dill weed

1. Combine sour cream and dill.

GARLIC SOUP WITH TOASTED BREAD

45 *A beaten egg is often stirred into this Mexican soup before serving.*

4 first-course servings (about 1 cup each)

4 slices French or sourdough bread
Vegetable cooking spray
6–8 cloves garlic, finely chopped
½ teaspoon each: ground cumin, dried oregano leaves
1 tablespoon olive oil
2 cans (14½ ounces each) reduced-sodium fat-free chicken broth
Salt and cayenne pepper, to taste
Chopped cilantro, as garnish

1. Spray both sides of bread slices generously with cooking spray; cook in large skillet, over medium heat, until golden, about 2 minutes on each side.

2. Sauté garlic and herbs in oil in medium saucepan until lightly browned, about 3 minutes. Add broth and heat to boiling; reduce heat and simmer, covered, 5 minutes. Season to taste with salt and cayenne pepper. Place slices of bread in bottoms of soup bowls; ladle soup over and sprinkle with cilantro.

Per Serving:
Calories: 162
% calories from fat: 28
Protein (g): 3.2
Carbohydrate (g): 20.6
Fat (g): 5
Saturated fat (g): 0.7
Cholesterol (mg): 0
Sodium (mg): 202

Exchanges:
Milk: 0.0
Vegetable: 1.0
Fruit: 0.0
Bread: 1.5
Meat: 0.0
Fat: 0.5

WINTER GAZPACHO

45 *This hot version of gazpacho brings vegetable-garden flavors and a bright assortment of garnishes to the winter dinner table.*

6 first-course servings

1 cup each: water, packed spinach
½ cup each: chopped carrots, celery, green bell pepper
4 cups reduced-sodium tomato juice, divided
2 teaspoons low-sodium Worcestershire sauce
1 teaspoon beef bouillon crystals
¼ teaspoon dried tarragon leaves
Salt and cayenne pepper, to taste
1 each: chopped small onion, hard-cooked egg, cubed small avocado
1½ cups Garlic or Herb Croutons (½ recipe) (see p. 637, 636)

Per Serving:
Calories: 115
% calories from fat: 27
Protein (g): 4.2
Carbohydrate (g): 18.3
Fat (g): 3.8
Saturated fat (g): 0.7
Cholesterol (mg): 35.3
Sodium (mg): 221

Exchanges:
Milk: 0.0
Vegetable: 2.0
Fruit: 0.0
Bread: 0.5
Meat: 0.0
Fat: 0.5

1. Heat water, spinach, carrots, celery, and bell pepper to boiling in large saucepan. Heat to boiling; reduce heat and simmer, covered, until carrots are tender, about 8 minutes. Process vegetable mixture, 2 cups tomato juice, Worcestershire sauce, bouillon crystals, and tarragon in food processor or blender until smooth; return to saucepan. Add remaining 2 cups tomato juice and cook over medium heat until hot, about 5 minutes. Season to taste with salt and cayenne pepper. Serve in shallow bowls; sprinkle with chopped onion, egg, avocado, and Garlic Croutons.

LENTIL SOUP

This satisfying soup is good on a cold, snowy day.

6 first-course servings

1 pound dry brown lentils

1 cup finely chopped onion

½ cup each: finely chopped celery and carrot

2 quarts water

1 large smoked pork hock

2 teaspoons each: sugar, beef bouillon crystals

¼ teaspoon dry mustard

½ teaspoon dried thyme leaves

Salt and cayenne pepper, to taste

Per Serving:
Calories: 89
% calories from fat: 12
Protein (g): 6.7
Carbohydrate (g): 16.5
Fat (g): 1.4
Saturated fat (g): 0.3
Cholesterol (mg): 6.5
Sodium (mg): 277

Exchanges:
Milk: 0.0
Vegetable: 0.0
Fruit: 0.0
Bread: 1.0
Meat: 0.0
Fat: 0.5

1. Heat all ingredients, except salt and pepper, to boiling in large saucepan; reduce heat and simmer, covered, until lentils are very tender and soup has thickened, about 45 minutes. Discard pork hock; skim fat from soup and season to taste with salt and pepper.

LEMON MUSHROOM SOUP

Fresh and dried mushrooms combine in this delicious lemon-accented soup.

6 first-course servings

1½ cups hot water

1 ounce dried porcini mushrooms

¾ cup thinly sliced onion

1½ tablespoons minced garlic

2 teaspoons flour

1 quart Rich Chicken Stock (see p. 4)

¼ cup dry white wine (optional)

4 ounces cremini mushrooms, quartered

1 tablespoon fresh or 1 teaspoon dried rosemary leaves

¼ cup each: chopped fresh lemon pulp, minced parsley, divided

Salt and pepper, to taste

6 Bruschetta (½ recipe) (see p. 637)

Per Serving:
Calories: 90
% calories from fat: 10
Protein (g): 3.7
Carbohydrate (g): 14.9
Fat (g): 1
Saturated fat (g): 0.1
Cholesterol (mg): 0
Sodium (mg): 86

Exchanges:
Milk: 0.0
Vegetable: 2.0
Fruit: 0.0
Bread: 0.5
Meat: 0.0
Fat: 0.0

1. Pour hot water over porcini mushrooms in bowl; let stand until softened, about 20 minutes. Remove mushrooms with slotted spoon; strain liquid through double layer of cheesecloth and reserve 2 tablespoons liquid. Inspect porcini carefully, rinsing if necessary, to remove grit. Chop coarsely.

2. Sauté onion and garlic in lightly greased large saucepan until tender, about 5 minutes. Sprinkle with flour and cook 1 minute. Add stock, wine, porcini and cremini mushrooms, reserved porcini liquid, and rosemary; heat to boiling. Reduce heat and simmer, covered, until mushrooms are tender, about 15 minutes, adding lemon pulp and parsley during last 5 minutes. Season to taste with salt and pepper. Place Bruschetta in bottoms of soup bowls; ladle soup over.

FRESH MOREL SOUP

45 *Make this elegant soup with any fragrant wild mushroom, or a mixture of mushrooms.*

4 first-course servings

1½ cups chopped morel mushrooms

1–2 teaspoons margarine or butter

1 quart reduced-sodium fat-free beef broth

1 cup water

1–2 tablespoons dry sherry (optional)

Salt and pepper, to taste

Crumbled blue cheese, as garnish

Per Serving:
Calories: 35
% calories from fat: 26
Protein (g): 5.6
Carbohydrate (g): 1.2
Fat (g): 1.1
Saturated fat (g): 0.2
Cholesterol (mg): 0
Sodium (mg): 172

Exchanges:
Milk: 0.0
Vegetable: 0.0
Fruit: 0.0
Bread: 0.0
Meat: 0.5
Fat: 0.0

1. Cook mushrooms in margarine in medium saucepan over medium heat until lightly browned, about 5 minutes. Add broth and water and heat to boiling; reduce heat and simmer, uncovered, 15 minutes. Stir in sherry; season to taste with salt and pepper. Sprinkle each bowl of soup with blue cheese.

BLACK MUSHROOM SOUP

45 *Chinese black mushrooms (dried shiitake mushrooms) add a fragrant, woodsy flavor to this soup.*

6 first-course servings

2 cups boiling water

1½ ounces dried Chinese black mushrooms

1 ounce dried cloud ear mushrooms

¼ cup each: chopped onion, green onions

5 cups reduced-sodium fat-free chicken broth

3 cups sliced cremini mushrooms

Salt and white pepper, to taste

Per Serving:
Calories: 72
% calories from fat: 16
Protein (g): 2.9
Carbohydrate (g): 11.1
Fat (g): 1.4
Saturated fat (g): 0.1
Cholesterol (mg): 0
Sodium (mg): 10

Exchanges:
Milk: 0.0
Vegetable: 3.0
Fruit: 0.0
Bread: 0.0
Meat: 0.0
Fat: 0.0

1. Pour boiling water over dried mushrooms in bowl; let stand until mushrooms are softened, about 15 minutes. Drain, reserving liquid. Slice mushrooms, discarding tough stems from black mushrooms.

2. Sauté onion and green onions in lightly greased large saucepan until tender, about 5 minutes. Add dried mushrooms, reserved liquid and broth; heat to boiling. Reduce heat and simmer, covered, 20 minutes, adding cremini mushrooms during last 10 minutes. Season to taste with salt and white pepper.

VIDALIA ONION SOUP

The mild sweetness of Vidalia onions makes this soup special, but try it with other flavorful onion varieties too.

8 first-course servings

6 cups thinly sliced Vidalia onions

2 cloves garlic, minced

1 teaspoon sugar

⅓ cup all-purpose flour

6 cups reduced-sodium fat-free chicken or
    vegetable broth

1½ teaspoons dried sage leaves

2 bay leaves

Salt and white pepper, to taste

Snipped chives or sliced green onions, as garnish

Per Serving:
Calories: 88
% calories from fat: 3
Protein (g): 2.2
Carbohydrate (g): 16.4
Fat (g): 0.3
Saturated fat (g): 0.1
Cholesterol (mg): 0
Sodium (mg): 13

Exchanges:
Milk: 0.0
Vegetable: 2.0
Fruit: 0.0
Bread: 0.5
Meat: 0.0
Fat: 0.0

1. Cook onions and garlic in lightly greased large saucepan, covered, over medium-low heat until softened, 8 to 10 minutes. Stir in sugar and continue cooking, uncovered, until onions are lightly browned, about 10 minutes. Stir in flour; cook 1 minute. Add broth and herbs; heat to boiling. Reduce heat and simmer, covered, 30 minutes. Discard bay leaves. Process half the soup in food processor or blender until smooth; return to saucepan and season to taste with salt and white pepper. Serve warm or chilled; sprinkle each bowl of soup with chives.

VARIATION

Baked Onion Soup with Sun-Dried Tomato Pesto — Make soup as above, adding ¼ cup dry sherry in Step 2. Spread 8 Bruschetta (see p. 637) with ½ cup Sun-Dried Tomato Pesto (see p. 662). Place in bottoms of 8 oven-proof soup bowls and sprinkle with 1 cup shredded reduced-fat Italian-blend cheese. Ladle soup over and bake at 425 degrees, 10 to 15 minutes, or until cheese is melted.

THREE-ONION SOUP WITH MUSHROOMS

Mushrooms are a flavorful addition to this onion soup.

6 first-course servings

3 cups thinly sliced onions

1½ cups thinly sliced leeks

½ cup chopped shallots or green onions

1 tablespoon margarine or butter

1 teaspoon sugar

2 cups sliced mushrooms

6½ cups reduced-sodium fat-free chicken broth

Salt and pepper, to taste

Per Serving:
Calories: 119
% calories from fat: 21
Protein (g): 2.7
Carbohydrate (g): 18.5
Fat (g): 3
Saturated fat (g): 0.5
Cholesterol (mg): 0
Sodium (mg): 218

Exchanges:
Milk: 0.0
Vegetable: 3.0
Fruit: 0.0
Bread: 0.0
Meat: 0.0
Fat: 0.5

1. Cook onions, leeks, and shallots in margarine in large saucepan, covered, over medium-low heat until onions are softened, about 15 minutes. Stir in sugar; cook, uncovered, until onion mixture is golden, about 15 minutes. Stir in mushrooms; cook over medium heat until tender, about 5 minutes. Add broth and heat to boiling; reduce heat and simmer, uncovered, 15 minutes. Season to taste with salt and pepper.

RED ONION AND APPLE SOUP WITH CURRY

Red onions, cooked until sweet and tender, lend a special flavor to this autumn soup.

6 first-course servings

1¼ pounds red onions (about 4 medium), thinly sliced

1 tablespoon margarine or butter

1½ quarts Rich Chicken Stock (see p. 4)

2 cups coarsely grated peeled tart cooking apples, divided

½ cup coarsely shredded carrots

1 large bay leaf

1 teaspoon each: curry and chili powder

¼ teaspoon each: dried thyme leaves, ground allspice

Salt and pepper, to taste

Mango chutney, as garnish

1. Sauté onions in margarine in large saucepan until tender and lightly browned, about 15 minutes. Stir in stock, 1 cup apples, carrots, and seasonings; heat to boiling. Reduce heat and simmer, covered, until vegetables are tender, about 20 minutes, adding remaining 1 cup apples during last 5 minutes. Discard bay leaf; season to taste with salt and pepper. Serve with chutney to stir into soup.

Per Serving:
Calories: 106
% calories from fat: 18
Protein (g): 6.4
Carbohydrate (g): 16.4
Fat (g): 2.3
Saturated fat (g): 0.4
Cholesterol (mg): 0
Sodium (mg): 393

Exchanges:
Milk: 0.0
Vegetable: 2.0
Fruit: 0.5
Bread: 0.0
Meat: 0.0
Fat: 0.5

HOT CHILI VICHYSSOISE

Potato soup will never be boring if served Tex-Mex style. This version, prepared with chilies, packs a punch!

6 first-course servings

1 each: medium leek (white part only), poblano and jalapeño chili

1 pound new red potatoes, unpeeled, halved

6 cloves garlic, peeled

Vegetable cooking spray

1½ teaspoons ground cumin

½ teaspoon each: chili powder, dried oregano leaves

4 cups reduced-sodium fat-free chicken broth, divided

½–¾ cup fat-free half-and-half or fat-free milk

¼ cup chopped cilantro

Salt, to taste

Per Serving:
Calories: 113
% calories from fat: 2
Protein (g): 6.6
Carbohydrate (g): 20.9
Fat (g): 0.3
Saturated fat (g): 0
Cholesterol (mg): 0
Sodium (mg): 169

Exchanges:
Milk: 0.0
Vegetable: 1.0
Fruit: 0.0
Bread: 1.0
Meat: 0.0
Fat: 0.0

1. Cut leek and chilies into ¾-inch pieces; arrange in single layer on greased foil-lined jelly roll pan; spray with cooking spray and sprinkle with herbs. Roast at 425 degrees until browned and tender, about 40 minutes, removing garlic when tender, about 30 minutes. Process vegetables and 2 cups broth in food processor or blender until smooth. Heat vegetable mixture and remaining broth to boiling in large saucepan; reduce heat to medium. Stir in half-and-half and cook until hot, 3 to 4 minutes. Stir in cilantro; season with salt. Serve warm or chilled.

GINGER PUMPKIN SOUP

Substitute 2½ cups canned pumpkin if you can't get a fresh pumpkin.

6 first-course servings

1 small pumpkin, peeled, seeded, cubed
1 cup chopped onion
1 tablespoon chopped gingerroot
1 teaspoon minced garlic
3 cups Chicken Stock (see p. 2)
½ cup dry white wine or Chicken Stock
½ teaspoon ground cloves
Salt and pepper, to taste

Per Serving:
Calories: 83
% calories from fat: 6
Protein (g): 2.8
Carbohydrate (g): 15.3
Fat (g): 0.6
Saturated fat (g): 0.2
Cholesterol (mg): 1.7
Sodium (mg): 8

Exchanges:
Milk: 0.0
Vegetable: 0.0
Fruit: 0.0
Bread: 1.0
Meat: 0.0
Fat: 0.0

1. Heat all ingredients, except salt and pepper, to boiling in large saucepan; reduce heat and simmer, covered, until pumpkin is tender, about 20 minutes. Process soup in food processor or blender until smooth. Return to saucepan and heat until hot; season to taste with salt and pepper.

SPINACH SOUP

This soup is best eaten as soon as its cooked, as the color will change as it stands.

10 first-course servings

1 large leek (white part only) thinly sliced
⅓ cup each: sliced carrot, celery
1 tablespoon olive oil
2 quarts Rich Chicken Stock (see p. 4)
2 pounds fresh spinach
Salt and pepper, to taste
½ cup (2 ounces) grated Parmesan cheese
Croutons (see p. 636)

Per Serving:
Calories: 113
% calories from fat: 31
Protein (g): 9.1
Carbohydrate (g): 9.9
Fat (g): 3.8
Saturated fat (g): 1.2
Cholesterol (mg): 4
Sodium (mg): 229

Exchanges:
Milk: 0.0
Vegetable: 2.0
Fruit: 0.0
Bread: 0.0
Meat: 0.5
Fat: 0.5

1. Sauté leek, carrot, and celery in oil in large saucepan until tender, about 8 minutes; add stock and heat to boiling. Add spinach and cook, uncovered, until wilted, about 2 minutes. Process soup in food processor or blender until smooth; season to taste with salt and pepper. Sprinkle each bowl of soup with Parmesan cheese and croutons.

APPLE SQUASH SOUP

This soup is the perfect autumn offering.

8 first-course servings

1½ cups chopped onions

2 teaspoons ground cinnamon

¼ teaspoon each: ground ginger, cloves

⅛ teaspoon ground nutmeg

1½ tablespoons margarine or butter

1 large butternut squash, peeled, seeded, cubed (about 2½ pounds)

2 tart cooking apples, peeled, cored, chopped

1⅓ cups apple cider

3 cups Chicken Stock (see p. 2)

Salt and pepper, to taste

Spiced Sour Cream (recipe follows)

Per Serving:
Calories: 155
% calories from fat: 15
Protein (g): 3.3
Carbohydrate (g): 32.6
Fat (g): 2.8
Saturated fat (g): 0.5
Cholesterol (mg): 1.3
Sodium (mg): 48

Exchanges:
Milk: 0.0
Vegetable: 0.0
Fruit: 0.0
Bread: 2.0
Meat: 0.0
Fat: 0.5

1. Cook onions and spices in margarine in large saucepan over low heat until onions are very tender and golden, about 20 minutes, stirring frequently; add squash, apples, cider, and stock. Heat to boiling; reduce heat and simmer, covered, until tender, about 25 minutes. Process soup in food processor or blender until smooth; season to taste with salt and pepper. Serve with Spiced Sour Cream.

Spiced Sour Cream
Makes about 1 cup

½ cup fat-free sour cream
1 teaspoon sugar
½ teaspoon ground cinnamon
⅛ teaspoon ground ginger
1–2 teaspoons lemon juice

1. Combine all ingredients.

SUMMER SQUASH SOUP

45 *Use any summer squash in this soup.*

6 first-course servings

4 medium zucchini, chopped
1 cup peeled, cubed Idaho potato
⅓ cup each: chopped shallots, green onions
2 cloves garlic, minced
4 cups reduced-sodium fat-free chicken broth
1 cup chopped kale or spinach
1–½ teaspoons dried tarragon leaves
¼–½ cup fat-free half-and-half or fat-free milk
Salt and white pepper, to taste
Cayenne pepper, as garnish
1½ cups Sourdough Croutons (½ recipe) (see p. 636)

Per Serving:
Calories: 100
% calories from fat: 7
Protein (g): 3.8
Carbohydrate (g): 20.6
Fat (g): 0.8
Saturated fat (g): 0.1
Cholesterol (mg): 0
Sodium (mg): 65

Exchanges:
Milk: 0.0
Vegetable: 1.0
Fruit: 0.0
Bread: 1.0
Meat: 0.0
Fat: 0.0

1. Sauté zucchini, potato, shallots, green onions, and garlic in lightly greased saucepan until lightly browned, about 8 minutes. Add broth, kale, and tarragon. Heat to boiling; reduce heat and simmer, covered, until vegetables are tender, 10 to 15 minutes. Process soup in food processor or blender until smooth; stir in half-and-half and season to taste with salt and white pepper. Serve warm or chilled; sprinkle each of bowl soup with cayenne pepper and top with Sourdough Croutons.

VARIATION

Squash and Fennel Bisque — Make soup as above, adding 1 sliced fennel bulb and ½ cup sliced celery, and substituting spinach for kale. Omit tarragon. Thin with additional broth if necessary.

FRESH TOMATO SOUP

To peel tomatoes, place a few at a time into a pan of boiling water for about 30 seconds. Remove and slip off skins. Halve the tomatoes and remove seeds.

6 first-course servings

4 each: sliced green onions, minced cloves garlic

1 teaspoon olive oil

2½ pounds tomatoes, peeled, seeded, chopped, divided

2½ cups Rich Chicken Stock (see p. 4)

¼ cup chopped fresh or 1 tablespoon dried basil leaves

1 bay leaf

2 teaspoons sugar

½ cup dry white wine (optional)

Salt and pepper, to taste

Chopped parsley, as garnish

Per Serving:
Calories: 87
% calories from fat: 17
Protein (g): 4
Carbohydrate (g): 11.6
Fat (g): 1.8
Saturated fat (g): 0.3
Cholesterol (mg): 0.4
Sodium (mg): 36

Exchanges:
Milk: 0.0
Vegetable: 2.0
Fruit: 0.0
Bread: 0.0
Meat: 0.0
Fat: 0.5

1. Sauté green onions and garlic in oil in large saucepan until transparent, about 2 minutes. Reserve 2 cups tomatoes; process remaining tomatoes in food processor or blender until smooth; stir into saucepan and cook 5 minutes. Stir in stock, basil, bay leaf, and sugar. Heat to boiling; reduce heat and simmer, uncovered, 40 minutes, adding wine and reserved 2 cups tomatoes during last 15 minutes. Discard bay leaf; season to taste with salt and pepper. Garnish each bowl of soup with parsley.

TOMATO BISQUE

Smoked pork hocks give a rich flavor to this tomato soup.

8 first-course servings

1 each: chopped large onion, small carrot, small red bell pepper

2 each: sliced ribs celery, minced garlic cloves

1½ teaspoons olive oil

2 tablespoons flour

2½ cups Beef Stock (see p. 5)

1 can (28 ounces) crushed tomatoes

1 can (6 ounces) tomato paste

2 small smoked pork hocks (about 1¼ pounds)

½ cup diced peeled potatoes

1 teaspoon dried thyme leaves

½ teaspoon each: ground allspice, curry powder

1½ cups 1% low-fat milk

1 teaspoon sugar

Salt and pepper, to taste

Per Serving:
Calories: 123
% calories from fat: 13
Protein (g): 6.5
Carbohydrate (g): 20.1
Fat (g): 1.8
Saturated fat (g): 0.6
Cholesterol (mg): 4.1
Sodium (mg): 500

Exchanges:
Milk: 0.0
Vegetable: 0.0
Fruit: 0.5
Bread: 1.5
Meat: 0.0
Fat: 0.5

1. Sauté onion, carrot, bell pepper, celery, and garlic in oil in large saucepan until softened, about 5 minutes. Stir in flour; cook 1 to 2 minutes. Stir in stock, tomatoes, tomato paste, pork hocks, potato, and seasonings; heat to boiling. Reduce heat and simmer, covered, 15 minutes. Discard pork hocks. Process soup in food processor or blender until smooth; return mixture to saucepan and add milk and sugar. Cook, covered, over medium heat until hot; do not boil. Season to taste with salt and pepper.

TOMATO ESSENCE

Use three or four of your favorite herbs in this soup.

6 first-course servings

1 medium onion, chopped
1 cup loosely packed mixed herbs, coarsely chopped
1 teaspoon olive oil
4 tomatoes, chopped
½ cup reduced-sodium tomato paste
2 cups Chicken Stock (see p. 2)
1 cup fat-free milk
2 tablespoons sugar
Salt and white pepper, to taste
¼ cup (1 ounce) grated Parmesan cheese

Per Serving:
Calories: 110
% calories from fat: 22
Protein (g): 5.9
Carbohydrate (g): 17
Fat (g): 3
Saturated fat (g): 1.2
Cholesterol (mg): 5.8
Sodium (mg): 153

Exchanges:
Milk: 0.0
Vegetable: 3.0
Fruit: 0.0
Bread: 0.0
Meat: 0.0
Fat: 0.5

1. Sauté onion and herbs in oil in large saucepan until onion is tender, about 5 minutes. Stir in tomatoes, tomato paste, and stock; heat to boiling. Reduce heat and simmer, covered, 15 minutes. Process soup in food processor or blender until smooth; return to saucepan and stir in milk and sugar. Heat over medium heat until hot; do not boil. Season to taste with salt and white pepper. Sprinkle each bowl with Parmesan cheese.

TOMATO-ORANGE SOUP

45

This light and refreshing soup requires no cooking—a bonus for a busy or hot weather day!

6 first-course servings

2 small oranges, peeled, finely chopped
3 medium tomatoes, peeled, seeded, cubed
¾ cup chopped onion
1 can (14½ ounces) reduced-sodium fat-free
   chicken broth
1 cup reduced-sodium tomato juice
½ cup dry white wine or water
1 tablespoon each: red wine vinegar, sugar

Finely grated zest of 1 orange

Salt and pepper, to taste

Per Serving:
Calories: 78
% calories from fat: 3
Protein (g): 3.2
Carbohydrate (g): 13.7
Fat (g): 0.3
Saturated fat (g): 0
Cholesterol (mg): 0
Sodium (mg): 157

1. Combine all ingredients, except orange zest, salt, and pepper. Refrigerate until chilled; season to taste with salt and pepper. Sprinkle each bowl of soup with orange zest.

Exchanges:
Milk: 0.0
Vegetable: 3.0
Fruit: 0.0
Bread: 0.0
Meat: 0.0
Fat: 0.0

TWO-TOMATO SOUP

45 *The concentrated flavor of sun-dried tomatoes enhances the taste of garden-ripe tomato soup.*

6 first-course servings

Per Serving:
Calories: 117
% calories from fat: 5
Protein (g): 3.7
Carbohydrate (g): 22.6
Fat (g): 0.8
Saturated fat (g): 0.1
Cholesterol (mg): 0
Sodium (mg): 150

1 cup chopped onion

½ cup each: chopped celery, carrot

2 teaspoons minced roasted garlic

4 cups each: reduced-sodium fat-free chicken broth, chopped ripe or canned tomatoes

1 large Idaho potato, peeled, cubed

½ cup sun-dried tomatoes (not in oil), softened

½ teaspoon dried basil leaves

½ cup fat-free half-and-half or fat-free milk

2–3 teaspoons sugar

Salt and pepper, to taste

Exchanges:
Milk: 0.0
Vegetable: 2.0
Fruit: 0.0
Bread: 1.0
Meat: 0.0
Fat: 0.0

1. Sauté onion, celery, carrot, and garlic in lightly greased large saucepan until lightly browned, 5 to 8 minutes. Add broth, tomatoes, potato, sun-dried tomatoes, and basil; heat to boiling. Reduce heat and simmer, covered, until vegetables are tender, 10 to 15 minutes. Process soup in food processor or blender until smooth; return to saucepan. Stir in half-and-half and cook over medium heat until hot, 3 to 5 minutes; season to taste with sugar, salt, and pepper.

VARIATION

Baked Two-Tomato Soup — Make soup as above. Ladle into oven-proof bowls. Thaw 1 sheet (½ package) frozen puff pastry according to package directions. Cut 6 rounds the size of tops of bowls and place on top of soup, pressing gently to rim of bowls. Brush with beaten egg, and sprinkle each with 1 to 2 teaspoons grated Parmesan cheese. Bake at 375 degrees until dough is puffed and golden, about 20 minutes.

ZESTY TOMATO-VEGETABLE SOUP

45 | *Italian tomatoes make this full-flavored vegetable soup especially good.*

6 first-course servings

1 each: chopped medium onion, large rib celery, medium carrot, red bell pepper

1½ teaspoons olive oil

1 cup reduced-sodium beef broth

1 can (28 ounces) Italian plum tomatoes, undrained

¼ cup dry white wine or beef broth

1 teaspoon lemon juice

¾ teaspoon celery salt

Pinch crushed red pepper

Salt and pepper, to taste

Per Serving:
Calories: 81
% calories from fat: 15
Protein (g): 3.1
Carbohydrate (g): 11.6
Fat (g): 1.3
Saturated fat (g): 0.2
Cholesterol (mg): 0
Sodium (mg): 608

Exchanges:
Milk: 0.0
Vegetable: 2.0
Fruit: 0.0
Bread: 0.0
Meat: 0.0
Fat: 0.5

1. Sauté onion, celery, carrot, and bell pepper in oil in large saucepan until vegetables are tender, about 10 minutes. Stir in remaining ingredients, except salt and pepper; heat to boiling. Reduce heat and simmer, covered, until vegetables are tender, about 15 minutes. Process soup in food processor or blender until smooth; season to taste with salt and pepper. Refrigerate until chilled.

SUN-DRIED TOMATO AND LINGUINE SOUP

45 *Great soup in less than 45 minutes! One-half cup uncooked orzo can be substituted for the linguine, if preferred.*

4 first-course servings

½ cup thinly sliced celery

2 tablespoons thinly sliced green onions

2 cloves garlic, minced

2 cans (14½ ounces each) reduced-sodium chicken broth

2 ounces uncooked linguine, broken into pieces (3-inch)

2 sun-dried tomatoes (not in oil), softened, finely chopped

1–2 teaspoons lemon juice

Salt and pepper, to taste

Per Serving:
Calories: 111
% calories from fat: 10
Protein (g): 3.3
Carbohydrate (g): 16.8
Fat (g): 1.3
Saturated fat (g): 0.1
Cholesterol (mg): 0
Sodium (mg): 155

Exchanges:
Milk: 0.0
Vegetable: 1.0
Fruit: 0.0
Bread: 1.0
Meat: 0.0
Fat: 0.0

1. Sauté celery, onions, and garlic in lightly greased medium saucepan until tender, 5 to 7 minutes. Stir in broth and heat to boiling; add linguine and sun-dried tomatoes. Reduce heat and simmer, uncovered, until pasta is *al dente*, about 10 minutes. Season with lemon juice, salt, and pepper.

LIGHTLY CREAMED VEGETABLE SOUP

45

Fat-free milk, whipped with an immersion blender, lends a wonderful rich texture to this fragrant creamed soup. Or, if desired, just stir the milk into the soup near the end of the cooking time.

6 first-course servings

1 cup each: sliced onion, carrots, yellow
  summer squash
⅔ cup each: chopped green and red bell pepper, celery
1 clove garlic, minced
1½ tablespoons margarine or butter
4 cups reduced-sodium fat-free chicken broth
4 peppercorns
3 whole cloves
1 bay leaf
⅓ cup all-purpose flour
⅔ cup water
Salt and pepper, to taste
½ cup fat-free milk

Per Serving:
Calories: 112
% calories from fat: 27
Protein (g): 3.4
Carbohydrate (g): 18
Fat (g): 3.6
Saturated fat (g): 0.7
Cholesterol (mg): 0.3
Sodium (mg): 73

Exchanges:
Milk: 0.0
Vegetable: 2.0
Fruit: 0.0
Bread: 0.5
Meat: 0.0
Fat: 0.5

1. Sauté vegetables in margarine in large saucepan until onion is tender, 8 to 10 minutes. Add broth and herbs, tied in a cheesecloth bag; heat to boiling. Reduce heat and simmer, covered, until vegetables are tender, 10 to 15 minutes; discard cheesecloth bag. Heat soup to boiling; stir in combined flour and water, stirring, until thickened, about 1 minute. Season to taste with salt and pepper. Just before serving, whip fat-free milk with an immersion blender or process in blender at high speed 30 seconds; stir into soup.

LIME-SCENTED VEGETABLE SOUP

A soup with a fresh flavor, accented with lime and cilantro.

6 first-course servings

2 cups sliced carrots
¾ cup each: chopped red bell pepper, sliced celery
½ cup sliced green onions

6 cloves garlic, minced

1 small jalapeño chili, finely chopped

6 cups reduced-sodium fat-free chicken broth

½–¾ cup lime juice

½ teaspoon ground cumin

1 cup chopped tomato

½ cup each: chopped cucumber, avocado

Finely chopped cilantro

1½ cups Herb Croutons (½ recipe) (see p. 636)

Per Serving:
Calories: 106
% calories from fat: 29
Protein (g): 3.3
Carbohydrate (g): 17.6
Fat (g): 3.9
Saturated fat (g): 0.1
Cholesterol (mg): 0
Sodium (mg): 100

Exchanges:
Milk: 0.0
Vegetable: 2.0
Fruit: 0.0
Bread: 0.5
Meat: 0.0
Fat: 0.5

1. Sauté carrots, bell pepper, celery, green onions, garlic, and jalapeño chili in lightly greased saucepan 5 minutes. Add broth, lime juice, and cumin to saucepan; heat to boiling. Reduce heat and simmer, covered, until vegetables are tender, 10 to 15 minutes. Add tomato, cucumber, and avocado to each bowl of soup; sprinkle with cilantro and Herb Croutons.

GARDEN SOUP

A light, colorful soup showcasing an appealing blend of vegetables and herbs.

6 first-course servings

1 cup chopped onion

½ cup each: diced red bell pepper, celery, carrots

2 garlic cloves, minced

1 tablespoon olive oil

1½ quarts Chicken Stock (see p. 2)

1 cup cooked dried or rinsed, drained canned
  cannellini beans

1 bay leaf

1½ teaspoons dried Italian seasoning

½ cup each: diced yellow summer squash, zucchini

2 medium tomatoes, diced

Salt and pepper, to taste

Per Serving:
Calories: 124
% calories from fat: 19
Protein (g): 8.8
Carbohydrate (g): 17.8
Fat (g): 2.7
Saturated fat (g): 0.4
Cholesterol (mg): 0
Sodium (mg): 366

Exchanges:
Milk: 0.0
Vegetable: 1.0
Fruit: 0.0
Bread: 1.0
Meat: 0.0
Fat: 0.5

1. Sauté onion, bell pepper, celery, carrots, and garlic in oil in large saucepan until onion is tender, about 5 minutes. Add stock, beans, and herbs; heat to boiling. Reduce heat and simmer, covered, 30 minutes, adding squash and tomatoes during last 10 minutes. Discard bay leaf; season to taste with salt and pepper.

STRACCIATELLE WITH TINY MEATBALLS

Stracciatelle means "torn rags," which is what the egg whites look like when you stir them into the hot soup.

8 first-course servings

1 quart Chicken Stock (see p. 2)

2 cups water

½ cup each: pastina or other small soup pasta, chopped celery, onion, sliced carrot

8 ounces spinach, sliced

Turkey Meatballs (recipe follows)

Salt and pepper, to taste

2 egg whites, lightly beaten

Shredded Parmesan cheese, as garnish

Per Serving:
Calories: 87
% calories from fat: 28
Protein (g): 7.3
Carbohydrate (g): 8.8
Fat (g): 2.7
Saturated fat (g): 0.7
Cholesterol (mg): 10.8
Sodium (mg): 94

Exchanges:
Milk: 0.0
Vegetable: 1.0
Fruit: 0.0
Bread: 0.0
Meat: 1.0
Fat: 0.0

1. Heat stock, water, pastina, and vegetables to boiling in large in large saucepan; add Turkey Meatballs. Reduce heat and simmer, uncovered, or until meatballs are cooked and pasta is *al dente*, about 10 minutes. Season to taste with salt and pepper. Slowly stir egg whites into soup; garnish each bowl of soup with Parmesan cheese.

Turkey Meatballs
Makes 24 small meatballs

8 ounces ground lean turkey

½ small onion, minced

2 tablespoons seasoned dry bread crumbs

1 tablespoon each: chopped parsley, grated Parmesan cheese

2 tablespoons tomato paste

1. Mix all ingredients; form into small meatballs using about 2 teaspoons mixture for each.

PASTA SOUP WITH GREENS

Use any of your favorite greens in this soup, or try a combination of greens.

4 first-course servings

1 each: chopped medium leek (white part only),
  small onion
1–2 teaspoons olive oil
1 quart Low-Salt Chicken Stock (see p. 3)
1½ teaspoons dried marjoram leaves
¼ cup acini de pepe or stellini
1½ cups chopped escarole or kale
Salt and pepper, to taste
2–3 tablespoons grated Parmesan cheese, as garnish

Per Serving:
Calories: 88
% calories from fat: 23
Protein (g): 4.2
Carbohydrate (g): 13
Fat (g): 2.3
Saturated fat (g): 0.7
Cholesterol (mg): 5.4
Sodium (mg): 61

Exchanges:
Milk: 0.0
Vegetable: 0.0
Fruit: 0.0
Bread: 1.0
Meat: 0.0
Fat: 0.5

1. Sauté leek and onion in oil in large saucepan until lightly browned. Add stock, marjoram, pasta, and escarole; heat to boiling. Reduce heat and simmer, uncovered, until pasta is tender, about 10 minutes. Season to taste with salt and pepper; sprinkle each bowl of soup with Parmesan cheese.

SUMMER SNOW PEA SOUP

45 *Make this soup a day in advance so that flavors can blend.*

6 first-course servings

½ cup each: chopped green onions, yellow onion
1 tablespoon margarine or butter
4 cups reduced-sodium fat-free chicken broth
1 pound snow peas, trimmed
4 cups coarsely chopped romaine lettuce
½ teaspoon each: dried tarragon and mint leaves
Salt and white pepper, to taste
6 tablespoons plain fat-free sour cream

Per Serving:
Calories: 76
% calories from fat: 28
Protein (g): 4.3
Carbohydrate (g): 9.8
Fat (g): 2.5
Saturated fat (g): 0.5
Cholesterol (mg): 0.3
Sodium (mg): 47

Exchanges:
Milk: 0.0
Vegetable: 2.0
Fruit: 0.0
Bread: 0.0
Meat: 0.0
Fat: 0.5

1. Sauté onions in margarine in large saucepan until tender, about 5 minutes. Add remaining ingredients, except salt, pepper, and sour cream; heat to boiling. Reduce heat and simmer, covered, until snow peas are very tender, about 15 minutes. Process soup in food processor or blender until smooth; strain and discard solids. Season to taste with salt and white pepper. Serve warm or chilled; garnish each bowl of soup with a dollop of sour cream.

VEGETABLE-BARLEY SOUP

Any vegetables you like can be substituted in this versatile soup.

8 first-course servings

2 quarts Beef Stock (see p. 5)
1 can (15 ounces) tomato sauce
½ cup finely chopped parsley
2 cups each: cubed potatoes, cut green beans, thinly sliced cabbage
⅓ cup quick-cooking barley
1 tablespoon dried Italian seasoning
1 to 2 teaspoons chili powder
Salt and pepper, to taste

Per Serving:
Calories: 108
% calories from fat: 9
Protein (g): 3.5
Carbohydrate (g): 22.7
Fat (g): 1.1
Saturated fat (g): 0.2
Cholesterol (mg): 0.3
Sodium (mg): 111

Exchanges:
Milk: 0.0
Vegetable: 0.0
Fruit: 0.0
Bread: 1.5
Meat: 0.0
Fat: 0.0

1. Heat all ingredients, except salt and pepper, to boiling in Dutch oven; reduce heat and simmer until vegetables are tender, about 20 minutes. Season to taste with salt and pepper.

ONION AND LEEK SOUP WITH PASTA

Soup pasta, small shells, or bow ties can be alternate pasta choices.

6 first-course servings

4 cups sliced onions
2 cups sliced leeks (white parts only)
6 cloves garlic, minced
1 teaspoon sugar
7 cups reduced-sodium fat-free chicken broth
4 ounces uncooked small pasta rings
Salt and white pepper, to taste
6 teaspoons grated Parmesan cheese

1. Cook onions, leeks, and garlic in lightly greased large saucepan, covered, over medium heat until onions are wilted, 5 to 8 minutes. Stir in sugar; cook, uncovered, over medium-low heat until onion mixture is very soft and golden, 15 to 20 minutes. Add broth to saucepan and heat to boiling; add pasta, reduce heat, and simmer, uncovered, until pasta is *al dente*, 6 to 8 minutes. Season to taste with salt and white pepper. Sprinkle each bowl of soup with 1 teaspoon Parmesan cheese over each.

Per Serving:
Calories: 211
% calories from fat: 3
Protein (g): 12.9
Carbohydrate (g): 37.1
Fat (g): 0.8
Saturated fat (g): 0.1
Cholesterol (mg): 0
Sodium (mg): 234

Exchanges:
Milk: 0.0
Vegetable: 2.0
Fruit: 0.0
Bread: 2.0
Meat: 0.0
Fat: 0.0

BEAN AND BARLEY SOUP WITH KALE

Serve this nutritious soup with Tomato-Basil Focaccia (see p. 642).

8 first-course servings

1½ cups chopped onions
1 cup chopped carrots
8 ounces mushrooms, sliced
1 teaspoon minced garlic
¼ teaspoon crushed red pepper
2 teaspoons each: dried thyme leaves, olive oil
7 cups Fragrant Beef Stock (see p. 6)
½ cup quick-cooking barley
2 cans (15 ounces each) Great Northern beans, rinsed, drained
3–4 cups sliced kale
1 tablespoon lemon juice
Salt and pepper, to taste

Per Serving:
Calories: 183
% calories from fat: 10
Protein (g): 11.7
Carbohydrate (g): 35.6
Fat (g): 2.3
Saturated fat (g): 0.5
Cholesterol (mg): 2.6
Sodium (mg): 350

Exchanges:
Milk: 0.0
Vegetable: 1.0
Fruit: 0.0
Bread: 2.0
Meat: 0.0
Fat: 0.5

1. Sauté onions, carrots, mushrooms, garlic, red pepper, and thyme in olive oil in large saucepan until tender, about 10 minutes. Stir in remaining ingredients, except lemon juice, salt, and pepper. Heat to boiling; reduce heat and simmer, covered, until barley is tender, about 15 minutes. Stir in lemon juice; season to taste with salt and pepper.

NAVY BEAN AND SPINACH SOUP

A delicious, hearty soup with the meaty taste of smoked pork.

6 first-course servings

1½ cups dried navy beans

1 large onion, chopped

2 garlic cloves, minced

2 teaspoons olive oil

2 quarts Low-Salt Chicken Stock (see p. 3)

¼ cup pearl barley

1 smoked pork hock (optional)

2 each: sliced large carrots, ribs celery, bay leaves

¾ teaspoon each: dried marjoram, thyme, and
   basil leaves

1 can (14½ ounces) reduced-sodium stewed tomatoes

1 package (10 ounces) frozen chopped spinach, thawed

Salt and cayenne pepper, to taste

Per Serving:
Calories: 225
% calories from fat: 8
Protein (g): 16
Carbohydrate (g): 37.6
Fat (g): 2.2
Saturated fat (g): 0.4
Cholesterol (mg): 1.3
Sodium (mg): 385

Exchanges:
Milk: 0.0
Vegetable: 1.0
Fruit: 0.0
Bread: 2.0
Meat: 1.0
Fat: 0.0

1. Cover beans with 2 inches water in large saucepan and heat to boiling. Reduce heat and boil 2 minutes. Remove from heat; let stand, covered, 1 hour. Drain.

2. Sauté onion and garlic in olive oil in large saucepan until onion is tender, about 5 minutes. Add beans and remaining ingredients, except tomatoes, spinach, salt, and cayenne pepper; heat to boiling. Reduce heat and simmer, covered, until beans are tender, about 1 hour. Discard pork hock and bay leaves. Add tomatoes with liquid and spinach; simmer, until hot, about 5 minutes. Season to taste with salt and cayenne pepper.

LENTIL SOUP WITH ORZO

For a hearty vegetarian dinner, make this soup with Roasted Vegetable Stock (see p. 11).

6 first-course servings

1½ cups chopped onions

¾ cup chopped carrot, celery

1 tablespoon minced garlic

1 teaspoon dried oregano leaves

⅛–¼ teaspoon crushed red pepper

2 teaspoons olive oil

2 cups Quick-Spiced Beef Stock (see p. 6)

2 cans (14½ ounces each) Italian-style
  stewed tomatoes

1 cup water

8 ounces dried lentils

4 ounces uncooked orzo or other small soup pasta

2 cups packed spinach, sliced

Salt and pepper, to taste

Per Serving:
Calories: 212
% calories from fat: 9
Protein (g): 12.3
Carbohydrate (g): 45 7
Fat (g): 24
Saturated fat (g): 0.3
Cholesterol (mg): 0
Sodium (mg): 293

Exchanges:
Milk: 0.0
Vegetable: 2.0
Fruit: 0.0
Bread: 2 0
Meat: 1.0
Fat: 0.0

1. Sauté onions, carrot, celery, garlic, oregano, and crushed red pepper in oil in large saucepan until onion is tender, about 8 minutes. Stir in stock, tomatoes with liquid, water, and lentils. Heat to boiling; reduce heat and simmer, covered, until lentils are tender, about 30 minutes. Stir in orzo and simmer, uncovered, until tender, about 10 minutes. Stir in spinach; season to taste with salt and pepper.

SAUSAGE AND LENTIL SOUP

Thick, hearty, and accented with the robust flavor of Italian sausage.

10 first-course servings

8–12 ounces reduced-fat Italian-style turkey sausage, casing removed
1½ cups chopped onions
¾ cup chopped carrots
1 pound dried lentils
3 quarts Beef Stock (see p. 5)
1 can (28 ounces) reduced-sodium crushed tomatoes
½ teaspoon each: dried marjoram and thyme leaves
1 bay leaf
2–3 teaspoons lemon juice
Salt and pepper, to taste

Per Serving:
Calories: 192
% calories from fat: 15
Protein (g): 14.3
Carbohydrate (g): 28.8
Fat (g): 3.4
Saturated fat (g): 0.8
Cholesterol (mg): 12.5
Sodium (mg): 202

Exchanges:
Milk: 0.0
Vegetable: 0.0
Fruit: 0.0
Bread: 2.0
Meat: 1.0
Fat: 0.0

1. Cook sausage, onions, and carrots in large saucepan over medium heat until sausage is browned, about 8 minutes; crumble sausage with a fork. Add lentils, stock, tomatoes, and herbs; heat to boiling. Reduce heat and simmer, covered, until lentils are tender, about 30 minutes. Discard bay leaf; season to taste with lemon juice, salt, and pepper.

VARIATION

Lentil Soup with Fennel — Make recipe as above, omitting Italian sausage. Sauté ½ cup sliced fennel bulb with the onions and carrots. Substitute 1 teaspoon lightly crushed fennel seeds for the marjoram and thyme. Process soup in food processor or blender until smooth; garnish soup with finely chopped fennel tops.

SPLIT-PEA SOUP JARDINIERE

This "gardener's style" split-pea soup is flavored the old-fashioned way with a ham bone and leeks, turnips, and carrots.

8 first-course servings

1 pound dried split green peas

2½ quarts water

1 each: meaty ham bone, quartered small onion, bay leaf

4 whole cloves

2 teaspoons dried thyme leaves

2 each: sliced leeks (white parts only), ribs celery, carrots, cubed small turnips, chopped large tomatoes, minced cloves garlic

Salt and pepper, to taste

Per Serving:
Calories: 175
% calories from fat: 6
Protein (g): 11.6
Carbohydrate (g): 31.5
Fat (g): 1.2
Saturated fat (g): 0.3
Cholesterol (mg): 4.8
Sodium (mg): 156

Exchanges:
Milk 0.0
Vegetable: 2.0
Fruit: 0.0
Bread: 1.0
Meat: 1.0
Fat: 0.0

1. Heat split peas, water, ham bone, quartered onion, bay leaf, cloves, and thyme, to boiling in large saucepan; reduce heat and simmer, covered, 2 hours. Remove ham bone; remove and shred meat. Discard bone. Strain broth and discard solids. Return broth and ham to pan; add vegetables and garlic and heat to boiling. Reduce heat and simmer until vegetables are tender and soup is thick, 20 to 30 minutes. Season to taste with salt and pepper.

VARIATIONS

Canadian Pea Soup — Make soup as above, substituting yellow split peas for the green split peas, 2 to 4 ounces diced lean salt pork for the ham bone and ham, and 2 parsnips, diced, for the turnip. Omit celery.

Dutch Split-Pea Soup — Make soup as above, omitting ham bone, onion, and cloves and substituting ½ cup diced celery root for the parsnips. When vegetables are tender, purée soup in food processor or blender; season to taste with salt and pepper and stir in 8 ounces sliced and browned reduced-fat smoked sausage.

SPINACH-PASTA SOUP WITH BASIL

Serve this fragrant soup with Garlic Bread or Spinach Mushroom Flatbread (see pp. 645, 640).

4 first-course servings

1 each: finely chopped small onion, minced
   garlic clove
2 teaspoons olive oil
1½ quarts Chicken Stock (see p. 2)
1 cup water
¾ cup uncooked broken vermicelli (2-inch)
1 package (10 ounces) frozen chopped spinach, thawed
¼ cup chopped fresh or 1 tablespoon dried
   basil leaves
1 cup each: chopped plum tomatoes, rinsed drained
   canned garbanzo beans
Salt and pepper, to taste
2 tablespoons grated Parmesan cheese, as garnish

Per Serving:
Calories: 193
% calories from fat: 18
Protein (g): 13.3
Carbohydrate (g): 27.6
Fat (g): 3.9
Saturated fat (g): 0.9
Cholesterol (mg): 2
Sodium (mg): 563

Exchanges:
Milk: 0.0
Vegetable: 0.0
Fruit: 0.0
Bread: 2.0
Meat: 1.0
Fat: 0.0

1. Sauté onion and garlic in oil in large saucepan until tender, about 5 minutes. Add stock and water; heat to boiling. Add vermicelli; reduce heat, and simmer, uncovered, until tender, 7 to 10 minutes. Add remaining ingredients, except salt, pepper, and Parmesan cheese; simmer, uncovered, 5 minutes. Season to taste with salt and pepper. Sprinkle each bowl of soup with Parmesan cheese.

THREE

Chowders

SHRIMP-CORN CHOWDER

45 *A quick and easy soup to make, thanks to canned and frozen ingredients.*

6 entrée servings

2 slices reduced-sodium bacon

⅓ cup each: chopped onion, celery

1 can (10½ ounces) cream of shrimp soup

1½ cups fat-free milk

2 cups cubed frozen potatoes

1½ cups whole kernel corn

12 ounces small shrimp, peeled, deveined

Salt and cayenne pepper, to taste

Per Serving:
Calories: 176
% calories from fat: 18
Protein (g): 14.9
Carbohydrate (g): 22.4
Fat (g): 3.6
Saturated fat (g): 1.8
Cholesterol (mg): 96
Sodium (mg): 577

Exchanges:
Milk: 0.0
Vegetable: 0.0
Fruit: 0.0
Bread: 1.5
Meat: 1.0
Fat: 0.0

1. Fry bacon in medium saucepan until crisp; drain well. Drain all but 2 teaspoons fat from saucepan; add onion and celery and sauté until tender, about 5 minutes. Stir in soup and milk until smooth. Stir in potatoes and corn and heat to boiling; reduce heat and simmer, covered, until potatoes are tender, about 5 minutes. Add shrimp and simmer until cooked, about 5 minutes. Season to taste with salt and cayenne pepper.

PARSLEY CHOWDER

Use Italian parsley for the boldest herb flavor in this unusual chowder.

6 first-course servings

1 quart Rich Chicken Stock (see p. 4)

2 cups packed parsley sprigs

½ cup each: chopped onion, celery

1 tablespoon margarine or butter

2 teaspoons sugar

2 cups diced peeled potatoes

1 cup fat-free milk

¼ cup all-purpose flour

2 tablespoons dry sherry (optional)

¼ cup finely chopped parsley

Salt and pepper, to taste

Per Serving:
Calories: 140
% calories from fat: 18.1
Protein (g): 6.9
Carbohydrate (g): 21.3
Fat (g): 2.8
Saturated fat (g): 0.5
Cholesterol (mg): 1.5
Sodium (mg): 87

Exchanges:
Milk: 0.0
Vegetable: 0.0
Fruit: 0.0
Bread: 1.5
Meat: 0.0
Fat: 0.5

1. Heat stock and 2 cups parsley to boiling in large saucepan; reduce heat and simmer, covered, 30 minutes. Strain; reserve stock. Sauté onion and celery in margarine in large saucepan until tender, about 8 minutes. Sprinkle with sugar and cook 1 minute. Stir in reserved stock and potatoes and heat to boiling; reduce heat and simmer, covered, until potatoes are tender, about 10 minutes. Heat to boiling; stir in combined milk and flour, stirring until thickened, about 1 minute. Reduce heat and add sherry; simmer 2 to 3 minutes. Stir in chopped parsley; season to taste with salt and pepper.

VARIATION

Pesto Chowder — Make recipe as above, substituting basil for the parsley and olive oil for the margarine; omit celery and sherry. Sprinkle each bowl of soup with freshly grated Parmesan cheese.

LEEK CHOWDER WITH HAM

45 *Horseradish mustard and Worcestershire sauce team up to give this dish a flavor that's especially pleasing and memorable.*

4 entrée servings

8 ounces lean ham, cubed

3 leeks (white parts only) sliced

1 teaspoon olive oil

1 can (14½ ounces) fat-free chicken broth

2 large Idaho potatoes, peeled, cubed (¼-inch)

1 bay leaf

1 teaspoon each: horseradish mustard, Worcestershire sauce

½ cup fat-free milk

Salt and white pepper, to taste

Per Serving:
Calories: 281
% calories from fat: 16
Protein (g): 21.2
Carbohydrate (g): 37.7
Fat (g): 5
Saturated fat (g): 1.5
Cholesterol (mg): 32.3
Sodium (mg): 881

Exchanges:
Milk: 0.0
Vegetable: 0.0
Fruit: 0.0
Bread: 2.5
Meat: 2.0
Fat: 0.0

1. Cook ham and leeks in oil in large saucepan over medium heat until leeks are translucent, 6 to 8 minutes. Remove from saucepan and reserve. Add broth, potatoes, and bay leaf; heat to boiling. Reduce heat and simmer, covered, until potatoes are tender, about 15 minutes; discard bay leaf. Process soup in food processor or blender until smooth; return to saucepan. Stir in mustard, Worcestershire sauce, milk, and reserved ham and leeks. Cook over medium heat until hot, about 5 minutes; season to taste with salt and white pepper.

FLORIDA AVOCADO AND TOMATO CHOWDER

45 | *In this easy recipe, colorful ingredients create a kaleidoscope of fresh colors and flavors.*

4 entrée servings

3 cups cubed, peeled potatoes

1 can (14 ounces) reduced-sodium fat-free chicken broth

1 teaspoon dried thyme leaves

8 ounces smoked turkey breast, cubed

1 cup each: whole kernel corn, chopped plum tomatoes, cubed avocado

Juice of 1 lime

3 slices bacon, cooked, crumbled

Salt and pepper, to taste

Per Serving:
Calories: 333
% calories from fat: 26
Protein (g): 21
Carbohydrate (g): 44.7
Fat (g): 10.2
Saturated fat (g): 2.4
Cholesterol (mg): 51.1
Sodium (mg): 765

Exchanges:
Milk: 0.0
Vegetable: 2.0
Fruit: 0.0
Bread: 2.0
Meat: 2.0
Fat: 1.5

1. Heat potatoes, broth, and thyme to boiling in medium saucepan; reduce heat and simmer, covered, until potatoes are tender, about 10 minutes. Using slotted spoon, transfer ½ the potatoes to a medium bowl. Process remaining mixture in food processor or blender until smooth; return to saucepan. Add turkey, corn, and reserved potatoes; heat to boiling. Reduce heat and simmer 5 minutes. Stir in tomatoes, avocado, lime juice, and bacon. Season to taste with salt and pepper.

FRESH TOMATO-ZUCCHINI CHOWDER

45 *Savor summer's bounty in this lively chowder of basil, tomatoes, and zucchini. Bacon adds a delightful smoky accent.*

4 first-course servings

1 cup chopped onion

1 can (14½ ounces) vegetable broth

1 medium potato, cubed

1 cup cubed zucchini

¼ cup whole kernel corn

1 pound plum tomatoes, chopped

¼ cup finely chopped fresh or 1 tablespoon dried basil leaves

Salt and cayenne pepper, to taste

2 slices turkey bacon, fried crisp, crumbled

Per Serving:
Calories: 138
% calories from fat: 12
Protein (g): 4.9
Carbohydrate (g): 28.8
Fat (g): 2
Saturated fat (g): 0.4
Cholesterol (mg): 5
Sodium (mg): 463

Exchanges:
Milk: 0.0
Vegetable: 1.0
Fruit: 0.0
Bread: 1.5
Meat: 0.0
Fat: 0.0

1. Sauté onion in lightly greased large saucepan until tender, 3 to 4 minutes. Add remaining ingredients, except basil, salt, cayenne pepper, and bacon; heat to boiling. Reduce heat and simmer, covered, until potatoes are tender, about 15 minutes. Stir in basil; season to taste with salt and cayenne pepper. Sprinkle each bowl of soup with crumbled bacon.

VARIATION

Green Garden Chowder — Make chowder as above, omitting corn, and adding 1 cup each small broccoli florets, and cut green beans. Stir in 1 cup sliced spinach or kale during last 3 to 4 minutes cooking time. Sprinkle each bowl of soup with crumbled bacon and grated Parmesan cheese.

POTATO CHOWDER

45 *Substitute any desired vegetables in this versatile soup, such as carrots, zucchini, green beans, or corn for a delectable vegetable chowder.*

6 entrée servings (about 1 cup each)

1 cup chopped onion

¼ cup thinly sliced celery

2 tablespoons margarine or butter

3 tablespoons flour

2 cups reduced-sodium chicken broth

3½ cups peeled, cubed Idaho potatoes

¼–½ teaspoon celery seeds

2 cups fat-free milk

Salt and pepper, to taste

Per Serving:
Calories: 212
% calories from fat: 17
Protein (g): 7.5
Carbohydrate (g): 37.1
Fat (g): 4.2
Saturated fat (g): 0.9
Cholesterol (mg): 1.3
Sodium (mg): 210

Exchanges:
Milk: 0.0
Vegetable: 1.0
Fruit: 0.0
Bread: 2.0
Meat: 0.0
Fat: 1.0

1. Sauté onion and celery in margarine or butter in large saucepan until tender, 5 to 8 minutes; stir in flour and cook 1 minute longer. Add broth, potatoes, and celery seeds to saucepan; heat to boiling. Reduce heat and simmer, covered, until potatoes are tender, 10 to 15 minutes. Stir in milk and cook until hot, 2 to 3 minutes. Season to taste with salt and pepper.

VARIATIONS

Easy Vichyssoise — Make recipe as above, substituting chopped leek for half the onion and omitting celery and celery seeds. Cool; process soup in food processor or blender until smooth. Refrigerate until chilled. Serve in bowls; sprinkle with minced fresh chives.

Potato Chowder au Gratin — Make recipe as above. Process half the chowder in food processor or blender until almost smooth; return to saucepan and heat 2 to 3 minutes. Pour into 6 ovenproof bowls; top each with 2 tablespoons shredded Cheddar cheese and sprinkle lightly with ground nutmeg. Bake at 500 degrees until cheese is melted, about 5 minutes.

POTATO CURRY CHOWDER

The curry flavor in this chowder is subtle; increase the amount if you prefer.

4 entrée servings

1 cup chopped green onions

3 each: minced cloves garlic, cubed large red potatoes

1 quart Chicken Stock (see p. 2)

1 can (12 ounces) evaporated fat-free milk

1 cup fat-free milk

¾ teaspoon curry powder

½ teaspoon ground cumin

Salt and pepper, to taste

Per Serving:
Calories: 183
% calories from fat: 6
Protein (g): 12.2
Carbohydrate (g): 33.1
Fat (g): 1.2
Saturated fat (g): 0.3
Cholesterol (mg): 8
Sodium (mg): 186

Exchanges:
Milk: 1.0
Vegetable: 0.0
Fruit: 0.0
Bread: 1.5
Meat: 0.0
Fat: 0.0

1. Sauté green onions and garlic in lightly greased large saucepan over medium-low heat, 4 minutes. Add potatoes and stock; heat to boiling. Reduce heat and simmer, covered, until potatoes are tender, about 15 minutes. Stir in remaining ingredients, except salt and pepper, and heat to boiling. Reduce heat and simmer, covered, 10 minutes, stirring occasionally. Season to taste with salt and pepper.

IDAHO CHOWDER WITH CHEESE

Rosemary gives this soup an aromatic flavor.

8 entrée servings

4 cups chopped onions

1 cup chopped celery

2 tablespoons minced garlic

½ teaspoon dried rosemary leaves

6 large Idaho potatoes, peeled, cubed (½-inch)

2 cups Chicken Stock (see p. 2)

4 cups fat-free milk

¼ cup all-purpose flour

⅛ teaspoon ground nutmeg

2 teaspoons low-sodium Worcestershire sauce

1 cup (4 ounces) shredded Swiss cheese

Salt and white pepper, to taste

Per Serving:
Calories: 241
% calories from fat: 17
Protein (g): 11.9
Carbohydrate (g): 38
Fat (g): 4.7
Saturated fat (g): 2.8
Cholesterol (mg): 18.1
Sodium (mg): 111

Exchanges:
Milk: 0.0
Vegetable: 1.0
Fruit: 0.0
Bread: 2.0
Meat: 0.5
Fat: 1.0

1. Cook onions, celery, garlic, and rosemary in lightly greased large saucepan, covered, over low heat until onions are golden brown, about 20 minutes. Add potatoes and stock. Heat to boiling; reduce heat and simmer, covered, until potatoes are tender, about 15 minutes. Heat to boiling; add combined milk, flour, nutmeg, and Worcestershire sauce, stirring until thickened, about 1 minute. Remove chowder from heat; add cheese, stirring until melted; season to taste with salt and white pepper.

VARIATION

Three-Cheese and Potato Chowder — Make recipe as above, substituting ½ cup (2 ounces) each reduced-fat shredded mozzarella and Cheddar cheese and 2 to 4 tablespoons crumbled blue cheese for the Swiss cheese. Sprinkle each bowl of soup with chopped chives.

SMOKY POTATO CHOWDER

A packaged potato mix adds preparation convenience speed to this easy chowder.

4 entrée servings

1 medium onion, coarsely chopped

1–2 tablespoons canola oil

1 package (5½ ounces) au gratin potatoes

2½ cups water

2¼ cups fat-free milk, divided

2–4 ounces reduced-fat smoked sausage

¼ teaspoon dried thyme leaves

Salt and pepper, to taste

Chopped dill weed or parsley, as garnish

Per Serving:
Calories: 248
% calories from fat: 23
Protein (g): 10.1
Carbohydrate (g): 38.5
Fat (g): 6.4
Saturated fat (g): 0.8
Cholesterol (mg): 9.1
Sodium (mg): 928

Exchanges:
Milk: 0.5
Vegetable: 0.0
Fruit: 0.0
Bread: 2.0
Meat: 0.0
Fat: 1.5

1. Sauté onion in oil in large saucepan until tender, about 5 minutes. Stir in potatoes and sprinkle with sauce mix. Stir in water and ¾ cup milk; heat to boiling. Reduce heat and simmer, covered, 30 minutes or until potatoes are tender, stirring occasionally. Add sausage, remaining 1½ cups milk, and thyme; simmer 5 minutes. Season to taste with salt and pepper. Sprinkle each bowl with dill weed.

POTATO, CORN, AND CANADIAN BACON CHOWDER

45 *The Canadian bacon can be sautéed in 1 teaspoon margarine or butter or sautéed until crisp and "frizzled," then sprinkled on the chowder as a garnish.*

6 entrée servings

1 each: chopped large onion, minced garlic clove

2 teaspoons olive oil

3½ cups each: fat-free chicken broth, cubed peeled red potatoes

1 large bay leaf

¾ teaspoon dried thyme leaves

¼ teaspoon dry mustard

2½ cups each: 1% low-fat milk, whole kernel corn

6 ounces Canadian bacon, julienned

Salt and white pepper, to taste

Per Serving:
Calories: 282
% calories from fat: 19
Protein (g): 13.8
Carbohydrate (g): 45.9
Fat (g): 6
Saturated fat (g): 1.7
Cholesterol (mg): 19.3
Sodium (mg): 824

Exchanges:
Milk: 0.0
Vegetable: 0.0
Fruit: 0.0
Bread: 3.0
Meat: 1.0
Fat: 0.5

1. Sauté onion and garlic in oil in large saucepan until tender, about 5 minutes. Add broth, potatoes, bay leaf, thyme, and mustard; heat to boiling. Reduce heat and simmer, covered, until potatoes are tender, about 10 minutes. Add milk and corn; heat to boiling. Reduce heat and simmer, covered, 5 minutes; discard bay leaf. Process half the vegetables and liquid in food processor or blender until smooth; return to saucepan. Stir in Canadian bacon and simmer, covered, 5 minutes. Season to taste with salt and white pepper.

VARIATION

Colcannon Chowder — Make recipe as above, sautéing 2 cups thinly sliced cabbage with the onion and garlic, reducing milk to 2 cups, and omitting corn. Do not purée the mixture. Combine ½ cup reduced-fat sour cream and 1 tablespoon flour; stir into the chowder with the Canadian bacon.

HEARTY CORN AND POTATO CHOWDER

45 *If a thicker soup is desired, mix 2 tablespoons flour with ¼ cup water; stir into boiling soup. Boil, stirring until thickened, about 1 minute.*

4 entrée servings

2 cups whole kernel corn

1 medium onion, chopped

1 tablespoon canola oil

2 cups each: reduced-sodium chicken broth,
   cubed potatoes

½ cup sliced celery

½ teaspoon dried thyme leaves

1¾ cups fat-free half-and-half or fat-free milk

Salt and pepper, to taste

Per Serving:
Calories: 248
% calories from fat: 19
Protein (g): 8.2
Carbohydrate (g): 44.7
Fat (g): 5.6
Saturated fat (g): 1.5
Cholesterol (mg): 5.3
Sodium (mg): 447

Exchanges:
Milk: 0.0
Vegetable: 0.0
Fruit: 0.0
Bread: 3.0
Meat: 0.0
Fat: 1.0

1. Sauté corn and onion in oil in large saucepan until onion is tender, 5 to 8 minutes. Process ½ the vegetable mixture and the broth in food processor or blender until finely chopped; return to saucepan. Add potatoes, celery, and thyme; heat to boiling. Reduce heat and simmer, covered, until vegetables are tender, 10 to 15 minutes. Stir in half-and-half and cook 2 to 3 minutes; season to taste with salt and pepper.

CHEESE AND CORN CHOWDER

45 *A satisfying whole-meal chowder, rich with sausage, cheese, and the flavor of corn.*

6 entrée servings

8 ounces reduced-fat smoked sausage, sliced

1 each: medium chopped onion, red bell pepper, potato, minced clove garlic

3 tablespoons flour

3 cups fat-free milk

2–3 teaspoons chicken bouillon crystals

16 ounces whole kernel corn

1 can (16 ounces) cream-style corn

½–¾ cup (2–3 ounces) shredded Cheddar cheese

1½ cups chopped tomatoes

Salt and pepper, to taste

1½ cups Chili Croutons (½ recipe) (see p. 636)

Per Serving:
Calories: 326
% calories from fat: 16
Protein (g): 18
Carbohydrate (g): 54.7
Fat (g): 6.2
Saturated fat (g): 2.8
Cholesterol (mg): 29.8
Sodium (mg): 786

Exchanges:
Milk: 0.0
Vegetable: 2.0
Fruit: 0.0
Bread: 3.0
Meat: 1.0
Fat: 0.0

1. Stir sausage, onion, bell pepper, potato, and garlic into lightly greased large saucepan and cook until sausage is lightly browned, about 5 minutes; sprinkle with flour and cook 1 to 2 minutes longer. Stir in milk, bouillon crystals, and corn. Heat to boiling; reduce heat and simmer, covered, until tender, about 10 minutes. Add cheese and tomatoes, stirring until cheese is melted. Season to taste with salt and pepper. Serve in bowls; sprinkle with Chili Croutons.

QUICK GNOCCHI CHOWDER WITH SMOKED TURKEY

45 *Often served with butter and Parmesan cheese as a side dish, gnocchi becomes the main attraction in this chowder!*

4 entrée servings

1 cup reduced-sodium fat-free chicken broth

1 can (14½ ounces) reduced-sodium crushed tomatoes

10 ounces smoked turkey breast, cubed

1 package (12 ounces) potato gnocchi

1 teaspoon poultry seasoning

2 cups each: broccoli and cauliflower florets

½ cup chopped fresh or 2 tablespoons dried
    basil leaves

¼ cup (1 ounce) shredded provolone cheese

Salt and pepper, to taste

Per Serving:
Calories: 221
% calories from fat: 17
Protein (g): 16.8
Carbohydrate (g): 30
Fat (g): 4.2
Saturated fat (g): 2.1
Cholesterol (mg): 24.3
Sodium (mg): 7

Exchanges:
Milk: 0.0
Vegetable: 1.0
Fruit: 0.0
Bread: 1.5
Meat: 2.0
Fat: 0.0

1. Heat chicken broth, tomatoes, turkey, gnocchi, and poultry seasoning to boiling in large saucepan; reduce heat and simmer, covered, 5 minutes. Stir in broccoli and cauliflower; simmer until tender, 5 to 8 minutes. Add basil and cheese, stirring until cheese is melted. Season to taste with salt and pepper.

BLACK-EYED PEA AND CORN CHOWDER

45 *Roasted red peppers and bacon enliven this fuss-free, ready-in-a-flash chowder.*

4 first-course servings

1 cup each: fat-free chicken broth, chopped onion

1 can (15 ounces) black-eyed peas, rinsed, drained

1 can (14 ounces) cream-style corn

2 teaspoons minced garlic

1 teaspoon dried savory leaves

1 cup coarsely chopped roasted red peppers

Salt and pepper, to taste

4 slices turkey bacon, cooked, drained, crumbled

Per Serving:
Calories: 153
% calories from fat: 14
Protein (g): 11.3
Carbohydrate (g): 25.5
Fat (g): 2.7
Saturated fat (g): 0.6
Cholesterol (mg): 10
Sodium (mg): 576

Exchanges:
Milk: 0.0
Vegetable: 1.0
Fruit 0.0
Bread: 1.0
Meat: 1.0
Fat: 1.0

1. Heat all ingredients, except roasted peppers, salt, pepper, and bacon, to boiling in large saucepan; reduce heat and simmer, covered, 15 minutes, adding roasted peppers the last 5 minutes. Season to taste with salt and pepper; sprinkle each bowl of soup with bacon.

VARIATION

Red Beans 'n' Greens Chowder — Make recipe as above, substituting red beans for the black-eyed peas, 1½ cups frozen cut okra for the corn, and 1 cup sliced turnip greens or kale for the roasted red peppers.

CARAMELIZED ONION AND BEAN CHOWDER

The onions are cooked very slowly until golden, giving a sweet flavor to the chowder.

8 entrée servings

1½ pounds onions, thinly sliced

2 tablespoons margarine or butter

2 teaspoons sugar

1 quart each: reduced-sodium fat-free chicken
   and beef broth

2 medium potatoes, peeled, cubed

¾ teaspoon dried thyme leaves

1 can (15½ ounces) Great Northern beans,
   rinsed, drained

¼–½ cup dry sherry (optional)

Salt and pepper, to taste

1½ cups Garlic Croutons (½ recipe) (see p. 636)

Per Serving:
Calories: 159
% calories from fat: 17
Protein (g): 10.1
Carbohydrate (g): 25
Fat (g): 3.2
Saturated fat (g): 0.6
Cholesterol (mg): 0
Sodium (mg): 443

Exchanges:
Milk: 0.0
Vegetable: 2.0
Fruit: 0.0
Bread: 1.0
Meat: 0.0
Fat: 0.5

1. Sauté onions in margarine or butter in large saucepan over low heat until tender, about 15 minutes. Stir in sugar; cook until golden brown, about 20 minutes, stirring frequently. Add chicken and beef broth, potatoes, and thyme; heat to boiling. Reduce heat and simmer, covered, until potatoes are tender, about 15 minutes. Stir in beans and sherry; simmer 5 minutes. Season to taste with salt and pepper; sprinkle each bowl of chowder with Garlic Croutons.

NAVY BEAN AND BACON CHOWDER

Use 3 cans (15½ ounces each) navy or Great Northern beans to speed preparation of this flavor-packed dish.

8 entrée servings

1½ cups dried navy beans, rinsed

½ cup each: chopped carrots, onion

2 large cloves garlic, minced

½ teaspoon each: dried oregano, basil, and
   rosemary leaves

1½ quarts Chicken Stock (see p. 2)

1 cup fat-free half-and-half or fat-free milk

Salt and pepper, to taste

8 slices bacon, cooked, crumbled

Per Serving:
Calories: 216
% calories from fat: 18
Protein (g): 13.2
Carbohydrate (g): 31.4
Fat (g): 4.2
Saturated fat (g): 1.3
Cholesterol (mg): 7.9
Sodium (mg): 153

Exchanges:
Milk: 0.0
Vegetable: 0.0
Fruit: 0.0
Bread: 2.0
Meat: 1.0
Fat: 0.5

1. Cover beans with 2 inches cold water in large saucepan; heat to boiling and boil, uncovered, 2 minutes. Remove from heat and let stand, covered, 1 hour; drain.

2. Combine beans and remaining ingredients except half-and-half, salt, pepper, and bacon in large saucepan. Heat to boiling; reduce heat and simmer, covered, until beans are tender, 45 to 60 minutes. Process about 2 cups chowder in food processor or blender until smooth; return to saucepan. Add half-and-half and heat to simmering; season to taste with salt and pepper. Sprinkle each bowl of chowder with bacon.

VARIATION

Mixed Bean Chowder — Make recipe as above, substituting ½ cup each dried Great Northern, pinto, and kidney beans for the navy beans. Do not purée mixture. Heat chowder to boiling; stir in combined ½ cup water and ¼ cup all-purpose flour. Stir until thickened, about 1 minute.

TEX-MEX CHICKEN AND CHEESE CHOWDER

45 *For less heat, plain Jack cheese can be substituted for all or part of the Pepper-Jack cheese.*

4 entrée servings

½ cup finely chopped onion
1 cup cubed zucchini
1½ cups cubed, cooked chicken breast
2 cans (17 ounces) cream-style corn
3 cups fat-free milk
1½ cups (6 ounces) shredded reduced-fat
    Pepper-Jack cheese
Salt and pepper, to taste
Baked Tortilla Chips

Per Serving:
Calories: 279
% calories from fat: 14
Protein (g): 18.2
Carbohydrate (g): 8.9
Fat (g): 6.3
Saturated fat (g): 2.9
Cholesterol (mg): 60.8
Sodium (mg): 673

Exchanges:
Milk: 1.0
Vegetable: 0.0
Fruit: 0.0
Bread: 1.5
Meat: 3.0
Fat: 0.0

1. Sauté onion in lightly greased large saucepan until tender, about 5 minutes; add chicken, corn, and milk and heat to boiling. Reduce heat and simmer, covered, 5 minutes. Reduce heat to low and add cheese, stirring until melted. Season to taste with salt and pepper.

VARIATION

Chicken and Creamed Chowder — Make recipe as above, substituting ½ cup each thinly sliced celery and carrots for the zucchini and Colby cheese for the Pepper-Jack cheese; increase cream-style corn to 2 cans.

CHICKEN CORN CHOWDER

This hearty chowder is thickened in a healthful way—a portion of the ingredients is puréed, then added to the rest of the chowder.

8 entrée servings

3 cups whole kernel corn, thawed
½ cup each: chopped onion, green bell pepper, carrots
1–2 teaspoons each: minced jalapeño chili, garlic
1½ quarts Chicken Stock (see p. 2)
1 pound boneless skinless chicken breast, cubed (½-inch)
2 medium tomatoes, chopped

½ teaspoon each: dried savory and thyme leaves
1–2 cups fat-free half-and-half or fat-free milk
Salt and pepper, to taste

1. Sauté corn, onion, bell pepper, carrots, jalapeño chili, and garlic in lightly greased large saucepan until onion is tender, about 5 minutes. Process half the mixture and 2 cups stock in food processor or blender until smooth; return to saucepan. Add remaining 1 quart stock, chicken, tomatoes, and herbs; heat to boiling. Reduce heat and simmer, covered, until chicken is cooked, about 15 minutes. Stir in half and half; cook over medium heat until hot; season to taste with salt and pepper.

Per Serving:
Calories: 171
% calories from fat: 11
Protein (g): 17.6
Carbohydrate (g): 22
Fat (g): 2.1
Saturated fat (g): 0.8
Cholesterol (mg): 37.7
Sodium (mg): 130

Exchanges:
Milk: 0.0
Vegetable: 1.0
Fruit: 0.0
Bread: 1.0
Meat: 2.0
Fat: 0.0

HEARTY CHICKEN CORN CHOWDER

45 *Salsa and black olives are surprising flavor accents in this hearty chowder.*

6 entrée servings

1 pound boneless, skinless chicken breast, cubed
½ cup each: chopped onion, red bell pepper
2 teaspoons minced garlic
1 teaspoon olive oil
2 cups cubed, peeled potatoes
1–1½ cups reduced-sodium fat-free chicken broth
2 cans (15 ounces each) cream-style corn
⅓ cup mild or hot salsa
Salt and pepper, to taste
Chopped black olives, as garnish

Per Serving:
Calories: 291
% calories from fat: 17
Protein (g): 22
Carbohydrate (g): 45.6
Fat (g): 3.9
Saturated fat (g): 0.7
Cholesterol (mg): 46
Sodium (mg): 536

Exchanges:
Milk: 0.0
Vegetable: 0.0
Fruit: 0.0
Bread: 2.5
Meat: 2.0
Fat: 0.0

1. Sauté chicken, onion, bell pepper, and garlic in oil in large saucepan until vegetables are tender, about 8 minutes; Add potatoes and broth; heat to boiling. Reduce heat and simmer, covered, until potatoes are tender, about 10 minutes. Stir in corn and salsa; simmer, uncovered, until slightly thickened, about 5 minutes. Season to taste with salt and pepper. Sprinkle each bowl of chowder with olives.

VARIATION

Mediterranean-Style Chicken and Shrimp Chowder — Make recipe as above, using 8 ounces chicken and substituting 1 can (19 ounces) garbanzo beans for 1 can of corn, and 1 chopped roasted red pepper for the bell pepper. Omit salsa. Add ¾ teaspoon dried oregano leaves and 8 ounces peeled, deveined shrimp to chowder.

CHICKEN-VEGETABLE CHOWDER

A delicious chowder, ready in less than 30 minutes, that uses canned and frozen ingredients for convenience.

6 entrée servings

1 pound boneless, skinless chicken breast, cubed (¾-inch)

1 cup sliced carrots

½ cup chopped onion

2 cloves garlic, minced

1 tablespoon margarine or butter

2 cups small broccoli florets

½ cup Mexican-style whole kernel corn

2 cups Chicken Stock (see p. 2)

1 can (10¼ ounces) reduced-sodium cream of potato soup

1 teaspoon dried thyme leaves

3 tablespoons flour

½ cup fat-free half-and-half or fat-free milk

Salt and pepper, to taste

Per Serving:
Calories: 207
% calories from fat: 21
Protein (g): 21.3
Carbohydrate (g): 19.1
Fat (g): 4.8
Saturated fat (g): 1.3
Cholesterol (mg): 47.1
Sodium (mg): 107

Exchanges:
Milk: 0.0
Vegetable: 1.0
Fruit: 0.0
Bread: 2.0
Meat: 2.0
Fat: 0.0

1. Sauté chicken, carrots, onion, and garlic in margarine in large saucepan until chicken is lightly browned, 8 to 10 minutes. Add remaining ingredients except flour, half-and-half, salt, and pepper; heat to boiling. Reduce heat and simmer, covered, until chicken is cooked and vegetables are tender, about 10 minutes. Heat soup to boiling; add combined flour and half-and-half, stirring until thickened, about 1 minute. Season to taste with salt and pepper.

CHICKEN AND FRESH VEGETABLE CHOWDER

This delicious chowder is very easy to prepare; use a food processor to chop all the vegetables quickly.

8 entrée servings

½ cup each: chopped onion, green bell pepper, celery, carrots, zucchini

2 cloves garlic, minced

2 tablespoons olive oil

1½ pounds boneless, skinless chicken breast, cubed (1-inch)

¼ cup all-purpose flour

1 quart Chicken Stock (see p. 2)

¾ teaspoon each: dried thyme and marjoram leaves

1 bay leaf

¾ cup fat-free half-and-half or fat-free milk

Salt and pepper, to taste

Per Serving:
Calories: 188
% calories from fat: 27
Protein (g): 21.8
Carbohydrate (g): 11.3
Fat (g): 5.6
Saturated fat (g): 1.3
Cholesterol (mg): 53.5
Sodium (mg): 118

Exchanges:
Milk: 0.0
Vegetable: 3.0
Fruit: 0.0
Bread: 0.0
Meat: 2.0
Fat: 0.0

1. Sauté vegetables and garlic in oil in large saucepan until tender, about 8 minutes; stir in chicken and sauté until lightly browned, about 5 minutes. Sprinkle with flour and cook 2 minutes. Stir in stock and herbs. Heat to boiling; reduce heat and simmer, covered, until chicken is tender, about 15 minutes. Stir in half-and-half and simmer until hot, 2 to 3 minutes. Discard bay leaf; season to taste with salt and pepper.

CHICKEN CHOWDER HISPANIOLA

45 *This enticing chowder boasts sofrito, a popular Cuban seasoning found in the ethnic section of many supermarkets.*

4 entrée servings

12 ounces boneless, skinless chicken breast, cubed (¾-inch)

1 medium onion, chopped

1 teaspoon olive oil

1 can (15 ounces) each: rinsed drained garbanzo beans

1 can (14½ ounces) each: undrained, reduced-sodium diced tomatoes, reduced-sodium fat-free chicken broth

2 cups packed spinach

2 tablespoons sofrito sauce (optional)

Salt and pepper, to taste

¼ cup slivered almonds, toasted

Per Serving:
Calories: 346
% calories from fat: 29
Protein (g): 30.5
Carbohydrate (g): 28.2
Fat (g): 10.5
Saturated fat (g): 1.9
Cholesterol (mg): 54.3
Sodium (mg): 639

Exchanges:
Milk: 0.0
Vegetable: 3.0
Fruit: 0.0
Bread: 1.0
Meat: 3.0
Fat: 1.0

1. Sauté chicken and onion in oil in large saucepan until chicken is lightly browned, about 8 minutes. Add beans, tomatoes with liquid, and broth and heat to boiling; reduce heat and simmer, covered, 10 minutes. Stir in spinach and sofrito; simmer until spinach is wilted, 5 minutes. Season to taste with salt and pepper. Sprinkle each bowl of stew with almonds.

CHICKEN AND SHRIMP CHOWDER WITH LIME

45 *Lime provides the flavor accent in this soup, while tomatoes and avocados contribute crisp color contrasts.*

4 entrée servings

8 ounces boneless, skinless chicken breast, cubed (¾-inch)

2 cans (14½ ounces each) reduced-sodium fat-free chicken broth

½ cup uncooked rice

Juice of 1 lime

⅛ teaspoon celery seeds

8 ounces peeled, deveined shrimp, halved crosswise

4 scallions, sliced

¼–½ teaspoon crushed red pepper

3 plum tomatoes, coarsely chopped

1 teaspoon grated lime zest

1 avocado, cubed

Salt and pepper, to taste

Per Serving:
Calories: 331
% calories from fat: 25
Protein (g): 30.9
Carbohydrate (g): 30.9
Fat (g): 9.2
Saturated fat (g): 2
Cholesterol (mg): 121.2
Sodium (mg): 290

Exchanges:
Milk: 0.0
Vegetable: 0.0
Fruit: 0.0
Bread: 2.0
Meat: 3.5
Fat: 0.0

1. Heat chicken, broth, rice, lime juice, and celery seeds to boiling in large saucepan; reduce heat and simmer, covered, until chicken is cooked, about 20 minutes. Add remaining ingredients, except lime zest, avocado, salt, and pepper; simmer until rice is tender and shrimp are cooked, about 5 minutes. Stir in avocado and zest; season to taste with salt and pepper.

BEAN AND SHRIMP CHOWDER

You can make a meal out of this high-protein chowder; just add a slice of Hearty Vegetable-Rye Bread (see p. 646).

8 entrée servings

¼ cup chopped onion

1 tablespoon margarine or butter

3 tablespoons flour

½–¾ teaspoon dried thyme leaves

¼ teaspoon dry mustard

1½ cups Chicken Stock (see p. 2)

2 cups fat-free milk

1 can (16 ounces) cream-style corn

2 cans (15½ ounces each) Great Northern beans, rinsed, drained

1½ pounds peeled, deveined medium shrimp

Salt and cayenne pepper, to taste

Per Serving:
Calories: 218
% calories from fat: 10
Protein (g): 22.9
Carbohydrate (g): 30.9
Fat (g): 2.7
Saturated fat (g): 0.6
Cholesterol (mg): 131.8
Sodium (mg): 658

Exchanges:
Milk: 0.0
Vegetable: 0.0
Fruit: 0.0
Bread: 2.0
Meat: 2.0
Fat: 0.0

1. Sauté onion in margarine in large saucepan until tender, about 3 minutes; stir in flour, thyme, and dry mustard and cook 1 minute.

Stir in stock and milk and heat to boiling, stirring until thickened, 1 to 2 minutes. Add corn and beans, reduce heat, and simmer 10 minutes. Stir in shrimp; simmer until shrimp are cooked, about 5 minutes. Season to taste with salt and cayenne pepper.

LOBSTER AND SHRIMP CHOWDER

45 *For easiest preparation, purchase cooked lobster and shrimp in the seafood department of your supermarket.*

4 entrée servings

2 large Yukon gold potatoes, peeled, cubed

1 medium onion, chopped

1 can (14½ ounces) reduced-sodium diced tomatoes, undrained

1½ cups clam juice

8 ounces cooked lobster tail, cut into small chunks

4 ounces cooked, peeled, deveined small shrimp

1 teaspoon dried tarragon leaves

1 cup 1% low-fat milk

¼ cup chopped parsley

Salt and pepper, to taste

Per Serving:
Calories: 210
% calories from fat: 9
Protein (g): 22.4
Carbohydrate (g): 25.7
Fat (g): 2.1
Saturated fat (g): 0.9
Cholesterol (mg): 100.7
Sodium (mg): 519

Exchanges:
Milk: 0.0
Vegetable: 1.0
Fruit: 0.0
Bread: 1.0
Meat: 2.0
Fat: 0.0

1. Heat potatoes, onion, tomatoes with liquid, and clam juice to boiling in large saucepan; reduce heat and simmer, covered, until potatoes are tender, about 10 minutes. Add remaining ingredients, except salt and pepper, and simmer, uncovered, until hot, about 5 minutes. Season to taste with salt and pepper.

VARIATION

Crabmeat Chowder — Make recipe as above, substituting 1½ cups Fish Stock (p. 8) for the clam juice, ½ teaspoon dried thyme leaves for the tarragon, and 3 cans (4 ounces each) lump crabmeat for the lobster and shrimp; drain crabmeat and remove any shells.

CURRIED SCALLOP AND POTATO CHOWDER

45 *This chowder has a lively curry flavor and a bright yellow color!*

4 entrée servings

1½ cups clam juice
½ cup dry white wine or water
1 pound potatoes, peeled, cubed
1 teaspoon curry powder
½ teaspoon minced garlic
1 pound sea scallops
1 cup frozen peas
¼–½ cup 1% low-fat milk
Salt and pepper, to taste

Per Serving:
Calories: 251
% calories from fat: 7
Protein (g): 25.6
Carbohydrate (g): 29.4
Fat (g): 1.8
Saturated fat (g): 0.2
Cholesterol (mg): 49.3
Sodium (mg): 482

Exchanges:
Milk: 0.0
Vegetable: 0.0
Fruit: 0.0
Bread: 2.0
Meat: 3.0
Fat: 0.0

1. Heat clam juice, wine, potatoes, curry powder, and garlic to boiling in large saucepan; reduce heat and simmer, covered, until potatoes are tender, about 10 minutes. Process about half the mixture in food processor or blender until smooth; return to pan. Stir in scallops, peas and milk; cook over medium heat until scallops are cooked, about 5 minutes. Season to taste with salt and pepper.

CRAB CHOWDER WITH SNOW PEAS

45 *This aromatic chowder gets its flavor essence from jasmine rice, gingerroot, and sorrel.*

4 first-course servings

2 cups clam juice
2½ cups water
½ cup jasmine or basmati rice
2 green onions, sliced
1 tablespoon minced gingerroot
2 cans (4 ounces each) lump crabmeat
2 cups each: snow peas, halved crosswise, torn sorrel or kale leaves
1 tablespoon dry sherry (optional)
½ cup 2% reduced-fat milk
Salt and pepper, to taste

Per Serving:
Calories: 209
% calories from fat: 8
Protein (g): 17.6
Carbohydrate (g): 28.8
Fat (g): 1.9
Saturated fat (g): 0.5
Cholesterol (mg): 52.7
Sodium (mg): 491

Exchanges:
Milk: 0.0
Vegetable: 1.0
Fruit: 0.0
Bread: 1.0
Meat: 2.0
Fat: 0.0

1. Heat clam juice and water to boiling in large saucepan. Stir in rice, green onions, and gingerroot; reduce heat and simmer, covered, until rice is tender, about 25 minutes. Stir in remaining ingredients, except salt and pepper; simmer until snow peas are crisp-tender, 3 to 4 minutes. Season to taste with salt and pepper.

SHERRIED CRAB AND MUSHROOM CHOWDER

Succulent, sweet crabmeat and fresh mushrooms complement one another in this elegant dish.

4 entrée servings

1 pound mushrooms, sliced

⅔ cup chopped onion

¼ cup each: finely chopped celery, carrot

1 tablespoon margarine or butter

1½ tablespoons flour

2½ cups Chicken Stock (see p. 2)

¾ cup diced, peeled red potatoes

⅛ teaspoon dried thyme leaves

1 tablespoon tomato paste

1½ teaspoons reduced-sodium soy sauce

1⅓ cups whole milk

6 ounces fresh lump crabmeat, coarsely chopped

2 tablespoons dry sherry (optional)

Salt and white pepper, to taste

Per Serving:
Calories: 159
% calories from fat: 27
Protein (g): 10.8
Carbohydrate (g): 18.1
Fat (g): 5
Saturated fat (g): 1.7
Cholesterol (mg): 33.8
Sodium (mg): 371

Exchanges:
Milk: 0.0
Vegetable: 0.0
Fruit: 0.0
Bread: 1.0
Meat: 1.0
Fat: 0.5

1. Sauté mushrooms, onion, celery, and carrot in margarine in large saucepan until tender, about 8 minutes. Remove and reserve about ⅓ of the mushroom mixture. Stir flour into saucepan; cook 1 minute. Stir in 1½ cups stock, potatoes, and thyme; heat to boiling. Reduce heat and simmer, covered, until potatoes are tender, about 10 minutes. Process chowder in food processor or blender until smooth; return to saucepan. Add reserved mushroom mixture and remaining ingredients, except salt and pepper; heat to simmering. Simmer, covered until crab is cooked, 5 to 8 minutes. Season to taste with salt and white pepper.

SPICY CRAB AND SCALLOP CHOWDER

45 *The flavor kick in this seafood chowder comes from pickling spice!*

4 entrée servings

1 medium onion, chopped

1 rib celery, chopped

1 tablespoon margarine or butter

1½ cups clam juice

1 can (14½ ounces) reduced-sodium stewed tomatoes

2 teaspoons pickling spice

1 can (4 ounces) lump crabmeat, drained

8 ounces bay scallops

¼–½ cup 2% reduced-fat milk

Salt and pepper, to taste

Per Serving:
Calories: 144
% calories from fat: 26
Protein (g): 18.2
Carbohydrate (g): 8.9
Fat (g): 4.3
Saturated fat (g): 0.8
Cholesterol (mg): 50.4
Sodium (mg): 485

Exchanges:
Milk: 0.0
Vegetable: 1.0
Fruit: 0.0
Bread: 0.0
Meat: 2.0
Fat: 0.0

1. Sauté onion and celery in margarine or butter in large saucepan until softened. Add clam juice, tomatoes, and pickling spice, tied in a cheesecloth bag. Heat to boiling; stir in crabmeat, scallops, and milk. Reduce heat and simmer, covered, until scallops are cooked and opaque, about 5 minutes. Discard spice bag. Season to taste with salt and pepper.

SEAFOOD SAMPLER CHOWDER

45 *This sensibly seasoned chowder is great with Croutons (see p. 636).*

4 entrée servings

½ cup each: chopped yellow bell pepper,
   chopped onion
1 teaspoon olive oil
1 can (14½ ounces) reduced-sodium diced
   tomatoes, undrained
2 medium potatoes, cubed
½ cup dry white wine or water
½ teaspoon celery seeds
1 teaspoon herbes de Provence or dried
   Italian seasoning
8 ounces haddock or halibut, cubed (1-inch)
4 ounces each: bay scallops, peeled deveined shrimp
½ teaspoon hot pepper sauce
Salt, to taste

Per Serving:
Calories: 231
% calories from fat: 10
Protein (g): 23.7
Carbohydrate (g): 24.7
Fat (g): 2.5
Saturated fat (g): 0.4
Cholesterol (mg): 88
Sodium (mg): 172

Exchanges:
Milk: 0.0
Vegetable: 1.0
Fruit: 0.0
Bread: 1.0
Meat: 3.0
Fat: 0.0

1. Sauté pepper and onion in oil in large saucepan until lightly browned, about 5 minutes. Add tomatoes with liquid, potatoes, wine, and herbs; heat to boiling. Reduce heat and simmer, covered, until potatoes are tender, about 10 minutes. Add seafood; simmer until haddock is tender and flakes with a fork, about 5 minutes. Stir in hot pepper sauce; season to taste with salt.

SEAFOOD CHOWDER

45 *If you prefer, Fish Stock (see p. 8) can be used in place of the clam juice.*

8 entrée servings

4 slices bacon
1 cup each: sliced onions, celery
1 can (28 ounces) reduced-sodium diced tomatoes, undrained
4 cups chopped, peeled potatoes
2 cups clam juice
½–1 cup tomato sauce

1 tablespoon low-sodium Worcestershire sauce

1 teaspoon dried rosemary leaves

⅓ cup all-purpose flour

1 cup fat-free half-and-half or fat-free milk

1½ pounds halibut or whitefish steaks, cubed (1-inch)

Salt and pepper, to taste

Per Serving:
Calories: 300
% calories from fat: 12
Protein (g): 24.2
Carbohydrate (g): 41.6
Fat (g): 3.9
Saturated fat (g): 0.9
Cholesterol (mg): 29.8
Sodium (mg): 395

Exchanges:
Milk: 0.0
Vegetable: 2.0
Fruit: 0.0
Bread: 2.0
Meat: 2.0
Fat: 0.0

1. Fry bacon in large saucepan until crisp; drain, crumble, and reserve. Discard all but 1 tablespoon bacon fat; add onions and celery and sauté until tender, about 8 minutes. Add tomatoes with liquid, potatoes, clam juice, tomato sauce, Worcestershire sauce, and rosemary; heat to boiling. Reduce heat and simmer, covered, until vegetables are tender, about 10 minutes. Heat chowder to boiling; stir in combined flour and half-and-half, stirring, until thickened, about 1 minute. Add fish; reduce heat and simmer, covered, until fish is tender and flakes with a fork, about 5 minutes. Season to taste with salt and pepper. Sprinkle each bowl of chowder with reserved bacon.

VARIATION

Rich Shrimp Chowder — Make recipe as above, substituting 1½ pounds peeled, deveined shrimp for the halibut. Decrease potatoes to 2 cups and add 1 cup frozen peas.

FRESH SALMON CHOWDER WITH POTATOES

Farmed salmon is always a good choice.

4 entrée servings

3 cups Fish Stock (see p. 8) or clam juice, divided
4 salmon steaks (4 ounces each)
1 cup chopped onion
1 tablespoon each: margarine or butter, flour
3¼ cups cubed, peeled potatoes
½ teaspoon each: dry mustard, dried marjoram leaves
1 cup whole milk
Salt and white pepper, to taste

Per Serving:
Calories: 418
% calories from fat: 20
Protein (g): 30.1
Carbohydrate (g): 50.1
Fat (g): 9.1
Saturated fat (g): 2.5
Cholesterol (mg): 70.3
Sodium (mg): 158

Exchanges:
Milk: 0.0
Vegetable: 0.0
Fruit: 0.0
Bread: 35
Meat: 3.0
Fat: 0.0

1. Heat 1 cup stock to simmering in large saucepan over medium-low heat; add salmon and simmer, covered, until salmon flakes with a fork, 8 to 10 minutes. Remove to plate; break fish into bite-sized pieces, discarding skin and bones. Strain stock and reserve.

2. Sauté onion in margarine in large saucepan until tender, about 5 minutes. Stir in flour; cook 1 to 2 minutes. Stir in remaining 2 cups stock, reserved stock, potatoes, dry mustard, and marjoram; heat to boiling. Reduce heat and simmer, covered, until potatoes are tender, about 10 minutes. Process half the chowder in food processor or blender until smooth; return to saucepan. Stir in milk and salmon; cook over medium heat until hot. Season to taste with salt and white pepper.

SALMON AND ROASTED PEPPER CHOWDER

45 *Salmon is paired with corn and seasoned with jalapeño chilies, cumin, and oregano for a fast and fabulous feast.*

4 entrée servings

2 cups each: whole kernel corn, reduced-sodium vegetable broth
2 medium potatoes, peeled, cubed
1 cup chopped roasted red pepper
½–1 jalapeño chili, minced

2 teaspoons minced garlic

1 teaspoon each: cumin seeds, dried oregano leaves

12 ounces salmon steaks, cubed (1-inch)

Salt and pepper, to taste

Per Serving:
Calories: 259
% calories from fat: 12
Protein (g): 20.5
Carbohydrate (g): 36.4
Fat (g): 3.4
Saturated fat (g): 0.5
Cholesterol (mg): 42.8
Sodium (mg): 197

1. Combine all ingredients, except salmon, salt, and pepper in large saucepan. Heat to boiling; reduce heat and simmer, covered, until potatoes are tender, about 10 minutes. Add salmon; simmer until salmon is tender and flakes with a fork, about 5 minutes. Season to taste with salt and pepper.

Exchanges:
Milk: 0.0
Vegetable: 0.0
Fruit: 0.0
Bread: 2.0
Meat: 2.0
Fat: 0.0

SHRIMP AND VEGETABLE CHOWDER

45 *The rich flavor of this chowder comes from a combination of herbs, spices, tomato sauce, and milk.*

6 entrée servings

1 cup each: chopped onion, green or red bell pepper

2 garlic cloves, minced

2 teaspoons olive oil

3 cups each: reduced-sodium fat-free chicken broth, whole kernel corn

2 cups diced, peeled red potatoes

⅓ cup dry sherry (optional)

2 teaspoons dried Italian seasoning

¼ teaspoon each: chili powder, dry mustard

3–4 drops hot pepper sauce

1½ tablespoons cornstarch

¼ cup cold water

1½ cups cooked, peeled, deveined medium shrimp

1 can (8 ounces) tomato sauce

½ cup whole milk

Salt and pepper, to taste

Per Serving:
Calories: 270
% calories from fat: 9
Protein (g): 15.9
Carbohydrate (g): 45.2
Fat (g): 2.9
Saturated fat (g): 0.8
Cholesterol (mg): 72
Sodium (mg): 455

Exchanges:
Milk: 0.0
Vegetable: 3.0
Fruit: 0.0
Bread: 2.0
Meat: 1.0
Fat: 0.0

1. Sauté onion, bell pepper, and garlic in oil in large saucepan until onion is soft, about 5 minutes. Add broth, corn, potatoes, sherry,

Italian seasoning, chili powder, mustard, and hot pepper sauce; heat to boiling. Reduce heat and simmer, covered, until potatoes are tender, 12 to 15 minutes. Heat chowder to boiling; stir in combined cornstarch and water, stirring until thickened, about 1 minute. Reduce heat and add shrimp, tomato sauce, and milk; simmer, covered, 2 to 3 minutes. Season to taste with salt and pepper.

BERMUDA FISH CHOWDER

Like Manhattan-style chowders, Bermuda chowders typically contain tomatoes. They have a wonderful flavor and robustness all their own.

6 entrée servings

1 cup each: chopped onion, celery, carrots

½ cup chopped green bell pepper

1 tablespoon canola oil

1 quart Fish Stock (see p. 8) or clam juice

2½ teaspoons Worcestershire sauce

2 large bay leaves

½–¾ teaspoon dried thyme leaves

1 teaspoon curry powder

2 small smoked pork hocks

3¼ cups cubed, peeled boiled potatoes

1 can (14½ ounces) Italian plum tomatoes, undrained, chopped

⅓ cup catsup

1 pound lean fish fillets (whitefish, flounder, haddock, cod), cubed (1-inch)

Salt and pepper, to taste

Per Serving:
Calories: 282
% calories from fat: 23
Protein (g): 20.2
Carbohydrate (g): 32.8
Fat (g): 7.2
Saturated fat (g): 1
Cholesterol (mg): 45.5
Sodium (mg): 742

Exchanges:
Milk: 0.0
Vegetable: 0.0
Fruit: 0.0
Bread: 2.0
Meat: 2.0
Fat: 0.5

1. Sauté onion, celery, carrots, and bell pepper in oil in large saucepan until tender, about 10 minutes. Add remaining ingredients, except fish, salt, and pepper, and heat to boiling. Reduce heat and simmer, covered, 30 minutes. Stir in fish and simmer, covered, until fish is tender and flakes with a fork, about 10 minutes. Discard bay leaves and pork hocks; season to taste with salt and pepper.

CANADIAN CHOWDER

45 *Mace is the secret flavor in this quick and easy chowder.*

6 entrée servings

1 cup each: finely chopped onion, carrots, celery

2 leeks (white parts only), thinly sliced

1 can (28 ounces) crushed tomatoes

2 cups water

1 pound cod or halibut, cubed (1-inch)

1 cup 2% reduced-fat or fat-free milk

¼–½ teaspoon ground mace

Salt and white pepper, to taste

¼ cup thinly sliced green onions

Per Serving:
Calories: 176
% calories from fat: 8
Protein (g): 18.4
Carbohydrate (g): 22.3
Fat (g): 1.6
Saturated fat (g): 0.6
Cholesterol (mg): 35.4
Sodium (mg): 311

Exchanges:
Milk: 0.0
Vegetable: 2.0
Fruit: 0.0
Bread: 0.0
Meat: 2.0
Fat: 0.0

1. Sauté onion, carrots, celery, and leeks in lightly greased large saucepan until tender, about 10 minutes. Add tomatoes and water; heat to boiling. Reduce heat and simmer, covered, until vegetables are tender, 10 to 15 minutes. Add fish; simmer, covered, until fish is tender and flakes with a fork, about 5 minutes. Stir in milk and mace and simmer until hot; season to taste with salt and white pepper. Sprinkle each bowl of chowder with green onions.

MONKFISH-CHEDDAR CHOWDER

45 *Use any favorite firm-textured fish in this creamy, cheesy chowder.*

4 entrée servings

½ cup each: chopped onion, sliced carrots

2 teaspoons margarine or butter

1 pound potatoes, peeled, cubed

1 can (14 ounces) reduced-sodium fat-free chicken broth

1 pound monkfish, cubed (¾-inch)

½ cup each: fat-free milk, shredded reduced-fat Cheddar cheese (2 ounces)

½–1 teaspoon hot pepper sauce

Salt, to taste

Per Serving:
Calories: 274
% calories from fat: 19
Protein (g): 24.9
Carbohydrate (g): 29.5
Fat (g): 5.9
Saturated fat (g): 1.8
Cholesterol (mg): 35.4
Sodium (mg): 344

Exchanges:
Milk: 0.0
Vegetable: 0.0
Fruit: 0.0
Bread: 1.5
Meat: 3.0
Fat: 0.0

1. Sauté onion and carrots in margarine in large saucepan until tender, 3 to 4 minutes; add potatoes and broth. Heat to boiling; reduce heat and simmer, covered, until potatoes are tender, about 10 minutes. Process about ½ the chowder in food processor or blender until smooth; return to saucepan and heat to boiling. Add fish and milk; reduce heat and simmer, covered, until fish is tender and flakes with a fork, about 5 minutes. Stir in cheese and hot pepper sauce; stir over low heat until cheese is melted. Season to taste with salt.

VARIATION

Cod and Vegetable Chowder — Make recipe as above, substituting cod for the monkfish. Decrease potatoes to 2 cups; add 1 cup small broccoli florets, ½ cup frozen peas, and ½ cup cut green beans.

NOVA SCOTIA SEAFOOD CHOWDER

Hearty chowders are a hallmark of the cuisine in Canada's Atlantic provinces. They are milk-based like their New England counterparts. The type and combination of seafood used depends on the day's catch.

4 entrée servings

1 each: large chopped onion, carrot, rib celery, garlic clove

2 teaspoons margarine or butter

2 cups each: Fish Stock (see p. 8), whole milk, divided, cubed peeled potatoes, small cauliflower florets

1½ teaspoons dried basil leaves

½ teaspoon dried marjoram leaves

¼ teaspoon dry mustard

1 tablespoon cornstarch

8 ounces skinless flounder or whitefish fillets, cubed

4 ounces each: peeled deveined cooked shrimp, crabmeat

Salt and white pepper, to taste

Per Serving:
Calories: 255
% calories from fat: 19
Protein (g): 20.3
Carbohydrate (g): 31.1
Fat (g): 5.3
Saturated fat (g): 2.2
Cholesterol (mg): 80
Sodium (mg): 317

Exchanges:
Milk: 0.0
Vegetable: 0.0
Fruit: 0.0
Bread: 2.0
Meat: 2.0
Fat: 0.0

1. Sauté onion, carrot, celery, and garlic in margarine in large saucepan until onion is tender, about 8 minutes. Add stock, 1½ cups milk, potatoes, cauliflower, and herbs; heat to boiling. Reduce heat and simmer, covered, until potatoes are tender, about 15 minutes. Heat soup to boiling; stir in combined cornstarch and remaining ½ cup of milk, stirring, until thickened, about 1 minute. Reduce heat; add seafood and simmer, covered, until flounder is tender and flakes with a fork, about 10 minutes. Season to taste with salt and white pepper.

POTATO SEAFOOD CHOWDER

45 *Substitute clam juice for half the milk, if you like.*

4 entrée servings

1 cup sliced onion
½ cup sliced celery
3 medium russet potatoes, unpeeled, cubed
1 teaspoon margarine or butter
2 tablespoons flour
1 quart fat-free milk
⅛ teaspoon crushed saffron (optional)
8 ounces each: haddock or cod fillets
½ cup peeled, deveined small shrimp
Salt and white pepper, to taste

Per Serving:
Calories: 254
% calories from fat: 7
Protein (g): 22.8
Carbohydrate (g): 36.2
Fat (g): 2
Saturated fat (g): 0.6
Cholesterol (mg): 37
Sodium (mg): 245

Exchanges:
Milk: 1.0
Vegetable: 0.0
Fruit: 0.0
Bread: 1.0
Meat: 2.0
Fat: 0.0

1. Sauté onion, celery, and potatoes in margarine in large saucepan 5 minutes; stir in flour and cook 1 minute. Add milk and saffron and heat to boiling; reduce heat and simmer, covered, until vegetables are tender, about 15 minutes. Add haddock and shrimp; simmer until haddock is tender and flakes with a fork, about 5 minutes. Season to taste with salt and white pepper.

HALIBUT AND POTATO CHOWDER

45 *This chunky chowder has a thick, flavorful base of puréed vegetables.*

4 entrée servings

1 each: chopped large onion, rib celery
1½ cups clam juice
4 cups cubed, peeled potatoes
1 pound halibut, cubed (¾-inch)
1 small carrot, shredded
1 cup 1% low-fat milk
1 teaspoon dried savory leaves
½–1 teaspoons hot pepper sauce
Salt, to taste
2 slices bacon, cooked crisp, crumbled

Per Serving:
Calories: 394
% calories from fat: 12
Protein (g): 31.4
Carbohydrate (g): 55.4
Fat (g): 5.4
Saturated fat (g): 1.4
Cholesterol (mg): 45.7
Sodium (mg): 430

Exchanges:
Milk: 0.0
Vegetable: 1.0
Fruit: 0.0
Bread: 3.0
Meat: 3.0
Fat: 0.0

1. Sauté onion and celery in lightly greased large saucepan until light browned, about 5 minutes. Stir in clam juice and potatoes and heat to boiling; reduce heat and simmer, covered, until potatoes are tender, about 15 minutes. Process half the mixture in food processor or blender until smooth; return to saucepan. Heat to boiling; add remaining ingredients, except salt and bacon. Reduce heat and simmer, covered, until halibut is tender and flakes with a fork, about 5 minutes. Season to taste with salt; sprinkle each bowl of soup with bacon.

FISH AND SWEET POTATO CHOWDER

45 *Cod, orange roughy, and red snapper are other possible fish choices for this herb-scented chowder.*

8 entrée servings

½ cup chopped onion, green bell pepper
2 cloves garlic, minced
1–2 tablespoons margarine or butter
1 tablespoon flour
2 cans (14½ ounces each) reduced-sodium diced tomatoes, undrained
2 cups water
½ cup dry white wine or water

1 teaspoon each: dried basil and oregano leaves

¼ teaspoon dried thyme leaves

4 cups cooked cubed sweet potatoes

½ cup whole kernel corn

12 ounces each: cubed salmon steaks (1-inch),
  peeled deveined shrimp

Salt and pepper, to taste

Per Serving:
Calories: 261
% calories from fat: 23
Protein (g): 19.8
Carbohydrate (g): 25.3
Fat (g): 6.7
Saturated fat (g): 1.7
Cholesterol (mg): 85.7
Sodium (mg): 184

Exchanges:
Milk: 0.0
Vegetable: 0.0
Fruit: 0.0
Bread: 2.0
Meat: 2.0
Fat: 0.0

1. Sauté onion, bell pepper, and garlic in margarine in large saucepan until tender, 3 to 4 minutes; add flour and cook 1 minute. Add remaining ingredients, except salmon, shrimp, salt, and pepper; heat to boiling. Reduce heat and simmer, covered, until vegetables are tender, about 15 minutes. Add salmon and shrimp; simmer, covered, until salmon flakes with a fork and shrimp are cooked, 5 to 8 minutes. Season to taste with salt and pepper.

SCANDINAVIAN FISH CHOWDER

This fish soup features cod, with accents of dill, cucumber, and hard-cooked eggs.

8 entrée servings

1 cup chopped celery

½ cup chopped onion

1 tablespoon margarine or butter

¼ cup all-purpose flour

2 cups each: water, diced peeled potatoes

1 teaspoon dried dill weed

¼ teaspoon ground allspice

2 cups fat-free milk

1 pound skinless cod fillets, sliced

1 cup chopped, seeded cucumber

½ teaspoon paprika

2 tablespoons lemon juice

Salt and pepper, to taste

Hard-cooked egg slices, as garnish

Per Serving:
Calories: 159
% calories from fat: 11
Protein (g): 14.2
Carbohydrate (g): 21
Fat (g): 2.1
Saturated fat (g): 0.5
Cholesterol (mg): 25.4
Sodium (mg): 99

Exchanges:
Milk: 0.0
Vegetable: 1 0
Fruit: 0.0
Bread 1.0
Meat: 1.0
Fat: 0.0

1. Sauté celery and onion in margarine in large saucepan until tender, about 5 minutes; sprinkle with flour and cook 1 to 2 minutes. Stir in water, potatoes, dill weed, and allspice. Heat to boiling; reduce heat and simmer, covered, until potatoes are tender, about 10 minutes. Stir in milk, cod, cucumber, and paprika; simmer, covered, until fish is tender and flakes with a fork, about 8 minutes. Stir in lemon juice; season to taste with salt and pepper. Garnish bowls of soup with egg slices.

WHITE CHEDDAR CLAM CHOWDER

45   *White Cheddar cheese adds a new flavor dimension to this classic clam chowder.*

8 entrée servings

½ cup each: chopped carrot, celery, onion

3 tablespoons flour

3 cans (8 ounces each) minced clams, drained, liquor reserved

2 cups clam juice

4 cups fat-free milk

1 teaspoon dried thyme leaves

1 cup each: cubed cooked peeled potatoes, shredded white Cheddar cheese (4 ounces)

Salt and cayenne pepper, to taste

Cooked, crumbled bacon, as garnish

Per Serving:
Calories: 276
% calories from fat: 22
Protein (g): 30.6
Carbohydrate (g): 22
Fat (g): 6.7
Saturated fat (g): 3.3
Cholesterol (mg): 74
Sodium (mg): 396

Exchanges:
Milk: 0.0
Vegetable: 1.0
Fruit: 0.0
Bread: 1.0
Meat: 3.0
Fat: 0.0

1. Sauté carrot, celery, and onion in lightly greased large saucepan until tender, about 8 minutes. Sprinkle with flour and cook 1 to 2 minutes. Stir in clam liquor, clam juice, milk, and thyme and heat to boiling, stirring until thickened, about 1 minute. Stir in clams and potatoes; reduce heat and simmer, covered, 5 minutes. Add cheese, stirring until cheese melted. Season to taste with salt and cayenne pepper; sprinkle each bowl of soup with bacon.

RED CLAM CHOWDER

45 *For variation, sweet potatoes can be substituted for the russets.*

8 first-course servings

1 cup chopped onion

½ cup each: chopped green bell pepper, celery

1 clove garlic

2 tablespoons olive oil

2 cans (6½ ounces each) chopped clams, drained, liquor reserved

2 cups clam juice

1 can (14½ ounces) diced reduced-sodium tomatoes, undrained

1–2 cups tomato juice

2 cups diced peeled russet potatoes

¾ cup sliced carrots

1 bay leaf

1 teaspoon dried basil leaves

½ teaspoon each: dried oregano leaves, sugar

Salt and cayenne pepper, to taste

Per Serving:
Calories: 154
% calories from fat: 20
Protein (g): 6.3
Carbohydrate (g): 26.1
Fat (g): 3.7
Saturated fat (g): 0.5
Cholesterol (mg): 7.6
Sodium (mg): 651

Exchanges:
Milk: 0.0
Vegetable: 2.0
Fruit: 0.0
Bread: 2.0
Meat: 0.0
Fat: 0.5

1. Sauté onion, green pepper, celery, and garlic in oil in large saucepan until onion is tender, about 8 minutes. Add enough water to reserved clam liquor make 1¾ cups; add liquor and remaining ingredients, except clams, salt, and cayenne pepper to saucepan and heat to boiling. Reduce heat and simmer, covered, until potatoes are tender, about 15 minutes, adding clams last 5 minutes. Discard bay leaf; season to taste with salt and cayenne pepper.

EASY MANHATTAN CLAM CHOWDER

45 *Enjoy this quick version of the popular clam chowder.*

4 first-course servings

4 slices bacon, diced
1 cup each: chopped onion, cubed peeled potatoes
¾ cup sliced carrots
2 tablespoons flour
1 cup clam juice
1 can (14½ ounces) reduced-sodium diced
   tomatoes, undrained
½ teaspoon dried thyme leaves
2 cans (6 ounces each) minced clams, undrained
Salt and pepper, to taste

Per Serving:
Calories: 187
% calories from fat: 11
Protein (g): 14.9
Carbohydrate (g): 27.5
Fat (g): 2.4
Saturated fat (g): 0.4
Cholesterol (mg): 33.4
Sodium (mg): 305

Exchanges:
Milk: 0.0
Vegetable: 2.0
Fruit: 0.0
Bread: 1.0
Meat: 1.0
Fat: 0.0

1. Cook bacon and onion in lightly greased large saucepan over medium heat until bacon is crisp and onion tender, about 5 minutes. Add potatoes and carrots and cook 5 minutes; add flour and cook 1 minute. Add remaining ingredients, except salt and pepper, and heat to boiling; reduce heat and simmer, covered, until vegetables are tender, about 15 minutes. Season to taste with salt and pepper.

MANHATTAN-STYLE CLAM CHOWDER WITH CORN

45 *The mild smokiness of Canadian bacon adds subtle flavor to this version of the chowder.*

4 entrée servings

1 cup finely chopped large onion
½ cup each: chopped celery, green bell pepper
1 clove garlic, minced
2 teaspoons margarine or butter
1 cup each: fat-free chicken broth, cubed peeled potatoes
2 ounces Canadian bacon, julienned
2 cans (6½ ounces each) chopped clams, undrained
2 cans (14½ ounces each) reduced-sodium diced tomatoes, undrained
1 cup whole kernel corn

1 bay leaf

½ teaspoon each: dried thyme and basil leaves, sugar

Salt, and cayenne pepper, to taste

1. Sauté onion, celery, bell pepper, and garlic in margarine in large saucepan until onion is tender, about 5 minutes. Add broth, potatoes, and Canadian bacon; heat to boiling. Reduce heat and simmer, covered, until potatoes are tender, 10 to 12 minutes. Add remaining ingredients, except salt and cayenne pepper; heat to boiling. Reduce heat and simmer, covered, until hot, about 8 minutes. Discard bay leaf; season to taste with salt and cayenne pepper.

Per Serving:
Calories: 206
% calories from fat: 14
Protein (g): 9.8
Carbohydrate (g): 37.3
Fat (g): 3.6
Saturated fat (g): 0.8
Cholesterol (mg): 9.5
Sodium (mg): 488

Exchanges:
Milk: 0.0
Vegetable: 1.0
Fruit: 0.0
Bread: 2.0
Meat: 0.5
Fat: 0.0

MANHATTAN-STYLE FISH AND VEGETABLE CHOWDER

45 *A delicious chowder, with its flavor of the sea and vegetable-rich texture.*

6 entrée servings

1 cup chopped onion

½ cup each: chopped celery, carrot

2 teaspoons margarine or butter

2 cups reduced-sodium fat-free chicken broth

1 quart reduced-sodium tomato juice

1 cup each: frozen French-style green beans, whole
   kernel corn, cubed potato

1 bay leaf

½ teaspoon each: dried thyme and marjoram leaves

¼ teaspoon each: dry mustard, black pepper

10–12 ounces skinless flounder or halibut fillets,
   cubed (¾-inch)

Salt and cayenne pepper, to taste

Per Serving:
Calories: 198
% calories from fat: 20
Protein (g): 17.9
Carbohydrate (g): 24.4
Fat (g): 4.8
Saturated fat (g): 1.2
Cholesterol (mg): 39
Sodium (mg): 692

Exchanges:
Milk: 0.0
Vegetable: 0.0
Fruit: 0.0
Bread: 1.5
Meat: 2.0
Fat: 0.0

1. Sauté onion, celery, and carrot in margarine in large saucepan until tender, about 8 minutes. Add remaining ingredients, except fish, salt, and cayenne pepper; heat to boiling. Reduce heat and simmer, covered, until vegetables are tender, about 15 minutes. Add fish and simmer, covered, until fish is tender and flakes with a fork, about 8 minutes. Discard bay leaf; season to taste with salt and cayenne pepper.

NEW YORK CITY CLAM CHOWDER

Serve this chowder with Hearty Vegetable-Rye Bread (see p. 646).

6 entrée servings

36 littleneck or other small clams
Olive oil cooking spray
4 medium potatoes, peeled, cubed
1 cup sliced onion
½ cup each: chopped carrots, clam juice
1 can (28 ounces) crushed tomatoes
⅓ cup chopped parsley
½ teaspoon dried thyme leaves
2 bay leaves
¼ teaspoon hot pepper sauce
Salt and pepper, to taste

Per Serving:
Calories: 228
% calories from fat: 5
Protein (g): 19
Carbohydrate (g): 34.8
Fat (g): 1.3
Saturated fat (g): 0.2
Cholesterol (mg): 38.2
Sodium (mg): 332

Exchanges:
Milk: 0.0
Vegetable: 1.0
Fruit: 0.0
Bread: 2.0
Meat: 1.0
Fat: 0.0

1. Heat clams and water to boiling in large saucepan; reduce heat and simmer, covered, until clams open, 5 to 8 minutes. Discard any clams that do not open. Strain liquid through double layer of cheesecloth and reserve.

2. Sauté potatoes, onion, and carrots in lightly greased Dutch oven until onion is tender, about 5 minutes. Mix in reserved clam liquid and remaining ingredients, except clams, salt and pepper. Heat chowder to boiling; reduce heat and simmer, covered, until vegetables are tender, about 15 minutes, adding clams the last 5 minutes. Discard bay leaves; season to taste with salt and pepper.

LIGHTHOUSE CLAM CHOWDER

45 *Enjoy this mouth-watering New England-style chowder, creamy and loaded with clams and potatoes.*

4 first-course servings

1½ cups clam juice

2 cans (6½ ounces each) minced clams, drained, liquor reserved

1 cup cubed potatoes (1-inch)

½ cup chopped onion

¼ cup sliced celery

1½ cups 2% reduced-fat milk

2 ounces lean ham, chopped

2 teaspoons Worcestershire sauce

¾ teaspoon dried thyme leaves

Salt and pepper, to taste

Per Serving:
Calories: 136
% calories from fat: 15
Protein (g): 7
Carbohydrate (g): 22.4
Fat (g): 2.3
Saturated fat (g): 1.3
Cholesterol (mg): 13.5
Sodium (mg): 568

Exchanges:
Milk: 0.0
Vegetable: 1.0
Fruit: 0.0
Bread: 1.0
Meat: 0.0
Fat: 0.5

1. Heat clam juice, reserved clam liquor, potatoes, onion, and celery to boiling in large saucepan; reduce heat and simmer, covered, until potatoes are tender, about 15 minutes. Using slotted spoon, remove half the vegetables; reserve. Process remaining chowder in food processor or blender until smooth; return to saucepan. Stir in reserved vegetables, clams, milk, ham, Worcestershire sauce, and thyme; cook over medium heat until hot, about 5 minutes. Season to taste with salt and pepper.

MAINE CLAM CHOWDER

For convenience, make this chowder a day in advance, steam the clams (Step 1) and add to the chowder just before serving.

6 entrée servings

36 littleneck or other clams

6 cups water

1 cup chopped onion

½ cup chopped celery, sliced carrot

4 medium red potatoes, peeled, cubed

2 cups fat-free milk, divided

½ cup clam juice

¼ cup all-purpose flour

Salt and white pepper, to taste

Per Serving:
Calories: 158
% calories from fat: 4
Protein (g): 11.6
Carbohydrate (g): 27.5
Fat (g): 0.8
Saturated fat (g): 0.2
Cholesterol (mg): 19.6
Sodium (mg): 164

Exchanges:
Milk: 0.0
Vegetable: 0.0
Fruit: 0.0
Bread: 1.5
Meat: 1.0
Fat: 0.0

1. Heat clams and water to boiling in large saucepan; reduce heat and simmer, covered, until clams open, 5 to 8 minutes. Discard any clams that do not open. Remove clams from shells, chop, and reserve. Strain liquid through double layer of cheesecloth and reserve.

2. Sauté onion, celery, and carrot in lightly greased saucepan until onion is tender, about 5 minutes. Add potatoes, 1½ cups milk, reserved clam liquid, and clam juice and heat to boiling. Reduce heat and simmer, covered, until vegetables are tender, about 15 minutes. Heat chowder to boiling; stir in combined flour and remaining ½ cup milk, stirring until thickened, about 1 minute. Stir in reserved clams and cook over medium heat 2 to 3 minutes; season to taste with salt and white pepper.

NEW ENGLAND CLAM CHOWDER

45 *Fresh clams can be used in this fragrant clam chowder. Soak 3 dozen clams in cold water for 30 minutes. Heat clams to boiling in a covered skillet with 1½ cups water; boil until clams have opened, 6 to 8 minutes. Remove clams from shells and add to chowder; discard any that do not open. Strain broth through a double layer of cheesecloth and add to chowder.*

6 entrée servings

1 cup each: chopped onion, celery

¼ cup all-purpose flour

2 cups clam juice

2 cans (6½ ounces each) diced clams, undrained

2 cans (6 ounces) whole clams, undrained

1¾ cups peeled russet potatoes, cubed

1 teaspoon dried thyme leaves

1 bay leaf

1½–2 cups fat-free half-and-half or fat-free milk

Salt and pepper, to taste

2 slices bacon, fried crisp, crumbled

Per Serving:
Calories: 195
% calories from fat: 11
Protein (g): 13.4
Carbohydrate (g): 30.3
Fat (g): 2.3
Saturated fat (g): 0.6
Cholesterol (mg): 59.2
Sodium (mg): 261

Exchanges:
Milk 0.0
Vegetable: 0.0
Fruit: 0.0
Bread: 1.5
Meat: 1.0
Fat: 0.0

1. Sauté onion and celery in lightly greased large saucepan until tender, 5 to 8 minutes; stir in flour and cook 1 minute. Stir in clam juice, diced and whole clams, potatoes, and herbs; heat to boiling. Reduce heat and simmer, covered, until potatoes are tender, about 15 minutes. Stir in half-and-half; cook over medium heat until hot, about 5 minutes. Discard bay leaf; season to taste with salt and pepper. Sprinkle each bowl of chowder with bacon.

WHITE CLAM AND CORN CHOWDER

45 *This hearty chowder is savory and rich in flavor.*

4 entrée servings

1 each: chopped medium onion, large rib celery

1 tablespoon each: margarine or butter, flour

1 cup clam juice or fat-free chicken broth

1 can (10½ ounces) minced clams, undrained, liquor reserved

1 large bay leaf

½ teaspoon dried marjoram leaves

2 cups cubed peeled red potatoes (¼-inch)

1 cup whole kernel corn

1 cup 2% reduced-fat milk

Salt and pepper, to taste

Per Serving:
Calories: 281
% calories from fat: 18
Protein (g): 27.9
Carbohydrate (g): 33.5
Fat (g): 5.9
Saturated fat (g): 1.5
Cholesterol (mg): 54.7
Sodium (mg): 554

Exchanges:
Milk: 0.0
Vegetable: 0.0
Fruit: 0.0
Bread: 2.0
Meat: 3.0
Fat: 0.0

1. Sauté onion and celery in margarine in large saucepan until onion is tender, about 5 minutes. Stir in flour; cook 1 minute longer. Stir in clam juice and reserved clam liquor, herbs, potatoes, and corn; heat to boiling. Reduce heat and simmer, covered, until potatoes are tender, about 15 minutes. Discard bay leaf. Process half the chowder in food processor or blender until smooth; return to saucepan. Stir in milk and minced clams; cook over medium heat 5 minutes. Season to taste with salt and pepper.

FLOUNDER CHOWDER

Although this dish calls for flounder, orange roughy or halibut may be substituted.

6 entrée servings

1 each: large chopped onion, rib celery, minced
  garlic clove

2 teaspoons margarine or butter

2 cups each: Fish Stock (see p. 8) or vegetable broth,
  2% reduced-fat milk, cubed peeled
  potatoes (¾-inch)

1 cup frozen lima beans

1 large carrot, diced

1½ teaspoons dried basil leaves

½ teaspoon dried marjoram leaves

¼ teaspoon each: dry mustard, crushed celery seeds

1 tablespoon plus 1 teaspoon cornstarch

¼ cup water

1 pound skinless flounder fillets, cubed (1-inch)

½ cup whole kernel corn

Salt and pepper, to taste

Per Serving:
Calories: 252
% calories from fat: 28
Protein (g): 21.2
Carbohydrate (g): 23.7
Fat (g): 7.9
Saturated fat (g): 2.4
Cholesterol (mg): 48
Sodium (mg): 179

Exchange:
Milk: 0.0
Vegetable: 0.0
Fruit: 0.0
Bread: 1.5
Meat: 3.0
Fat: 0.0

1. Sauté onion, celery, and garlic in margarine in large saucepan until onion is tender, 5 to 8 minutes. Add stock, milk, vegetables, and herbs and heat to boiling; reduce heat and simmer, covered, until vegetables are tender, about 15 minutes. Heat soup to boiling; stir in combined cornstarch and water; stirring, until thickened, about 1 minute Reduce heat and stir in fish and corn; simmer, uncovered, until fish is tender and flakes with a fork, about 5 minutes. Season to taste with salt and pepper.

LIGHT FISH CHOWDER

Use any kind of fish you like in this nutritious fish chowder.

4 entrée servings

1 large onion, chopped

⅓ cup each: sliced carrots, celery

2 teaspoons margarine or butter

3 tablespoons flour

2 cups water

1 large potato, peeled, cubed

½ teaspoon dried thyme leaves

1 bay leaf

1 pound skinless whitefish fillets, cubed

2 cups fat-free milk

¼ cup chopped parsley

Salt and white pepper, to taste

Per Serving:
Calories: 258
% calories from fat: 13
Protein (g): 28.1
Carbohydrate (g): 27.3
Fat (g): 3.8
Saturated fat (g): 0.9
Cholesterol (mg): 62.3
Sodium (mg): 219

Exchanges:
Milk: 0.5
Vegetable: 1.0
Fruit: 0.0
Bread: 1.0
Meat: 2.0
Fat: 0.0

1. Sauté onion, carrots, and celery in margarine in large saucepan until tender, about 10 minutes. Sprinkle with flour and cook 1 to 2 minutes. Add water and heat to boiling stir in potato, thyme, and bay leaf. Reduce heat and simmer, covered, until potato is tender, about 15 minutes. Stir in fish and milk; simmer, covered, until fish is tender and flakes with a fork, about 5 minutes. Discard bay leaf. Stir in parsley; season to taste with salt and white pepper.

FOUR

Chili

FAMILY-FAVORITE CHILI

45 *This very easy chili will appeal to all ages.*

8 entrée servings

1½ pounds lean ground beef or turkey

2 cans (15 ounces each) pinto beans, rinsed, drained

2 cans (14½ ounces each) reduced-sodium
   stewed tomatoes

2 cups whole kernel corn

1 cup chopped onion

½ cup chopped green bell pepper

2 tablespoons taco seasoning mix

1 tablespoon light ranch salad dressing mix

Salt and pepper, to taste

Fat-free sour cream

Tortilla chips

Per Serving:
Calories: 268
% calories from fat: 13
Protein (g): 23.3
Carbohydrate (g): 36.4
Fat (g): 4.1
Saturated fat (g): 1.2
Cholesterol (mg): 41.2
Sodium (mg): 566

Exchanges:
Milk: 0.0
Vegetable: 1.0
Fruit: 0.0
Bread: 2.0
Meat: 2.0
Fat: 0.0

1. Cook ground beef in lightly greased large saucepan over medium heat until browned, about 10 minutes; crumble with a fork. Add remaining ingredients, except salt, pepper, sour cream, and tortilla chips, and heat to boiling. Reduce heat and simmer, covered, 20 minutes. Season to taste with salt and pepper. Serve with sour cream and tortilla chips.

VARIATION

Chili-Stuffed Potatoes — Scrub 8 medium Idaho potatoes; wrap in aluminum foil and bake at 400 degrees until tender, 45 to 60 minutes. Make chili recipe as above, cutting recipe in half and deleting tortilla chips. Split potatoes lengthwise and fluff with a fork; spoon chili over potatoes. Sprinkle each with 2 tablespoons shredded reduced-fat Cheddar cheese and garnish with dollops of sour cream.

SPEEDY CHILI

45 *Easy for those tired mid-week evenings.*

8 entrée servings

1 pound each: lean ground beef, ground turkey

2 large onions, chopped

3 cloves garlic, minced

1 can (6 ounces) reduced-sodium tomato paste

2 cans (10½ ounces each) zesty tomato sauce

2 cans (15½ ounces each) kidney beans,
    rinsed, drained

2 tablespoons chili powder

1 teaspoon dried oregano leaves

Salt and pepper, to taste

Per Serving:
Calories: 293
% calories from fat: 14
Protein (g): 33.6
Carbohydrate (g): 29.2
Fat (g): 4.4
Saturated fat (g): 1.7
Cholesterol (mg): 57.7
Sodium (mg): 902

Exchanges:
Milk: 0.0
Vegetable: 0.0
Fruit: 0.0
Bread: 2.0
Meat: 3.0
Fat: 0.0

1. Cook ground beef, turkey, onions, and garlic in lightly greased large saucepan over medium heat until meat is browned, 10 to 12 minutes; crumble meat with a fork. Stir in remaining ingredients, except salt and pepper and heat to boiling; reduce heat and simmer, covered, 15 minutes. Season to taste with salt and pepper.

CHILI CON CARNE

A flavorful chili that will satisfy the heartiest of appetites!

8 entrée servings

1 pound very lean ground beef

1 cup each: chopped onions, green bell pepper

2 cloves garlic, minced

1–2 tablespoons chili powder

2 teaspoons each: ground cumin, dried
   oregano leaves

2 cans (14½ ounces each) reduced-sodium diced
   tomatoes, undrained

1 can (15 ounces) red kidney beans, rinsed, drained

1 can (6 ounces) reduced-sodium tomato paste

¾ cup beer or water

1 tablespoon each: packed light brown sugar,
   unsweetened cocoa

Salt and pepper, to taste

½ cup each: shredded fat-free or reduced-fat Cheddar cheese
   (2 ounces), sliced green onions, fat-free sour cream

Per Serving:
Calories: 220
% calories from fat: 13
Protein (g): 21.9
Carbohydrate (g): 28.7
Fat (g): 3.6
Saturated fat (g): 1
Cholesterol (mg): 32.5
Sodium (mg): 224

Exchanges:
Milk: 0.0
Vegetable: 2.0
Fruit: 0.0
Bread: 1.0
Meat: 2.0
Fat: 0.0

1. Cook ground beef, onions, bell pepper, garlic, and herbs in lightly greased large saucepan over medium heat until meat is browned, 8 to 10 minutes; crumble beef with a fork. Add tomatoes with liquid, beans, tomato paste, beer, brown sugar, and cocoa; heat to boiling. Reduce heat and simmer, covered, 30 to 45 minutes. Simmer, uncovered, to thicken, if desired. Season to taste with salt and pepper. Sprinkle each bowl of chili with cheese, green onions, and sour cream.

VARIATIONS

Chili Mac — Make chili as above, adding 1 cup uncooked elbow macaroni or chili mac pasta and ½ cup water to chili during last 15 minutes of cooking time.

Southwestern Chili — Make recipe as above, substituting black or pinto beans for the red kidney, and adding 1 minced jalapeño chili. Garnish each bowl with chopped cilantro.

CORN AND BEAN CON CARNE

Cornmeal Crisps are a perfect chili complement!

8 entrée servings

12 ounces ground beef round

1 large onion, finely chopped

1 quart reduced-sodium fat-free beef broth

2 cans (14½ ounces each) reduced-sodium diced
   tomatoes, undrained

2 cans (15 ounces each) reduced-sodium kidney
   beans, rinsed, drained

2 cups whole kernel corn

1–2 tablespoons chili powder

1 teaspoon each: ground cumin, sugar

Salt and pepper, to taste

Cornmeal Crisps (recipe follows)

Per Serving:
Calories: 364
% calories from fat: 21
Protein (g): 22.2
Carbohydrate (g): 52.2
Fat (g): 8.8
Saturated fat (g): 2
Cholesterol (mg): 21.6
Sodium (mg): 422

Exchanges:
Milk: 0.0
Vegetable: 1.0
Fruit: 0.0
Bread: 3.0
Meat: 2.0
Fat: 0.5

1. Cook beef and onion in lightly greased large saucepan over medium heat until beef is browned, 5 to 8 minutes; crumble beef with a fork. Stir in remaining ingredients, except salt, pepper, and Cornmeal Crisps; heat to boiling. Reduce heat and simmer, covered, 20 to 25 minutes. Season to taste with salt. Serve with Cornmeal Crisps.

Cornmeal Crisps

Makes about 12

1 cup self-rising flour

⅓ cup yellow cornmeal

1 tablespoon sugar

4 tablespoons cold margarine or butter, cut into pieces

1 tablespoon distilled white vinegar

¼ cup ice water

1 egg white, beaten

2–3 tablespoons grated Parmesan cheese

1. Combine flour, cornmeal, and sugar in small bowl; cut in margarine with pastry cutter until mixture resembles coarse crumbs. Mix in vinegar and enough ice water for mixture to form a dough.

Roll dough on floured surface to scant ¼ inch thickness; cut into rounds and place on greased cookie sheet. Brush with egg white and sprinkle with Parmesan cheese. Bake at 375 degrees until golden, 7 to 10 minutes. Cool on wire rack.

BAKED CHILI CON CARNE

45

A colorful chili with oven-baked goodness.

6 entrée servings

16 ounces beef round or skirt steak, fat trimmed, sliced (1-inch)

1 teaspoon minced garlic

1 cup chopped onion

½ cup each: chopped green, red, and yellow bell peppers

1 jalapeño chili, minced

1 can (14½ ounces) reduced-sodium diced tomatoes, undrained

1 can (16 ounces) tomato sauce

1 can (6 ounces) reduced-sodium tomato paste

1 can (15½ ounces) each: light red and dark red kidney beans, rinsed, drained

1 teaspoon each: chili powder, ground cumin

1 bay leaf

Salt and pepper, to taste

Toppings: shredded reduced-fat Cheddar cheese, fat-free sour cream, chopped green onions, and tomatoes

Per Serving:
Calories: 306
% calories from fat: 11
Protein (g): 29.3
Carbohydrate (g): 48.9
Fat (g): 4.4
Saturated fat (g): 0.9
Cholesterol (mg): 36.5
Sodium (mg): 1081

Exchanges:
Milk: 0.0
Vegetable: 3.0
Fruit: 0.0
Bread: 2.0
Meat: 2.0
Fat: 0.0

1. Cook beef and garlic in lightly greased Dutch oven over medium heat until beef is browned, 8 to 10 minutes; crumble beef with a fork. Stir in remaining ingredients, except salt, pepper, and toppings. Bake, covered, at 350 degrees for 1¼ hours, stirring occasionally. Discard bay leaf; season to taste with salt and pepper. Serve with Toppings (not included in nutritional data).

CHUNKY CHILI FOR A CROWD

Make this big batch of chili for a party, and serve it with a do-it-yourself array of garnishes. Or make it for dinner, and freeze some for later use.

16 entrée servings

4 pounds lean beef stew meat, cubed (1-inch)

1–2 tablespoons canola oil

2 cups sliced onions

¼ cup each: minced garlic, chopped jalapeño chili

2 cans (28 ounces each) reduced-sodium diced tomatoes, undrained

3 cans (15 ounces each) pinto beans, rinsed, drained

1 can (6 ounces) reduced-sodium tomato paste

3–4 tablespoons chili powder

1 teaspoon beef bouillon crystals

2 green bell peppers, sliced

⅓ cup water

¼ cup cornstarch

Salt and pepper, to taste

Hot pepper sauce, to taste

Toppings: baked tortilla chips, grated reduced-fat Cheddar cheese, fat-free sour cream, chopped tomatoes, diced avocado, sliced black olives

Per Serving:
Calories: 301
% calories from fat: 22
Protein (g): 34.3
Carbohydrate (g): 24.5
Fat (g): 7.4
Saturated fat (g): 2.3
Cholesterol (mg): 70.9
Sodium (mg): 304

Exchanges:
Milk: 0.0
Vegetable: 2.0
Fruit: 0.0
Bread: 1.0
Meat: 3.0
Fat: 0.0

1. Cook beef in oil in large Dutch oven over medium heat until browned, 10 to 12 minutes. Stir in onions, garlic, and jalapeño chili and cook until onions are tender, about 8 minutes. Stir in tomatoes with liquid, beans, tomato paste, chili powder, and bouillon crystals. Heat to boiling; reduce heat and simmer, covered, until meat is very tender, 1½ to 2 hours, adding green peppers the last 10 minutes. Heat chili to boiling; stir in combined water and cornstarch, stirring until thickened, about 1 minute. Season to taste with salt, pepper, and hot pepper sauce. Serve with Toppings (not included in nutritional data).

SPICED BEAN CHILI WITH FUSILLI

45 *Use your favorite beans and any shaped pasta in this versatile chili.*

8 entrée servings

1 pound lean ground beef

2 cups chopped onions

1 cup sliced cremini or white mushrooms

½ cup each: sliced celery, dry white wine or water

2 cans (14½ ounces each) diced tomatoes with roasted garlic, undrained

1 can (15 ounces) each: garbanzo and dark red kidney beans, rinsed, drained

2 tablespoons chili powder

¾ teaspoon each: dried oregano and thyme leaves, ground cumin

8 ounces fusilli, cooked

Salt and pepper, to taste

3–4 tablespoons sliced green or ripe olives

Per Serving:
Calories: 367
% calories from fat: 26
Protein (g): 21.3
Carbohydrate (g): 47.3
Fat (g): 10.6
Saturated fat (g): 3.2
Cholesterol (mg): 35.2
Sodium (mg): 759

Exchanges:
Milk: 0.0
Vegetable: 1.0
Fruit: 0.0
Bread: 3.0
Meat: 1.0
Fat: 1.5

1. Cook ground beef, onions, mushrooms, and celery in lightly greased large saucepan over medium heat until beef is browned, 8 to 10 minutes; crumble beef with a fork. Add wine, tomatoes with liquid, beans, and herbs; heat to boiling. Reduce heat and simmer, covered, 10 minutes. Add pasta and cook until hot, 2 to 3 minutes. Season to taste with salt and pepper; sprinkle each bowl of soup with olives.

CINCINNATI CHILI

5-Way Cincinnati Chili gained fame in the chili parlors of Cincinnati. The sauce is seasoned with sweet spices and generally has a hint of dark chocolate. The chili is served alone, 1 way; 2 ways, over spaghetti; 3 ways, with added beans; 4 ways, with chopped onions; and 5 ways, with shredded cheese!

8 entrée servings

12 ounces lean ground turkey or beef

½ cup chopped onion

4 cloves garlic, minced

1 can (28 ounces) reduced-sodium crushed tomatoes

1 can (8 ounces) tomato sauce

½ cup water

2–3 tablespoons chili powder

1 tablespoon cocoa

2 teaspoons dried oregano leaves

1 teaspoon each: ground cinnamon, allspice

Salt and pepper, to taste

16 ounces spaghetti, cooked, warm

Toppings: canned, drained pinto beans, chopped onions, shredded reduced-fat Cheddar cheese

Per Serving:
Calories: 381
% calories from fat: 13
Protein (g): 19.6
Carbohydrate (g): 62
Fat (g): 5.7
Saturated fat (g): 1.3
Cholesterol (mg): 31.6
Sodium (mg): 454

Exchanges:
Milk: 0.0
Vegetable: 3.0
Fruit: 0.0
Bread: 3.0
Meat: 1.0
Fat: 0.5

1. Sauté ground turkey in lightly greased large saucepan over medium heat until turkey is browned, about 5 minutes; crumble with a fork. Add onion and garlic and sauté until onion is tender, about 5 minutes. Stir in remaining ingredients except spaghetti and toppings; heat to boiling. Reduce heat and simmer, covered, 15 minutes; simmer, uncovered, until thickened to desired consistency, about 15 minutes. Serve with spaghetti and Toppings (not included in nutritional data).

MALE CHAUVINIST CHILI

A real man's chili—but women will love it too!

8 entrée servings

8 ounces each: sliced (½-inch) low-sodium, reduced-fat Italian-style turkey sausage, lean ground beef eye of round

1½ cups coarsely chopped onions

1 green bell pepper, coarsely chopped

2 cloves garlic, minced

1 small jalapeño chili, minced

1½ quarts chopped tomatoes

1 can (15 ounces) each: rinsed drained pinto and black beans, chickpeas

1 cup dry red wine or tomato juice

¼–½ cup low-sodium Worcestershire sauce

1 teaspoon each: dry mustard, celery seeds

1–2 tablespoons chili powder

½ teaspoon ground cumin

Salt and pepper, to taste

8 slices reduced-sodium bacon, fried crisp, crumbled

Per Serving:
Calories: 332
% calories from fat: 21
Protein (g): 21.8
Carbohydrate (g): 43.4
Fat (g): 8.4
Saturated fat (g): 2.2
Cholesterol (mg): 33.9
Sodium (mg): 789

Exchanges:
Milk: 0.0
Vegetable: 2.0
Fruit: 0.0
Bread: 2.0
Meat: 2.0
Fat: 0.5

1. Cook Italian sausage and ground beef in lightly greased Dutch oven over medium heat until meats are browned; crumble with a fork. Add onions, bell pepper, garlic, and jalapeño chili to Dutch oven and sauté 5 minutes. Add remaining ingredients, except salt, pepper, and bacon and heat to boiling; reduce heat and simmer, covered, 45 minutes. Stir in bacon; season to taste with salt and pepper.

OLD HICKORY CHILI WITH WHITE BEANS

45 *This quick hickory-smoked turkey chili is made without wood chips or a grill. The cook's flavor trick—natural hickory seasoning.*

4 entrée servings

8 ounces ground turkey

1 cup each: chopped onion, mild or medium salsa

2 cups coarsely chopped tomatoes

1 can (15 ounces) white kidney beans, rinsed, drained

1 tablespoon white wine vinegar

2 tablespoons each: chili powder, finely chopped fresh cilantro

1 teaspoon natural hickory seasoning (optional)

Salt and pepper, to taste

Per Serving:
Calories: 212
% calories from fat: 10
Protein (g): 17.3
Carbohydrate (g): 31.4
Fat (g): 2.5
Saturated fat (g): 0.6
Cholesterol (mg): 22.4
Sodium (mg): 630

Exchanges:
Milk: 0.0
Vegetable: 0.0
Fruit: 0.0
Bread: 2.0
Meat: 1.0
Fat: 0.0

1. Cook turkey and onion in lightly greased large saucepan over medium heat until turkey is browned, about 5 minutes; crumble turkey with a fork. Add remaining ingredients, except cilantro, hickory seasonings, salt, and pepper; heat to boiling. Reduce heat and simmer, covered, 10 minutes. Stir in cilantro and hickory seasoning. Season to taste with salt and pepper.

BLIZZARD CHILI

A great chili for snowbound winter evenings.

6 entrée servings

1 pound lean ground beef round

2 cups finely chopped onions

1 clove garlic, minced

2 cups each: cooked dry or rinsed drained canned kidney, black, and cannellini beans

2 cans (15 ounces each) tomato sauce

1 bay leaf

1 tablespoon chili powder

2 teaspoons sugar

1 teaspoon ground cumin

Salt and pepper, to taste

Per Serving:
Calories: 457
% calories from fat: 10.4
Protein (g): 33
Carbohydrate (g): 59
Fat (g): 10.4
Saturated fat (g): 3.8
Cholesterol (mg): 47
Sodium (mg): 98

Exchanges:
Milk: 0.0
Vegetable: 3.0
Fruit: 0.0
Bread: 2.5
Meat: 3.0
Fat: 0.5

1. Cook ground beef, onions, and garlic in lightly greased large saucepan over medium heat until beef is browned, 8 to 10 minutes; crumble beef with a fork. Stir in remaining ingredients, except salt and pepper, and heat to boiling. Reduce heat and simmer, covered, 20 to 30 minutes. Discard bay leaf; season to taste with salt and pepper.

MICROWAVE CHICKEN AND PINTO BEAN CHILI

45 *Enjoy microwave speed in the preparation of this great chili.*

4 entrée servings

12 ounces ground chicken breast
½ cup each: chopped medium onion, green bell pepper
2 cloves garlic, minced
1 can (14½ ounces) Mexican-style stewed tomatoes
½ teaspoon ground cumin
1-2 tablespoons chili powder
1 can (15½ ounces) pinto beans, rinsed, drained
Salt and pepper, to taste

Per Serving:
Calories: 197
% calories from fat: 9
Protein (g): 19.7
Carbohydrate (g): 26
Fat (g): 2.1
Saturated fat (g): 0.5
Cholesterol (mg): 34.5
Sodium (mg): 555

Exchanges:
Milk: 0.0
Vegetable: 2.0
Fruit: 0.0
Bread: 1.0
Meat: 1.5
Fat: 0.0

1. Microwave chicken, onion, bell pepper, and garlic in 2-quart glass casserole, loosely covered, on Medium power, until chicken is cooked, 4 to 5 minutes. Drain; crumble chicken with a fork. Stir in remaining ingredients, except salt, pepper, and cilantro; microwave, covered, on Medium power 10 minutes, stirring halfway through cooking time. Season to taste with salt and pepper; garnish each bowl with cilantro.

MESQUITE CHICKEN CHILI

A differently delicious Tex-Mex dish that will appeal to the adventurous and not-so-adventurous alike.

4 entrée servings

12 ounces boneless, skinless chicken breast, cubed
¾ cup each: chopped onion, poblano chili
1 teaspoon olive oil
1 can (28 ounces) reduced-sodium crushed tomatoes

8 ounces tomatillos, husked, coarsely chopped

1 can (15 ounces) red beans, rinsed, drained

2 tablespoons chili powder

2 teaspoons minced garlic

1 teaspoon mesquite smoke flavoring

Salt and pepper, to taste

Per Serving:
Calories: 293
% calories from fat: 15
Protein (g): 28.1
Carbohydrate (g): 36.3
Fat (g): 5.3
Saturated fat (g): 1.1
Cholesterol (mg): 51.7
Sodium (mg): 469

Exchanges:
Milk: 0.0
Vegetable: 2.0
Fruit: 0.0
Bread: 2.0
Meat: 2.0
Fat: 0.0

1. Sauté chicken, onion, and poblano chili in oil in large saucepan until chicken is browned, about 8 minutes; add remaining ingredients, except salt and pepper. Heat to boiling; reduce heat and simmer, covered, 10 minutes. Season to taste with salt and pepper.

VARIATION

Hominy Chili — Make chili as above, substituting boneless lean beef for the chicken and 1 can (15 ounces) hominy, drained, for the tomatillos; omit mesquite smoke flavoring. Sprinkle each bowl of chili with shredded Cheddar cheese and dollops of reduced-fat sour cream.

SANTA FE SKILLET CHILI WITH CHILI-CHEESE DUMPLINGS

45

Fluffy cheese and chili-flavored dumplings top this skillet-easy chili.

6 entrée servings

1 pound lean ground beef

1 cup chopped onion

1 teaspoon minced garlic

1 tablespoon each: chili powder, ground cumin

½ teaspoon crushed red pepper

1 can (15 ounces) chili beans in spicy sauce, undrained

1 can (14½ ounces) Mexican-style stewed tomatoes

1 can (4 ounces) chopped green chilies, undrained

Salt and pepper, to taste

Chili-Cheese Dumplings (see p. 592)

Per Serving:
Calories: 307
% calories from fat: 23
Protein (g): 23.1
Carbohydrate (g): 37.7
Fat (g): 8.3
Saturated fat (g): 2.6
Cholesterol (mg): 40.4
Sodium (mg): 909

Exchanges:
Milk: 0.0
Vegetable: 2.0
Fruit: 0.0
Bread: 3.0
Meat: 3.0
Fat: 0.5

1. Cook ground beef, onion, garlic, and seasonings in lightly greased large saucepan over medium heat until beef is browned, about 5 minutes; crumble beef with a fork. Stir in beans with liquid, tomatoes, and green chilies; heat to boiling. Reduce heat and simmer, covered, 10 minutes; season to taste with salt and pepper.

2. Heat stew to boiling. Spoon Chili Cheese Dumplings dough into 6 mounds on top of chili. Reduce heat and simmer, uncovered, 10 minutes; simmer, covered, until dumplings are dry on top, about 10 minutes.

CHILI VERDE

This "green chili" is made with tomatillos, which are also called Mexican green tomatoes. Use canned tomatillos if fresh are not available.

8 entrée servings

1 pound boneless lean pork, cubed (1-inch)
2 large onions, thinly sliced
6–8 cloves garlic, chopped
1 cup water
2 pounds tomatillos, husked
2 cans (14½ ounces each) reduced-sodium
  fat-free chicken broth
2 cans (15 ounces each) Great Northern beans,
  rinsed, drained
2 cans (4 ounces each) diced green chilies
2 teaspoons ground cumin
½ cup lightly packed cilantro, chopped
Cilantro-Chili Sour Cream (recipe follows)

Per Serving:
Calories: 276
% calories from fat: 19
Protein (g): 24.4
Carbohydrate (g): 31.2
Fat (g): 5.8
Saturated fat (g): 1.6
Cholesterol (mg): 32.2
Sodium (mg): 550

Exchanges:
Milk: 0.0
Vegetable: 1.0
Fruit: 0.0
Bread: 2.0
Meat: 2.0
Fat: 0.0

1. Heat pork, onions, garlic, and water to boiling in large saucepan; reduce heat and simmer, covered, 30 minutes, adding more water if necessary to prevent sticking. Cook, uncovered, over medium-high heat until all liquid is gone and meat is browned. Add tomatillos and broth; heat to boiling. Reduce heat and simmer, covered, until tomatillos are tender, about 20 minutes. Break tomatillos apart, using two forks. Add beans, green chilies, and cumin. Simmer, covered, until meat is very tender, 20 to 30 minutes; stir in cilantro. Serve with Cilantro-Chili Sour Cream.

Cilantro-Chili Sour Cream
Makes about ½ cup

½ cup fat-free sour cream
1 tablespoon chopped cilantro
1 teaspoon chopped pickled jalapeño chili

1. Combine all ingredients.

CHILI WITH BEANS AND BEER

This chili is very easy to make—the longer it simmers, the better the flavor.

6 entrée servings

1 pound lean ground beef
1 tablespoon minced garlic, ground cumin
3 tablespoons chili powder
1 teaspoon dried oregano leaves
3 tablespoons flour
2 cans (10½ ounces each) reduced-sodium fat-free
   beef broth
1 can (12 ounces) beer or reduced-sodium beef broth
1 can (15 ounces) each: undrained chili beans in
   spicy sauce, rinsed drained pinto beans
Salt and pepper, to taste

Per Serving:
Calories: 320
% calories from fat: 29
Protein (g): 25
Carbohydrate (g): 30.8
Fat (g): 10.7
Saturated fat (g): 3.9
Cholesterol (mg): 47
Sodium (mg): 609

Exchanges:
Milk: 0.0
Vegetable: 0.0
Fruit: 0.0
Bread: 2.0
Meat: 2.5
Fat: 1.0

1. Cook ground beef in lightly greased large saucepan over medium heat until browned; crumble with a fork. Add garlic, herbs, and flour and cook 1 to 2 minutes. Stir in beef broth and beer and heat to boiling; reduce heat and simmer, covered, 1 hour, adding beans during last 15 minutes. Season to taste with salt and pepper.

VARIATIONS

Ranchero Chili — Make recipe as above, cooking 4 ounces sliced reduced-fat smoked sausage and ½ cup chopped onion with the ground beef. Serve bowls of chili with dollops of sour cream.

Mexican Chili Potatoes — Cook beef as above, adding herbs. Omit flour, beef broth, and beer. Stir beans into beef mixture; season to taste with salt and pepper; reserve. Cut 6 medium Idaho potatoes lengthwise into quarters. Place potatoes on greased foil-lined cookie sheet and spray with vegetable cooking spray; sprinkle lightly with salt and pepper. Bake at 400 degrees until golden and tender, 30 to 45 minutes. Spoon reserved chili over potatoes and sprinkle each with 2 tablespoons shredded reduced-fat Co-Jack cheese and bake until melted, about 5 minutes. Serve with fat-free sour cream; sprinkle with sliced green onions.

CHILI RIO GRANDE

Lots of onions, and a combination of ground and cubed meats give this chili loads of flavor and texture.

12 entrée servings

4 cups chopped onions
1 tablespoon olive oil
2 pounds lean pork, cubed (¾-inch)
1 pound lean ground beef
2 tablespoons minced garlic
¼ cup chili powder
1 tablespoon ground cumin
2 teaspoons dried oregano leaves
2 cans (14½ ounces each) reduced-sodium diced
    tomatoes, undrained
1¾ cups Quick-Spiced Beef Stock (see p. 6)
1 can (12 ounces) beer or tomato juice
1 can (4 ounces) chopped green chilies
2 cans (15 ounces each) red kidney beans, rinsed, drained
Salt and pepper, to taste
¾ cup Cilantro-Chili Sour Cream (1½ recipes) (see p. 121)

Per Serving:
Calories: 344
% calories from fat: 30
Protein (g): 32.7
Carbohydrate (g): 25.3
Fat (g): 11.5
Saturated fat (g): 3.8
Cholesterol (mg): 66.4
Sodium (mg): 352

Exchanges:
Milk: 0.0
Vegetable: 2.0
Fruit: 0.0
Bread: 1.0
Meat: 4.0
Fat: 0.0

1. Cook onions in oil in large saucepan over medium-low heat until golden brown, about 20 minutes. Add meats and cook over medium heat until browned, about 10 minutes, crumbling beef with a fork; stir in remaining ingredients, except beans, salt, pepper, and Cilantro-Chili Sour Cream. Heat to boiling; reduce heat and simmer, covered, 45 to 60 minutes, adding beans during last 10 minutes. Season to taste with salt and pepper; serve with dollops of Cilantro-Chili Sour Cream.

FIERY PINTO BEAN CHILI

45 *Adjust the heat in this quick chili to suit your taste. Quesadillas help quench the fire!*

6 entrée servings

1 can (15 ounces) pinto beans, rinsed, drained
2 cups shredded, cooked chicken (8 ounces)
1 clove garlic, minced
3–6 jalapeño chilies, minced
3 green onions, sliced
2 medium tomatoes, chopped
½–1 cup tomato juice
1 teaspoon dried whole coriander
Salt, to taste
Quesadillas (recipe follows)

Per Serving:
Calories: 298
% calories from fat: 21
Protein (g): 22.4
Carbohydrate (g): 36.5
Fat (g): 7.2
Saturated fat (g): 3
Cholesterol (mg): 35.4
Sodium (mg): 564

Exchanges:
Milk: 0.0
Vegetable: 1.0
Fruit. 0.0
Bread: 2.0
Meat: 2.5
Fat: 0.0

1. Combine all ingredients, except salt and Quesadillas, in large saucepan; heat to boiling. Reduce heat and simmer, covered, 20 to 25 minutes. Season to taste with salt. Serve with Quesadillas.

Quesadillas
Makes 6

1 poblano chili, thinly sliced
1 medium onion, finely chopped
½ teaspoon ground cumin
2 tablespoons finely chopped cilantro
1 cup (4 ounces) shredded reduced-fat Monterey Jack or Pepper Jack
  cheese
6 flour tortillas (6-inch)
Vegetable cooking spray

1. Sauté poblano chili and onion in lightly greased large skillet until tender, about 5 minutes; stir in cumin and cilantro. Sprinkle cheese on half of each tortilla; spoon vegetable mixture over cheese and fold tortillas in half. Cook quesadillas in lightly greased large skillet over medium to medium-high heat until browned on the bottoms, 2 to 3 minutes. Spray tops of quesadillas with cooking spray; turn and cook until browned on the other side.

VARIATION

Slow-Burn Chili — Make recipe as above, decreasing jalapeño chilies to 2, and adding ½ teaspoon each black and cayenne pepper and ¼ to ½ teaspoon crushed red pepper. Season to taste with salt and hot pepper sauce.

TEXAS HOT CHILI

Hot sausage, hot chilies, and lots of spices make this chili extra good.

8 entrée servings

12 ounces hot Italian-style turkey sausage, casing removed

1¼ pounds coarsely ground lean beef

1 large onion, chopped

1 can (4 ounces) chopped green chilies, undrained

1 jalapeño chili, chopped

1 can (14½ ounces) each: undrained reduced-sodium diced tomatoes, reduced-sodium fat-free beef broth

1 can (15 ounces) each: tomato sauce, rinsed drained red kidney and garbanzo beans

2 tablespoons hot chili powder

½ teaspoon each: ground cumin and coriander

1 tablespoon low-sodium Worcestershire sauce

Salt and cayenne pepper, to taste

Hot pepper sauce, to taste

Per Serving:
Calories: 300
% calories from fat: 24
Protein (g): 28.9
Carbohydrate (g): 29.8
Fat (g): 8.3
Saturated fat (g): 2.2
Cholesterol (mg): 57.1
Sodium (mg): 744

Exchanges:
Milk: 0.0
Vegetable: 0.0
Fruit: 0.0
Bread: 2.0
Meat: 3.0
Fat: 0.0

1. Cook sausage and ground beef in lightly greased large saucepan over medium heat until browned, about 5 minutes; crumble with a fork. Add onion, green chilies, and jalapeño chili and cook until onion is tender, about 5 minutes. Stir in remaining ingredients, except salt, cayenne pepper, and hot pepper sauce, and heat to boiling. Reduce heat and simmer, covered, 20 to 30 minutes or until thickened. Season to taste with salt, cayenne pepper, and hot pepper sauce.

VARIATION

Italian-Style Chili — Make recipe as above, deleting green chilies and jalapeño chilies and substituting 4 ounces sliced pepperoni for 4 ounces of the ground beef and 1 to 1½ teaspoons dried Italian seasoning for the cumin and coriander.

VEAL CHILI POBLANO

45 *Ground veal, poblano chili, and purchased seasoning mix make this fast-track chili an almost-instant favorite.*

4 entrée servings

1 pound ground lean veal or turkey
1 each: chopped large onion, small poblano chili, rib celery
1 can (14½ ounces) reduced-sodium crushed tomatoes
1 can (15 ounces) Great Northern beans, rinsed, drained
½–1 package (1¼ ounce-size) chili seasoning mix
Tortilla Wedges (recipe follows)

Per Serving:
Calories: 282
% calories from fat: 18
Protein (g): 34.2
Carbohydrate (g): 26.4
Fat (g): 6.1
Saturated fat (g): 1.6
Cholesterol (mg): 99.5
Sodium (mg): 659

Exchanges:
Milk: 0.0
Vegetable: 0.0
Fruit: 0.0
Bread: 2.0
Meat: 3.0
Fat: 0.0

1. Cook veal in lightly greased large saucepan over medium heat, until browned, about 8 minutes; crumble with a fork. Add onion, poblano chili, and celery, and sauté until tender, about 5 minutes. Stir in tomatoes, beans, and seasoning mix; heat to boiling. Reduce heat and simmer, uncovered, 15 minutes. Serve with Tortilla Wedges.

Tortilla Wedges
Makes 12 wedges

2 flour tortillas (6-inch)
¼ cup each: (1 ounce) shredded reduced-fat pepper-Jack and Cheddar cheese, sliced green onions, mild or hot salsa
Reduced-fat sour cream, as garnish

1. Place tortillas on baking sheet; sprinkle with combined cheeses and green onions. Bake at 450 degrees until edges of tortillas are browned and cheese is melted, 5 to 7 minutes. Cut each tortilla into 6 wedges; top each with 1 teaspoon salsa and small dollop of sour cream.

BIG RED CHILI

45 *A spicy chili that sports red onions, red kidney beans, red bell peppers, and crushed tomatoes.*

4 entrée servings

8 ounces ground beef sirloin
1 each: large chopped red onion, red bell pepper
1 can (28 ounces) reduced-sodium crushed tomatoes
1 can (15 ounces) red kidney beans, rinsed, drained
2 tablespoons each: red wine vinegar, chili powder
¼ teaspoon ground allspice
⅔ cup mild or medium picante sauce
Salt and pepper, to taste

Per Serving:
Calories: 197
% calories from fat: 16
Protein (g): 17.5
Carbohydrate (g): 25.3
Fat (g): 3.6
Saturated fat (g): 1.1
Cholesterol (mg): 29.7
Sodium (mg): 652

Exchanges:
Milk: 0.0
Vegetable: 2.0
Fruit: 0.0
Bread: 1.0
Meat: 1.0
Fat: 0.5

1. Cook beef, onion, and red pepper in lightly greased large saucepan over medium heat until beef is browned, about 5 minutes; crumble beef with a fork. Add remaining ingredients, except picante sauce, salt, and pepper; heat to boiling. Reduce heat and simmer, covered, 30 minutes, adding picante sauce the last 10 minutes. Season to taste with salt and pepper.

VARIATION

Farmhouse Chili — Make recipe as above, substituting home-style turkey sausage for the ground beef and tomato juice for the picante sauce. Decrease chili powder to 1 tablespoon. Omit allspice; add 1 to 2 tablespoons maple syrup and ¾ teaspoon each ground cumin and dried sage leaves.

LIGHTNING-FAST TEXAS CHILI

45 *Get Texas-size flavor in this recipe. Cilantro adds a captivating pungency.*

4 entrée servings

8 ounces each: lean ground pork, ground turkey breast
1 cup sliced green onions
1 pound tomatoes, chopped
1 can (15 ounces) chili beans, undrained

1 small cayenne or jalapeño chili, seeded, chopped

Salt, to taste

Finely chopped cilantro, as garnish

Per Serving:
Calories: 262
% calories from fat: 19
Protein (g): 30.5
Carbohydrate (g): 25.3
Fat (g): 5.9
Saturated fat (g): 1.6
Cholesterol (mg): 54.9
Sodium (mg): 404

Exchanges:
Milk: 0.0
Vegetable: 2.0
Fruit: 0.0
Bread: 1.0
Meat: 2.5
Fat: 0.0

1. Cook pork, turkey, and green onions in lightly greased large saucepan over medium heat until meats are browned, about 8 minutes; and crumble meats with a fork. Stir in tomatoes, chili beans with liquid, and cayenne chili; heat to boiling. Reduce heat and simmer, covered, 15 minutes. Season to taste with salt and pepper; sprinkle each bowl of soup with cilantro.

EASY TORTILLA CHILI

45 *Baked tortilla chips add crunch and texture to this flavorful chili.*

8 entrée servings

8 ounces ground beef round

2 cups chopped onions

3¾ cups reduced-sodium fat-free beef broth

1 jar (16 ounces) reduced-sodium mild or medium salsa

1 can (15 ounces) kidney beans, rinsed, drained

1½ cups whole kernel corn

1 teaspoon chili powder

2 cups crushed, baked tortilla chips

Salt and pepper, to taste

½ cup (2 ounces) shredded reduced-fat Cheddar cheese

Per Serving:
Calories: 280
% calories from fat: 12
Protein (g): 20
Carbohydrate (g): 42
Fat (g): 3.9
Saturated fat (g): 1.1
Cholesterol (mg): 23.3
Sodium (mg): 622

Exchanges:
Milk: 0.0
Vegetable: 2.0
Fruit: 0.0
Bread: 2.0
Meat: 1.5
Fat: 0.0

1. Cook ground beef and onions in lightly greased large saucepan over medium heat until beef is browned, about 5 minutes; crumble beef with a fork. Stir in broth, salsa, beans, corn, and chili powder; heat to boiling. Reduce heat and simmer, covered, 15 to 20 minutes. Stir in tortilla chips; season to taste with salt and pepper. Sprinkle each bowl of chili with cheese.

SOUTH-OF-THE-BORDER CHILI

45 *A chili that's a little different, made with canned soup!*

6 entrée servings

⅓–½ cup: chopped onion, green onions, red
     bell pepper
1 small jalapeño chili, seeded, finely chopped
2 cloves garlic, minced
1–2 tablespoons olive oil
1 pound boneless, skinless chicken breast, cubed
     (¾-inch)
1 can (10¾ ounces) reduced-sodium, reduced-fat
     cream of chicken soup
½ cup tomato sauce
1–1½ cups fat-free milk
1 can (4 ounces) chopped green chilies, drained
1 tablespoon chili powder
½ teaspoon ground cumin
Salt and pepper, to taste
½ cup (2 ounces) shredded reduced-fat Monterey Jack cheese
Baked Tortilla Chips (recipe follows)

Per Serving:
Calories: 259
% calories from fat: 27
Protein (g): 24.4
Carbohydrate (g): 23.5
Fat (g): 7.8
Saturated fat (g): 2.6
Cholesterol (mg): 59.8
Sodium (mg): 467

Exchanges:
Milk: 0.0
Vegetable: 2.0
Fruit: 0.0
Bread: 1.0
Meat: 2.5
Fat: 0.0

1. Sauté onions, bell pepper, jalapeño chili, and garlic in oil in large
saucepan 5 minutes; add chicken and cook until browned, 5 to 8
minutes. Stir in remaining ingredients, except salt, pepper, cheese,
and Baked Tortilla Chips; heat to boiling. Reduce heat and simmer,
covered, 10 minutes; season to taste with salt and pepper. Sprinkle
each serving with cheese; serve with Baked Tortilla Chips.

Baked Tortilla Chips

Makes 6 servings (8 chips each)

6 corn tortillas (6-inch)
Vegetable cooking spray
⅛ teaspoon each: ground cumin, chili powder, dried
     oregano leaves, paprika
Salt and cayenne pepper, to taste

1. Cut each tortilla into 8 wedges; arrange in single layer on jelly roll pan. Spray tortillas with cooking spray; sprinkle lightly with combined herbs, salt, and cayenne pepper. Bake at 350 degrees until lightly browned, 5 to 7 minutes.

CHILI MOLE

This chili boasts the intriguing flavor of traditional Mexican mole sauce; use chicken, pork, or beef or a combination of the 3 meats.

6 entrée servings

1 pound lean pork, fat trimmed, cubed

1 cup each: reduced-sodium fat-free chicken broth, chopped onion

1 tablespoon minced roasted garlic

½–1 teaspoon chopped seeded jalapeño chili

¼ cup slivered, blanched almonds

1 can (15 ounces) caliente-style chili beans, undrained

¼ cup tomato sauce

2–3 teaspoons low-sodium Worcestershire sauce

¼ teaspoon ground cinnamon

1 can (14½ ounces) reduced-sodium diced tomatoes, undrained

1 can (15 ounces) black beans, rinsed, drained

½ ounce unsweetened chocolate

Salt and pepper, to taste

Guacamole (recipe follows)

Finely chopped cilantro, as garnish

Per Serving:
Calories: 328
% calories from fat: 28
Protein (g): 28.8
Carbohydrate (g): 32.5
Fat (g): 10.6
Saturated fat (g): 3
Cholesterol (mg): 42.9
Sodium (mg): 671

Exchanges:
Milk: 0.0
Vegetable: 1.0
Fruit: 0.0
Bread: 2.0
Meat: 2.0
Fat: 1.0

1. Heat pork and chicken broth to boiling in medium saucepan; reduce heat and simmer, covered, until pork is tender, 20 to 30 minutes; drain, reserving liquid. Sauté onion, garlic, jalapeño chili, and almonds in small skillet until onion is tender, 5 to 8 minutes. Process onion mixture, chili beans with liquid, tomato sauce, Worcestershire sauce, and cinnamon in food processor or blender until smooth; return to saucepan and add pork. Stir in tomatoes with liquid and black beans; heat to boiling. Reduce heat and simmer, covered, 10 minutes, stirring in enough reserved cooking liquid to make desired consistency. Add chocolate, stirring until melted; season to taste with salt and pepper. Top each bowl of chili with Guacamole; sprinkle generously with cilantro.

Guacamole
Makes about ⅔ cup

1 medium avocado, coarsely mashed
½ each: small finely chopped onion, seeded minced jalapeño chili
1 tablespoon finely chopped cilantro
Hot pepper sauce, to taste
Salt, to taste

1. Mix avocado, onion, jalapeño chili, and cilantro; season to taste with hot pepper sauce and salt.

CHORIZO CHILI

This chili begins with our flavorful low-fat version of Chorizo, to which beans, tomatoes, and onions are added. The Chorizo can be used in many of your favorite Mexican recipes, or formed into patties and cooked for a dinner entrée.

8 entrée servings

Chorizo (recipe follows)
½ cup chopped onion
2 cans (15 ounces each) pinto or black beans, rinsed, drained
2 cans (14½ ounces each) reduced-sodium diced tomatoes, undrained
Salt and pepper to taste

Per Serving:
Calories: 229
% calories from fat: 17
Protein (g): 24.4
Carbohydrate (g): 24.2
Fat (g): 4.3
Saturated fat (g): 1.3
Cholesterol (mg): 49.3
Sodium (mg): 414

Exchanges:
Milk: 0.0
Vegetable: 2.0
Fruit: 0.0
Bread: 1.0
Meat: 2.0
Fat: 0.0

1. Cook Chorizo and onion in lightly greased large saucepan over medium heat until Chorizo is browned, 8 to 10 minutes; crumble chorizo with a fork. Stir in beans and tomatoes with liquid and heat to boiling; reduce heat and simmer, covered, 30 to 45 minutes. Season to taste with salt and pepper.

Chorizo
Makes 1½ pounds

½ teaspoon each: crushed coriander and cumin seeds
2 dried ancho chilies
1½ pounds pork tenderloin, finely chopped or ground
4 cloves garlic, minced
2 tablespoons each: paprika, cider vinegar, water
1 teaspoon dried oregano leaves
½ teaspoon salt

1. Cook coriander and cumin seeds in lightly greased small skillet over medium heat, stirring frequently until toasted, 2 to 3 minutes. Remove from skillet; reserve. Add ancho chilies to skillet; cook over medium heat until softened, about 1 minute on each side, turning chilies often so they do not burn. Remove and discard stems, veins, and seeds; chop finely. Combine all ingredients; refrigerate 4 hours or overnight for flavors to blend.

CHEESY CHILI BLANCO WITH RED TOMATO SALSA

This white chili is made extra-creamy with the addition of sour cream and Monterey Jack cheese.

8 entrée servings

2 cups chopped onions
1 tablespoon each: chopped garlic, canola oil
1½ pounds boneless, skinless chicken breasts, cubed
2 cans (15 ounces each) Great Northern beans, rinsed, drained
1 can (14½ ounces) reduced-sodium fat-free chicken broth
1 can (4 ounces) diced green chilies, drained
1 tablespoon dried oregano leaves
1 teaspoon ground cumin
1 cup fat-free sour cream
2 cups (8 ounces) shredded reduced-fat Monterey Jack cheese
Salt and cayenne pepper, to taste
Red Tomato Salsa (recipe follows)

Per Serving:
Calories: 331
% calories from fat: 24
Protein (g): 37.5
Carbohydrate (g): 27.7
Fat (g): 9.3
Saturated fat (g): 4.4
Cholesterol (mg): 72
Sodium (mg): 674

Exchanges:
Milk: 0.0
Vegetable: 0.0
Fruit: 0.0
Bread: 2.0
Meat: 3.5
Fat: 0.0

1. Sauté onions and garlic in oil in large saucepan until tender, about 8 minutes. Add chicken and sauté until lightly browned, about 5 minutes. Stir in beans, broth, green chilies, oregano, and cumin. Heat to boiling; reduce heat and simmer, covered, 30 minutes. Stir in sour cream and cheese, stirring until cheese is melted. Season to taste with salt and cayenne pepper. Serve with Red Tomato Salsa.

Red Tomato Salsa
Makes about 2 cups

2 large tomatoes, chopped
⅓ cup each: finely chopped onion, poblano chili
1 clove garlic, minced
2 tablespoons finely chopped cilantro
Salt, to taste

1. Mix all ingredients, except salt; season to taste with salt.

WHITE CHILI

There's lots of flavor in this chicken and white bean chili.

8 entrée servings

1 cup each: chopped red or green bell peppers, onion
2 teaspoons each: minced garlic, jalapeño chili, gingerroot
1 teaspoon each: dried thyme and oregano leaves
1 tablespoon canola oil
1 pound boneless, skinless chicken breast, cubed (¾-inch)
2 tablespoons flour
2 cups Chicken Stock (see p. 2)
2 cans (15 ounces each) Great Northern beans, rinsed, drained
Salt and pepper, to taste
Tomatillo Salsa (recipe follows)
Fat-free sour cream, as garnish

Per Serving:
Calories: 195
% calories from fat: 16
Protein (g): 19.6
Carbohydrate (g): 25.1
Fat (g): 4
Saturated fat (g): 0.8
Cholesterol (mg): 35.4
Sodium (mg): 322

Exchanges:
Milk: 0.0
Vegetable: 2.0
Fruit: 0.0
Bread: 1.0
Meat: 1.5
Fat: 0.0

1. Sauté peppers, onion, garlic, jalapeño chili, gingerroot, thyme, and oregano in oil in large saucepan until onion is tender, about 8 minutes. Add chicken and sauté 5 minutes; sprinkle with flour and cook 1 to 2 minutes. Add stock and beans; heat to boiling. Reduce heat and simmer, covered, until chicken is tender, about 10 minutes. Season to taste with salt and pepper. Serve with Tomatillo Salsa and sour cream.

Tomatillo Salsa
Makes about 1 cup

12 ounces tomatillos, husked
½ small onion, chopped
1 tablespoon finely chopped cilantro
1 teaspoon each: minced jalapeño chili, garlic
¼ teaspoon ground cumin
⅛ teaspoon sugar
Salt, to taste

1. Simmer tomatillos in water to cover in large saucepan until tender, 5 to 8 minutes. Cool; drain, reserving liquid. Process tomatillos, and remaining ingredients, except salt, in food processor or blender until almost smooth, adding enough reserved liquid to make medium dipping consistency. Season to taste with salt.

BLACK AND WHITE BEAN CHILI

Made with black and white beans, this chili is uniquely accented in flavor and color with sun-dried tomatoes.

4 entrée servings (about 1¼ cups each)

12 ounces very lean ground beef

1 cup chopped onion

½ cup chopped green bell pepper

1 medium jalapeño chili, finely chopped

2 teaspoons minced garlic

2 cans (14½ ounces) each: reduced-sodium diced tomatoes, undrained

1 can (15 ounces each): Great Northern and black beans, rinsed, drained

¼ cup chopped sun-dried tomatoes (not in oil)

2–3 tablespoons chili powder

1–1½ teaspoons each: ground cumin, dried oregano leaves

1 bay leaf

Salt and pepper, to taste

¼ cup finely chopped cilantro

Per Serving:
Calories: 386
% calories from fat: 14
Protein (g): 34
Carbohydrate (g): 55.2
Fat (g): 6.5
Saturated fat (g): 2.2
Cholesterol (mg): 52.7
Sodium (mg): 604

Exchanges:
Milk: 0.0
Vegetable: 2.0
Fruit: 0.0
Bread: 3.0
Meat: 2.0
Fat: 0.0

1. Cook ground beef, onion, bell pepper, jalapeño chili, and garlic in lightly greased large saucepan over medium heat until beef is browned, 8 to 10 minutes; crumble beef with a fork. Stir in remaining ingredients, except salt, pepper, and cilantro. Heat to boiling; reduce heat and simmer, covered, 30 minutes. Discard bay leaf; season to taste with salt and pepper. Stir in cilantro.

PRAIRIE CHILI WITH CHICKEN

45

Bean sprouts add a unique "crunch" to this flavorful chicken-based chili.

4 entrée servings

12 ounces cooked chicken breast, shredded

1 can (14½ ounces) reduced-sodium stewed tomatoes, undrained

1 can (15½ ounces) pinto beans, rinsed, drained

¾ cup mild picante sauce

2 ancho chilies, softened, chopped

2 tablespoons dried onion flakes

¼–½ teaspoon crushed red pepper

1 teaspoon paprika

1 cup fresh or rinsed, drained canned bean sprouts

Salt, to taste

Per Serving:
Calories: 352
% calories from fat: 29
Protein (g): 34.2
Carbohydrate (g): 28.8
Fat (g): 11.5
Saturated fat (g): 2.9
Cholesterol (mg): 70.5
Sodium (mg): 689

Exchanges:
Milk: 0.0
Vegetable: 3.0
Fruit: 0.0
Bread: 1.0
Meat: 4.0
Fat: 0.0

1. Heat all ingredients, except bean sprouts and salt, to boiling in large saucepan; reduce heat and simmer, covered, 15 minutes, adding bean sprouts the last 5 minutes. Season to taste with salt.

TENDERLOIN CHILI

45 *This super-easy, super-fast chili sports tender, lean pork and fresh tomatoes.*

4 entrée servings

12 ounces cooked pork tenderloin, shredded

1 can (15 ounces) each: reduced-sodium fat-free beef broth, rinsed drained pinto beans

1 pound plum tomatoes, sliced

2 jalapeño chilies, minced

1 tablespoon chili powder

1 teaspoon each: toasted cumin seeds, Worcestershire sauce

Salt and pepper, to taste

Per Serving:
Calories: 274
% calories from fat: 19
Protein (g): 32.7
Carbohydrate (g): 23.4
Fat (g): 5.8
Saturated fat (g): 1.7
Cholesterol (mg): 67.1
Sodium (mg): 475

Exchanges:
Milk: 0.0
Vegetable: 2.0
Fruit: 0.0
Bread: 1.0
Meat: 3.0
Fat: 0.0

1. Heat all ingredients, except salt and pepper, to boiling in large saucepan; reduce heat and simmer, covered, 15 minutes. Season to taste with salt and pepper.

LENTIL CHILI WITH BACON AND BEER

45 *Lime, beer, and bacon make this chili differently delicious. So give it a try; it's a snap to make.*

4 entrée servings

1 medium onion, chopped

1½ cups cooked lentils

1 can (15 ounces) black beans, rinsed, drained

1 cup each: canned crushed tomatoes, beer, or tomato juice

1 tablespoon each: minced garlic, chili powder

1 jalapeño chili, seeded, chopped

1 teaspoon each: ground cumin, crushed dried rosemary leaves

Juice of 1 lime

Salt and pepper, to taste

4 slices bacon, cooked crisp, crumbled

Per Serving:
Calories: 244
% calories from fat: 1
Protein (g): 15
Carbohydrate (g): 43
Fat (g): 3.7
Saturated fat (g): 0.9
Cholesterol (mg): 5
Sodium (mg): 631

Exchanges:
Milk: 0.0
Vegetable: 0.0
Fruit: 0.0
Bread: 3.0
Meat: 0.0
Fat: 0.5

1. Sauté onion in lightly greased large saucepan until tender, about 5 minutes. Stir in remaining ingredients, except lime juice, salt, pepper, and bacon; heat to boiling. Reduce heat and simmer, covered, 15 minutes. Stir in lime juice; season to taste with salt and pepper. Sprinkle each bowl of chili with bacon.

ROASTED PEPPER CHILI

45 *Here's a mild-mannered chili with a lean and healthful profile. For crunch, serve it topped with broken baked tortilla chips.*

4 entrée servings

8 ounces ground turkey

1 cup chopped red onion

1 can (14½ ounces) each: undrained stewed tomatoes, rinsed, drained black beans

1 tablespoon chili powder

½ teaspoon ground cumin

¼ teaspoon ground allspice

1 small jalapeño chili, seeded, minced
½ cup coarsely chopped roasted red peppers
Salt and pepper, to taste

1. Cook turkey and onion in lightly greased large saucepan over medium heat until turkey is browned, about 5 minutes; crumble turkey with a fork. Add remaining ingredients, except roasted red peppers, salt, and pepper; heat to boiling. Reduce heat and simmer, covered, 15 minutes. Add roasted red peppers during last 5 minutes. Season to taste with salt and pepper.

Per Serving:
Calories: 170
% calories from fat: 11
Protein (g): 15.7
Carbohydrate (g): 29.7
Fat (g): 2.5
Saturated fat (g): 0.4
Cholesterol (mg): 22.4
Sodium (mg): 692

Exchanges:
Milk: 0.0
Vegetable: 2.0
Fruit: 0.0
Bread: 1.0
Meat: 1.0
Fat: 0.0

CHILI WITH SQUASH AND BEANS

A squeeze of lime adds a cooling touch to this spicy chili.

6 entrée servings

1 pound lean ground beef
2 medium onions, sliced (1-inch)
2 cups chopped celery
1 red bell pepper, sliced (1-inch)
½ jalapeño chili, finely chopped
2 cloves garlic, minced
2 cups butternut squash, peeled, cubed (1-inch)
1 can (15 ounces) each: reduced-sodium chunky
   tomato sauce, rinsed drained red kidney beans
3 cups reduced-sodium tomato juice
1 medium zucchini, cubed
1 cup sliced mushrooms
1½ teaspoons each: chili powder, ground cumin
Salt and pepper, to taste
6 lime wedges

Per Serving:
Calories: 317
% calories from fat: 30
Protein (g): 21.2
Carbohydrate (g): 36.1
Fat (g): 10.8
Saturated fat (g): 4
Cholesterol (mg): 46.6
Sodium (mg): 357

Exchanges:
Milk: 0.0
Vegetable: 1.0
Fruit: 0.0
Bread: 2.0
Meat: 2.0
Fat: 1.0

1. Cook ground beef in lightly greased large saucepan over medium heat until browned, about 8 minutes; crumble with a fork. Add onions, celery, bell pepper, jalapeño chili, and garlic. Sauté until tender, 8 to 10 minutes. Add remaining ingredients, except salt, pepper, and lime wedges; heat to boiling. Reduce heat and simmer, uncovered, until vegetables are tender and chili is thickened, 20 to 25 minutes. Season to taste with salt and pepper. Serve with lime wedges.

PORK CHILI WITH GREENS

Kale adds nutrients and color to this tasty chili.

8 entrée servings

1½ pounds lean ground pork or turkey

2 cans (15 ounces each) kidney beans, rinsed, drained

2 cans (14½ ounces each) reduced-sodium petite-diced tomatoes, undrained

½ cup chopped onion

½ teaspoon each: ground cinnamon, cumin

8 ounces kale or spinach, coarsely chopped

Salt and pepper, to taste

Per Serving:
Calories: 261
% calories from fat: 21
Protein (g): 28
Carbohydrate (g): 23.8
Fat (g): 6.1
Saturated fat (g): 2
Cholesterol (mg): 48.3
Sodium (mg): 332

Exchanges:
Milk: 0.0
Vegetable: 2.0
Fruit: 0.0
Bread: 1.0
Meat: 2.5
Fat: 0.0

1. Cook pork in lightly greased large saucepan; stir in beans, tomatoes with liquid, onion, cinnamon, and cumin. Heat to boiling; reduce heat and simmer, covered, 45 minutes, stirring in kale the last 10 minutes. Season to taste with salt and pepper.

VARIATION

Chili with Rajas — Make chili as above, substituting lean ground beef for the pork. Omit cinnamon and kale; add 1 to 2 tablespoons chili powder. Cook 2 thinly sliced poblano chilies and 1 sliced medium onion in 1 to 2 tablespoons olive oil in large skillet over medium to medium-low heat until chilies are very tender and onions are caramelized, 15 to 20 minutes; season to taste with salt. Serve chili in bowls; top with chili and onion mixture.

SWEET AND SPICY CHILI

45 *Sweet potatoes and sweet spices, combined with jalapeño chili and ginger-root, make a chili that is sure to please.*

6 entrée servings

1½ cups chopped onions

8 ounces mushrooms, quartered

2 teaspoons each: minced garlic, gingerroot, jalapeño chili

1 tablespoon olive oil

2 tablespoons flour

1 pound boneless, skinless chicken breast, cubed (¾-inch)

1 can (14½ ounces) chicken broth

2 medium sweet potatoes, peeled, cubed (¾-inch)

2 cans (15 ounces each) Great Northern beans, rinsed, drained

1 teaspoon each: dried oregano leaves, ground cumin

½ teaspoon ground coriander and cinnamon

Salt and white pepper; to taste

Fat-free sour cream, as garnish

Per Serving:
Calories: 274
% calories from fat: 16
Protein (g): 26.5
Carbohydrate (g): 36.7
Fat (g): 5.2
Saturated fat (g): 1
Cholesterol (mg): 46
Sodium (mg): 716

Exchanges:
Milk: 0.0
Vegetable: 0.0
Fruit: 0.0
Bread: 2.5
Meat: 2.0
Fat: 0.0

1. Sauté onions, mushrooms, garlic, gingerroot, and jalapeño chili in oil in large saucepan until tender, about 8 minutes; sprinkle with flour and cook 1 to 2 minutes. Add remaining ingredients, except salt, pepper, and sour cream; heat to boiling. Reduce heat and simmer, covered, until chicken is cooked and sweet potatoes are tender, about 20 minutes. Season to taste with salt and white pepper. Serve with sour cream.

CALIFORNIA CHILI

45 *This zesty chili sports familiar West Coast ingredients.*

6 entrée servings

1 pound boneless, skinless chicken breast, cubed (1-inch)
1 teaspoon crushed mixed peppercorns
4 cups sliced plum tomatoes
1 cup each: diced softened sun-dried tomatoes (not in oil), zinfandel or other dry red wine
¼–½ teaspoon dried red pepper
1–2 tablespoons chili powder
1 avocado, chopped
2 tablespoons sunflower seeds, toasted
Salt, to taste
6 tablespoons chopped basil

Per Serving:
Calories: 258
% calories from fat: 30
Protein (g): 21.5
Carbohydrate (g): 19.7
Fat (g): 9.2
Saturated fat (g): 1.8
Cholesterol (mg): 46
Sodium (mg): 272

Exchanges:
Milk: 0.0
Vegetable: 4.0
Fruit: 0.0
Bread: 0.0
Meat: 2.0
Fat: 1.0

1. Sauté chicken and peppercorns in lightly greased large saucepan until chicken is browned, 8 to 10 minutes. Add plum and sun-dried tomatoes, wine, red pepper, and chili powder; heat to boiling. Reduce heat and simmer, covered, 10 minutes; simmer, uncovered, until thickened to desired consistency, 5 to 10 minutes. Stir in avocado and sunflower seeds; season to taste with salt. Sprinkle each bowl of chili with basil.

YELLOW SQUASH AND WHITE BEAN CHILI

45 *For convenience, drained, rinsed beans can be substituted for the cooked dried beans.*

6 entrée servings

1 pound lean ground pork
1 cup each: chopped onion, thinly sliced leek (white part only), yellow bell pepper
1 jalapeño chili, finely chopped
2 teaspoons each: minced garlic, cumin seeds
1 tablespoon olive oil

¾ cup each: cubed yellow summer squash,
   peeled red potatoes
2 cups each: cooked, dried Great Northern and
   garbanzo beans
1 can (14½ ounces) reduced-sodium chicken broth
½ cup dry white wine or reduced-sodium
   chicken broth
1 teaspoon each: dried oregano leaves, chili powder
½ teaspoon each: ground coriander, cinnamon
1 bay leaf
Salt and pepper, to taste
1 small tomato, finely chopped
2 green onions, thinly sliced
3 tablespoons finely chopped cilantro

Per Serving:
Calories: 350
% calories from fat: 23
Protein (g): 32.7
Carbohydrate (g): 41.2
Fat (g): 10
Saturated fat (g): 2.7
Cholesterol (mg): 49.3
Sodium (mg): 719

Exchanges:
Milk: 0.0
Vegetable: 2.0
Fruit: 0.0
Bread: 2.0
Meat: 3.0
Fat: 0.0

1. Sauté pork, onion, leek, bell pepper, jalapeño chili, garlic, and cumin seeds in oil in large saucepan until pork is browned and vegetables tender, about 10 minutes. Add squash, potatoes, beans, broth, wine, herbs, and spices and heat to boiling. Reduce heat and simmer, covered, until vegetables are tender, about 10 minutes. Simmer, uncovered, until thickened to desired consistency, 5 to 10 minutes. Season to taste with salt and pepper; discard bay leaf. Sprinkle each bowl of soup with tomato, green onions, and cilantro.

VARIATION

Med-Rim Chili — Make chili as above, substituting ground lamb or beef for the pork and adding ¼ cup sliced Greek or ripe olives. Make 1 package (5.6 ounces) couscous according to package directions. Serve chili over couscous; sprinkle each serving with 1 tablespoon crumbled feta cheese.

CHICKEN CHILI WITH ORANGE CILANTRO RICE

An aromatic chili, with a perfect rice accompaniment.

6 entrée servings

1 pound boneless, skinless chicken breast, cubed
½ cup chopped onion
1 clove garlic, minced
1–2 tablespoons canola oil
1 can (28 ounces) diced tomatoes, undrained
1 can (15 ounces) Great Northern beans, rinsed, drained
2 teaspoons chili powder
½ teaspoon ground cumin
¼ teaspoons ground allspice
1 strip orange zest (2 x ½-inch)
Salt and pepper, to taste
Orange Cilantro Rice (recipe follows)
Chopped cilantro, as garnish

Per Serving:
Calories: 295
% calories from fat: 14
Protein (g): 24.1
Carbohydrate (g): 41.3
Fat (g): 4.8
Saturated fat (g): 0.9
Cholesterol (mg): 46
Sodium (mg): 765

Exchanges:
Milk: 0.0
Vegetable: 2.0
Fruit: 0.0
Bread: 2.0
Meat: 2.0
Fat: 0.0

1. Sauté chicken, onion, and garlic in oil in large saucepan until chicken is browned, 8 to 10 minutes. Stir in tomatoes with liquid, beans, spices, and orange zest; heat to boiling. Reduce heat and simmer, covered, 20 to 30 minutes; season to taste with salt and pepper. Serve over Orange Cilantro Rice; sprinkle with cilantro.

Orange Cilantro Rice
Makes 6 servings

½ cup sliced green onions
1 cup long-grain rice
Grated zest of 1 small orange
2¼ cups water
2 tablespoons finely chopped cilantro
Salt and pepper, to taste

1. Sauté onions in lightly greased medium saucepan until tender, 3 to 5 minutes. Add rice and orange zest; stir over medium heat until rice is lightly browned, 2 to 3 minutes. Add water and heat to boiling; reduce heat and simmer, covered, until rice is tender, 20 to 25 minutes. Stir in cilantro; season to taste with salt and pepper.

HABANERO CHILI

45 *This chili gets its firepower from the habanero chili; substitute jalapeño chili for a milder flavor.*

4 entrée servings

1 each: large onion, medium green bell pepper, chopped

¼–½ habanero chili, chopped

4 ounces turkey sausage, halved lengthwise, sliced

1 teaspoon olive oil

1 can (14½ ounces) reduced-sodium diced tomatoes, undrained

2 cups refried beans

1 tablespoon chili powder

1 teaspoon ground cumin

Salt, to taste

1 cup fat-free sour cream

Per Serving:
Calories: 293
% calories from fat: 18
Protein (g): 17.1
Carbohydrate (g): 43.8
Fat (g): 5.9
Saturated fat (g): 1
Cholesterol (mg): 25.6
Sodium (mg): 767

Exchanges:
Milk: 0.0
Vegetable: 0.0
Fruit: 0.0
Bread: 3.0
Meat: 1.0
Fat: 0.5

1. Sauté onion, bell pepper, habanero chili, and sausage in oil in large saucepan until sausage is browned, about 5 minutes. Stir in remaining ingredients, except salt and sour cream; heat to boiling. Reduce heat and simmer, covered, 15 minutes; simmer, uncovered, 5 to 10 minutes if thicker consistency is desired. Season to taste with salt. Serve with sour cream.

FIVE

Lunch
and
Supper Soups

VELVET VICHYSSOISE

45

Although typically served chilled, this soup is also delicious served warm.

6 first-course servings

½ cup each: chopped onion, leek (white part only)

2 tablespoons margarine or butter

3 tablespoons flour

2 cups reduced-sodium fat-free chicken broth

3½ cups cubed, peeled Idaho potatoes

2 cups fat-free milk

Salt and pepper, to taste

Minced chives, as garnish

Per Serving:
Calories: 227
% calories from fat: 16
Protein (g): 8.3
Carbohydrate (g): 39.4
Fat (g): 4.2
Saturated fat (g): 0.9
Cholesterol (mg): 1.5
Sodium (mg): 151

Exchanges:
Milk: 0.0
Vegetable: 2.0
Fruit: 0.0
Bread: 2.0
Meat: 0.0
Fat: 1.0

1. Sauté onion and leek in margarine in large saucepan until tender, 5 to 8 minutes. Stir in flour; cook 1 minute. Add broth and potatoes; heat to boiling. Reduce heat and simmer, covered, until potatoes are tender, 10 to 15 minutes. Stir in milk; simmer until hot, 3 to 4 minutes. Season to taste with salt and pepper. Process soup in food processor or blender until smooth. Refrigerate until chilled. Sprinkle each bowl of soup with chives.

VARIATION

Creamy Cauliflower Soup — Make recipe as above, substituting 2½ cups coarsely chopped cauliflower for 2½ cups potatoes; add ½ cup (2 ounces) grated Parmesan cheese to the soup with the milk. Omit chives; sprinkle each bowl of soup with ground nutmeg.

QUICK VICHYSSOISE

45

When you need a really fast version of vichyssoise, this is it!

4 first-course servings

1½ cups chopped leeks (white parts only) or green onions

½ teaspoon celery seeds

1 cup each: reduced-sodium fat-free chicken broth, cubed peeled Idaho potatoes

2 cups fat-free milk

Salt and cayenne pepper, to taste

1. Sauté leeks and celery seeds in lightly greased large saucepan until leeks are tender, about 5 minutes; add chicken broth and potatoes and heat to boiling. Reduce heat and simmer, covered, until potatoes are tender, about 10 minutes; process soup and milk in food processor or blender until smooth. Season to taste with salt and cayenne pepper; refrigerate until chilled.

Per Serving:
Calories: 150
% calories from fat: 4
Protein (g): 8.3
Carbohydrate (g): 27.9
Fat (g): 0.8
Saturated fat (g): 0.4
Cholesterol (mg): 3.4
Sodium (mg): 126

Exchanges:
Milk: 0.5
Vegetable: 0.0
Fruit: 0.0
Bread: 1.5
Meat: 0.0
Fat: 0.0

VARIATION

Sweet Potato Vichyssoise — Make recipe as above, substituting ¾ cup chopped green onions for the leeks, sweet potatoes for the Idaho potatoes, and ½ cup orange juice for ½ cup of the milk. Omit celery seeds; add ½ teaspoon each ground cinnamon and mace. Sprinkle each bowl of soup with grated orange zest.

CREAMY CARROT SOUP

45 *Orange and ginger flavor this quick soup. The soup is also excellent served chilled.*

4 first-course servings

2 cups sliced carrots

½ teaspoon chopped gingerroot

2 teaspoons canola oil

1 tablespoon flour

2 cups reduced-sodium fat-free chicken broth

1 cup fat-free milk

¼ cup frozen orange juice concentrate

¼ teaspoon each: dried tarragon and thyme leaves

Salt and pepper, to taste

Sour cream, as garnish

Per Serving:
Calories: 104
% calories from fat: 22
Protein (g): 7.3
Carbohydrate (g): 12.7
Fat (g): 2.6
Saturated fat (g): 0.3
Cholesterol (mg): 1.9
Sodium (mg): 159

Exchanges:
Milk: 0.5
Vegetable: 1.0
Fruit: 0.0
Bread: 0.0
Meat: 0.0
Fat: 0.5

1. Sauté carrots and gingerroot in oil in large saucepan until lightly browned, about 8 minutes; sprinkle with flour and cook 1 minute.

Stir in remaining ingredients, except salt, pepper, and sour cream, and heat to boiling; reduce heat and simmer, covered, until carrots are tender, about 10 minutes. Process soup in food processor or blender until smooth. Season to taste with salt and pepper; garnish each bowl of soup with a dollop of sour cream.

CAULIFLOWER SOUP

45 *This velvety soup is flavored with a combination of curry powder, caraway seeds, and crushed red pepper—delicious!*

4 first-course servings

1 quart cauliflower florets

⅓ cup each: diced carrot, onion, sliced celery

2½ cups water

1 teaspoon each: chicken bouillon granules, curry powder, caraway seeds

¼–½ teaspoon crushed red pepper

Juice of ½ lemon

Salt and pepper, to taste

Paprika, as garnish

Per Serving:
Calories: 67
% calories from fat: 10
Protein (g): 4.3
Carbohydrate (g): 12.4
Fat (g): 0.8
Saturated fat (g): 0.1
Cholesterol (mg): 0.8
Sodium (mg): 316

Exchanges:
Milk: 0.0
Vegetable: 2.0
Fruit: 0.0
Bread: 0.0
Meat: 0.0
Fat: 0.0

1. Heat all ingredients, except lemon juice, salt, pepper, and paprika, to boiling in large saucepan; reduce heat and simmer, covered, until cauliflower is tender, about 10 minutes.

2. Process soup in food processor or blender until smooth. Season to taste with lemon juice, salt, and pepper; sprinkle each bowl of soup with paprika.

CURRIED CORN SOUP

45 *A variety of spices and coconut milk make this soup an exotic treat.*

6 first-course servings

1½ cups chopped onions

1 jalapeño chili, finely chopped

1 tablespoon each: minced garlic, gingerroot, canola oil

2 tablespoons flour

½ teaspoon each: ground cumin, cinnamon

2 cups each: reduced-sodium fat-free chicken broth, whole kernel corn

1 can (14 ounces) light coconut milk

1 cup fat-free half-and-half or fat-free milk

Salt and pepper, to taste

Chopped cilantro, as garnish

Per Serving:
Calories: 161
% calories from fat: 27
Protein (g): 6.2
Carbohydrate (g): 23.5
Fat (g): 4.9
Saturated fat (g): 0.3
Cholesterol (mg): 0
Sodium (mg): 117

Exchanges:
Milk: 0.0
Vegetable: 1.0
Fruit: 0.0
Bread: 1.0
Meat: 0.0
Fat: 1.0

1. Sauté onions, jalapeño chili, garlic, and gingerroot in oil until tender, about 8 minutes. Stir in flour and spices and cook 1 minute. Add chicken broth and corn and heat to boiling; reduce heat and simmer, covered, 10 minutes. Stir in coconut milk and half-and-half and cook over medium heat until hot, about 5 minutes; season to taste with salt and pepper. Sprinkle each bowl of soup with cilantro.

CREAM OF MUSHROOM SOUP

45 *For a richer texture, use fat-free half-and-half instead of fat-free milk.*

4 first-course servings

1 pound mushrooms

2 tablespoons margarine or butter, divided

1 cup chopped onion

2½ cups each: reduced-sodium chicken broth, fat-free milk, divided

2 tablespoons

Salt and pepper, to taste

Per Serving:
Calories: 207
% calories from fat: 29
Protein (g): 8.6
Carbohydrate (g): 25.3
Fat (g): 7
Saturated fat (g): 1.4
Cholesterol (mg): 2.5
Sodium (mg): 185

Exchanges:
Milk: 0.5
Vegetable: 2.5
Fruit: 0.0
Bread: 0.5
Meat: 0.0
Fat: 1.5

1. Slice enough mushroom caps to make 2 cups; finely chop stems and remaining mushrooms. Sauté sliced mushroom caps in 1 tablespoon margarine in large saucepan until tender, about 5 minutes; remove and reserve. Add onion and chopped mushrooms to saucepan and sauté in remaining 1 tablespoon margarine until onion is tender, about 5 minutes. Add broth and 2 cups milk and heat to boiling. Stir in combined remaining ½ cup milk and cornstarch, stirring until thickened, about 1 minute. Stir in reserved sliced mushrooms; season to taste with salt and pepper.

CREAMY MUSHROOM-BASIL SOUP

45 *This wonderful creamy soup takes only minutes to make because it's thickened with instant mashed potatoes.*

4 first-course servings

8 ounces fresh mushrooms, sliced
1 teaspoon chopped garlic
1 tablespoon margarine or butter
1 quart reduced-sodium fat-free chicken broth
½ cup whole milk
2 tablespoons dry sherry (optional)
1–1¼ cups instant mashed potatoes
¼ cup chopped fresh or 2 tablespoons dried
    basil leaves
Salt and white pepper, to taste

Per Serving:
Calories: 166
% calories from fat: 22
Protein (g): 10.2
Carbohydrate (g): 21
Fat (g): 4.1
Saturated fat (g): 1.2
Cholesterol (mg): 4.2
Sodium (mg): 230

Exchanges:
Milk: 0.0
Vegetable: 1.0
Fruit: 0.0
Bread: 1.0
Meat: 0.0
Fat: 1.0

1. Sauté mushrooms and garlic in margarine in large saucepan until mushrooms are tender, about 8 minutes. Stir in broth, milk, sherry, mashed potatoes, and basil; heat to boiling. Reduce heat and simmer 10 minutes; season to taste with salt and white pepper.

MUSHROOM SOUP

45 *Use your favorite mushroom—portobello or shiitake are flavorful choices.*

4 first-course servings

1 pound mushrooms, finely chopped
4 teaspoons margarine or butter
2 tablespoons flour
2 cups reduced-sodium fat-free chicken broth

1 can (13 ounces) evaporated fat-free milk

Salt and pepper, to taste

1. Sauté mushrooms in margarine in large saucepan until tender, about 8 minutes. Sprinkle with flour and cook 1 minute. Add chicken broth and heat to boiling; stir in evaporated milk, reduce heat and simmer, covered, 5 minutes. Season to taste with salt and pepper.

Per Serving:
Calories: 175
% calories from fat: 29
Protein (g): 1.5
Carbohydrate (g): 17.9
Fat (g): 6.1
Cholesterol (mg): 1.2
Sodium (mg): 254

Exchanges:
Milk: 1.0
Vegetable: 1.0
Fruit: 0.0
Bread: 0.0
Meat: 0.0
Fat: 1.5

ASPARAGUS-TOMATO SOUP WITH CHEESE

45 *This delicious soup combines flavors of asparagus, tomatoes, and Cheddar cheese, accented with mustard.*

6 first-course servings

1 each: chopped medium onion, carrot

2 teaspoons margarine or butter

½ cup instant rice

3 cups reduced-sodium fat-free chicken broth, divided

½ teaspoon dried marjoram leaves

¼ teaspoon each: dry mustard, white pepper

1 cup (4 ounces) shredded reduced-fat Cheddar cheese

1 can (14½ ounces) diced tomatoes, undrained

1¼ pounds asparagus spears, sliced, cooked

Salt, to taste

Per Serving:
Calories: 141
% calories from fat: 26
Protein (g): 10.2
Carbohydrate (g): 17.3
Fat (g): 4.2
Saturated fat (g): 2
Cholesterol (mg): 12.7
Sodium (mg): 558

Exchanges:
Milk: 0.0
Vegetable: 2.0
Fruit: 0.0
Bread: 0.5
Meat: 1.0
Fat: 0.0

1. Sauté onion and carrot in margarine in large saucepan until onion is tender, about 5 minutes. Add rice, broth, marjoram, dry mustard, and white pepper; heat to boiling. Reduce heat and simmer, covered, until rice is cooked, about 10 minutes. Process soup and cheese in food processor or blender until smooth; return to saucepan. Add tomatoes and asparagus; cook over medium heat until hot. Season to taste with salt.

RIPE TOMATO AND LEEK SOUP

45 *Use the summer's ripest tomatoes for this soup, cooking only briefly to maintain their sweetness. Peel the tomatoes, or not, as you prefer.*

6 first-course servings

2 cups sliced leeks (white parts only)
3 cloves garlic, minced
1 tablespoon olive oil
6 large tomatoes. chopped
1 quart reduced-sodium fat-free chicken broth
1 teaspoon dried basil leaves
Salt and white pepper, to taste
6 tablespoons fat-free sour cream or fat-free plain yogurt
Basil sprigs, as garnish

Per Serving:
Calories: 120
% calories from fat: 19
Protein (g): 7.3
Carbohydrate (g): 17.7
Fat (g): 2.6
Saturated fat (g): 0.5
Cholesterol (mg): 0
Sodium (mg): 173

Exchanges:
Milk: 0.0
Vegetable: 3.0
Fruit: 0.0
Bread: 0.0
Meat: 0.5
Fat: 0.5

1. Sauté leeks and garlic in oil in large saucepan until tender, about 8 minutes. Add tomatoes, broth, and basil; heat to boiling. Reduce heat and simmer, covered, 10 minutes. Process soup in food processor or blender until smooth; season to taste with salt and white pepper. Serve warm or chilled. Garnish each bowl of soup with a dollop of sour cream and a basil sprig.

EASY CURRIED POTATO SOUP

45 *This healthy, hearty soup can be made when the pantry is nearly bare.*

4 entrée servings

1 large onion, chopped
2 teaspoons minced gingerroot
2 large garlic cloves, minced
½ teaspoon caraway seeds
2 teaspoons margarine or butter
4 cups cubed, peeled baking potatoes
1 medium sweet apple, peeled, diced
1¼ quarts reduced-sodium fat-free chicken broth
2–3 teaspoons curry powder

Per Serving:
Calories: 254
% calories from fat: 9
Protein (g): 8.8
Carbohydrate (g): 52
Fat (g): 2.7
Saturated fat (g): 1.3
Cholesterol (mg): 5.1
Sodium (mg): 1049

Exchanges:
Milk: 0.0
Vegetable: 1.0
Fruit: 0.0
Bread: 3.0
Meat: 0.0
Fat: 0.5

½ teaspoon ground allspice

1 can (14½ ounces) stewed tomatoes

Salt and pepper, to taste

1. Sauté onion, gingerroot, garlic, and caraway seeds in margarine in large saucepan until onion is tender, about 5 minutes; add potatoes, apple, broth, curry powder, and allspice. Heat to boiling; reduce heat and simmer, covered, until potatoes are tender, about 10 minutes. Process 2 cups potato mixture in food processor or blender until smooth. Return to saucepan; add tomatoes and simmer, covered, 5 minutes. Season to taste with salt and pepper.

POTATO AND CABBAGE SOUP

45 *Purchased prepared ingredients make this soup extra-easy to make.*

6 entrée servings

4 ounces reduced-fat, reduced-sodium smoked sausage, thinly sliced

1 medium onion, chopped

2 cups coleslaw mix

1–2 tablespoons canola oil

1 tablespoon flour

1 package (8 ounces) frozen hash brown potatoes

1 quart reduced-sodium fat-free chicken broth

⅓ cup reduced-fat sour cream

Salt and pepper, to taste

Per Serving:
Calories: 353
% calories from fat: 9
Protein (g): 15.7
Carbohydrate (g): 68.5
Fat (g): 4
Saturated fat (g): 1.4
Cholesterol (mg): 13.1
Sodium (mg): 536

Exchanges:
Milk: 0.0
Vegetable: 2.0
Fruit: 0.0
Bread: 4.0
Meat: 0.0
Fat: 0.5

1. Cook sausage, onion, and coleslaw mix in oil in large saucepan over medium heat until sausage is browned and onion is tender, about 5 minutes; add flour and cook 1 minute. Add potatoes and broth and heat to boiling. Reduce heat and simmer, covered, 10 minutes. Stir in combined sour cream and simmer 2 minutes; stir in water, if thinner consistency is desired. Season to taste with salt and pepper.

CHEDDAR POTATO AND VEGETABLE SOUP

45 *Instant mashed potatoes are the secret ingredient in this quick and creamy soup.*

4 entrée servings

1 quart reduced-sodium fat-free chicken broth
5 cups small cauliflower or broccoli florets
1 medium onion, chopped
2 garlic cloves, minced
½ teaspoon dry mustard
1½ cups 1% low-fat milk
½ to 1 cup instant mashed potatoes
1 cup (4 ounces) reduced-fat Cheddar cheese
Salt and white pepper, to taste

Per Serving:
Calories: 285
% calories from fat: 23
Protein (g): 18.4
Carbohydrate (g): 37.8
Fat (g): 7.3
Saturated fat (g): 4.7
Cholesterol (mg): 24.8
Sodium (mg): 893

Exchanges:
Milk: 0.0
Vegetable: 1.0
Fruit: 0.0
Bread: 2.0
Meat: 2.0
Fat: 0.0

1. Heat broth, cauliflower, onion, garlic, and dry mustard to boiling in large saucepan. Reduce heat and simmer, covered, until cauliflower is tender, about 8 minutes. Add milk and mashed potatoes; cook over medium heat until hot, about 5 minutes; stir in cheese until melted. Season to taste with salt and pepper.

CHICKEN AND CORN SOUP

45 *This quick soup makes an easy workday meal.*

6 entrée servings

2 cups diced, peeled potatoes
¾ cup chopped onion
3 cups fat-free milk
1½ cups cubed cooked chicken breast
1 can (16 ounces) cream-style corn
Salt and pepper, to taste

Per Serving:
Calories: 244
% calories from fat: 9
Protein (g): 18
Carbohydrate (g): 38.9
Fat (g): 2.5
Saturated fat (g): 0.6
Cholesterol (mg): 32
Sodium (mg): 295

Exchanges:
Milk: 0.5
Vegetable: 0.0
Fruit: 0.0
Bread: 2.0
Meat: 1.0
Fat: 0.0

1. Heat potatoes and onion in 2 inches water in large saucepan to boiling. Reduce heat and simmer, covered, until potatoes are tender, about 10 minutes; drain. Add milk, chicken, and corn;

cook, covered, over medium heat until hot, about 8 minutes. Season to taste with salt and pepper.

HAMBURGER GOULASH SOUP

45 *This is a good, easy, meal-in-a-bowl soup. Be sure to use extra-lean ground beef.*

6 entrée servings

12 ounces very lean ground beef

⅔ cup each: chopped onion, red or green bell pepper

¾ teaspoon each: caraway seeds, dried thyme leaves

3 tablespoons paprika

¾ teaspoon each: chili and garlic powder

1 quart reduced-sodium fat-free beef broth

1 tablespoon Worcestershire sauce

3 cups diced potatoes

1 cup reduced-sodium canned stewed tomatoes

¼ cup catsup

Salt and pepper, to taste

Per Serving:
Calories: 202
% calories from fat: 16
Protein (g): 16.6
Carbohydrate (g): 27
Fat (g): 3.6
Saturated fat (g): 1.4
Cholesterol (mg): 35.2
Sodium (mg): 259

Exchanges:
Milk: 0.0
Vegetable: 0.0
Fruit: 0.0
Bread: 1.5
Meat: 2.0
Fat: 0.0

1. Cook beef, onion, bell pepper, and seasonings in lightly greased large saucepan over medium heat until beef is browned, about 5 minutes; crumble beef with a fork. Add remaining ingredients, except salt and pepper; heat to boiling. Reduce heat and simmer, covered, until potatoes are tender, about 10 minutes. Season to taste with salt and pepper.

HAM, SPINACH, AND PASTA SOUP

45 *Leaf spinach and angel hair pasta are excellent ingredients for fast soups since they both cook so quickly.*

4 entrée servings

1 medium onion, chopped
1¼ quarts reduced-sodium fat-free chicken broth
1 can (15 ounces) tomato sauce
6 ounces lean reduced-sodium ham, cubed
2 teaspoons dried Italian seasoning
1 cup uncooked angel hair pasta, broken (2-inch)
3 cups loosely packed sliced spinach
Salt and pepper to taste

Per Serving:
Calories: 188
% calories from fat: 10
Protein (g): 14.7
Carbohydrate (g): 29.5
Fat (g): 2.3
Saturated fat (g): 0.3
Cholesterol (mg): 19.1
Sodium (mg): 653

Exchanges:
Milk: 0.0
Vegetable: 2.0
Fruit: 0.0
Bread: 1.0
Meat: 1.0
Fat: 0.0

1. Sauté onion in lightly greased large saucepan until tender, about 5 minutes; stir in broth, tomato sauce, ham, and dried Italian seasoning; heat to boiling. Add pasta, reduce heat and simmer, uncovered, until pasta is *al dente*, 2 to 3 minutes. Stir in spinach; simmer, covered, 2 minutes. Season to taste with salt and pepper.

CHUNKY CHICKEN AND PASTA SOUP

45 *This colorful, fast-to-make soup always gets an enthusiastic reception!*

4 entrée servings

8 ounces boneless, skinless chicken breast, cubed
1 cup chopped onion
½ cup each: diced green and red bell pepper
1 garlic clove, minced
1 tablespoon olive oil
3½ cups fat-free chicken broth
1 can (14½ ounces) diced tomatoes, undrained
¼ cup chopped parsley
¾ teaspoon each: dried basil and oregano leaves
1 cup uncooked vermicelli, broken (2-inch)
Salt and pepper, to taste

Per Serving:
Calories: 305
% calories from fat: 15
Protein (g): 22.8
Carbohydrate (g): 41.7
Fat (g): 5.1
Saturated fat (g): 0.7
Cholesterol (mg): 32.9
Sodium (mg): 650

Exchanges:
Milk: 0.0
Vegetable: 0.0
Fruit: 0.0
Bread: 3.0
Meat: 2.0
Fat: 0.0

1. Sauté chicken, onion, bell peppers, and garlic in oil in large saucepan until onion is tender; about 8 minutes. Add broth, tomatoes with liquid, and herbs; heat to boiling. Add vermicelli and simmer, uncovered, until vermicelli is *al dente*, about 8 minutes. Season to taste with salt and pepper.

RICE AND ADZUKI BEANS WITH VEGETABLES

45 *In this easy khichuri, a classic Indian grain-and-bean stew, slightly sweet adzuki beans replace the usual dal or legume.*

6 entrée servings

1 can (15 ounces) adzuki beans, rinsed, drained
½ cup uncooked rice
2 cans (14½ ounces each) reduced-sodium fat-free
  chicken broth
1 teaspoon each: ground cumin, minced gingerroot
1 teaspoon ground turmeric
1 small jalapeño chili, minced
3 carrots, thinly sliced
2 cups each: cut waxed beans, chopped
  plum tomatoes
Salt and pepper, to taste
¼ cup toasted sunflower seeds

Per Serving:
Calories: 323
% calories from fat: 10
Protein (g). 10.3
Carbohydrate (g): 62.4
Fat (g): 3.5
Saturated fat (g): 04
Cholesterol (mg): 0
Sodium (mg): 209

Exchanges:
Milk: 0.0
Vegetable: 3.0
Fruit: 0.0
Bread: 3.0
Meat: 0.0
Fat: 0.0

1. Heat all ingredients, except tomatoes, salt, pepper, and sunflower seeds, to boiling in medium saucepan; reduce heat and simmer, covered, until vegetables and rice are tender, about 25 minutes, adding tomatoes during last 5 minutes. Season to taste with salt and pepper; sprinkle each bowl of soup with sunflower seeds.

TURKEY CON SALSA SOUP

45 *Use your favorite salsa to give this soup its picante flavor!*

6 entrée servings

12 ounces ground turkey breast

1 large onion, chopped

2 garlic cloves, minced

2 teaspoons chili powder

1 teaspoon ground cumin

1¼ quarts reduced-sodium fat-free beef broth

2 cups reduced-sodium mild or hot salsa

1 can (15½ ounces) kidney beans, rinsed, drained

2 cups whole kernel corn

½ cup instant mashed potatoes

Salt and pepper, to taste

Per Serving:
Calories: 296
% calories from fat: 6
Protein (g): 21.8
Carbohydrate (g): 44.8
Fat (g): 1.7
Saturated fat (g): 0.4
Cholesterol (mg): 22.5
Sodium (mg): 633

Exchanges:
Milk: 0.0
Vegetable: 0.0
Fruit: 0.0
Bread: 3.0
Meat: 2.0
Fat: 0.0

1. Cook turkey, onion, garlic, chili powder, and cumin over medium heat in lightly greased large saucepan until turkey is browned, about 5 minutes; crumble turkey with a fork. Add broth, salsa, beans, and corn; heat to boiling. Reduce heat and simmer, covered, 15 minutes, adding instant mashed potatoes the last 5 minutes; season to taste with salt and pepper.

ROASTED RED PEPPER, CORN, AND BLACK BEAN SOUP

45 *Jarred roasted red peppers and canned black beans are great time-savers in this hearty, colorful soup.*

4 entrée servings

2 cups chopped onions

1 tablespoon olive oil

⅔ cup instant rice

1 quart reduced-sodium fat-free chicken broth

¾ teaspoon dried thyme leaves

⅛ teaspoon each: crushed red pepper, ground allspice

1 jar (12 ounces) roasted red peppers, drained, diced, divided

1 cup whole kernel corn

1 can (15 ounces) black beans, rinsed, drained

½ cup diced lean ham

Salt and pepper, to taste

1. Sauté onions in oil in large saucepan until tender, about 8 minutes, Add rice, broth, and seasonings; heat to boiling. Reduce heat and simmer, covered, until rice is tender, about 5 minutes. Process soup and 8 ounces roasted red peppers in food processor or blender until smooth. Return to saucepan; add remaining ingredients, except salt and pepper. Cook over medium heat until hot, about 5 minutes. Season to taste with salt and pepper.

Per Serving:
Calories: 286
% calories from fat: 13
Protein (g): 13.3
Carbohydrate (g): 55.2
Fat (g): 4.4
Saturated fat (g): 0.7
Cholesterol (mg): 8.4
Sodium (mg): 1325

Exchanges:
Milk: 0.0
Vegetable: 0.0
Fruit: 0.0
Bread: 3.5
Meat: 1.0
Fat: 0.0

GARBANZO AND PASTA SOUP

Quick, easy, and good, this soup makes a nice luncheon entrée.

4 entrée servings

1 each: chopped medium onion, minced clove garlic

¼ cup each: finely chopped celery, carrot

2 teaspoons olive oil

1 quart Chicken Stock (see p. 2)

1 can (8 ounces) tomato sauce

2 cups cooked dried or 1 can (15 ounces) rinsed, drained garbanzo beans

½ cup diced zucchini

1 bay leaf

½ teaspoon each: dried thyme and basil leaves

⅓ cup uncooked small soup pasta

Salt and pepper, to taste

Per Serving:
Calories: 209
% calories from fat: 16
Protein (g): 12.4
Carbohydrate (g): 32.5
Fat (g): 3.8
Saturated fat (g): 0.4
Cholesterol (mg): 0
Sodium (mg): 333

Exchanges:
Milk: 0.0
Vegetable: 0.0
Fruit: 0.0
Bread: 2.0
Meat: 1.0
Fat: 0.0

1. Sauté onion, garlic, celery, and carrot in oil in large saucepan until onion is tender, about 5 minutes. Add remaining ingredients, except pasta, salt, and pepper; heat to boiling. Reduce heat and simmer, covered, 10 minutes. Heat soup to boiling; add pasta. Reduce heat and simmer, uncovered, until pasta is *al dente*, 4 to 5 minutes. Discard bay leaf; season to taste with salt and pepper.

CURRIED BEAN SOUP

45 *Use any white bean, such as cannellini, navy, soy, lima, or garbanzo in this creamy, rich soup.*

6 entrée servings

1 cup each: chopped onion, sliced leek (white part only)

1 tablespoon each: minced garlic, curry powder

2 tablespoons olive oil

2 cans (15 ounces each) Great Northern beans, rinsed, drained

3½ cups reduced-sodium vegetable broth

½ cup fat-free half-and-half or fat-free milk

Salt and pepper, to taste

6 tablespoons fat-free sour cream or plain yogurt

Chopped cilantro, as garnish

Per Serving:
Calories: 263
% calories from fat: 16
Protein (g): 13.7
Carbohydrate (g): 42.5
Fat (g): 4.9
Saturated fat (g): 1
Cholesterol (mg): 0
Sodium (mg): 393

Exchanges:
Milk: 0.0
Vegetable: 1.5
Fruit: 0.0
Bread: 2.5
Meat: 0.5
Fat: 0.5

1. Sauté onion, leek, garlic, and curry powder in oil in large saucepan until onion is tender, 5 to 8 minutes. Add beans and broth and heat to boiling; reduce heat and simmer, covered, 5 minutes. Process soup in food processor or blender until smooth; return to saucepan. Stir in half-and-half; cook over medium heat until hot, 2 to 3 minutes; season to taste with salt and pepper. Top each bowl of soup with a tablespoon of sour cream; sprinkle with cilantro.

ARTICHOKE BISQUE WITH SHRIMP

This elegant soup can be made up to 3 days in advance.

6 entrée servings

1 can (14 ounces) artichoke hearts, rinsed, drained, divided

¼ cup sliced green onions

1 tablespoon margarine or butter

¼ cup all-purpose flour

3 cups Chicken Stock (see p. 2)

1½ cups fat-free milk

1 cup fat-free half-and-half or fat-free milk

8–12 ounces peeled, deveined small shrimp

⅛ teaspoon ground nutmeg

Salt and cayenne pepper, to taste

Per Serving:
Calories: 147
% calories from fat: 18
Protein (g): 12.6
Carbohydrate (g): 15.9
Fat (g): 2.7
Saturated fat (g): 0.6
Cholesterol (mg): 60.6
Sodium (mg): 329

Exchanges:
Milk: 0.0
Vegetable: 3.0
Fruit: 0.0
Bread: 0.0
Meat: 1.0
Fat: 0.0

1. Quarter half the artichokes; process remaining artichokes in food processor until smooth. Reserve. Sauté green onions in margarine until tender, about 3 minutes. Stir in flour and cook 2 minutes. Add stock and milk and heat to boiling, stirring until thickened, about 1 minute. Stir in reserved artichokes, half-and-half, shrimp, and nutmeg; simmer, covered, until shrimp are cooked and soup is hot, about 5 minutes. Season to taste with salt and cayenne pepper.

HERBED BROCCOLI AND PASTA SOUP

45 *A versatile soup, as any vegetable in season and favorite herb can be substituted for the broccoli and thyme.*

6 first-course servings

3 cans (14½ ounces each) reduced-sodium fat-free chicken broth

4 cloves garlic, minced

2 teaspoons dried thyme leaves

3 cups small broccoli florets

1 cup uncooked fusilli (spirals)

2–3 tablespoons lemon juice

Salt and pepper, to taste

Per Serving:
Calories: 151
% calories from fat: 7.8
Protein (g): 6.4
Carbohydrate (g): 29
Fat (g): 1.3
Saturated fat (g): 0.1
Cholesterol (mg): 0.0
Sodium (mg): 801

Exchanges:
Milk: 0.0
Vegetable: 3.0
Fruit: 0.0
Bread: 1.0
Meat: 0.0
Fat: 0.0

1. Heat broth, garlic, and thyme to boiling in medium saucepan. Stir in broccoli and fusilli. Reduce heat and simmer, uncovered, until broccoli is tender and pasta is *al dente*, about 10 minutes. Season to taste with lemon juice, salt, and pepper.

CHEESY BROCCOLI-POTATO SOUP

45

To save preparation time, frozen broccoli and hash brown potatoes can be substituted for the fresh.

6 entrée servings

1 cup chopped onion
½ cup each: finely chopped celery, carrots
1–2 tablespoons margarine or butter
1 quart reduced-sodium fat-free chicken or beef broth
2 cups each: broccoli florets, cubed unpeeled
   Idaho potatoes
½ teaspoon each: celery seeds, dried thyme leaves
3 cups fat-free half-and-half or fat-free milk, divided
⅓ cup all-purpose flour
1½–2 cups (6–8 ounces) shredded reduced-fat mild
   Cheddar cheese
Salt and pepper, to taste

Per Serving:
Calories: 299
% calories from fat: 20
Protein (g): 17.9
Carbohydrate (g): 38
Fat (g): 6.3
Saturated fat (g): 2.5
Cholesterol (mg): 15.2
Sodium (mg): 670

Exchanges:
Milk: 0.0
Vegetable: 2.0
Fruit: 0.0
Bread: 2.0
Meat: 1.0
Fat: 1.0

1. Sauté onion, celery and carrots in margarine in large saucepan until onion is tender, about 5 minutes. Add broth, broccoli, potatoes, and herbs; heat to boiling. Reduce heat and simmer, covered, until vegetables are tender, 10 to 15 minutes. Heat soup to boiling; stir in combined 1 cup half-and-half and flour, stirring, until thickened, about 1 minute. Stir in remaining 2 cups half-and-half, reduce heat to medium and add cheese, stirring until melted. Season to taste with salt and pepper.

CHILLED PEA SOUP

45
❄

A refreshing soup for hot sultry days; serve with a ripe tomato salad and crusty bread or rolls.

6 entrée servings

½ cup chopped onion
½ teaspoon each: dried marjoram and thyme leaves
2 cups reduced-sodium fat-free chicken broth
2 packages (20 ounces each) frozen peas

2 cups sliced romaine lettuce

Salt and white pepper, to taste

½ cup fat-free sour cream

Paprika, as garnish

Per Serving:
Calories: 257
% calories from fat: 4
Protein (g): 17.4
Carbohydrate (g): 46.6
Fat (g): 1.1
Saturated fat (g): 0.2
Cholesterol (mg): 0
Sodium (mg): 274

Exchanges:
Milk: 0.0
Vegetable: 0.0
Fruit: 0.0
Bread: 3.0
Meat: 0.5
Fat: 0.0

1. Sauté onion and herbs in lightly greased large saucepan until onion is tender, about 5 minutes. Stir in broth, peas, and lettuce; heat to boiling. Reduce heat and simmer, covered, 10 minutes. Process soup in food processor or blender until smooth; season to taste with salt and pepper. Refrigerate until chilled; stir in sour cream before serving. Sprinkle each bowl of soup with paprika.

EGGPLANT SOUP WITH ROASTED RED PEPPER SAUCE

Grilling gives eggplant a distinctive smoky flavor. For indoor cooking, eggplant can be oven roasted. Pierce the eggplant in several places with a fork and place in a baking pan. Bake at 350 degrees until soft, 45 to 50 minutes.

4 entrée servings

2 medium eggplants

¾ cup chopped onion

¼ cup chopped green bell pepper

2 cloves garlic, minced

1 tablespoon olive oil

4–5 cups reduced-sodium fat-free chicken broth

Salt and white pepper, to taste

Roasted Red Pepper Sauce (recipe follows)

Per Serving:
Calories: 250
% calories from fat: 19
Protein (g): 6.8
Carbohydrate (g): 44.8
Fat (g): 6
Saturated fat (g): 0.7
Cholesterol (mg): 0
Sodium (mg): 25

Exchanges:
Milk: 0.0
Vegetable: 2.0
Fruit: 0.0
Bread: 2.0
Meat: 0.0
Fat: 1.0

1. Pierce eggplant in several places with fork. Grill over medium hot coals, turning frequently, until eggplant is very soft, about 30 minutes; cool slightly. Cut eggplant in half, scoop out pulp, and chop coarsely.

2. Sauté onion, pepper, and garlic in oil in large saucepan until tender, 5 to 8 minutes. Add broth and eggplant and heat to boiling.

Reduce heat and simmer, covered, 15 minutes. Process soup in food processor or blender until smooth. Season to taste with salt and white pepper. Serve warm or chilled; swirl about ¼ cup Roasted Red Pepper Sauce into each bowl of soup.

Roasted Red Pepper Sauce
Makes about ¾ cup

2 large red bell peppers, halved
1 teaspoon sugar

1. Place peppers, skin sides up, on broiler pan. Broil 4 to 6 inches from heat source until skins are blistered and blackened. Place peppers in plastic bag for 5 minutes; remove and peel off skins. Process peppers and sugar in food processor or blender until smooth.

NOTE: 1 jar (12 ounces) roasted red peppers, drained, can be substituted for the peppers in the recipe.

BRANDIED ONION SOUP

This soup is best if you allow it to simmer slowly to meld flavors.

8 first-course servings

4 cups thinly sliced onions
2–3 teaspoons each: margarine or butter, olive oil
2 tablespoons flour
2 quarts Fragrant Beef Stock (see p. 6)
2–4 tablespoons brandy (optional)
Salt and pepper, to taste

Per Serving:
Calories: 186
% calories from fat: 30
Protein (g): 10.2
Carbohydrate (g): 22.4
Fat (g): 6.5
Saturated fat (g): 2.7
Cholesterol (mg): 10.9
Sodium (mg): 394

Exchanges:
Milk: 0.0
Vegetable: 1.0
Fruit: 0.0
Bread: 1.0
Meat: 1.0
Fat: 0.5

1. Cook onions in margarine and oil in Dutch oven over medium to medium-low heat until golden, 15 to 20 minutes; stir in flour and cook 2 minutes. Add stock and heat to boiling; reduce heat and simmer, covered, 35 to 45 minutes. Add brandy; season to taste with salt and pepper.

VARIATION

Onion and Potato Soup — Make recipe as above, adding 3 cups cubed, peeled potatoes, ¼ teaspoon each dried marjoram and thyme leaves with the stock; sprinkle each bowl of soup with 2 tablespoons shredded Swiss cheese.

CURRIED ONION-POTATO SOUP

Sip this delicious soup cold from soup cups in the summer; in winter, serve it hot.

4 first-course servings

3 cups coarsely chopped onions

1 garlic clove, minced

1¼ teaspoons each: ground cumin, ground turmeric, curry powder

2 teaspoons margarine or butter

1 quart Chicken Stock (see p. 2) or fat-free chicken broth

¾ cup whole milk

2 cups peeled, diced potatoes

Salt and pepper, to taste

Per Serving:
Calories: 206
% calories from fat: 21
Protein (g): 7.5
Carbohydrate (g): 31.9
Fat (g): 4.7
Saturated fat (g): 1.6
Cholesterol (mg): 14.6
Sodium (mg): 61

Exchanges:
Milk: 0.0
Vegetable: 0.0
Fruit: 0.0
Bread: 2.0
Meat: 0.0
Fat: 1.0

1. Sauté onions, garlic, and seasonings in margarine in large saucepan until onions are soft, about 10 minutes. Add stock, milk, and potatoes; heat to boiling; reduce heat and simmer, covered, until potatoes are tender, about 15 minutes. Process soup in food processor or blender until smooth. Season to taste with salt and pepper; serve warm or chilled.

TOMATO SOUP WITH PASTA

Freeze ripe tomatoes from your garden for making this soup in the winter, too.

6 first-course servings

½ cup each: chopped onion, carrot

¼ cup chopped celery

1 clove garlic, minced

1 teaspoon each: dried basil and oregano leaves

½ teaspoon anise seeds, lightly crushed

1–2 tablespoons olive oil

3 pounds tomatoes, coarsely chopped

3 cups Rich Chicken Stock (see p. 4)

1 cup small soup pasta (stelline, orzo, or rings)

Salt and pepper, to taste

Shredded Parmesan cheese, as garnish

Per Serving:
Calories: 164
% calories from fat: 20
Protein (g): 7
Carbohydrate (g): 26.3
Fat (g): 3.8
Saturated fat (g): 0.6
Cholesterol (mg): 0.5
Sodium (mg): 45

Exchanges:
Milk: 0.0
Vegetable: 2.0
Fruit: 0.0
Bread: 1.0
Meat: 0.0
Fat: 0.5

1. Sauté onion, carrot, celery, garlic, and herbs in oil in large saucepan until tender, about 5 minutes. Add tomatoes and stock; heat to boiling. Reduce heat and simmer, covered, 25 minutes. Process soup in food processor or blender until smooth. Return to saucepan and heat to boiling; stir in pasta. Simmer, uncovered, until pasta is tender, about 8 minutes. Season to taste with salt and pepper. Sprinkle each bowl of soup with Parmesan cheese.

CREAMY TOMATO SOUP WITH CHUNKY VEGETABLES

A grown-up version of that comforting soup we know so well.

4 first-course servings

1 medium onion, fincly chopped

1 large garlic clove, minced

2 teaspoons olive oil

1 quart Chicken Stock (see p. 2)

2 small unpeeled new potatoes, cubed

1½ cups small cauliflower florets

1 cup each: diced zucchini, green bell pepper

2 to 4 tablespoons dry sherry (optional)

¾ teaspoon dried basil leaves

¼ teaspoon each: dried thyme and marjoram leaves

⅛ teaspoon dry mustard

1 can (8 ounces) tomato sauce

¾ cup whole milk

1½ tablespoons cornstarch

¼ cup cold water

Salt and pepper, to taste

Per Serving:
Calories: 207
% calories from fat: 22
Protein (g): 8.6
Carbohydrate (g): 31.6
Fat (g): 5.1
Saturated fat (g): 1.6
Cholesterol (mg): 14.6
Sodium (mg): 356

Exchanges:
Milk: 0.0
Vegetable: 0.0
Fruit: 0.0
Bread: 2.0
Meat: 0.0
Fat: 1.0

1. Sauté onion and garlic in oil in large saucepan until onion is soft, about 5 minutes. Add stock, vegetables, sherry, herbs, and mustard; heat to boiling. Reduce heat and simmer, covered, until vegetables are tender, about 15 minutes. Add tomato sauce and milk and heat to boiling; whisk in combined cornstarch and water, stirring until thickened, about 1 minute. Season to taste with salt and pepper.

TWO-SEASON SQUASH SOUP

Winter butternut squash and summer garden zucchini are combined in this perfect soup. Delicious with Hearty Vegetable-Rye Bread (see p. 646).

6 first-course servings

1 cup chopped onion

2 cloves garlic, minced

2 teaspoons olive oil

3 cups Quick-Spiced Beef Stock (see p. 5)

1 medium butternut squash, peeled, seeded, cubed

2 medium zucchini, sliced

1 can (28 ounces) reduced-sodium diced tomatoes, undrained

1 can (15 ounces) Great Northern beans, drained, rinsed

1 teaspoon each: low-sodium Worcestershire sauce, dried marjoram leaves

½ teaspoon dried rosemary leaves

Salt and pepper, to taste

Per Serving:
Calories: 136
% calories from fat: 9
Protein (g): 83
Carbohydrate (g): 27.3
Fat (g): 1.7
Saturated fat (g): 0.3
Cholesterol (mg): 0
Sodium (mg): 296

Exchanges:
Milk: 0.0
Vegetable: 3.0
Fruit: 0.0
Bread: 0.5
Meat: 0.0
Fat: 0.5

1. Sauté onion and garlic in oil in large saucepan until tender, about 5 minutes. Add remaining ingredients, except salt and pepper and heat to boiling. Reduce heat and simmer, covered, until squash is tender, about 15 minutes. Season to taste with salt and pepper.

CHICKEN VEGETABLE SOUP WITH ORZO

45 *Escarole lends a unique taste to this hearty soup; kale or spinach can also be used.*

4 entrée servings

12 ounces boneless, skinless chicken breast, cubed
1 cup each: chopped onion, sliced carrots, celery
4 cloves garlic, minced
5 cups reduced-sodium fat-free chicken broth
2 medium zucchini or summer yellow squash, sliced
1 cup sliced mushrooms
½ teaspoon each: dried thyme and oregano leaves
½ cup uncooked orzo
½ cup frozen peas
6 medium leaves escarole or kale, sliced or
   coarsely chopped
Salt and pepper, to taste
2 tablespoons grated Romano cheese

Per Serving:
Calories: 265
% calories from fat: 10
Protein (g): 9.1
Carbohydrate (g): 44.3
Fat (g): 2.9
Saturated fat (g): 0.9
Cholesterol (mg): 3.6
Sodium (mg): 298

Exchanges:
Milk: 0.0
Vegetable: 3.0
Fruit: 0.0
Bread: 2.0
Meat: 0.0
Fat: 1.0

1. Sauté chicken in lightly greased large saucepan until cooked, about 8 minutes; remove from saucepan. Add onion, carrots, celery, and garlic to saucepan and sauté until onion is tender, about 5 minutes. Add broth, zucchini, mushrooms, and herbs; heat to boiling. Stir in orzo, peas, and escarole; reduce heat and simmer, uncovered, until orzo is *al dente*, about 7 minutes. Season with salt and pepper. Sprinkle each bowl of soup with cheese.

GARDEN HARVEST SOUP

45 *Vary the vegetables according to your garden's or greengrocer's bounty.*

6 first-course servings

2 small onions, sliced

2 cloves garlic, minced

¾ cup each: sliced carrots, red and yellow bell pepper

1 tablespoon olive oil

5 cups reduced-sodium fat-free chicken broth

½ cup whole kernel corn

1 cup each: cut green beans, sliced zucchini, yellow summer squash

½ teaspoon each: dried basil and oregano leaves

⅓ cup fat-free half-and-half or fat-free milk

Salt and pepper, to taste

Per Serving:
Calories: 136
% calories from fat: 17
Protein (g): 8.4
Carbohydrate (g): 21.3
Fat (g): 2.8
Saturated fat (g): 0.4
Cholesterol (mg): 0
Sodium (mg): 161

Exchanges:
Milk: 0.0
Vegetable: 4.0
Fruit: 0.0
Bread: 0.0
Meat: 0.0
Fat: 0.5

1. Sauté onions, garlic, carrots, and bell peppers in oil in large saucepan until tender, about 5 minutes. Add broth, remaining vegetables, and herbs; heat to boiling. Reduce heat and simmer, covered, until vegetables are tender, about 15 minutes, adding half-and-half during last 5 minutes. Season to taste with salt and pepper.

SUMMER SOUP WITH TOMATO RELISH

A fresh tomato relish adds flavor highlights to this colorful soup.

4 first-course servings

2 large onions, coarsely chopped

1 large garlic clove, chopped

1 tablespoon each: margarine or butter, flour

1 quart Chicken Stock (see p. 2) or fat-free chicken broth

1 pound yellow summer squash, chopped

1½ cups whole kernel corn, divided

½ cup diced, peeled boiling potato

¼ teaspoon dry mustard

½ cup whole milk

1–2 teaspoons lemon juice

Salt and pepper, to taste

Chopped cilantro, as garnish

Fresh Tomato Relish (recipe follows)

Per Serving:
Calories: 169
% calories from fat: 18
Protein (g): 7.6
Carbohydrate (g): 29.7
Fat (g): 3.7
Saturated fat (g): 1.1
Cholesterol (mg): 3.3
Sodium (mg): 357

Exchanges:
Milk: 0.0
Vegetable: 2.0
Fruit: 0.0
Bread: 2.0
Meat: 0.0
Fat: 0.5

1. Sauté onions and garlic in margarine in large saucepan until onions are tender, 8 to 10 minutes; stir in flour and cook 1 minute. Add stock, squash, 1 cup corn, potato, and dry mustard; heat to boiling. Reduce heat and simmer, covered, until potato is tender, about 10 minutes. Process soup in food processor or blender until smooth; return to saucepan. Stir in remaining ½ cup corn and milk; simmer, uncovered, 5 minutes. Season to taste with lemon juice, salt, and pepper. Sprinkle each bowl of soup with cilantro; serve with Fresh Tomato Relish to stir into soup.

Fresh Tomato Relish

1 large, ripe tomato, peeled, finely diced

¼ cup chopped cilantro

1 tablespoon red wine vinegar

¼ teaspoon salt

1. Combine all ingredients.

VEGETABLE SOUP WITH COUNTRY HAM

Country ham, beef broth, and chicken are a unique combination in this delicious soup.

6 entrée servings

1 package (8 ounces) country ham, fat trimmed, diced

½ cup each: chopped onion, leek (white part only), sliced carrot, celery

2 large garlic cloves, minced

1 teaspoon dried thyme leaves

2 teaspoons olive oil

2 quarts reduced-sodium fat-free beef broth

1 can (15 ounces) lima or navy beans, rinsed, drained

12 ounces boneless, skinless chicken breast, cubed half

1 cup each: cubed red potatoes, cut green beans, sliced asparagus spears

Salt and pepper, to taste

Per Serving:
Calories: 263
% calories from fat: 20
Protein (g): 31
Carbohydrate (g): 20.7
Fat (g): 5.7
Saturated fat (g): 1.5
Cholesterol (mg): 59.3
Sodium (mg): 1406

Exchanges:
Milk: 0.0
Vegetable: 1.0
Fruit: 0.0
Bread: 1.0
Meat: 3.0
Fat: 0.0

1. Sauté country ham, onion, leek, carrot, celery, garlic, and thyme in olive oil in Dutch oven until vegetables are tender, about 5 minutes. Add remaining ingredients, except asparagus, salt, and pepper; heat to boiling. Reduce heat and simmer, covered, until chicken is cooked and vegetables are tender, about 15 minutes, adding asparagus during the last 5 minutes. Season to taste with salt and pepper.

LIMA BEAN AND BARLEY SOUP

An excellent winter soup, with robust seasonings.

4 entrée servings

1 cup chopped onion
½ cup each thinly sliced celery, cubed turnip
2 teaspoons canola oil
1½ quarts Chicken Stock (see p. 2)
1 medium pork hock
1 can (14½ ounces) diced tomatoes, undrained
1 cup frozen lima beans
¼ cup quick-cooking barley
¾ teaspoon each: dried thyme and marjoram leaves
1 bay leaf
½–1 teaspoon sugar
Salt and pepper, to taste

Per Serving:
Calories: 226
% calories from fat: 18
Protein (g): 11.4
Carbohydrate (g): 33.1
Fat (g): 4.4
Saturated fat (g): 0.8
Cholesterol (mg): 16.4
Sodium (mg): 281

Exchanges:
Milk: 0.0
Vegetable: 1.0
Fruit: 0.0
Bread: 2.0
Meat: 1.0
Fat: 0.0

1. Sauté onion, celery, and turnip in oil in large saucepan until onion is tender, about 5 minutes. Add remaining ingredients, except sugar, salt, and pepper and heat to boiling; reduce heat and simmer, covered, until vegetables and barley are tender, 15 to 20 minutes. Discard pork hock and bay leaf; skim fat from top of soup. Season to taste with sugar, salt, and pepper.

SPICY OATMEAL SOUP

Oatmeal adds interesting texture to this vegetable soup; fresh bread crumbs can be substituted.

4 entrée servings

2 large leeks (white parts only), thinly sliced
2 teaspoons each: margarine or butter, canola oil
1 cup each: sliced carrots, zucchini, diced
  unpeeled potatoes
½ cup thinly sliced celery
1½ quarts Rich Chicken Stock (see p. 4)
2 teaspoons dried basil leaves
2–4 drops hot pepper sauce

½ cup quick-cooking oatmeal

½ cup dry white wine (optional)

Salt and pepper, to taste

Per Serving:
Calories: 299
% calories from fat: 14
Protein (g): 12.9
Carbohydrate (g): 40.2
Fat (g): 4.4
Saturated fat (g): 0.9
Cholesterol (mg): 1.5
Sodium (mg): 129

1. Sauté leeks in margarine and canola oil in large saucepan until tender, about 5 minutes. Add remaining ingredients, except oatmeal, wine, salt, and pepper; heat to boiling. Reduce heat and simmer, covered, 30 minutes, adding oatmeal and wine during last 15 minutes; season to taste with salt and pepper.

Exchanges:
Milk: 0.0
Vegetable: 2.0
Fruit: 0.0
Bread: 2.0
Meat: 0.0
Fat: 2.0

SWEET-AND-SOUR CABBAGE SOUP

This rich, tangy cabbage soup is made with both beef and turkey.

8 entrée servings

8 ounces each: ground beef round, turkey breast

1 large onion, chopped

½ cup sliced carrots

2 garlic cloves, minced

2 quarts Fragrant Beef Stock (see p. 6)

4 cups thinly sliced green cabbage

1 can (15 ounces) tomato sauce

2 tablespoons each: cider vinegar, brown sugar

1 bay leaf

1 teaspoon dried thyme leaves

⅛ teaspoon ground cinnamon

⅓ cup raisins

½ cup uncooked white rice

Salt and pepper, to taste

Per Serving:
Calories: 202
% calories from fat: 18
Protein (g): 16.1
Carbohydrate (g): 26.2
Fat (g): 4.2
Saturated fat (g): 1.7
Cholesterol (mg): 25.8
Sodium (mg): 425

Exchanges:
Milk: 0.0
Vegetable: 1.0
Fruit: 0.0
Bread: 1.0
Meat: 2.0
Fat: 0.0

1. Cook ground beef and turkey, onion, carrots, and garlic in Dutch oven over medium heat until meat is browned, about 5 minutes; crumble meat with a fork. Add remaining ingredients, except rice, salt, and pepper; heat to boiling. Reduce heat and simmer, covered, 40 minutes, adding rice during last 20 to 25 minutes. Discard bay leaf; season to taste with salt and pepper.

SPICY BEEF AND CABBAGE SOUP

45   *The combination of vinegar, sugar, and spices gives this easy soup its zest.*

6 first-course servings

12 ounces ground beef round

1 each: finely chopped large onion, minced garlic clove

1 quart beef broth

3 cups each: water, shredded cabbage

½ cup each: thinly sliced celery, carrots

1 can (15 ounces) tomato sauce

2 tablespoons each: cider vinegar, sugar

½ teaspoon each: dry mustard, dried thyme and marjoram leaves

¼ teaspoon ground cinnamon

⅛ teaspoon ground cloves

3 bay leaves

⅓ cup uncooked rice

Salt and pepper, to taste

Per Serving:
Calories: 136
% calories from fat: 13
Protein (g): 10.5
Carbohydrate (g): 20.2
Fat (g): 2
Saturated fat (g): 0.5
Cholesterol (mg): 20.5
Sodium (mg): 518

Exchanges:
Milk: 0.0
Vegetable: 2.0
Fruit: 0.0
Bread: 0.5
Meat: 1.0
Fat: 0.0

1. Cook beef, onion, and garlic in lightly greased large saucepan over medium heat until meat is browned, 5 to 8 minutes; crumble beef with a fork. Add remaining ingredients except rice, salt, and pepper; heat to boiling. Reduce heat and simmer, covered, 15 minutes. Add rice; simmer, covered, until rice is tender, 20 to 25 minutes. Discard bay leaves; season to taste with salt and pepper.

MEATBALL AND VEGETABLE SOUP

The meatballs are baked for easy preparation.

6 entrée servings

½ cup each: finely chopped onion, celery, carrots

1 garlic clove, minced

1 quart Beef Stock (see p. 5)

2 cups water

1 can (14½ ounces) reduced-sodium crushed tomatoes

1 can (8 ounces) tomato sauce

2 cups each: whole kernel corn, cut green beans, small cauliflower florets

¼ cup quick-cooking barley

2 teaspoons sugar

1 teaspoon dried basil leaves

½ teaspoon each: dried thyme leaves, dry mustard, chili powder

2 bay leaves

Meatballs (recipe follows)

Salt and pepper, to taste

Per Serving:
Calories: 188
% calories from fat: 13
Protein (g): 10
Carbohydrate (g): 29.6
Fat (g): 2.1
Saturated fat (g): 0.6
Cholesterol (mg): 20.5
Sodium (mg): 351

Exchanges:
Milk: 0.0
Vegetable: 2.0
Fruit: 0.0
Bread: 1.0
Meat: 1.0
Fat: 0.0

1. Sauté onion, celery, carrots, and garlic in lightly greased large saucepan until onion is tender, about 8 minutes. Add remaining ingredients, except salt and pepper, in large saucepan; heat to boiling. Reduce heat and simmer, covered, until vegetables and barley are tender, about 15 minutes. Discard bay leaves; season to taste with salt and pepper.

Meatballs

Makes 1½ dozen

1 pound ground beef round
2 tablespoons finely chopped onion
1 egg white
¼ cup quick-cooking oats
2 tablespoons catsup
⅛ teaspoon each: dried thyme leaves, dry mustard
¼ teaspoon each: salt, pepper

1. Combine all ingredients; roll into 18 meatballs. Bake in baking pan at 350 degrees until cooked and browned, about 10 minutes.

BEEF, VEGETABLE, AND BARLEY SOUP

Thick and hearty, this soup will warm you on a cold winter day.

6 entrée servings

12 ounces ground beef round
1 large onion, chopped
2 large garlic cloves, minced
3 cups coarsely shredded cabbage
½ cup each: sliced celery, carrots
1 cup cubed, peeled potato
1½ quarts Fragrant Beef Stock (see p. 6)
1 can (14½ ounces) reduced-sodium stewed tomatoes
1 teaspoon each: dried thyme and basil leaves, chili
     powder, paprika
½ teaspoon dry mustard
2 bay leaves
⅓ cup quick-cooking barley
Salt and pepper, to taste

Per Serving:
Calories: 116
% calories from fat: 11
Protein (g): 16.2
Carbohydrate (g): 24.3
Fat (g): 2.2
Saturated fat (g): 0.7
Cholesterol (mg): 23.4
Sodium (mg): 118

Exchanges:
Milk: 0.0
Vegetable: 2.0
Fruit: 0.0
Bread: 1.0
Meat: 1.0
Fat: 0.0

1. Cook beef, onion, and garlic in lightly greased medium saucepan over medium heat until beef is browned, about 5 minutes; crumble beef with a fork. Add remaining ingredients, except barley, salt, and pepper; heat to boiling. Reduce heat and simmer, covered, 30 minutes, adding barley during the last 15 minutes. Discard bay leaves; season to taste with salt and pepper.

VEGETABLE OXTAIL SOUP

Long simmering brings out the rich flavor of oxtails, making this vegetable soup a real treat.

6 entrée servings

1 pound oxtails, sliced (2-inch)
1 tablespoon canola oil
3 tablespoons flour
1½ quarts Beef Stock (see p. 5)
1 teaspoon dried thyme leaves

1 bay leaf

2 large tomatoes, chopped

1 cup sliced celery

¾ cup each: chopped onion, sliced carrot, diced
parsnip, diced potato

⅓ cup quick-cooking barley

Salt and pepper, to taste

Per Serving:
Calories: 219
% calories from fat: 28
Protein (g): 12.4
Carbohydrate (g): 28.1
Fat (g): 17
Saturated fat (g): 0.4
Cholesterol (mg): 0.3
Sodium (mg): 35

Exchanges:
Milk: 0.0
Vegetable: 2.0
Fruit: 0.0
Bread: 1.0
Meat: 1.0
Fat: 1.0

1. Brown oxtails in oil in large saucepan; sprinkle
with flour and cook 2 minutes. Stir in stock,
thyme, and bay leaf; heat to boiling. Reduce heat
and simmer, covered, until oxtails are very tender,
1½ to 2 hours; remove oxtails from soup. Remove
meat from bones and return to soup; discard
bones. Add vegetables and barley to soup;
simmer, covered, until vegetables and barley
are tender, 15 to 20 minutes. Discard bay leaf;
season to taste with salt and pepper.

OLD-FASHIONED CHICKEN-VEGETABLE SOUP

A homey, heartwarming soup like Grandma used to make.

6 entrée servings

6–8 scallions, coarsely chopped

⅓ cup chopped celery

1 tablespoon margarine or butter

1 cup shredded green cabbage

1½ quarts Chicken Stock (see p. 2)

1 pound boneless, skinless chicken breast,
cubed (¾-inch)

¾ cup each: sliced carrots, celery, cubed
peeled rutabaga

2 cups small cauliflower florets

1 cup diced, peeled red potatoes

2 ounces uncooked medium egg noodles

⅓ cup chopped parsley

Salt and pepper, to taste

Per Serving:
Calories: 197
% calories from fat: 18
Protein (g): 18.2
Carbohydrate (g): 22.9
Fat (g): 3.9
Saturated fat (g): 0.9
Cholesterol (mg): 38.2
Sodium (mg): 401

Exchanges:
Milk: 0.0
Vegetable: 0.0
Fruit: 0.0
Bread: 2.0
Meat: 1.0
Fat: 0.0

1. Sauté scallions and celery in margarine in large saucepan until tender, about 5 minutes. Add remaining ingredients, except noodles, parsley, salt, and pepper; heat to boiling. Reduce heat and simmer, covered, 10 minutes. Add noodles and parsley; simmer, uncovered, until vegetables are tender and noodles are cooked, about 7 minutes. Season to taste with salt and pepper.

CLASSIC CHICKEN NOODLE SOUP

Comfort food at its best!

4 entrée servings

4 ounces each: boneless, skinless chicken breast
   and thighs, fat trimmed, cubed (¾-inch)
1 cup each: sliced celery, carrots, chopped onion
2 cans (14½ ounces each) reduced-sodium
   chicken broth
1 teaspoon dried marjoram leaves
1 bay leaf
1 cup uncooked wide noodles
Salt and pepper, to taste

Per Serving:
Calories: 307
% calories from fat: 14
Protein (g): 22.8
Carbohydrate (g): 44.3
Fat (g): 5
Saturated fat (g): 0.8
Cholesterol (mg): 32.9
Sodium (mg): 409

Exchanges:
Milk: 0.0
Vegetable: 1.0
Fruit: 0.0
Bread: 2.5
Meat: 2.0
Fat: 0.0

1. Cook chicken, celery, carrots, and onion in lightly greased large saucepan over medium heat until chicken is browned, about 7 minutes. Add chicken broth and herbs; heat to boiling. Reduce heat and simmer, covered, until chicken and vegetables are tender, 15 to 20 minutes. Add noodles; cook, uncovered, until noodles are tender, 7 to 10 minutes. Discard bay leaf; season to taste with salt and pepper.

ALPHABET CHICKEN SOUP

Kids like the alphabet letters in this traditional chicken soup!

4 entrée servings

½ cup each: chopped onion carrots, celery
1 large garlic clove, minced
2 teaspoons canola oil

2 quarts Chicken Stock (see p. 2) or reduced-
    sodium fat-free chicken broth

1 pound skinless chicken breast halves

1 large bay leaf

½ teaspoon dried thyme leaves

⅛ teaspoon celery seeds

½ cup alphabet pasta

Salt and pepper, to taste

Per Serving:
Calories: 303
% calories from fat: 19
Protein (g): 36.5
Carbohydrate (g): 19.2
Fat (g): 5.9
Saturated fat (g): 1.2
Cholesterol (mg): 88.4
Sodium (mg): 139

Exchanges:
Milk: 0.0
Vegetable: 1.0
Fruit: 0.0
Bread: 1.0
Meat: 4.0
Fat: 0.0

1. Sauté onion and garlic in canola oil in large
saucepan until onion is tender, about 5 minutes.
Add remaining ingredients, except pasta, salt,
and pepper; heat to boiling. Reduce heat and
simmer, covered, until chicken is cooked, about
20 minutes. Remove chicken and remove meat
from bones; shred or cut into bite-sized pieces
and return to saucepan. Heat soup to boiling and
add pasta; reduce heat and simmer, uncovered,
until pasta is *al dente*, 8 to 10 minutes. Discard
bay leaf. Season to taste with salt and pepper.

CHICKEN-VEGETABLE NOODLE SOUP

*This chicken noodle soup is loaded with vegetables for extra goodness
and nutrition.*

6 entrée servings

1 cup each: chopped celery, carrots, chopped
    parsnip, onion

1 tablespoon olive oil

2 quarts Rich Chicken Stock (see p. 4)

1 cup each: small broccoli florets, cut green beans

½ cup frozen peas

¾ teaspoon each: dried thyme and rosemary leaves

1–2 teaspoons balsamic vinegar

4 ounces noodles

1½ cups shredded cooked chicken breast

Salt and pepper, to taste

Per Serving:
Calories: 262
% calories from fat: 18
Protein (g): 22.2
Carbohydrate (g): 28.7
Fat (g): 4.9
Saturated fat (g): 1.1
Cholesterol (mg): 28.3
Sodium (mg): 147

Exchanges:
Milk: 0.0
Vegetable: 3.0
Fruit: 0.0
Bread: 1.0
Meat: 2.0
Fat: 0.0

1. Sauté celery, carrots, parsnip, and onion in oil in large saucepan until tender, about 8 minutes. Stir in stock, broccoli, green beans, peas, herbs, and vinegar; heat to boiling. Stir in noodles and chicken; reduce heat and cook until noodles are tender, 7 to 10 minutes. Season to taste with salt and pepper.

CHICKEN-RICE SOUP

The combination of tarragon, turnip, and parsnip gives this soup its great flavor.

6 entrée servings

1 each: large finely chopped onion, minced
    garlic clove
2 teaspoons canola oil
2 quarts Chicken Stock (see p. 2)
½ cup each: coarsely shredded, peeled parsnip,
    turnip, sliced carrots, celery
2 bay leaves
½ teaspoon each: dried thyme and tarragon leaves
1½ pounds skinless chicken breasts
½ cup uncooked white rice
Salt and pepper, to taste

Per Serving:
Calories: 283
% calories from fat: 15
Protein (g): 32.7
Carbohydrate (g): 23.4
Fat (g): 4.4
Saturated fat (g): 0.9
Cholesterol (mg): 79.0
Sodium (mg): 116

Exchanges:
Milk: 0.0
Vegetable: 0.0
Fruit: 0.0
Bread: 1.5
Meat: 4.0
Fat: 0.0

1. Sauté onion and garlic in oil in large saucepan until onion is tender, about 5 minutes. Add remaining ingredients except salt, and pepper. Heat to boiling; reduce heat and simmer, covered, until chicken is cooked and rice is tender, about 25 minutes. Remove chicken; remove meat from bones; shred or cut into bite-sized pieces and return to soup. Discard bay leaves; season to taste with salt and pepper.

CHICKEN AND BARLEY SOUP

Quick-cooking barley requires about 15 minutes to cook, compared to pearl barley, which requires almost an hour.

6 entrée servings

12 ounces boneless, skinless chicken breast, cubed (¾-inch)

1 cup chopped onion

⅓ cup each: coarsely shredded carrot, sliced celery

1 clove garlic, minced

1 quart Chicken Stock (see p. 2)

1 cup water

⅓ cup quick-cooking barley

¼ cup chopped parsley

½ teaspoon dried thyme leaves

1 bay leaf

Salt and pepper, to taste

Per Serving:
Calories: 145
% calories from fat: 16
Protein (g): 18.1
Carbohydrate (g): 12
Fat (g): 2.5
Saturated fat (g): 0.7
Cholesterol (mg): 45.9
Sodium (mg): 327

Exchanges:
Milk: 0.0
Vegetable: 0.0
Fruit: 0.0
Bread: 0.5
Meat: 2.0
Fat: 0.0

1. Cook chicken breast, vegetables, and garlic over medium heat in lightly greased large saucepan until chicken is browned, about 8 minutes. Add remaining ingredients, except salt and pepper and heat to boiling. reduce heat and simmer, covered, until vegetables and barley are tender, about 15 minutes. Discard bay leaf; season to taste with salt and pepper.

MEATBALL AND VEGETABLE SOUP

Chicken Meatballs can be prepared in advance and refrigerated, covered, several hours before making the soup.

8 entrée servings

1 cup each: chopped onion, thickly sliced carrots, zucchini
2 quarts reduced-sodium chicken broth
Chicken Meatballs (recipe follows)
Salt and pepper, to taste

Per Serving:
Calories: 238
% calories from fat: 23
Protein (g): 35.4
Carbohydrate (g): 6.6
Fat (g): 5.5
Saturated fat (g): 1.9
Cholesterol (mg): 72.9
Sodium (mg): 545

Exchanges:
Milk: 0.0
Vegetable: 0.0
Fruit: 0.0
Bread: 0.5
Meat: 3.5
Fat: 0.0

1. Sauté vegetables in lightly greased large saucepan until tender, about 8 minutes. Add broth and heat to boiling. Add Chicken Meatballs; reduce heat and simmer, covered, until meatballs are cooked, about 8 minutes. Season to taste with salt and pepper.

Chicken Meatballs

Makes 40 meatballs

2 pounds ground chicken breast
1½ cups fresh whole wheat bread crumbs
¼ cup (1 ounce) grated Parmesan cheese
1 egg
2 teaspoons minced garlic
1½ teaspoons dried Italian seasoning
½ teaspoon each: salt, pepper

1. Combine all ingredients, form into 40 meatballs.

VARIATION

Garden Meatball Soup — Make meatballs as above, substituting lean ground beef for the chicken breast, and beef broth for the chicken broth. Stir 1 cup sliced cabbage and 1 can (15 ounces) each rinsed, drained kidney beans and stewed tomatoes into broth; heat to boiling and complete as above.

CHICKEN RAVIOLI SOUP

Wonton wrappers, found in the produce section of your supermarket, make ravioli easy to prepare.

6 entrée servings

½ cup julienned or shredded carrots
¼ cup sliced green onions
1 teaspoon canola oil
2⅓ quarts Rich Chicken Stock (see p. 4)
3 cups thinly sliced bok choy or Napa cabbage
Chicken Ravioli (recipe follows)
Salt and pepper, to taste

Per Serving:
Calories: 267
% calories from fat: 14
Protein (g): 22.2
Carbohydrate (g): 29.9
Fat (g): 3.8
Saturated fat (g): 0.9
Cholesterol (mg): 29
Sodium (mg): 420

Exchanges:
Milk: 0.0
Vegetable: 0.0
Fruit: 0.0
Bread: 2.0
Meat: 2.0
Fat: 0.0

1. Sauté carrots and green onions in oil in large saucepan until tender, about 5 minutes. Add stock and heat to boiling; reduce heat and simmer, covered, 5 minutes. Stir in bok choy and Chicken Ravioli and heat to boiling; reduce heat and simmer, covered, until bok choy is tender, about 5 minutes. Season to taste with salt and pepper.

Chicken Ravioli

Makes 1½ dozen

8 ounces ground chicken breast
1 tablespoon minced green onion
1 teaspoon each: minced garlic, grated gingerroot
¼ teaspoon each: salt, pepper
36 wonton wrappers

1. Combine all ingredients, except wonton wrappers, in small bowl. Place rounded teaspoon of chicken mixture in center of each wonton wrapper. Moisten edges of wrappers with water. Top with remaining wrappers; press edges to seal. Refrigerate, covered, until ready to cook.

CHICKEN AND CHILIES SOUP

The green chilies add spicy south-of-the-border flavor.

6 first-course servings

½ cup each: finely chopped onion, celery

1 large clove garlic, minced

1 teaspoon margarine or butter

1 quart Chicken Stock (see p. 2)

¾ cup cubed cooked chicken breast

1 can (4 ounces) chopped green chilies, drained

1½ cups small cauliflower florets

1 cup cooked kidney beans

2 tablespoons cornstarch

¼ cup cold water

½ cup (2 ounces) each: shredded mild Cheddar cheese, fat-free Cheddar cheese

Salt and pepper, to taste

Per Serving:
Calories: 139
% calories from fat: 22
Protein (g): 12.5
Carbohydrate (g): 14.2
Fat (g): 3.4
Saturated fat (g): 1.8
Cholesterol (mg): 17.9
Sodium (mg): 471

Exchanges:
Milk: 0.0
Vegetable: 0.0
Fruit: 0.0
Bread: 1.0
Meat: 1.0
Fat: 0.0

1. Sauté onion, celery, and garlic in margarine in large saucepan until onion is tender, about 5 minutes. Add stock, chicken, chilies, cauliflower, and beans; heat to boiling. Reduce heat and simmer, covered, until cauliflower is tender, about 10 minutes. Heat soup to boiling; stir in combined cornstarch and water, stirring, until thickened, about 1 minute. Reduce heat to low; add cheeses, stirring until melted. Season to taste with salt and pepper.

EASY TORTILLA SOUP

45

This quick version of Tortilla Soup uses many canned ingredients for speedy preparation.

6 first-course servings

¾ cup chopped onion

1 clove garlic, minced

⅛–¼ teaspoon crushed red pepper

1 teaspoon olive oil

1 can (4 ounces) chopped green chilies, drained

2 cans (14½ ounces each) reduced- sodium fat-free chicken broth

1 can (14½ ounces) reduced-sodium diced tomatoes, undrained

1 can (15 ounces) spicy chili beans, undrained

2 teaspoons red wine vinegar

¼ cup chopped cilantro

Salt, to taste

6 corn tortillas (6-inch), cut into ½-inch strips

Vegetable cooking spray

½ small avocado, peeled, cubed

Per Serving:
Calories: 181
% calories from fat: 18
Protein (g): 10
Carbohydrate (g): 30.2
Fat (g): 4.1
Saturated fat (g): 0.6
Cholesterol (mg): 0
Sodium (mg): 530

Exchanges:
Milk: 0.0
Vegetable: 0.0
Fruit: 0.0
Bread: 2.0
Meat: 0.0
Fat: 1.0

1. Sauté onion, garlic, and crushed red pepper in oil in large saucepan until tender, about 5 minutes. Add chilies, broth, tomatoes and beans with liquid, and vinegar; heat to boiling. Reduce heat and simmer, covered, 10 minutes. Stir in cilantro and season to taste with salt.

2. Place tortilla strips on baking sheet. Spray with cooking spray and toss; bake at 375 degrees until crisp, about 5 minutes. Place tortilla strips and avocado in each soup bowl; ladle soup over.

HAM AND SPLIT PEA SOUP

Thick and satisfying, this soup is a meal in a bowl.

6 entrée servings

2¼ quarts water

2 bouillon cubes

1 meaty ham bone or 2 large ham hocks

2 cups dried green split peas

½ cup each: finely chopped onion, thinly sliced carrots and celery

½ teaspoon each: dried thyme and marjoram, celery salt, pepper

2 bay leaves

Salt and pepper, to taste

Per Serving:
Calories: 165
% calories from fat: 25
Protein (g): 10.5
Carbohydrate (g): 21.5
Fat (g): 4.6
Saturated fat (g): 1.5
Cholesterol (mg): 23.2
Sodium (mg): 570

Exchanges:
Milk: 0.0
Vegetable: 0.0
Fruit: 0.0
Bread: 1.5
Meat: 1.0
Fat: 0.0

1. Heat all ingredients, except salt and pepper, to boiling in Dutch oven; reduce heat and simmer, covered, stirring occasionally, until split peas are tender and have thickened the soup, about 1 hour. Remove ham bone, cut meat into small pieces, and return to soup; discard bone. Discard bay leaves; season to taste with salt and pepper.

CREAM OF PEA SOUP

Dried split peas and fresh peas are combined in this rich-flavored soup.

12 entrée servings

½ cup each: coarsely shredded carrot, chopped
  onion, leek (white part only)
1–2 tablespoons margarine or butter
3 quarts Rich Chicken Stock (see p. 4)
1½ pounds dried split peas
1½ teaspoons sugar
2 cups frozen peas
1 can (13 ounces) evaporated fat-free milk
Salt and pepper, to taste
1½ cups Rye-Caraway Croutons (½ recipe)
  (see p. 636)

Per Serving:
Calories: 322
% calories from fat: 8
Protein (g): 23.8
Carbohydrate (g): 49.4
Fat (g): 2.8
Saturated fat (g): 0.6
Cholesterol (mg): 2.2
Sodium (mg): 131

Exchanges:
Milk: 0.0
Vegetable: 2.0
Fruit: 0.0
Bread: 3.0
Meat: 1.0
Fat: 0.0

1. Sauté carrot, onion, and leek in margarine in Dutch oven until tender, about 5 minutes; add stock, split peas, and sugar and heat to boiling. Reduce heat and simmer, covered, until peas are tender, about 1 hour, adding frozen peas during last 10 minutes. Process soup in food processor or blender until smooth; return to saucepan. Add evaporated milk and cook, covered over medium heat until hot, about 5 minutes. Season to taste with salt and pepper. Top each bowl of soup with Rye-Caraway Croutons.

HEARTY SPLIT PEA, BEAN, AND BARLEY SOUP

We love this stick-to-the-ribs soup for its variety of textures.

12 entrée servings

4 quarts water

1 meaty ham bone or 2 large smoked pork hocks

2 cups dried green split peas

½ cup each: pearl barley, dried black-eyed peas, navy beans

3 bay leaves

2–4 beef bouillon cubes

1 cup coarsely chopped onions

½ cup each: thinly sliced carrots, celery

2 cloves garlic, minced

½ teaspoon each: dried thyme leaves, crushed celery seeds

Salt and pepper, to taste

Per Serving:
Calories: 153
% calories from fat: 10
Protein (g): 8.4
Carbohydrate (g): 27.4
Fat (g): 1.8
Saturated fat (g): 0.5
Cholesterol (mg): 5.9
Sodium (mg): 205

Exchanges:
Milk: 0.0
Vegetable: 0.0
Fruit: 0.0
Bread: 2.0
Meat: 0.0
Fat: 0.0

1. Heat all ingredients, except salt and pepper, to boiling in large Dutch oven; reduce heat and simmer, covered, until beans, peas, and barley are tender, 1 to 1½ hours. Remove ham bone, cut meat into bite-sized pieces, and return to soup; discard bone. Discard bay leaves; season to taste with salt and pepper.

DOWN-HOME SOUP

Smoked pork hock, black-eyed peas, and barley combine to give this soup its down-home flavor and richness.

6 entrée servings

1 cup chopped onion

¼ cup each: sliced carrot, chopped celery

1 garlic clove, minced

2 teaspoons olive oil

2 quarts Chicken Stock (see p. 2) or
   reduced-sodium fat-free chicken broth

½ cup dried black-eyed peas

3 tablespoons pearl barley

2 small pork hocks

1 bay leaf

2 teaspoons dried basil leaves

½ teaspoon dried thyme leaves

2½ cups cut green beans

1 can (14½ ounces) reduced-sodium diced tomatoes, undrained

Pinch crushed red pepper

Salt and pepper, to taste

Per Serving:
Calories: 146
% calories from fat: 22
Protein (g): 7.8
Carbohydrate (g): 19.2
Fat (g): 3.4
Saturated fat (g): 0.8
Cholesterol (mg): 15.2
Sodium (mg): 61

Exchanges:
Milk: 0.0
Vegetable: 0.0
Fruit: 0.0
Bread: 1.0
Meat: 1.0
Fat: 0.5

1. Sauté onion, carrot, celery, and garlic in oil in large saucepan until onion is tender, about 5 minutes. Add stock, black-eyed peas, barley, pork hocks, and herbs and heat to boiling; reduce heat and simmer, covered, until black-eyed peas and barley are tender, about 1 hour. Add green beans, tomatoes with liquid, and red pepper; simmer, covered, until green beans are tender, about 10 minutes. Discard bay leaf and pork hocks; season to taste with salt and pepper.

BLACK-EYED PEA AND LENTIL SOUP

This soup is flavorful, economical, and full of protein. Use the food processor to chop the vegetables quickly.

10 entrée servings

½ cup each: chopped carrots, celery, onion

2 cloves garlic, minced

2 teaspoons olive oil

8 ounces lean smoked ham, cubed

1 can (14½ ounces) reduced-sodium diced
   tomatoes, undrained

2 quarts Beef Stock (see p. 5)

1½ cups dried lentils

1 cup dried black-eyed peas

½ teaspoon each: dried thyme and rosemary leaves

Salt and pepper, to taste

Per Serving:
Calories: 219
% calories from fat: 12
Protein (g): 15.4
Carbohydrate (g): 33.9
Fat (g): 3
Saturated fat (g): 0.7
Cholesterol (mg): 12.3
Sodium (mg): 300

Exchanges:
Milk: 0.0
Vegetable: 1.0
Fruit: 0.0
Bread: 2.0
Meat: 1.0
Fat: 0.0

1. Sauté carrots, celery, onion, and garlic in oil in large saucepan until tender, about 10 minutes. Stir in remaining ingredients, except salt and pepper, and heat to boiling. Reduce heat and simmer, covered, until black-eyed peas are tender, about 1 hour, stirring occasionally. Season to taste with salt and pepper.

RED LENTIL SOUP

Red lentils have a milder taste and finer texture than brown lentils.

6 entrée servings

1½ cups dried red lentils

1 cup finely chopped onion

⅓ cup each: diced celery, green bell pepper

1 garlic clove, minced

1½ quarts Low-Salt Chicken Stock (see p. 3)

1 teaspoon each: chili powder, paprika

1 bay leaf

1½ cups reduced-fat spaghetti sauce

1–2 teaspoons sugar

Salt and pepper, to taste

Per Serving:
Calories: 210
% calories from fat: 4
Protein (g): 17
Carbohydrate (g): 34.6
Fat (g): 1
Saturated fat (g): 0.1
Cholesterol (mg): 5
Sodium (mg): 335

Exchanges:
Milk: 0.0
Vegetable: 1.0
Fruit: 0.0
Bread: 2.0
Meat: 0.5
Fat: 0.0

1. Heat all ingredients, except spaghetti sauce, sugar, salt, and pepper to boiling in large saucepan; reduce heat and simmer, covered, until lentils are tender, about 30 minutes. Stir in spaghetti sauce and simmer, uncovered, 10 to 15 minutes. Discard bay leaf; season to taste with sugar, salt, and pepper.

LENTIL-VEGETABLE SOUP WITH HAM

Lentils lend a wonderful homey flavor and heartiness to this simple soup.

4 entrée servings

½ cup each: chopped onion, carrot, celery, ham
1 tablespoon olive oil
⅔ cup dried lentils
1 quart Rich Chicken Stock (see p. 4)
⅛–¼ teaspoon crushed red pepper
1 small smoked pork hock
1 can (14½ ounce) stewed tomatoes
Salt and pepper, to taste

Per Serving:
Calories: 237
% calories from fat: 24
Protein (g): 16.9
Carbohydrate (g): 27.3
Fat (g): 6.4
Saturated fat (g): 1.4
Cholesterol (mg): 11.6
Sodium (mg): 414

Exchanges:
Milk: 0.0
Vegetable: 2.0
Fruit: 0.0
Bread: 1.0
Meat: 2.0
Fat: 0.0

1. Sauté onion, carrot, celery, and ham in oil in Dutch oven until vegetables are tender, about 8 minutes. Stir in lentils, stock, crushed red pepper, and pork hock; heat to boiling. Reduce heat and simmer until lentils are tender, about 30 minutes. Add tomatoes; simmer, uncovered, 5 minutes. Discard pork hock; season to taste with salt and pepper.

RICH BEEF AND LENTIL SOUP

Browned beef and caramelized onions add richness to a favorite lentil soup.

10 entrée servings

1 pound lean beef stew cubes
1½ cups finely chopped onions
1 tablespoon olive oil
2 tablespoons flour
3 quarts reduced-sodium fat-free beef broth

3 cups dried lentils

½ cup each: finely chopped leek (white part only), carrots, celery

¼ cup dry white wine (optional)

Salt and pepper, to taste

Per Serving:
Calories: 313
% calories from fat: 12
Protein (g): 31.7
Carbohydrate (g): 37.3
Fat (g): 4.2
Saturated fat (g): 1.1
Cholesterol (mg): 28.4
Sodium (mg): 234

1. Cook beef and onions in oil in large saucepan over medium to medium-high heat until beef is browned and crusty and onions are well browned, about 10 minutes; stir in flour and cook 1 minute. Add broth, lentils, leek, carrots, and celery; heat to boiling. Reduce heat and simmer, covered, until lentils are tender, 30 to 45 minutes, stirring in wine during last 15 minutes. Season to taste with salt and pepper.

Exchanges:
Milk: 0.0
Vegetable: 1.0
Fruit: 0.0
Bread: 2.0
Meat: 2.5
Fat: 0.0

SPICY LENTIL-TOMATO SOUP WITH HAM

This easy, spicy lentil soup is seasoned with ham, tomatoes, and a lively blend of herbs.

6 entrée servings

3 cups chopped onions

2 large garlic cloves, minced

1 tablespoon olive oil

1½ quarts Chicken Stock (see p. 2)

2 pork hocks (optional)

1 cup each: finely chopped celery, carrots

½ cup dried red or brown lentils

1 tablespoon dried basil leaves

½ teaspoon each: dried oregano and thyme leaves

½ cup finely diced lean ham

1 can (28 ounces) Italian plum tomatoes, coarsely chopped, undrained

1 cup each: shredded green cabbage, rinsed, drained canned garbanzo beans

Salt and cayenne pepper, to taste

Per Serving:
Calories: 204
% calories from fat: 16
Protein (g): 14.3
Carbohydrate (g): 28.6
Fat (g): 3.7
Saturated fat (g): 0.6
Cholesterol (mg): 5
Sodium (mg): 671

Exchanges:
Milk: 0.0
Vegetable: 3.0
Fruit: 0.0
Bread: 1.0
Meat: 1.0
Fat: 0.0

1. Sauté onions and garlic in oil in large saucepan until onions are soft, 8 to 10 minutes. Add stock, pork hocks, celery, carrots, lentils, and herbs; heat to boiling. Reduce heat and simmer, covered, until lentils are tender, about 30 minutes; discard pork hocks. Add ham, tomatoes with liquid, cabbage, and beans; simmer, covered, 15 minutes. Season to taste with salt and cayenne pepper.

WHITE BEAN SOUP

Great Northern or navy beans can be substituted for the cannellini beams.

4 first-course servings

2 cups chopped celery
1 medium onion, chopped
3 scallions, chopped
1–2 cloves garlic, minced
2 tablespoons canola oil
2 cans (15 ounces each) cannellini beans,
    rinsed, drained
1 cup each: Quick Sage Chicken Stock
    (see p. 2), water
½ teaspoon each: dried dill weed and thyme leaves
3 whole allspice
Juice of 1 lemon
Salt and cayenne pepper, to taste

Per Serving:
Calories: 238
% calories from fat: 17
Protein (g): 11
Carbohydrate (g): 38.3
Fat (g): 4.6
Saturated fat (g): 0.3
Cholesterol (mg): 0
Sodium (mg): 399

Exchanges:
Milk: 0.0
Vegetable: 0.0
Fruit: 0.0
Bread: 2.5
Meat: 0.0
Fat: 1.0

1. Sauté celery, onion, scallions, and garlic in oil in large saucepan until tender, about 5 minutes. Add remaining ingredients, except salt and pepper and heat to boiling; reduce heat and simmer, covered, 15 minutes. Process soup in food processor or blender until smooth; season to taste with salt and pepper.

WHITE BEAN AND PASTA SOUP

Enjoy the combination of beans and pasta in this Italian-seasoned soup.

6 entrée servings

1 large onion, chopped

2 garlic cloves, chopped

2 teaspoons olive oil

2 cans (15 ounces each) Great Northern beans, rinsed, drained

2 quarts Chicken Stock (see p. 2) or reduced-sodium fat-free chicken broth

1 can (8 ounces) tomato sauce

½ cup each: sliced carrots, celery, chopped parsley

1 tablespoon dried Italian seasoning

2 cups broken angel hair pasta (3-inch)

Salt and pepper, to taste

Per Serving:
Calories: 401
% calories from fat: 10
Protein (g): 21.2
Carbohydrate (g): 66.7
Fat (g): 4.6
Saturated fat (g): 1.0
Cholesterol (mg): 15.2
Sodium (mg): 251

Exchanges:
Milk: 0.0
Vegetable: 1.0
Fruit: 0.0
Bread: 4.0
Meat: 1.0
Fat: 0.0

1. Sauté onion and garlic in oil in Dutch oven until onion is tender, about 5 minutes. Add remaining ingredients, except pasta, salt, and pepper; heat to boiling. Reduce heat and simmer, covered, 20 minutes. Heat soup to boiling and add pasta; reduce heat and simmer, uncovered, until pasta is *al dente*, 2 to 3 minutes. Season to taste with salt and pepper.

WHITE BEAN SOUP WITH SPINACH

This soup is a meal in a bowl. Serve with warm crusty bread and a crisp green salad.

8 first-course servings

1½ cups dried Great Northern beans

1 large onion, chopped

2 cloves garlic, minced

2 teaspoons olive oil

1½ quarts Chicken Stock (see p. 2)

2 cups water

¼ cup pearl barley

⅓ cup each: sliced carrots, celery

2 bay leaves

1 teaspoon each: dried marjoram and basil leaves

½ teaspoon dried thyme leaves

1 can (14½ ounces) diced tomatoes, undrained

1 package (10 ounces) frozen chopped spinach, thawed, drained

Salt and pepper, to taste

Per Serving:
Calories: 115
% calories from fat: 14
Protein (g): 5.4
Carbohydrate (g): 20.9
Fat (g): 1.9
Saturated fat (g): 1
Cholesterol (mg): 0
Sodium (mg): 806

Exchanges:
Milk: 0.0
Vegetable: 3.0
Fruit: 0.0
Bread: 0.5
Meat: 0.0
Fat: 0.0

1. Cover beans with 2 inches of water in large saucepan; heat to boiling. Boil 2 minutes; remove from heat and let stand, covered, 1 hour. Drain.

2. Sauté onion and garlic in oil in large saucepan oven until tender, about 5 minutes. Add beans and remaining ingredients, except tomatoes, spinach, salt, and pepper; heat to boiling. Reduce heat and simmer, covered, until beans and barley are tender, about 1 hour. Discard bay leaves. Add tomatoes with liquid and spinach; simmer, covered, until hot, about 5 minutes. Season to taste with salt and pepper.

HEARTY BEAN AND BARLEY SOUP

Bean and barley soup is hard to beat on a chilly evening; serve with Herbed-Garlic Breadsticks (see p. 638).

8 entrée servings

2 cups dried Great Northern beans

2¼ quarts water

1 meaty ham bone or 2 pork hocks

¼ cup pearl barley

2 cups chopped onions

⅓ cup each: sliced carrots, celery

3–4 beef bouillon cubes

1½ garlic cloves, minced

3 bay leaves

1½ teaspoons dried thyme leaves

3 cups thinly sliced cabbage

1 can (8 ounces) tomato sauce

Salt and pepper, to taste

Per Serving:
Calories: 225
% calories from fat: 4
Protein (g): 12.2
Carbohydrate (g): 43.1
Fat (g): 1.1
Saturated fat (g): 0.3
Cholesterol (mg): 1.4
Sodium (mg): 378

Exchanges:
Milk: 0.0
Vegetable: 0.0
Fruit: 0.0
Bread: 3.0
Meat: 1.0
Fat: 0.0

1. Cover beans with 2 inches of water in Dutch oven and heat to boiling; boil 2 minutes. Remove from heat and let stand, covered, 1 hour. Drain.

2. Heat beans and remaining ingredients, except cabbage, tomato sauce, salt, and pepper to boiling in Dutch oven; reduce heat and simmer, covered, until beans are very tender, 1 to 1½ hours. Remove ham bone; cut meat into small pieces and return to soup. Discard bone and bay leaves. Add cabbage and tomato sauce; simmer, covered, until cabbage is tender, about 10 minutes. Season to taste with salt and pepper.

EASY BARLEY AND GARBANZO SOUP

45 *A one-step soup—what could be easier!*

6 first-course servings

1½ quarts water
3 beef bouillon cubes
⅓ cup quick-cooking barley
1 can (15 ounces) tomato sauce
¼ cup each: finely chopped celery, carrot
2 tablespoons dried minced onion
2 teaspoons sugar
½ teaspoon each: dry mustard, dried thyme leaves
1 can (15 ounces) garbanzo beans, rinsed, drained
1 can (16 ounces) cut green beans, drained
Salt and pepper, to taste

Per Serving:
Calories: 122
% calories from fat: 5
Protein (g): 5.8
Carbohydrate (g): 26.9
Fat (g): 0.8
Saturated fat (g): 0.1
Cholesterol (mg): 0
Sodium (mg): 738

Exchanges:
Milk: 0.0
Vegetable: 0.0
Fruit: 0.0
Bread: 1.5
Meat: 0.0
Fat: 0.0

1. Heat all ingredients, except salt and pepper, to boiling in large saucepan; reduce heat and simmer, covered, until barley is tender, about 15 minutes. Season to taste with salt and pepper.

CHICKEN NOODLE SOUP

45 *Enjoy this quick and easy version of the comfort food we all enjoy.*

4 entrée servings

4 ounces each: boneless, skinless chicken breast and thighs, fat trimmed, cubed
1 cup each: sliced celery, carrots, onion
2 cans (14½ ounces each) reduced-sodium fat-free chicken broth
1 teaspoon dried marjoram leaves
1 bay leaf
1 cup uncooked broad noodles
Salt and pepper, to taste

Per Serving:
Calories: 307
% calories from fat: 14
Protein (g): 22.8
Carbohydrate (g): 44.3
Fat (g): 5
Saturated fat (g): 0.8
Cholesterol (mg): 32.9
Sodium (mg): 409

Exchanges:
Milk: 0.0
Vegetable: 1.0
Fruit: 0.0
Bread: 2.5
Meat: 2.0
Fat: 0.0

1. Sauté chicken and vegetables in lightly greased large saucepan until chicken is browned, 8 to 10 minutes. Add chicken broth and herbs; heat to boiling. Reduce heat and simmer, covered, until chicken is cooked, about 15 minutes. Heat soup to boiling; add noodles. Reduce heat and cook, uncovered, until noodles are tender, 7 to 10 minutes. Discard bay leaf; season to taste with salt and pepper.

COUNTRY CHICKEN-NOODLE SOUP

Made with a stewing hen and homemade egg noodles, this chicken soup tastes just like the one Grandma used to make.

10 entrée servings

1 stewing chicken (about 4 pounds), cut up
3 quarts water
1 quartered small onion
1 teaspoon dried marjoram leaves
2 cups each: sliced carrots, whole kernel corn
1 cup frozen peas
Country Noodles (recipe follows)
¼ cup chopped parsley
Salt and pepper, to taste

Per Serving:
Calories: 232
% calories from fat: 22
Protein (g): 23.2
Carbohydrate (g): 22.1
Fat (g): 5.6
Saturated fat (g): 1.5
Cholesterol (mg): 79
Sodium (mg): 138

Exchanges:
Milk 0.0
Fruit: 0.0
Vegetable: 2.0
Bread: 1.0
Meat: 2.0
Fat: 0.0

1. Heat chicken, water, onion, and herbs to boiling in large saucepan; reduce heat and simmer, covered, until chicken is tender, about 1 hour. Strain broth and return to saucepan; skim off fat. Remove meat from chicken, discarding skin and bones; cut meat into small cubes and return to saucepan. Discard onion and herbs. Add vegetables to saucepan; heat to boiling. Reduce heat and simmer, covered, until carrots are almost tender, about 10 minutes. Uncoil noodle dough and drop into soup; simmer until noodles are tender, 3 to 5 minutes. Stir in parsley; season to taste with salt and pepper.

Country Noodles

1 cup all-purpose flour
1 egg
1 tablespoon water
¼ teaspoon salt

1. Place flour in medium bowl. Make a well in center and add egg, water, and salt. Gradually mix in flour with a fork until dough is formed. Knead dough on floured surface until smooth, kneading in additional flour if dough is sticky. Let dough stand, covered, at room temperature 1 hour. Roll dough on lightly floured surface to ⅛-inch thickness. Loosely roll up dough like a jelly roll; cut into scant ½-inch slices.

CHUNKY CHICKEN SOUP

Try other grains in this soup—millet, wheat berries, or bulgur would be delicious!

6 entrée servings

1½ quarts reduced-sodium fat-free chicken broth
1 can (14½ ounces) stewed tomatoes
1 pound boneless, skinless chicken breast, cubed
½ cup uncooked rice
1 large onion, chopped
⅓ cup each: thinly sliced ribs celery, carrots
1 teaspoon each: dried basil, thyme, and
    marjoram leaves
2 cups each: rinsed, drained canned garbanzo
    beans, coarsely chopped cauliflower
Salt and pepper, to taste

Per Serving:
Calories: 293
% calories from fat: 8
Protein (g): 28.5
Carbohydrate (g): 39.4
Fat (g): 2.8
Saturated fat (g): 0.5
Cholesterol (mg): 43.8
Sodium (mg): 855

Exchanges:
Milk: 0.0
Vegetable: 2.0
Fruit: 0.0
Bread: 2.0
Meat: 2.0
Fat: 0.0

1. Heat all ingredients, except cauliflower, salt, and pepper to boiling in large saucepan; reduce heat and simmer, covered, until rice is tender, about 25 minutes, adding cauliflower during last 10 minutes. Season to taste with salt and pepper.

SAVORY CHICKEN SOUP

For a delicious flavor accent, stir 1 cubed avocado into the soup just before serving.

6 entrée servings

1 chicken, cut up (about 3 pounds)

3 cups sliced carrots, divided

1 cup each: sliced celery, onion

1 bay leaf

2½ quarts water

2 tablespoons finely chopped shallots

8 ounces mushrooms, sliced

1 tablespoon margarine or butter

3 tablespoons flour

1–2 teaspoons curry powder

½ cup quick-cooking barley

1 cup fat-free half-and-half or fat-free milk

2 tablespoons dry sherry (optional)

Salt and pepper, to taste

Per Serving:
Calories: 316
% calories from fat: 25
Protein (g): 28.4
Carbohydrate (g): 27.7
Fat (g): 8.6
Saturated fat (g): 2.1
Cholesterol (mg): 72.3
Sodium (mg): 171

Exchanges:
Milk: 0.0
Vegetable: 3.0
Fruit: 0.0
Bread: 1.0
Meat: 3.0
Fat: 0.0

1. Heat chicken, 1 cup carrots, celery, onion, bay leaf, and water to boiling in large saucepan; reduce heat and simmer, covered, until chicken is tender, about 45 minutes. Strain soup; reserve stock. Remove chicken from bones; cut into bite-size pieces and discard bones. Process vegetables with 2 cups stock in food processor or blender until smooth; reserve.

2. Sauté shallots and mushrooms in margarine in large saucepan until tender, about 8 minutes. Stir in flour and curry powder; cook 2 minutes. Stir in reserved stock, remaining 2 cups carrots, and barley; heat to boiling. Reduce heat and simmer, covered, until barley is tender, about 15 minutes. Stir in reserved vegetable purée and chicken, half-and-half, and sherry; simmer until hot, about 5 minutes. Season to taste with salt and pepper.

CHICKEN-VEGETABLE SOUP WITH ENDIVE

Kale, Swiss chard, watercress or spinach can be substituted for the endive.

6 entrée servings

1 each: large chopped onion, diced rib celery, carrot

2 large garlic cloves, minced

1 tablespoon olive oil

1½ quarts reduced-sodium fat-free chicken broth

1½ pounds boneless, skinless chicken breast, cubed

1 can (14½ ounces) reduced-sodium diced
   tomatoes, undrained

2 medium red potatoes, peeled, coarsely diced

1½ teaspoons dried marjoram leaves

½ teaspoon each: dried basil leaves, pepper

¼ cup uncooked orzo

4 cups coarsely chopped curly endive

Salt and pepper, to taste

Per Serving:
Calories: 256
% calories from fat: 16
Protein (g): 33.1
Carbohydrate (g): 20.3
Fat (g): 4.4
Saturated fat (g): 1.0
Cholesterol (mg): 67.2
Sodium (mg): 689

Exchanges:
Milk: 0.0
Vegetable: 1.0
Fruit: 0.0
Bread: 1.0
Meat: 3.0
Fat: 0.0

1. Sauté onion, celery, carrot, and garlic in oil in Dutch oven
until vegetables are tender, about 8 minutes. Add broth, chicken,
tomatoes with liquid, potatoes, marjoram, basil, and pepper and
heat to boiling; reduce heat and simmer, covered, until chicken
is cooked, about 20 minutes, adding orzo and endive the last 10
minutes. Season to taste with salt and pepper.

SLOW-COOKER CHICKEN GUMBO

*Black-eyed peas, okra, and succotash, all Southern favorites, combine nicely
in this nourishing gumbo.*

6 entrée servings

1 package (10 ounces) each: frozen black-eyed peas and succotash

1 cup frozen sliced okra

1 quart fat-free chicken broth

1 can (14½ ounces) diced tomatoes, undrained

2 large onions, finely chopped

⅓ cup each: chopped celery, red or green bell pepper

1 medium pork hock

1 pound boneless, skinless chicken breast, cubed

3 tablespoons uncooked rice

1 bay leaf

¼ teaspoon dried thyme leaves

Salt and pepper, to taste

Per Serving:
Calories: 269
% calories from fat: 7
Protein (g): 27.1
Carbohydrate (g): 36.6
Fat (g): 2.2
Saturated fat (g): 0.3
Cholesterol (mg): 44.7
Sodium (mg): 568

Exchanges:
Milk: 0.0
Vegetable: 1 0
Fruit: 0.0
Bread: 2.0
Meat: 3.0
Fat: 0.0

1. Rinse frozen vegetables under warm water to partially thaw. Combine all ingredients except salt and pepper in slow cooker. Cover and cook on High 30 minutes. Continue cooking on High 3 hours or change setting to Low and cook 7 hours. Discard pork hock and bay leaf. Season to taste with salt and pepper.

HERBED CHICKEN SOUP WITH SPLIT PEAS

This easy variation of split-pea soup uses chicken instead of the more traditional ham.

8 entrée servings

¼ cup each: sliced green onions, carrots, celery

½ teaspoon each: dried savory and marjoram leaves

2 teaspoons olive oil

2 quarts reduced-sodium fat-free chicken broth

1 package (16 ounces) dried green split peas

2 cups cubed, cooked boneless, skinless chicken breast

Salt and pepper, to taste

Per Serving:
Calories: 282
% calories from fat: 5
Protein (g): 28.6
Carbohydrate (g): 37.8
Fat (g) 1.6
Saturated fat (g): 0.3
Cholesterol (mg): 21.8
Sodium (mg): 203

Exchanges:
Milk: 0.0
Vegetable: 0.0
Fruit: 0.0
Bread: 2.5
Meat: 2.0
Fat: 0.0

1. Sauté green onions, carrots, celery, and herbs in oil in large saucepan until vegetables are tender, about 5 minutes. Add broth and split peas and heat until boiling; reduce heat and simmer, covered, until split peas are tender, 30 to 40 minutes, adding chicken during last 10 minutes. Season to taste with salt and pepper.

CHICKEN-VEGETABLE SOUP WITH ORZO

45 *This hearty vegetable soup is perfect for a light supper—serve with warm, homemade bread (see Index).*

4 entrée servings

12 ounces boneless, skinless chicken breast, cubed
1 medium onion, coarsely chopped
½ cup each: sliced carrots, celery
3 cloves garlic, minced
½ teaspoon each: dried thyme and oregano leaves
2 cans (15 ounces each) reduced-sodium chicken broth
1 cup water
½ cup each: uncooked orzo, frozen peas
Salt and pepper, to taste
2 tablespoons grated Romano cheese

Per Serving:
Calories: 260
% calories from fat: 15
Protein (g): 24
Carbohydrate (g): 29.9
Fat (g): 4.1
Saturated fat (g): 1.3
Cholesterol (mg): 47.1
Sodium (mg): 281

Exchanges:
Milk: 0.0
Vegetable: 1.5
Fruit: 0.0
Bread: 1.5
Meat: 2.0
Fat: 0.0

1. Cook chicken, onion, carrots, celery, and garlic in lightly greased large saucepan until chicken is browned, about 8 minutes; Add chicken broth and water; heat to boiling. Stir in orzo and peas; reduce heat and simmer, uncovered, until orzo is *al dente*, about 7 minutes. Season to taste with salt and pepper; stir in cheese.

TURKEY-NOODLE SOUP

The perfect soup for using that leftover holiday turkey!

6 entrée servings

1 cup each: chopped carrots, celery, onion,
  sliced mushrooms
1 tablespoon minced garlic
2 tablespoons margarine or butter
3 tablespoons flour
2½ quarts Turkey Stock (see p. 4)
¾ teaspoon each: dried marjoram and thyme leaves
4 ounces egg noodles
4 cups diced, cooked turkey
1 cup frozen peas
Salt and pepper, to taste

Per Serving:
Calories: 376
% calories from fat: 26
Protein (g): 36.7
Carbohydrate (g): 28.5
Fat (g): 10.4
Saturated fat (g): 2.7
Cholesterol (mg): 80.1
Sodium (mg): 182

Exchanges:
Milk: 0.0
Vegetable: 0.0
Fruit: 0.0
Bread: 1.0
Meat: 4.0
Fat: 0.0

1. Sauté carrots, celery, onion, mushrooms, and garlic in margarine in large saucepan until tender, about 10 minutes; sprinkle with flour and cook 1 to 2 minutes. Stir in stock and herbs and heat to boiling; reduce heat and simmer, covered, 15 minutes. Heat soup to boiling; stir in noodles, turkey, and peas. Reduce heat and simmer, uncovered, until noodles are tender, 7 to 10 minutes. Season to taste with salt and pepper.

VARIATION

Turkey-Wild Rice Soup — Make soup as above, omitting noodles and peas, and adding 2 cups cooked wild rice and 1 cup diced cooked turnips or parsnips with the turkey.

HOME-STYLE TURKEY-VEGETABLE SOUP

The recipe is designed to yield a lot of soup since it's great reheated.

12 entrée servings

4 pounds turkey wings

3 cups water

1¾ quarts reduced-sodium fat-free chicken broth

2 cups coarsely chopped onions

¼ teaspoon each: dried marjoram and thyme leaves

1 cup each: chopped peeled rutabaga or turnip, celery, cabbage, carrots

¼ cup quick cooking barley

¼ cup uncooked elbow macaroni

1½ cups whole kernel corn

1 can (14½ ounces) diced tomatoes, undrained

1 can (16 ounces) Great Northern beans, rinsed, drained

Salt and pepper, to taste

Per Serving:
Calories: 336
% calories from fat: 28
Protein (g): 31
Carbohydrate (g): 29.9
Fat (g): 10.6
Saturated fat (g): 2.8
Cholesterol (mg): 65.1
Sodium (mg): 610

Exchanges:
Milk: 0.0
Vegetable: 2.0
Fruit: 0.0
Bread: 1.0
Meat: 4.0
Fat: 0.0

1. Heat turkey, water, broth, onions, and herbs to boiling in large saucepan; reduce heat and simmer, covered, until turkey is tender, about 30 minutes. Remove turkey wings; remove and shred meat and return to soup. Discard bones; skim fat from soup. Heat soup to boiling; add remaining ingredients, except salt and pepper.

Reduce heat and simmer, uncovered, until vegetables, barley, and macaroni are tender, about 10 minutes. Season to taste with salt and pepper.

TURKEY SOUP WITH TARRAGON

45 *This chunky, mustard-spiked soup makes a great one-dish meal.*

4 entrée servings

1 pound boneless, skinless turkey breast, cubed
2 tablespoons flour
1½ tablespoons olive oil
1 cup coarsely chopped onion
⅓ cup each: thinly sliced celery, carrots
1 tablespoon dried tarragon leaves
2 large potatoes, peeled, cubed
1 quart reduced-sodium fat-free chicken broth
1½ tablespoons Dijon mustard
Salt and pepper, to taste

Per Serving:
Calories: 229
% calories from fat: 26
Protein (g): 21.7
Carbohydrate (g): 20.9
Fat (g): 6.6
Saturated fat (g): 1.2
Cholesterol (mg): 35.2
Sodium (mg): 381

Exchanges:
Milk: 0.0
Vegetable: 0.0
Fruit: 0.0
Bread: 1.5
Meat: 2.0
Fat: 0.0

1. Coat turkey cubes lightly with flour; cook in oil in Dutch oven over medium heat until lightly browned, about 8 minutes. Add onion, celery, carrots, and tarragon; cook until onion is tender, about 5 minutes. Add remaining ingredients, except salt and pepper, and heat to boiling. Reduce heat and simmer, covered, until potatoes are tender, about 15 minutes. Season to taste with salt and pepper.

QUICK DINNER SOUP

45 *This soup is easy to make with use of packaged and frozen ingredients.*

6 entrée servings

12–16 ounces reduced-sodium smoked sausage, sliced (½-inch)
½ cup each: sliced celery, carrots, chopped green bell pepper
1½ quarts water
1 package (1.5 ounces) low-sodium onion soup mix

1 can (28 ounces) reduced-sodium diced
   tomatoes, undrained
1 package (10 ounces) each: frozen hash brown
   potatoes and sliced okra
1–2 tablespoons sugar
1½ teaspoons dried Italian seasoning
Salt and pepper, to taste
Hot pepper sauce, to taste

Per Serving:
Calories: 282
% calories from fat: 9
Protein (g): 15.2
Carbohydrate (g): 53.4
Fat (grit): 2.9
Saturated fat (g): 0.8
Cholesterol (mg): 26.5
Sodium (mg): 617

Exchanges:
Milk: 0.0
Vegetable: 2.0
Fruit: 0.0
Bread: 2.5
Meat: 1.0
Fat: 0.0

1. Cook sausage, celery, carrots, and bell pepper in lightly greased large saucepan until sausage is browned, 7 to 8 minutes; add remaining ingredients, except salt, pepper, and hot pepper sauce and heat to boiling. Reduce heat and simmer, covered, 20 minutes. Season to taste with salt, pepper, and hot pepper sauce.

PAY DAY SOUP

45 *Use up what's on hand today—pay day is tomorrow!!*

8 entrée servings

1 cup chopped onion
2 cloves garlic, minced
2 teaspoons olive oil
2 tablespoons flour
1½ quarts reduced-sodium, fat-free chicken broth
2 cups each: cubed, peeled potatoes, cooked rice
1 can (15 ounces) garbanzo beans, rinsed, drained
2 tablespoons grated Parmesan cheese
Salt and pepper, to taste

Per Serving:
Calories: 359
% calories from fat: 21
Protein (g): 9.5
Carbohydrate (g): 61
Fat (g): 8.5
Saturated fat (g): 2
Cholesterol (mg): 4.3
Sodium (mg): 206

Exchanges:
Milk: 0.0
Vegetable: 3.0
Fruit: 0.0
Bread: 3.0
Meat: 0.0
Fat: 1.5

1. Sauté onion and garlic in oil in large saucepan until tender, about 5 minutes; add flour and cook 1 minute. Add remaining ingredients, except Parmesan cheese, salt, and pepper; heat to boiling. Reduce heat and simmer, covered, until potatoes are tender, about 15 minutes. Stir in Parmesan cheese; season to taste with salt and pepper.

SLOW-COOKER HAMBURGER AND VEGETABLE SOUP

This sweet-sour favorite simmers all day in a slow cooker.

4 entrée servings

12 ounces ground beef round

1 large onion, finely chopped

2 large garlic cloves, minced

⅓ cup each, sliced celery, carrots

1¼ quarts reduced-sodium fat-free beef broth

1 can (15 ounces) tomato sauce

1 each: diced medium potato, thinly sliced large carrot

1 cup each: whole kernel corn, baby lima beans

2 tablespoons pearl barley

2 tablespoons each: packed light brown sugar,
   apple cider vinegar

¾ teaspoon each: dry mustard, dried thyme leaves

1 large bay leaf

Salt and pepper, to taste

Per Serving:
Calories: 347
% calories from fat: 13
Protein (g): 25.3
Carbohydrate (g): 50
Fat (g): 5.1
Saturated fat (g): 2.1
Cholesterol (mg): 52.7
Sodium (mg): 596

Exchanges:
Milk: 0.0
Vegetable: 0.0
Fruit: 0.0
Bread: 3.0
Meat: 2.0
Fat: 0.0

1. Cook beef, onion, and garlic in lightly greased large saucepan over medium heat until beef is browned, about 5 minutes; crumble beef with a fork. Add remaining ingredients, except salt and pepper, and heat to boiling; transfer to slow cooker. Cover and cook on Low 7 to 9 hours until barley and vegetables are tender, 7 to 9 hours. Discard bay leaf; season to taste with salt and pepper.

BEEF-BARLEY SOUP

This hearty, rib-sticking soup is even better if made a day or so in advance.

8 entrée servings

1 pound lean beef stew meat, cubed

1 cup each: chopped onion, celery, carrots

1 clove garlic, minced

1 tablespoon flour

4 cups water

1 can (14½ ounces) each: reduced-sodium beef broth, undrained diced tomatoes

½ teaspoon each: dried marjoram and thyme leaves

1 bay leaf

1 cup each: cut green beans, cubed parsnips or potatoes

½ cup each: frozen peas, quick-cooking barley

Salt and pepper, to taste

Per Serving:
Calories: 187
% calories from fat: 16
Protein (g): 18.8
Carbohydrate (g): 21.1
Fat (g): 3.3
Saturated fat (g): 1.1
Cholesterol (mg): 35.4
Sodium (mg): 153

Exchanges:
Milk: 0.0
Vegetable: 2.0
Fruit: 0.0
Bread: 0.5
Meat: 2.0
Fat: 0.0

1. Cook beef in lightly greased Dutch oven over medium heat until browned, 8 to 10 minutes. Add onion, celery, carrots, and garlic; cook until onion is tender, about 5 minutes. Stir in flour; cook l minute. Add water, broth, tomatoes with liquid, and herbs; heat to boiling. Reduce heat and simmer, covered, until beef is very tender, about 1 hour, adding remaining vegetables and barley during last 15 minutes. Discard bay leaf; season to taste with salt and pepper.

BEEF WITH RED WINE SOUP

This soup is reminiscent of the classic Beef Burgundy.

6 entrée servings

1 pound lean beef stew meat, cubed

1 tablespoon flour

2 teaspoons olive oil

6 ounces Canadian bacon, diced

1 cup each: chopped onion, sliced mushrooms

⅓ cup each: sliced carrots, celery

1 garlic clove, minced

1 quart Beef Stock (see p. 5)

½ cup dry red wine

1 can (8 ounces) tomato sauce

1½ teaspoon dried thyme leaves

2 bay leaves

4 cups cubed red potatoes

Salt and pepper, to taste

Per Serving:
Calories: 336
% calories from fat: 17
Protein (g): 28.1
Carbohydrate (g): 32.5
Fat (g): 6.2
Saturated fat (g): 1.8
Cholesterol (mg): 51.8
Sodium (mg): 280

Exchanges:
Milk: 0.0
Vegetable: 1.0
Fruit: 0.0
Bread: 1.5
Meat: 4.0
Fat: 0.0

1. Coat beef cubes lightly with flour; cook in oil in Dutch oven over medium heat 5 minutes. Add Canadian bacon, onion, mushrooms, carrots, celery, and garlic until vegetables are tender, 8 to 10 minutes. Add stock, wine, tomato sauce, and herbs; heat to boiling. Reduce heat and simmer, covered, until beef is tender, 50 to 60 minutes, adding potatoes during last 15 minutes. Discard bay leaves; season to taste with salt and pepper.

CORNED BEEF AND CABBAGE SOUP

This unusual soup duplicates the flavor of a New England boiled dinner.

6 entrée servings

1 large onion, chopped
2 large garlic cloves, minced
½ tablespoon olive oil
1¾ quarts reduced-sodium fat-free chicken broth
8 ounces deli corned beef, fat trimmed, cut into small pieces
4 cups thinly sliced cabbage
12 baby carrots, halved
2 large bay leaves
1 tablespoon apple cider vinegar
2 teaspoons each: Dijon mustard, caraway seeds
4 cups cubed red potatoes
Salt and pepper, to taste

Per Serving:
Calories: 209
% calories from fat: 22
Protein (g): 14.1
Carbohydrate (g): 26.9
Fat (g): 5.3
Saturated fat (g): 1.8
Cholesterol (mg): 21.3
Sodium (mg): 1216

Exchanges:
Milk: 0.0
Vegetable: 2.0
Fruit: 0.0
Bread: 1.0
Meat: 1.0
Fat: 0.0

1. Sauté onion and garlic in oil in large saucepan until onion is tender, about 5 minutes. Add remaining ingredients, except potatoes, salt, and pepper; heat to boiling. Reduce heat and simmer, covered, 45 minutes, adding potatoes the last 15 minutes. Discard bay leaves; season to taste with salt and pepper.

BAKED VEGETABLE SOUP WITH CABBAGE ROLLS

Stuffed cabbage leaves are baked in this vegetable soup to make a hearty dinner treat!

4 entrée servings

1¼ quarts Chicken Stock (see p. 2)

4 ribs celery, sliced

1 each: peeled cubed large potato, sliced carrot, chopped onion

1 large tomato, peeled, seeded, chopped

1 cup whole kernel corn

Salt and pepper, to taste

Cabbage Rolls (recipe follows)

6 tablespoons shredded Gruyère or Swiss cheese

Per Serving:
Calories: 373
% calories from fat: 22
Protein (g): 35.4
Carbohydrate (g): 37.3
Fat (g): 9.6
Saturated fat (g): 3.4
Cholesterol (mg): 200.2
Sodium (mg): 765

Exchanges:
Milk: 0.0
Vegetable: 2.0
Fruit: 0.0
Bread: 2.0
Meat: 3.0
Fat: 0.0

1. Heat stock, celery, potato, carrot, and onion to boiling in large saucepan; reduce heat and simmer, covered, until vegetables are tender, about 15 minutes. Stir in tomato and corn; season to taste with salt and pepper.

2. Place Cabbage Rolls, seam sides down, in 2½-quart casserole; ladle soup over. Bake, covered, at 350 degrees for 30 minutes. Arrange Cabbage Rolls in bottoms of shallow soup bowls; ladle soup over and sprinkle with cheese.

Cabbage Rolls
Makes 8

12 medium cabbage leaves

12 ounces lean ground veal

½ cup fresh bread crumbs

2 eggs

¾–1 teaspoon each: dried marjoram and thyme leaves

½ teaspoon salt

1. Cook cabbage leaves in boiling, salted water until limp, about 5 minutes; rinse in cold water and pat dry on paper toweling. Mix veal, bread crumbs, eggs, herbs, and salt. Place cabbage leaves, vein sides down, on cutting board. Place about 2 tablespoons veal mixture on stem end of each leaf; fold end over veal mixture, fold sides in and roll to form packets. Secure with toothpicks.

VEGETABLE SOUP WITH CHILI MEATBALLS

Lightly spiced meatballs add the perfect touch to this simple vegetable soup.

8 entrée servings

1 cup thinly sliced onion
¾ cup thinly sliced carrots
2 teaspoons olive oil
2 quarts Chicken Stock (see p. 2)
1 cup Mexican-style whole kernel corn
1 package (10 ounces) frozen chopped spinach
¼ cup dry sherry (optional)
Chili Meatballs (recipe follows)
Salt and pepper, to taste

Per Serving:
Calories: 192
% calories from fat: 28
Protein (g): 20.6
Carbohydrate (g): 14.8
Fat (g): 6
Saturated fat (g): 1.6
Cholesterol (mg): 71.2
Sodium (mg): 279

Exchanges:
Milk: 0.0
Vegetable: 0.0
Fruit: 0.0
Bread: 1.0
Meat: 2.0
Fat: 0.0

1. Sauté onion and carrots in oil in large saucepan until tender, about 5 minutes. Stir in stock, corn, and spinach. Heat to boiling; reduce heat and simmer, covered, 5 minutes. Stir in sherry and Chili Meatballs; season to taste with salt and pepper.

Chili Meatballs

Makes 32 meatballs

1½ pounds ground beef round
⅓ cup finely chopped onion, unseasoned dried bread crumbs
1 teaspoon minced garlic
1 tablespoon chili powder
2 teaspoons ground cumin
½ teaspoon salt
1 egg

1. Combine all ingredients. Shape into 32 balls and place on jelly roll pan. Bake at 325 degrees until cooked, about 10 minutes.

LAMB AND WHITE BEAN SOUP

If you like bean soup, try this version with lamb shanks.

6 entrée servings

1½ cups dried Great Northern or navy beans,
   sorted, rinsed

2 lamb shanks (about 1¾ pounds)

2 quarts Beef Stock (see p. 5)

2 each: sliced large carrots, ribs celery

1 large onion, finely chopped

2 large garlic cloves, minced

3 bay leaves

1½ teaspoons dried thyme and marjoram leaves

½ teaspoon each: crushed celery seeds, dry mustard

3 cups thinly sliced cabbage

Salt and pepper, to taste

Per Serving:
Calories: 371
% calories from fat: 29
Protein (g): 28.8
Carbohydrate (g): 37.4
Fat (g): 11.8
Saturated fat (g): 5.4
Cholesterol (mg): 61.6
Sodium (mg): 110

Exchanges:
Milk: 0.0
Vegetable: 0.0
Fruit: 0.0
Bread: 2.5
Meat: 3.0
Fat: 0.5

1. Place beans in large saucepan, cover with 2 inches of water, and heat to boiling. Reduce heat and simmer, covered, 2 minutes. Remove pan from heat and let stand, covered, 1 hour. Drain.

2. Heat beans and remaining ingredients, except cabbage, salt, and pepper to boiling in large saucepan; reduce heat and simmer, covered, until beans are tender, about 1 hour, adding cabbage during last 20 minutes. Remove lamb shanks; cut meat into bite-sized pieces, and return to saucepan. Discard bones and bay leaves; season to taste with salt and pepper.

LAMB SOUP WITH BARLEY

This vegetable soup can also be made with lean pork or beef.

8 entrée servings

1½ pounds lean lamb stew meat, cubed

1 quart water

1 bay leaf

1½ cups each: sliced onions, carrots, turnips

1 cup sliced celery

1 tablespoon each: minced garlic, olive oil

1½ quarts Low-Salt Chicken Stock (see p. 3)

½ cup each: dry white wine (optional), quick-cooking
   pearl barley

1 teaspoon each: dried oregano and rosemary leaves

Salt and pepper, to taste

Per Serving:
Calories: 241
% calories from fat: 20
Protein (g): 16.1
Carbohydrate (g): 27.9
Fat (g): 5.5
Saturated fat (g): 1.5
Cholesterol (mg): 38.9
Sodium (mg): 70

Exchanges:
Milk: 0.0
Vegetable: 2.0
Fruit: 0.0
Bread: 1.0
Meat: 2.0
Fat: 0.0

1. Heat lamb, water, and bay leaf to boiling in large saucepan;
reduce heat and simmer, covered, until lamb is tender, about 1½
hours. Discard bay leaf. Sauté vegetables and garlic in oil in large
saucepan until lightly browned, about 10 minutes. Stir in lamb and
cooking liquid, stock, wine, barley, oregano, and rosemary; heat to
boiling. Reduce heat and simmer, covered, until barley is tender,
about 15 minutes. Season to taste with salt and pepper.

LAMB, SPLIT-PEA, BEAN, AND BARLEY SOUP

*If you like split-pea soup made with ham bone, try this slightly milder
variation, using lamb.*

8 entrée servings

2¾ quarts water

3 pounds lamb shanks

2 cups dry green split peas

¼ cup pearl barley

¾ cup dry navy or Great Northern beans

3 bay leaves

2–4 beef bouillon cubes

1 cup chopped onion

⅓ cup each: sliced carrots, celery

1 cloves garlic, minced

1 teaspoon each: dried thyme and basil leaves

½ teaspoon crushed celery seeds

Salt and pepper, to taste

Per Serving:
Calories: 331
% calories from fat: 11
Protein (g): 29
Carbohydrate (g): 46
Fat (g): 4.1
Saturated fat (g): 1.3
Cholesterol (mg): 41
Sodium (mg): 253

Exchanges:
Milk 0.0
Vegetable: 1.0
Fruit: 0.0
Bread: 2.5
Meat: 2.5
Fat: 0.0

1. Heat water, lamb, split peas, barley, and beans to boiling in large saucepan; add remaining ingredients, except salt and pepper. Reduce heat and simmer, covered, until beans are tender, about 1 hour; discard bay leaves. Remove lamb shanks; remove meat, cut into bite-sized pieces and return to soup. Discard bones. Season to taste with salt and pepper

FOUR-BEAN SOUP WITH SAUSAGE

45 *This hearty soup has a Mexican accent and spicy flavor, and it can be made very quickly.*

8 entrée servings

8 ounces reduced-sodium, reduced-fat smoked
  sausage, sliced

1 cup chopped onion

½ cup each: chopped green bell pepper, celery

1 teaspoon minced garlic

1 small jalapeño chili, chopped

2 teaspoons olive oil

1 can (15 ounces) each: rinsed drained garbanzo,
  pinto and black beans

1 package (10 ounces) frozen cut green beans

1 can (14½ ounces) each: reduced-sodium stewed
  tomatoes, reduced-sodium fat-free chicken broth

1 jar (8 ounces) mild salsa

1 can (6 ounces) spicy vegetable juice cocktail

2–3 teaspoons chili powder

1 teaspoon dried oregano leaves

Salt and hot pepper sauce, to taste

Per Serving:
Calories: 245
% calories from fat: 13
Protein (g): 15.3
Carbohydrate (g): 42.6
Fat (g): 4.1
Saturated fat (g): 0.7
Cholesterol (mg): 13.2
Sodium (mg): 911

Exchanges:
Milk: 0.0
Vegetable: 2.0
Fruit: 0.0
Bread: 2.0
Meat: 1.0
Fat: 0.0

1. Sauté sausage, onion, bell pepper, celery, garlic, and jalapeño chili in oil in large saucepan until lightly browned, about 8 minutes. Add remaining ingredients, except salt and hot pepper sauce, and heat to boiling. Reduce heat and simmer, covered, 10 minutes. Season to taste with salt and hot pepper sauce.

SMOKY SIX-BEAN SOUP

Beans are slowly simmered with smoked pork in this richly flavored soup. Use any bean combination your family enjoys.

12 entrée servings

2 pounds smoked pork shoulder, cubed

4 quarts Fragrant Beef Stock (see p. 6)

¾ cup each: chopped onion, dried red kidney, navy, baby lima, pinto, black, and garbanzo beans

⅓ cup low-sodium Worcestershire sauce

2 bay leaves

2 teaspoons dried Italian seasoning

1 cup chopped carrots

2 ribs celery, sliced

Salt and pepper, to taste

Hot pepper sauce, to taste

Per Serving:
Calories: 397
% calories from fat: 22
Protein (g): 34
Carbohydrate (g): 43.7
Fat (g): 10
Saturated fat (g): 3.5
Cholesterol (mg): 58.4
Sodium (mg): 146

Exchanges:
Milk: 0.0
Vegetable: 0.0
Fruit: 0.0
Bread: 3.0
Meat: 3.0
Fat: 0.0

1. Combine pork, stock, onion, beans, Worcestershire sauce, bay leaves, and Italian seasoning in Dutch oven. Heat to boiling; reduce heat and simmer, covered, until beans are tender, 1 to 1½ hours, adding carrots and celery during last 15 minutes. Discard bay leaves. Season to taste with salt, pepper, and hot pepper sauce.

VARIATIONS

Barley-Bean Soup — Make soup as above, substituting 1 cup pearl barley for the lima and garbanzo beans, ¾ teaspoon each dried rosemary and sage leaves for the Italian seasoning. Add 2 cups corn during last 10 minutes cooking time.

Smoky Red and Black Bean Soup — Make soup as above, using 2 cups each dried red and black beans for all the beans, and substituting 1 to 1½ pounds sliced reduced-sodium, reduced-fat smoked sausage for the pork shoulder. Reduce Italian seasoning to 1 teaspoon and add ½ teaspoon ground cumin. Stir in 1 to 2 cups cooked rice during last 10 minutes of cooking time.

BEEFY BEAN SOUP

Meaty beef shanks flavor this bean soup. Double or triple the recipe, and freeze some for comfort food on cold winter nights.

8 entrée servings

1 pound meaty beef shanks
2 quarts water
1 each: sliced rib celery, halved onion
1 teaspoon each: dried oregano and thyme leaves
1 bay leaf
2 cans (15 ounces each) kidney beans, rinsed, drained
1 can (14½ ounces) stewed tomatoes
1 cup each: sliced carrots, onion, diced turnips, cut
   green beans
Salt and pepper, to taste

Per Serving:
Calories: 158
% calories from fat: 10
Protein (g): 10.2
Carbohydrate (g): 26.8
Fat (g): 2
Saturated fat (g): 0.6
Cholesterol (mg): 8.7
Sodium (mg): 510

Exchanges:
Milk: 0.0
Vegetable: 1 0
Fruit: 0.0
Bread: 2.0
Meat: 0.0
Fat: 1.0

1. Heat beef shanks, water, celery, halved onion, and herbs to boiling in large saucepan; reduce heat and simmer, covered, until meat is tender, about 1 to 1½ hours. Strain soup and reserve broth; cut meat from bones and reserve. Discard bones, celery, onion, and bay leaf. Return broth and meat to saucepan. Stir in remaining ingredients, except salt and pepper; heat to boiling. Reduce heat and simmer, covered, until vegetables are tender, about 20 minutes. Season to taste with salt and pepper.

BEAN AND SPINACH SOUP PRONTO

45 *Beans and spinach are a classic Italian combination, which we've used in this hearty soup.*

6 entrée servings

1½ quarts chicken broth
6 ounces Canadian bacon, cut into strips
1 tablespoon dried Italian seasoning
1 garlic clove, minced
1 can (15 ounces) each: tomato sauce, rinsed, drained cannellini beans
1 package (10 ounces) frozen chopped spinach, partially thawed
½ cup uncooked orzo
Salt and pepper, to taste

Per Serving:
Calories: 207
% calories from fat: 11
Protein (g): 12.8
Carbohydrate (g): 30.5
Fat (g): 2.5
Saturated fat (g): 0.6
Cholesterol (mg): 16.4
Sodium (mg): 1524

Exchanges:
Milk 0.0
Vegetable: 0.0
Fruit: 0.0
Bread: 2.0
Meat: 1.0
Fat: 0.0

1. Heat all ingredients, except orzo, salt, and pepper to boiling in large saucepan; reduce heat and simmer 15 minutes. Add orzo and simmer, uncovered, until orzo is tender, about 10 minutes. Season to taste with salt and pepper.

NAVY BEAN SOUP WITH HAM

A quick-soak method is used for the beans. If you prefer soaking the beans overnight, omit step 1 and proceed with step 2 in the recipe, using the soaked beans.

6 entrée servings

8 ounces dried navy or Great Northern beans
Water
1½ cups cubed lean smoked ham
⅔ cup each: chopped onion, carrot, celery
2 cloves garlic, minced
1 tablespoon each: canola oil, flour
4 cups reduced-sodium chicken broth
1 cup water
¼ teaspoon dried thyme leaves

Per Serving:
Calories: 223
% calories from fat: 16
Protein (g): 20.1
Carbohydrate (g): 29.5
Fat (g): 4.0
Saturated fat (g): 0.9
Cholesterol (mg): 21.6
Sodium (mg): 639

Exchanges:
Milk: 0.0
Vegetable: 0.0
Fruit: 0.0
Bread: 2.0
Meat: 2.0
Fat: 0.0

1 bay leaf
Salt and pepper, to taste

1. Cover beans with 2 inches of water in large saucepan; heat to boiling; boil, uncovered, 2 minutes. Remove from heat and let stand, covered, 1 hour; drain.

2. Sauté ham, onion, carrot, celery, and garlic in oil in large saucepan until vegetables are tender, 5 to 8 minutes. Stir in flour; cook 1 minute. Add beans, broth, water, and herbs to saucepan; heat to boiling. Reduce heat and simmer, covered, until beans are tender, 1 to 1¼ hours. Discard bay leaf; season to taste with salt and pepper.

SLOW-COOKER WORKDAY BEAN SOUP

This easy, economical slow-cooker soup is designed to fit into a busy work schedule.

6 entrée servings

1 cup each: dried pinto or cranberry beans, Great Northern beans, soaked overnight, chopped onion
½ cup finely diced red or green bell pepper, onion, sliced celery
1 quart fat-free beef broth
1 cup water
1 bay leaf
3 tablespoons catsup
2 tablespoons sugar
1 tablespoon apple cider vinegar
2 teaspoons chili powder
¼ teaspoon each: dried thyme leaves, dry mustard, ground allspice, pepper
1 can (8 ounces) reduced-sodium tomato paste
Salt and pepper, to taste

Per Serving:
Calories: 325
% calories from fat: 4
Protein (g): 19
Carbohydrate (g): 61.7
Fat (g): 1.5
Saturated fat (g): 0.4
Cholesterol (mg): 0.9
Sodium (mg): 422

Exchanges:
Milk: 0.0
Vegetable: 0.0
Fruit: 0.0
Bread: 4.0
Meat: 1.0
Fat: 0.0

1. Add all ingredients, except tomato paste, salt, and pepper to slow cooker. Cover and cook on Low until beans are tender, 8 to 10 hours. Discard bay leaf. Stir in tomato paste. Cover and cook on High until hot, about 15 minutes.

SAUSAGE AND BLACK BEAN SOUP

Smoked sausage flavors this hearty black bean soup.

6 entrée servings

1 pound dried black beans
1 cup each: sliced carrots, chopped onion
½ cup chopped celery
1 tablespoon olive oil
2 quarts Low-Salt Chicken Stock (see p. 3)
2 tablespoons low-sodium Worcestershire sauce
2 teaspoons dried marjoram leaves
1 bay leaf
8 ounces smoked turkey sausage, sliced
Salt and pepper, to taste
Lemon wedges

Per Serving:
Calories: 370
% calories from fat: 16
Protein (g): 24.9
Carbohydrate (g): 55.7
Fat: (g): 6.7
Saturated fat (g): 1.7
Cholesterol (mg): 28.2
Sodium (mg): 403

Exchanges:
Milk 0.0
Vegetable: 1.0
Fruit: 0.0
Bread: 3.0
Meat: 2.0
Fat: 0.0

1. Place beans in large saucepan with water to cover by 2 inches. Heat to boiling; boil 2 minutes. Let stand, covered, 1 hour; drain.

2. Sauté carrots, onion, and celery in oil in large saucepan until lightly browned, about 8 minutes. Stir in beans, stock, Worcestershire sauce, marjoram, and bay leaf. Heat to boiling; reduce heat and simmer, covered, until beans are tender, 1 to 1½ hours, adding sausage during last 30 minutes. Discard bay leaf; season to taste with salt and pepper. Serve with lemon wedges.

VARIATION

Sherried Black Bean Soup — Make recipe as above, substituting crushed cumin seeds for the marjoram and adding 1 teaspoon dried oregano leaves and 1 to 2 teaspoons brown sugar. Before serving, season to taste with 1 to 2 tablespoons dry sherry.

LENTIL-BARLEY SOUP WITH BEEF

Very hearty, healthful, and economical, this soup features a savory blend of lentils, rice, barley, and corn.

6 entrée servings

1½ quarts Beef Stock (see p. 5)

1½ cups finely chopped onions, large ribs celery

⅓ cup each: finely chopped celery, parsley

¼ cup each: dried lentils, pearl barley, uncooked brown rice

1 teaspoon dried thyme leaves

½ cup each: chopped carrots, turnip

1 cup whole kernel corn

Salt and pepper, to taste

Per Serving:
Calories: 247
% calories from fat: 15
Protein (g): 21.9
Carbohydrate (g): 30.7
Fat (g): 4.2
Saturated fat (g): 1.3
Cholesterol (mg): 44
Sodium (mg): 90

Exchanges:
Milk: 0.0
Vegetable: 0.0
Fruit: 0.0
Bread: 2.0
Meat: 2.0
Fat: 0.0

1. Heat all ingredients except carrots, turnip, corn, salt, and pepper to boiling in Dutch oven; reduce heat and simmer, covered, 45 minutes. Add carrots, turnip and corn; simmer, covered, until vegetables, barley, and rice are tender, about 15 minutes. Season to taste with salt and pepper.

SPLIT-PEA SOUP WITH HAM

Serve this hearty soup with thick slices of Garlic Bread (see p. 645).

8 entrée servings

1½ cups cubed lean ham, chopped onions

1 cup chopped carrots

½ cup sliced celery

1 tablespoon olive oil

1½ quarts water

1 can (14½ ounces) reduced-sodium chicken broth

1 pound dried split peas

1–2 teaspoons beef bouillon crystals

1 teaspoon dried marjoram leaves

Salt and pepper, to taste

Per Serving:
Calories: 264
% calories from fat: 11
Protein (g): 21.6
Carbohydrate (g): 39.9
Fat (g): 3.4
Saturated fat (g): 0.6
Cholesterol (mg): 16.2
Sodium (mg): 513

Exchanges:
Milk: 0.0
Vegetable: 1.0
Fruit: 0.0
Bread: 2.0
Meat: 2.0
Fat: 0.0

1. Sauté ham, onions, carrots, and celery in oil in large saucepan until onions are tender, 8 to 10 minutes. Add water, chicken broth, split peas, bouillon crystals, and marjoram; heat to boiling. Reduce heat and simmer, covered, until split peas are tender, 45 to 60 minutes. Season to taste with salt and pepper.

VARIATIONS

Savory Pea Soup with Smoked Sausage — Make soup as above, substituting 8 ounces smoked turkey sausage, halved lengthwise and sliced, for the ham, and adding 2 cups diced potato, 1 teaspoon dried thyme leaves, and 1 bay leaf. Discard bay leaf; season to taste with hot pepper sauce.

Split-Pea Soup with Barley — Make soup as above, omitting ham. Increase water to 8 cups, and add ½ cup barley with the split peas. Cook until barley and peas are tender, 45 to 60 minutes.

SIX

Melting-Pot Soups

CHINESE SNOW PEA SOUP

45 | *This fresh-tasting soup has Oriental accents of soy sauce and gingerroot.*

4 first-course servings

1 quart reduced-sodium fat-free chicken broth
¼ cup each: thinly sliced scallions, finely
   chopped carrots
1 clove garlic, minced
1 teaspoon each: grated gingerroot, light soy sauce
½ cup sliced mushrooms
1 cup sliced snow peas

Per Serving:
Calories: 32
% calories from fat: 2
Protein (g): 4.2
Carbohydrate (g): 3.9
Fat (g): 0.1
Saturated fat (g): 0.0
Cholesterol (mg): 0.0
Sodium (mg): 603

Exchanges:
Milk: 0.0
Vegetable: 0.0
Fruit: 0.0
Bread: 0.5
Meat: 0.0
Fat: 0.0

1. Heat broth, scallions, carrots, garlic, ginger-root, and soy sauce to boiling in medium sauce-pan; reduce heat and simmer, covered, 5 minutes. Add mushrooms and snow peas; simmer until snow peas are crisp-tender, about 5 minutes.

ITALIAN MUSHROOM-BARLEY SOUP

45 | *For variation, substitute 1 can (15 ounces) drained, rinsed Great Northern beans for the barley.*

10 first-course servings

1½ cups quick-cooking barley
3 tomatoes, chopped
2 each: chopped carrots, minced cloves garlic
1 medium onion, chopped
1½ quarts chicken broth
2 cups tomato juice
1 tablespoon chopped fresh or 1 teaspoon dried
   basil and oregano leaves
1 cup thinly sliced mushrooms
Salt and pepper, to taste
Reduced-fat sour cream, as garnish

Per Serving:
Calories: 135
% calories from fat: 7
Protein (g): 5.3
Carbohydrate (g): 27.7
Fat (g): 1.1
Saturated fat (g): 0.2
Cholesterol (mg): 0
Sodium (mg): 208

Exchanges:
Milk: 0.0
Vegetable: 1.5
Fruit: 0.0
Bread: 1.5
Meat: 0.0
Fat: 0.0

1. Heat all ingredients, except salt, pepper, and sour cream to boiling in large saucepan; reduce heat and simmer, covered, until barley is tender, about 15 minutes, Season to taste with salt and pepper. Top each bowl of soup with a dollop of sour cream.

EGG DROP SOUP

45 *The easiest egg drop soup ever!*

4 first-course servings

1 quart reduced-sodium fat-free chicken broth
1½ tablespoons cornstarch
2 tablespoons cold water
2 each: chopped scallions, beaten egg whites
Salt and white pepper, to taste

1. Heat broth to boiling in medium saucepan; stir in combined cornstarch and water, stirring until thickened, about 1 minute. Stir in scallions; remove from heat and gradually stir in egg whites with a fork. Season to taste with salt and white pepper.

Per Serving:
Calories: 51
% calories from fat: 0
Protein (g): 7.8
Carbohydrate (g): 3.1
Fat (g): 0
Saturated fat (g): 0
Cholesterol (mg): 0
Sodium (mg): 198

Exchanges:
Milk: 0.0
Vegetable: 0.0
Fruit: 0.0
Bread: 0.0
Meat: 1.0
Fat: 0.0

GREEK LEMON-RICE SOUP

45 *Nicely tart; use fresh lemon juice for the best flavor. If making this soup in advance, do not add egg until reheating for serving.*

4 first-course servings

3½ cups reduced-sodium fat-free chicken broth
¼ cup uncooked rice
2 large cloves garlic, minced
¼–⅓ cup lemon juice
1 egg, lightly beaten
2 tablespoons chopped parsley
Salt and white pepper, to taste

Per Serving:
Calories: 106
% calories from fat: 20
Protein (g): 3
Carbohydrate (g): 14.4
Fat (g): 2.4
Saturated fat (g): 0.5
Cholesterol (mg): 53.3
Sodium (mg): 31

Exchanges:
Milk: 0.0
Vegetable: 0.0
Fruit: 0.0
Bread: 1.0
Meat: 0.0
Fat: 0.5

1. Heat broth to boiling in medium saucepan; stir in rice and garlic. Reduce heat and simmer, covered, until rice is tender, about 25 minutes; reduce heat to low; Mix lemon juice and egg; slowly stir mixture into soup. Stir in parsley; season to taste with salt and white pepper.

TORTELLINI SOUP

We rely on prepared tortellini from the dairy case for this flavorful and speedy soup.

4 entrée servings

1 each: chopped large onion, minced garlic clove
2 teaspoons olive oil
1¼ quarts Chicken Stock (see p. 2)
½ cup finely chopped parsley
2 tablespoons dry sherry (optional)
1 package (9 ounces) fresh cheese-and-garlic tortellini
2 teaspoons dried Italian seasoning
1 can (15 ounces) tomato sauce
1 teaspoon sugar
Salt and pepper, to taste

Per Serving:
Calories: 298
% calories from fat: 16
Protein (g): 17.3
Carbohydrate (g): 46.2
Fat (g): 5.5
Saturated fat (g): 1.9
Cholesterol (mg): 33.7
Sodium (mg): 659

Exchanges:
Milk: 0.0
Vegetable: 3.0
Fruit: 0.0
Bread: 2.0
Meat: 1.0
Fat: 0.5

1. Sauté onion and garlic in oil in large saucepan until onions are tender, about 5 minutes; add stock, parsley, sherry, tortellini, and Italian seasoning; heat to boiling. Reduce heat and simmer, uncovered, until tortellini float to the top and are *al dente,* 5 to 8 minutes. Stir in tomato sauce and simmer, covered, 5 minutes. Stir in sugar and season to taste with salt and pepper.

TORTELLINI AND BEAN SOUP

45 *Using purchased pasta sauce, refrigerated tortellini, and canned beans, you can make this flavorful soup in minutes.*

8 entrée servings

1½ quarts reduced-sodium fat-free chicken broth

2 cups reduced-fat garlic-and-herb spaghetti sauce

2 cans (15 ounces each) reduced-sodium red kidney beans, rinsed, drained

1 package (9 ounces) fresh cheese tortellini

Salt and pepper, to taste

Per Serving:
Calories: 206
% calories from fat: 10
Protein (g): 12.9
Carbohydrate (g): 33.5
Fat (g): 2.2
Saturated fat (g): 0.9
Cholesterol (mg): 9.0
Sodium (mg): 1006

Exchanges:
Milk: 0.0
Vegetable: 0.0
Fruit: 0.0
Bread: 2.0
Meat: 1.0
Fat: 0.0

1. Heat broth, spaghetti sauce, and beans to boiling in large saucepan; stir in tortellini. Reduce heat and simmer, uncovered, until tortellini are *al dente,* about 8 minutes. Season to taste with salt and pepper.

ASIAN SHIITAKE AND NOODLE SOUP

45 *Shiitake mushrooms and Japanese udon noodles give this soup its distinctive Asian flavor.*

6 first-course servings

2 cups thinly sliced shiitake or other wild mushrooms, tough stems discarded

1 cup each: diced red bell pepper, julienned carrots

2 green onions, sliced

1 teaspoon each: minced gingerroot, garlic

1–2 teaspoons Asian sesame oil

1 quart reduced-sodium fat-free beef broth

1 teaspoon reduced-sodium tamari soy sauce

1 cup packed fresh spinach, sliced

1 package (8½ ounces) Japanese udon noodles, cooked, warm

Salt and pepper, to taste

Per Serving:
Calories: 208
% calories from fat: 10
Protein (g): 10.7
Carbohydrate (g): 38
Fat (g): 2.4
Saturated fat (g): 0.1
Cholesterol (mg): 0
Sodium (mg): 215

Exchanges:
Milk: 0.0
Vegetable: 1.0
Fruit: 0.0
Bread: 2.0
Meat: 0.0
Fat: 0.5

1. Sauté mushrooms, bell pepper, carrots, green onions, gingerroot, and garlic in sesame oil in large saucepan until tender, about 8 minutes. Stir in beef broth and soy sauce and heat to boiling; reduce heat and simmer, covered, 5 minutes. Stir in spinach and simmer until wilted, about 5 minutes. Season to taste with salt and pepper. Place noodles in soup bowls and ladle soup over.

CHINESE BEEF AND NOODLE SOUP

45 *We've used Chinese lo mein noodles in this easy and flavorful soup.*

6 entrée servings

2 tablespoons each: light soy sauce, dry sherry (optional)
½ teaspoon ground ginger
1 garlic clove, minced
3–4 drops Asian hot chili oil or hot pepper sauce
1½ tablespoons cornstarch
12 ounces lean beef round steak, very thinly sliced
¼ cup chopped scallions
1 tablespoon Asian sesame oil
1¼ quarts reduced-sodium fat-free chicken broth
1 can (8 ounces) sliced water chestnuts, drained
⅔ package (10-ounce size) Chinese lo mein noodles
Salt and pepper, to taste

Per Serving:
Calories: 268
% calories from fat: 19
Protein (g): 20.4
Carbohydrate (g): 32.1
Fat (g): 5.5
Saturated fat (g): 1.2
Cholesterol (mg): 28
Sodium (mg): 498

Exchanges:
Milk: 0.0
Vegetable: 0.0
Fruit: 0.0
Bread: 2.0
Meat: 2.0
Fat: 0.0

1. Combine soy sauce, sherry, ginger, garlic, hot chili oil, and cornstarch in small bowl. Stir in beef and scallions, coating well. Sauté beef mixture in sesame oil in large saucepan until browned, 5 to 8 minutes. Add broth and heat to boiling, stirring until slightly thickened, about 1 minute. Stir in water chestnuts and noodles; reduce heat, and simmer 3 to 4 minutes or until noodles are tender. Season to taste with salt and pepper.

RED AND WHITE BEAN SOUP WITH BACON AND PASTA

45 *Any small soup pasta can be substituted for the orzo.*

6 entrée servings

6 ounces Canadian bacon, thinly sliced

1 large onion, chopped

2 large ribs celery, finely chopped

2 teaspoons olive oil

1½ quarts reduced-sodium fat-free chicken broth

1 can (19 ounces) cannellini beans, rinsed, drained

1 can (15 ounces) each: rinsed drained reduced-sodium red kidney beans, tomato sauce

2 teaspoons dried Italian seasoning

½ cup uncooked orzo

Salt and pepper, to taste

Per Serving:
Calories: 291
% calories from fat: 14
Protein (g): 18.9
Carbohydrate (g): 42.1
Fat (g): 4.3
Saturated fat (g): 0.8
Cholesterol (mg): 14.2
Sodium (mg): 1286

Exchanges:
Milk: 0.0
Vegetable: 0.0
Fruit: 0.0
Bread: 3.0
Meat: 1.5
Fat: 0.0

1. Sauté Canadian bacon, onion, and celery in oil in large saucepan until onion is tender, about 5 minutes. Add broth, beans, tomato sauce, and Italian seasoning; heat to boiling and add orzo. Reduce heat and simmer, uncovered, until pasta is *al dente,* about 10 minutes. Season to taste with salt and pepper.

CANNELLINI BEAN AND PASTA SOUP

45 *Parmesan Croutons (see p. 636) would be a flavorful garnish for this soup.*

4 entrée servings

¾ cup diced Canadian bacon

⅓ cup diced red bell pepper

2 cloves garlic, minced

2 teaspoons olive oil

1 quart reduced-sodium fat-free chicken broth

1 cup uncooked small elbow macaroni

½ teaspoon each: dried marjoram and sage leaves

1 can (19 ounces) cannellini beans, rinsed, drained, divided

¾ cup water

Salt and pepper, to taste

⅔ cup herbed croutons

Per Serving:
Calories: 235
% calories from fat: 14
Protein (g): 18.2
Carbohydrate (g): 39.4
Fat (g): 4.2
Saturated fat (g): 0.7
Cholesterol (mg): 8.1
Sodium (mg): 731

Exchanges:
Milk: 0.0
Vegetable: 0.0
Fruit: 0.0
Bread: 2.5
Meat: 1.0
Fat: 0.0

1. Sauté Canadian bacon, bell pepper, and garlic in oil in large saucepan until bacon begins to brown, about 5 minutes. Add broth and heat to boiling; stir in macaroni and herbs. Reduce heat and simmer until macaroni is *al dente*, about 7 minutes. Process 1½ cups beans and ¾ cup water in food processor or blender until smooth; add to saucepan with remaining ½ cup beans. Simmer until hot, about 5 minutes; season to taste with salt and pepper. Place croutons in soup bowls; ladle soup over.

SOUTHERN GUMBO

To please all palates, serve this soup with an assortment of hot sauces.

12 entrée servings

2 cups each: cubed lean ham, chopped onions

1 cup each: chopped celery, green bell peppers

1 teaspoon dried thyme leaves

1 tablespoon each: minced garlic, canola oil

¼ cup all-purpose flour

1½ quarts Rich Chicken Stock (see p. 4)

1 can (28 ounces) reduced-sodium diced
   tomatoes, undrained

12 ounces boneless, skinless chicken breast, cubed

1 cup uncooked rice

2 bay leaves

12 ounces small shrimp, peeled, deveined

2 teaspoons each: low-sodium Worcestershire sauce,
   gumbo file powder

Salt and hot pepper sauce, to taste

Per Serving:
Calories: 212
% calories from fat: 15
Protein (g): 21.2
Carbohydrate (g): 22.6
Fat (g): 3.3
Saturated fat (g): 0.5
Cholesterol (mg): 71.2
Sodium (mg): 353

Exchanges:
Milk: 0.0
Vegetable: 0.0
Fruit: 0.0
Bread: 1.5
Meat: 2.0
Fat: 0.0

1. Sauté ham, onions, celery, bell peppers, thyme, and garlic in oil in large Dutch oven until tender, about 10 minutes. Sprinkle with flour; cook 1 to 2 minutes. Add stock, tomatoes with liquid, chicken, rice, and bay leaves. Heat to boiling, reduce heat and simmer, covered, until rice is tender, about 25 minutes, stirring in shrimp, Worcestershire sauce, and file powder during last 5 minutes. Discard bay leaves; season to taste with salt and hot pepper sauce.

TORTELLINI CHICKEN SOUP

The homemade tortellini makes this soup extra-special. Tortellini can be made ahead of time and frozen for up to 2 months.

12 entrée servings

4 pounds chicken, cut up

2 quarts water

1 medium onion, quartered

⅓ cup sliced carrots, celery

1 teaspoon dried oregano leaves

1 bay leaf

Chicken Tortellini (recipe follows)

¼ cup chopped parsley

¼–½ cup (2 ounces) grated Parmesan cheese

Salt and pepper, to taste

Per Serving:
Calories: 227
% calories from fat: 27
Protein (g): 23.9
Carbohydrate (g): 15.7
Fat (g): 6.7
Saturated fat (g): 1.7
Cholesterol (mg): 95.7
Sodium (mg): 294

Exchanges:
Milk: 0.0
Vegetable: 0.0
Fruit: 0.0
Bread: 1.0
Meat: 3.0
Fat: 0.0

1. Heat chicken, water, onion, carrots, celery, oregano, and bay leaf to boiling in large saucepan; reduce heat and simmer, covered, until chicken is tender, about 40 minutes. Strain broth and return to saucepan. Remove meat from chicken bones and coarsely chop, reserving ¾ cup dark meat for the tortellini; return remaining chicken to saucepan. Discard bones, vegetables, and bay leaf. Heat broth to boiling; add Chicken Tortellini, uncovered, and simmer until they float to the top and are *al dente*, 5 to 7 minutes. Stir in parsley and cheese; season to taste with salt and pepper.

Chicken Tortellini
Makes 48 tortellini

1½ cups all-purpose flour
1 each: egg, egg white
2 teaspoons olive oil
1 teaspoon salt, divided
¾ cup chopped reserved dark chicken
2 tablespoons grated Parmesan cheese
1 egg yolk
1 teaspoon grated lemon zest
Generous pinch ground nutmeg
⅛ teaspoon pepper

1. Place flour in large bowl. Make well in center; add egg, egg white, oil, and ¾ teaspoon salt. Mix flour into egg with a fork, forming a dough. Knead on lightly floured surface until very smooth and elastic, about 10 minutes. Let stand, covered, 10 minutes. Combine remaining ingredients in bowl.

2. Divide dough in half. Roll one half on lightly floured surface into 10-inch round. Cut into twenty-four 2-inch circles. Place 1 teaspoon chicken mixture in center of each circle. Moisten edges with water. Fold in half; seal edges. Shape into rings, stretching slightly and shaping around finger. Press tips together to seal. Repeat with remaining dough and filling. Refrigerate, covered, until ready to use, up to 24 hours, or freeze no longer than 2 months.

CHICKEN WONTON SOUP

Ginger-spiced chicken wontons are a delicious addition to this soup. The wontons can be refrigerated, covered, several hours before cooking.

6 entrée servings

½ cup each: chopped red bell pepper, carrot

2 teaspoons minced gingerroot

1 teaspoon Asian sesame oil

1 quart Chicken Stock (see p. 2)

1 can (8 ounces) baby corn, rinsed, drained

1 cup packed spinach, sliced

2–3 teaspoons reduced-sodium soy sauce

Chicken Wontons (recipe follows)

Salt and cayenne pepper, to taste

Per Serving:
Calories: 187
% calories from fat: 13
Protein (g): 14.5
Carbohydrate (g): 25.1
Fat (g): 2.8
Saturated fat (g): 0.6
Cholesterol (mg): 28.2
Sodium (mg): 430

Exchanges:
Milk: 0.0
Vegetable: 2.0
Fruit: 0.0
Bread: 1.0
Meat: 1.0
Fat: 0.0

1. Sauté bell pepper, carrot, and gingerroot in sesame oil in Dutch oven 2 to 3 minutes; add remaining ingredients, except wontons, and heat to boiling. Stir in Chicken Wontons and simmer, uncovered, until wontons float to the top and are tender, about 5 minutes. Season to taste with salt and cayenne pepper.

Chicken Wontons

Makes 24 wontons

8 ounces boneless, skinless chicken breast

¼ cup sliced green onions

1 teaspoon minced gingerroot

24 wonton wrappers

1. Process all ingredients, except wonton wrappers, in food processor until finely chopped. Place 1 mounded teaspoon chicken mixture on each wonton wrapper; moisten edges with water, and fold in half diagonally to create triangles, sealing edges.

CHINESE HOT POT

45 *Enjoy the perfect blend of Oriental flavors in this fragrant soup.*

6 entrée servings

4 cans (14½ ounces each) reduced-sodium fat-free
  chicken broth

½ cup dry white wine (optional)

¼ cup reduced-sodium Tamari soy sauce

2 tablespoons sugar

2 packages (3½ ounces each) Oriental-style noodles,
  broken in half, seasoning packets discarded

½ cup each: small broccoli florets, sliced
  mushrooms, carrots

1 can (4 ounces) baby corn, drained

1 pound boneless, skinless chicken breast, cubed

1 cup snow peas, trimmed

1 bunch watercress, coarsely chopped

4 green onions, sliced

Salt and pepper, to taste

Per Serving:
Calories: 330
% calories from fat: 8
Protein (g): 30.2
Carbohydrate (g): 36.5
Fat (g): 2.9
Saturated fat (g): 0.6
Cholesterol (mg): 46
Sodium (mg): 850

Exchanges:
Milk: 0.0
Vegetable: 1.0
Fruit: 0.0
Bread: 2.0
Meat: 3.0
Fat: 0.0

1. Heat broth, wine, soy sauce, and sugar to boiling in large saucepan. Add noodles, broccoli, mushrooms, carrots, corn, and chicken; reduce heat and simmer, covered, until vegetables are crisp-tender and chicken is cooked, 8 to 10 minutes, adding snow peas during last 3 to 4 minutes. Stir in watercress and green onions; season to taste with salt and pepper.

VIETNAMESE CURRIED CHICKEN AND COCONUT SOUP

Rice noodles can be round or flat. They must be softened in water before cooking. Cooked angel hair pasta can be substituted.

6 entrée servings

⅔ cup sliced green onions

2 tablespoons minced gingerroot

1 tablespoon minced garlic

3–4 tablespoons curry powder

2 cans (14½ ounces each) reduced-sodium fat-free chicken broth

3 cups reduced-fat coconut milk

1 pound boneless, skinless chicken breast

1 tablespoon grated lime zest

½–1 teaspoon Oriental chili paste

¼ cup lime juice

⅓ cup minced cilantro

Salt and white pepper, to taste

½ package (8-ounce size) rice noodles

Per Serving:
Calories: 261
% calories from fat: 29
Protein (g): 23
Carbohydrate (g): 23.4
Fat (g): 8.5
Saturated fat (g): 0.6
Cholesterol (mg): 46
Sodium (mg): 347

Exchanges:
Milk: 0.0
Vegetable: 1.0
Fruit: 0.0
Bread: 1.0
Meat: 2.5
Fat: 0.5

1. Sauté green onions, gingerroot, and garlic in lightly greased large saucepan 2 to 3 minutes; stir in curry powder and cook, stirring, 30 seconds. Add chicken broth, coconut milk, chicken, lime zest, and chili paste; heat to boiling. Reduce heat and simmer, covered, until chicken is cooked, about 20 minutes. Remove chicken and shred with 2 forks; return to saucepan. Stir in lime juice and cilantro; season to taste with salt and white pepper. Simmer, uncovered, 5 minutes.

2. Place noodles in large bowl; pour cold water over to cover. Let stand until noodles are separate and soft, about 5 minutes; drain. Stir noodles into 4 quarts boiling water. Reduce heat and simmer, uncovered, until tender, about 5 minutes; drain. Spoon noodles into soup bowls; ladle soup over noodles.

SOUTHERN-STYLE SOUP WITH GREENS

A country-style soup—savory, substantial, and good.

4 entrée servings

2 medium onions, coarsely chopped
4 medium carrots, sliced
2 teaspoons canola oil
1 quart reduced-sodium chicken broth
2½ cups water
2 small ham hocks
1 large bay leaf
½ teaspoon each: dried thyme leaves
8 ounces collard or mustard greens, coarsely chopped
4 cups cubed potatoes
½ cup diced lean smoked ham
Salt and pepper, to taste

Per Serving:
Calories: 313
% calories from fat: 15
Protein (g): 11.6
Carbohydrate (g): 56.5
Fat (g): 5.6
Saturated fat (g): 1.3
Cholesterol (mg): 19.8
Sodium (mg): 651

Exchanges:
Milk: 0.0
Vegetable: 2.0
Fruit: 0.0
Bread: 3.0
Meat: 1.0
Fat: 0.0

1. Sauté onions and carrots in oil in large saucepan until soft, about 5 minutes. Add broth, water, and ham hocks and heat to boiling. Add herbs and collards; simmer, covered, 45 minutes, adding potatoes and ham the last 15 minutes. Discard bay leaf and ham hocks. Season to taste with salt and pepper.

SAUSAGE AND SUCCOTASH SOUP

Try this soup with hominy in place of the lima beans for something a little bit different.

6 entrée servings

⅔ cup each: sliced celery, chopped onion, red bell pepper
1 tablespoon margarine or butter
¼ cup all-purpose flour
2 cups each: fat-free milk, reduced-sodium fat-free chicken broth
12 ounces reduced-sodium reduced-fat smoked sausage, sliced, browned
1 can (15 ounces) cream-style corn
½ package (10 ounce-size) frozen baby lima beans
Hot pepper sauce, to taste

Salt and pepper, to taste

½–1 cup (2–4 ounces) shredded reduced-fat
Cheddar cheese

Per Serving:
Calories: 272
% calories from fat: 23
Protein (g): 17.2
Carbohydrate (g): 36.6
Fat (g): 7.0
Saturated fat (g): 2.7
Cholesterol (mg): 33.3
Sodium (mg): 833

Exchanges:
Milk: 0.0
Vegetable: 0.0
Fruit: 0.0
Bread: 2.5
Meat: 2.0
Fat: 0.0

1. Sauté celery, onion, and bell pepper in margarine in large saucepan until tender, about 10 minutes; sprinkle with flour and cook 1 to 2 minutes. Stir in milk and chicken broth; heat to boiling, stirring, until thickened, about 1 minute. Stir in sausage, corn, and lima beans; heat to boiling. Reduce heat and simmer, covered, until beans are tender, about 10 minutes. Season to taste with hot pepper sauce, salt, and pepper. Add cheese, stirring until melted.

MEXICAN CHICKEN-CORN SOUP

Monterey Jack cheese gives this chicken-based soup a rich flavor; use pepper-Jack cheese for a spicier soup.

8 entrée servings

1 pound boneless, skinless chicken breasts, cubed

1½ cups chopped onion

1 cup chopped red or green bell pepper

1 each: chopped small jalapeño chili, clove garlic

1 teaspoon ground cumin

1 tablespoon each: canola oil, flour

1 quart Rich Chicken Stock (see p. 4)

2 cups whole kernel corn

Salt and pepper, to taste

1–1½ cups (4–6 ounces) shredded reduced-fat
Monterey Jack cheese

Per Serving:
Calories: 194
% calories from fat: 30
Protein (g): 21.4
Carbohydrate (g): 12.3
Fat (g): 6.4
Saturated fat (g): 2.6
Cholesterol (mg): 45.1
Sodium (mg): 163

Exchanges:
Milk: 0.0
Vegetable: 0.0
Fruit: 0.0
Bread: 1.0
Meat: 2 0
Fat: 0.0

1. Sauté chicken, onion, bell pepper, jalapeño, garlic, and cumin in oil in large saucepan until chicken is lightly browned, about 10 minutes; sprinkle with flour and cook 1 to 2 minutes. Stir in stock and corn. Heat to boiling; reduce heat and simmer, covered, until chicken is cooked and vegetables are tender, about 15 minutes. Season to taste with salt and pepper. Add cheese, stirring until melted.

VARIATION

El Paso Pork and Hominy Soup — Make recipe as above, substituting lean pork for the chicken, rinsed, drained, canned hominy for the corn, and 1 small poblano chili for the bell pepper. Omit Monterey Jack cheese; sprinkle each serving of soup with 1 tablespoon crumbled Mexican white cheese or feta cheese.

MEXICAN VEGETABLE AND SALSA SOUP

Serve this spicy soup with guacamole and baked tortilla chips.

6 entrée servings

1 cup chopped onion

1 garlic clove, minced

2 teaspoons olive oil

1 quart reduced-sodium fat-free chicken broth

1½ cups 1% reduced-fat milk

5 cups cubed peeled boiling potatoes

1¼ cups (5 ounces) shredded reduced-fat
  Cheddar cheese

2 cans (15 ounces each) kidney beans, drained

1–1½ cups reduced-sodium mild or medium salsa

Salt, to taste

Per Serving:
Calories: 394
% calories from fat: 15
Protein (g): 21
Carbohydrate (g): 64
Fat (g): 6.8
Saturated fat (g): 3.4
Cholesterol (mg): 23
Sodium (mg): 793

Exchanges:
Milk: 0.0
Vegetable: 1.0
Fruit: 0.0
Bread: 3.5
Meat: 2.0
Fat: 0.5

1. Sauté onion and garlic in oil in large saucepan until onion is tender, about 5 minutes. Add broth, milk, and potatoes; heat to boiling. Reduce heat and simmer, covered, until potatoes are tender, about 15 minutes. Process soup in food processor or blender until smooth; return to saucepan. Add cheese, beans, and salsa; simmer until hot, 3 to 4 minutes. Season to taste with salt.

IRISH POTATO-KALE SOUP

Fresh kale adds a subtle and pleasant flavor to this creamy soup, which is based on a traditional Irish recipe.

4 servings

2 medium onions, finely chopped

1 large garlic clove, minced

2 teaspoons margarine or butter

1 quart Beef Stock (see p. 5)

4 cups cubed, peeled potatoes

½ teaspoon dried thyme leaves

¼ teaspoon dry mustard

⅛ teaspoon crushed celery seeds

2 cups whole milk

3 cups coarsely chopped kale

Salt and pepper, to taste

Per Serving:
Calories: 300
% calories from fat: 19
Protein (g): 9.4
Carbohydrate (g): 52.9
Fat (g): 6.5
Saturated fat (g): 2.8
Cholesterol (mg): 12.5
Sodium (mg): 106

Exchanges:
Milk: 0.0
Vegetable: 0.0
Fruit: 0.0
Bread: 3.5
Meat: 1.0
Fat: 0.0

1. Sauté onions and garlic in margarine in large saucepan until onion is tender, about 5 minutes. Add stock, potatoes, and seasonings; heat to boiling. Reduce heat and simmer, covered, until potatoes are very tender, about 15 minutes. Process half the soup in food processor or blender until smooth; return to saucepan. Add milk and kale; heat to boiling. Reduce heat and simmer, covered, until kale is tender, about 5 minutes. Season to taste with salt and pepper.

KALE AND RAVIOLI SOUP

45

Make this soup 2 to 3 days in advance, enhancing flavors. Add pasta to the soup when reheating for serving so that the pasta is fresh and perfectly cooked.

6 first-course servings

1 cup each: sliced carrots, chopped plum tomatoes, onions, celery
2 cloves garlic, minced
¾ teaspoon each: dried basil and rosemary leaves
2 cans (15 ounces each) reduced-sodium chicken broth
1½ cups water
1 package (9 ounces) fresh low-fat herb ravioli
3 cups coarsely chopped kale
2–3 teaspoons lemon juice
Salt and pepper, to taste

Per Serving:
Calories: 171
% calories from fat: 15
Protein (g): 11.1
Carbohydrate (g): 25
Fat (g): 2.8
Saturated fat (g): 1.5
Cholesterol (mg): 25.8
Sodium (mg): 285

Exchanges:
Milk: 0.0
Vegetable: 2.0
Fruit: 0.0
Bread: 1 0
Meat: 1 0
Fat: 0.0

1. Sauté carrots, tomatoes, onion, celery, garlic, and herbs until onions are tender, about 5 minutes. Add chicken broth and water; heat to boiling. Reduce heat and simmer, covered, 10 minutes. Heat broth mixture to boiling; stir in ravioli and kale. Reduce heat and simmer, uncovered, until ravioli are *al dente*, about 5 minutes. Stir in lemon juice, salt, and pepper.

QUICK BORSCHT

45

8 entrée servings

2 quarts reduced-sodium fat-free beef broth
12 ounces cooked shredded lean beef
3 cups coarsely shredded cabbage
1½ cups sliced carrot
1 cup chopped onion
1 can (16 ounces) shredded beets, undrained
2 tablespoons fresh or 1 tablespoon dried dill weed
⅓ cup cider vinegar

Salt and pepper, to taste

Sour cream, as garnish

1. Heat broth, beef, vegetables, dill weed, and vinegar to boiling in large saucepan; reduce heat and simmer, covered, until vegetables are tender, about 20 minutes. Season to taste with salt and pepper. Garnish each bowl of soup with a dollop of sour cream.

Per Serving:
Calories: 121
% calories from fat: 14
Protein (g): 15.7
Carbohydrate (g): 9.5
Fat (g): 1.9
Saturated fat (g): 0.6
Cholesterol (mg): 23.4
Sodium (mg): 301

Exchanges:
Milk: 0.0
Vegetable: 2.0
Fruit: 0.0
Bread: 0.0
Meat: 1.5
Fat: 0.0

RUSSIAN BORSCHT

This hearty Russian soup is traditionally made with beef shanks or beef brisket; our version uses lean stew meat, which cooks more quickly.

12 first-course servings

3 cans (14½ ounces each) reduced-sodium fat-free beef broth

1 pound lean beef stew meat, cubed

2 bay leaves

1 teaspoon dried thyme leaves

4 cups thinly sliced cabbage

2 cups each: shredded beets, carrots

1 cup each: chopped onion, shredded turnip

1 can (14½ ounces) diced tomatoes with roasted garlic, undrained

1 tablespoon sugar

3–4 tablespoons red wine vinegar

Salt and pepper, to taste

Fresh Dill Sour Cream (recipe follows)

Per Serving:
Calories: 137
% calories from fat: 21
Protein (g): 14.4
Carbohydrate (g): 12.8
Fat (g): 3.2
Saturated fat (g): 1.7
Cholesterol (mg): 28.7
Sodium (mg): 289

Exchanges:
Milk: 0.0
Vegetable: 3.0
Fruit: 0.0
Bread: 0.0
Meat: 1.0
Fat: 0.0

1. Heat broth, stew meat, bay leaves, and thyme to boiling in large saucepan; reduce heat and simmer, covered, until meat is tender, about 1 hour. Stir in vegetables, tomatoes with liquid, and sugar and heat to boiling; reduce heat and simmer, covered, until vegetables are tender, about 20 minutes. Season to taste with vinegar, salt, and pepper; discard bay leaves. Drizzle each bowl of soup with Fresh Dill Sour Cream.

Fresh Dill Sour Cream
Makes about ¾ cup

¾ cup reduced-fat sour cream
2 tablespoons fresh or 1 tablespoon dried dill weed
2–3 tablespoons fat-free milk

1. Mix all ingredients, using enough milk to make a thick, pourable consistency.

VARIATION

Ukrainian Borscht — Make soup as above, substituting 8 ounces each lean cubed pork and sliced, browned smoked turkey sausage for the beef. Add 1 can (15 ounces) rinsed, drained Great Northern beans.

EASTERN EUROPEAN BORSCHT WITH MEAT

Be sure to start the soup at least one day ahead of serving time, as the beets need to stand overnight.

12 entrée servings

3½ cups cooked, peeled, coarsely shredded
   beets, divided
2 tablespoons red wine vinegar
1 teaspoon sugar
1 pound lean beef stew meat, cubed
2 quarts water
2 teaspoons each: dried marjoram leaves, dill weed
4 cups shredded cabbage
2 cups shredded, peeled potatoes
1 cup each: shredded carrots, sliced onion
1½ pound reduced-sodium, reduced-fat smoked
   sausage, sliced
Salt and pepper, to taste

Per Serving:
Calories: 224
% calories from fat: 22
Protein (g): 18.6
Carbohydrate (g): 24.3
Fat (g): 5.6
Saturated fat (g): 2.0
Cholesterol (mg): 48.5
Sodium (mg): 575

Exchanges:
Milk: 0.0
Vegetable: 0.0
Fruit: 0.0
Bread: 1.5
Meat: 2.0
Fat: 0.0

1 cup fat-free sour cream

¼ cup chopped fresh dill weed

1. Combine ½ cup beets, vinegar, and sugar in small bowl; refrigerate, covered, overnight. Reserve and refrigerate remaining beets.

2. Heat beef, water, marjoram, and dill weed to boiling in large saucepan; heat to boiling. Reduce heat and simmer, covered, until beef is tender, about 1 hour. Stir in beet mixture, cabbage, potatoes, carrots, onion, and smoked sausage; simmer, covered, 30 minutes. Stir in remaining beets; simmer, covered, 10 minutes. Season to taste with salt and pepper. Garnish each bowl of soup with a generous dollop of sour cream; sprinkle with dill weed.

HEARTY CABBAGE AND VEGETABLE SOUP

A delicious and convenient use for left-over cooked beef.

8 entrée servings

1 quart Fragrant Beef Stock (see p. 6)

2 cups reduced-sodium tomato juice

3 cups shredded green or red cabbage

1 cup each: thinly sliced onion, carrots,
  mushrooms, cubed unpeeled potatoes

4 cups cubed, cooked lean beef

2 tablespoons raisins

1 tablespoon sugar

1 teaspoon each: caraway seeds, paprika

2–3 teaspoons vinegar

Salt and pepper, to taste

Dilled Sour Cream (recipe follows)

Per Serving:
Calories: 214
% calories from fat: 28
Protein (g): 20.2
Carbohydrate (g): 18.7
Fat (g): 6.9
Saturated fat (g): 3
Cholesterol (mg): 51.1
Sodium (mg): 83

Exchanges:
Milk: 0.0
Vegetable: 2.0
Fruit: 0.0
Bread: 0.5
Meat: 2.0
Fat: 0.0

1. Heat all ingredients, except salt, pepper, and Dilled Sour Cream, to boiling in large saucepan. Reduce heat and simmer, covered, until vegetables are tender, about 20 minutes. Season to taste with salt and pepper. Garnish bowls of soup with dollops of Dilled Sour Cream.

Dilled Sour Cream

Makes about ½ cup

½ cup reduced-fat sour cream
1 teaspoon dried dill weed
1–2 teaspoons lemon juice

1. Mix all ingredients.

VARIATION

Meatless Cabbage and Vegetable Soup — Make recipe as above, substituting Basic Vegetable Stock (see p. 9) for the Beef Stock, and omit beef. Add 1 can (15 ounces each) rinsed and drained navy and kidney beans. Serve with Garlic Croutons (see p. 636).

SLOW-COOKER GOULASH SOUP

This soup is delicious with Fresh Dill Sour Cream and Hearty Vegetable-Rye Bread (see pp. 240, 646).

6 entrée servings

2 cups diced, peeled potatoes
1 cup each: chopped onion, cut green beans (¾-inch)
⅓ cup each: thinly sliced carrot, diced celery
2 large garlic cloves, minced
2 tablespoons pearl barley
1 pound lean beef round, cubed
1¼ quarts hot water
4 beef bouillon cubes
1 bay leaf
1½ teaspoons paprika
½ teaspoon each: dry mustard, dried thyme leaves
1 can (15 ounces) tomato sauce
Salt and pepper, to taste

Per Serving:
Calories: 175
% calories from fat: 13
Protein (g): 13.9
Carbohydrate (g): 25.3
Fat (g): 2.5
Saturated fat (g): 0.7
Cholesterol (mg): 27.4
Sodium (mg): 547

Exchanges:
Milk: 0.0
Vegetable: 0.0
Fruit: 0.0
Bread: 1.5
Meat: 1.0
Fat: 0.0

1. Combine all ingredients, except tomato sauce, salt, and pepper, in slow cooker; cover and cook on High 1 hour. Change setting to Low and cook until beef is tender, 7 to 8 hours, stirring in tomato sauce during the last hour. Discard bay leaf; season to taste with salt and pepper.

BASQUE VEGETABLE SOUP

A marvelous chickpea soup with a Spanish accent!

8 entrée servings

2½ quarts reduced-sodium chicken broth

2 cans (15 ounces each) chickpeas, rinsed, drained

4 cups coarsely shredded cabbage

1 cup each: chopped onion, leeks (white parts only), cubed unpeeled potatoes

½ cup each: cubed turnip, chopped carrots, red and green bell peppers

5 large garlic cloves, chopped

1¼ pounds boneless, skinless chicken breast, cubed

2 teaspoons dried thyme leaves

½ cup dry red wine

Salt and pepper, to taste

1½ cups Sourdough Croutons (½ recipe) (see p. 636)

Per Serving:
Calories: 395
% calories from fat: 6
Protein (g): 29.7
Carbohydrate (g): 58.8
Fat (g): 2.7
Saturated fat (g): 0.5
Cholesterol (mg): 41.1
Sodium (mg): 1142

Exchanges:
Milk: 0.0
Vegetable: 0.0
Fruit: 0.0
Bread: 4.0
Meat: 3.0
Fat: 0.0

1. Heat all ingredients, except wine, salt, pepper, and croutons to boiling in large saucepan; reduce heat and simmer, covered, until vegetables are tender, about 20 minutes. Add wine and simmer, covered, 15 minutes. Season to taste with salt and pepper. Sprinkle each bowl of soup with Sourdough Croutons.

MINESTRONE PRIMAVERA

A chunky soup chock-full of vegetables often opens an Italian meal—or it can be the meal.

8 entrée servings

1 cup chopped onion, thinly sliced leeks (white parts only).

2 tablespoons olive oil

1¼ quarts reduced-sodium fat-free chicken broth, divided

3 cups coarsely shredded cabbage

4 cups quartered tomatoes

12 small new potatoes, quartered

2 cups each: sliced carrots, small cauliflower florets, frozen peas

1 cup each: sliced fennel bulb, cut green beans

1 can (15 ounces) rinsed, drained garbanzo beans

1½ teaspoons each: dried basil and oregano leaves

4 ounces uncooked macaroni

½ cup finely chopped parsley

Salt and pepper, to taste

Grated Parmesan cheese, as garnish

Per Serving:
Calories: 338
% calories from fat: 17
Protein (g): 11.5
Carbohydrate (g): 61.4
Fat (g): 6.8
Saturated fat (g): 1.2
Cholesterol (mg): 1.5
Sodium (mg): 189

Exchanges:
Milk: 0.0
Vegetable: 4.0
Fruit: 0.0
Bread: 2.5
Meat: 0.0
Fat: 1.0

1. Sauté onion and leeks in oil in large saucepan until onion is tender, about 5 minutes. Add cabbage and sauté 1 minute longer. Add remaining ingredients, except macaroni, parsley, salt, pepper, and Parmesan cheese; heat to boiling. Reduce heat and simmer, covered, until vegetables are tender, about 15 minutes. Heat soup to boiling; add macaroni, reduce heat, and simmer, uncovered, until macaroni is *al dente*, 8 to 10 minutes. Stir in parsley; season to taste with salt and pepper. Sprinkle each bowl of soup with Parmesan cheese.

CHICKPEA AND PASTA MINESTRONE

Substantial and wonderfully flavorful, this interesting minestrone is simple to make.

6 entrée servings

1 large onion, chopped

2 each: peeled thinly sliced large carrots, ribs celery, minced garlic cloves

2 cups chopped cabbage

1½ quarts reduced-sodium fat-free chicken broth

1 can (15 ounces) chickpeas, rinsed, drained

1 can (14½ ounces) tomatoes with Italian herbs, undrained, coarsely chopped

4–5 ounces reduced-sodium smoked ham, diced

1 tablespoon dried Italian seasoning

¼ cup uncooked orzo

Salt and pepper, to taste

Per Serving:
Calories: 220
% calories from fat: 11
Protein (g): 14.0
Carbohydrate (g): 34.8
Fat (g): 2.7
Saturated fat (g): 0.7
Cholesterol (mg): 11.7
Sodium (mg): 998

Exchanges:
Milk: 0.0
Vegetable: 2.0
Fruit: 0.0
Bread: 2.5
Meat: 1.0
Fat: 0.0

1. Heat all ingredients, except orzo, salt, and pepper to boiling in large saucepan. Reduce heat and simmer, covered, until vegetables are tender, about 20 minutes. Add pasta and simmer, uncovered, until *al dente*, 8 to 10 minutes. Season to taste with salt and pepper.

BEEFY MINESTRONE

Make this chunky soup the centerpiece of an Italian-style family supper. Serve with a tossed salad and crusty bread.

8 entrée servings

1 pound lean beef round, cubed (¾-inch)

Flour

1 large onion, chopped

2 garlic cloves, minced

1 teaspoon olive oil

1 can (6 ounces) tomato paste

2 quarts Beef Stock (see p. 5)

2 cups chopped green cabbage

2 each: thinly sliced medium carrots, bay leaves

1 tablespoon dried Italian seasoning

1 can (19 ounces) cannellini beans, rinsed, drained

2 cups coarsely diced zucchini

3 cups cooked elbow macaroni

Salt and pepper, to taste

Per Serving:
Calories: 220
% calories from fat: 13
Protein (g): 22.1
Carbohydrate (g): 31.2
Fat (g): 3.4
Saturated fat (g): 0.8
Cholesterol (mg): 27.4
Sodium (mg): 388

Exchanges:
Milk: 0.0
Vegetable: 2.0
Fruit: 0.0
Bread: 1.0
Meat: 2.0
Fat: 0.0

1. Coat beef cubes lightly with flour. Cook beef, onion, and garlic in oil in Dutch oven over medium heat until beef is browned and onion is tender, 8 to 10 minutes. Add tomato paste, stock, cabbage, carrots, and herbs; heat to boiling. Reduce heat and simmer, covered, until beef is tender, about 45 to 60 minutes. Add beans and zucchini; simmer, covered, until zucchini is tender, about 10 minutes. Discard bay leaves. Add pasta and simmer 2 to 3 minutes; season to taste with salt and pepper.

MEATY MINESTRONE

The combination of beef and Italian sausage make this easy vegetable soup extra-hearty.

8 entrée servings

1¼ pounds lean beef stew meat, cubed

1 each: chopped large onion, sliced rib celery

2 each: sliced carrots, minced cloves garlic

1–2 teaspoons olive oil

1½ quarts Beef Stock (see p. 5)

2 teaspoons dried basil leaves

1 teaspoon dried oregano leaves

1 bay leaf

1 can (15 ounces) Great Northern beans, rinsed, drained

1 can (14½ ounces) reduced-sodium diced tomatoes, undrained

1 package (10 ounces) frozen Italian green beans

4 ounces Italian-style turkey sausage, cooked, drained, sliced

2 ounces uncooked rotini or shell pasta

Salt and pepper, to taste

Shredded Parmesan cheese, as garnish

Per Serving:
Calories: 235
% calories from fat: 30
Protein (g): 24
Carbohydrate (g): 19
Fat (g): 8.5
Saturated fat (g): 2.6
Cholesterol (mg): 52
Sodium (mg): 280

Exchanges:
Milk: 0.0
Vegetable: 1.0
Fruit: 0.0
Bread: 1.0
Meat: 2.0
Fat: 0.5

1. Sauté beef, onion, celery, carrots, and garlic in oil in large saucepan until lightly browned, about 15 minutes. Stir in stock and herbs; heat to boiling. Reduce heat and simmer, covered, until meat is tender, about 1 hour. Stir in remaining ingredients, except salt, pepper, and Parmesan cheese. Heat to boiling; reduce heat and simmer, uncovered, until pasta is *al dente*, about 15 minutes. Discard bay leaf; season to taste with salt and pepper. Sprinkle each bowl of soup with Parmesan cheese.

VARIATION

Vegetarian Minestrone Gratin — Make recipe as above, adding 1 can (15 ounces) rinsed, drained kidney beans and 1 large cubed zucchini; omit beef, Beef Stock, and Italian-style turkey sausage. Toast 8 slices (½-inch) French bread under broiler; sprinkle each with 2 tablespoons shredded reduced-fat mozzarella cheese and broil until melted, 1 to 2 minutes. Top each bowl of soup with a bread slice and sprinkle with chopped parsley.

HEARTY MINESTRONE WITH PEPPERONI

Pepperoni adds great flavor to this full-bodied soup. Serve with crusty bread and a salad for an easy, satisfying supper.

4 entrée servings

1 each: chopped large onion, coarsely diced rib celery, red bell pepper

2 each: coarsely chopped medium carrots, zucchini, minced garlic cloves

1 tablespoon olive oil

¼ cup finely diced pepperoni or hard salami

1 quart reduced-sodium fat-free chicken broth

2 cups water

1 can (28 ounces) reduced-sodium Italian plum tomatoes, undrained

1 can (15 ounces) cannellini beans or Great Northern beans, rinsed, drained

1 tablespoon dried Italian seasoning

½ cup uncooked elbow macaroni

Salt and pepper, to taste

Per Serving:
Calories: 327
% calories from fat: 21
Protein (g): 15.5
Carbohydrate (g): 48.1
Fat (g): 7.7
Saturated fat (g): 1.7
Cholesterol (mg): 5.6
Sodium (mg): 1067

Exchanges:
Milk: 0.0
Vegetable: 0.0
Fruit: 0.0
Bread: 3.0
Meat: 2.0
Fat: 0.0

1. Sauté fresh vegetables and garlic in oil in large saucepan until tender, about 8 minutes; add pepperoni and cook 2 to 3 minutes. Add broth, water, tomatoes with liquid, beans, and Italian seasoning; heat to boiling. Reduce heat and simmer, covered, until vegetables are tender, about 15 minutes. Heat soup to boiling and add macaroni; reduce heat and simmer, uncovered, until macaroni is *al dente*, 8 to 10 minutes. Season to taste with salt and pepper.

ITALIAN MEATBALL SOUP

45 *Substitute other pastas for the spaghetti, if you like, such as orecchiette (little ears) or conchiglie (shells).*

8 entrée servings

4 cans (14½ ounces each) reduced-sodium chicken broth

3 cups water

2 cups each: cut green beans, sliced carrots, chopped onions

5 plum tomatoes, coarsely chopped

2 cloves garlic, minced

1–2 teaspoons dried Italian seasoning

Italian Turkey Meatballs (recipe follows)

8 ounces uncooked thin spaghetti, broken into pieces (3-inch)

Salt and pepper, to taste

Per Serving:
Calories: 270
% calories from fat: 28
Protein (g): 19
Carbohydrate (g): 30.2
Fat (g): 8.7
Saturated fat (g): 2
Cholesterol (mg): 31.7
Sodium (mg): 174

Exchanges:
Milk: 0.0
Vegetable: 1.0
Fruit: 0.0
Bread: 1.5
Meat: 2.0
Fat: 0.5

1. Heat all ingredients, except Italian Turkey Meatballs, spaghetti, salt, and pepper to boiling in large saucepan; reduce heat and simmer, covered, until vegetables are tender, about 8 minutes. Heat soup to boiling; add Turkey Meatballs and pasta; reduce heat and simmer, uncovered, until meatballs are cooked and pasta is *al dente*, about 7 minutes. Season to taste with salt and pepper.

Italian Turkey Meatballs
Makes 32

1½ pounds ground turkey

1 egg

¼ cup seasoned dry bread crumbs

2 cloves garlic, minced

1 tablespoon dried Italian seasoning

¾ teaspoon salt

½ teaspoon pepper

1. Mix all ingredients; shape into 32 meatballs. Sauté in lightly greased large skillet until browned, 5 to 7 minutes.

MEXICAN MEATBALL SOUP

45

A great favorite in Mexico, this soup is traditionally seasoned with mint; we've offered oregano as an addition or alternative, if you like.

4 entrée servings

½ cup each: chopped onion, sliced carrots

2 cloves garlic, minced

1 small jalapeño chili, seeds and veins discarded, minced

1 tablespoon flour

2 cups each: reduced-sodium tomato juice, water

2 cans (14½ ounces each) reduced-sodium fat-free chicken broth

2 medium zucchini, sliced

1½ teaspoons dried mint and/or oregano leaves

Mexican Meatballs (recipe follows)

Salt and pepper, to taste

Per Serving:
Calories: 227
% calories from fat: 16
Protein (g): 28
Carbohydrate (g): 20.2
Fat (g): 4.1
Saturated fat (g): 1.4
Cholesterol (mg): 54.7
Sodium (mg): 426

Exchanges:
Milk: 0.0
Vegetable: 3.0
Fruit: 0.0
Bread: 0.0
Meat: 3.0
Fat: 0.0

1. Sauté onion, carrots, garlic, and jalapeño chili in lightly greased large saucepan until tender, about 5 minutes. Stir in flour; cook 1 to 2 minutes. Add tomato juice, water, broth, zucchini, and mint; heat to boiling. Add Mexican Meatballs; reduce heat and simmer, covered, until vegetables are tender and Mexican Meatballs are cooked, 10 to 15 minutes. Season to taste with salt and pepper.

Mexican Meatballs
Makes 24

1 pound ground beef eye of round

¼ cup cooked rice

⅓ cup finely chopped onion

1 clove garlic, minced

½ teaspoon each: dried mint and oregano leaves, ground cumin, salt

¼ teaspoon pepper

1. Mix all ingredients; form into 24 small meatballs.

CURRY SOUP WITH MEATBALLS

This lightly thickened soup is delicately flavored with curry powder.

4 entrée servings

½ cup chopped onion
2 teaspoons each: minced garlic, curry powder
1 teaspoon canola oil
2 tablespoons flour
1¼ quarts Beef Stock (see p. 5)
Curry Meatballs (recipe follows)
2 ounces uncooked vermicelli, broken into pieces
  (2-inch)
Salt and pepper, to taste
1 tablespoon chopped mint

Per Serving:
Calories: 216
% calories from fat: 37
Protein (g): 13.8
Carbohydrate (g): 19.9
Fat (g): 8.8
Saturated fat (g): 3
Cholesterol (mg): 35.6
Sodium (mg): 49

Exchanges:
Milk: 0.0
Vegetable: 0.0
Fruit: 0.0
Bread: 1.0
Meat: 2.0
Fat: 0.5

1. Sauté onion, garlic, and curry powder in oil in large skillet until onion is tender, about 5 minutes; sprinkle with flour and cook 1 to 2 minutes. Stir in stock and heat to boiling, stirring until thickened, about 1 minute. Stir in Curry Meatballs and pasta; simmer, uncovered, until meatballs are cooked and pasta is *al dente*, about 10 minutes. Season to taste with salt and pepper. Stir in mint.

Curry Meatballs
Makes 12

8 ounces lean ground beef
⅓ cup minced onion
1½ teaspoons curry powder
½ teaspoon salt
¼ teaspoon pepper

1. Combine all ingredients; shape into 12 meatballs.

SLOW-COOKER CREOLE-STYLE LAMB SOUP

Let this luscious soup cook all day while you're away.

6 entrée servings

1 cup each: chopped onion, zucchini, water

½ cup each: chopped green bell pepper, celery

2 large garlic cloves, minced

2 cans (15 ounces each) tomato sauce

3 cups fat-free beef broth

1 pound lean lamb for stew, cubed (½-inch)

⅓ cup uncooked rice

1 bay leaf

1 teaspoon dried marjoram leaves

½ teaspoon each: dried thyme and basil leaves

¼ teaspoon dry mustard

Salt and pepper, to taste

Hot pepper sauce, to taste

Per Serving:
Calories: 217
% calories from fat: 10
Protein (g): 16.1
Carbohydrate (g): 34.6
Fat (g): 2.5
Saturated fat (g): 0.7
Cholesterol (mg): 27.4
Sodium (mg): 383

Exchanges:
Milk: 0.0
Vegetable: 0.0
Fruit: 0.0
Bread: 2.5
Meat: 1.0
Fat: 0.0

1. Combine all ingredients, except salt, pepper, and hot pepper sauce, in slow cooker. Cover and cook on High for 1 hour. Change setting to Low and cook 7 to 9 hours or until meat and vegetables are tender. Discard bay leaf; season to taste with salt and pepper. Serve with hot pepper sauce.

YANKEE BEAN SOUP

This soup can also be made the old-fashioned way, with trimmings from a holiday ham, and 1 cup dried beans soaked in water overnight with the ham bone.

6 entrée servings

8–12 ounces reduced-sodium lean ham

1 each: chopped large onion, rib celery

2 each: chopped carrots, minced cloves garlic

1 tablespoon olive oil

1 quart Chicken Stock (see p. 2)

2 cans (15 ounces each) navy beans, rinsed, drained

1 can (14½ ounces) reduced-sodium diced
  tomatoes, undrained

1 teaspoon dried Italian seasoning

Salt and pepper, to taste

Per Serving:
Calories: 284
% calories from fat: 17
Protein (g): 20.9
Carbohydrate (g): 39.2
Fat (g): 5.7
Saturated fat (g): 1.3
Cholesterol (mg): 22.4
Sodium (mg): 836

Exchanges:
Milk: 0.0
Vegetable: 2.0
Fruit: 0.0
Bread: 2 0
Meat: 2.0
Fat: 0.0

1. Sauté ham, onion, celery, carrots, and garlic in oil in large saucepan until ham is lightly browned, about 8 minutes. Add remaining ingredients, except salt and pepper. Heat to boiling; reduce heat and simmer, covered, until vegetables are tender, about 20 minutes. Season to taste with salt and pepper.

SOUTHERN CORN AND BEAN SOUP WITH BEAN BISCUITS

Smoky chipotle chilies give this soup a unique flavor; biscuits made with puréed beans are extra moist.

6 entrée servings

1 cup each: chopped onion, red bell pepper

1 teaspoon each: chopped garlic, olive oil

2 cans (15 ounces each) Great Northern beans,
  rinsed, drained, coarsely mashed

1½ quarts Rich Chicken Stock (see p. 4)

2 cups whole kernel corn

¼–½ small chipotle chili in adobo, chopped

1 teaspoon dried thyme leaves

Salt and pepper, to taste

½ cup fat-free sour cream

Bean Biscuits (recipe follows)

Per Serving:
Calories: 361
% calories from fat: 23
Protein (g): 18.3
Carbohydrate (g): 55.2
Fat (g): 10
Saturated fat (g): 2.4
Cholesterol (mg): 1.1
Sodium (mg): 789

Exchanges:
Milk: 0.0
Vegetable: 1.0
Fruit: 0.0
Bread: 3.0
Mcat: 1.0
Fat: 1.5

1. Sauté onion, bell pepper, and garlic in oil in large saucepan until tender, about 5 minutes. Stir in beans, stock, corn, chipotle chili, and thyme. Heat to boiling; reduce heat and simmer, uncovered, 10 minutes. Season to taste with salt and pepper. Garnish each bowl of soup with dollops of sour cream and serve with Bean Biscuits.

Bean Biscuits
Makes 6

¾ cup all-purpose flour
2 teaspoons baking powder
1½ teaspoons sugar
¼ teaspoon salt
¼ cup vegetable shortening
½ can (15 ounces) Great Northern beans, rinsed, drained
3 tablespoons fat-free milk

1. Combine flour, baking powder, sugar, and salt in medium bowl; cut in shortening until mixture resembles coarse crumbs. Process beans and milk in food processor or blender until almost smooth; add to flour mixture and mix just until dough comes together. Drop dough by spoonfuls onto ungreased baking sheet. Bake at 375 degrees until light brown, about 12 minutes.

RED BEANS, RICE, AND SAUSAGE SOUP

Low-fat sausage gives this easy but satisfying soup its zip. The sausage retains its flavor best when it is added near the end of the cooking time.

6 entrée servings

1 each: large finely chopped onion, minced
garlic clove
1 teaspoon olive oil
1¼ quarts chicken broth
⅓ cup each: diced carrot, celery, red bell pepper
1 can (15 ounces) tomato sauce
2 cans (16 ounces each) dark red kidney beans,
rinsed, drained
¼ teaspoon dried thyme leaves
1 bay leaf
⅓ cup uncooked rice
6 ounces reduced-fat smoked sausage, sliced
Salt and pepper, to taste

Per Serving:
Calories: 221
% calories from fat: 221
Protein (g): 15.4
Carbohydrate (g): 34.7
Fat (g): 2.7
Saturated fat (g): 0.5
Cholesterol (mg): 13.5
Sodium (mg): 417

Exchanges:
Milk: 0.0
Vegetable: 1.0
Fruit: 0.0
Bread: 2.0
Meat: 1.0
Fat: 0.0

1. Sauté onion and garlic in oil in large saucepan until onion begins to brown, about 5 minutes. Add remaining ingredients, except sausage, salt, and pepper; heat to boiling. Reduce heat and simmer, covered, until rice is tender, about 25 minutes. Add sausage and simmer, uncovered, 10 minutes or until soup has thickened slightly; discard bay leaf and season to taste with salt and pepper.

PINTO SOUP WITH CHILI CRISPS

The flavor of this vegetable soup is enhanced with a garnish of fresh tomatoes and chili-flavored tortilla strips.

8 entrée servings

2 quarts reduced-sodium chicken broth
2 cups each: sliced onions, carrots, mushrooms, cubed unpeeled red potatoes
1 tablespoon minced garlic
2 teaspoons dried oregano leaves
1 teaspoon ground cumin
¼ teaspoon crushed red pepper
2 cans (15 ounces each) pinto beans, rinsed, drained
Salt and pepper, to taste
Chili Crisps (recipe follows)
2 cups chopped, peeled, seeded tomatoes
¼ cup chopped cilantro

Per Serving:
Calories: 206
% calories from fat: 7
Protein (g): 8.1
Carbohydrate (g): 38.2
Fat (g): 1.6
Saturated fat (g): 0.3
Cholesterol (mg): 0
Sodium (mg): 277

Exchanges:
Milk: 0.0
Vegetable: 2.0
Fruit: 0.0
Bread: 2.0
Meat: 0.0
Fat: 0.0

1. Heat broth, onions, carrots, mushrooms, potatoes, garlic, herbs, and red pepper to boiling in Dutch oven; reduce heat and simmer, covered, until vegetables are tender, about 20 minutes, adding beans during last 5 minutes. Season to taste with salt and pepper. Sprinkle each bowl of soup with Chili Crisps, tomatoes, and cilantro.

Chili Crisps
Makes about 3 cups

3 corn tortillas (6-inch)
Olive oil cooking spray
½ teaspoon each: garlic powder, chili powder

1. Spray both sides of tortillas with cooking spray; sprinkle tops with garlic and chili powder. Cut tortillas in half; cut halves into thin strips. Arrange on cookie sheet and bake at 425 degrees until crisp, about 10 minutes.

GOULASH BEAN SOUP

Caraway seeds and paprika give a Hungarian twist to this vegetable and bean soup.

8 entrée servings

1½ pounds lean beef round steak, cubed

2 cups chopped onions

1 cup each: chopped carrots, red bell pepper

1 tablespoon minced garlic

2 tablespoons flour

1 tablespoon paprika

2 teaspoons caraway seeds, crushed

1 teaspoon dried thyme leaves

1 quart Beef Stock (see p. 5)

1 can (14½ ounces) diced tomatoes, undrained

3 cups sliced cabbage

2 cans (15 ounces each) light red kidney beans

Salt and pepper, to taste

½ cup fat-free sour cream

Per Serving:
Calories: 253
% calories from fat: 13
Protein (g): 24.1
Carbohydrate (g): 31.6
Fat (g): 3.7
Saturated fat (g): 1.1
Cholesterol (mg): 41.4
Sodium (mg): 512

Exchanges:
Milk: 0.0
Vegetable: 0.0
Fruit: 0.0
Bread: 2.0
Meat: 2.0
Fat: 0.0

1. Cook beef in lightly greased large saucepan over medium heat until browned, about 10 minutes; remove and reserve. Add onions, carrots, bell pepper, and garlic to saucepan; sauté until lightly browned, about 5 minutes. Return reserved beef to saucepan and sprinkle with flour, paprika, caraway seeds, and thyme; cook 1 to 2 minutes. Stir in stock and tomatoes with liquid. Heat to boiling; reduce heat and simmer, covered, until beef is tender, 45 to 60 minutes, adding cabbage and beans during last 20 minutes. Season to taste with salt and pepper. Top each bowl of soup with dollops of sour cream.

GARBANZO AND COUSCOUS SOUP

45 *Couscous, a quick cooking, mild-flavored wheat pasta used in Middle Eastern cuisine, combines very pleasantly with garbanzo beans.*

6 entrée servings

1 medium onion, chopped

1 clove garlic, minced

2 teaspoons olive oil

1¼ quarts reduced-sodium fat-free chicken broth

1 each: finely chopped rib celery, large carrot

1 cup each: diced zucchini, small cauliflower florets

½ medium green bell pepper, diced

1 can (14½ ounces) diced tomatoes, undrained

1 can (15 ounces) garbanzo beans, rinsed, drained

1 bay leaf

¾ teaspoon each: ground cumin, dried thyme leaves

Generous pinch ground cloves

⅓ cup uncooked couscous

Salt and pepper, to taste

Per Serving:
Calories: 202
% calories from fat: 15
Protein (g): 11.8
Carbohydrate (g): 33
Fat (g): 3.4
Saturated fat (g): 0.4
Cholesterol (mg): 0
Sodium (mg): 413

Exchanges:
Milk: 0.0
Vegetable: 1.0
Fruit: 0.0
Bread: 2 0
Meat: 0.0
Fat: 0.5

1. Sauté onion and garlic in oil in Dutch oven until tender, about 5 minutes. Add remaining ingredients except couscous, salt, and pepper; heat to boiling. Reduce heat and simmer, covered, until vegetables are tender, 15 to 20 minutes. Heat soup to boiling; stir in couscous and boil 1 minute. Remove from heat and let stand, covered, 5 minutes. Discard bay leaf; season to taste with salt and pepper.

GARBANZO BEAN SOUP

45 *Cumin adds a Mexican flavor to this soup; curry powder can be substituted for an Indian variation.*

4 entrée servings

2 each: finely chopped medium onions, garlic cloves

2 cans (15 ounces each) garbanzo beans, rinsed, drained

2 cans (14 ½ ounces each) reduced-sodium fat-free chicken broth

1 teaspoon ground cumin

½–¾ teaspoon dried thyme leaves

Salt and pepper, to taste

¼ cup fat-free sour cream

Paprika or chili powder, as garnish

Per Serving:
Calories: 267
% calories from fat: 15
Protein (g): 12.4
Carbohydrate (g): 46.4
Fat (g): 4.6
Saturated fat (g): 0.6
Cholesterol (mg): 0
Sodium (mg): 627

Exchanges:
Milk: 0.0
Vegetable: 1.0
Fruit: 0.0
Bread: 3.0
Meat: 0.0
Fat: 0.0

1. Sauté onions and garlic in lightly greased large saucepan until tender, about 5 minutes. Add beans, broth, cumin, and thyme and heat to boiling; reduce heat and simmer, covered, 10 minutes. Process soup in food processor or blender until smooth; season to taste with salt and pepper. Top each bowl of soup with a dollop of sour cream and sprinkle with paprika.

SICILIAN SUMMER TOMATO SOUP

Perfect for a summer day, when tomatoes are at their best. Orange zest adds a pleasant accent.

10 first-course servings

2 each: medium red and yellow onions, finely chopped

2 tablespoons olive oil

1 cup sliced mushrooms

½ cup each: chopped green onions, carrots, celery

¼ cup chopped garlic

1 quart Chicken Stock (see p. 2)

½ cup dry white wine or Chicken Stock

18 plum tomatoes, peeled, seeded, chopped

1½ pounds spinach, coarsely chopped

¼ cup orange juice

2 tablespoons tomato paste

1 cup chopped parsley

½ cup chopped fresh or 2 tablespoons dried basil leaves

1 teaspoon sugar

Grated zest of 1 orange

Salt and pepper, to taste

Per Serving:
Calories: 146
% calories from fat: 22
Protein (g): 5.8
Carbohydrate (g): 22.2
Fat (g): 4.1
Saturated fat (g): 0.6
Cholesterol (mg): 0
Sodium (mg): 103

Exchanges:
Milk: 0.0
Vegetable: 4.0
Fruit: 0.0
Bread: 0.0
Meat: 0.0
Fat: 1.0

1. Sauté red and yellow onions in olive oil in large saucepan until tender, about 5 minutes. Add green onions, carrots, celery, mushrooms, and garlic; sauté 2 to 3 minutes. Add remaining ingredients, except salt and pepper and heat to boiling, reduce heat and simmer, covered, 10 minutes. Process soup in food processor or blender until smooth; season to taste with salt and pepper.

CREOLE TOMATO SOUP

45 *Tomatoes, green pepper, and spices combine to give this soup a Creole flavor.*

4 first-course servings

1 each: diced medium green bell pepper, chopped medium onion, minced garlic clove

2 teaspoons olive oil

2 cups reduced-sodium fat-free chicken or vegetable broth

1 can (28 ounces) tomato purée

2 teaspoons sugar

¾ teaspoon each: dried marjoram and basil leaves

2 bay leaves

Salt and pepper, to taste

Per Serving:
Calories: 98
% calories from fat: 21
Protein (g): 4.9
Carbohydrate (g): 16.1
Fat (g): 2 5
Saturated fat (g): 0.5
Cholesterol (mg): 0
Sodium (mg): 526

Exchanges:
Milk: 0.0
Vegetable: 3.0
Fruit: 0.0
Bread: 1.0
Meat: 0.0
Fat: 0.5

1. Sauté bell pepper, onion, and garlic in oil in large saucepan 5 minutes. Add remaining ingredients except salt and pepper and heat to boiling; reduce heat and simmer, covered, until green pepper is very tender, about 10 minutes. Discard bay leaves; season to taste with salt and pepper.

BEET BORSCHT

45 *This delicious soup is flavored in the traditional way with Polish sausage.*

8 entrée servings

8 ounces low-fat smoked Polish sausage,
  sliced (½-inch)
2 teaspoons margarine or butter
6 cups reduced-sodium fat-free beef broth
1 small head red cabbage, thinly sliced
4 medium beets, peeled, julienned or cubed
2 carrots, julienned or cubed
1 clove garlic, minced
1 bay leaf
2–3 teaspoons sugar
2 tablespoons cider vinegar
Salt and pepper, to taste
Chopped dill weed, as garnish

Per Serving:
Calories: 120
% calories from fat: 25
Protein (g): 10.9
Carbohydrate (g): 13.1
Fat (g): 0.4
Saturated fat (g): 0.6
Cholesterol (mg): 17.2
Sodium (mg): 437

Exchanges:
Milk: 0.0
Vegetable: 3.0
Fruit: 0.0
Bread: 0.0
Meat: 1.0
Fat: 0.0

1. Sauté sausage in margarine in Dutch oven until browned, about 5 minutes. Add remaining ingredients, except salt, pepper, and dill weed; heat to boiling. Reduce heat and simmer, covered, until vegetables are tender, about 15 minutes. Discard bay leaf. Season to taste with salt and pepper; sprinkle each bowl of soup with dill weed.

INDIAN LENTIL SOUP

45 *This soup (Dal Shorba) from India is flavored with curry powder and sweet coriander. Red, green, or brown lentils can be used.*

8 entrée servings

½ cup chopped onion
1 clove garlic, minced
2 teaspoons curry powder
1 teaspoon each: crushed coriander and cumin seeds
½ teaspoon ground turmeric
⅛–¼ teaspoon crushed red pepper flakes
1 tablespoon olive oil

5 cups reduced-sodium fat-free chicken broth

4 cups water

2 cups dried red or brown lentils

Salt and pepper, to taste

6 tablespoons fat-free plain yogurt

Per Serving:
Calories: 193
% calories from fat: 11
Protein (g): 16
Carbohydrate (g): 27.6
Fat (g): 2.4
Saturated fat (g): 0.3
Cholesterol (mg): 0.3
Sodium (mg): 121

Exchanges:
Milk: 0.0
Vegetable: 0.0
Fruit: 0.0
Bread: 2.0
Meat: 1.0
Fat: 0.0

1. Sauté onion, garlic, curry powder, herbs, and red pepper in oil in large saucepan until onion is tender, about 5 minutes. Add broth, water, and lentils; heat to boiling. Reduce heat and simmer, covered, until lentils are tender, about 30 minutes. Season to taste with salt and pepper. Top each bowl of soup with a tablespoon of yogurt.

TORTELLINI AND MUSHROOM SOUP

45 *Porcini mushrooms, a Tuscan delicacy found fresh in the fall, are available in dried form year round. Porcini impart a wonderful earthy flavor to recipes. Other dried mushrooms can be substituted for a similar flavor.*

6 first-course servings

Hot water

2 ounces dried porcini mushrooms

8 ounces white mushrooms, sliced

2 tablespoons finely chopped shallots or green onions

2 cloves garlic, minced

½ teaspoon dried tarragon leaves

2 cans (14½ ounces each) reduced-sodium beef broth

2–4 tablespoons dry sherry (optional)

1 package (9 ounces) fresh tomato-and-cheese tortellini

Salt and pepper, to taste

Per Serving:
Calories: 110
% calories from fat: 16
Protein (g): 5
Carbohydrate (g): 17.1
Fat (g): 2
Saturated fat (g): 0.4
Cholesterol (mg): 4.2
Sodium (mg): 184

Exchanges:
Milk: 0.0
Vegetable: 1.0
Fruit: 0.0
Bread: 1.0
Meat: 0.0
Fat: 0.5

1. Pour hot water over porcini mushrooms in bowl; let stand until softened, about 15 minutes; drain. Slice mushrooms, discarding any tough parts.

2. Sauté dried and white mushrooms, shallots, garlic, and tarragon in lightly greased large saucepan until mushrooms are tender, about

5 minutes. Add broth and sherry and heat to boiling; add tortellini. Reduce heat and simmer, uncovered, until tortellini are *al dente*, about 5 minutes; season to taste with salt and pepper.

FRENCH ONION SOUP

45 *This classic soup is topped with Bruschetta and fat-free cheese for healthful, delicious dining.*

8 first-course servings

6 cups (1½ pounds) thinly sliced Spanish onions
2 cloves garlic, minced
1 teaspoon sugar
6 cups reduced-sodium fat-free beef broth
2 bay leaves
Salt and white pepper, to taste
8 Bruschetta (⅓ recipe) (see p. 637)
8 tablespoons (2 ounces) shredded fat-free
    Swiss cheese

Per Serving:
Calories: 126
% calories from fat: 7
Protein (g): 4.9
Carbohydrate (g): 25
Fat (g): 1
Saturated fat (g): 0.1
Cholesterol (mg): 0.0
Sodium (mg): 542

Exchanges:
Milk: 0.0
Vegetable: 0.0
Fruit: 0.0
Bread: 1.5
Meat: 0.0
Fat: 0.0

1. Cook onions and garlic in lightly greased Dutch oven, covered, over medium-low heat until softened, 8 to 10 minutes. Stir in sugar and continue cooking, uncovered, until onions are lightly browned, about 10 minutes. Stir in broth and bay leaves; heat to boiling. Reduce heat and simmer, covered, 30 minutes. Discard bay leaves; season to taste with salt and white pepper. Top each Bruschetta with 1 tablespoon cheese; broil 6 inches from heat source until cheese is melted. Top each bowl of soup with a Bruschetta.

POBLANO CHILI SOUP

Poblano chilies give this soup extraordinary flavor. Taste the peppers, as they can vary in flavor from mild to very hot; if they are too hot for your taste, substitute some green bell peppers.

8 first-course servings

2 medium onions, chopped
4 medium poblano chilies, seeded, chopped
½–1 small jalapeño chili, seeded, finely chopped

2 cans (14½ ounces each) reduced-sodium
fat-free chicken broth

3 cups tomato juice

½ teaspoon ground cumin

Salt, to taste

Chopped cilantro, as garnish

Per Serving:
Calories: 88
% calories from fat: 3
Protein (g): 6.4
Carbohydrate (g): 18.2
Fat (g): 0.4
Saturated fat (g): 0
Cholesterol (mg): 0
Sodium (mg): 498

Exchanges:
Milk: 0.0
Vegetable: 3.5
Fruit: 0.0
Bread: 0.0
Meat: 0.0
Fat: 0.0

1. Sauté onions and chilies in lightly greased large saucepan until onions are tender, about 5 minutes. Add broth, tomato juice, and cumin and heat to boiling; reduce heat and simmer, covered, until chilies are very tender, about 10 minutes. Process in food processor or blender until smooth; season to taste with salt. Serve warm or chilled; sprinkle each bowl of soup with cilantro.

CHAYOTE SQUASH SOUP WITH CILANTRO CREAM

45 *Chayote squash, often called a "vegetable pear," is native to Mexico and readily available here. The squash is light green in color and delicate in flavor.*

6 first-course servings

1 large onion, chopped

2 cloves garlic, minced

3 tablespoons flour

3 large chayote squash, peeled, seeded, sliced

3 cans (14½ ounces each) reduced-sodium fat-free
chicken broth, divided

½ cup water

Salt and white pepper, to taste

Cilantro Cream (recipe follows)

Chopped cilantro, as garnish

Per Serving:
Calories: 68
% calories from fat: 11
Protein (g): 2.9
Carbohydrate (g): 13.3
Fat (g): 0.9
Saturated fat (g): 0.1
Cholesterol (mg): 0.2
Sodium (mg): 27

Exchanges:
Milk: 0.0
Vegetable: 2.5
Fruit: 0.0
Bread: 0.0
Meat: 0.0
Fat: 0.0

1. Sauté onion and garlic in lightly greased medium skillet until tender, about 5 minutes. Stir in flour; cook over medium heat 2 minutes, stirring constantly. Add squash and broth to saucepan; heat to boiling. Reduce heat and simmer, covered, until squash is tender, 15 to 20 minutes. Process soup in food processor or blender until smooth; season to taste with salt and white pepper. Serve warm or chilled; drizzle each bowl of soup with Cilantro Cream and sprinkle with cilantro.

Cilantro Cream

Makes about ½ cup

⅓ cup fat-free sour cream
1 tablespoon finely chopped cilantro
¼–⅓ cup fat-free milk

1. Mix sour cream and cilantro in small bowl, adding enough milk for desired consistency.

ORIENTAL WATERCRESS SOUP

45 *Spinach can be substituted for the watercress in this fragrant Cantonese offering.*

6 first-course servings

6 cups reduced-sodium fat-free chicken broth
2 cups loosely packed torn watercress
3 slices gingerroot (¼-inch)
Salt and white pepper, to taste
2 sliced green onions
2 tablespoons shredded carrot

Per Serving:
Calories: 11
% calories from fat: 9
Protein (g): 0.9
Carbohydrate (g): 1.8
Fat (g): 0.1
Saturated fat (g): 0
Cholesterol (mg): 0
Sodium (mg): 116

Exchanges:
Milk: 0.0
Vegetable: 0.0
Fruit: 0.0
Bread: 0.0
Meat: 0.0
Fat: 0.0

1. Heat broth, watercress, and gingerroot to boiling in large saucepan; reduce heat and simmer, covered, 15 minutes. Discard gingerroot; season to taste with salt and white pepper. Sprinkle each bowl of soup with green onions and carrot.

POTSTICKER SOUP

The potstickers can be assembled several hours in advance; refrigerate, covered, on a lightly greased cookie sheet.

6 first-course servings

6 cups reduced-sodium fat-free chicken broth
24 Five-Spice Potstickers (recipe follows)
1 cup sliced spinach
⅓ cup sliced green onions
Reduced-sodium tamari soy sauce
Pepper, to taste

Per Serving:
Calories: 139
% calories from fat: 5
Protein (g): 10.7
Carbohydrate (g): 20.3
Fat (g): 0.8
Saturated fat (g): 0.1
Cholesterol (mg): 2.9
Sodium (mg): 426

Exchanges:
Milk: 0.0
Vegetable: 1.0
Fruit: 0.0
Bread: 1.0
Meat: 1.0
Fat: 0.0

1. Heat chicken broth to boiling in Dutch oven; add potstickers and simmer, uncovered, until potstickers rise to the surface, 2 to 3 minutes. Stir in spinach and green onions; simmer 2 to 3 minutes. Season to taste with soy sauce and pepper.

Five-Spice Potstickers
Makes 24

1 cup sliced Chinese cabbage
¼ cup shredded carrot, green onions
2 teaspoons minced gingerroot
1 small clove garlic, minced
1 teaspoon each: reduced-sodium tamari soy sauce, five-spice powder
¼ teaspoon hot chili paste
1 ounce light tofu, coarsely crumbled
24 wonton or gyoza wrappers
1 egg white, beaten

1. Stir-fry cabbage, carrot, green onions, gingerroot, and garlic in lightly greased wok or large skillet until cabbage is wilted, 2 to 3 minutes. Remove from heat; stir in soy sauce, five-spice powder, hot chili paste, and tofu. Cool. Spoon ½ tablespoon filling on each wonton wrapper; brush edges of wrapper with egg white. Fold wrapper in half and press edges to seal. Repeat with remaining filling, wrappers, and egg white.

CHINESE PORK AND WATERCRESS SOUP

The watercress is stirred into the soup, but not cooked, which helps retain its bright color and fresh, peppery taste.

6 first-course servings

3 ounces boneless pork loin, fat trimmed, cut into strips (1 x ¼-inch)

1 small garlic clove, halved

1 slice fresh gingerroot (¼-inch)

5½ cups Chicken Stock (see p. 2) or fat-free chicken broth, divided

4 green onions, quartered lengthwise and sliced (1-inch)

1 tablespoon dry sherry (optional)

2 teaspoons reduced-sodium soy sauce

⅔ cup cooked rice

1½ cups lightly packed watercress

Salt and pepper, to taste

Per Serving:
Calories: 68
% calories from fat: 11
Protein (g): 7.4
Carbohydrate (g): 6.9
Fat (g): 0.8
Saturated fat (g): 0.3
Cholesterol (mg): 6.2
Sodium (mg): 374

Exchanges:
Milk: 0.0
Vegetable: 0.0
Fruit: 0.0
Bread: 1.0
Meat: 0.0
Fat: 0.0

1. Heat pork, garlic, gingerroot, and ½ cup stock to boiling in large saucepan; reduce heat and simmer, covered, until pork is cooked, about 5 minutes. Using a slotted spoon, remove pork strips and reserve. Strain broth and return to saucepan; discard garlic and gingerroot. Add remaining 5 cups stock, reserved pork, green onions, sherry, soy sauce, and rice; heat to boiling. Reduce heat and simmer, covered, until pork is tender, about 5 minutes. Stir in watercress; remove from heat and let stand until watercress is wilted, about 30 seconds. Season to taste with salt and pepper; serve immediately.

HOT SOUR SOUP

The contrast in hot and sour flavors makes this Mandarin soup a unique offering. The hot chili sesame oil and Sour Sauce are intensely flavored, so use sparingly.

6 first-course servings

Per Serving:
Calories: 176
% calories from fat: 28
Protein (g): 11
Carbohydrate (g): 21
Fat (g): 6
Saturated fat (g): 0.8
Cholesterol (mg): 35
Sodium (mg): 630

Exchanges:
Milk: 0.0
Vegetable: 0.0
Fruit: 0.0
Bread: 1.5
Meat: 1.5
Fat: 0.0

1 ounce dried Chinese black mushrooms
¾ cup boiling water
1 quart reduced-sodium fat-free chicken broth
1½ cups cubed tempeh or light extra-firm tofu
½ cup bamboo shoots
¼ cup distilled white vinegar
2 tablespoons reduced-sodium tamari soy sauce
1 tablespoon each: finely chopped gingerroot, brown
   sugar, cornstarch
3 tablespoons water
Salt and pepper, to taste
1 egg, lightly beaten
1 teaspoon Asian sesame oil
12–18 drops hot chili sesame oil or Szechwan chili sauce
Sour Sauce (recipe follows)

1. Combine mushrooms and boiling water in small bowl; let stand until mushrooms are softened, 15 to 20 minutes. Drain, reserving liquid. Slice mushrooms, discarding tough stems.

2. Heat broth, mushrooms and reserved liquid, tempeh, bamboo shoots, vinegar, soy sauce, gingerroot, and brown sugar to boiling in large saucepan. Reduce heat and simmer, uncovered, 10 minutes. Heat soup to boiling; stir in combined cornstarch and water, stirring until thickened, about 1 minute. Season to taste with salt and pepper. Slowly stir egg into soup; stir in sesame oil. Serve with hot chili oil and Sour Sauce.

Sour Sauce

Makes about ⅓ cup

3 tablespoons distilled white vinegar
1 tablespoon reduced-sodium tamari soy sauce
2 tablespoons packed light brown sugar

1. Mix all ingredients.

INDIAN-SPICED CHICKEN SOUP

This flavorful chicken soup is delicious with Pita Bread (p. 639) for a light lunch.

8 entrée servings

2 quarts water
6 peppercorns
1 chicken (about 3½ pounds), cut up
2 teaspoons ground coriander
1 teaspoon each: ground turmeric, ginger
⅛–¼ teaspoon crushed red pepper
1½ teaspoons cider vinegar
½ cup thinly sliced onion
1 tablespoon canola oil
Salt and pepper, to taste
Chopped cilantro, as garnish

Per Serving:
Calories: 179
% calories from fat: 26
Protein (g): 30.2
Carbohydrate (g): 1.4
Fat (g): 4.9
Saturated fat (g): 1.3
Cholesterol (mg): 82.1
Sodium (mg): 89

Exchanges:
Milk: 0.0
Vegetable: 0.0
Fruit: 0.0
Bread: 0.0
Meat: 3.0
Fat: 0.0

1. Combine water, peppercorns, and chicken in Dutch oven. Heat to boiling; reduce heat and simmer, covered, until chicken is tender, about 35 minutes. Strain broth into large bowl; skim off fat. Remove meat from bones, cutting into pieces; discard bones and skin. Add meat to broth.

2. Mix spices, red pepper, and vinegar, making a paste. Sauté onion in oil in large saucepan over low heat until tender, but not brown, about 10 minutes. Stir spice paste into onion; cook, stirring, 5 minutes. Add broth and chicken and heat to boiling; reduce heat and simmer, covered, 10 minutes. Season to taste with salt and pepper; garnish each bowl of soup with chopped cilantro.

MARRAKECH SOUP

This light, clear soup, delicately flavored with Moroccan spices, makes a perfect first course for a Middle Eastern dinner. Use your richest homemade chicken stock for the best results.

8 first-course servings

2½ quarts Rich Chicken Stock (see p. 4)

¾ cup each: sliced celery, onions

2 each: halved cloves garlic, quartered lemons

8 sprigs parsley

½ teaspoon each: ground ginger, turmeric, cinnamon

Pinch saffron (optional)

Salt and pepper, to taste

8 thin lemon slices

Chopped cilantro, as garnish

Per Serving:
Calories: 57
% calories from fat: 19
Protein (g): 6.5
Carbohydrate (g): 3.6
Fat (g): 1.1
Saturated fat (g): 0.3
Cholesterol (mg): 1.3
Sodium (mg): 48

Exchanges:
Milk: 0.0
Vegetable: 2.0
Fruit: 0.0
Bread: 0.0
Meat: 0.0
Fat: 0.0

1. Heat all ingredients except salt, pepper, lemon slices, and cilantro, to boiling in large saucepan; reduce heat and simmer, covered, 45 minutes. Strain, discarding vegetables and lemons. Season to taste with salt and pepper; garnish each bowl of soup with lemon slices and cilantro.

WHITE BEAN SOUP PROVENÇAL

Serve Focaccia (see p. 642) as a perfect accompaniment to this herb-infused soup.

8 entrée servings

1 pound dried cannellini or navy beans
1 cup each: chopped onion, celery
3 cloves garlic, minced
2 teaspoons dried sage leaves
1½ quarts Low-Salt Chicken Stock (see p. 3)
   or reduced-sodium fat-free chicken broth
2 cups water
3 large plum tomatoes, chopped
2 teaspoons lemon juice
Salt and pepper, to taste
Mixed Herb Pesto (recipe follows)

Per Serving:
Calories: 283
% calories from fat: 21
Protein (g): 16.2
Carbohydrate (g): 41.9
Fat (g): 6.9
Saturated fat (g): 1.2
Cholesterol (mg): 3.6
Sodium (mg): 199

Exchanges:
Milk: 0.0
Vegetable: 2.0
Fruit: 0.0
Bread: 2.0
Meat: 1.0
Fat: 1.0

1. Cover beans with 2 inches water in large saucepan and heat to boiling; boil, uncovered, 2 minutes. Remove from heat and let stand, covered, 1 hour; drain.

2. Sauté onion, celery, garlic, and sage in lightly greased large saucepan until tender, about 5 minutes. Stir in beans, stock, and water; heat to boiling. Reduce heat and simmer, covered, until beans are tender, 45 to 60 minutes. Process in food processor or blender until smooth; return to saucepan. Stir in tomatoes and lemon juice; cook, covered, over medium heat 5 minutes. Season to taste with salt and pepper. Stir 1 tablespoon Mixed Herb Pesto into each bowl of soup.

Mixed Herb Pesto

Makes about ½ cup

½ cup each: packed basil leaves, parsley sprigs
¼ cup packed oregano leaves
3 cloves garlic
2 tablespoons each: grated Parmesan cheese, walnut pieces, olive oil
2 teaspoons lemon juice
Salt and pepper, to taste

1. Process herbs, garlic, Parmesan cheese, and walnuts in food processor, adding oil and lemon juice gradually, until mixture is very finely chopped. Season to taste with salt and pepper.

MEXICAN CORN SOUP

45 *Serve this soup with warm tortillas or a delicious cornbread (see Index).*

4 first-course servings

¼ cup each: shredded carrot, chopped green bell
   pepper, green onions
¼ teaspoon celery seeds
1 teaspoon olive oil
1 cup whole kernel corn
2 cups reduced-sodium fat-free chicken broth
1 cup fat-free milk
⅛ teaspoon crushed red pepper
Salt and pepper, to taste

Per Serving:
Calories: 103
% calories from fat: 13
Protein (g): 7.6
Carbohydrate (g): 15.8
Fat (g): 1.5
Saturated fat (g): 0.2
Cholesterol (mg): 1.6
Sodium (mg): 141

Exchanges:
Milk: 0.0
Vegetable: 0.0
Fruit: 0.0
Bread: 1.0
Meat: 0.0
Fat: 0.5

1. Sauté carrot, green pepper, and green onions in oil in large saucepan until tender, about 8 minutes. Add remaining ingredients, except salt and pepper; heat to boiling. Reduce heat and simmer, covered, 5 minutes. Process soup in food processor or blender until smooth; season to taste with salt and pepper.

ITALIAN CANNELLINI AND CABBAGE SOUP

45

Any white bean, such as Great Northern or navy, may be substituted for the cannellini.

8 first-course servings

3 cups thinly sliced or chopped cabbage

1 small onion, coarsely chopped

3 cloves garlic, minced

1 teaspoon crushed caraway seeds

2 cans (14 ½ ounces each) reduced-sodium chicken broth

1 cup water

1 can (15 ounces) cannellini or Great Northern beans, rinsed, drained

½ cup uncooked mostaccioli (penne)

Salt and pepper, to taste

Per Serving:
Calories: 107
% calories from fat: 7
Protein (g): 6.9
Carbohydrate (g): 21.9
Fat (g): 1
Saturated fat (g): 0.1
Cholesterol (mg): 0
Sodium (mg): 175

Exchanges:
Milk: 0.0
Vegetable: 1.0
Fruit: 0.0
Bread: 1.0
Meat: 0.5
Fat: 0.0

1. Sauté cabbage, onion, garlic, and caraway seeds in lightly greased large saucepan until cabbage is wilted, 8 to 10 minutes. Add chicken broth, water, and beans and heat to boiling. Stir in pasta; reduce heat and simmer, uncovered, until pasta is *al dente*, about 12 minutes; season to taste with salt and pepper.

BEET BORSCHT WITH SMOKED SAUSAGE

For convenience, 2 cups canned, drained, shredded beets can be substituted for the fresh; reduce cooking time to 10 to 15 minutes.

8 first-course servings

2 cups julienned or diced peeled beets

½ small head red cabbage, shredded

2 carrots, quartered lengthwise, sliced

1 clove garlic, minced

1½ quarts reduced-sodium fat-free beef broth

1 bay leaf

2–3 teaspoons sugar

1–2 tablespoons cider vinegar

4 ounces reduced-sodium, reduced-fat smoked sausage, thinly sliced

Per Serving:
Calories: 91
% calories from fat: 4
Protein (g): 7.5
Carbohydrate (g): 15.1
Fat (g): 0.4
Saturated fat (g): 0.1
Cholesterol (mg): 3.2
Sodium (mg): 248

Exchanges:
Milk: 0.0
Vegetable: 3.0
Fruit: 0.0
Bread: 0.0
Meat: 0.0
Fat: 0.0

Salt and pepper, to taste

½ cup fat-free sour cream

1. Sauté beets in lightly greased large saucepan 2 to 3 minutes; stir in cabbage, carrots, garlic, broth, bay leaf, sugar, and vinegar. Heat to boiling; reduce heat and simmer, uncovered, 30 minutes, adding sausage during last 10 minutes of cooking. Discard bay leaf; season to taste with salt and pepper. Garnish each bowl of soup with sour cream.

SOUP À L'OIGNON

The flavor secret to this soup is cooking the onions slowly until they are deeply browned and caramelized.

4 entrée servings

1 pound onions, thinly sliced

4 teaspoons margarine or butter

½ teaspoon dry mustard

2 teaspoons flour

1 quart Fragrant Beef Stock (see p. 6)

½ cup dry white wine (optional)

Salt and pepper, to taste

4 slices French bread, toasted

½ cup (2 ounces) shredded Parmesan cheese

Per Serving:
Calories: 243
% calories from fat: 30
Protein (g): 10.7
Carbohydrate (g): 25.2
Fat (g): 8.3
Saturated fat (g): 3.1
Cholesterol (mg): 10.9
Sodium (mg): 430

Exchanges:
Milk: 0.0
Vegetable: 2.0
Fruit: 0.0
Bread: 1.0
Meat: 0.5
Fat: 2.0

1. Cook onions in margarine in large saucepan over medium to medium-low heat until golden, 15 to 20 minutes; stir in mustard and flour and cook 1 to 2 minutes. Add stock and wine; heat to boiling. Reduce heat and simmer, covered, 30 minutes. Season to taste with salt and pepper. Sprinkle bread with cheese; broil until melted, 1 to 2 minutes. Top each bowl of soup with bread slices.

VARIATION

Onion and White Bean Soup — Make recipe as above, adding 1 can (15 ounces) rinsed, drained navy or Great Northern beans, ½ teaspoon dried savory leaves, and ¼ teaspoon dried thyme leaves with broth. Omit French bread and Parmesan cheese. Sprinkle top of each serving with 1 tablespoon grated Manchego cheese.

TUSCAN TOMATO SOUP

Every Tuscan cook has a different way of preparing this soup, but each version has two basic elements—ripe tomatoes and crusty bread.

6 first-course servings

1 large onion, chopped

2 cloves garlic, chopped

2 tablespoons olive oil

1 quart Chicken Stock (see p. 2)

3 pounds very ripe tomatoes, peeled, seeded, coarsely chopped

1 cup chopped fresh or 2 to 3 tablespoons dried basil leaves

Salt and pepper, to taste

6 slices Italian bread, toasted

Per Serving:
Calories: 195
% calories from fat: 25
Protein (g): 6.3
Carbohydrate (g): 31.4
Fat (g): 5.6
Saturated fat (g): 0.8
Cholesterol (mg): 0
Sodium (mg): 199

Exchanges:
Milk: 0.0
Vegetable: 3.0
Fruit: 0.0
Bread: 1.0
Meat: 0.0
Fat: 1.0

1. Sauté onion and garlic in olive oil in large saucepan until tender, about 5 minutes. Add stock and tomatoes; heat to boiling. Reduce heat and simmer, covered, 20 minutes. Process soup in food processor or blender until coarsely puréed; stir in basil; season to taste with salt and pepper. Place bread slices in bottoms of soup bowls; ladle soup over.

MATZO BALL AND VEGETABLE SOUP

We've added a variety of vegetables to this traditional Jewish soup.

6 first-course servings

1½–2 quarts Chicken Stock (see p. 2)

¼ cup each: sliced celery, carrot

1 cup frozen lima beans

1½ cups small cauliflower florets

Matzo Balls (recipe follows)

Salt and pepper, to taste

Per Serving:
Calories: 159
% calories from fat: 26
Protein (g): 8.7
Carbohydrate (g): 20.6
Fat (g): 4.7
Saturated fat (g): 0.8
Cholesterol (mg): 44.7
Sodium (mg): 765

Exchanges:
Milk: 0.0
Vegetable: 0.0
Fruit: 0.0
Bread: 1.5
Meat: 0.0
Fat: 1.0

1. Heat all ingredients, except Matzo Balls, salt, and pepper to boiling in large saucepan; reduce heat and simmer, covered, until vegetables are tender about 15 minutes. Add Matzo Balls; simmer, covered, 5 minutes. Season to taste with salt and pepper.

Matzo Balls
Makes 12

2 eggs
1 tablespoon canola oil
½ cup matzo meal
¼ teaspoon salt
2½ tablespoons Chicken Stock (see p. 2)

1. Mix all ingredients; refrigerate, covered, 1 hour. Form dough into 12 balls; drop into simmering water and cook, uncovered, 30 to 35 minutes. Remove with slotted spoon and drain.

ASIAN MUSHROOM SOUP WITH NOODLES

Thin egg noodles or spaghetti can be substituted for the soba noodles.

6 entrée servings

3 cups boiling water
1 ounce dried shiitake mushrooms
1½ pounds cremini mushrooms, minced, divided
½ small onion, minced
1 clove garlic, minced
1–2 tablespoons margarine or butter
¼ teaspoon dried thyme leaves
1 quart Low-Salt Chicken Stock (see p. 3)
½ cup dry white wine (optional)
4 ounces soba noodles
8 ounces snow peas, trimmed
½ cup sliced radishes
1 tablespoon red wine vinegar
Salt and pepper, to taste

Per Serving:
Calories: 195
% calories from fat: 10
Protein (g): 11.3
Carbohydrate (g): 27.7
Fat (g): 2.3
Saturated fat (g): 0.5
Cholesterol (mg): 2.3
Sodium (mg): 118

Exchanges:
Milk: 0.0
Vegetable: 3.0
Fruit: 0.0
Bread: 1.0
Meat: 0.0
Fat: 1.0

1. Pour boiling water over shiitake mushrooms in bowl and let stand until softened, about 15 minutes. Drain; strain liquid through fine strainer and reserve. Finely chop mushrooms, discarding tough stems.

2. Sauté shiitake mushrooms, 1 pound cremini mushrooms, onion, and garlic in margarine in large saucepan until soft, 5 to 8 minutes. Add thyme, stock, wine, and reserved mushroom liquid; heat to boiling. Reduce heat and simmer, covered, 30 minutes. Strain soup, reserving mushrooms for another use. Add remaining ingredients, except salt and pepper; simmer, uncovered, until noodles are *al dente*, about 5 minutes. Season to taste with salt and pepper.

EAST MEETS WEST SOUP

This creamy, hotly spiced soup is garnished with crisp Chili-Seasoned Wontons.

6 first-course servings

1 cup each: thinly sliced onions, celery
1 small jalapeño chili, minced
1 tablespoon each: minced gingerroot, garlic
1 teaspoon ground cumin
2 teaspoons margarine or butter
¼ cup all-purpose flour
3 cups Low-Salt Chicken Stock (see p. 3)
2½ cups fat-free milk
2 cans (4 ounces each) chopped green chilies, drained
Salt and pepper, to taste
¼ cup chopped cilantro
Chili-Seasoned Wontons (recipe follows)

Per Serving:
Calories: 192
% calories from fat: 18
Protein (g): 8.2
Carbohydrate (g): 31.2
Fat (g): 3.7
Saturated fat (g): 0.7
Cholesterol (mg): 5.7
Sodium (mg): 369

Exchanges:
Milk: 0.0
Vegetable: 0.0
Fruit: 0.0
Bread: 2.0
Meat: 0.0
Fat: 1.0

1. Sauté onions, celery, jalapeño chili, gingerroot, garlic, and cumin in margarine in large saucepan until tender, about 5 minutes. Stir in flour and cook 2 minutes. Stir in stock, milk, and green chilies and heat to boiling, stirring until thickened, about 1 minute; reduce heat and simmer, uncovered, 5 minutes. Season to taste with salt and pepper; stir in cilantro. Serve with Chili-Seasoned Wontons.

Chili-Seasoned Wontons

Makes 36

1 teaspoon hot chili powder
½ teaspoon garlic powder
¼ teaspoon cayenne pepper
2 teaspoons canola oil
2 teaspoons water
18 wonton wrappers, cut diagonally into halves

1. Combine all ingredients, except wonton wrappers; brush both sides of wonton wrappers with mixture and place on cookie sheet. Bake at 375 degrees until crisp, about 5 minutes; cool on wire racks.

FRENCH VEGETABLE SOUP

Made with a traditional French veal stock, cubes of veal, and lots of fresh vegetables, this soup is a special treat.

8 entrée servings

1 pound lean veal, cubed
½ cup each: chopped onion, sliced celery, carrot
1 teaspoon dried thyme leaves
½ teaspoon dried savory leaves
2 teaspoons olive oil
2 quarts Veal Stock (see p. 7)
1 can (14½ ounces) reduced-sodium diced
   tomatoes, undrained
1½ cups cubed, peeled potatoes
1 cup each: small broccoli and cauliflower florets,
   cut green beans, frozen peas
Salt and pepper, to taste

Per Serving:
Calories: 199
% calories from fat: 18
Protein: (g): 21.5
Carbohydrate (g): 19.4
Fat (g): 4.2
Saturated fat (g): 1.2
Cholesterol (mg): 66.1
Sodium (mg): 84

Exchanges:
Milk: 0.0
Vegetable: 1.0
Fruit: 0.0
Bread: 1.0
Meat: 2.0
Fat: 0.0

1. Sauté veal, onion, celery, carrot, thyme, and savory in oil in large saucepan until veal is browned, about 10 minutes. Stir in stock and heat to boiling; reduce heat and simmer, covered, until veal is tender, about 30 minutes. Stir in remaining ingredients, except salt and pepper; heat to boiling. Reduce heat and simmer, covered, until vegetables are tender, about 15 minutes; season to taste with salt and pepper.

MINESTRONE

45 *Minestrone does not always contain pasta, nor is it always a heavy, hearty soup. Enjoy this light version of an old favorite.*

8 first-course servings

1 cup sliced carrots

½ cup each: chopped onion, celery, sliced fennel bulb

2 cloves garlic, minced

1 tablespoon olive oil

5 cups reduced-sodium fat-free beef broth

1 small zucchini, sliced

1 cup each: snap peas, broccoli florets

1 cup halved cherry tomatoes

¾–1 teaspoon each: dried basil and oregano leaves

¼ cup finely chopped parsley

Salt and pepper, to taste

1½ cups Parmesan Croutons (½ recipe) (see p. 636)

Per Serving:
Calories: 146
% calories from fat: 21
Protein (g): 7.3
Carbohydrate (g): 4.9
Fat (g): 3.5
Saturated fat (g): 0.6
Cholesterol (mg): 0.5
Sodium (mg): 447

Exchanges:
Milk: 0.0
Vegetable: 1.0
Fruit: 0.0
Bread: 1.0
Meat: 0.0
Fat: 0.5

1. Sauté carrots, onion, celery, fennel, and garlic in oil in Dutch oven until onion is tender, about 8 minutes. Add broth, vegetables, and herbs; heat to boiling. Reduce heat and simmer, covered, until vegetables are tender, 10 to 15 minutes; season to taste with salt and pepper. Sprinkle each bowl of soup with croutons.

MINESTRONE WITH PESTO

In the basil-loving town of Genoa, the addition of pungent pesto distinguishes the local version of minestrone.

12 entrée servings

¾ cup each: chopped leeks (white parts only), carrots, celery, chopped yellow bell pepper

2 large cloves garlic, minced

3 quarts Chicken Stock (see p. 2)

1 pound yellow summer squash, cubed

1 cup frozen peas

2 cans (15 ounces each) cannellini beans, rinsed, drained

2 cups uncooked elbow macaroni
Fat-Free Pesto (recipe follows), divided
Salt and pepper, to taste
Shredded Parmesan cheese, as garnish

Per Serving:
Calories: 224
% calories from fat: 19
Protein (g): 14
Carbohydrate (g): 37.6
Fat (g): 5.2
Saturated fat (g): 5
Cholesterol (mg): 23.8
Sodium (mg): 1269

Exchanges:
Milk: 0.0
Vegetable: 1.0
Fruit: 0.0
Bread: 2.0
Meat: 1.0
Fat: 0.0

1. Sauté leeks, carrots, celery, bell pepper, and garlic in lightly greased Dutch oven until vegetables are tender, about 10 minutes. Add stock and heat to boiling; add squash, peas, beans, and macaroni. Reduce heat and simmer, uncovered, until squash is tender and macaroni is *al dente*, 7 to 10 minutes. Stir in ½ cup Fat-Free Pesto; season to taste with salt and pepper. Sprinkle each bowl of soup with Parmesan cheese; pass remaining Pesto.

Fat-Free Pesto

Makes about 1¼ cups

2 cups loosely packed basil leaves
4 large cloves garlic
½ cup reduced-sodium fat-free chicken broth
Salt and pepper, to taste

1. Process basil and garlic in food processor or blender until finely chopped; gradually add chicken broth, processing until almost smooth. Season to taste with salt and pepper.

RUSSIAN CABBAGE SOUP

Use red or green cabbage and fresh or canned beets in this savory soup.

8 first-course servings

2 medium onions, sliced

1 tablespoon margarine or butter

7 cups reduced-sodium fat-free beef broth

1 can (14½ ounces) reduced-sodium diced
  tomatoes, undrained

6 cups thinly sliced red cabbage

4 large beets, peeled, cubed

1 cup each: sliced carrots, cubed turnip, potato

1 tablespoon cider vinegar

Salt and pepper, to taste

8 tablespoons fat-free sour cream

Per Serving:
Calories: 109
% calories from fat: 17
Protein (g): 4
Carbohydrate (g): 20.7
Fat (g): 2.2
Saturated fat (g): 0.4
Cholesterol (mg): 0
Sodium (mg): 91

Exchanges:
Milk: 0.0
Vegetable: 3.0
Fruit: 0.0
Bread: 0.5
Meat: 0.0
Fat: 0.0

1. Sauté onions in margarine in Dutch oven until tender, about 5
minutes. Add broth, tomatoes with liquid, vegetables, and vinegar;
heat to boiling. Reduce heat and simmer, covered, until beets are
tender, 20 to 30 minutes; season to taste with salt and pepper. Top
each bowl of soup with a tablespoon of sour cream.

BOURBON STREET SOUP

*Okra, rice, tomatoes, and crushed red pepper add Southern accents to
this vegetable beef soup. Serve with hot pepper sauce for added hotness,
if you like!*

6 entrée servings

1 pound lean beef stew meat, cubed (1-inch)

1 quart water

1½ cups chopped onions

¾ cup chopped green bell pepper

3 cloves garlic, minced

1 can (28 ounces) reduced-sodium diced tomatoes, undrained

1 can (14½ ounces) reduced-sodium stewed tomatoes

1 teaspoon dried thyme leaves

¼–½ teaspoon crushed red pepper

1 bay leaf

1½ cups each: whole kernel corn, sliced okra

⅓ cup uncooked rice

Salt and pepper, to taste

Per Serving:
Calories: 264
% calories from fat: 15
Protein (g): 24.1
Carbohydrate (g): 34.5
Fat (g): 4.4
Saturated fat (g): 1.4
Cholesterol (mg): 47.3
Sodium (mg): 77

1. Heat all ingredients, except corn, okra, rice, salt, and pepper to boiling in large saucepan. Reduce heat and simmer, covered, until meat is very tender, 1 to 1½ hours, adding corn, okra, and rice during the last 25 minutes. Discard bay leaf; season to taste with salt and pepper.

Exchanges:
Milk: 0.0
Vegetable: 1.0
Fruit: 0.0
Bread: 2.0
Meat: 2.0
Fat: 0.0

PORTUGUESE SOUP

This flavorful kale soup is a simplified version of the Portuguese favorite, Caldo Verde. Linguiça, a Portuguese sausage, can be used for the most authentic flavor; brown it in a skillet and drain well.

4 entrée servings

8 ounces reduced-fat smoked sausage, sliced, browned

1 cup chopped onion

½ cup chopped red bell pepper

2 tablespoons minced garlic

2 teaspoons olive oil

1 quart Beef Stock (see p. 5)

3 medium potatoes, peeled, cubed

1 can (15 ounces) red kidney beans, rinsed, drained

¼ cup tomato sauce

3 cups sliced kale or spinach

Salt and pepper, to taste

Hot pepper sauce, to taste

Per Serving:
Calories: 326
% calories from fat: 15
Protein (g): 18.7
Carbohydrate (g): 53
Fat (g): 5.7
Saturated fat (g): 1.2
Cholesterol (mg): 26.8
Sodium (mg): 850

Exchanges:
Milk: 0.0
Vegetable: 2.0
Fruit: 0.0
Bread: 3.0
Meat: 1.0
Fat: 0.5

1. Cook sausage, onion, bell pepper, and garlic in oil in large saucepan over medium heat until sausage is browned and onion tender, about 8 minutes. Stir in stock, potatoes, beans, and tomato sauce; heat to boiling; reduce heat and simmer, covered, until potatoes are tender, about 15 minutes, adding kale during last 5 minutes. Season to taste with salt, pepper, and hot pepper sauce.

POZOLE

This Mexican soup is traditionally made with a pig's head or pork hocks; our version contains lean pork tenderloin and chicken breast instead. The soup always contains hominy and is served with a variety of crisp vegetable garnishes.

4 entrée servings

2 ancho chilies, stems, seeds, and veins discarded

1 cup each: boiling water, chopped onion

1 clove garlic, minced

2 cans (14½ ounces each) reduced-sodium fat-free chicken broth

8 ounces each: cubed pork tenderloin and boneless, skinless chicken breast (1-inch)

1 can (15 ounces) hominy, drained

1 can (14½ ounces) reduced-sodium diced tomatoes, undrained

½ teaspoon each: dried oregano and thyme leaves

Salt and pepper, to taste

6 lime wedges

¼ cup each: thinly sliced lettuce, cabbage, green onion, radish, shredded carrot

Per Serving:
Calories: 181
% calories from fat: 16
Protein (g): 21.2
Carbohydrate (g): 16.7
Fat (g): 3.2
Saturated fat (g): 0.9
Cholesterol (mg): 44.8
Sodium (mg): 244

Exchanges:
Milk: 0.0
Vegetable: 1.0
Fruit: 0.0
Bread: 1.0
Meat: 2.5
Fat: 0.0

1. Cover chilies with boiling water in small bowl; let stand until softened, about 10 minutes. Process chilies and water in food processor or blender until smooth; reserve.

2. Sauté onion and garlic in lightly greased large saucepan until tender; add broth and meats and heat to boiling. Reduce heat and simmer, covered, until meats are tender, 10 to 15 minutes; strain, returning broth to saucepan. Shred meats with fork and return to saucepan. Add reserved chili mixture, hominy, tomatoes with liquid, and herbs; cook, covered, over medium heat 10 minutes. Season to taste with salt and pepper. Serve with lime wedges and fresh vegetables for each person to add to the soup.

INDIAN-STYLE POTATO-SPINACH SOUP WITH CHICKEN

An unusual combination of herbs and spices gives this hearty soup an exotic flavor and aroma.

6 entrée servings

12 ounces diced boneless skinless chicken breast

1 cup chopped onion

2 large garlic cloves, minced

1 teaspoon canola oil

½ teaspoon each: caraway seeds, ground cardamom

1½ tablespoons mild or hot curry powder

2 teaspoons ground coriander

1½ quarts Chicken Stock (see p. 2)

3 cups coarsely cubed, peeled baking potatoes

½ package (10 ounce-size) frozen chopped spinach

1 can (14½ ounces) diced tomatoes, undrained

Salt and pepper, to taste

Per Serving:
Calories: 209
% calories from fat: 13
Protein (g): 19.5
Carbohydrate (g): 23.9
Fat (g): 2.9
Saturated fat (g): 0.6
Cholesterol (mg): 42.9
Sodium (mg): 167

Exchanges:
Milk: 0.0
Vegetable: 0.0
Fruit: 0.0
Bread: 1.5
Meat: 2.0
Fat: 0.0

1. Cook chicken, onion, and garlic, over medium heat in oil in large saucepan until chicken is browned, about 5 minutes. Add spices and cook 1 minute. Add stock and potatoes; heat to boiling. Reduce heat and simmer until potatoes are tender, 10 to 15 minutes. Add spinach and tomatoes with liquid; simmer, covered, until spinach is cooked, about 8 minutes. Season to taste with salt and pepper.

MULLIGATAWNY

Colorful and lightly spiced with curry powder, this popular soup originated in India.

4 entrée servings

1½ cups each: coarsely chopped onions, tart apples

½ cup each: sliced celery, carrots, red bell pepper

1 large garlic clove, minced

2 teaspoons canola oil

2½ teaspoons curry powder

1 teaspoon chili powder

½ teaspoon each: ground allspice, dried thyme leaves

1 quart Chicken Stock (see p. 2)

1 cup water

½ cup diced, peeled red potatoes

1 pound boneless, skinless chicken breast halves

1 can (14½ ounces) diced tomatoes, undrained

¼ cup coarsely chopped parsley

Salt and pepper, to taste

Per Serving:
Calories: 189
% calories from fat: 19
Protein (g): 17.4
Carbohydrate (g): 22.3
Fat (g): 4
Saturated fat (g): 0.7
Cholesterol (mg): 33.5
Sodium (mg): 363

Exchanges:
Milk: 0.0
Vegetable: 0.0
Fruit: 0.5
Bread: 1.3
Meat: 1.0
Fat: 0.0

1. Sauté onions, apples, celery, carrots, bell pepper, and garlic in oil in large saucepan until tender, about 10 minutes. Add spices and cook 1 minute; add remaining ingredients, except parsley, salt, and pepper and heat to boiling. Reduce heat and simmer, covered, until chicken is cooked, about 20 minutes. Remove chicken and shred coarsely; reserve. Process soup in food processor or blender until smooth; return to saucepan. Add reserved chicken; cook, covered, over medium heat until hot, about 5 minutes. Stir in parsley; season to taste with salt and pepper.

SPICY NORTH AFRICAN-STYLE CHICKEN SOUP

The tangy flavors and hearty textures of North African cuisine combine in this chicken soup.

6 entrée servings

3 cups coarsely chopped onions

2 large garlic cloves, minced

2 teaspoons olive oil

1½ quarts Chicken Stock (see p. 2) or reduced-sodium fat-free chicken broth

1 pound boneless, skinless chicken breast halves, fat trimmed, cubed

½ cup each: bulgur wheat, celery

1 can (14½ ounces) reduced-sodium stewed tomatoes, undrained

1 cinnamon stick

2 large bay leaves

¾ teaspoon each: dried marjoram and thyme leaves

⅛ teaspoon ground cloves

Salt and pepper, to taste

Per Serving:
Calories: 165
% calories from fat: 16
Protein (g): 17.5
Carbohydrate (g): 18.1
Fat (g): 3
Saturated fat (g): 0.6
Cholesterol (mg): 29.6
Sodium (mg): 335

Exchanges:
Milk: 0.0
Vegetable: 1.0
Fruit: 0.0
Bread: 1.0
Meat: 1.0
Fat: 0.0

1. Sauté onions and garlic in oil in large saucepan until onions are soft, about 12 minutes. Add remaining ingredients, except salt and pepper, and heat to boiling. Reduce heat, and simmer, covered, 25 to 30 minutes or until bulgur is tender. Discard cinnamon stick and bay leaves; season to taste with salt and pepper.

WEST AFRICAN CURRIED CHICKEN SOUP

Pineapple and curry team up to give this soup its pleasing flavor.

4 entrée servings

⅓ cup each: diced celery, finely chopped onion

1 clove garlic, minced

2 teaspoons margarine or butter

1–2 teaspoons curry powder

3 tablespoons flour

1 quart Chicken Stock (see p. 2)

8 ounces boneless, skinless chicken breast, cubed

1 can (8 ounces) crushed pineapple, drained

¾ cup whole milk

Salt and pepper, to taste

Per Serving:
Calories: 168
% calories from fat: 22
Protein (g): 16.6
Carbohydrate (g): 16.3
Fat (g): 4.1
Saturated fat (g): 1.4
Cholesterol (mg): 34.2
Sodium (mg): 310

Exchanges:
Milk: 0.0
Vegetable: 0.0
Fruit: 0.0
Bread: 1.0
Meat: 2.0
Fat: 0.0

1. Sauté celery, onion, and garlic in margarine in large saucepan over medium heat until onion is soft, about 5 minutes; stir in curry powder and flour and cook 1 minute. Add stock and chicken and heat to boiling; reduce heat and simmer, covered, until chicken is cooked, about 20 minutes. Stir in pineapple and milk; season to taste with salt and pepper. Refrigerate until chilled.

ORIENTAL SOUP WITH NOODLES AND CHICKEN

The dried chow mein noodles in this soup are not the fried ones we have used with chop suey for many years. Be sure the correct noodles are used.

4 entrée servings

1 ounce dried cloud ear or shiitake mushrooms

½ cup each: sliced white mushrooms, julienned or sliced carrots

6 ounces cooked, shredded chicken breast

2 cans (14½ ounces each) reduced-sodium chicken broth

2 tablespoons dry sherry (optional)

1½ teaspoons light soy sauce

½ teaspoon five-spice powder

2 ounces snow peas, trimmed

½ package (5ounce-size) dried chow mein noodles

Salt and pepper, to taste

1. Place dried mushrooms in bowl; pour hot water over to cover. Let stand until mushrooms are soft, about 15 minutes; drain. Slice mushrooms, discarding any tough parts.

2. Sauté dried and white mushrooms, carrots, and chicken in lightly greased medium skillet until chicken is browned, about 5 minutes. Add broth, sherry, soy sauce, and five-spice powder. Heat to boiling; reduce heat and simmer, covered, 20 minutes, adding snow peas and noodles during last 10 minutes. Season to taste with salt and pepper.

Per Serving:
Calories: 213
% calories from fat: 30
Protein (g): 16.4
Carbohydrate (g): 19.7
Fat (g): 7.6
Saturated fat (g): 1.2
Cholesterol (mg): 29.2
Sodium (mg): 259

Exchanges:
Milk: 0.0
Vegetable: 0.5
Fruit: 0.0
Bread: 1.0
Meat: 1.5
Fat: 1.0

SOPA DE CASA

45 *Chicken, green chilies, and Monterey Jack cheese offer a pleasing flavor combination.*

6 entrée servings

3 cups whole kernel corn, thawed, divided
1 can (14½ ounces) reduced-sodium fat-free chicken broth
1 pound boneless, skinless chicken breast, cubed (¾-inch)
1 cup chopped onion
½ jalapeño chili, minced
2 large cloves garlic, minced
1 tablespoon olive oil
1 cup fat-free half-and-half or fat-free milk
1 can (4 ounces) chopped green chilies, undrained
1 large tomato, chopped
¾ teaspoon dried oregano leaves
½ teaspoon ground cumin
1 cup (4 ounces) shredded reduced-fat Monterey Jack cheese
Salt and pepper, to taste

Per Serving:
Calories: 281
% calories from fat: 24
Protein (g): 28.8
Carbohydrate (g): 24.5
Fat (g): 7.7
Saturated fat (g): 3.4
Cholesterol (mg): 59.5
Sodium (mg): 376

Exchanges:
Milk: 0.0
Vegetable: 2.0
Fruit: 0.0
Bread: 1.0
Meat: 3.0
Fat: 0.0

1. Process 1½ cups corn and chicken broth in food processor or blender until smooth; reserve. Cook chicken, onion, jalapeño chili, and garlic in oil in large saucepan over medium heat until chicken is browned, 8 to 10 minutes. Stir in reserved corn purée, remaining 1½ cups corn, half-and-half, chilies with liquid, tomato, and herbs and heat to boiling. Reduce heat and simmer, covered, 10 minutes; add cheese, stirring until melted. Season to taste with salt and pepper.

MEXICAN-STYLE CHICKEN AND LIME SOUP

Lightly seasoned with lime, this soup has an abundance of chicken and vegetables.

8 entrée servings

½ cup each: chopped onion, green bell pepper

2 teaspoons olive oil

2 quarts Low-Salt Chicken Stock (see p. 3)

1½ pounds boneless, skinless chicken breast, cubed

2 large tomatoes, peeled, seeded, chopped

1 cup each: whole kernel corn, diced zucchini

¼ cup each: chopped cilantro, lime juice

Salt and pepper, to taste

4 each: corn tortillas (6-inch), each cut into 10 wedges

Vegetable cooking spray

Thin lime slices, as garnish

Per Serving:
Calories: 185
% calories from fat: 13
Protein (g): 24.9
Carbohydrate (g): 15.5
Fat (g): 2.8
Saturated fat (g): 0.5
Cholesterol (mg): 49.3
Sodium (mg): 609

Exchanges:
Milk: 0.0
Vegetable: 0.0
Fruit: 0.0
Bread: 1.0
Meat: 2.0
Fat: 0.0

1. Sauté onion and bell pepper in oil in large saucepan until tender, about 5 minutes. Add stock, chicken, tomatoes, corn, and zucchini; heat to boiling. Reduce heat and simmer, covered, until chicken is cooked, about 20 minutes. Add cilantro and lime juice; season to taste with salt and pepper.

2. Spray tortillas lightly with cooking spray and toss; cook in lightly greased large skillet over medium heat until browned and crisp, about 5 minutes. Add tortilla wedges to soup bowls; ladle soup over. Float lime slices on top of soup.

TORTILLA SOUP

45 *Crisply fried tortilla chips add "crunch" to this soup.*

6 first-course servings

2 corn or flour tortillas (6-inch), cut into strips
(2 x ¼-inch)
Vegetable cooking spray
¾ cup each: chopped onion, celery, tomato
½ teaspoon each: dried basil leaves, ground cumin
5 cups reduced-sodium fat-free chicken broth
1 can (15 ounces) pinto beans, rinsed, drained
6 ounces cooked chicken breast, shredded or cubed
¼ cup finely chopped cilantro
1–2 teaspoons lime juice
Salt and cayenne pepper, to taste

Per Serving:
Calories: 176
% calories from fat: 10
Protein (g): 19.1
Carbohydrate (g): 22.6
Fat (g): 2
Saturated fat (g): 0.3
Cholesterol (mg): 24.1
Sodium (mg): 386

Exchanges:
Milk: 0.0
Vegetable: 1.0
Fruit: 0.0
Bread: 1.0
Meat: 2.0
Fat: 0.0

1. Spray tortillas lightly with cooking spray and toss; cook in lightly greased medium skillet over medium heat until browned and crisp, about 5 minutes; reserve.

2. Sauté onion, celery, tomato, basil, and cumin in lightly greased saucepan until onion is tender, 3 to 5 minutes. Add broth, beans, and chicken and heat to boiling; reduce heat and simmer, uncovered, 5 minutes. Stir in cilantro; season to taste with lime juice, salt and cayenne pepper. Add tortilla strips to soup bowls; ladle soup over.

TUSCAN LENTIL SOUP

A basic lentil soup at its best—a real cold weather comfort food!

10 entrée servings

1 large onion, diced

½ cup each: chopped red bell pepper, sliced carrots

2 cloves garlic, minced

2 tablespoons olive oil

1 pound dried lentils

1 quart Chicken Stock (see p. 2)

3 cups water

1 can (14½ ounces) crushed tomatoes

Salt and pepper, to taste

Grated Parmesan cheese, as garnish

Per Serving:
Calories: 211
% calories from fat: 15
Protein (g): 13.3
Carbohydrate (g): 33.6
Fat (g): 3.6
Saturated fat (g): 0.5
Cholesterol (mg): 0
Sodium (mg): 409

Exchanges:
Milk: 0.0
Vegetable: 1.5
Fruit: 0.0
Bread: 1.5
Meat: 1.0
Fat: 0.5

1. Sauté onion, bell pepper, carrots, and garlic in oil in large sauce-pan until tender, about 5 minutes; add lentils, stock, and water, and heat to boiling. Reduce heat and simmer, covered, until lentils are tender, about 30 minutes, adding tomatoes during last 5 minutes. Season to taste with salt and pepper; sprinkle each bowl of soup with Parmesan cheese.

ITALIAN-STYLE VEGETABLE SOUP

Convenience foods help put this soup on the table in record time.

8 entrée servings

1 each: chopped large onion, minced garlic clove

2 teaspoons olive oil

1½ quarts Rich Chicken Stock (see p. 4)

1 can (15 ounces) tomato sauce

2 large carrots, peeled, chopped

1 can (19 ounces) cannellini beans, rinsed, drained

1 package (16 ounces) frozen mixed broccoli, corn, and red bell peppers

1½ cups chopped cabbage

1 teaspoon each: dried Italian seasoning

Per Serving:
Calories: 178
% calories from fat: 9
Protein (g): 12.5
Carbohydrate (g): 33.9
Fat (g): 2.1
Saturated fat (g): 0.2
Cholesterol (mg): 0
Sodium (mg): 529

Exchanges:
Milk: 0.0
Vegetable: 3.0
Fruit: 0.0
Bread: 1.0
Meat: 0.0
Fat: 0.5

Salt and pepper, to taste

2 cups seasoned crouton stuffing mix

1. Sauté onion and garlic in olive oil in Dutch oven until onion is tender, about 5 minutes. Add remaining ingredients, except salt, pepper, and stuffing mix; heat to boiling. Reduce heat and simmer, covered, until cabbage is tender, about 20 minutes. Season to taste with salt and pepper. Spoon ¼ cup stuffing mix into each soup bowl; ladle soup over.

PASTA FAGIOLI OLE!

A traditional Pasta Fagioli, with some Mexican-style flavor twists!

6 first-course servings

2 cans (15 ounces each) pinto beans, rinsed, drained

3 cups Low-Salt Chicken Stock (see p. 3)

2½ cups diced tomatoes

1 cup each: chopped onions, green bell pepper, sliced carrots

½ cup chopped celery

1 clove garlic, minced

1 medium jalapeño chili, finely chopped

2 teaspoons dried oregano leaves

1 cup cooked elbow macaroni

¼ cup chopped cilantro

Salt and cayenne pepper, to taste

Per Serving:
Calories: 211
% calories from fat: 7
Protein (g): 11.3
Carbohydrate (g): 39.6
Fat (g): 1.7
Saturated fat (g): 0.3
Cholesterol (mg): 0.0
Sodium (mg): 725

Exchanges:
Milk: 0.0
Vegetable: 0.0
Fruit: 0.0
Bread: 2.5
Meat: 1.0
Fat: 0.0

1. Heat all ingredients, except macaroni, cilantro, salt, and pepper to boiling in large saucepan; reduce heat and simmer, covered, 20 minutes. Add macaroni and cilantro and simmer until hot, about 5 minutes. Season to taste with salt and cayenne pepper.

SHRIMP AND BLACK BEAN SOUP

45 *In Mexico, leaves from the avocado tree are used for seasoning this favorite Oaxacan soup. We've substituted a bay leaf, which is somewhat stronger in flavor.*

6 entrée servings

2 medium onions, chopped

4 cloves garlic, minced

2 medium tomatoes, cut into wedges

3 cans (14½ ounces each) reduced-sodium fat-free chicken broth, divided

2 cans (15 ounces each) black beans, rinsed, drained

1 teaspoon each: dried oregano and thyme leaves, ground cumin

1 bay leaf

8 ounces peeled, deveined shrimp

Salt and pepper, to taste

Chopped cilantro, as garnish

Per Serving:
Calories: 162
% calories from fat: 4
Protein (g): 17.0
Carbohydrate (g): 26.6
Fat (g): 0.9
Saturated fat (g): 0.2
Cholesterol (mg): 57.5
Sodium (mg): 1071

Exchanges:
Milk: 0.0
Vegetable: 0.0
Fruit: 0.0
Bread: 1.5
Meat: 1.0
Fat: 0.0

1. Sauté onions and garlic in lightly greased large saucepan until tender, about 5 minutes. Process onion mixture, tomatoes, and 1 can chicken broth in food processor or blender until smooth; return to saucepan. Add remaining 2 cans broth, beans, and herbs; heat to boiling. Reduce heat and simmer, covered, 15 minutes, adding shrimp during last 5 minutes. Discard bay leaf. Season to taste with salt and pepper; sprinkle each bowl of soup with cilantro.

ITALIAN MUSHROOM SOUP

This is a very sophisticated soup that is ideal for entertaining.

4 first-course servings

2 medium onions, chopped

1 pound cremini mushrooms, thinly sliced

1 quart Rich Chicken Stock (see p. 4)

⅓ cup each: tomato purée, sweet vermouth
  or chicken broth

1 tablespoon minced fresh or 1 teaspoon dried
  basil leaves

¼ cup minced chives or green onions

Shredded Parmesan cheese, as garnish

Per Serving:
Calories: 139
% calories from fat: 19
Protein (g): 9.8
Carbohydrate (g): 13.3
Fat (g): 3
Saturated fat (g): 0.5
Cholesterol (mg): 1
Sodium (mg): 138

Exchanges:
Milk: 0.0
Vegetable: 3.0
Fruit: 0.0
Bread: 0.0
Meat: 0.0
Fat: 1.0

1. Sauté onions and mushrooms in lightly greased large saucepan until tender, about 10 minutes. Add stock, tomato purée, and vermouth; heat to boiling. Reduce heat and simmer, covered, 5 minutes. Stir in basil and chives; sprinkle each bowl of soup with Parmesan cheese.

SEVEN

Seafood Soups

CLAM SOUP

45

You can make this dish with mussels as well, or make the soup with 1 pound peeled, deveined shrimp, simmering just until shrimp are cooked and tender, about 5 minutes.

4 entrée servings

3 large garlic cloves

2 tablespoons olive oil

4 dozen clams (littlenecks or cherrystones), scrubbed

1 cup each: tomato sauce, dry white wine

¼ cup minced parsley

⅛–¼ teaspoon crushed red pepper

1 teaspoon each: dried oregano and thyme leaves

Salt and pepper, to taste

4 slices Italian bread, toasted

Per Serving:
Calories: 275
% calories from fat: 26
Protein (g): 15.2
Carbohydrate (g): 25.9
Fat (g): 7.9
Saturated fat (g): 1.1
Cholesterol (mg): 28.9
Sodium (mg): 575

Exchanges:
Milk: 0.0
Vegetable: 0.0
Fruit: 0.0
Bread: 2.0
Meat: 2.0
Fat: 0.5

1. Sauté garlic in oil in large saucepan until browned, 2 to 3 minutes; discard garlic. Add remaining ingredients, except salt, pepper, and bread, and heat to boiling; reduce heat and simmer, covered, 5 minutes or until clams have opened. Discard any unopened clams; season to taste with salt and pepper. Serve broth and clams in shallow bowls with toasted bread.

FIFTEEN-MINUTE CLAM SOUP

Serve this delicious soup with crusty bread and dry white wine.

6 first-course servings

½ medium onion, finely chopped

2 cloves garlic, chopped

4 thin slices day-old bread, cubed (½-inch)

2 medium tomatoes, peeled, seeded, finely chopped

3 cups each: clam juice or Fish Stock
   (see p. 8), water

2–4 tablespoons dry sherry (optional)

1 teaspoon paprika

24 clams, or mussels, scrubbed

Per Serving:
Calories: 101
% calories from fat: 8
Protein (g): 6.6
Carbohydrate (g): 12.8
Fat (g): 0.9
Saturated fat (g): 0.1
Cholesterol (mg): 12.1
Sodium (mg): 374

Exchanges:
Milk: 0.0
Vegetable: 1.0
Fruit: 0.0
Bread: 0.5
Meat: 0.0
Fat: 0.5

Salt and pepper, to taste

Chopped parsley, as garnish

1. Sauté onion, garlic, and bread in lightly greased large saucepan until onion is soft, about 5 minutes. Add remaining ingredients, except salt, pepper, and parsley, and simmer, covered, until clams or mussels have opened, about 10 minutes. Discard any unopened shellfish. Season broth to taste with salt and pepper. Sprinkle each bowl of soup with parsley.

SEA SCALLOP AND PASTA SOUP

45 *Small bay scallops or other seafood can be used in this colorful soup.*

6 entrée servings

½ cup each: chopped onion, diced green and red pepper

½ teaspoon minced garlic

8 ounces mushrooms, sliced

2 tablespoons olive oil

1 can (14½ ounces) Italian plum tomatoes, undrained, chopped

2 cups reduced-sodium fat-free chicken broth

½ cup dry white wine or chicken broth

1 pound sea scallops, halved

¼ cup finely chopped parsley

8 ounces uncooked small soup pasta, cooked

¼–½ cup (1–2 ounces) grated Parmesan cheese

Salt and pepper, to taste

Per Serving:
Calories: 323
% calories from fat: 20
Protein (g): 24.1
Carbohydrate (g): 37.4
Fat (g): 74
Saturated fat (g): 1.3
Cholesterol (mg): 34.8
Sodium (mg): 382

Exchanges:
Milk: 0.0
Vegetable: 1.0
Fruit: 0.0
Bread: 2.0
Meat: 2.5
Fat: 0.0

1. Sauté onion, bell peppers, garlic, and mushrooms in oil in large saucepan until mushrooms are tender, about 10 minutes. Add remaining ingredients, except Parmesan cheese, salt, and pepper; heat to boiling. Remove from heat and let stand, covered, until scallops are opaque, about 5 minutes. Stir in Parmesan cheese; season to taste with salt and pepper.

SHRIMP CREOLE SOUP

45 *Canned ingredients makes this shrimp soup easy to prepare.*

4 entrée servings

1 can (14½ ounces) stewed tomatoes
1 can (10¾ ounces) condensed chicken gumbo soup
1 cup each: water, chopped onion
1 small red bell pepper, chopped
¼ cup uncooked rice
2 cloves garlic, minced
1 teaspoon each: dried basil and thyme leaves
1 bay leaf
1 pound peeled, deveined shrimp
Salt and hot pepper sauce, to taste

Per Serving:
Calories: 209
% calories from fat: 9
Protein (g): 22.1
Carbohydrate (g): 24.5
Fat (g): 2.2
Saturated fat (g): 0.6
Cholesterol (mg): 179.7
Sodium (mg): 956

Exchanges:
Milk: 0.0
Vegetable: 1.0
Fruit: 0.0
Bread: 1.0
Meat: 2.0
Fat: 0.0

1. Combine all ingredients, except shrimp, salt, and hot pepper sauce, in large saucepan; heat to boiling. Reduce heat and simmer, covered, until rice is tender, about 20 minutes. Stir in shrimp; simmer until shrimp are cooked, about 5 minutes. Discard bay leaf. Season to taste with salt and hot pepper sauce.

CURRIED SHRIMP AND BROCCOLI SOUP

45 *This creamy-textured soup takes advantage of the quick thickening ability of instant mashed potatoes.*

4 entrée servings

4 cups small broccoli florets and chopped stems
1 quart reduced-sodium fat-free chicken broth
1 garlic clove, minced
2½ teaspoons mild curry powder
¼ teaspoon ground allspice
1 cup 2% reduced-fat milk
1–1¼ cups instant mashed potatoes
16 ounces peeled, deveined shrimp
Salt and pepper, to taste

Per Serving:
Calories: 145
% calories from fat: 12
Protein (g): 19.4
Carbohydrate (g): 13.3
Fat (g): 1.9
Saturated fat (g): 0.8
Cholesterol (mg): 108.6
Sodium (mg): 440

Exchanges:
Milk: 0.0
Vegetable: 0.0
Fruit: 0.0
Bread: 1.0
Meat: 2.0
Fat: 0.0

1. Heat broccoli, broth, garlic, and spices to boiling in large saucepan; reduce heat and simmer, covered, until broccoli is tender, 5 to 7 minutes. Stir in milk and potatoes; cook over medium heat, stirring, until hot. Add shrimp and simmer until cooked, about 5 minutes; season to taste with salt and pepper.

RED SNAPPER SOUP

45 *This flavorful soup is incredibly easy to prepare.*

6 entrée servings

5 cups water

1 cup each: finely chopped onions, peeled potatoes

1 can (14½ ounces) reduced-sodium diced tomatoes, undrained

2 pounds skinless red snapper fillets, cubed (1-inch)

Salt and cayenne pepper, to taste

1. Heat water, onions, potatoes, and tomatoes with liquid to boiling in large saucepan; reduce heat and simmer, covered, until potatoes are tender, about 15 minutes. Add fish and simmer until fish is tender and flakes with a fork, 5 to 8 minutes. Season to taste with salt and cayenne pepper.

Per Serving:
Calories: 241
% calories from fat: 8
Protein (g): 33.4
Carbohydrate (g): 20.5
Fat (g): 2.2
Saturated fat (g): 0.3
Cholesterol (mg): 55.4
Sodium (mg): 352

Exchanges:
Milk: 0.0
Vegetable: 0.0
Fruit: 0.0
Bread: 1.0
Meat: 3.0
Fat: 0.0

CLAM BISQUE

45   *Substitute canned lobster, crabmeat, or shrimp for the clams to create variations of this bisque.*

4 entrée servings

2 tablespoons grated onion
2 teaspoons margarine or butter
2 cups fat-free milk
2 tablespoons flour
½ teaspoon celery salt
1 cup reduced-sodium fat-free chicken broth or water
2 cans (6½ ounces each) minced clams, undrained
Salt and pepper, to taste
Chopped parsley, as garnish

Per Serving:
Calories: 208
% calories from fat: 17
Protein (g): 28.8
Carbohydrate (g): 12.9
Fat (g): 3.8
Saturated fat (g): 0.7
Cholesterol (mg): 12.9
Sodium (mg): 506

Exchanges:
Milk: 0.0
Vegetable: 0.0
Fruit: 0.0
Bread: 1.0
Meat: 3.0
Fat: 0.0

1. Sauté onion in margarine in large saucepan 1 minute; stir in combined milk, flour, and celery salt and heat to boiling, stirring until slightly thickened, about 1 minute. Stir in clams and liquor; cook over medium heat until hot, about 5 minutes. Season to taste with salt and pepper. Sprinkle each bowl of bisque with parsley.

LINGUINE CLAM SOUP

45   *Buy only clams that are tightly closed, and after cooking, discard any that have not opened.*

6 entrée servings

36 little neck or cherrystone clams, scrubbed
6 cloves garlic, minced
1 cup dry white wine or clam juice
1 quart clam juice
⅛–¼ teaspoon crushed red pepper
Salt and black pepper, to taste
8 ounces linguine, broken into pieces, cooked
¼ cup minced parsley

Per Serving:
Calories: 210
% calories from fat: 8
Protein (g): 17.1
Carbohydrate (g): 25.2
Fat (g): 1.8
Saturated fat (g): 0.1
Cholesterol (mg): 34
Sodium (mg): 501

Exchanges:
Milk: 0.0
Vegetable: 0.0
Fruit: 0.0
Bread: 1.5
Meat: 2.0
Fat: 0.0

1. Heat clams, garlic, and wine to boiling in large saucepan. Reduce heat and simmer, covered, 4 to 5 minutes or until clams have opened. Remove clams from shells and reserve; discard any unopened clams. Add clam juice and red pepper to saucepan and heat to boiling; reduce heat and simmer, covered, 4 to 5 minutes. Stir in reserved clams; simmer, covered, 1 to 2 minutes. Season to taste with salt and pepper. Serve over linguine in shallow bowls; sprinkle with parsley.

MUSSEL SOUP WITH SAFFRON

45 *Brightly colored bits of vegetables and a savory broth bring out the flavor of the mussels in this tempting, eye-catching soup.*

4 first-course servings

1¼ cups clam juice

¾ cup water

⅔ cup dry white wine

2¼ pounds mussels, scrubbed

⅓ cup each: finely chopped carrot, celery

1 large garlic clove, minced

4 green onions, sliced

2 teaspoons margarine or butter

1 bay leaf

10 saffron threads, crumbled (optional)

¼ cup finely chopped tomatoes

Salt and cayenne pepper, to taste

Per Serving:
Calories: 146
% calories from fat: 25
Protein (g): 16
Carbohydrate (g): 5.8
Fat (g): 3.9
Saturated fat (g): 0.3
Cholesterol (mg): 58.3
Sodium (mg): 402

Exchanges:
Milk: 0.0
Vegetable: 0.0
Fruit: 0.0
Bread: 0.5
Meat: 2.0
Fat: 0.0

1. Heat clam juice, water, and wine to boiling in large saucepan; add mussels, reduce heat, and simmer, covered, 5 minutes or until mussels open. Drain and reserve cooking liquid. Remove mussels from shells and reserve; discard any unopened mussels.

2. Sauté carrot, celery, garlic, and green onions in margarine in large saucepan 5 minutes. Stir in reserved mussel liquid, bay leaf, and saffron and heat to boiling. Reduce heat and simmer, covered, 10 minutes. Add tomatoes and reserved mussels; simmer, covered, until hot, 2 to 3 minutes. Discard bay leaf; season to taste with salt and cayenne pepper.

GREEN LIP MUSSEL AND SAFFRON SOUP

45 *Green lip mussels are from New Zealand. Larger in size than many mussels, they are about two inches long and very delicious.*

4 entrée servings

1 each: sliced medium onion, chopped carrot

½ cup dry white wine or water

½ teaspoon dried thyme leaves

2 bay leaves

Pinch saffron (optional)

2 pounds green lip mussels, scrubbed

2 cups clam juice, divided

2 tablespoons cornstarch

2 cups 2% reduced-fat milk

Salt and pepper, to taste

Per Serving:
Calories: 218
% calories from fat: 21
Protein (g): 18.3
Carbohydrate (g): 19.5
Fat (g): 5
Saturated fat (g): 2
Cholesterol (mg): 40.9
Sodium (mg): 675

Exchanges:
Milk: 0.0
Vegetable: 1.0
Fruit: 0.0
Bread: 0.5
Meat: 2.0
Fat: 1.0

1. Heat onion, carrot, wine, thyme, bay leaves, and saffron to boiling in large saucepan; add mussels, reduce heat and simmer, covered, until mussels open, 3 to 5 minutes. Remove mussels from shells and reserve; discard any unopened mussels and bay leaves. Process soup with 1½ cups clam juice in food processor or blender until smooth; return to saucepan and heat to boiling. Stir in combined remaining ½ cup clam juice and cornstarch, stirring, until thickened, about 1 minute. Add reserved mussels and milk; reduce heat and simmer, covered, until hot, about 5 minutes. Season to taste with salt and pepper.

POTATO-MUSSEL SAFFRON SOUP

Saffron lends a beautiful color and flavor to this soup.

8 first-course servings

3 each: medium peeled diced potatoes, thinly sliced carrots,
    small leeks (white parts only), minced cloves garlic, shallots

1 quart water

1 can (14½ ounces) crushed tomatoes

½ cup chopped parsley

2 bay leaves

1 teaspoon fennel seeds

¼ teaspoon saffron (optional)

32 mussels, scrubbed

Salt and white pepper, to taste

Per Serving:
Calories: 222
% calories from fat: 30
Protein (g): 8.3
Carbohydrate (g): 31.4
Fat (g): 7.6
Saturated fat (g): 1.9
Cholesterol (mg): 45.9
Sodium (mg): 401

Exchanges:
Milk: 0.0
Vegetable: 3.0
Fruit: 0.0
Bread: 1 0
Meat: 0.0
Fat: 1.5

1. Sauté potatoes, carrots, leeks, garlic, and shallots in lightly greased large saucepan until leeks are tender, about 5 minutes. Add water and remaining ingredients, except mussels, salt, and white pepper; heat to boiling. Reduce heat and simmer, covered, until vegetables are tender, about 15 minutes. Add mussels and simmer until mussels open, 3 to 5 minutes; discard any unopened mussels and bay leaves; season to taste with salt and white pepper.

OYSTER SOUP

45 *A classic first course for Christmas dinner, or any month with an "r"! You can buy fresh shucked oysters at most large supermarkets during the holiday season.*

4 entrée servings

⅔ cup each: chopped celery, onion, carrots

2 teaspoons margarine or butter

3 tablespoons flour

1 pint shucked oysters, undrained

3 cups fat-free milk

1 cup fat-free half-and-half or fat-free milk

Salt and pepper, to taste

2 tablespoons chopped chives

Oyster crackers

Per Serving:
Calories: 190
% calories from fat: 16
Protein (g): 12.4
Carbohydrate (g). 25.6
Fat (g): 3.2
Saturated fat (g): 0.9
Cholesterol (mg): 17.5
Sodium (mg): 300

Exchanges:
Milk: 1.0
Vegetable: 0.0
Fruit: 1.0
Bread: 0.5
Meat: 1.0
Fat: 0.0

1. Sauté celery, onion, and carrots in margarine in medium saucepan until softened, about 5 minutes; sprinkle with flour and cook 2 minutes. Drain oysters and add liquor to pan, stirring well. Stir in milk and half-and-half; heat just to boiling. Reduce heat and simmer, covered, until vegetables are tender, about 10 minutes.

Stir in oysters and simmer, covered, until edges of oysters curl, 2 to 4 minutes; do not boil. Season to taste with salt and pepper; stir in chives. Serve with oyster crackers (not included in nutritional data).

OYSTER AND MUSHROOM BISQUE

45 *A creamy mushroom soup is enhanced with oysters and sherry.*

4 first-course servings

8 ounces mushrooms, sliced
1 teaspoon margarine or butter
1 tablespoon flour
1 cup reduced-sodium fat-free chicken broth
1 egg yolk
1 cup fat-free half-and-half or fat-free milk
1 pint oysters, undrained
2–3 tablespoons dry sherry (optional)
Salt and white pepper, to taste
Oyster crackers

Per Serving:
Calories: 140
% calories from fat: 23
Protein (g): 8.6
Carbohydrate (g): 14.2
Fat (g): 3.4
Saturated fat (g): 0.9
Cholesterol (mg): 67.4
Sodium (mg): 219

Exchanges:
Milk: 0.0
Vegetable: 0.0
Fruit: 0.0
Bread: 1.0
Meat: 0.5
Fat: 1.0

1. Sauté mushrooms in margarine in medium saucepan until tender, about 5 minutes; stir in flour and cook 1 minute. Process mushrooms, chicken broth, and egg yolk in food processor or blender until smooth; return to saucepan and stir in half-and-half. Cook, stirring, over medium heat until lightly thickened; do not boil. Add oysters and liquor and cook, covered, until edges of oysters curl, 2 to 4 minutes. Stir in sherry; season to taste with salt and white pepper. Serve with oyster crackers (not included in nutritional data).

MARDI GRAS OYSTER SOUP

45 *Oysters, a New Orleans favorite, are combined with clam juice and wine in this special celebration soup.*

6 first-course servings

1½ pounds shucked fresh or canned oysters, liquor reserved

⅔ cup chopped onion

1–2 teaspoons margarine or butter

¼ cup all-purpose flour

1 quart clam juice

2 egg yolks, lightly beaten

½ cup dry white wine or water

Salt and cayenne pepper, to taste

Chopped chives, as garnish

Per Serving:
Calories: 132
% calories from fat: 29
Protein (g): 7.6
Carbohydrate (g): 12
Fat (g): 4.2
Saturated fat (g): 1.2
Cholesterol (mg): 99.4
Sodium (mg): 586

Exchanges:
Milk: 0.0
Vegetable: 0.0
Fruit: 0.0
Bread: 0.5
Meat: 1.0
Fat: 1.0

1. Coarsely chop about 1 cup oysters; cut remaining oysters in half. Sauté onion in margarine in large saucepan until tender, about 5 minutes. Stir in flour and cook 1–2 minutes. Stir in oyster liquor and clam juice; heat to simmering. Whisk about 1 cup clam juice mixture into egg yolks; whisk mixture back into saucepan, whisking until thickened, 1 to 2 minutes. Stir in wine and oysters and simmer, covered, until edges of oysters curl, 2 to 4 minutes. Season to taste with salt and cayenne pepper. Sprinkle each bowl of soup with chives.

CHINESE OYSTER SOUP

Enjoy the Oriental flavor accents in this oyster soup.

4 first-course servings

2½ cups Oriental Stock (see p. 12)
2 tablespoons reduced-sodium soy sauce
1 tablespoon grated gingerroot
1 pint shucked fresh or canned oysters, undrained
2 cups sliced Napa cabbage
8 ounces mushrooms, sliced
½ cup fresh or canned bean sprouts
4 green onions, sliced
Salt and pepper, to taste

Per Serving:
Calories: 72
% calories from fat: 15
Protein (g): 6.2
Carbohydrate (g): 10.2
Fat (g): 1.3
Saturated fat (g): 0.3
Cholesterol (mg): 14.2
Sodium (mg): 444

Exchanges:
Milk: 0.0
Vegetable: 0.0
Fruit: 0.0
Bread: 0.5
Meat: 1.0
Fat: 0.0

1. Heat stock, soy sauce, and gingerroot to boiling in large saucepan; add oysters and liquor, cabbage, mushrooms, bean sprouts, and green onions. Heat to boiling; reduce heat and simmer, covered, until cabbage is tender and edges of oysters curl, about 5 minutes. Season to taste with salt and pepper.

SQUASH AND SCALLOP SOUP

45

Acorn or Hubbard squash can also be used in this recipe.

6 entrée servings

1 cup chopped celery
½ cup chopped onion
1 tablespoon margarine or butter
¼ cup all-purpose flour
1 cup reduced-sodium fat-free chicken broth
2 cups each: fat-free milk, cubed, peeled
   butternut squash
¼ teaspoon ground ginger
1 pound bay scallops
1–2 teaspoons low-sodium Worcestershire sauce
Salt and white pepper, to taste

Per Serving:
Calories: 161
% calories from fat: 17
Protein (g): 19.3
Carbohydrate (g): 14.5
Fat (g): 3.1
Saturated fat (g): 0.5
Cholesterol (mg): 33.6
Sodium (mg): 276

Exchanges:
Milk: 0.0
Vegetable: 0.0
Fruit: 0.0
Bread: 1.0
Meat: 2.0
Fat: 0.0

1. Sauté celery and onion in margarine in large saucepan until tender, about 5 minutes; sprinkle with flour and cook 1 to 2 minutes. Stir in broth, milk, squash, and ginger and heat to boiling; reduce heat and simmer, covered, until squash is tender, about 15 minutes. Stir in scallops; simmer, covered, until scallops are opaque, about 5 minutes. Season to taste with Worcestershire sauce, salt, and white pepper.

SHERRIED CRABMEAT SOUP

This delicately seasoned soup can be made with canned crabmeat.

4 entrée servings

1½ cups Easy Fish Stock (see p. 8)

1 cup sliced celery

2 cans (6½ ounces each) crabmeat, drained, divided

1 cup 2% reduced-fat milk

¼ teaspoon ground mace

1 tablespoon cornstarch

3 tablespoons dry sherry or water

Salt and cayenne pepper, to taste

Per Serving:
Calories: 168
% calories from fat: 20
Protein (g): 19.9
Carbohydrate (g): 7.8
Fat (g): 3.5
Saturated fat (g): 1.2
Cholesterol (mg): 100.4
Sodium (mg): 524

Exchanges:
Milk: 0.0
Vegetable: 0.0
Fruit: 0.0
Bread: 0.5
Meat: 2.0
Fat: 0.0

1. Heat stock, celery and 1 can crabmeat to boiling in large saucepan; reduce heat and simmer, covered, until celery is tender, about 10 minutes. Process soup in food processor or blender until smooth; return to saucepan. Stir in milk and mace and heat to boiling; stir in combined cornstarch and sherry, stirring until thickened, about 1 minute. Stir in remaining 1 can crabmeat; reduce heat and simmer, covered, until hot, 2 to 3 minutes. Season to taste with salt and cayenne pepper.

MARYLAND CRAB SOUP

Old Bay is a popular herb and spice blend used with crab and other seafood in the Chesapeake region. If not available, its flavor can be approximated by substituting ½ teaspoon each: celery salt, paprika, dry mustard; ¼ teaspoon each: black and crushed red pepper; ⅛ teaspoon ground cloves; and a pinch each ground mace and ground ginger.

6 entrée servings

2 slices bacon, finely diced

1 teaspoon canola oil

2 each: large finely chopped onions, carrots, ribs celery

1½ quarts fat-free beef broth

2½ cups clam juice

2 bay leaves

½ teaspoon dry mustard

1–2 tablespoons Old Bay seasoning

3 cups diced, peeled red potatoes

2½ cups coarsely chopped canned undrained plum tomatoes

1 cup whole kernel corn

12 ounces fresh backfin crabmeat, cartilage and shell discarded, cut into ½-inch pieces

½ cup finely chopped parsley

Salt and pepper, to taste

Per Serving:
Calories: 206
% calories from fat: 12
Protein (g): 22.8
Carbohydrate (g): 29.7
Fat (g): 3.0
Saturated fat (g): 0.6
Cholesterol (mg): 36.7
Sodium (mg): 1371

Exchanges:
Milk: 0.0
Vegetable: 0.0
Fruit: 0.0
Bread: 2.0
Meat: 2.0
Fat: 0.0

1. Cook bacon in large saucepan until crisp; drain fat and reserve bacon. Add oil, onions, carrots, and celery to saucepan; sauté until onions are tender, 8 to 10 minutes. Add remaining ingredients, except crabmeat, parsley, salt, and pepper; heat to boiling. Reduce heat and simmer, covered, until vegetables are tender, about 10 minutes. Stir in crabmeat and parsley; simmer, covered, until hot, about 5 minutes. Discard bay leaves; season to taste with salt and pepper.

EGG DROP CRAB SOUP

A kitchen tip—gingerroot does not have to be peeled before using!

4 first-course servings

4 green onions, sliced
2 teaspoons each: minced garlic, gingerroot
1–2 teaspoons Asian sesame oil
1 quart Rich Chicken Stock (see p. 4)
1 can (15 ounces) cream-style corn
1 can (6 ounces) crabmeat, drained
2 eggs, lightly beaten
2 tablespoons chopped cilantro
Salt and pepper, to taste

Per Serving:
Calories: 160
% calories from fat: 25
Protein (g): 18.8
Carbohydrate (g): 9.4
Fat (g): 4.3
Saturated fat (g): 1
Cholesterol (mg): 96.5
Sodium (mg): 313

Exchanges:
Milk: 0.0
Vegetable: 0.0
Fruit: 0.0
Bread: 0.5
Meat: 2.0
Fat: 0.0

1. Sauté green onions, garlic, and gingerroot in oil in large saucepan 2 minutes. Stir in stock, corn, and crabmeat. Heat to boiling; reduce heat and simmer, covered, 5 minutes. Slowly stir beaten egg into soup. Stir in cilantro; season to taste with salt and pepper.

SHRIMP BISQUE

1½ cups each clam juice and water can be substituted for the Fish Stock.

4 entrée servings

¾ cup chopped onion
2 teaspoons margarine or butter
12 ounces peeled, deveined shrimp
3 tablespoons each: flour, tomato paste
3 cups Fish Stock (see p. 8)
½ cup fat-free half-and-half or fat-free milk
2 teaspoons curry powder
¼ teaspoon paprika
¾ cup chopped tomato
Salt and cayenne pepper, to taste
1 cup Garlic Croutons (⅓ recipe) (see p. 636)

Per Serving:
Calories: 219
% calories from fat: 17
Protein (g): 23.0
Carbohydrate (g): 20.8
Fat (g): 4.1
Saturated fat (g): 0.8
Cholesterol (mg): 134.3
Sodium (mg): 482

Exchanges:
Milk: 0.0
Vegetable: 0.0
Fruit: 0.0
Bread: 1.5
Meat: 2.0
Fat: 0.0

1. Sauté onion in margarine in large saucepan until tender, about 5 minutes; stir in shrimp and sauté 2 to 3 minutes. Sprinkle with flour and cook 1 to 2 minutes. Stir in stock, half-and-half, curry powder, and paprika and heat to boiling, stirring until thickened, about 1 minute.

2. Process soup in food processor or blender until almost smooth; return to saucepan; stir in tomato and cook, covered, over medium heat until hot, 2 to 3 minutes. Season to taste with salt and cayenne pepper. Sprinkle each bowl of soup with Garlic Croutons.

LIGHT SALMON BISQUE WITH DILL

Dill weed compliments the flavor of fresh salmon nicely in this light, tempting bisque.

4 entrée servings

2½ cups Fish Stock (see p. 8), divided
8 ounces skinless salmon fillets
1 cup chopped onion
¼ cup each: chopped celery, carrot
2 teaspoons margarine or butter
1 tablespoon flour
1½ cups chopped, peeled potatoes
1 tablespoon tomato paste
¼–½ teaspoon dry mustard
1¼ cups whole milk
2–3 teaspoons lemon juice
1½ teaspoons dried dill weed
Salt and white pepper, to taste

Per Serving:
Calories: 213
% calories from fat: 28
Protein (g): 20.3
Carbohydrate (g): 22.5
Fat (g): 6.7
Saturated fat (g): 2
Cholesterol (mg): 38.7
Sodium (mg): 508

Exchanges:
Milk: 0.0
Vegetable: 0.0
Fruit: 0.0
Bread: 1 5
Meat: 2.0
Fat: 0.0

1. Heat ½ cup stock to simmering in medium skillet; add salmon fillets, skin side down. Simmer, covered, until salmon is tender and flakes with a fork, 5 to 7 minutes. Remove fish and lay skin side up on a plate and cool; remove and discard skin. Flake fish into small pieces; strain stock and reserve.

2. Sauté onion, celery, and carrot in margarine in large saucepan until onion is tender, about 5 minutes. Stir in flour and cook 1 minute. Stir in remaining 2 cups stock, potatoes, tomato paste, and dry mustard; heat to boiling. Reduce heat and simmer, covered, until potatoes are tender, about 10 minutes. Process soup in food processor or blender until smooth; return to saucepan and heat to boiling. Add reserved salmon and stock, milk, lemon juice, and dill weed; reduce heat and simmer, covered, until hot, 3 to 4 minutes. Season to taste with salt and white pepper.

SALMON WILD RICE SOUP

A very special soup—the rich flavors of salmon and wild rice are perfect complements.

6 entrée servings

1½ cups sliced mushrooms

¾ cup chopped onion

½ cup sliced celery

1 teaspoon minced garlic

2 tablespoons flour

½ teaspoon each: dry mustard, dried rosemary leaves

3 cups Easy Fish Stock (see p. 8) or fat-free chicken broth

1 pound skinless salmon steaks, cubed

1 cup each: cooked wild rice, fat-free half-and-half or fat-free milk

Salt and cayenne pepper, to taste

2 slices bacon, fried crisp, crumbled

Per Serving:
Calories: 200
% calories from fat: 20
Protein (g): 20.3
Carbohydrate (g): 15.5
Fat (g): 3.9
Saturated fat (g): 0.8
Cholesterol (mg): 44.7
Sodium (mg): 142

Exchanges:
Milk: 0.0
Vegetable: 0.0
Fruit: 0.0
Bread: 1.0
Meat: 2.0
Fat: 0.0

1. Sauté mushrooms, onion, celery and garlic in lightly greased large saucepan until tender, about 8 minutes. Stir in flour, mustard, and rosemary and cook 1 to 2 minutes. Add stock and heat to boiling; reduce heat and simmer, covered, 5 minutes. Stir in salmon, wild rice, and half-and-half; simmer, covered, until salmon is tender and flakes with a fork, about 5 minutes. Season to taste with salt and cayenne pepper. Sprinkle each bowl of soup with reserved bacon.

VARIATION

Tuna-Rice Soup — Make soup as above, substituting tarragon for the rosemary, tuna steaks for the salmon, and white rice for the wild rice. Omit dry mustard; season to taste with lemon juice.

ZUCCHINI AND TUNA SOUP

An easy soup, made with canned tuna—also delicious with canned salmon.

4 entrée servings

¾ cup chopped onion
½ cup chopped celery
2 teaspoons minced garlic
2 tablespoons flour
1 can (6½ ounces) tuna in water, drained
2½ cups Low-Salt Chicken Stock (see p. 3)
1 cup fat-free milk
½–1 cup (2–4 ounces) shredded Cheddar cheese
1 cup shredded zucchini
1–2 teaspoons lemon juice
Salt and pepper, to taste
Hot pepper sauce

Per Serving:
Calories: 174
% calories from fat: 28
Protein (g): 19.6
Carbohydrate (g): 11.5
Fat (g): 5.4
Saturated fat (g): 3.2
Cholesterol (mg): 32
Sodium (mg): 292

Exchanges:
Milk: 0.0
Vegetable: 0.0
Fruit: 0.0
Bread: 1.0
Meat: 2.0
Fat: 0.0

1. Sauté onion, celery, and garlic in lightly greased large saucepan until tender, about 5 minutes. Sprinkle with flour and cook 1 to 2 minutes. Stir in tuna, stock, and milk. Heat to boiling; reduce heat and simmer 5 minutes. Add cheese, stirring until melted. Process soup in food processor or blender until smooth; return to saucepan. Stir in zucchini and cook over medium heat until hot, about 5 minutes. Season to taste with lemon juice, salt, and pepper; serve with hot pepper sauce.

SEAFOOD WONTON SOUP

Wonton wrappers can be found in the produce department of the supermarket.

4 first-course servings

1½ quarts Fish Stock
Seafood Wontons (recipe follows)
1 cup sliced spinach
¼ cup minced parsley or cilantro
Salt and pepper, to taste

Per Serving:
Calories: 178
% calories from fat: 6
Protein (g): 13.2
Carbohydrate (g): 21.5
Fat (g): 0.9
Saturated fat (g): 0.1
Cholesterol (mg): 18.2
Sodium (mg): 283

Exchanges:
Milk: 0.0
Vegetable: 1.0
Fruit: 0.0
Bread: 1.0
Meat: 1.5
Fat: 0.0

1. Heat stock to boiling in large saucepan; reduce heat and add Seafood Wontons, spinach, and parsley. Simmer, uncovered, until wontons are cooked and float to the surface, 5 to 7 minutes. Season to taste with salt and pepper.

Seafood Wontons

Makes 16 wontons

4 ounces skinless orange roughy fillets, very finely chopped
2 green onions, finely chopped
1 teaspoon each: light soy sauce, ground ginger
16 wonton wrappers

1. Mix all ingredients, except wonton wrappers. Place heaping teaspoon fish mixture on each wonton wrapper; moisten edges with water, fold opposite corners together, and seal.

CANTONESE FISH SOUP

Use any desired fresh or frozen fish in this delicate soup.

4 entrée servings

1 quart Fish Stock (see p. 8)
1 pound skinless haddock steaks, cubed (1-inch)
2 tablespoons dry white wine (optional)
2 teaspoons minced fresh gingerroot
3 green onions, thinly sliced
1 teaspoon Asian sesame oil
1 cup sliced kale or spinach
Salt and pepper, to taste

Per Serving:
Calories: 138
% calories from fat: 8
Protein (g): 24.1
Carbohydrate (g): 1.8
Fat (g): 1
Saturated fat (g): 0.2
Cholesterol (mg): 71.7
Sodium (mg): 100

Exchanges:
Milk: 0.0
Vegetable: 0.0
Fruit: 0.0
Bread: 0.0
Meat: 3.0
Fat: 0.0

1. Heat stock to boiling in a large saucepan; add remaining ingredients, except salt and pepper. Reduce heat and simmer, covered, until fish is tender and flakes with a fork, about 10 minutes. Season to taste with salt and pepper.

THAI FISH SOUP

Oriental ingredients combine with flounder in this lovely soup.

4 entrée servings

1½ quarts Fish Stock (see p. 8)
2 teaspoons reduced-sodium soy sauce
1 teaspoon each: minced garlic, gingerroot
Generous pinch ground Szechuan peppercorns
8 ounces skinless flounder fillets, cubed
½ cup each: sliced mushrooms, trimmed snow peas
¼ cup chopped cilantro
Salt and pepper, to taste

Per Serving:
Calories: 114
% calories from fat: 10
Protein (g): 15.1
Carbohydrate (g): 3.5
Fat (g): 0.9
Saturated fat (g): 0.2
Cholesterol (mg): 39.8
Sodium (mg): 444

Exchanges:
Milk: 0.0
Vegetable: 0.0
Fruit: 0.0
Bread: 0.0
Meat: 2.0
Fat: 0.0

1. Heat stock, soy sauce, garlic, gingerroot, and peppercorns to boiling in large saucepan; reduce heat and simmer, covered, 5 minutes. Add flounder, mushrooms, snow peas, and cilantro; simmer, covered, until fish is tender and flakes with a fork, 4 to 5 minutes. Season to taste with salt and pepper.

GINGER FISH SOUP

Aromatic gingerroot accents this delicious fish soup.

4 entrée servings

1 quart Easy Fish Stock (see p. 8)

1 cup water

1 tablespoon each: reduced-sodium soy sauce,
  minced gingerroot

1 teaspoon minced garlic

2 ounces vermicelli, broken (2-inch)

8 ounces skinless fish fillets (flounder, whitefish, or
  perch), cubed

4 ounces small peeled, deveined shrimp

1 small cucumber, peeled, seeded, thinly sliced

1 cup sliced mushrooms

¼ cup sliced green onions

4 cups packed spinach, sliced

Salt and cayenne pepper, to taste

Per Serving:
Calories: 203
% calories from fat: 19
Protein (g): 23.6
Carbohydrate (g): 16.9
Fat (g): 4.2
Saturated fat (g): 0.6
Cholesterol (mg): 75.8
Sodium (mg): 416

Exchanges:
Milk: 0.0
Vegetable: 0.0
Fruit: 0.0
Bread: 1.0
Meat: 2.0
Fat: 0.0

1. Heat stock, water, soy sauce, gingerroot, and garlic to boiling
in large saucepan; stir in remaining ingredients, except salt and
cayenne pepper. Reduce heat and simmer, uncovered, until fish is
tender and flakes with a fork and pasta is *al dente*, 4 to 5 minutes.
Season to taste with salt and cayenne pepper.

FISH SOUP WITH ROMAINE LETTUCE

Romaine lettuce adds a delicate flavor dimension to this easy fish soup.

4 entrée servings

8 ounces skinless whitefish fillets, cubed

2 teaspoons canola oil

1 teaspoon each: cornstarch, reduced-sodium soy sauce, Asian sesame oil

1 quart Easy Fish Stock (see p. 8)

4 cups thinly sliced romaine lettuce leaves

2 green onions, thinly sliced

Salt and white pepper, to taste

1. Toss fish with combined canola oil, cornstarch, soy sauce, and Asian sesame oil in medium bowl; refrigerate, covered, 30 minutes. Heat stock to boiling in medium saucepan; stir in lettuce, green onions, and fish. Reduce heat and simmer, covered, until fish is tender and flakes with a fork, 2 to 3 minutes. Remove from heat; season to taste with salt and white pepper.

Per Serving:
Calories: 136
% calories from fat: 30
Protein (g): 15.2
Carbohydrate (g): 3.2
Fat (g): 3.5
Saturated fat (g): 0.5
Cholesterol (mg): 58.6
Sodium (mg): 95

Exchanges:
Milk: 0.0
Vegetable: 1.0
Fruit: 0.0
Bread: 0.0
Meat: 1.0
Fat: 0.0

SOUTHERN GUMBO WITH SHRIMP

This classic Southern soup is updated to a lighter, healthier low-fat version.

6 entrée servings

¾ cup each: sliced onion, green bell pepper

2 cups sliced okra

3 cups chopped tomatoes

1 quart Fish Stock (see p. 8)

1 bay leaf

⅛–¼ teaspoon crushed red pepper

12 ounces each: cubed, skinless red snapper fillets, peeled, deveined large shrimp

1 teaspoon gumbo file powder

Salt and pepper, to taste

2 cups cooked rice, warm

Per Serving:
Calories: 239
% calories from fat: 8
Protein (g): 25.9
Carbohydrate (g): 26
Fat (g): 2
Saturated fat (g): 0.4
Cholesterol (mg): 111.8
Sodium (mg): 146

Exchanges:
Milk: 0.0
Vegetable: 2.0
Fruit: 0.0
Bread: 1.0
Meat: 2.0
Fat: 0.0

1. Sauté onion, bell pepper, and okra in lightly greased large saucepan until onions are tender, about 5 minutes. Add tomatoes, stock, bay leaf and red pepper; heat to boiling. Reduce heat and simmer, covered, 5 minutes. Add fish and shrimp; simmer, covered, until shrimp is cooked and fish is tender and flakes with a fork, 5 to 8 minutes. Discard bay leaf; stir in gumbo file and season to taste with salt and pepper. Serve over rice.

GEORGIA FISH SOUP

45 *Peanut butter is the surprise ingredient in this unusual fish soup.*

6 entrée servings

1 cup thinly sliced onion

½ cup chopped green bell pepper

2 teaspoons each: minced garlic, chili powder

½ teaspoon dried thyme leaves

1 can (28 ounces) reduced-sodium diced
   tomatoes, undrained

⅓–½ cup reduced-fat peanut butter

1 package (10 ounces) frozen sliced okra

1 pound skinless cod fillets, sliced

Salt and pepper, to taste

Hot pepper sauce

Per Serving:
Calories: 210
% calories from fat: 28
Protein (g): 19.9
Carbohydrate (g): 19.2
Fat (g): 6.7
Saturated fat (g): 1.3
Cholesterol (mg): 32.4
Sodium (mg): 166

Exchanges:
Milk: 0.0
Vegetable: 3.0
Fruit: 0.0
Bread: 0.0
Meat: 2.0
Fat: 0.5

1. Sauté onion, green pepper, garlic, chili powder, and thyme in lightly greased large saucepan until onion is tender, about 5 minutes. Stir in tomatoes with liquid, peanut butter, and okra; heat to boiling. Reduce heat and simmer, covered, until okra is tender, about 10 minutes. Add cod; simmer, covered, until fish is tender and flakes with a fork, 6 to 8 minutes. Season to taste with salt and pepper; serve with hot pepper sauce.

CARIBBEAN-STYLE FLOUNDER

45 *Annatto seeds, often used in Caribbean and Mexican cooking, impart a subtle flavor and deep yellow color to foods they are cooked with. They are available in Mexican groceries and in many large supermarkets.*

4 entrée servings

2 teaspoons canola oil

1 tablespoon annatto seeds (optional)

1 medium onion, thinly sliced

2 cups reduced-sodium fat-free chicken broth

1 sweet potato, peeled, cubed

1 can (14½ ounces) reduced-sodium diced
   tomatoes, undrained

1 teaspoon dried thyme leaves

1 cup frozen peas

1 pound skinless flounder fillets, cubed (¾-inch)

3–4 teaspoons lemon juice

Salt and pepper, to taste

Per Serving:
Calories: 240
% calories from fat: 16
Protein (g): 28.5
Carbohydrate (g): 21.4
Fat (g): 4.2
Saturated fat (g): 0.8
Cholesterol (mg): 60.1
Sodium (mg): 227

Exchanges:
Milk: 0.0
Vegetable: 0.0
Fruit: 0.0
Bread: 1.0
Meat: 3.0
Fat: 0.0

1. Heat oil in large saucepan over medium-high heat; add annatto seeds and sauté for 3 minutes. Remove seeds with slotted spoon and discard. Add onion to saucepan; sauté 2 minutes. Add broth, potato, tomatoes with liquid, and thyme. Heat to boiling; reduce heat and simmer, covered, until potato is tender, about 10 minutes. Add peas and flounder; simmer until fish is tender and flakes with a fork, about 10 minutes. Season to taste with lemon, salt, and pepper.

SOPA AZTECS

This soup is reminiscent of the fare you'll find in a Mexican cafe.

4 entrée servings

2 corn tortillas (6-inch), cut into thin strips

Olive oil cooking spray

1 cup sliced red onion

4 cloves garlic, minced

1½ quarts Easy Fish Stock (see p. 8)

12 ounces skinless red snapper fillets, sliced (1-inch)

½ teaspoon cumin seeds

⅛–¼ teaspoon crushed red pepper

¼ cup each: chopped cilantro, avocado

Lime juice, to taste

Salt, to taste

6 tablespoons (1½ ounces) shredded reduced-fat
   Cheddar cheese

Per Serving:
Calories: 237
% calories from fat: 26
Protein (g): 26
Carbohydrate (g): 12.7
Fat (g): 5.9
Saturated fat (g): 2
Cholesterol (mg): 48.6
Sodium (mg): 163

Exchanges:
Milk: 0.0
Vegetable: 0.0
Fruit: 0.0
Bread: 1.0
Meat: 3.0
Fat: 0.0

1. Spray tortillas with cooking spray and cook over medium heat in large saucepan until crisp. Remove from saucepan and reserve. Add onion and garlic to skillet and sauté until tender, about 5 minutes. Add stock, red snapper, cumin seeds, and red pepper; heat to boiling. Reduce heat and simmer, covered, until fish is tender and flakes with a fork, 5 to 10 minutes. Stir in cilantro and avocado; season to taste with lime juice and salt. Sprinkle each bowl of soup with reserved tortilla strips and cheese.

MAGYAR FISH SOUP

Hungarian paprika and caraway seeds flavor this interesting soup.

8 entrée servings

2 quarts Easy Fish Stock (see p. 8)

1 teaspoon caraway seeds

1 tablespoon Hungarian paprika

1 pound each: skinless bass and halibut fillets, cubed

1 each: chopped tomato, red bell pepper

Salt and pepper, to taste

Per Serving:
Calories: 198
% calories from fat: 18
Protein (g): 30.6
Carbohydrate (g): 2.9
Fat (g): 3.3
Saturated fat (g): 0.7
Cholesterol (mg): 65.8
Sodium (mg): 112

Exchanges:
Milk: 0.0
Vegetable: 0.0
Fruit: 0.0
Bread: 0.0
Meat: 4.0
Fat: 0.0

1. Heat stock, caraway seeds, and paprika to boiling in large saucepan; reduce heat and simmer, covered, 10 minutes. Add fish, tomato, and bell pepper and simmer, covered, until fish is tender and flakes with a fork, about 10 minutes. Season to taste with salt and pepper.

FISH SOUP WITH VEGETABLES

This soup is delicious served with Roasted Red Pepper Bread (see p. 647).

8 entrée servings

1 cup chopped onion
½ cup each: chopped celery, bell pepper, sliced
   carrots, mushrooms
4 cloves garlic, minced
2 tablespoons olive oil
2 cans (28 ounces each) crushed tomatoes
1 can (16 ounces) reduced-sodium tomato juice
¾ cup clam juice
3 medium potatoes, peeled, diced
1 teaspoon dried oregano leaves
8 ounces each: cubed skinless halibut, sole, snapper
½ cup dry white wine (optional)
Salt and pepper, to taste

Per Serving:
Calories: 245
% calories from fat: 19
Protein (g): 20.3
Carbohydrate (g): 25.1
Fat (g): 5.2
Saturated fat (g): 0.8
Cholesterol (mg): 32.8
Sodium (mg): 275

Exchanges:
Milk: 0.0
Vegetable: 2.5
Fruit: 0.0
Bread: 1.0
Meat: 2.0
Fat: 0.0

1. Sauté onion, celery, bell pepper, carrots, mushrooms, and garlic in oil in large saucepan until onion is tender, about 5 minutes. Add tomatoes, tomato juice, clam juice, potatoes, and oregano; heat to boiling. Reduce heat and simmer, covered, until potatoes are tender, about 15 minutes. Add fish and wine; simmer, covered, until fish is tender and flakes with a fork, about 10 minutes. Season to taste with salt and pepper.

HEARTY FISH SOUP

This soup makes a hearty meal when served with salad and warm, crusty bread.

6 entrée servings

⅓ cup each: finely chopped onion, carrots, green bell pepper
3 cans (14½ ounces each) reduced-sodium diced tomatoes, undrained
¾ cup clam juice
3 medium potatoes, peeled, diced

1 cup whole kernel corn

1 teaspoon dried oregano leaves

8 ounces each: cubed, skinless cod, flounder and orange roughy fillets

½ cup dry white wine (optional)

¼ cup finely chopped fresh or 1 tablespoon dried basil leaves

Salt and pepper, to taste

Per Serving:
Calories: 242
% calories from fat: 6
Protein (g). 23.3
Carbohydrate (g): 28.6
Fat (g): 1.7
Saturated fat (g): 0.3
Cholesterol (mg): 46.7
Sodium (mg): 204

Exchanges:
Milk: 0.0
Vegetable: 2.0
Fruit: 0.0
Bread: 1.0
Meat: 2.0
Fat: 0.0

1. Sauté onion, carrots, and bell pepper in lightly greased large saucepan until tender, about 5 minutes. Add tomatoes with liquid, clam juice, potatoes, corn, and oregano and heat to boiling; reduce heat and simmer, covered, until potatoes are tender, about 10 minutes. Add fish and wine; simmer, covered, until fish is tender and flakes with a fork, 8 to 10 minutes. Stir in basil; season to taste with salt and pepper.

FISHERMAN'S CATCH

Choose 2 or 3 kinds of fish for this soup, selecting from cod, flounder, red snapper, salmon, halibut, or haddock.

6 entrée servings

½ cup each: chopped onion, celery, carrot

1 teaspoon dried rosemary leaves

1 tablespoon olive oil

3 tablespoons flour

1 can (14½ ounces) diced tomatoes, undrained

1 cup dry white wine or water

¾ cup clam juice

1½ pounds skinless fish fillets or steaks, cubed

⅓ cup chopped parsley

⅓ cup fat-free half-and-half or fat-free milk

Salt and pepper, to taste

6 slices Italian bread, toasted

Per Serving:
Calories: 302
% calories from fat: 13
Protein (g): 26.4
Carbohydrate (g): 25.1
Fat (g): 4.2
Saturated fat (g): 0.9
Cholesterol (mg): 48.7
Sodium (mg): 662

Exchanges:
Milk: 0.0
Vegetable: 2.0
Fruit: 0.0
Bread: 1.0
Meat 3.0
Fat: 0.0

1. Sauté onion, celery, carrot, and rosemary in oil in large saucepan until onion is tender, about 10 minutes; sprinkle with flour and cook 1 to 2 minutes. Stir in tomatoes with liquid, wine, and clam juice; heat to boiling. Reduce heat and simmer, covered, 10 minutes. Add fish and parsley; simmer, covered, until fish is tender and flakes with a fork, about 10 minutes. Stir in half-and-half; simmer until hot, 2 to 3 minutes. Season to taste with salt and pepper. Place bread in soup bowls; ladle soup over.

VARIATION

Pesto Fish Soup — Make soup as above, adding 1 cup cooked cannellini or Great Northern beans, and omitting half-and-half. Stir ½ cup Fennel Pesto (see p. 663) into soup before serving.

FISH-OF-THE-DAY SOUP

The great fish soups are made with the fresh catch of the day.

6 entrée servings

1 cup chopped onion
4 each: minced cloves garlic, chopped large tomatoes
3 bay leaves
1 teaspoon each: dried oregano and basil leaves
1¼ quarts Fish Stock (see p. 8)
½ cup dry white wine (optional)
1 cup tomato juice
1 pound cod or halibut fillets cubed
8 ounces each: cubed, skinless red snapper and halibut fillets, peeled deveined jumbo shrimp
Salt and pepper, to taste
1½ cups Garlic Croutons (½ recipe) (see p. 636)

Per Serving:
Calories: 203
% calories from fat: 10
Protein (g): 26.8
Carbohydrate (g): 15.0
Fat (g): 2.0
Saturated fat (g): 0.4
Cholesterol (mg): 87.3
Sodium (mg): 437

Exchanges:
Milk: 0.0
Vegetable: 0.0
Fruit: 0.0
Bread: 1.0
Meat: 3.0
Fat: 0.0

1. Sauté onion and garlic in lightly greased large saucepan until tender, about 5 minutes. Add tomatoes, herbs, stock, wine, and tomato juice and heat to boiling; reduce heat and simmer, covered, 5 minutes. Add seafood and simmer, covered, until shrimp is cooked and fish is tender and flakes with a fork, 5 to 7 minutes. Discard bay leaves, season to taste with salt and pepper. Sprinkle each bowl of soup with Garlic Croutons.

NIÇOISE FISH SOUP

45 *Fennel seeds add a special flavor dimension to this great soup.*

8 entrée servings

1 cup chopped onion

1 tablespoon each: minced garlic, olive oil

3 cups water

1 cup clam juice

2 cups chopped tomatoes

½ teaspoon each: dried thyme leaves, crushed
    fennel seeds, ground turmeric

1 bay leaf

2 pounds assorted lean skinless fish fillets or steaks
    (halibut, haddock, red snapper, cod, etc.), cubed

Salt and cayenne pepper, to taste

Bruschetta (see p. 637)

Per Serving:
Calories: 240
% calories from fat: 20
Protein (g): 27
Carbohydrate (g): 19.9
Fat (g): 5.4
Saturated fat (g): 0.8
Cholesterol (mg): 36.1
Sodium (mg): 309

Exchanges:
Milk: 0.0
Vegetable: 1.0
Fruit: 0.0
Bread: 1.0
Meat: 2.5
Fat: 0.0

1. Sauté onion and garlic in oil in large saucepan until tender, about
5 minutes. Stir in water, clam juice, tomatoes, and herbs. Heat to
boiling; reduce heat and simmer, covered, 10 minutes. Add fish
and heat to boiling; reduce heat and simmer, covered, until fish
is tender and flakes with a fork, 5 to 8 minutes. Discard bay leaf.
Season to taste with salt and cayenne pepper. Place Bruschetta in
soup bowls; ladle soup over.

FISH SOUP MARSEILLES

Fresh fennel gives this soup its authentic South-of-France flavor; substitute 2 teaspoons fennel seeds if you prefer.

6 entrée servings

½ cup each: chopped onion, sliced fennel bulb

1 tablespoon minced garlic

2 teaspoons olive oil

1 can (14½ ounces) Italian-style stewed tomatoes

3–4 cups Mediterranean Stock (see p. 12)

1 cup uncooked orzo or other small soup pasta

8 ounces skinless whitefish fillets, cubed

8 ounces peeled, deveined shrimp

Salt and pepper, to taste

Per Serving:
Calories: 231
% calories from fat: 14
Protein (g): 16.5
Carbohydrate (g): 29.9
Fat (g): 3.4
Saturated fat (g): 0.5
Cholesterol (mg): 63.4
Sodium (mg): 227

Exchanges:
Milk: 0.0
Vegetable: 0.0
Fruit: 0.0
Bread: 2.0
Meat: 2.0
Fat: 0.0

1. Sauté onion, fennel, and garlic in oil in large saucepan until tender, about 8 minutes. Stir in tomatoes and stock. Heat to boiling; stir in orzo, fish, and shrimp. Reduce heat, and simmer, covered, until orzo and shrimp are cooked and fish is tender and flakes with a fork, about 8 minutes. Season to taste with salt and pepper.

SHORTCUT FISH SOUP

45

This easy soup has a base of prepared spaghetti sauce.

6 entrée servings

1 medium onion, thinly sliced

2 cloves garlic, minced

⅛–¼ teaspoon crushed red pepper

1 teaspoon olive oil

1 jar (20 ounces) spaghetti sauce with herbs

1 cup each: clam juice, water

½ cup dry white wine (optional)

1 pound assorted skinless lean fish fillets (whitefish, cod, snapper, or flounder)

1 can (6 ounces) whole clams, undrained

Salt and pepper, to taste

Per Serving:
Calories: 227
% calories from fat: 24
Protein (g): 22.4
Carbohydrate (g): 17.6
Fat (g): 6.1
Saturated fat (g): 0.9
Cholesterol (mg): 49.4
Sodium (mg): 695

Exchanges:
Milk: 0.0
Vegetable: 3.0
Fruit: 0.0
Bread: 0.0
Meat: 3.0
Fat: 0.0

1. Sauté onion, garlic, and crushed red pepper in oil in large saucepan until onion is tender, about 5 minutes. Stir in spaghetti sauce, clam juice, water, and wine; heat to boiling. Reduce heat and simmer, covered, 10 minutes. Stir in fish and clams with liquor; heat to boiling. Reduce heat and simmer, covered, until fish is tender and flakes with a fork, about 10 minutes. Season to taste with salt and pepper.

TUSCAN FISH SOUP

Along the Tuscan coast, each town boasts its own incomparable fish soup. The pride of Livorno is known as cacciucco. Each usually has five different kinds of fish, one for each of the cs in the dish's name.

6 entrée servings

3 cloves garlic, minced

2 medium onions, chopped

¼–½ teaspoon crushed red pepper

1 teaspoon olive oil

3 pounds tomatoes, peeled, seeded, chopped

1 quart chicken broth

½ cup dry red wine (optional)

1½ pounds assorted skinless fish fillets or steaks
   (sole, salmon, red snapper, tuna, or halibut), cubed

6 ounces peeled, deveined shrimp

2 tablespoons fresh or 1 teaspoon dried oregano,
   sage, and rosemary leaves

Salt and pepper, to taste

6 slices Italian bread, toasted

2 cloves garlic, halved

Per Serving:
Calories: 337
% calories from fat: 19
Protein (g): 28.6
Carbohydrate (g): 33.7
Fat (g): 7.1
Saturated fat (g): 1.1
Cholesterol (mg): 82.2
Sodium (mg): 337

Exchanges:
Milk: 0.0
Vegetable: 2.5
Fruit: 0.0
Bread: 1.5
Meat: 3.0
Fat: 0.0

1. Sauté garlic, onions, and crushed red pepper in olive oil in large saucepan until onions are tender, about 5 minutes. Add tomatoes, broth, and wine and heat to boiling. Reduce heat and simmer, covered, 20 minutes; add fish and shrimp and simmer, covered, until shrimp are cooked and fish is tender and flakes with a fork, about 10 minutes. Stir in herbs; season to taste with salt and pepper. Rub bread with garlic cloves; place in soup bowls and ladle soup over.

CIOPPINO

Our version of this classic Italian soup is made with shellfish. Clams in their shells are traditionally used, but canned whole clams may be substituted, if you prefer.

6 entrée servings

1 cup each: thinly sliced onion, green onions, green bell pepper

1 tablespoon each: minced garlic, olive oil

1 can (14½ ounces) reduced-sodium diced tomatoes, undrained

1 cup each: clam juice, water

½ cup dry white wine or clam juice

½ teaspoon each: dried tarragon, thyme, and rosemary leaves

1 bay leaf

1 pound crabmeat or firm white fish, cubed

12 ounces peeled, deveined shrimp

18 clams in shells, scrubbed

Salt and pepper, to taste

Per Serving:
Calories: 210
% calories from fat: 19
Protein (g): 24.1
Carbohydrate (g): 10.2
Fat (g): 4.3
Saturated fat (g): 0.6
Cholesterol (mg): 130.6
Sodium (mg): 276

Exchanges:
Milk: 0.0
Vegetable: 2.0
Fruit: 0.0
Bread: 0.0
Meat: 3.0
Fat: 0.0

1. Sauté onion, green onions, bell pepper, and garlic in oil in large saucepan, over low heat, until tender, 5 to 8 minutes. Add tomatoes with liquid, clam juice, water, wine, and herbs. Heat to boiling; reduce heat and simmer, covered, 20 minutes. Add crabmeat, shrimp, and clams; heat to boiling. Reduce heat and simmer, covered, until shrimp are cooked and clams have opened, about 8 minutes. Discard bay leaf and any clams that have not opened. Season to taste with salt and pepper.

CIOPPINO MEDITERRANEAN

This popular California fish soup is given an Italian accent.

6 entrée servings

¼ cup each: chopped green bell pepper, onion

1 clove garlic, minced

1 tablespoon olive oil

2 cans (14½ ounces each) diced tomatoes, undrained

1 can (6 ounces) low-sodium tomato paste

1 cup water

½ cup dry red wine (optional)

1 teaspoon each: dried oregano and basil leaves

8 ounces each: cubed skinless sole fillet, peeled
  deveined shrimp

2 cans (6 ½ ounces each) minced clams, undrained

Salt and pepper, to taste

Per Serving:
Calories: 206
% calories from fat: 19
Protein (g): 24.5
Carbohydrate (g): 14.9
Fat (g): 4.3
Saturated fat (g): 0.6
Cholesterol (mg): 95.3
Sodium (mg): 345

Exchanges:
Milk: 0.0
Vegetable: 0.0
Fruit: 0.0
Bread: 1.0
Meat: 3.0
Fat: 0.0

1. Sauté bell pepper, onion, and garlic in oil in large saucepan until tender, about 5 minutes. Add remaining ingredients, except seafood, salt, and pepper, and heat to boiling. Reduce heat and simmer, covered, 20 minutes. Add seafood and simmer until shrimp are cooked, and sole is tender and flakes with a fork, 5 to 7 minutes. Season to taste with salt and pepper.

MEDITERRANEAN-STYLE SHRIMP AND VEGETABLE SOUP

45 *A fragrant vegetable soup with a citrus accent.*

6 first-course servings

2 cups sliced mushrooms

½ cup each: chopped onion, green bell pepper

3 cloves garlic, minced

1 can (14½ ounces) reduced-sodium diced
  tomatoes, undrained

1 can (8 ounces) tomato sauce

2 cups vegetable broth

½ cup dry white wine or orange juice

2 strips orange zest (3 x ½ inches)

2 bay leaves

¾ teaspoon each: dried marjoram and savory leaves

½ teaspoon crushed fennel seeds

1 pound peeled, deveined shrimp

Salt and pepper, to taste

Per Serving:
Calories: 121
% calories from fat: 8
Protein (g): 14.8
Carbohydrate (g): 10.7
Fat (g): 1.1
Saturated fat (g): 0.2
Cholesterol (mg): 115.6
Sodium (mg): 211

Exchanges:
Milk: 0.0
Vegetable: 2.0
Fruit: 0.0
Bread: 0.0
Meat: 1.0
Fat: 0.0

1. Sauté mushrooms, onion, bell pepper, and garlic in lightly greased large saucepan until vegetables are tender, 8 to 10 minutes. Add remaining ingredients, except shrimp, salt and pepper, and heat to boiling; reduce heat and simmer, covered, 10 to 15 minutes. Add shrimp and simmer, covered, until cooked, 3 to 5 minutes. Discard bay leaves and orange zest; season to taste with salt and pepper.

KAKAVIA

What the French call bouillabaisse, the Greeks call kakavia.

12 entrée servings

2 cups chopped onions

2 ribs celery, chopped

1 tablespoon minced garlic

2 leeks (white parts only) sliced

3 large carrots, chopped

1 can (28 ounces) crushed tomatoes

1 quart clam juice

½ cup dry white wine (optional)

2 pounds skinless fish fillets (halibut, salmon, cod, or red snapper), cubed

12 each: scrubbed clams and mussels

12 ounces peeled, deveined shrimp

3 bay leaves

1 teaspoon dried thyme leaves

3 to 4 tablespoons lemon juice

Salt and pepper, to taste

Per Serving:
Calories: 203
% calories from fat: 14
Protein (g): 32.6
Carbohydrate (g): 11.2
Fat (g): 3.3
Saturated fat (g): 0.6
Cholesterol (mg): 121.0
Sodium (mg): 805

Exchanges:
Milk: 0.0
Vegetable: 0.0
Fruit: 0.0
Bread: 0.5
Meat: 4.0
Fat: 0.0

1. Sauté onions, celery garlic, leeks, and carrots in lightly greased large saucepan until onions are tender, about 10 minutes. Add tomatoes, clam juice, and wine; heat to boiling. Add remaining ingredients, except lemon juice, salt, and pepper; reduce heat and simmer, covered, until shrimp are cooked, fish is tender and flakes with a fork, and clams and mussels open, about 10 minutes. Discard any unopened clams and mussels and bay leaves. Season to taste with lemon juice, salt, and pepper.

CALDO DE PESCADO

This South American fish soup includes a medley of vegetables, with a flavor accent of orange.

10 entrée servings

2 cups chopped onions

3 cloves garlic, minced

1 large red bell pepper, chopped

1 tablespoon olive oil

2 cups peeled, sliced potatoes

3 cups Easy Fish Stock (see p. 8)

1 can (28 ounce) crushed tomatoes, undrained

2 large ears corn, sliced (1-inch pieces)

1 teaspoon each: grated orange zest, ground turmeric

1 pound skinless red snapper fillets, cubed

12 ounces large shrimp, peeled, deveined

Salt and cayenne pepper, to taste

Per Serving:
Calories: 173
% calories from fat: 15
Protein (g): 19.4
Carbohydrate (g): 17.9
Fat (g): 2.8
Saturated fat (g): 0.5
Cholesterol (mg): 68
Sodium (mg): 389

Exchanges:
Milk: 0.0
Vegetable: 0.0
Fruit: 0.0
Bread: 1.0
Meat: 2.0
Fat: 0.0

1. Sauté onions, garlic, and bell pepper in olive oil in large saucepan until onions are tender, about 10 minutes. Add remaining ingredients, except seafood, salt, and cayenne pepper; heat to boiling. Reduce heat and simmer, covered, 15 to 20 minutes. Add seafood and simmer, covered, until shrimp are cooked and fish is tender and flakes with a fork, 5 to 10 minutes; season to taste with salt and cayenne pepper.

SPANISH FISH SOUP

This unique soup is flavored with ground almonds and thickened with bread.

8 entrée servings

1 cup chopped onion
1 teaspoon paprika
½ teaspoon crushed cumin seeds
3½ cups each: water, clam juice
1 cup dry white wine or clam juice
⅓ cup ground almonds
2 slices firm white bread, crusts removed, cubed
1 cup fat-free milk
2 pounds skinless halibut, cubed
2 hard-cooked egg yolks, finely chopped
1 cup fat-free half-and-half or fat-free milk
Salt and cayenne pepper, to taste
8 thin slices lemon
Chopped parsley, as garnish

Per Serving:
Calories: 275
% calories from fat: 23
Protein (g): 28.1
Carbohydrate (g): 11.5
Fat (g): 6.5
Saturated fat (g): 1
Cholesterol (mg): 90
Sodium (mg): 356

Exchanges:
Milk: 0.0
Vegetable: 0.0
Fruit: 0.0
Bread: 1.0
Meat: 3.0
Fat: 1.0

1. Sauté onion, paprika, and cumin seeds in lightly greased large saucepan until tender, about 5 minutes. Stir in water, clam juice, wine, and almonds. Heat to boiling; reduce heat and simmer, covered, 20 minutes. Soak bread in milk; mash until smooth. Stir bread mixture into soup; simmer, uncovered, 10 minutes. Stir halibut and egg yolk into soup; simmer, covered, until fish is tender and flakes with a fork, about 5 minutes. Stir in half-and-half; simmer until hot, 2 to 3 minutes. Season to taste with salt and pepper. Float lemon slices on top of bowls of soup; sprinkle with parsley.

PORTUGUESE-STYLE FISHERMAN'S POT

This soup is attractive and robustly seasoned.

6 entrée servings

2 large onions, finely chopped

⅓ cup each: chopped carrot, celery, red bell pepper

1 large garlic clove, minced

1 tablespoon olive oil

1½ cups fat-free chicken broth

3–4 medium red potatoes, unpeeled, cubed

2 cans (14½ ounces each) diced tomatoes, undrained

¾ cup dry white wine or water

1 bay leaf

2 teaspoons each: chili powder, paprika

Pinch saffron threads, crumbled (optional)

½ teaspoon each: celery seeds, dried thyme leaves

Pinch crushed red pepper

24 fresh mussels, scrubbed

1½ pounds skinless cod, haddock, or whitefish
   fillets, cubed

8 ounces peeled, deveined shrimp

Salt and cayenne pepper, to taste

Per Serving:
Calories: 362
% calories from fat: 16
Protein (g): 43.1
Carbohydrate (g): 27.3
Fat (g): 6.4
Saturated fat (g): 1.1
Cholesterol (mg): 132.5
Sodium (mg): 736

Exchanges:
Milk: 0.0
Vegetable: 0.0
Fruit: 0.0
Bread: 2.0
Meat: 4.0
Fat: 0.0

1. Sauté onions, carrot, celery, bell pepper, and garlic in oil in large saucepan until onions are tender, about 10 minutes. Add broth and potatoes and heat to boiling. Reduce heat and simmer, covered, until potatoes are tender, about 10 minutes.

2. Add tomatoes with liquid, wine, and seasonings; simmer, uncovered, until slightly thickened, about 20 minutes. Add seafood and simmer, covered, until shrimp are cooked, mussels are opened, and fish is tender and flakes with a fork, 5 to 8 minutes. Discard bay leaf and any unopened mussels; season to taste with salt and cayenne pepper.

GAZPACHO WITH SHRIMP

45

The perfect mid-summer treat, made with garden-ripe tomatoes.

4 entrée servings

3 cups chopped, peeled, seeded tomatoes

1½ cups reduced-sodium tomato juice

¾ cup chopped, peeled, seeded cucumber

⅓ cup each: chopped onion, green bell pepper

1 clove garlic, minced

1–2 tablespoons balsamic vinegar

¼ teaspoon hot pepper sauce

12 ounces peeled, deveined medium shrimp, cooked

Salt and pepper, to taste

8 thin cucumber slices

Per Serving:
Calories: 143
% calories from fat: 8
Protein (g): 20.1
Carbohydrate (g): 13.4
Fat (g): 1.3
Saturated fat (g): 0.3
Cholesterol (mg): 165.8
Sodium (mg): 210

Exchanges:
Milk: 0.0
Vegetable: 2.0
Fruit: 0.0
Bread: 0.0
Meat: 2.0
Fat: 0.0

1. Process all ingredients, except shrimp, salt, pepper, and cucumber slices, in food processor or blender until almost smooth. Stir in shrimp and season to taste with salt and pepper; refrigerate until chilled. Garnish each bowl of soup with cucumber slices.

MEXICAN CORN AND SHRIMP SOUP

45

Epazote is a popular Mexican herb that can be purchased in Mexican groceries. It's easy to grow but must be planted annually in northern climates. A combination of fresh cilantro and oregano makes a flavorful substitute.

4 entrée servings

¾ cup chopped onion

1 each: minced medium jalapeño chili, clove garlic

1 tablespoon olive oil

3½ cups reduced-sodium vegetable broth

5 cups whole kernel corn

2 tablespoons chopped fresh or 2 teaspoons dried
   epazote leaves

Salt and cayenne pepper, to taste

12 ounces peeled, deveined shrimp

¾ cup Roasted Red Pepper Sauce (½ recipe, see p. 164)

Per Serving:
Calories: 190
% calories from fat: 14
Protein (g): 22.6
Carbohydrate (g): 19.3
Fat (g): 3.1
Saturated fat (g): 0.5
Cholesterol (mg): 130.8
Sodium (mg): 332

Exchanges:
Milk: 0.0
Vegetable: 0.0
Fruit: 0.0
Bread: 1.0
Meat: 2.0
Fat: 0.0

1. Sauté onion, jalapeño chili, and garlic in oil in large saucepan until tender, about 5 minutes. Add broth and corn; heat to boiling. Reduce heat and simmer, covered, 10 minutes. Process soup mixture in food processor or blender until almost smooth; stir in epazote and season to taste with salt and cayenne pepper. Return soup to saucepan and heat to simmering; add shrimp and cook, covered, over medium heat until shrimp are cooked, 3 to 5 minutes. Serve warm or chilled; swirl about 3 tablespoons Roasted Red Pepper Sauce into each bowl of soup.

EIGHT

Vegetarian Soups

VERY BERRY SOUP WITH BERRY CRÈME

L

45

❄

A garden of berries in a bowl of soup! When fresh berries are out of season, frozen unsweetened berries can be substituted.

4 first-course servings

1½ cups each: raspberries, quartered
   strawberries, water
¾ cup dry red wine or cranberry juice
3–4 tablespoons sugar
½ cup fat-free half-and-half or fat-free milk
Berry Crème (recipe follows)
¼ cup blueberries
Mint sprigs, as garnish

Per Serving:
Calories: 141
% calories from fat: 3
Protein (g): 2.9
Carbohydrate (g): 25.1
Fat (g): 0.5
Saturated fat (g): 0
Cholesterol (mg): 0
Sodium (mg): 69

Exchanges:
Milk: 0.0
Vegetable: 0.0
Fruit: 2.0
Bread: 0.0
Meat: 0.0
Fat: 0.0

1. Heat raspberries, strawberries, water, wine, and sugar to boiling in large saucepan. Reduce heat and simmer, covered, until berries are tender, 5 to 8 minutes. Process soup mixture in food processor or blender until smooth; strain, discarding seeds. Mix in half-and-half; refrigerate until chilled. Top each bowl of soup with Berry Crème, blueberries, and mint.

Berry Crème
Makes about ½ cup

½ cup light whipped topping
¼ cup powdered sugar
2 tablespoons seedless raspberry or strawberry jam
1 teaspoon finely grated orange zest

1. Mix all ingredients.

SUMMER FRUIT SOUP

This beautiful pink soup, lightly spiced, will cool you on a hot day.

6 first-course servings

3 cups coarsely chopped seeded watermelon

2 cups quartered strawberries

½ cup orange juice

1½ teaspoons lemon juice

2 tablespoons sugar

1 tablespoon cornstarch

½ teaspoon ground cinnamon

⅛ teaspoon each: ground ginger, mace

¾ cup fat-free milk

Lemon slices, as garnish

Per Serving:
Calories: 83
% calories from fat: 7
Protein (g): 2
Carbohydrate (g): 18.6
Fat (g): 0.7
Saturated fat (g): 0.1
Cholesterol (mg): 0.6
Sodium (mg): 18

Exchanges:
Milk: 0.0
Vegetable: 0.0
Fruit: 1.5
Bread: 0.0
Meat: 0.0
Fat: 0.0

1. Process watermelon and strawberries in food processor or blender until smooth; pour into large saucepan. Stir in combined orange and lemon juice, sugar, cornstarch, and spices; heat to boiling, stirring, until thickened, 1 to 2 minutes. Remove from heat; stir in milk. Refrigerate until chilled; garnish each bowl of soup with lemon slices.

SPICY APPLE-WINE SOUP

L

This sweet and spicy soup is delicious as a luncheon first-course or as a dessert.

45

❄

4 first-course servings

6 whole cloves

2 thick lemon slices, seeds removed

½ cup burgundy wine or white grape juice

2 cups each: white grape juice, coarsely chopped, peeled tart apples

1 large cinnamon stick

2 tablespoons honey

1 tablespoon sugar

2 tablespoons golden raisins

1½ tablespoons cornstarch

¼ cup water

4 tablespoons reduced-fat sour cream

Per Serving:
Calories: 173
% calories from fat: 2
Protein (g): 1
Carbohydrate (g): 39.9
Fat (g): 0.4
Saturated fat (g): 0.1
Cholesterol (mg): 0
Sodium (mg): 20

Exchanges:
Milk: 0.0
Vegetable: 0.0
Fruit: 3.0
Bread: 0.0
Meat: 0.0
Fat: 0.0

1. Stick cloves into rind on lemon slices. Heat lemon slices, wine, grape juice, apples, cinnamon stick, honey, and sugar to boiling in medium saucepan; reduce heat and simmer, covered, until apples are tender, about 10 minutes. Remove cinnamon stick and lemon slices; stir in raisins and combined cornstarch and water, heat to boiling, stirring until thickened, about 1 minute. Garnish each bowl of soup with a tablespoon of sour cream.

BLUEBERRY SOUP

L

A light and pretty soup, combining whole and puréed blueberries.

45

❄

6 first-course servings

4 cups fresh or frozen blueberries, divided

¼ cup lemon juice

1 cup each: cranberry juice, dry white wine or cranberry juice

½- ¾ cup sugar, divided

2 tablespoons cornstarch

⅛ teaspoon ground cinnamon

½–1 teaspoon vanilla, divided
¾ cup low-fat vanilla yogurt

1. Heat 2 cups blueberries and lemon juice to boiling in medium saucepan; reduce heat and simmer 2 minutes or until berries soften. Process mixture in food processor or blender until smooth. Strain mixture into medium saucepan; whisk in cranberry juice, wine, and combined ½ cup sugar, cornstarch, and cinnamon. Heat to boiling, whisking until thickened, about 1 minute. Stir in vanilla and remaining ¼ cup sugar to taste; refrigerate until chilled; stir in remaining 2 cups blueberries. Garnish each bowl of soup with dollops of yogurt.

Per Serving:
Calories: 212
% calories from fat: 3
Protein (g): 2.3
Carbohydrate (g): 44.0
Fat (g): 0.7
Saturated fat (g): 0.3
Cholesterol (mg): 1.5
Sodium (mg): 22

Exchanges:
Milk: 0.5
Vegetable: 0.0
Fruit: 3.0
Bread: 0.0
Meat: 0.0
Fat: 0.0

CANTALOUPE-LIME SOUP

V

This nutritious soup is a tangy refresher on a hot day.

45
❄

4 first-course servings

¼ cup sugar
1 tablespoon cornstarch
Dash salt
¾ cup cold water
4 cups cubed cantaloupe (1-inch)
Zest from 1 lime, grated
1 tablespoon fresh lime juice
Lime slices, as garnish

Per Serving:
Calories: 90
% calories from fat: 3
Protein (g): 1.1
Carbohydrate (g): 22.5
Fat (g): 0.4
Saturated fat (g): 0
Cholesterol (mg): 0
Sodium (mg): 12

Exchanges:
Milk: 0.0
Vegetable: 0.0
Fruit: 1.5
Bread: 0.0
Meat: 0.0
Fat: 0.0

1. Combine sugar, cornstarch, and salt in small saucepan; whisk in water and heat to boiling, whisking until thickened, about 1 minute. Process sugar mixture and cantaloupe in food processor or blender until smooth; stir in lime zest and juice. Refrigerate until chilled; garnish each bowl of soup with lime slices.

SWEET CHERRY SOUP

L

45
❄️

Serve as a first course — or a dessert! For year-round enjoyment, frozen cherries can be substituted for the fresh.

4 first-course servings

1½ pounds dark sweet cherries, pitted
3–4 tablespoons sugar
3 cups plus ¼ cup water, divided
12 whole cloves
1 large cinnamon stick, broken into pieces
1½ tablespoons cornstarch
Ground nutmeg, as garnish
4 tablespoons fat-free sour cream

Per Serving:
Calories: 179
% calories from fat: 8
Protein (g): 3
Carbohydrate (g): 41.9
Fat (g): 1.6
Saturated fat (g): 0.4
Cholesterol (mg): 0
Sodium (mg): 10

Exchanges:
Milk: 0.0
Vegetable: 0.0
Fruit: 3.0
Bread: 0.0
Meat: 0.0
Fat: 0.0

1. Heat cherries, sugar, and 3 cups water to boiling in medium saucepan; add spices, tied in cheesecloth bag. Reduce heat and simmer, covered, until cherries are tender, 15 to 20 minutes; remove and discard spices. Process soup mixture in food processor or blender until smooth;. strain into saucepan, discarding cherry skins. Heat to boiling; whisk in combined cornstarch and remaining ¼ cup water, whisking until thickened, about 1 minute. Refrigerate until chilled; sprinkle each bowl of soup with nutmeg and top with a tablespoon of sour cream.

PEAR, MELON, AND MANGO SOUP

L

45
❄️

Delicate flavors combine in a beautiful, pale green soup.

8 first-course servings

2 cups chopped, peeled pears (1-inch)
½ cup apple juice
¼ cup lime juice
8 cups cubed honeydew melon (1-inch)
¼ teaspoon ground nutmeg
1 mango, peeled, pitted, chopped
1 cup blueberries
Honey-Lime Cream (recipe follows)
Mint sprigs, as garnish

1. Heat pears, apple juice, and lime juice to boiling in medium saucepan; reduce heat and simmer, covered, until pears are tender, about 5 minutes. Process pear mixture, melon, and nutmeg in food processor or blender until smooth; refrigerate until chilled. Sprinkle each bowl of soup with mango and blueberries and top with a dollop of Honey-Lime Cream; garnish with mint sprigs.

Per Serving:
Calories: 123
% calories from fat: 3
Protein (g): 2.5
Carbohydrate (g): 30.2
Fat (g): 0.5
Saturated fat (g): 0.1
Cholesterol (mg): 0.5
Sodium (mg): 33

Exchanges:
Milk: 0.0
Vegetable: 0.0
Fruit: 2.0
Bread: 0.0
Meat: 0.0
Fat: 0.0

Honey-Lime Cream

Makes about 1 cup

1 cup fat-free plain yogurt
2 tablespoons honey
2 teaspoons lime juice
1 teaspoon grated lime zest

1. Combine all ingredients.

ICED RED PLUM SOUP WITH CHERRY LIQUEUR

L

This tangy fruit soup takes advantage of summer's abundance of plums.

45

8 first-course servings

1¾ pounds ripe red plums halved, pitted
1–1⅓ cups sugar, divided
½ cup cranberry juice cocktail
1½ cups low-fat vanilla yogurt
2 tablespoons cherry liqueur or cranberry juice
1 teaspoon vanilla
Thinly sliced plum, as garnish

Per Serving:
Calories: 175
% calories from fat: 4
Protein (g): 2.6
Carbohydrate (g): 38.6
Fat (g): 0.7
Saturated fat (g): 0.4
Cholesterol (mg): 2.3
Sodium (mg): 31

Exchanges:
Milk: 0.5
Vegetable: 0.0
Fruit: 2.0
Bread: 0.0
Meat: 0.0
Fat: 0.0

1. Heat halved plums, 1 cup sugar, and cranberry juice to boiling in large saucepan; reduce heat and simmer, covered, until plums are soft, about 6 minutes. Process mixture in food processor or blender until smooth. Transfer to large bowl and stir in yogurt, liqueur, and vanilla; stir in

remaining ⅓ cup sugar to taste. Place soup in freezer until ice crystals begin to form around the edges, 2 to 3 hours; stir well and ladle into bowls; garnish with plum slices.

ICED STRAWBERRY-BUTTERMILK SOUP

L

45

Pretty and refreshing, this soup is a great addition to a warm-weather brunch or luncheon menu.

6 first-course servings

3 cups sliced fresh or frozen rhubarb
¾–1 cup granulated sugar, divided
½ cup cranberry juice, divided
1 tablespoon lemon juice
1½ tablespoons cornstarch
3 tablespoons orange or cherry liqueur or orange juice
2⅔ cups fresh or partially thawed, frozen strawberries
1½ cups buttermilk, divided
1 teaspoon vanilla
Strawberry slices, as garnish

Per Serving:
Calories: 198
% calories from fat: 4
Protein (g): 3.0
Carbohydrate (g): 42.1
Fat (g): 0.9
Saturated fat (g): 0.4
Cholesterol (mg): 2.5
Sodium (mg): 68

Exchanges:
Milk: 0.0
Vegetable: 0.0
Fruit: 3.0
Bread: 0.0
Meat: 0.0
Fat: 0.0

1. Heat rhubarb, ¾ cup sugar, and ¼ cup cranberry juice to boiling in large saucepan; reduce heat and simmer, stirring occasionally, until rhubarb is very tender, 8 to 10 minutes. Stir in combined remaining ¼ cup cranberry juice, lemon juice, cornstarch, and liqueur, stirring until thickened, about 1 minute. Process mixture in food processor or blender until smooth; transfer to large bowl.

2. Process strawberries, 1¼ cups buttermilk, and vanilla in food processor or blender until smooth. Strain into rhubarb mixture; discard seeds. Stir in remaining ¼ cup sugar to taste. Place soup in freezer until ice crystals begin to form around the edges, 2 to 3 hours; stir well and ladle into bowls. Pour scant tablespoon buttermilk in center of soup in each bowl; stir with small spoon to swirl. Garnish with strawberry slices.

CRANBERRY FRUIT SOUP

A sweet and colorful first course for holiday dining.

4 first-course servings

1 cup sugar
¼ cup cornstarch
1 quart reduced-calorie cranberry juice
Cranberry Cream (recipe follows)

1. Whisk combined sugar and cornstarch into cranberry juice in medium saucepan; heat to boiling, whisking until thickened, about 1 minute. Refrigerate until chilled; garnish each bowl of soup with Cranberry Cream.

Per Serving:
Calories: 200
% calories from fat: 3
Protein (g): 0
Carbohydrate (g): 49
Fat (g): 0.7
Saturated fat (g): 0.7
Cholesterol (mg): 0
Sodium (mg): 51

Exchanges:
Milk: 0.0
Vegetable: 0.0
Fruit: 3.3
Bread: 0.0
Meat: 0.0
Fat: 0.0

Cranberry Cream
Makes about ½ cup

1 cup light non-dairy whipped topping
2–3 teaspoons powdered sugar
2–4 tablespoons chopped fresh or frozen cranberries

1. Mix all ingredients.

CIDER SOUP

L *An unusual soup, and a great choice for fall dining.*

45 **6 first-course servings**

2½ cups thinly sliced leek (white part only)

¼ cup chopped celery

2 tablespoons chopped green bell pepper

2–3 teaspoons margarine or butter

2 tablespoons flour

¼ teaspoon dry mustard

1½ cups reduced-sodium vegetable broth

2–3 teaspoons low-sodium Worcestershire sauce

1 cup (4 ounces) shredded reduced-fat Cheddar
   cheese

1 cup apple cider

⅓ cup fat-free half-and-half or fat-free milk

Salt and white pepper, to taste

Per Serving:
Calories: 123
% calories from fat: 35
Protein (g): 8.6
Carbohydrate (g): 11.4
Fat (g): 4.8
Saturated fat (g): 2.6
Cholesterol (mg): 13.5
Sodium (mg): 234

Exchanges:
Milk: 0.0
Vegetable: 0.0
Fruit: 1.0
Bread: 0.0
Meat: 1.0
Fat: 0.5

1. Sauté leek, celery, and bell pepper in margarine in medium saucepan until tender, about 5 minutes. Stir in flour and dry mustard; cook 1 minute. Stir in chicken broth and Worcestershire sauce and heat to boiling; reduce heat and simmer, stirring, until slightly thickened, about 1 minute. Remove from heat; add cheese and stir until melted. Process soup mixture in food processor or blender until smooth; return to saucepan. Stir in cider and half-and-half; cook over medium heat until hot, 3 to 5 minutes. Season to taste with salt and white pepper.

VARIATION

Caramel Apple Soup — Make soup as above. Sauté 2 cups peeled, sliced apples in 1 to 2 tablespoons margarine 2 minutes; sprinkle with ⅓ cup packed light brown sugar. Cook over medium heat, stirring occasionally, until apples are tender, 3 to 4 minutes. Spoon apples into bottoms of soup bowls; ladle warm soup over.

TROPICAL MELON SOUP

V

45
❄

Enjoy this refreshing soup as a first course, a light dessert, or a midday snack.

4 first-course servings

4 cups cubed cantaloupe (1-inch)
1½ cups cubed honeydew melon (1-inch)
¼ cup each: fresh lemon juice, dry white wine
1 tablespoon sugar
Shredded coconut, as garnish
Grated lime zest, as garnish

1. Process melon, lemon juice, wine, and sugar in food processor or blender until smooth; refrigerate until chilled. Sprinkle each bowl of soup with coconut and lime zest.

Per Serving:
Calories: 97
% calories from fat: 2
Protein (g): 1.7
Carbohydrate (g): 22.7
Fat (g): 0.2
Saturated fat (g): 0
Cholesterol (mg): 0
Sodium (mg): 38

Exchanges:
Milk: 0.0
Vegetable: 0.0
Fruit: 1.5
Bread: 0.0
Meat: 0.0
Fat: 0.0

FRAGRANT MELON SOUP

V

45
❄

The flavor of the soup is determined by the ripeness and flavor of the melon.

4 first-course servings

4 cups cubed cantaloupe (1-inch)
½ cup orange juice
3–4 tablespoons lemon or lime juice
2 tablespoons honey
¼–½ cup fat-free half-and-half or fat-free milk
4 thin lemon or lime slices
Mint or lemon balm sprigs, as garnish

1. Process cantaloupe, orange and lemon juice, honey, and half-and-half in food processor or blender until smooth; refrigerate until chilled; garnish each bowl of soup with a lemon slice and mint sprig.

Per Serving:
Calories: 116
% calories from fat: 4
Protein (g): 2.2
Carbohydrate (g): 28
Fat (g): 0.5
Saturated fat (g): 0
Cholesterol (mg): 0
Sodium (mg): 30

Exchanges:
Milk: 0.0
Vegetable: 0.0
Fruit: 2.0
Bread: 0.0
Meat: 0.0
Fat: 0.0

GAZPACHO WITH AVOCADO SOUR CREAM

L

45

❄

Easy to make and served cold, gazpacho is a wonderful soup to keep on hand in summer months.

6 first-course servings

5 large tomatoes, halved, seeded
2 cups reduced-sodium tomato juice
2 cloves garlic
2 tablespoons lime juice
1 teaspoon dried oregano leaves
1 cup each: chopped yellow bell pepper, celery, cucumber
6 green onions, thinly sliced
2 tablespoons finely chopped cilantro
Salt and pepper, to taste
Avocado Sour Cream (recipe follows)
Hot pepper sauce

Per Serving:
Calories: 76
% calories from fat: 17
Protein (g): 3.3
Carbohydrate (g): 15.1
Fat (g): 1.6
Saturated fat (g): 0.3
Cholesterol (mg): 0.1
Sodium (mg): 46

Exchanges:
Milk: 0.0
Vegetable: 2.0
Fruit: 0.0
Bread: 0.0
Meat: 0.0
Fat: 0.5

1. Chop tomatoes, reserving 1 cup. Process remaining tomatoes, tomato juice, garlic, lime juice, and oregano in food processor or blender until smooth. Mix tomato mixture, reserved tomatoes, bell pepper, celery, cucumber, green onions, and cilantro in large bowl; season to taste with salt and pepper. Serve chilled; top each bowl of soup with a dollop of Avocado Sour Cream. Serve with hot pepper sauce.

Avocado Sour Cream

Makes about ⅔ cup

½ medium avocado, chopped
¼ cup fat-free sour cream
2 tablespoons fat-free milk
Salt and white pepper, to taste

1. Process all ingredients in food processor until smooth; season to taste with salt and white pepper.

SPANISH GAZPACHO

V

45

❄

Add additional tomato juice if a thinner consistency is desired. For flavor variation, serve this gazpacho with Garlic Croutons (see pg. 636).

6 first-course servings

1 quart reduced-sodium tomato juice

2–3 tablespoons lemon juice

1 cup each: chopped green bell peppers, zucchini, seeded cucumber

½ cup each: sliced green onions, celery

3 cloves garlic, minced

2 teaspoons olive oil

1 teaspoon dried basil leaves

Salt and pepper, to taste

Hot pepper sauce to taste

Per Serving:
Calories: 63
% calories from fat: 21
Protein (g): 2.3
Carbohydrate (g): 12.1
Fat (g): 1.8
Saturated fat (g): 0.3
Cholesterol (mg): 0.0
Sodium (mg): 28

Exchanges:
Milk: 0.0
Vegetable: 2.0
Fruit: 0.0
Bread: 0.0
Meat: 0.0
Fat: 0.5

1. Combine all ingredients, except salt, pepper, and hot pepper sauce, in large bowl. Season to taste with salt, pepper, and hot pepper sauce. Refrigerate until chilled.

EASY GAZPACHO

V

45

❄

If the yen for gazpacho strikes and good ripe tomatoes are unavailable, try this version, using canned tomatoes.

4 first-course servings

2 cans (14½ ounces each) plum tomatoes, undrained

1 small clove garlic, minced

1–2 tablespoons chopped scallions or chives

1 medium cucumber, peeled, seeded, chopped

½ cup each: chopped green bell pepper, celery

2–3 drops hot pepper sauce

¼ teaspoon pepper

Salt, to taste

Parsley sprigs, as garnish

Per Serving:
Calories: 38
% calories from fat: 9
Protein (g): 1.8
Carbohydrate (g): 8.2
Fat (g): 0.4
Saturated fat (g): 0.1
Cholesterol (mg): 0
Sodium (mg): 230

Exchanges:
Milk: 0.0
Vegetable: 2.0
Fruit: 0.0
Bread: 0.0
Meat: 0.0
Fat: 0.0

1. Process tomatoes with liquid and garlic in food processor or blender until smooth. Transfer to bowl and add remaining ingredients except salt and parsley. Season to taste with salt; refrigerate until chilled. Garnish each bowl of soup with parsley.

WHITE GAZPACHO

L

Something different that is sure to please!

45
❄

4 first-course servings

1 large onion, sliced
4 cloves garlic, minced
2 cups fat-free milk
1 vegetable bouillon cube
1–1 ½ cups plain fat-free yogurt
2 teaspoons lemon juice
2 dashes hot pepper sauce
Salt and white pepper, to taste
⅓ cup each: chopped seeded cucumber,
    yellow tomato, avocado
Finely chopped cilantro, as garnish

Per Serving:
Calories: 109
% calories from fat: 27
Protein (g): 6.7
Carbohydrate (g): 14.3
Fat (g): 3.4
Saturated fat (g): 0.6
Cholesterol (mg): 2
Sodium (mg): 196

Exchanges:
Milk: 0.5
Vegetable: 2.0
Fruit: 0.0
Bread: 0.0
Meat: 0.0
Fat: 0.5

1. Sauté onion and garlic in lightly greased skillet over medium-low heat until very tender, about 15 minutes. Add milk and bouillon cube; cook over medium-high heat until hot. Process milk mixture, yogurt, lemon juice, and hot pepper sauce in food processor or blender until smooth. Season to taste with salt and white pepper. Refrigerate until chilled; stir in cucumber, tomato, and avocado. Sprinkle each bowl of soup with cilantro.

BEAN GAZPACHO

L

45

❄

*Puréed beans contribute nutritional value, plus a velvety texture, to this
delicious gazpacho.*

8 entrée servings

2 cans (15 ounces each) pinto beans, rinsed, drained
1 quart reduced-sodium tomato juice
3–4 tablespoons lime juice
2 teaspoons each: reduced-sodium Worcestershire
    sauce, minced roasted garlic
1 cup each: thick and chunky salsa, peeled, seeded,
    chopped cucumber, sliced celery
½ cup each: sliced green onions, chopped green
    bell pepper
½ cup each: chopped avocado, fat-free sour cream
1½ cups (½ recipe) Herb Croutons (see p. 636)

Per Serving:
Calories: 260
% calories from fat: 13
Protein (g): 12.9
Carbohydrate (g): 47.1
Fat (g): 3.8
Saturated fat (g): 0.2
Cholesterol (mg): 0
Sodium (mg): 642

Exchanges:
Milk: 0.5
Vegetable: 2.0
Fruit: 0.0
Bread: 2.5
Meat: 0.5
Fat: 0.0

1. Process beans, tomato juice, lime juice, Worcestershire sauce,
and garlic in food processor or blender until smooth; pour into
large bowl. Mix in remaining ingredients, except avocado, sour
cream, and Herb Croutons. Refrigerate until chilled. Mix avocado
into soup; garnish each bowl of soup with a dollop of sour cream
and croutons.

45-MINUTE PREPARATION TIP: Bake Herb Croutons while
preparing the soup.

BEER SOUP

L

45

A first-course soup with spunky beer flavor. Use a flavorful micro-brewery beer.

4 first-course servings

2 tablespoons flour
1 tablespoon sugar
2 cups fat-free half-and-half or 2% reduced-fat milk
1 cup beer
1 tablespoon dark corn syrup
1 cup (4 ounces) shredded reduced-fat Swiss cheese
Ground ginger or nutmeg, as garnish

Per Serving:
Calories: 194
% calories from fat: 7
Protein (g): 12.3
Carbohydrate (g): 25.1
Fat (g): 1.4
Saturated fat (g): 0.9
Cholesterol (mg): 9.5
Sodium (mg): 197

Exchanges:
Milk: 0.0
Vegetable: 0.0
Fruit: 0.0
Bread: 2.0
Meat: 1.0
Fat: 0.0

1. Mix flour and sugar in medium saucepan; whisk in half-and-half. Heat to boiling, whisking until thickened, about 1 minute. Whisk in beer and corn syrup and simmer 1 to 2 minutes. Spoon cheese into bottoms of soup bowls and ladle hot soup over; sprinkle lightly with ginger or nutmeg.

FRESH BASIL SOUP

L

45

For flavor variation, try another favorite garden herb, such as rosemary, oregano, lemon thyme, or marjoram.

6 first-course servings

4 cups reduced-sodium vegetable broth
1 cup each: firmly packed basil and parsley
½ cup chopped onion
1 teaspoon sugar
2 cups potatoes, peeled, cubed
1 cup fat-free milk
¼ cup all-purpose flour
1 tablespoon margarine or butter
Salt and white pepper, to taste
Basil sprigs, as garnish

Per Serving:
Calories: 128
% calories from fat: 17
Protein (g): 4
Carbohydrate (g): 22.7
Fat (g): 2.5
Saturated fat (g): 0.5
Cholesterol (mg): 0.8
Sodium (mg): 355

Exchanges:
Milk: 0.0
Vegetable: 0.0
Fruit: 0.0
Bread: 1.5
Meat: 0.0
Fat: 0.5

1. Heat broth, basil, parsley, onion, and sugar to boiling in medium saucepan; reduce heat and simmer, covered, 30 minutes. Strain; return broth to saucepan. Add potatoes and heat to boiling; reduce heat and simmer, covered, until potatoes are tender, about 15 minutes. Stir in combined milk and flour, stirring, until thickened, about 1 minute; stir in margarine. Season to taste with salt and white pepper; sprinkle each bowl of soup with basil sprigs.

SHIITAKE-PORTOBELLO CHOWDER

L

Celebrate the rich mushroom, cheese and wine flavors in this chowder.

45 **4 entrée servings**

4 shallots, thinly sliced

2 teaspoons margarine or butter, divided

2 large potatoes, cubed (¼-inch)

3 cups reduced-sodium vegetable broth

2 cups each: sliced shiitake mushroom caps, cubed portobello mushrooms

¼ cup (1 ounce) shredded Gruyère or Swiss cheese

2 tablespoons Marsala wine (optional)

Salt and white pepper, to taste

Per Serving:
Calories: 162
% calories from fat: 26
Protein (g): 5.6
Carbohydrate (g): 24.7
Fat (g): 5
Saturated fat (g): 1.8
Cholesterol (mg): 7.8
Sodium (mg): 114

Exchanges:
Milk: 0.0
Vegetable: 2.0
Fruit: 0.0
Bread: 1.0
Meat: 0.0
Fat: 1.0

1. Sauté shallots in 1 teaspoon margarine in large saucepan 2 to 3 minutes; add potatoes and broth and heat to boiling. Reduce heat and simmer, covered, until potatoes are tender, about 15 minutes. Process soup in food processor or blender until smooth; return to saucepan.

2. Sauté mushrooms in remaining 1 teaspoon margarine or butter in large skillet until lightly browned, about 8 minutes; stir into potato mixture. Cook, uncovered, over medium heat until hot, about 5 minutes. Remove from heat; add cheese and wine, stirring until cheese is melted. Season to taste with salt and white pepper.

BLACK MAGIC GARLIC CHOWDER

L

45

Garlic lovers take note—this is a colorful chowder with plenty of palate-appealing garlic flavor.

4 first-course servings

1 can (15 ounces) black beans, rinsed, drained, divided
1 can (14 ounces) reduced-sodium vegetable broth, divided
1 garlic bulb, cloves peeled and thinly sliced
2 small serrano chilies, seeded, minced
2 teaspoons olive oil
1 pound plum tomatoes, coarsely chopped
Salt and pepper, to taste
1½ cups Chili Croutons (½ recipe) (see p. 637)
¼ cup each: chopped parsley, fat-free sour cream

Per Serving:
Calories: 195
% calories from fat: 15
Protein (g): 9.2
Carbohydrate (g): 39.9
Fat (g): 3.9
Saturated fat (g): 0.4
Cholesterol (mg): 0
Sodium (mg): 503

Exchanges:
Milk: 0.0
Vegetable: 1.0
Fruit: 0.0
Bread: 2.0
Meat: 0.0
Fat: 0.5

1. Process ¾ cup beans and ¾ cup broth in food processor or blender until smooth. Sauté garlic and serrano chilies in oil in large saucepan until garlic is golden, about 5 minutes; stir in puréed beans and broth, remaining beans and broth and tomatoes. Heat to boiling; reduce heat and simmer, covered, 10 minutes. Season to taste with salt and pepper. Top each bowl of chowder with Chili Croutons, parsley, and a dollop of sour cream.

FRENCH VEGETABLE CHOWDER WITH PISTOU

L

45

Pistou, the French version of Italy's pesto, gives this chowder a lively flavor boost. Bon appétit!

4 entrée servings

1 cup each: cut wax beans, small cauliflower florets, cubed zucchini and potato
2 carrots, thinly sliced
1 can (14½ ounces) reduced-sodium vegetable broth, divided
1 can (15 ounces) Great Northern or navy beans, rinsed, drained
1 cup cooked elbow macaroni

3 plum tomatoes, coarsely chopped
4 scallions, sliced
Pistou (recipe follows)
Salt and pepper, to taste

1. Heat wax beans, cauliflower, zucchini, potato, carrots, and 1 cup broth to boiling in large saucepan; reduce heat and simmer, covered, until vegetables are tender, about 15 minutes. Process remaining broth and beans in food processor or blender until smooth; add to soup. Add macaroni, tomatoes, and scallions; heat to boiling; Reduce heat and simmer, covered, until hot, about 5 minutes. Stir in Pistou; season to taste with salt and pepper.

Pistou

Makes about ⅔ cup

1 tablespoon minced garlic
2 teaspoons olive oil
½ cup finely chopped basil
¼ cup (1 ounce) crumbled blue cheese

1. Combine all ingredients in bowl; mash with fork.

Per Serving:
Calories: 254
% calories from fat: 17
Protein (g): 12
Carbohydrate (g): 46.7
Fat (g): 5.2
Saturated fat (g): 1.8
Cholesterol (mg): 5.3
Sodium (mg): 581

Exchanges:
Milk: 0.0
Vegetable: 3.0
Fruit: 0.0
Bread: 2.0
Meat: 0.0
Fat: 1.0

BARLEY-VEGETABLE CHOWDER

L

A perfect dish for crisp autumn days; substitute any desired vegetables.

45

4 entrée servings

2 small onions, chopped

1 leek (white part only), sliced

2 cloves garlic, minced

1 cup each: fresh or frozen lima beans, whole kernel corn, finely chopped cabbage, sliced carrots

1 teaspoon dried savory leaves

½ teaspoon dried thyme leaves

1 bay leaf

2 cans (14½ ounces each) reduced-sodium vegetable broth, divided

⅔ cup quick-cooking barley

2 tablespoons flour

½ cup fat-free milk

Salt and pepper, to taste

Per Serving:
Calories: 322
% calories from fat: 6
Protein (g): 12.4
Carbohydrate (g): 63.9
Fat (g): 2.3
Saturated fat (g): 1.1
Cholesterol (mg): 0
Sodium (mg): 585

Exchanges:
Milk: 0.0
Vegetable: 2.0
Fruit: 0.0
Bread: 3.5
Meat: 0.5
Fat: 0.0

1. Sauté onions, leek, and garlic in lightly greased large saucepan until tender, about 5 minutes. Add remaining vegetables and herbs; sauté 2 to 3 minutes. Add broth and barley and heat to boiling; reduce heat and simmer, covered, until vegetables and barley are tender, about 15 minutes. Heat chowder to boiling; stir in combined flour and milk, stirring until thickened, about 1 minute. Discard bay leaf; season to taste with salt and pepper.

PIGEON PEA CHOWDER WITH SPANISH ONIONS

V

45

This hearty chowder reflects the Spanish colonial culinary tradition that makes Cuban and Puerto Rican cooking delightfully distinctive. Sofrito, a popular Cuban seasoning, can be found in the ethnic section of many supermarkets.

4 entrée servings

1 large Spanish onion, coarsely chopped

4 shallots, thinly sliced

2 teaspoons canola oil

2 cups shredded zucchini

6 tomatillos, husked, diced

1 large potato, unpeeled, cubed

1 can (15 ounces) green pigeon peas, rinsed, drained

2 cups reduced-sodium vegetable broth

¼ cup sofrito sauce (optional)

Salt and pepper, to taste

Per Serving:
Calories: 262
% calories from fat 22
Protein (g): 10.7
Carbohydrate (g): 42.1
Fat (g): 6.7
Saturated fat (g): 1.7
Cholesterol (mg): 5
Sodium (mg): 350

Exchanges:
Milk: 0.0
Vegetable: 0.0
Fruit: 0.0
Bread: 3.0
Meat: 0.0
Fat: 1.0

1. Sauté onion and shallots in oil in large saucepan until translucent, about 5 minutes. Add zucchini and sauté 2 to 3 minutes. Add remaining ingredients, except sofrito sauce, salt, and pepper; heat to boiling. Reduce heat and simmer, covered, until potatoes are tender, about 15 minutes. Stir in sofrito sauce; season to taste with salt and pepper.

VEGETARIAN CHILI IN BLACK AND WHITE

V

45

Black and white beans give this vegetarian chili a great texture. Its warm flavor comes from toasted cumin seeds. Toasting, a technique used by Indian cooks, enhances herb flavor.

4 entrée servings

1 medium onion, chopped

1 teaspoon olive oil

2 cups reduced-sodium tomato juice

2 tablespoons reduced-sodium tomato paste

1 can (15 ounces) each: rinsed drained black beans, Great Northern or navy beans

1½ cups cooked wild rice

1 anaheim chili, seeded, minced

1 teaspoon each: paprika, toasted cumin seeds

Salt and pepper, to taste

Per Serving:
Calories: 300
% calories from fat: 6
Protein (g): 16.3
Carbohydrate (g): 60.6
Fat (g): 2.2
Saturated fat (g): 0.4
Cholesterol (mg): 0
Sodium (mg): 427

Exchanges:
Milk: 0.0
Vegetable: 0.0
Fruit: 0.0
Bread: 4.0
Meat: 0.0
Fat: 0.5

1. Sauté onion in oil in large saucepan until translucent, about 5 minutes. Stir in remaining ingredients, except salt and pepper; heat to boiling. Reduce heat and simmer, covered, 5 to 10 minutes.

SAGEBRUSH CHILI WITH FRESH TOMATOES

V

45

For a fresh take on an old Southwestern favorite, this high-flavor chili sports ripe tomatoes and sage leaves.

4 entrée servings

4 scallions, sliced

8 cloves garlic, thinly sliced

2 teaspoons olive oil

1 quart tomato wedges

2 cans (15 ounces each) pinto beans, rinsed, drained

1 large cayenne chili, roasted, seeded, minced

2 tablespoons chili powder

1 teaspoon each: ground cumin and coriander

2 teaspoons finely chopped fresh or ½ teaspoon dried sage leaves

Salt and pepper, to taste

Per Serving:
Calories: 269
% calories from fat: 17
Protein (g): 13.4
Carbohydrate (g): 46.1
Fat (g): 5.2
Saturated fat (g): 0.9
Cholesterol (mg): 0
Sodium (mg): 680

Exchanges:
Milk: 0.0
Vegetable: 0.0
Fruit: 0.0
Bread: 3.0
Meat: 1.0
Fat: 0.0

1. Sauté scallions and garlic in oil in large saucepan 3 minutes. Add remaining ingredients, except salt and pepper; heat to boiling. Reduce heat and simmer, covered, until tomatoes soften, about 5 minutes. Season to taste with salt and pepper.

SWEET POTATO CHIPOTLE CHILI

V

45

Chipotle chilies are dried, smoked jalapeño chilies. When canned, they are in adobo sauce, which is made with ground chilies and spices. The chilies have a distinctive smoky flavor; taste before adding more, as they can be fiercely hot!

4 entrée servings

1 cup each: chopped onion, green bell pepper

2 teaspoons minced gingerroot

1 teaspoon each: minced garlic, crushed cumin seeds

1 tablespoons peanut or canola oil

3 cups cubed, peeled sweet potatoes

2 cans (15 ounces each) black beans, rinsed, drained

1 can (14 ½ ounces) chili-style chunky tomatoes, undrained

½–1 chipotle chili in adobo sauce, chopped

1 cup water or vegetable broth

Salt, to taste

Per Serving:
Calories: 213
% calories from fat: 14
Protein (g): 8.6
Carbohydrate (g): 44.8
Fat (g): 3.9
Saturated fat (g): 0.6
Cholesterol (mg): 0
Sodium (mg): 452

Exchanges:
Milk: 0.0
Vegetable: 0.0
Fruit: 0.0
Bread: 3.0
Meat: 0.0
Fat: 0.5

1. Sauté onion, bell pepper, gingerroot, garlic, and cumin seeds in oil in large saucepan until tender, about 5 minutes. Add remaining ingredients, except salt, and heat to boiling. Reduce heat and simmer, covered, until sweet potatoes are tender, about 15 minutes. Season to taste with salt.

MONTEREY CHILI ACINI DE PEPE

L

45

Bulgur or cracked wheat can be substituted for the acini de pepe, in this flavorful chili.

4 entrée servings

½ cup each: chopped onion, green bell pepper

1 teaspoon olive oil

1 can (15 ounces) pinto beans, rinsed, drained

1 can (14½ ounces) reduced-sodium diced tomatoes, undrained

1 tablespoon chili powder

1 teaspoon each: dried oregano leaves, unsweetened cocoa

½ cup acini de pepe, cooked

¼ cup chopped cilantro

Salt and pepper, to taste

¾ cup (3 ounces) shredded Monterey Jack cheese

Per Serving:
Calories: 275
% calories from fat: 29
Protein (g): 14
Carbohydrate (g): 36
Fat (g): 9.2
Saturated fat (g): 4.5
Cholesterol (mg): 18.9
Sodium (mg): 461

Exchanges:
Milk: 0.0
Vegetable: 1.0
Fruit: 0.0
Bread: 2.0
Meat: 1.0
Fat: 1.0

1. Sauté onion and bell pepper in oil in large saucepan until tender, 3 to 4 minutes. Add beans, tomatoes with liquid, chili powder, oregano, and cocoa. Heat to boiling; reduce heat and simmer, covered, 10 minutes. Stir in acini de pepe and cilantro; season to taste with salt and pepper. Sprinkle each bowl of chili with cheese.

BLACK BEAN, RICE, AND CORN CHILI

V

45

This vegetarian chili is simple, speedy, and tastes superb.

4 entrée servings

1½ cups chopped onions

1 tablespoon minced garlic

1 teaspoon olive oil

1 can (28 ounces) reduced-sodium crushed tomatoes, undrained

1 can (16 ounces) black beans, rinsed, drained

½ cup each: whole kernel corn, cooked rice

1 each: large chopped red bell pepper, minced jalapeño chili

1 tablespoon chili powder

1 teaspoon ground allspice

Salt and pepper, to taste

Per Serving:
Calories: 219
% calories from fat: 9
Protein (g): 10.1
Carbohydrate (g): 49.2
Fat (g): 2.7
Saturated fat (g): 0.3
Cholesterol (mg): 0
Sodium (mg): 726

1. Sauté onions and garlic in oil in large saucepan until tender, about 8 minutes. Stir in remaining ingredients, except salt and pepper, and heat to boiling. Reduce heat and simmer, covered, 15 minutes; season to taste with salt and pepper.

Exchanges:
Milk: 0.0
Vegetable: 3.0
Fruit: 0.0
Bread: 3.0
Meat: 0.0
Fat: 0.0

CINCINNATI CHILI WITH AN ATTITUDE

V

45

Midwesterners have a penchant for chili that's thick and spicy and served over spaghetti. Here's a vegetarian version with lentils, tomatoes, and easy-to-find seasonings.

6 entrée servings

Per Serving:
Calories: 277
% calories from fat: 7
Protein (g): 13.4
Carbohydrate (g): 53
Fat (g): 2.5
Saturated fat (g): 0.2
Cholesterol (mg): 0
Sodium (mg): 308

1 medium onion, chopped

1 tablespoon minced garlic

1 teaspoon olive oil

1 can (14½ ounces) crushed tomatoes, undrained

2 cups cooked lentils

1 tablespoon chili powder, unsweetened cocoa

½ teaspoon ground cinnamon

¼ teaspoon ground allspice

Salt and pepper, to taste

12 ounces linguine, cooked, warm

Toppings: kidney beans, chopped onion and bell pepper, shredded reduced-fat Cheddar cheese

Exchanges:
Milk: 0.0
Vegetable: 2.0
Fruit: 0.0
Bread: 3.0
Meat: 0.0
Fat: 0.0

1. Sauté onion and garlic in oil in large saucepan until tender, about 5 minutes. Add remaining ingredients, except salt, pepper, linguine, and Toppings; heat to boiling. Reduce heat and simmer, covered, 20 minutes. Season to taste with salt and pepper. Serve over linguine with a choice of Toppings (not included in nutritional data).

CHILI SIN CARNE

L   *The variety of toppings makes this chili fun to serve—add other toppings too, such as chopped bell peppers and tomatoes, and chopped fresh oregano or cilantro.*

6 entrée servings

⅔ package (12-ounce size) vegetarian ground beef

1 cup each: chopped onions, green bell pepper

2 cloves garlic, minced

1–2 tablespoons chili powder

1–2 teaspoons each: ground cumin, dried oregano leaves

¼ teaspoon ground cloves

6 cans (14½ ounces each) reduced-sodium diced tomatoes, undrained

1 can (15 ounces) red kidney beans, rinsed, drained

1 can (6 ounces) reduced-sodium tomato paste

¾ cup beer or water

1 tablespoon each: packed light brown sugar, unsweetened cocoa

Salt and pepper, to taste

Toppings: shredded fat-free or reduced-fat Cheddar cheese, thinly sliced green onions, fat-free or reduced-fat sour cream

Per Serving:
Calories: 245
% calories from fat: 5
Protein (g): 19.2
Carbohydrate (g): 40.3
Fat (g): 1.4
Saturated fat (g): 0.2
Cholesterol (mg): 0
Sodium (mg): 723

Exchanges:
Milk: 0.0
Vegetable: 2.0
Fruit: 0.0
Bread: 2.0
Meat: 1.0
Fat: 0.0

1. Cook vegetarian ground beef, onions, bell pepper, and garlic in lightly greased large saucepan over medium heat until vegetables are tender, 5 to 8 minutes. Add chili powder, cumin, oregano, and cloves; cook 1 to 2 minutes longer. Add remaining ingredients, except salt and pepper and toppings; heat to boiling. Reduce heat and simmer, covered, 45 minutes; simmer, uncovered, to thicken, if desired. Season to taste with salt and pepper. Serve with Toppings (not included in nutritional data).

VARIATIONS

Veggie Mac — Make recipe as above, adding 1 cup uncooked elbow macaroni or chili mac pasta and ½ cup water to chili after 30 minutes cooking time; heat to boiling. Reduce heat and simmer, covered, until macaroni is tender, about 15 minutes.

Southwest Chili — Make recipe as above, substituting black or pinto beans for the kidney beans and adding 1 minced jalapeño chili. Garnish each serving with a sprinkling of crushed tortilla chips and chopped cilantro leaves.

CARIBBEAN CHILI

This hearty meatless three-bean chili is accented with Mango Salsa; serve with brown rice if you like.

6 entrée servings

2 cups red or green bell peppers, chopped

1 cup chopped onion

1 jalapeño chili, chopped

2 teaspoons minced gingerroot

1 tablespoon each: minced garlic, canola oil

2 tablespoons each: paprika, chili powder

1 tablespoon ground cumin

¼ teaspoon ground cloves

2 teaspoons sugar

2 cans (14½ ounces each) reduced-sodium diced tomatoes, undrained

1 can (15 ounces) each: rinsed, drained pinto, Great Northern, and black beans

1 tablespoon lime juice

Salt and pepper, to taste

Mango Salsa (recipe follows)

Per Serving:
Calories: 331
% calories from fat: 13
Protein (g): 15.2
Carbohydrate (g): 67
Fat (g): 5.2
Saturated fat (g): 0.8
Cholesterol (mg): 0
Sodium (mg): 442

Exchanges:
Milk: 0.0
Vegetable: 3.0
Fruit: 0.0
Bread: 3.0
Meat: 0.0
Fat: 1.0

1. Sauté bell peppers, onion, jalapeño chili, gingerroot, and garlic in oil in large saucepan until tender, about 10 minutes. Add spices, herbs, and sugar; cook 1 minute. Stir in tomatoes with liquid, beans, and lime juice; heat to boiling. Reduce heat and simmer, covered, 20 minutes. Season to taste with salt and pepper. Serve with Mango Salsa.

Mango Salsa
Makes about 1¼ cups

1 cup each: cubed mango, banana
¼ cup chopped cilantro
½ small jalapeño chili, finely chopped
1 tablespoon frozen pineapple or orange juice concentrate, thawed
1 teaspoon lime juice

1. Combine all ingredients.

VEGETARIAN CHILI

V *Cooked, crumbled vegetarian burgers can be added to this chili for additional texture.*

6 entrée servings

1 cup each: chopped onion, carrots mushrooms
½ cup each: chopped green bell pepper, celery
2 cloves garlic, minced
1–2 tablespoons olive oil
2 cans (15 ounces each) kidney beans, rinsed, drained
1 can (15 ounces) garbanzo beans, rinsed, drained
1 cup tomato purée
2 large tomatoes, peeled, seeded
1 teaspoon ground cumin
1–2 tablespoons chili powder
½ teaspoon pepper
Salt, to taste

Per Serving:
Calories: 266
% calories from fat: 13
Protein (g): 12.8
Carbohydrate (g): 47.5
Fat (g): 4.1
Saturated fat (g): 0.5
Cholesterol (mg): 0
Sodium (mg): 646

Exchanges:
Milk: 0.0
Vegetable: 1.0
Fruit: 0.0
Bread: 3.0
Meat: 0.0
Fat: 0.5

1. Sauté onion, carrots, mushrooms, bell pepper, celery, and garlic in oil in Dutch oven until tender, 5 to 8 minutes. Stir in remaining ingredients, except salt, and heat to boiling; reduce heat and simmer 30 minutes, adding water, if necessary, for desired consistency. Season to taste with salt.

VEGETABLE-LENTIL CHILI

V *Lentils add great texture to this meatless chili.*

4 entrée servings

1 cup each: chopped onion, red or green bell pepper
⅓ cup each: sliced carrot, celery
1 clove garlic, minced
2 teaspoons olive oil
1 quart vegetable broth
1 cup water
1 can (14½ ounces) reduced-sodium diced tomatoes, undrained
¾–1 cup brown lentils
1 tablespoon chili powder
¾ teaspoon ground cumin
1 bay leaf
1 cup whole kernel corn
Salt and pepper, to taste

Per Serving:
Calories: 271
% calories from fat: 13
Protein (g): 13.3
Carbohydrate (g): 48.4
Fat (g): 3.9
Saturated fat (g): 0.5
Cholesterol (mg): 0
Sodium (mg): 541

Exchanges:
Milk: 0.0
Vegetable: 0.0
Fruit: 0.0
Bread: 3.0
Meat: 1.0
Fat: 0.0

1. Sauté onion, bell pepper, carrot, celery, and garlic in oil in large saucepan until tender, 3 to 4 minutes. Add remaining ingredients, except salt and pepper; heat to boiling. Reduce heat and simmer, covered, until lentils are tender, about 30 minutes. Discard bay leaf. Season to taste with salt and pepper.

SALSA CHILI

L

Salsa seasons this healthy, meatless chili.

45   **4 entrée servings**

1 can (16 ounces) reduced-sodium crushed
    tomatoes, undrained
1 can (15½ ounces) red kidney beans, rinsed, drained
1½ cups cooked barley
½ cup medium or hot salsa, whole kernel corn
1 tablespoon chili powder
½–1 teaspoon minced jalapeño chili
Salt and pepper, to taste
½ cup (2 ounces) shredded extra-sharp
    Cheddar cheese

Per Serving:
Calories: 317
% calories from fat: 16
Protein (g): 14.8
Carbohydrate (g): 55.2
Fat (g): 5.8
Saturated fat (g): 3.2
Cholesterol (mg): 14.9
Sodium (mg): 790

Exchanges:
Milk: 0.0
Vegetable: 2.0
Fruit: 0.0
Bread: 3.0
Meat: 0.0
Fat: 1.0

1. Heat all ingredients, except salt, pepper, and cheese, to boiling in large saucepan; reduce heat and simmer, covered, 10 to 15 minutes. Season to taste with salt and pepper. Sprinkle each bowl of chili with shredded cheese.

BRUSSELS SPROUTS SOUP

L

A perfect fall soup, when tiny fresh Brussels sprouts are available; serve Roasted Red Pepper Bread (see p. 647) as a flavorful accompaniment.

45

4 first-course servings

½ cup chopped onion
2 teaspoons minced garlic
1 tablespoon margarine or butter
2 tablespoons flour
1⅔ cups fat-free milk
1 pound Brussels sprouts, halved
1 teaspoon dried rosemary leaves
Salt and white pepper, to taste
Ground nutmeg, as garnish

Per Serving:
Calories: 136
% calories from fat: 23
Protein (g): 7.6
Carbohydrate (g): 21.3
Fat (g): 3.8
Saturated fat (g): 0.9
Cholesterol (mg): 1.9
Sodium (mg): 113

Exchanges:
Milk: 0.0
Vegetable: 4.0
Fruit: 0.0
Bread: 0.0
Meat: 0.0
Fat: 0.5

1. Sauté onion and garlic in margarine in large saucepan until tender, about 5 minutes; sprinkle with flour and cook 1 minute. Whisk in milk and heat to boiling, whisking until smooth. Add Brussels sprouts and rosemary; reduce heat and simmer until Brussels sprouts are tender, about 15 minutes. Process soup in food processor or blender until smooth; season to taste with salt and white pepper. Sprinkle each bowl of soup lightly with nutmeg.

CREAM OF ARTICHOKE AND MUSHROOM SOUP

L

45

Shiitake or cremini mushrooms can be substituted for the portobello mushrooms.

4 first-course servings

¾ cup chopped portobello mushrooms

2 tablespoons chopped onion

1 tablespoon each: margarine or butter, flour

3 cups fat-free milk

1 vegetable bouillon cube

1 package (9 ounces) frozen artichoke hearts, thawed, finely chopped

Salt and white pepper, to taste

Paprika, as garnish

Per Serving:
Calories: 135
% calories from fat: 22
Protein (g): 9.2
Carbohydrate (g): 18.9
Fat (g): 3.6
Saturated fat (g): 0.8
Cholesterol (mg): 3
Sodium (mg): 422

Exchanges:
Milk: 1.0
Vegetable: 1.0
Fruit: 0.0
Bread: 0.0
Meat: 0.0
Fat: 0.5

1. Sauté mushrooms and onion in margarine in medium saucepan until tender, about 5 minutes. Stir in flour; cook 1 minute. Stir in milk and bouillon cube and heat to boiling; add artichoke hearts. Reduce heat and simmer, uncovered, 5 minutes; season to taste with salt and white pepper. Sprinkle each bowl of soup with paprika.

PASILLA BLACK BEAN SOUP

L

For a hot and smoky flavor accent, add 1 to 2 teaspoons chopped canned chipotle peppers in adobo sauce to the soup.

4 entrée servings

1 cup each: chopped onion, carrots

2 teaspoons each: minced jalapeño chili, garlic

¾ teaspoon each: dried oregano leaves, ground cumin

¼ teaspoon dried thyme leaves

1 tablespoon olive oil

1 quart Basic Vegetable Stock (see p. 9)

6 dried pasilla chilies, stems and seeds removed, torn into pieces

1 can (14½ ounces) diced tomatoes, undrained

1 can (15 ounces) black beans, rinsed, drained

Salt and pepper, to taste

1 cup (4 ounces) shredded reduced-fat Mexican cheese blend

Chopped cilantro, as garnish

Per Serving:
Calories: 291
% calories from fat: 23
Protein (g): 16
Carbohydrate (g): 40
Fat (g): 7
Saturated fat (g): 4
Cholesterol (mg): 15
Sodium (mg): 1234

Exchanges:
Milk: 0.0
Vegetable: 0.0
Fruit: 0.0
Bread: 2.5
Meat: 2.0
Fat: 0.0

1. Sauté onion, carrots, jalapeño chili, garlic, and herbs in oil in large saucepan until onion is tender, about 5 minutes. Add stock, pasilla chilies, tomatoes with liquid, and beans; heat to boiling. Reduce heat and simmer, covered, 10 minutes. Process soup in food processor or blender until smooth. Season to taste with salt and pepper. Sprinkle each bowl of soup with cheese and cilantro.

CUCUMBER VICHYSSOISE WITH ROASTED RED PEPPER SWIRL

L

Buttermilk gives this soup a refreshing tang and roasted peppers add a flavor perk.

6 first-course servings

1 cup each: chopped onion, cubed peeled potato, sliced peeled cucumber

1½ cups Basic Vegetable Stock (see p. 9)

1 cup water

1 teaspoon ground cumin

1 cup buttermilk

Salt and white pepper, to taste

Roasted Red Pepper Swirl (recipe follows)

Per Serving:
Calories: 87
% calories from fat: 7
Protein (g): 3.3
Carbohydrate (g): 17.7
Fat (g): 0.7
Saturated fat (g): 0.3
Cholesterol (mg): 1.4
Sodium (mg): 49

Exchanges:
Milk: 0.0
Vegetable: 2.0
Fruit: 0.0
Bread: 0.5
Meat: 0.0
Fat: 0.0

1. Heat onion, potato, cucumber, stock, water, and cumin to boiling in large saucepan; reduce heat and simmer, covered, until tender, about 20 minutes. Process mixture in food processor or blender until smooth; pour into large bowl. Stir in buttermilk and season to taste with salt and white pepper. Refrigerate until chilled. Spoon 2 tablespoons Roasted Red Pepper Swirl into each bowl of soup and swirl with knife.

Roasted Red Pepper Swirl

Makes about ¾ cup

3 medium red bell peppers, halved

1 small serrano or jalapeño chili, halved

Vegetable cooking spray

½ cup water

1 clove garlic

2 teaspoons balsamic vinegar

1. Arrange red pepper and serrano chili in single layer on greased foil-lined jelly-roll pan; spray with cooking spray. Roast at 425 degrees until lightly browned, about 25 minutes. Process pepper mixture, water, garlic, and vinegar in food processor or blender until smooth.

VARIATION

Avocado and Chipotle Vichyssoise — Make recipe as above, omitting cucumber. Add 2 medium avocados, ¼–½ small chipotle chili in adobo, and 2 tablespoons dry sherry to mixture in food processor. Garnish each bowl of soup with 1 tablespoon each crumbled feta cheese and chopped cilantro.

SWEET RED PEPPER SOUP

L

45

Use jarred roasted peppers for this soup, or roast 3 medium red bell peppers. (See Roasted Pepper Swirl, p. 367, for roasting directions).

4 first-course servings

1 medium onion, chopped
½ small jalapeño chili, seeded, minced
1 clove garlic, minced
1 jar (15 ounces) roasted red bell peppers, drained
1 cup reduced-sodium tomato juice
1 can (14 ½ ounces) vegetable broth
½ teaspoon dried marjoram leaves
Salt and pepper, to taste
¼ cup fat-free sour cream
Sliced green onions, as garnish

Per Serving:
Calories: 77
% calories from fat: 5
Protein (g): 2.9
Carbohydrate (g): 13.4
Fat (g): 0.4
Saturated fat (g): 0.1
Cholesterol (mg): 0
Sodium (mg): 264

Exchanges:
Milk: 0.0
Vegetable: 3.0
Fruit: 0.0
Bread: 0.0
Meat: 0.0
Fat: 0.0

1. Sauté onion, jalapeño chili, and garlic in lightly greased saucepan until tender, about 5 minutes. Process onion mixture, roasted peppers, and tomato juice in food processor or blender until smooth. Return mixture to saucepan and add broth and marjoram; heat to boiling. Reduce heat and simmer, covered, 15 minutes. Season to taste with salt and pepper. Serve warm or chilled; top each bowl of soup with a dollop of sour cream and sprinkle with green onions.

GREEN VEGETABLE SOUP

V

45

Fresh herbs make this soup especially flavorful. Purchased pesto can be substituted for the Mixed Herb Pesto, but nutritional data will change.

6 first-course servings

½ cup each: chopped green cabbage, celery, onion, broccoli florets, cut green beans, diced zucchini, potato

1 each: chopped medium onion, diced medium potato

1 quart water

½ cup uncooked ditalini

Salt and pepper, to taste

¼ cup (½ recipe) Mixed Herb Pesto (see p. 270)

Per Serving:
Calories: 96
% calories from fat: 26
Protein (g): 2.9
Carbohydrate (g): 15.6
Fat (g): 2.8
Saturated fat (g): 0.4
Cholesterol (mg): 0.7
Sodium (mg): 29

Exchanges:
Milk: 0.0
Vegetable: 1.5
Fruit: 0.0
Bread: 0.5
Meat: 0.0
Fat: 0.5

1. Heat all ingredients, except ditalini, salt, pepper, and Mixed Herb Pesto, to boiling in large saucepan; stir in ditalini. Reduce heat and simmer, covered, until vegetables and pasta are tender, about 15 minutes. Season to taste with salt and pepper. Stir in Mixed Herb Pesto.

SUMMER POTATO-BUTTERMILK SOUP

L

45

This refreshing cold soup is perfect for lunch on a hot summer day.

4 first-course servings

3 medium red potatoes, cooked, peeled, cubed

2 cups chopped, peeled, seeded cucumber

¼ cup chopped fresh or 2 to 3 teaspoons dried dill weed

1 teaspoon dry mustard

½ teaspoon each: sugar, ground cumin

1 quart low-fat buttermilk

Salt and pepper to taste

Dill sprigs, as garnish

Per Serving:
Calories: 199
% calories from fat: 11
Protein (g): 10.4
Carbohydrate (g): 34.1
Fat (g): 2.6
Saturated fat (g): 1.4
Cholesterol (mg): 8.6
Sodium (mg): 264

Exchanges:
Milk: 1.0
Vegetable: 0.0
Fruit: 0.0
Bread: 1.5
Meat: 0.0
Fat: 0.5

1. Combine all ingredients, except salt, pepper, and dill springs, in large bowl; season to taste with salt and pepper. Refrigerate until chilled. Garnish each bowl of soup with dill sprigs.

TOMATO VEGETABLE SOUP

V *Puréed tomatoes provide the base for this tasty soup.*

45 **4 first-course servings**

1 can (28 ounces) Italian plum tomatoes,
  undrained, puréed
2 tablespoons minced scallions
2 whole cloves
1 bay leaf
½ cup each: frozen peas, whole kernel corn
Salt and pepper, to taste

Per Serving:
Calories: 78
% calories from fat: 2
Protein (g): 3.1
Carbohydrate (g): 14.9
Fat (g): 0.2
Saturated fat (g): 0
Cholesterol (mg): 0
Sodium (mg): 350

Exchanges:
Milk: 0.0
Vegetable: 3.0
Fruit: 0.0
Bread: 0.0
Meat: 0.0
Fat: 0.0

1. Heat all ingredients, except salt and pepper, to boiling in medium saucepan; reduce heat and simmer, covered, 10 minutes. Discard bay leaf and cloves; season to taste with salt and pepper.

HERBED CUCUMBER SOUP

L *Use a serrated grapefruit spoon to seed cucumbers quickly and easily.*

6 first-course servings

½ cup chopped onion
6 medium cucumbers, peeled, seeded, chopped
3 tablespoons flour
4 cups Basic Vegetable Stock (see p. 9)
1 teaspoon dried mint or dill weed
½ cup fat-free half-and-half or fat-free milk
Salt and white pepper, to taste
Paprika and thin slices cucumber, as garnish

Per Serving:
Calories: 70
% calories from fat: 8
Protein (g): 3.1
Carbohydrate (g): 13.7
Fat (g): 0.6
Saturated fat (g): 0.1
Cholesterol (mg): 0
Sodium (mg): 33

Exchanges:
Milk: 0.0
Vegetable: 1.0
Fruit: 0.0
Bread: 0.5
Meat: 0.0
Fat: 0.0

1. Sauté onion in lightly greased skillet until tender, 3 to 5 minutes. Add cucumbers and cook over medium heat 5 minutes; stir in flour and cook 1 minute longer. Add stock and mint to saucepan and heat to boiling; reduce heat and simmer, covered, 10 minutes. Process soup in food processor or blender until smooth; stir in half-and-half and season to taste with salt and pepper. Serve warm or chilled; garnish each bowl of soup with paprika and cucumber slices.

CUCUMBER-YOGURT SOUP

L

If possible, use Greek yogurt for this delicious and refreshing no-cook soup.

45

4 first-course servings

3 cups low-fat plain yogurt
1½ cups finely grated, seeded, peeled cucumber
¾ cup water
3 tablespoons minced chives
1 tablespoon each: minced dill weed, garlic
Salt and white pepper, to taste
Thinly sliced cucumber, as garnish

Per Serving:
Calories: 119
% calories from fat: 20
Protein (g): 9.5
Carbohydrate (g): 14.4
Fat (g): 2.7
Saturated fat (g):
Cholesterol (mg): 1.7
Sodium (mg): 121

Exchanges:
Milk: 1.0
Vegetable: 1.0
Fruit: 0.0
Bread: 0.0
Meat: 0.0
Fat: 0.5

1. Combine all ingredients, except salt, white pepper, and cucumber slices in bowl; season to taste with salt and white pepper. Refrigerate until chilled; garnish each bowl of soup with cucumber slices.

BEET SOUP WITH MASHED POTATOES AND YOGURT

The concept of cold soup served with hot mashed potatoes is interesting and surprising; the flavors meld unusually well.

8 first-course servings

1½ pounds beets, cooked, peeled
1 quart water
2 teaspoons sugar
1 tablespoon red wine vinegar
Salt and pepper, to taste
4 large Idaho potatoes
2 cups fat-free plain yogurt

Per Serving:
Calories: 126
% calories from fat: 2
Protein (g): 5.6
Carbohydrate (g): 26.1
Fat (g): 0.3
Saturated fat (g): 0.1
Cholesterol (mg): 1
Sodium (mg): 103

Exchanges:
Milk: 0.0
Vegetable: 2.0
Fruit: 0.0
Bread: 1.0
Meat: 0.0
Fat: 0.0

1. Process beets and 2 cups water in food processor or blender until smooth; transfer to bowl. Mix in remaining water, sugar, and vinegar; season to taste with salt and pepper. Refrigerate until chilled.

2. Bake potatoes at 425 degrees until tender, 45 to 60 minutes. Peel and mash potatoes; season to taste with salt and pepper. Ladle soup into bowls; spoon hot mashed potatoes into center of each bowl and spoon yogurt to the side.

ORANGE-SCENTED SQUASH SOUP

L

45

Subtly seasoned with orange and spices, this delicious soup can be served warm or chilled.

6 first-course servings

¾ cup chopped onion
1 teaspoon ground cinnamon
¼ teaspoon each: ground nutmeg, cloves
1½ cups water
3 pounds winter yellow squash (Hubbard, butternut, or acorn), peeled, cubed
1 large, tart cooking apple, peeled, cored, cubed

1 strip orange zest (3 x ½ inch)

¼–½ cup orange juice

1½–2 cups fat-free half-and-half or fat-free milk

Salt and white pepper, to taste

6 thin orange slices

Snipped chives, as garnish

Per Serving:
Calories: 144
% calories from fat: 8
Protein (g): 4.1
Carbohydrate (g): 30.2
Fat (g): 1.4
Saturated fat (g): 0.3
Cholesterol (mg): 0
Sodium (mg): 64

Exchanges:
Milk: 0.0
Vegetable: 0.0
Fruit: 0.0
Bread: 2.0
Meat: 0.0
Fat: 0.0

1. Sauté onion in lightly greased saucepan until tender, about 5 minutes. Stir in spices; cook 1 minute. Add water, squash, apple, and orange zest to saucepan; heat to boiling. Reduce heat and simmer, covered, until squash is tender, 10 to 15 minutes; discard orange zest. Process soup and orange juice in food processor or blender until smooth; add half-and-half. Season to taste with salt and white pepper. Serve warm or chilled; garnish each bowl of soup with an orange slice and chives.

VARIATION

Winter Squash Soup — Make recipe as above, deleting cloves, orange zest, and orange juice. Add ¼ teaspoon each ground ginger and cumin, and 1 cup apple cider; reduce fat-free half-and-half to ½–1 cup.

VICHYSSOISE

L

45
❄

This classic French potato soup is traditionally served chilled, although it's good warm too!

4 entrée servings

¾ cup each: sliced leeks or green onions, celery

2 tablespoons margarine or butter

6 cups reduced-sodium vegetable broth

2 pounds Idaho potatoes, peeled, cubed

¼ teaspoon dried thyme leaves

Salt and white pepper, to taste

6 tablespoons fat-free sour cream

Snipped chives, as garnish

Per Serving:
Calories: 282
% calories from fat: 20
Protein (g): 6.2
Carbohydrate (g): 51.5
Fat (g): 6.6
Saturated fat (g): 1.2
Cholesterol (mg): 0
Sodium (mg): 134

Exchanges:
Milk: 0.0
Vegetable: 1.0
Fruit: 0.0
Bread: 3.0
Meat: 0.0
Fat: 1.0

1. Sauté leeks and celery in margarine in large saucepan until tender, about 8 minutes. Stir in broth, potatoes, and thyme and heat to boiling; reduce heat and simmer, covered, until potatoes are tender, about 15 minutes. Process soup in food processor or blender until smooth; season to taste with salt and white pepper. Refrigerate until chilled; top each bowl of soup with 1 tablespoon sour cream and sprinkle with chives.

VARIATION

Celery Vichyssoise — Make soup as above, adding 3 large ribs sliced celery to the vegetables. Garnish each bowl with a dollop of Dilled Sour Cream (see p. 242) and celery leaves.

SAVORY MUSHROOM AND BARLEY SOUP

V

45

Use of quick-cooking barley speeds preparation. Other grains, such as wild rice or oat groats, can be substituted for the barley; cook before adding to the soup.

4 entrée servings

1 cup each: chopped onion, celery, carrots

1 teaspoon dried savory leaves

¾ teaspoon fennel seeds, crushed

1 quart water

1 can (14½ ounces) reduced-sodium diced
tomatoes, undrained

½ cup quick-cooking barley

2 cups sliced cremini or white mushrooms

¼ cup chopped parsley

Salt and pepper, to taste

Per Serving:
Calories: 151
% calories from fat: 8
Protein (g): 5.6
Carbohydrate (g): 32.1
Fat (g): 1.4
Saturated fat (g): 0.1
Cholesterol (mg): 0
Sodium (mg): 53

Exchanges:
Milk: 0.0
Vegetable: 2.0
Fruit: 0.0
Bread: 1.5
Meat: 0.0
Fat: 0.0

1. Sauté onion, celery, and carrots in lightly
greased saucepan until onion is tender, about
5 minutes. Stir in herbs; cook 1 minute. Add
water, tomatoes with liquid, barley, and mushrooms to saucepan; heat to boiling. Cook, covered,
until barley is tender, 10 to 15 minutes. Stir in
parsley; season to taste with salt and pepper.

SPINACH SOUP WITH ONION FLOWERS

V

*An attractive and unusual first-course offering. Roasted Vegetable or
Oriental Stock (see pp. 11, 12) can also be used to make
this soup.*

8 first-course servings

8 small onions, peeled

2¼ quarts Canned Vegetable Stock (1½ recipes)
(see p. 10), divided

1 package (10 ounces) frozen spinach

Salt and white pepper, to taste

Green onions, thinly sliced, as garnish

Per Serving:
Calories: 107
% calories from fat: 9
Protein (g): 2.6
Carbohydrate (g): 15.7
Fat (g): 1.1
Saturated fat (g): 0.1
Cholesterol (mg): 0
Sodium (mg): 85

Exchanges:
Milk: 0.0
Vegetable: 2.0
Fruit: 0.0
Bread: 0.5
Meat: 0.0
Fat: 0.0

1. Cut onions into ¼-inch slices from top to
bottom, cutting to, but not through, the bottoms.
Turn onions a quarter turn; cut into ¼-inch
slices, intersecting previous slices and cutting to,
but not through, the bottoms. Heat 6 cups stock
to boiling in large saucepan; add onions. Reduce
heat and simmer, covered, until onions are
tender, about 20 minutes. Remove onions with
slotted spoon; reserve stock.

2. Heat spinach and remaining 3 cups stock to boiling in medium saucepan; reduce heat and simmer, covered, 10 minutes. Strain, pressing lightly on spinach to extract all juice. Discard spinach, or reserve for other use. Combine stock from onions and spinach; heat until hot. Season to taste with salt and white pepper. Arrange onions in bowls; pour soup around onions and sprinkle with green onions. Serve with knives, forks, and spoons.

CREAMED CORN SOUP

L

Garnish bowls of soup generously with finely chopped cilantro or parsley.

4 entrée servings

½ cup chopped onion

1 medium Idaho potato, peeled, cubed

2 cloves garlic, minced

3 tablespoons all-purpose flour

½ teaspoon ground coriander

⅛ teaspoon cayenne pepper

3½ cups Canned Vegetable Stock (see p. 10)

1 cup fat-free milk

1 can (15½ ounces) whole kernel corn, drained

2 medium tomatoes, chopped

Salt and pepper, to taste

Paprika, as garnish

Per Serving:
Calories: 238
% calories from fat: 8
Protein (g): 7.7
Carbohydrate (g): 45.7
Fat (g): 2.3
Saturated fat (g): 0.4
Cholesterol (mg): 1
Sodium (mg): 443

Exchanges:
Milk: 0.0
Vegetable: 3.0
Fruit: 0.0
Bread: 2.0
Meat: 0.0
Fat: 0.5

1. Sauté onion, potato, and garlic in lightly greased saucepan until onion is tender, about 5 minutes. Stir in flour, coriander, and cayenne pepper; cook 1 minute. Stir in stock and heat to boiling; reduce heat and simmer, covered, until potato is tender, about 10 minutes. Process soup mixture in food processor or blender until almost smooth; return to saucepan. Stir in milk, corn, and tomatoes and heat to boiling; reduce heat and simmer, uncovered, 5 minutes. Season to taste with salt and pepper; sprinkle each bowl of soup with paprika.

VARIATION

Latin-American Corn and Avocado Soup — Make soup as above, omitting tomatoes and adding ½ teaspoon crushed saffron with the stock. Beat 2 eggs with 4 ounces fat-free cream cheese and 2 tablespoons prepared chili sauce. Gradually whisk into puréed soup. Garnish each bowl of soup with avocado slices.

EASY MEXICAN CORN AND BEAN SOUP

V   *This spicy soup is quick and easy to prepare.*

45   **4 entrée servings**

¾ cup each: finely chopped large onion, green bell pepper

1 garlic clove, minced

1 tablespoon canola oil

2½ cups reduced-sodium tomato juice

1 can (14½ ounces) reduced-sodium tomatoes, undrained, puréed

2 cups each: whole kernel corn, cooked kidney beans or 1 can (16 ounces) rinsed drained kidney beans

1 tablespoon chili powder

1 teaspoon each: ground cumin, sugar

Salt and pepper, to taste

Per Serving:
Calories: 232
% calories from fat: 14
Protein (g): 10.6
Carbohydrate (g): 44.2
Fat (g): 3.8
Saturated fat (g): 0.3
Cholesterol (mg): 0
Sodium (mg): 45

Exchanges:
Milk: 0.0
Vegetable: 2.0
Fruit: 0.0
Bread: 2.0
Meat: 0.0
Fat: 0.5

1. Sauté onion, bell pepper, and garlic in oil in large saucepan until tender, about 5 minutes; add remaining ingredients, except salt and pepper, and heat to boiling. Reduce heat and simmer, covered, 20 to 25 minutes, Season to taste with salt and pepper.

SOUTHWEST-STYLE POTATO-CORN CHOWDER CON QUESO

L

Add jalapeño chilies to this satisfying soup, if you like a fiery tang.

4 entrée servings

⅔ cup chopped onion

2 teaspoons margarine or butter

1 tablespoon flour

3 cups Basic Vegetable Stock (see p. 9)

3½ cups cubed, peeled potatoes

1 package (10 ounces) frozen whole kernel corn

1 bay leaf

½ teaspoon each: dry mustard, dried marjoram leaves

3 ounces reduced-fat sharp Cheddar cheese, cubed

2½ cups 2% reduced-fat milk

1 can (4 ounces) chopped mild green chilies, drained

Salt and white pepper, to taste

Finely chopped fresh chives, as garnish

Per Serving:
Calories: 324
% calories from fat: 18
Protein (g): 12.8
Carbohydrate (g): 55.3
Fat (g): 6.8
Saturated fat (g): 3
Cholesterol (mg): 18.1
Sodium (mg): 648

Exchanges:
Milk: 0.5
Vegetable: 0.0
Fruit: 0.0
Bread: 3.0
Meat: 0.0
Fat: 1.0

1. Sauté onion in margarine in large saucepan until soft. Stir in flour and cook 1 minute. Add stock, potatoes, corn, bay leaf, dry mustard, and marjoram; heat to boiling. Reduce heat and simmer, covered, until potatoes are tender, about 15 minutes. Discard bay leaf. Process 1 cup mixture with cheese in food processor or blender until smooth. Return to saucepan; add milk and chilies. Stir over medium heat until hot, 5 to 8 minutes; do not boil. Season to taste with salt and pepper. Garnish each bowl of soup with chives.

GARLIC SOUP

L

45

Serve this soup with a colorful tossed vegetable salad and small wedges of reduced-fat Swiss cheese.

4 first-course servings

1½ quarts water

3 tablespoons tomato paste

18 cloves garlic, crushed

1 cup finely chopped parsley
1 tablespoon dried Italian seasoning
1 bay leaf
Salt and pepper, to taste
4 slices crusty Italian bread, toasted
½ cup (2 ounces) grated Parmesan cheese

Per Serving:
Calories: 166
% calories from fat: 23
Protein (g): 8.7
Carbohydrate (g): 23.9
Fat (g): 4.4
Saturated fat (g): 2.2
Cholesterol (mg): 7.9
Sodium (mg): 469

Exchanges:
Milk: 0.0
Vegetable: 0.0
Fruit: 0.0
Bread: 1.5
Meat: 0.0
Fat: 1.0

1. Heat water, tomato paste, garlic, parsley, and herbs to boiling in large saucepan. Reduce heat and simmer 15 minutes. Discard bay leaf; season to taste with salt and pepper. Place toasted bread slices in bottoms of soup bowls and sprinkle with cheese; ladle soup over.

GOULASH SOUP

L *Caraway seeds and paprika flavor this easy vegetable soup.*

4 entrée servings

1½ cups chopped onions
1 cup each: sliced green bell pepper, carrots, parsnip, celery
1 tablespoon canola oil
1½ quarts water
2 cups tomato juice
2 large red potatoes, peeled, chopped
¼ teaspoon paprika
1 teaspoon caraway seeds
Salt and pepper, to taste
½ cup low-fat plain yogurt

Per Serving:
Calories: 216
% calories from fat: 15
Protein (g): 6
Carbohydrate (g): 41
Fat (g): 3.9
Saturated fat (g): 0.9
Cholesterol (mg): 1.7
Sodium (mg): 507

Exchanges:
Milk: 0.0
Vegetable: 2.0
Fruit: 0.0
Bread: 2.0
Meat: 0.0
Fat: 0.5

1. Sauté onions, bell pepper, carrots, parsnip, and celery in oil in large saucepan until tender, about 10 minutes. Stir in remaining ingredients, except salt, pepper, and yogurt; heat to boiling. Reduce heat and simmer, covered, until vegetables are tender, 15 to 20 minutes. Season to taste with salt and pepper. Garnish each bowl of soup with a dollop of yogurt.

CABBAGE SOUP

L

45

Easy to make and satisfying to eat. Serve with Peasant Bread (see p. 650) for a pleasing contrast of flavors and textures.

6 entrée servings

1 small head cabbage, shredded
2 large onions, thinly sliced
2 carrots, sliced
1 large potato, peeled, sliced
1 bay leaf
½ teaspoon each: dried dill weed, rosemary leaves
1 cup water
3 cups fat-free milk
2 tablespoons low-fat plain yogurt
Salt and pepper, to taste

Per Serving:
Calories: 134
% calories from fat: 5
Protein (g): 8.7
Carbohydrate (g): 25.8
Fat (g): 0.8
Saturated fat (g): 0.2
Cholesterol (mg): 2.5
Sodium (mg): 112

Exchanges:
Milk: 0.5
Vegetable: 1.0
Fruit: 0.0
Bread: 1.0
Meat: 0.0
Fat: 0.0

1. Heat vegetables, herbs, and water to boiling in large saucepan; reduce heat and simmer, covered, until vegetables are tender, about 15 minutes. Add milk and yogurt; cook until hot, about 5 minutes. Discard bay leaf; season to taste with salt and pepper.

SHERRIED WINTER SQUASH SOUP

V

Any type of winter squash can be used in this Italian-accented soup.

4 entrée servings

½ cup chopped onion
2 cloves garlic, minced
2 teaspoons olive oil
1 can (28 ounces) reduced-sodium diced tomatoes, undrained
5 cups Roasted Vegetable Stock (see p. 11)
1 large butternut squash, peeled, seeded, cubed
4 medium potatoes, cubed
1 teaspoon dried basil leaves
½ teaspoon dried thyme leaves
½ cup chopped parsley

Per Serving:
Calories: 260
% calories from fat: 10
Protein (g): 5.9
Carbohydrate (g): 51.4
Fat (g): 2.9
Saturated fat (g): 0.4
Cholesterol (mg): 0
Sodium (mg): 51

Exchanges:
Milk: 0.0
Vegetable: 1.0
Fruit: 0.0
Bread: 3.0
Meat: 0.0
Fat: 0.5

2 to 4 tablespoons dry sherry (optional)

Salt and pepper, to taste

1. Sauté onion and garlic in oil in large saucepan until tender, about 5 minutes. Stir in remaining ingredients, except sherry, salt, and pepper. Heat to boiling; reduce heat and simmer, covered, until vegetables are tender, about 15 minutes. Stir in sherry; season to taste with salt and pepper.

CINNAMON-SPICED PUMPKIN SOUP

L

45

For convenience, 2 cans (16 ounces each) pumpkin can be substituted for the fresh pumpkin. Any yellow winter squash such as butternut, Hubbard, or acorn can also be used.

4 first-course servings

4 cups cubed, seeded, peeled pumpkin

2 cups fat-free half-and-half or fat-free milk

1–2 tablespoons light brown sugar

½ teaspoon ground cinnamon

¼ teaspoon ground nutmeg

Snipped chives, as garnish

Per Serving:
Calories: 125
% calories from fat: 1
Protein (g): 5.2
Carbohydrate (g): 23.2
Fat (g): 0.2
Saturated fat (g): 0.1
Cholesterol (mg): 0
Sodium (mg): 122

Exchanges:
Milk: 1.0
Vegetable: 0.0
Fruit: 0.0
Bread: 0.5
Meat: 0.0
Fat: 0.0

1. Cook pumpkin in covered medium saucepan in 1 inch simmering water until tender, about 15 minutes; drain. Process pumpkin and half-and-half in food processor or blender; return to saucepan. Stir in brown sugar and spices; cook over medium heat until hot, about 5 minutes. Sprinkle each bowl of soup with chives.

PURÉED ROASTED VEGETABLE SOUP

L

45

This soup is also delicious served without rice and topped with Garlic Croutons (see p. 636).

6 entrée servings

2 pattypan squash or zucchini

1 each: small poblano chili or green bell pepper, medium red bell pepper, red onion, peeled eggplant

3 cloves garlic, peeled

Olive oil cooking spray

1½ tablespoons herbs de Provence

1 quart reduced-sodium vegetable broth, divided

1–2 tablespoons lemon juice

Salt and pepper, to taste

3 cups cooked rice, warm

¾ cup fat-free plain yogurt

Per Serving:
Calories: 219
% calories from fat: 4
Protein (g): 6.7
Carbohydrate (g): 47.4
Fat (g): 1.1
Saturated fat (g): 0.2
Cholesterol (mg): 0.5
Sodium (mg): 87

Exchanges:
Milk: 0.0
Vegetable: 3.0
Fruit: 0.0
Bread: 2.0
Meat: 0.0
Fat: 0.0

1. Cut vegetables, except garlic, into 1-inch pieces; arrange in single layer on greased foil-lined jelly roll pan. Spray vegetables with cooking spray; sprinkle with herbs. Roast vegetables at 425 degrees until browned and tender, about 40 minutes, removing garlic when soft, after about 20 minutes. Process vegetables and 2 cups broth in food processor or blender until smooth. Heat vegetable mixture, remaining 2 cups broth, and lemon juice in large saucepan to boiling; reduce heat and simmer, uncovered, 5 minutes. Season to taste with salt and pepper. Serve soup over rice in bowls; garnish with dollops of yogurt.

EVERYTHING-BUT-CABBAGE SOUP

V *Load your shopping cart with healthy vegetables to make this tasty soup—*
go ahead and add cabbage, if you insist!

6 entrée servings

¾ cup minced onion

2 tablespoons olive oil

1½ quarts low-sodium vegetable broth

3 cups diced, peeled baking potatoes

3 ears corn, each cut into 2-inch pieces

¾ cup each: cut green beans, diced carrots, celery,
  sweet potatoes, butternut squash, zucchini

1 can (14½ ounces) reduced-sodium tomatoes,
  undrained, coarsely chopped

¾ cup frozen peas

1 tablespoon tomato paste

1 teaspoon each: white wine vinegar, sugar

1 bay leaf

½ teaspoon dried thyme and marjoram leaves

Salt and pepper, to taste

Per Serving:
Calories: 324
% calories from fat: 10
Protein (g): 9.9
Carbohydrate (g): 70
Fat (g): 4
Saturated fat (g): 0.6
Cholesterol (mg): 0
Sodium (mg): 567

Exchanges:
Milk: 0.0
Vegetable: 5.0
Fruit: 0.0
Bread: 2.5
Meat: 0.0
Fat: 0.0

1. Sauté onion in oil in large saucepan until soft. Add vegetable
broth and remaining ingredients, except salt and pepper, and heat
to boiling. Reduce heat and simmer, covered, until vegetables are
tender, about 15 minutes. Discard bay leaf. Season to taste with
salt and pepper.

SPRING SOUP

V *A perfect spring soup, when asparagus is in season!*

6 entrée servings

½ cup finely chopped onion

2 tablespoons olive or canola oil

1 cup chopped tomatoes

1 quart water

1 cup diced potatoes

¼ cup rice, uncooked

1½ cups cut asparagus (1-inch)

1 cup each: fresh or frozen peas, coarsely chopped
    scallions

Salt and pepper, to taste

Per Serving:
Calories: 151
% calories from fat: 29
Protein (g): 4.6
Carbohydrate (g): 23.6
Fat (g): 5
Saturated fat (g): 0.6
Cholesterol (mg): 0
Sodium (mg): 32

Exchanges:
Milk: 0.0
Vegetable: 1.5
Fruit: 0.0
Bread: 1.0
Meat: 0.0
Fat: 1.0

1. Sauté onion in oil in large saucepan until lightly browned, about 5 minutes. Add tomatoes; cook, covered, over medium heat 5 minutes. Add water, potatoes, and rice and heat to boiling; reduce heat and simmer, covered, until rice is tender, 20 to 25 minutes, adding asparagus, peas, and scallions during last 5 to 7 minutes. Season to taste with salt and pepper.

MOTHER HUBBARD'S SOUP

V *Use this opportunity to clean out the refrigerator and pantry!*

45 | **8 entrée servings**

4 small potatoes, cubed

1 sweet potato, peeled, cubed

2 ribs celery, sliced

2 cups sliced cabbage

8 ounces broccoli

1 cup each: frozen peas, whole kernel corn,
    sliced carrots

1 can (14½ ounces) diced tomatoes with roasted
    garlic, undrained

Per Serving:
Calories: 172
% calories from fat: 2
Protein (g): 6.4
Carbohydrate (g): 37.9
Fat (g): 0.5
Saturated fat (g): 0.1
Cholesterol (mg): 0
Sodium (mg): 337

Exchanges:
Milk: 0.0
Vegetable: 1.0
Fruit: 0.0
Bread: 2.0
Meat: 0.0
Fat: 0.0

4 cans (14½ ounces each) reduced-sodium
   vegetable broth
1 teaspoon dried rosemary leaves
½ teaspoon each: dried thyme and oregano leaves
Salt and pepper, to taste

1. Heat all ingredients, except salt and pepper, to boiling in large saucepan; reduce heat and simmer, covered, until vegetables are tender, about 15 minutes. Season to taste with salt and pepper.

POTATO PISTOU

L

A rich and flavorful soup with a velvety texture.

45 **6 entrée servings**

2 quarts water
2 cups chopped onions
5 tomatoes, peeled, seeded, chopped
4 red potatoes, peeled, diced
¾ cup halved green beans
2 medium zucchini, sliced
½ teaspoon dried marjoram leaves,
1½ cups packed basil leaves
5 cloves garlic, minced
¼ cup (1 ounce) grated Parmesan cheese
Salt and pepper, to taste

Per Serving:
Calories: 136
% calories from fat: 10
Protein (g): 5.1
Carbohydrate (g): 28.4
Fat (g): 1.6
Saturated fat (g): 0.7
Cholesterol (mg): 2.6
Sodium (mg): 106

Exchanges:
Milk: 0.0
Vegetable: 2.0
Fruit: 0.0
Bread: 1.0
Meat: 0.0
Fat: 0.0

1. Heat water, vegetables, and dried herbs to boiling in large saucepan; reduce heat and simmer, covered, until vegetables are tender, about 15 minutes. Process soup mixture in food processor or blender until smooth; return to saucepan and simmer, covered, 15 minutes. Process basil, garlic, and Parmesan cheese in food processor until smooth; stir into soup. Season to taste with salt and pepper.

SPINACH AND TORTELLINI SOUP

LO

45

Soups can be made 2 to 3 days in advance, enhancing flavors. If the soup contains pasta, cook it separately and add to the soup when reheating so it's fresh and perfectly cooked.

6 entrée servings

2 cups sliced carrots

¼ cup sliced green onions

2 cloves garlic, minced

1 teaspoon dried basil leaves

2 cans (14 ½ ounces) reduced-sodium vegetable broth

1½ cups water

1 package (9 ounces) fresh tomato-cheese tortellini

3 cups torn spinach leaves

2–3 teaspoons lemon juice

⅛–¼ teaspoon ground nutmeg

Salt and pepper, to taste

Per Serving:
Calories: 290
% calories from fat: 9
Protein (g): 12.1
Carbohydrate (g): 48
Fat (g): 2.8
Saturated fat (g): 1
Cholesterol (mg): 3.8
Sodium (mg): 395

Exchanges:
Milk: 0.0
Vegetable: 2.0
Fruit: 0.0
Bread: 2.5
Meat: 1.0
Fat: 0.0

1. Sauté carrots, green onions, garlic, and basil in lightly greased large saucepan until onions are tender, about 5 minutes. Add broth and water and heat to boiling; reduce heat and simmer, covered, 10 minutes. Heat soup to boiling; stir in tortellini and spinach; reduce heat and simmer, uncovered, until tortellini are *al dente*, about 5 minutes. Season with lemon juice, nutmeg, salt, and pepper.

TORTELLINI SOUP WITH KALE

LO

When there's no time to cook, canned vegetable broth can be used in place of the homemade stock.

8 first-course servings

1 cup each: sliced mushrooms, leek (white part only) or green onions

3 cloves garlic, minced

1 tablespoon olive oil

3 quarts Roasted Vegetable or Rich Mushroom Stock (see pp. 11, 13)

2 cups packed kale, coarsely chopped

½ package (9-ounce size) fresh mushroom or herb tortellini

Salt and pepper, to taste

1. Sauté mushrooms, leek, and garlic in oil in Dutch oven until leek is tender, 5 to 8 minutes. Add stock and heat to boiling; stir in kale and tortellini; reduce heat and simmer, covered, until tortellini are *al dente*, about 7 minutes. Season to taste with salt and pepper.

Per Serving:
Calories: 105
% calories from fat: 24
Protein (g): 3
Carbohydrate (g): 11.6
Fat (g): 3.1
Saturated fat (g): 0.8
Cholesterol (mg): 8.4
Sodium (mg): 69

Exchanges:
Milk: 0.0
Vegetable: 2.0
Fruit: 0.0
Bread: 0.0
Meat: 0.0
Fat: 1.0

TOMATO-VEGETABLE SOUP WITH SOUR CREAM

L

Homemade croutons are delicious and easy to make (see Index).

45 **6 entrée servings**

1 large onion, thinly sliced

2 tablespoons each: olive oil, flour

1¼ quarts water

½ cup dry white wine or water

5–6 vegetable bouillon cubes

8 large tomatoes, peeled, quartered

1 bay leaf

2 teaspoons dried basil leaves

1 cup each: cubed peeled cooked potatoes and butternut squash, frozen peas

1½ cups fat-free sour cream, divided

Salt and pepper, to taste

Plain croutons, as garnish

Per Serving:
Calories: 302
% calories from fat: 10
Protein (g): 12.2
Carbohydrate (g): 54.3
Fat (g): 3.8
Saturated fat (g): 0.6
Cholesterol (mg): 0.1
Sodium (mg): 684

Exchanges:
Milk: 0.0
Vegetable: 2.0
Fruit: 0.0
Bread: 3.0
Meat: 2.0
Fat: 0.5

1. Sauté onion in oil in large saucepan until soft; stir in flour and cook 1 minute. Add water, wine, bouillon cubes, tomatoes, bay leaf, and basil. Heat to boiling; reduce heat and simmer, covered, 20 minutes; discard bay leaf. Process soup in food processor or blender until smooth. Return soup to saucepan, add vegetables, and heat to boiling; reduce heat and simmer, covered, until vegetables are tender, about 10 minutes. Stir in 1 cup sour cream; cook over medium heat until hot, about 5 minutes. Season to taste with salt and pepper. Garnish each bowl of soup with remaining ½ cup sour cream and croutons.

GARLICKY LIMA BEAN SOUP

L *For those who love garlic! Of course the garlic can be reduced in amount if you prefer a more subtle dish.*

6 first-course servings

2 cups coarsely chopped onions
10 large cloves garlic, peeled, quartered
¼–½ teaspoon crushed red pepper
2 cans (17 ounces each) lima beans, rinsed, drained
3 cups Basic Vegetable Stock (see p. 9)
1 teaspoon dried thyme leaves
½ cup fat-free half-and-half
Salt and cayenne pepper, to taste

Per Serving:
Calories: 169
% calories from fat 5
Protein (g): 9.2
Carbohydrate (g): 31.5
Fat (g): 0.9
Saturated fat (g): 0.2
Cholesterol (mg): 0
Sodium (mg): 429

Exchanges:
Milk: 0.0
Vegetable: 1.0
Fruit: 0.0
Bread: 2.0
Meat: 0.0
Fat: 0.0

1. Sauté onions, garlic, and crushed red pepper in lightly greased large saucepan until onions are tender, 8 to 10 minutes. Add beans, stock, and thyme; heat to boiling. Reduce heat and simmer, covered, 10 minutes. Process soup in food processor or blender until smooth; return to saucepan. Stir in half-and-half; cook over medium heat 5 minutes. Season to taste with salt and cayenne pepper.

DITALINI WITH WHITE BEANS AND COLLARDS

L

45

Create a stir with this knockout entrée that's full of beans, pasta, and healthful greens. Kale or cabbage can be substituted for the collards.

4 entrée servings

1 cup chopped onion
2 teaspoons olive oil
1 can (14½ ounces) diced tomatoes, undrained
1 can (14 ounces) reduced-sodium vegetable broth

1 can (15 ounces) small white beans, rinsed, drained

⅔ cup uncooked ditalini

1 teaspoon dried oregano leaves

2 cups packed torn collard greens

2 tablespoons shredded provolone cheese

Salt and hot pepper sauce, to taste

Per Serving:
Calories: 234
% calories from fat: 14
Protein (g): 12.8
1 teaspoon olive oil
Carbohydrate (g): 44.1
Fat (g): 4
Saturated fat (g): 1.4
Cholesterol (mg): 4.9
Sodium (mg): 826

Exchanges:
Milk: 0.0
Vegetable: 3.0
Fruit: 0.0
Bread: 2.0
Meat: 0.0
Fat: 0.5

1. Sauté onion in oil in large saucepan until tender, about 5 minutes. Add tomatoes with liquid, broth, beans, ditalini, and oregano; heat to boiling. Reduce heat and simmer, covered, until ditalini are *al dente*, 10 to 12 minutes. Stir in collard greens; simmer, covered, until tender, about 5 minutes. Stir in provolone cheese; season to taste with salt and hot pepper sauce.

GARLIC VEGETABLE SOUP

V

A real garlic lover's soup—add more garlic, if you like!

45   **8 entrée servings**

1 cup chopped leeks (white parts only)

6 large garlic cloves, minced

1 tablespoon olive oil

2½ quarts water

1 can (15 ounces) navy or Great Northern beans, rinsed, drained

1 pound tomatoes, peeled, seeded, coarsely chopped

1 cup each: diced new potatoes, coarsely chopped carrots, cut green beans (½-inch)

½ cup chopped celery

2 tablespoons each: tomato paste, dried basil leaves

Salt and pepper, to taste

Per Serving:
Calories: 148
% calories from fat: 14
Protein (g): 6.4
Carbohydrate (g): 27.5
Fat (g): 2.4
Saturated fat (g): 0.4
Cholesterol (mg): 0
Sodium (mg): 222

Exchanges:
Milk: 0.0
Vegetable: 2.0
Fruit: 0.0
Bread: 2.0
Meat: 0.0
Fat: 0.5

1. Sauté leeks and garlic in oil in large saucepan until tender but not browned, 6 to 8 minutes. Add remaining ingredients, except salt and pepper, and heat to boiling; reduce heat and simmer, covered, 20 minutes. Season to taste with salt and pepper.

ALSATIAN PEASANT SOUP

L

45

Root vegetables, cabbage, and beans combine for a robust soup that is almost a stew. Serve with a crusty rye bread and a good beer.

6 entrée servings

½ cup each: chopped onion, celery

1 tablespoon olive oil

1 teaspoon dried thyme leaves

½ teaspoon crushed caraway seeds

1 bay leaf

3 cups reduced-sodium vegetable broth

2 cups thinly sliced cabbage

1 cup each: cubed potato, parsnip, sliced carrots

2 cans (15 ounces each) Great Northern beans, rinsed, drained

Salt and pepper, to taste

¾ cup (3 ounces) shredded reduced-fat Swiss cheese

1½ cups Rye Caraway Croutons (½ recipe, see p. 636)

Per Serving:
Calories: 300
% calories from fat: 13
Protein (g): 17
Carbohydrate (g): 50
Fat (g): 4.3
Saturated fat (g): 1
Cholesterol (mg): 5
Sodium (mg): 352

Exchanges:
Milk: 0.0
Vegetable: 1.0
Fruit: 0.0
Bread: 3.0
Meat: 1.0
Fat: 0.0

1. Sauté onion and celery in oil in large saucepan until tender, about 5 minutes. Add herbs; cook 2 minutes. Add broth, vegetables, and beans; heat to boiling. Reduce heat and simmer, covered, until vegetables are tender, 10 to 15 minutes. Discard bay leaf; season to taste with salt and pepper. Sprinkle each bowl of soup with 2 tablespoons shredded cheese and Rye Caraway Croutons.

LIGHT MINESTRONE

L

45

Minestrone does not always contain pasta, nor is it always a heavy, hearty soup. Enjoy this light version of an old favorite, selecting vegetables that are freshest and most plentiful.

8 entrée servings

1 cup sliced carrots

½ cup each: chopped onion, celery, fennel bulb

2 cloves garlic, minced

1 tablespoon olive oil

5 cups reduced-sodium vegetable broth

1 can (19 ounces) garbanzo beans, rinsed, drained

1 cup each: snap peas, broccoli florets, sliced zucchini

¾–1 teaspoon each: dried basil and oregano leaves

1 cup halved cherry tomatoes

¼ cup finely chopped parsley

Salt and pepper, to taste

1½ cups Parmesan Croutons (½ recipe) (see p. 636)

Per Serving:
Calories: 146
% calories from fat: 21
Protein (g): 8.6
Carbohydrate (g): 21.3
Fat (g): 3.5
Saturated fat (g): 0.6
Cholesterol (mg): 0.5
Sodium (mg): 447

Exchanges:
Milk: 0.0
Vegetable: 1.0
Fruit: 0.0
Bread: 1.0
Meat: 0.0
Fat: 0.5

1. Sauté carrots, onion, celery, fennel, and garlic in oil in Dutch oven until onion is tender, 5 to 8 minutes. Add broth, beans, peas, broccoli, zucchini, and herbs; heat to boiling. Reduce heat and simmer, covered, until vegetables are tender, 10 to 15 minutes, adding tomatoes and parsley during last 5 minutes. Season to taste with salt and pepper; sprinkle each bowl of soup with Parmesan Croutons.

PASTA E FAGIOLI

L *Perhaps the only soup that's better than a good pasta e fagioli is e fagioli the second day. If you make it a day ahead, wait to add the pasta until just before you serve it.*

12 first-course servings

1 cup chopped onion

½ cup each: diced celery, carrot

1½ tablespoons minced garlic

2 tablespoons olive oil

2 cups dried Great Northern or cannellini beans, soaked overnight, drained

2¼ quarts water

4½ cups diced, peeled, seeded tomatoes

5 ounces elbow macaroni, uncooked

Salt and pepper, to taste

Grated Parmesan cheese, as garnish

Per Serving:
Calories: 124
% calories from fat: 21
Protein (g): 5
Carbohydrate (g): 20.4
Fat (g): 3.1
Saturated fat (g): 1.1
Cholesterol (mg): 10.2
Sodium (mg): 126

Exchanges:
Milk: 0.0
Vegetable: 1.0
Fruit: 0.0
Bread: 1.0
Meat: 0.0
Fat: 0.5

1. Sauté onion, celery, carrot, and garlic in oil in Dutch oven until soft, about 5 minutes. Add beans and water; heat to boiling. Reduce heat and simmer, covered, until beans are tender, 45 to 60 minutes. Add tomatoes and pasta; simmer, covered, until pasta is *al dente*, about 10 minutes. Season to taste with salt and pepper. Sprinkle each bowl of soup with Parmesan cheese.

ROASTED VEGETABLE MINESTRONE

V *Oven roasting enhances the natural flavors of vegetables, making this soup a favorite in our repertoire.*

6 entrée servings

1 each: unpeeled medium eggplant, large Idaho potato, bell pepper
2 each: medium zucchini, tomatoes, onions
½ small butternut squash, peeled
Vegetable cooking spray
2 teaspoons dried Italian seasoning
4 cloves garlic, minced
1 can (15½ ounces) cannellini or Great Northern beans, rinsed, drained
1¾ quarts vegetable broth
2–3 tablespoons white balsamic vinegar
Salt and pepper, to taste

Per Serving:
Calories: 203
% calories from fat: 6
Protein (g): 7.7
Carbohydrate (g): 42.3
Fat (g): 1.5
Saturated fat (g): 0.1
Cholesterol (mg): 0
Sodium (mg): 706

Exchanges:
Milk: 0.0
Vegetable: 2.0
Fruit: 0.0
Bread: 2.0
Meat: 0.0
Fat: 0.0

1. Cut fresh vegetables into ¾-inch pieces; arrange in single layer on greased foil-lined jelly roll pan. Spray vegetables generously with cooking spray and sprinkle with Italian seasoning. Roast at 425 degrees until vegetables are browned and tender, about 40 minutes. Combine roasted vegetables, garlic, beans, and broth in large saucepan; heat to boiling. Reduce heat and simmer, covered, 10 minutes. Season to taste with vinegar, salt, and pepper.

GREEN VEGETABLE MINESTRONE

LO *This green soup is wonderful in spring, when fresh asparagus and peas are in season, but make it whenever you're in the mood for delicious soup!*

6 entrée servings

1½ quarts Basic Vegetable Stock (see p. 9)

1 cup each: thinly sliced onion, uncooked broken spinach fettuccine

2 cans (15 ounces each) Great Northern beans, rinsed, drained

2 cups sliced zucchini

1½ cups each: small broccoli florets, cut asparagus (1-inch)

1 cup each: cut green beans, fresh or frozen peas

2 tablespoons each: chopped fresh or 2 teaspoons dried basil and rosemary leaves

2 large cloves garlic

Salt and pepper, to taste

Shredded Parmesan cheese, as garnish

Per Serving:
Calories: 186
% calories from fat: 6
Protein (g): 13.1
Carbohydrate (g): 38.8
Fat (g): 1.4
Saturated fat (g): 0.3
Cholesterol (mg): 14
Sodium (mg): 478

Exchanges:
Milk: 0.0
Vegetable: 2.0
Fruit: 0.0
Bread: 2.0
Meat: 0.0
Fat: 0.0

1. Heat stock and onion to boiling in large saucepan; stir in fettuccine. Reduce heat and simmer 5 minutes. Stir in canned beans, vegetables, herbs, and garlic; simmer, covered, until vegetables are tender and pasta is *al dente*, about 10 minutes. Season to taste with salt and pepper. Sprinkle each bowl of soup with Parmesan cheese.

SUMMER MINESTRONE

LO *Thick and savory, this traditional Italian soup is always a favorite.*

8 entrée servings

2 cups each: cubed potatoes, sliced carrots

1 cup each: halved green beans, sliced zucchini, carrots, cabbage, chopped onion

½ cup sliced celery

3–4 cloves garlic, minced

2 teaspoons dried Italian seasoning

4 cups reduced-sodium vegetable broth

1 can (15 ounces) kidney beans, rinsed, drained

1 can (14½ ounces) reduced-sodium stewed tomatoes

2 cups water

1½ cups uncooked mostaccioli

Salt and pepper, to taste

2 tablespoons grated Parmesan or Romano cheese

Per Serving:
Calories: 177
% calories from fat: 9
Protein (g): 8.1
Carbohydrate (g): 33.7
Fat (g): 1.8
Saturated fat (g): 0.6
Cholesterol (mg): 1.2
Sodium (mg): 256

Exchanges:
Milk: 0.0
Vegetable: 2.0
Fruit: 0.0
Bread: 1.5
Meat: 0.5
Fat: 0.0

1. Sauté fresh vegetables and garlic in lightly greased large saucepan until crisp-tender, 10 to 12 minutes. Stir in Italian seasoning; cook 1 minute. Add broth, beans, tomatoes, and water; heat to boiling. Reduce heat and simmer, covered, 10 minutes. Heat soup to boiling and add pasta; reduce heat and simmer, uncovered, until pasta is *al dente*, about 10 minutes. Season to taste with salt and pepper; sprinkle each bowl of soup with Parmesan cheese.

TWO-BEAN MINESTRONE

LO *Cannellini beans and chickpeas enrich this soup with protein, fiber, and vitamins.*

8 entrée servings

2 cloves garlic, minced

½ cup chopped onion

2 tablespoons olive oil

1 cup each: diced potato, sliced leek

½ cup each: sliced carrots, celery, chopped parsley

1½ quarts water

1 can (14½ ounces) plum tomatoes,
undrained, chopped

½ cup dry red wine

1 tablespoon each: dried oregano and basil leaves

½ cup uncooked small elbow macaroni

1 can (15 ounces) each: rinsed drained cannellini or
Great Northern beans, chickpeas

1½ cups each: sliced zucchini, shredded cabbage

Salt and pepper, to taste

8 teaspoons grated Parmesan cheese

Per Serving:
Calories: 267
% calories from fat: 17
Protein (g): 9
Carbohydrate (g): 43.1
Fat (g): 5.3
Saturated fat (g): 0.9
Cholesterol (mg): 1.3
Sodium (mg): 331

Exchanges:
Milk: 0.0
Vegetable: 2.0
Fruit: 0.0
Bread: 2.0
Meat: 0.0
Fat: 1.5

1. Sauté garlic and onion in olive oil in large saucepan until onion is tender. Add potato, leek, carrots, celery, parsley, water, tomatoes with liquid, red wine, and herbs; heat to boiling. Reduce heat and simmer, covered, until vegetables are tender, about 10 minutes. Add remaining ingredients, except salt, pepper, and Parmesan cheese, and simmer until pasta is *al dente*, about 7 minutes. Season to taste with salt and pepper. Sprinkle each bowl of soup with 1 teaspoon Parmesan cheese.

ITALIAN BEAN SOUP

V *For a creamy textured soup, purée ½ the cooked bean mixture before adding the macaroni and garbanzo beans.*

6 entrée servings

1 cup dried cannellini beans

2 quarts water

1 cup each: chopped onion, green bell pepper, carrots

½ cup chopped celery

1 teaspoon each: dried basil and oregano leaves,
low-sodium vegetable bouillon crystals

¼ teaspoon dry mustard

2 cloves garlic, minced

3 cans (8 ounces) tomato sauce

½ cup uncooked whole-wheat elbow macaroni

1 can (15 ounces) garbanzo beans, rinsed, drained

Salt and pepper, to taste

Per Serving:
Calories: 291
% calories from fat: 4
Protein (g): 14.1
Carbohydrate (g): 56.6
Fat (g): 1.4
Saturated fat (g): 0.2
Cholesterol (mg): 0
Sodium (mg): 280

Exchanges:
Milk: 0.0
Vegetable: 3.0
Fruit: 0.0
Bread: 3.0
Meat: 0.0
Fat: 0.0

1. Cover dried beans with 2 inches water in Dutch oven; heat to boiling. Boil 2 minutes. Remove from heat, and let stand, covered, 1 hour. Drain, discarding liquid.

2. Return beans to Dutch oven with 2 quarts water and remaining ingredients, except tomato sauce, macaroni, garbanzo beans, salt, and pepper. Heat to boiling; reduce heat and simmer, covered, until beans are tender, 45 to 60 minutes. Add tomato sauce, macaroni, and garbanzo beans and cook until macaroni is tender, about 10 minutes; season to taste with salt and pepper.

FOUR-BEAN AND VEGETABLE SOUP

V *Any kind of dried beans can be used in the soup.*

12 entrée servings

8 ounces each: dried black, navy, pinto, and
  garbanzo beans
Water
2 cups chopped green bell pepper
1 cup chopped onion
6–8 cloves garlic, minced
2 tablespoons olive oil
6 cups reduced-sodium vegetable broth
2–3 teaspoons dried thyme leaves
2 cans (14½ ounces each) reduced-sodium diced
  tomatoes, undrained
2 cups each: sliced carrots, cut green beans
Salt and pepper, to taste

Per Serving:
Calories: 342
% calories from fat: 11
Protein (g): 18.1
Carbohydrate (g): 58.5
Fat (g): 4.3
Saturated fat (g): 0.5
Cholesterol (mg): 0
Sodium (mg): 35

Exchanges:
Milk: 0.0
Vegetable: 3.0
Fruit: 0.0
Bread: 3.0
Meat: 1.0
Fat: 0.0

1. Cover dried beans with 2 inches water in Dutch oven; heat to boiling. Boil 2 minutes. Remove from heat, and let stand, covered, 1 hour. Drain, discarding liquid.

2. Sauté bell pepper, onion, and garlic in oil in Dutch oven until tender, 4 to 5 minutes. Add beans, broth, and herbs and heat to boiling; reduce heat and simmer, covered, until beans are tender, 1 to 1½ hours, adding tomatoes with liquid, carrots, and green beans during last 15 to 20 minutes. Season to taste with salt and pepper.

TUSCAN BEAN SOUP

V *A hearty well-seasoned bean soup that is sure to please.*

45 **8 entrée servings**

1 cup chopped onion

½ cup each: chopped celery, green bell pepper

2 teaspoons minced roasted garlic

2 tablespoons olive oil

1 tablespoon flour

1½ teaspoons dried Italian seasoning

7 cups reduced-sodium fat-free vegetable broth

2 cans (15 ounces each) cannellini or Great Northern
   beans, rinsed, drained

2 tablespoons reduced-sodium tomato paste

½ cup quick-cooking barley

1 cup each: cubed unpeeled potato, sliced carrots,
   packed baby spinach leaves

Salt and pepper, to taste

Per Serving:
Calories: 233
% calories from fat: 18
Protein (g): 10.7
Carbohydrate (g): 40.8
Fat (g): 5.6
Saturated fat (g): 0.7
Cholesterol (mg): 0
Sodium (mg): 245

Exchanges:
Milk: 0.0
Vegetable: 2.0
Fruit: 0.0
Bread: 2.0
Meat: 0.0
Fat: 1.0

1. Sauté onion, celery, bell pepper, and garlic in oil in Dutch oven until tender, about 5 minutes. Add flour and herbs; cook 1 minute. Add broth, beans, and tomato paste and heat to boiling; reduce heat and simmer, covered, 15 minutes. Add barley, potato, carrots, and spinach; simmer until vegetables are tender, about 10 minutes. Season to taste with salt and pepper.

BEAN-THICKENED SOUP

V *Puréed beans contribute a hearty texture and subtle flavor to this soup.*

45 **4 first-course servings**

⅓ cup each: sliced carrots, onion

2 large cloves garlic, minced

1¾ cups vegetable broth

1 can (14½ ounces) petite-diced tomatoes, undrained

1 can (15 ounces) Great Northern beans, rinsed, drained, puréed

½ teaspoon each: dried thyme and sage leaves

Salt and pepper, to taste

1. Sauté carrots, onion, and garlic in lightly greased large saucepan until onion is tender, about 5 minutes. Stir in broth, tomatoes with liquid, puréed beans, and herbs. Heat to boiling; reduce heat and simmer, covered, until carrots are tender, about 10 minutes. Season to taste with salt and pepper.

Per Serving:
Calories: 176
% calories from fat: 5
Protein (g): 9.8
Carbohydrate (g): 34
Fat (g): 1
Saturated fat (g): 0.2
Cholesterol (mg): 0
Sodium (mg): 208

Exchanges:
Milk: 0.0
Vegetable: 2.0
Fruit: 0.0
Bread: 1.5
Meat: 0.5
Fat: 0.0

CHICKPEA AND PASTA SOUP

V

45

Use any fresh vegetables for the zucchini and celery in this soup—carrots, cauliflower or broccoli florets, mushrooms, peas, and green beans are possible choices.

4 entrée servings

¾ cup each: chopped onion, cubed zucchini, sliced celery

3–4 cloves garlic, minced

1 teaspoon each: dried rosemary and thyme leaves

⅛ teaspoon crushed red pepper

1 can (15 ounces) each: reduced-sodium vegetable broth, rinsed drained chickpeas

1 can (14½ ounces) reduced-sodium stewed tomatoes

1 cup uncooked farfalle (bow ties)

Salt, to taste

2–3 teaspoons lemon juice

Per Serving:
Calories: 322
% calories from fat: 10
Protein (g): 11.5
Carbohydrate (g): 56.4
Fat (g): 3.7
Saturated fat (g): 0.5
Cholesterol (mg): 0
Sodium (mg): 514

Exchanges:
Milk: 0.0
Vegetable: 3.0
Fruit: 0.0
Bread: 3.0
Meat: 0.0
Fat: 0.5

1. Sauté onion, zucchini, celery, garlic, herbs, and red pepper in lightly greased large saucepan until onion is tender, about 5 minutes; add broth, chickpeas, and tomatoes and heat to boiling. Reduce heat and simmer, covered, 10 minutes. Heat soup to boiling and add pasta; reduce heat and simmer, uncovered, until pasta is *al dente*, about 8 minutes; season to taste with salt and lemon juice.

TWO-BEAN AND PASTA SOUP

V

45

This substantial soup thickens upon standing; thin with additional broth or water, if necessary.

6 entrée servings

1½ cups cubed carrots

½ cup each: chopped green bell pepper, sliced green onions

3 cloves garlic, minced

2 teaspoons each: dried basil and oregano leaves

2 cans (15 ounces each) reduced-sodium vegetable broth

1 cup water

1 can (14½ ounces) reduced-sodium stewed tomatoes

1 can (15 ounces) each: cannellini and pinto beans, rinsed, drained

1½ cups uncooked rigatoni

2–3 teaspoons lemon juice

Salt and pepper, to taste

Per Serving:
Calories: 225
% calories from fat: 7
Protein (g): 13.6
Carbohydrate (g): 45.7
Fat (g): 2
Saturated fat (g): 0
Cholesterol (mg): 0
Sodium (mg): 522

Exchanges:
Milk: 0.0
Vegetable: 2.0
Fruit: 0.0
Bread: 2.5
Meat: 0.0
Fat: 0.0

1. Sauté carrots, bell pepper, green onions, garlic and herbs in lightly greased large saucepan until vegetables are tender, about 7 minutes. Add broth, water, tomatoes, and beans to saucepan; heat to boiling. Reduce heat and simmer, covered, 10 minutes. Heat soup to boiling and add pasta; reduce heat and simmer, uncovered, until pasta is *al dente*, 12 to 15 minutes. Season with lemon juice, salt, and pepper.

MEDITERRANEAN VEGETABLE SOUP

V *A fragrant vegetable soup with a citrus accent.*

6 first-course servings

2 cups sliced mushrooms

½ cup each: chopped onion, green bell pepper

3 cloves garlic, minced

3½ cups Mediterranean Stock (see p. 12)

1 can (14½ ounces) reduced-sodium diced tomatoes, undrained

1 can (8 ounces) tomato sauce

16 ounces light firm tofu, drained, cubed (¾-inch)

½ cup dry white wine (optional)

2 strips orange zest (3 x ½ inch)

2 bay leaves

1 teaspoon dried marjoram leaves

¼–½ teaspoon crushed fennel seeds

Salt and pepper, to taste

Per Serving:
Calories: 109
% calories from fat: 15
Protein (g): 8.1
Carbohydrate (g): 13.8
Fat (g): 2
Saturated fat (g): 0.1
Cholesterol (mg): 0
Sodium (mg): 104

Exchanges:
Milk: 0.0
Vegetable: 2.5
Fruit: 0.0
Bread: 0.0
Meat: 0.5
Fat: 0.0

1. Sauté mushrooms, onion, bell pepper, and garlic in lightly greased large saucepan until vegetables are tender, 8 to 10 minutes. Add remaining ingredients, except salt and pepper; heat to boiling. Reduce heat and simmer, covered, 10 to 15 minutes. Discard bay leaves; season to taste with salt and pepper.

WHITE BEAN AND SWEET POTATO SOUP WITH CRANBERRY COULIS

V *A wonderful combination of colors and flavors!*

6 entrée servings

1 cup chopped onion, peeled tart apple
1 pound sweet potatoes, peeled, cubed
1½ teaspoons minced gingerroot
2 cans (15 ounces each) navy or Great Northern
   beans rinsed, drained
3 cups reduced-sodium vegetable broth
½ teaspoon dried marjoram leaves
Salt and white pepper, to taste
Cranberry Coulis (recipe follows)

Per Serving:
Calories: 310
% calories from fat: 3
Protein (g): 12.6
Carbohydrate (g): 64.6
Fat (g): 1.2
Saturated fat (g): 0.3
Cholesterol (mg): 0
Sodium (mg): 650

Exchanges:
Milk: 0.0
Vegetable: 1.0
Fruit: 1.0
Bread: 3.0
Meat: 0.0
Fat: 0.0

1. Sauté onion, apple, sweet potatoes, and gingerroot in lightly greased large saucepan 5 minutes. Add beans, broth, and marjoram and heat to boiling; reduce heat and simmer, covered, until vegetables are tender, 10 to 15 minutes. Process soup in food processor or blender until smooth; season to taste with salt and white pepper. Swirl 2 tablespoons Cranberry Coulis into each bowl of soup.

Cranberry Coulis

6 servings (about 3 tablespoons each)

1½ cups fresh or frozen cranberries
1 cup orange juice
2 tablespoons each sugar, honey

1. Heat cranberries and orange juice to boiling in small saucepan; reduce heat and simmer, covered, until cranberries are tender, 5 to 8 minutes. Process with sugar and honey in food processor or blender until almost smooth. Serve warm or room temperature.

TANGY THREE-BEAN SOUP

V *The spicy barbecue flavor of this dish is a nice change of pace from the usual "tamer" bean soups.*

6 entrée servings

½ cup each: dried black-eyed peas, baby lima and
  Great Northern beans
2 quarts water
1 each: minced garlic clove, chopped large onion,
  sliced carrot and rib celery
⅛ teaspoon ground cloves
1 bay leaf
1 can (15 ounces) tomato sauce
1–2 tablespoons brown sugar
1 tablespoon each: apple cider vinegar, light molasses
½ teaspoon each: dry mustard, chili powder
¼ teaspoon each: ground celery seeds, dried thyme
  leaves, paprika, black pepper
Salt and cayenne pepper, to taste

Per Serving:
Calories: 167
% calories from fat: 5
Protein (g): 9.2
Carbohydrate (g): 33
Fat (g): 0.9
Saturated fat (g): 0.2
Cholesterol (mg): 0
Sodium (mg): 447

Exchanges:
Milk: 0.0
Vegetable: 1.0
Fruit: 0.0
Bread: 2.0
Meat: 0.0
Fat: 0.0

1. Cover beans with 2 inches water in Dutch oven and heat to boiling. Boil 2 minutes. Remove from heat and let stand, covered, 1 hour. Drain beans, discarding soaking liquid.

2. Return beans to Dutch oven; add 2 quarts water, garlic, onion, carrot, celery, cloves, and bay leaf and heat to boiling. Reduce heat and simmer, covered until beans are very tender and have thickened soup, 1 to 1½ hours, adding remaining ingredients, except salt and cayenne pepper, during last 30 minutes. Discard bay leaf; season to taste with salt and cayenne pepper.

DOWN EAST BEAN CHOWDER

V *This soup combines the flavors of Boston baked beans with old-fashioned New England potato chowder.*

8 entrée servings

2 cups chopped onions

1 cup each: sliced celery, carrots

1 tablespoon olive oil

2 cups diced peeled potatoes

1½ quarts Basic Vegetable Stock (see p. 9)

1 teaspoon dried thyme leaves

1 can (15 ounces) each: rinsed drained coarsely mashed navy beans, tomato sauce

1 can (14 ounces) vegetarian baked beans in molasses sauce

Liquid smoke, salt, and pepper, to taste

Per Serving:
Calories: 221
% calories from fat: 11
Protein (g): 8.9
Carbohydrate (g): 41.7
Fat (g): 3
Saturated fat (g): 0.8
Cholesterol (mg): 0
Sodium (mg): 397

Exchanges:
Milk: 0.0
Vegetable: 2.0
Fruit: 0.0
Bread: 2.0
Meat: 0.0
Fat: 0.5

1. Sauté onions, celery, and carrots in oil in large saucepan until tender, about 10 minutes. Add potatoes, stock and thyme. Heat to boiling; reduce heat and simmer, covered, until potatoes are tender, about 15 minutes. Stir in navy beans, tomato sauce, and baked beans; simmer, uncovered, until slightly thickened, about 10 minutes. Season to taste with liquid smoke, salt, and pepper.

BLACK BEAN SOUP

L *Dried beans can also be "quick cooked" rather than soaked overnight; see directions in Navy Bean Soup with Ham (p. 216). Or substitute three cans (15 ounces each) rinsed, drained canned black beans.*

4 entrée servings

1½ cups dried black beans
1 large onion, chopped
4 cloves garlic, minced
¾ teaspoon each: dried oregano and thyme leaves
1 large tomato, chopped
Salt and pepper, to taste
6 tablespoons fat-free sour cream
Chopped oregano or parsley, as garnish

Per Serving:
Calories: 200
% calories from fat: 4
Protein (g): 13.8
Carbohydrate (g): 39
Fat (g): 0.9
Saturated fat (g): 0.2
Cholesterol (mg): 0
Sodium (mg): 20

Exchanges:
Milk: 0.0
Vegetable: 1.0
Fruit: 0.0
Bread: 2.0
Meat: 0.5
Fat: 0.0

1. Cover beans with 4 inches water in large saucepan; soak overnight and drain.

2. Sauté onion, garlic and herbs in lightly greased large saucepan until softened, about 4 minutes. Add beans; cover with 2 inches water and heat to boiling. Reduce heat and simmer, covered, until beans are tender, 1½ to 2 hours, adding tomato during last 30 minutes. Process soup in food processor or blender until smooth. Return soup to saucepan; heat over medium heat until hot, 3 to 4 minutes. Season to taste with salt and pepper. Top each bowl of soup with dollop of sour cream and sprinkle with oregano.

BLACK BEAN SOUP WITH SUN-DRIED TOMATOES AND CILANTRO-LEMON CREAM

L *Cilantro-Lemon Cream adds a fresh accent to this south-of-the-border favorite.*

4 entrée servings

1 cup chopped onion
2 cloves garlic, minced
1 jalapeño chili, minced

3 cups Basic Vegetable Stock (see p. 9)

3 cups cooked dried black beans or 2 cans (15 ounces each) black beans, rinsed, drained

¾ cup sun-dried tomatoes (not in oil), softened

¾ teaspoon ground cumin, dried oregano leaves

¼–½ teaspoon hot pepper sauce

Salt and pepper, to taste

¼ cup chopped cilantro

Cilantro-Lemon Cream (recipe follows)

Per Serving:
Calories: 239
% calories from fat: 5
Protein (g): 15.2
Carbohydrate (g): 44.0
Fat (g): 1.5
Saturated fat (g): 0.3
Cholesterol (mg): 0
Sodium (mg): 256

Exchanges:
Milk: 0.0
Vegetable: 1.0
Fruit: 0.0
Bread: 3.0
Meat: 0.0
Fat: 0.0

1. Sauté onion, garlic, and jalapeño chili in lightly greased large saucepan until tender, 5 to 8 minutes. Add stock, beans, sun-dried tomatoes, cumin, and oregano to saucepan; heat to boiling. Reduce heat and simmer, covered, 10 minutes. Process soup in food processor or blender until smooth. Season to taste with hot pepper sauce, salt, and pepper; stir in cilantro. Garnish each bowl of soup with dollops of Cilantro Cream.

Cilantro-Lemon Cream
Makes about ⅓ cup

⅓ cup fat-free sour cream

2 tablespoons minced cilantro

1 teaspoon lemon or lime juice

¾ teaspoon ground coriander

2–3 dashes white pepper

1. Combine all ingredients.

VARIATION

Ancho Black Bean and Pumpkin Soup — Make soup as above, omitting sun-dried tomatoes, and Cilantro Cream. Heat 1 ancho chili in dry skillet over medium heat until softened; remove chili and discard veins and seeds. Purée chili and 1 can (15 ounces) pumpkin with the beans.

CUBAN BLACK BEAN SOUP

V

Although a number of steps are required to make this soup, the spicy, authentic Caribbean flavor is ample reward. Black beans can vary in cooking time, so check them for doneness after the first hour.

8 entrée servings

2 cups dried black beans

1¾ quarts water

3 each: chopped medium onions, minced
   garlic cloves

4–5 drops hot pepper sauce

1 large green bell pepper, finely chopped

1 tablespoon olive oil

2 teaspoons each: ground cumin, dried oregano leaves

Salt and pepper, to taste

Cuban Rice, warm (recipe follows)

Per Serving:
Calories: 274
% calories from fat: 11
Protein (g): 11.8
Carbohydrate (g): 50.1
Fat (g): 3.5
Saturated fat (g): 0.5
Cholesterol (mg): 0
Sodium (mg): 480

Exchanges:
Milk: 0.0
Vegetable: 1.0
Fruit: 0.0
Bread: 3.0
Meat: 0.0
Fat: 0.5

1. Cover beans with 2 inches of water in Dutch oven and heat to boiling. Boil for 2 minutes; remove from heat and let stand, covered, 1 hour. Drain beans, discarding liquid.

2. Return beans to Dutch oven; add 1¾ quarts water, onions, garlic, and hot pepper sauce and heat to boiling. Reduce heat and simmer, covered, until beans have are tender, 1½ to 2 hours, adding bell peppers, oil, and herbs during last 30 minutes. Season to taste with salt and pepper. Serve soup over rice in bowls.

Cuban Rice

Makes about 4 cups

1 cup uncooked long-grain white rice

1 tablespoon finely chopped onion

2 cups water

2 teaspoons olive oil

1½ tablespoons apple cider vinegar

1. Combine rice, onion, and water in saucepan; heat to boiling. Reduce heat and simmer, covered, 20 minutes or until rice is tender. Stir in oil and vinegar.

SPLIT-PEA SOUP WITH THREE ACCOMPANIMENTS

v *This thick and beautiful green soup is served with cubed sweet potatoes, fresh peas, and croutons.*

6 entrée servings

½ cup minced onion

1 rib celery, chopped

2 tablespoons margarine

1½ quarts water

½ cup dry white wine (optional)

1 pound dry split peas

2 vegetable bouillon cubes

¾ teaspoon dried thyme leaves

1 bay leaf

Salt and pepper, to taste

1 cup each: cooked warm peas and cubed peeled
   sweet potatoes, plain croutons

Per Serving:
Calories: 374
% calories from fat: 8
Protein (g): 21.5
Carbohydrate (g): 60.7
Fat (g): 3.4
Saturated fat (g): 0.5
Cholesterol (mg): 0.1
Sodium (mg): 441

Exchanges:
Milk: 0.0
Vegetable: 0.0
Fruit: 0.0
Bread: 4.0
Meat: 1.0
Fat: 0.5

1. Sauté onion and celery in margarine in large saucepan until tender, about 5 minutes. Stir in remaining ingredients, except salt, pepper, peas, sweet potatoes, and croutons. Heat to boiling; reduce heat and simmer, covered, until split peas are tender, about 45 minutes. Discard bay leaf. Process soup in food processor or blender until smooth; season to taste with salt and pepper. Pass green peas, sweet potatoes, and croutons to sprinkle on soup.

EASIEST BLACK-EYED PEA AND LENTIL SOUP

V *This soup will thicken if made in advance; stir in additional broth when reheating.*

6 entrée servings

½ cup each: chopped carrots, celery, onion
1 teaspoon minced garlic
2 tablespoons olive oil
6–8 cups reduced-sodium vegetable broth
¾ cup dried black-eyed peas
¾ teaspoon each: dried thyme and oregano leaves
1 bay leaf
3 medium tomatoes, chopped
1½ cups dried lentils
Salt and pepper, to taste

Per Serving:
Calories: 356
% calories from fat: 14
Protein (g): 20.7
Carbohydrate (g): 58.3
Fat (g): 5.9
Saturated fat (g): 0.9
Cholesterol (mg): 0
Sodium (mg): 119

Exchanges:
Milk: 0.0
Vegetable: 2.0
Fruit: 0.0
Bread: 3.0
Meat: 1.0
Fat: 1.0

1. Sauté carrots, celery, onion, and garlic in oil in large saucepan 5 minutes. Add 6 cups broth, black-eyed peas, and herbs; heat to boiling. Reduce heat and simmer, covered, 30 minutes; add tomatoes and lentils and simmer, covered, until peas and lentils are tender, about 30 minutes, adding additional broth if necessary. Discard bay leaf; season to taste with salt and pepper.

COUNTRY LENTIL SOUP

L *A light soup that is wholesome in flavor and texture. This soup freezes well, so make extra.*

6 entrée servings

1½ cups chopped onions
1 cup each: sliced celery, carrots
2 teaspoons minced garlic
1 tablespoon olive oil
3 cups vegetable broth
2 cups water
1 cup dried lentils
1 can (14½ ounces) reduced-sodium crushed tomatoes, undrained

½ teaspoon each: dried marjoram, oregano,
and thyme leaves

Salt and pepper, to taste

4 tablespoons grated fat-free Parmesan cheese

Per Serving:
Calories: 275
% calories from fat: 14
Protein (g): 15.8
Carbohydrate (g): 42.8
Fat (g): 4.4
Saturated fat (g): 0.6
Cholesterol (mg): 0
Sodium (mg): 109

Exchanges:
Milk: 0.0
Vegetable: 3.0
Fruit: 0.0
Bread: 2.0
Meat: 0.5
Fat: 0.5

1. Sauté onions, celery, carrots, and garlic in oil in large saucepan 5 to 8 minutes. Add broth, water, lentils, tomatoes, and herbs; heat to boiling. Reduce heat and simmer, covered, until lentils are tender, about 30 minutes. Season to taste with salt and pepper. Sprinkle each bowl of soup with 1 tablespoon cheese.

EASY INDIAN LENTIL SOUP

V *This hearty but very easy soup tastes best made with tiny beige Indian lentils available in Indian specialty food stores. However, regular brown lentils can also be used.*

4 entrée servings

1 large onion, finely chopped

1 garlic clove, minced

2 teaspoons canola oil

2½ quarts water

2 cups dried Indian lentils

⅓ cup each: thinly sliced celery, carrot

2–3 teaspoons mild curry powder

1 teaspoon sugar

Salt and pepper, to taste

Per Serving:
Calories: 306
% calories from fat: 18
Protein (g): 20.8
Carbohydrate (g): 51.2
Fat (g): 3
Saturated fat (g): 2
Cholesterol (mg): 0
Sodium (mg): 28

Exchanges:
Milk: 0.0
Vegetable: 0.0
Fruit: 0.0
Bread: 4.0
Meat: 0.0
Fat: 0.0

1. Sauté onion and garlic in oil in Dutch oven until onion is soft. Add remaining ingredients, except salt and pepper, and heat to boiling. Reduce heat and simmer, covered, until lentils soften and thicken the soup, about 45 minutes. Season to taste with salt and pepper.

CURRIED LENTIL-SPINACH SOUP

V   *Lentils and spinach lend delicious flavor and texture to this soup.*

6 entrée servings

2 cups chopped onions

2 large garlic cloves, minced

2 teaspoons olive oil

1¼ quarts reduced-sodium vegetable broth

2 cups water

¼ cup each: thinly sliced celery, carrot

1 cup dried brown lentils

2–2½ teaspoons mild curry powder

½ teaspoon chili powder

1 package (10 ounces) frozen chopped spinach, thawed, well-drained

1 can (14½ ounces) reduced-sodium petite-diced tomatoes, undrained

Salt and pepper, to taste

Per Serving:
Calories: 181
% calories from fat: 10
Protein (g): 10.5
Carbohydrate (g): 32.6
Fat (g): 2
Saturated fat (g): 0.3
Cholesterol (mg): 0
Sodium (mg): 104

Exchanges:
Milk: 0.0
Vegetable: 2.0
Fruit: 0.0
Bread: 1.5
Meat: 0.5
Fat: 1.0

1. Sauté onions and garlic in oil in large saucepan until onion is soft. Add remaining ingredients, except spinach, tomatoes, salt, and pepper; heat to boiling. Reduce heat and simmer, covered, 45 minutes, adding spinach and tomatoes with liquid during last 10 minutes. Season to taste with salt and pepper.

BEAN AND BARLEY SOUP

V   *A soup that can be easily increased to serve a crowd; make it 1 to 2 days in advance for best flavor.*

6 entrée servings

¾ cup each: chopped onion, red bell pepper

2 teaspoons minced garlic

2 tablespoons olive oil

1 tablespoon flour

1½ teaspoons dried Italian seasoning

7 cups low-sodium vegetable broth

2 cans (15 ounces) cannellini or Great Northern
    beans, rinsed, drained
2 tablespoons reduced-sodium tomato paste
½ cup quick-cooking barley
1 cup each: cubed unpeeled Idaho potato, sliced
    carrots, packed baby spinach leaves
Salt and pepper, to taste

1. Sauté onion, bell pepper, and garlic in oil
in Dutch oven 5 minutes. Add flour and Italian
seasoning; cook 1 minute. Add remaining
ingredients, except spinach, salt, and pepper;
heat to boiling. Reduce heat and simmer,
uncovered, 20 to 25 minutes, adding spinach
during last 5 minutes of cooking time. Season
to taste with salt and pepper.

Per Serving:
Calories: 297
% calories from fat: 17
Protein (g): 10
Carbohydrate (g): 52.1
Fat (g): 5.6
Saturated fat (g): 0.7
Cholesterol (mg): 0
Sodium (mg): 325

Exchanges:
Milk: 0.0
Vegetable: 1.0
Fruit: 0.0
Bread: 3.0
Meat: 0.0
Fat: 1.0

POTATO BARLEY SOUP

V *You can vary the flavor of this homey soup by using different stocks, as well
as different vegetables.*

8 entrée servings

1 cup chopped onion
3 cloves garlic, minced
3 cups chopped, peeled potatoes
½ cup each: sliced carrots, celery, parsnip
2 bay leaves
1 cup tomato juice
¾ cup quick-cooking barley
1 quart No-Salt Vegetable Stock (see p. 10)
½ teaspoon each: dried thyme and marjoram leaves
Salt and pepper, to taste

Per Serving:
Calories: 186
% calories from fat: 3
Protein (g): 5.1
Carbohydrate (g): 41.8
Fat (g): 0.7
Saturated fat (g): 0.1
Cholesterol (mg): 0
Sodium (mg): 285

Exchanges:
Milk: 0.0
Vegetable: 0.0
Fruit: 0.0
Bread: 2.5
Meat: 0.0
Fat: 0.0

1. Sauté onion, garlic, and potatoes in lightly greased Dutch oven 5
minutes; add remaining ingredients, except salt and pepper, and
heat to boiling. Reduce heat and simmer, covered, until vegetables
and barley are tender, about 20 minutes. Discard bay leaves; season
to taste with salt and pepper.

POLISH-STYLE MUSHROOM-BARLEY SOUP

L *Dried mushrooms add a woodsy flavor to the soup.*

4 entrée servings

¼ ounce dried mushrooms

2¼ quarts water, divided

5 vegetable bouillon cubes

½ cup pearl barley

3 medium potatoes, peeled, diced

1 small onion, coarsely chopped

1 rib celery, sliced

½ cup each: quartered baby carrots, dry white
    wine (optional)

1 cup frozen peas

Salt and white pepper, to taste

½ cup fat-free sour cream

4 teaspoons chopped fresh dill, as garnish

Per Serving:
Calories: 293
% calories from fat: 4
Protein (g): 9.9
Carbohydrate (g): 54.7
Fat (g): 1.5
Saturated fat (g): 0.1
Cholesterol (mg): 0
Sodium (mg): 777

Exchanges:
Milk: 0.0
Vegetable: 3.0
Fruit: 0.0
Bread: 3.0
Meat: 0.0
Fat: 0.0

1. Heat mushrooms and 2 cups water to boiling in small saucepan. Remove from heat and let stand until mushrooms are softened, about 15 minutes; drain, reserving liquid. Chop mushrooms coarsely.

2. Heat remaining 1 ¼ quarts water, bouillon, and barley to boiling in large saucepan; reduce heat and simmer, covered, 40 minutes. Stir in reserved mushroom liquid, chopped mushrooms, and remaining ingredients, except peas, salt, white pepper, sour cream and dill. Simmer until vegetables and barley are tender. 15 to 20 minutes, adding peas the last 5 minutes. Season to taste with salt and white pepper; garnish each bowl of soup with sour cream and dill.

SPICY BARLEY SOUP

45 *Herbs and dry mustard give this barley soup its savory flavor.*

6 first-course servings

1½ cups each: chopped onions, sliced mushrooms

1 large garlic clove, minced

1 tablespoon canola oil

2 quarts vegetable broth

½ cup each: sliced carrot, celery, turnip

3 tablespoons reduced-sodium tomato paste

¼ cup pearl barley

2 bay leaves

1 teaspoon dried marjoram leaves

½ teaspoon each: dried thyme leaves, celery seeds,
   dry mustard

Salt and pepper, to taste

Per Serving:
Calories: 95
% calories from fat: 25
Protein (g): 2.6
Carbohydrate (g): 16.5
Fat (g): 2.8
Saturated fat (g): 0.2
Cholesterol (mg): 0
Sodium (mg): 492

Exchanges:
Milk: 0.0
Vegetable: 0.0
Fruit: 0.0
Bread: 1.0
Meat: 0.0
Fat: 0.5

1. Sauté onions, mushrooms, and garlic in oil in large saucepan until onion is soft. Add remaining ingredients, except salt and pepper, and heat to boiling. Reduce heat and simmer, covered, until barley is tender and has thickened the soup, about 1 hour. Discard bay leaves; season to taste with salt and pepper.

NINE

Meat Stews

SKILLET BEEF STEW

Make this stew in an attractive skillet that can go to the table for serving.

6 entrée servings

1 pound lean beef round steak, cubed
2 tablespoons canola oil
8 ounces thinly sliced mushrooms
¼ cup chopped onion
1 clove garlic, minced
2 cups reduced-sodium fat-free beef broth
1 tablespoon dried Italian seasoning
1½ tablespoons cornstarch
½ cup dry white wine or beef broth
Salt and pepper, to taste
4 cups cooked wide noodles, warm

Per Serving:
Calories: 495
% calories from fat: 23
Protein (g): 36.4
Carbohydrate (g): 47.6
Fat (g): 12.5
Saturated fat (g): 1.9
Cholesterol (mg): 95.3
Sodium (mg): 264

Exchanges:
Milk: 0.0
Vegetable: 0.0
Fruit: 0.0
Bread: 3.0
Meat: 3.0
Fat: 1.5

1. Cook beef in oil in large skillet over medium heat until browned, about 8 minutes. Add mushrooms, onion, and garlic and cook 5 minutes. Stir in broth and Italian seasoning; heat to boiling. Reduce heat and simmer, covered, until beef is tender, about 45 to 60 minutes. Heat stew to boiling; add combined cornstarch and wine, stirring until thickened, about 3 minutes. Season to taste with salt and pepper; serve over noodles.

CUBED STEAK STEW

45 *Beef cubed steaks are quick-cooking and make it possible to have beef stew in less than 45 minutes.*

6 entrée servings

1½ pounds lean beef cubed steaks, cut into strips
    (2 x ½-inch)
3 tablespoons flour
½ teaspoon garlic powder
1 tablespoon olive oil
1 large onion, thinly sliced
1 can (14½ ounces) diced tomatoes with Italian herbs, undrained

1 can (8 ounces) tomato sauce
4 medium potatoes, cubed
1 package (10 ounces) frozen peas and carrots
Salt and pepper, to taste

Per Serving:
Calories: 307
% calories from fat: 19
Protein (g): 26.6
Carbohydrate (g): 35.5
Fat (g): 6.3
Saturated fat (g): 1.6
Cholesterol (mg): 55
Sodium (mg): 372

Exchanges:
Milk: 0.0
Vegetable: 1.0
Fruit: 0.0
Bread: 2.0
Meat: 2.5
Fat: 0.0

1. Coat beef with combined flour and garlic powder; cook in oil in large skillet over medium heat until browned, about 10 minutes. Add onion, tomatoes with liquid, and tomato sauce; heat to boiling. Reduce heat and simmer, uncovered, until meat is tender, about 30 minutes, adding potatoes, peas, and carrots during last 10 minutes. Season to taste with salt and pepper.

TERIYAKI BEEF STEW

The stew can also be served over whole-wheat thin spaghetti or any cooked grain.

4 entrée servings

12–16 ounces lean beef round steak, cut into
   thin strips
1 medium onion, cut into thin wedges
1 tablespoon minced gingerroot
2 teaspoons olive oil
1½ cups fat-free beef broth
2 tablespoons low-sodium teriyaki sauce
2 carrots, thinly sliced
2 cups small broccoli florets
Salt and pepper, to taste
8 ounces noodles, cooked, warm

Per Serving:
Calories: 332
% calories from fat: 25
Protein (g): 26
Carbohydrate (g): 44.4
Fat (g): 10.3
Saturated fat (g): 1.7
Cholesterol (mg): 45.6
Sodium (mg): 1081

Exchanges:
Milk: 0.0
Vegetable: 1.0
Fruit: 0.0
Bread: 2.0
Meat: 3.0
Fat: 0.0

1. Sauté beef, onion, and gingerroot in oil in Dutch oven over medium heat until meat is browned, 5 to 8 minutes. Add broth and teriyaki sauce; heat to boiling. Reduce heat and simmer, covered, until beef is tender, about 45 minutes, adding carrots and broccoli during last 10 minutes. Season to taste with salt and pepper; serve over noodles.

LIGHT BEEF STROGANOFF

Serve in shallow bowls with Roasted Red Pepper Bread (see p. 647).

4 entrée servings

1 pound lean beef round steak, cut into thin strips

8 ounces mushrooms, sliced

½ cup chopped onion

¼ cup chopped shallots or green onions

1 clove garlic, minced

1 tablespoon margarine or butter

3 tablespoons flour

2 cups beef broth

½ to 1 cup fat-free sour cream

Salt and pepper, to taste

Per Serving:
Calories: 281
% calories from fat: 30
Protein (g): 32.7
Carbohydrate (g): 15.4
Fat (g): 9.3
Saturated fat (g): 2.6
Cholesterol (mg): 69.5
Sodium (mg): 317

Exchanges:
Milk: 0.0
Vegetable: 0.0
Fruit: 0.0
Bread: 1.0
Meat: 4.0
Fat: 0.0

1. Cook beef, mushrooms, onion, shallots, and garlic in margarine in large saucepan over medium heat until meat is browned and onions are tender, about 10 minutes. Sprinkle with flour and cook 1 to 2 minutes. Add beef broth and heat to boiling; reduce heat and simmer, covered, until tender, about 45 minutes. Stir in sour cream and cook until hot, 2 to 3 minutes. Season to taste with salt and pepper.

BEEF GOULASH

In Hungary, this paprika-seasoned stew is called "gulyas" and it's often served with dollops of sour cream.

4 entrée servings

12–16 ounces lean beef round steak, cubed (¾-inch)

1 teaspoon olive oil

3 medium onions, cut into thin wedges

1 cup chopped portobello mushrooms

1 can (14½) diced tomatoes, undrained

1 tablespoon paprika

1 teaspoon unsweetened cocoa

2 cups coarsely sliced cabbage

1 tablespoon caraway seeds

Salt and pepper, to taste

8 ounces medium egg noodles, cooked, warm

Per Serving:
Calories: 407
% calories from fat: 17
Protein (g): 29.9
Carbohydrate (g): 55.2
Fat (g): 7.7
Saturated fat (g): 2
Cholesterol (mg): 90.9
Sodium (mg): 473

Exchanges:
Milk: 0.0
Vegetable: 2.0
Fruit: 0.0
Bread: 3.0
Meat: 2.0
Fat: 0.5

1. Cook beef in oil in large saucepan over medium until browned, about 5 minutes; add onions and mushrooms and cook 5 minutes. Add tomatoes with liquid, paprika, and cocoa and heat to boiling; reduce heat and simmer, covered, until beef is tender, 45 to 60 minutes, adding cabbage and caraway seeds during last 10 minutes. Season to taste with salt and pepper; serve over noodles.

PAPRIKA-SIRLOIN STEW WITH SOUR CREAM

45 *Tender beef and vegetables in a paprika-spiked sour cream sauce are ready to eat in less than 45 minutes.*

4 entrée servings

1 pound boneless beef sirloin steak, fat trimmed, cut into strips (1 x ½-inch)

1 cup each: peeled pearl onions, reduced-sodium fat-free beef broth

8 ounces Italian green beans

12 ounces red potatoes, cubed

1 can (14½ ounces) diced tomatoes, undrained

2 bay leaves

1 tablespoon paprika

½ cup fat-free sour cream

Salt and pepper, to taste

Per Serving:
Calories: 286
% calories from fat: 17
Protein (g): 27.4
Carbohydrate (g): 32.9
Fat (g): 5.4
Saturated fat (g): 2
Cholesterol (mg): 59.5
Sodium (mg): 768

Exchanges:
Milk: 0.0
Vegetable: 0.0
Fruit: 0.0
Bread: 2.0
Meat: 3.0
Fat: 0.0

1. Cook beef and onions in lightly greased large skillet over medium heat until beef is lightly browned, 8 to 10 minutes; add remaining ingredients, except sour cream, salt and pepper and heat to boiling. Reduce heat and simmer until beef and vegetables are tender, about 15 minutes. Stir in sour cream; season to taste with salt and pepper.

GROUND BEEF AND VEGETABLE STROGANOFF

45 *Fat-free half-and-half and sour cream contribute rich flavor and creamy texture to this favorite.*

8 entrée servings

1½ pounds lean ground beef

2 medium onions, thinly sliced

2 cloves garlic, minced

12 ounces each: sliced mixed wild mushrooms
  (shiitake, oyster, enoki, or cremini), broccoli florets

½ cup water

¼ cup dry red wine or water

1 cup fat-free half-and-half or fat-free milk

2 tablespoons flour

1½ teaspoons Dijon mustard

1 cup fat-free sour cream

½ teaspoon dried dill weed

Salt and pepper, to taste

16 ounces noodles, cooked, warm

Per Serving:
Calories: 467
% calories from fat: 22
Protein (g): 27.7
Carbohydrate (g): 61.5
Fat (g): 11.3
Saturated fat (g): 4.1
Cholesterol (mg): 52.9
Sodium (mg): 468

Exchanges:
Milk: 0.0
Vegetable: 3.0
Fruit: 0.0
Bread: 3.0
Meat: 2.0
Fat: 1.0

1. Cook ground beef in lightly greased large skillet over medium heat until browned, about 10 minutes; crumble with a fork. Add onions, garlic, and mushrooms and cook until tender, about 5 minutes. Add broccoli, water, and wine and heat to boiling. Reduce heat and simmer, covered, until broccoli is tender, about 8 minutes. Stir in combined half-and-half, flour, and mustard and heat to boiling, stirring until thickened, about 1 minute. Reduce heat to low; stir in sour cream and dill weed and cook until hot, 2 to 3 minutes. Season to taste with salt and pepper; serve over noodles.

GREEK BEEF AND LENTIL STEW

45 *Lentils and fresh vegetables partner deliciously in this easy stew.*

6 entrée servings

1 cup each: chopped onion, green bell pepper, cubed zucchini

2 teaspoons minced garlic

2 cups each: cubed Idaho potatoes, cut green beans

1 cup dry lentils

1 can (14½ ounces) reduced-sodium diced tomatoes, undrained

3 cups reduced-sodium fat-free beef broth

1 teaspoon each: dried oregano and mint leaves

½ teaspoon each: ground turmeric, coriander

12 ounces cooked, cubed lean beef eye of round

Salt and pepper, to taste

Per Serving:
Calories: 302
% calories from fat: 7
Protein (g): 25.5
Carbohydrate (g): 46.7
Fat (g): 2.6
Saturated fat (g): 0.8
Cholesterol (mg): 27.5
Sodium (mg): 122

Exchanges:
Milk: 0.0
Vegetable: 3.0
Fruit: 0.0
Bread: 2.0
Meat: 1.5
Fat: 0.0

1. Sauté onion, bell pepper, zucchini, and garlic in lightly greased large saucepan until tender, about 5 minutes. Add remaining ingredients, except salt and pepper; heat to boiling. Reduce heat and simmer, covered, until lentils are tender and stew is thickened, 20 to 30 minutes. Season to taste with salt and pepper.

VEAL STEW WITH SAGE

45 *Sage and dry white wine give this stew an Italian flair!*

6 entrée servings

1¼ pounds lean veal leg, cubed (½-inch)

¾ cup chopped onion

3 carrots, sliced

2 each: sliced ribs celery, chopped cloves garlic

½ teaspoon each: dried sage and thyme leaves

1½ cups reduced-sodium fat-free chicken broth

½ cup dry white wine or chicken broth

Salt and pepper, to taste

12 ounces egg noodles, cooked, warm

Per Serving:
Calories: 389
% calories from fat: 14
Protein (g): 35.2
Carbohydrate (g): 43.3
Fat (g): 5.9
Saturated fat (g): 1.8
Cholesterol (mg): 144.3
Sodium (mg): 126

Exchanges:
Milk: 0.0
Vegetable: 0.0
Fruit: 0.0
Bread: 3.0
Meat: 3.0
Fat: 0.0

1. Cook veal in lightly greased large skillet over medium heat until lightly browned, about 5 minutes; remove and reserve; add onion, carrots, celery, and garlic and cook until tender, about 5 minutes. Stir in remaining ingredients, except salt, pepper, and noodles; heat to boiling. Reduce heat and simmer, covered, until veal is tender, about 30 minutes. Season to taste with salt and pepper; serve over noodles.

VEAL STEW MARSALA

45 *Marsala wine flavors this easy stew. It tastes wonderful served over rice or pasta.*

4 entrée servings

1 pound lean veal leg, cubed
1 teaspoon olive oil
2 cups sliced mushrooms
2 cloves garlic, minced
2 tablespoons flour
1½ cups reduced-sodium fat-free chicken broth
½ cup Marsala wine or chicken broth
½ teaspoon dried rosemary leaves, crushed
Salt and pepper, to taste

Per Serving:
Calories: 213
% calories from fat: 24
Protein (g): 32.4
Carbohydrate (g): 3.2
Fat (g): 5.6
Saturated fat (g): 1.8
Cholesterol (mg): 114.4
Sodium (mg): 74

Exchanges:
Milk: 0.0
Vegetable: 1.0
Fruit: 0.0
Bread: 0.0
Meat: 3.0
Fat: 0.0

1. Cook veal in oil in large skillet over medium heat until browned, about 8 minutes; stir in mushrooms and garlic and cook until tender, about 5 minutes. Add flour and cook 1 to 2 minutes. Stir in broth, wine, and rosemary; heat to boiling. Reduce heat and simmer, covered, until meat is tender, about 30 minutes, adding more broth if needed. Season to taste with salt and pepper.

VEAL AND VEGETABLE PAPRIKASH

45 *Your preference of hot or sweet paprika can be used in this recipe.*

6 entrée servings

1½ pounds veal scallopine, cut into thin strips
1 tablespoon olive oil
2 cups thinly sliced cabbage
1 cup each: sliced onion, zucchini, carrots,
    green bell peppers, chopped tomato, mushrooms
2 tablespoons flour
1 tablespoon paprika
1 cup reduced-sodium chicken broth
½ cup fat-free sour cream
Salt and pepper, to taste
12 ounces noodles, cooked, warm

1. Sauté veal in oil in large skillet until browned, about 5 minutes; remove from skillet. Add vegetables to skillet and sauté until tender, 8 to 10 minutes. Stir in flour and paprika; cook 1 minute. Stir in veal and broth and heat to boiling, stirring until thickened, about 1 minute. Stir in sour cream; season to taste with salt and pepper. Serve over noodles.

Per Serving:
Calories: 419
% calories from fat: 20
Protein (g): 33.5
Carbohydrate (g): 49.8
Fat (g): 9.1
Saturated fat (g): 3.2
Cholesterol (mg): 138.5
Sodium (mg): 264

Exchanges:
Milk: 0.0
Vegetable: 2.0
Fruit: 0.0
Bread: 3.0
Meat: 3.0
Fat: 0.0

VEAL STEW WITH WINE

45 *Serve this stew over rice or pasta, with a green salad and warm crusty bread.*

6 entrée servings

1 each: large chopped onion, minced garlic clove
1½ pounds veal scallopine, cut into thin strips
1 tablespoon flour
1 cup water
½ cup each: tomato sauce, dry white wine
Salt and pepper, to taste

Per Serving:
Calories: 256
% calories from fat: 31
Protein (g): 32.5
Carbohydrate (g): 4.3
Fat (g): 8.5
Saturated fat (g): 3.1
Cholesterol (mg): 128.1
Sodium (mg): 243

Exchanges:
Milk: 0.0
Vegetable: 1.0
Fruit: 0.0
Bread 0.0
Meat: 4.0
Fat: 0.0

1. Cook onion, garlic, and veal in lightly greased large skillet over medium heat until vegetables are tender and veal is browned, about 10 minutes; add flour and cook 1 minute. Add water, tomato sauce, and wine and heat to boiling, reduce heat and simmer, covered, until veal is tender, about 15 to 20 minutes. Season to taste with salt and pepper.

PORK AND SQUASH RAGOUT

45 *Serve this hearty stew with Garlic Bread (see p. 645).*

4 entrée servings

1 pound pork tenderloin, cubed
1½ cups each: chopped onions, green bell peppers
2 teaspoons minced roasted garlic
1 tablespoon flour
2 cups cubed, peeled butternut or acorn squash
2 cans (14½ ounces each) reduced-sodium diced
    tomatoes, undrained
1 can (15 ounces) red kidney beans, rinsed, drained
¾ teaspoon dried Italian seasoning
Salt and pepper, to taste

Per Serving:
Calories: 344
% calories from fat: 10
Protein (g): 33.2
Carbohydrate (g): 46.2
Fat (g): 3.8
Saturated fat (g): 1.3
Cholesterol (mg): 73.1
Sodium (mg): 504

Exchanges:
Milk: 0.0
Vegetable: 0.0
Fruit: 0.0
Bread: 3.0
Meat: 3.0
Fat: 0.0

1. Cook pork in lightly greased large saucepan over medium heat until browned, 8 to 10 minutes; remove from skillet. Add onions, bell peppers, and garlic and sauté until tender, about 8 minutes; stir in flour and cook 1 minute. Add pork and remaining ingredients, except salt and pepper. Heat to boiling; reduce heat and simmer until pork is cooked, 15 to 20 minutes. Season to taste with salt and pepper.

PORK STEW WITH PEPPERS AND ZUCCHINI

45 *Flavorful pork tenderloin is low in saturated fat and cooks very quickly.*

4 entrée servings

1 pound pork tenderloin, cut into thin strips
2 teaspoons olive oil
1 each: chopped large onion, minced garlic clove
1 can (15 ounces) tomato sauce
½ cup chicken broth
1 cup each: sliced red and green bell peppers
1½ cups thinly sliced zucchini
3 tablespoons dry sherry (optional)
¾ teaspoon each: dried basil and thyme leaves

Per Serving:
Calories: 480
% calories from fat: 15
Protein (g): 34.8
Carbohydrate (g): 63.9
Fat (g): 7.8
Saturated fat (g): 1.9
Cholesterol (mg): 65.4
Sodium (mg): 91

Exchanges:
Milk: 0.0
Vegetable: 4.0
Fruit: 0.0
Bread: 3.0
Meat: 3.0
Fat: 0.0

1 bay leaf

Salt and pepper, to taste

4 cups cooked fusilli, warm

1. Cook pork in oil in large skillet over medium heat until browned, about 5 minutes; add onion and garlic and cook until tender, about 5 minutes. Add remaining ingredients, except salt, pepper, and fusilli; heat to boiling. Reduce heat and simmer, covered, until meat is tender, about 15 minutes. Discard bay leaf; season to taste with salt and pepper. Serve over fusilli.

ROSEMARY PORK AND WHITE BEAN STEW

45 *An elegant and flavorful stew with Tuscan flavors.*

6 entrée servings

1½ pounds pork tenderloin, cubed

2 cloves garlic, minced

2 teaspoons olive oil

1 tablespoon flour

1 can (14½ ounces) reduced-sodium diced tomatoes, undrained

1 can (14 ounces) artichoke hearts, rinsed, drained, quartered

1 can (15 ounces) cannellini or navy beans, rinsed, drained

⅔ cup reduced-sodium fat-free chicken broth

2 teaspoons each: dried rosemary leaves, grated orange zest

Salt and pepper, to taste

Per Serving:
Calories: 254
% calories from fat: 22
Protein (g): 29.3
Carbohydrate (g): 18.7
Fat (g): 5.9
Saturated fat (g): 1.6
Cholesterol (mg): 65.7
Sodium (mg): 341

Exchanges:
Milk: 0.0
Vegetable: 1.0
Fruit: 0.0
Bread: 1.0
Meat: 3.0
Fat: 0.0

1. Cook pork and garlic in oil in large saucepan over medium heat until browned, about 8 minutes; sprinkle with flour and cook 1 minute. Stir in remaining ingredients, except salt and pepper; heat to boiling. Reduce heat and simmer, covered, until pork is cooked, about 15 minutes. Season to taste with salt and pepper.

PEPPERED PORK AND WINE STEW

45

Enjoy medallions of pork tenderloin, coated with crushed peppercorns and simmered in a flavorful sauce.

4 entrée servings

1 pound pork tenderloin, sliced (½-inch)
1 tablespoon finely crushed peppercorns
1 medium onion, finely chopped
½ cup chopped red bell pepper
1 clove garlic, minced
1½ cups reduced-sodium fat-free beef broth
½ cup dry white wine or water
¼ cup all-purpose flour
1 tablespoon red wine vinegar
Salt and pepper, to taste
¼ cup minced chives or parsley

Per Serving:
Calories: 214
% calories from fat: 18
Protein (g): 26.9
Carbohydrate (g): 11
Fat (g): 4.2
Saturated fat (g): 1.4
Cholesterol (mg): 65.7
Sodium (mg): 110

Exchanges:
Milk: 0.0
Vegetable: 2.0
Fruit: 0.0
Bread: 0.0
Meat: 3.0
Fat: 0.0

1. Sprinkle pork slices with peppercorns, pressing into surface of meat; cook in lightly greased large skillet over medium heat until browned, 2 to 3 minutes on each side. Remove from skillet and reserve. Add onion, bell pepper, and garlic to skillet and sauté until tender, about 5 minutes. Add broth and heat to boiling; add reserved pork, reduce heat, and simmer, covered, until pork is tender, about 15 minutes. Heat stew to boiling; stir in combined wine, flour, and vinegar, stirring, until thickened, about 1 minute. Season to taste with salt and pepper; sprinkle with chives.

AUSTRIAN PORK STEW WITH APPLES AND CRANBERRY SAUCE

45

Enjoy this tangy medley of lean pork, fruit, and thyme.

4 entrée servings

1 pound boneless pork loin, sliced (¼-inch)
½ teaspoon dried thyme leaves
2 teaspoons margarine or butter
1 cup chopped onion

2 large tart apples, peeled, cored, thinly sliced

1 can (16 ounces) whole-berry cranberry sauce

1 tablespoon each: Worcestershire sauce, apple cider vinegar

2 tablespoons brown sugar

Salt and pepper, to taste

8 ounces egg noodles, cooked, warm

Per Serving:
Calories: 460
% calories from fat: 17
Protein (g): 19
Carbohydrate (g): 79
Fat (g): 8.5
Saturated fat (g): 2.4
Cholesterol (mg): 77
Sodium (mg): 123

Exchanges:
Milk: 0.0
Vegetable: 0.0
Fruit: 3.0
Bread: 2.0
Meat: 2.0
Fat: 0.5

1. Sprinkle pork with thyme; cook in margarine in Dutch oven over medium heat until browned, about 5 minutes. Add remaining ingredients, except salt, pepper, and noodles; heat to boiling. Reduce heat and simmer, covered, until pork is tender, about 30 minutes. Season to taste with salt and pepper; serve over noodles.

ORANGE PORK RAGOUT

Orange juice and cloves give this easy dish a distinct flavor.

4 entrée servings

1 pound boneless pork loin, cut into thin strips

2 teaspoons olive oil

1 cup each: sliced onion, red and green bell peppers

1½ cups orange juice

2 teaspoons sugar

1 teaspoon dried thyme leaves

¼ teaspoon ground cloves

Salt and pepper, to taste

3 cups cooked white rice, warm

Per Serving:
Calories: 428
% calories from fat: 23
Protein (g): 25.5
Carbohydrate (g): 57.3
Fat (g): 10.8
Saturated fat (g): 3.1
Cholesterol (mg): 42.4
Sodium (mg): 50

Exchanges:
Milk: 0.0
Vegetable: 2.0
Fruit: 0.5
Bread: 2.5
Meat: 3.0
Fat: 0.0

1. Cook pork in oil in large skillet over medium heat until lightly browned, about 5 minutes; remove and reserve. Add onion and bell peppers and sauté until tender, about 8 minutes. Add reserved pork and remaining ingredients, except salt, pepper, and rice, and heat to boiling. Reduce heat and simmer, covered, until pork is tender, about 30 minutes. Simmer, uncovered, until stew is thickened, about 10 minutes. Season to taste with salt and pepper; serve over rice.

BARBECUE PORK STEW

45 *Barbecue sauce and apple cider are the flavor secrets in this tasty stew.*

4 entrée servings

1 pound pork tenderloin, cubed (¾-inch)
1 medium onion, coarsely chopped
1 large tart apple, peeled, coarsely chopped
1 teaspoon crushed caraway seeds
1½ cups apple cider or apple juice, divided
½ cup honey-mustard barbecue sauce
2 tablespoons cornstarch
4 cups thinly sliced cabbage
Salt and pepper; to taste
8 ounces noodles, cooked, warm

Per Serving:
Calories: 521
% calories from fat: 8
Protein (g): 34
Carbohydrate (g): 82.9
Fat (g): 5
Saturated fat (g): 1.4
Cholesterol (mg): 65.7
Sodium (mg): 444

Exchanges:
Milk: 0.0
Vegetable: 1.0
Fruit: 2.0
Bread: 3.0
Meat: 3.0
Fat: 0.0

1. Cook pork in lightly greased large saucepan over medium heat until browned, about 8 minutes. Add onion, apple, and caraway seeds and cook until onion is tender, about 5 minutes. Add 1 cup apple cider and heat to boiling; reduce heat and simmer, covered, 5 minutes. Stir in combined remaining ½ cup apple cider, barbecue sauce, and cornstarch, stirring until thickened, about 1 minute. Stir in cabbage; simmer, covered, until cabbage and pork are tender, 10 to 15 minutes. Season to taste with salt and pepper. Serve over noodles.

BEAN AND CANADIAN BACON STEW WITH PASTA

45 *Canadian bacon adds a great smoked meat flavor to this stew.*

6 entrée servings

1 each: large finely chopped onion, minced garlic clove
2 teaspoons olive oil
1 can (15 ounces) tomato sauce
¾ cup fat-free beef broth
2½ cups cooked dried or drained, rinsed canned Great Northern beans
½ cup each: large green and red bell pepper, diced
¾ teaspoon each: dried thyme and basil leaves

¼ teaspoon dry mustard

1 bay leaf

6 ounces Canadian bacon, cut into thin strips

¼ cup fat-free ricotta cheese

Salt and pepper, to taste

12 ounces fusilli, cooked, warm

Per Serving:
Calories: 401
% calories from fat: 11
Protein (g): 22
Carbohydrate (g): 67.5
Fat (g): 5.0
Saturated fat (g): 1.2
Cholesterol (mg): 16.7
Sodium (mg): 815

Exchanges:
Milk: 0.0
Vegetable: 0.0
Fruit: 0.0
Bread: 4.0
Meat: 2.0
Fat: 0.0

1. Sauté onion and garlic in oil in Dutch oven until tender, about 5 minutes. Add remaining ingredients, except Canadian bacon, ricotta, salt, pepper, and fusilli; heat to boiling. Reduce heat and simmer, covered, 20 minutes, adding Canadian bacon during the last 10 minutes. Stir in ricotta; discard bay leaf and season to taste with salt and pepper. Serve over pasta.

CORNED BEEF AND RED CABBAGE STEW

45 *Don't wait until St. Patrick's Day to enjoy this luck-of-the-Irish stew. It's fast, easy, and delicious.*

4 entrée servings

8–12 ounces cooked lean corned beef, cubed

4 medium red potatoes, cubed

1 cup each: sliced carrots, cubed turnips

1 tablespoon apple cider vinegar

1 teaspoon pickling spice

1 pound cabbage, coarsely sliced

1 can (14½ ounces) reduced-sodium fat-free chicken broth, divided

1½ tablespoons flour

Salt and pepper, to taste

Per Serving:
Calories: 259
% calories from fat: 29
Protein (g): 13.6
Carbohydrate (g): 34.1
Fat (g): 8.5
Saturated fat (g): 2.8
Cholesterol (mg): 42.3
Sodium (mg): 646

Exchanges:
Milk: 0.0
Vegetable: 1.0
Fruit: 0.0
Bread: 2.0
Meat: 1.0
Fat: 1.0

1. Heat all ingredients, except cabbage, ½ cup broth, flour, salt, and pepper to boiling in large saucepan; reduce heat and simmer, covered, 10 minutes. Add cabbage and cook until vegetables are tender, about 10 minutes. Heat stew to boiling; stir in combined remaining ½ cup broth and flour, stirring, until thickened, about 1 minute. Season to taste with salt and pepper.

GERMAN-STYLE STEW

45 *Serve this stew with Hearty Vegetable-Rye Bread (see p. 646).*

4 entrée servings

2 cups each: fresh sauerkraut, thinly sliced peeled
  potatoes
1 cup each: thinly sliced peeled apples,
  chopped onion
1½ cups cubed, peeled rutabaga
12 ounces reduced-sodium ham steak, cubed (¼-inch)
1 tablespoon flour
2 bay leaves
1 cup apple cider
1½ tablespoons brown sugar
Salt and pepper, to taste

Per Serving:
Calories: 334
% calories from fat: 19
Protein (g): 21.3
Carbohydrate (g): 41.8
Fat (g): 6.9
Saturated fat (g): 2.3
Cholesterol (mg): 48.5
Sodium (mg): 1282

Exchanges:
Milk: 0.0
Vegetable: 2.0
Fruit: 0.0
Bread: 2.0
Meat: 3.0
Fat: 0.0

1. Heat all ingredients, except salt and pepper, to boiling in large saucepan; reduce heat and simmer, covered, until vegetables are tender, about 20 minutes. Discard bay leaves; season to taste with salt and pepper.

ONE-STEP HAM AND BEAN STEW

45 *Making a stew doesn't get much easier than this!*

6 entrée servings

6 ounces reduced-sodium baked ham, diced
1 can (15 ounces) each: rinsed, drained black, pinto,
  and navy beans
1 can (14½ ounces each) reduced-sodium fat-free
  beef broth
1 can (28 ounces) reduced-sodium diced
  tomatoes, undrained
⅓ cup quick-cooking barley
1 large onion, chopped
2 cloves garlic, minced
1 tablespoon chili powder

Per Serving:
Calories: 296
% calories from fat: 9
Protein (g): 20.6
Carbohydrate (g): 54.4
Fat (g): 3.3
Saturated fat (g): 0.8
Cholesterol (mg): 13.5
Sodium (mg): 922

Exchanges:
Milk 0.0
Vegetable: 1.0
Fruit: 0.0
Bread: 3.0
Meat: 1.0
Fat: 0.0

2 teaspoons dried oregano leaves

¼–½ teaspoon crushed red pepper

Salt and pepper, to taste

1. Heat all ingredients, except salt and pepper, to boiling in large saucepan; reduce heat and simmer, covered, until barley is cooked, about 20 minutes. Season to taste with salt and pepper.

SOUTHERN STEWED BLACK EYES, CHICKPEAS, AND HAM

45 *A hearty stew that can be made in less than 45 minutes with ingredients on hand. Serve with warm biscuits or corn bread (see Index).*

6 entrée servings

12 ounces reduced-sodium baked ham, cubed

½ cup chopped onion

2 cloves garlic, minced

1 tablespoon olive oil

2 cups halved small okra

1 can (14½ ounces) reduced-sodium stewed tomatoes

1 can (15 ounces) each: chickpeas and black-eyed peas, rinsed, drained

½ package (10-ounce size) frozen spinach, partially thawed

1 teaspoon each: dried marjoram and thyme leaves

¼ teaspoon hot pepper sauce

Salt and pepper, to taste

Per Serving:
Calories: 320
% calories from fat: 23
Protein (g): 21.8
Carbohydrate (g): 41.6
Fat (g): 8.2
Saturated fat (g): 2
Cholesterol (mg): 32.3
Sodium (mg): 841

Exchanges:
Milk: 0.0
Vegetable: 2.0
Fruit: 0.0
Bread: 2.0
Meat: 0.5
Fat: 0.0

1. Sauté ham, onion, and garlic in oil in large saucepan until onion is tender, 5 to 8 minutes. Stir in remaining ingredients, except salt and pepper; heat to boiling. Reduce heat and simmer, covered, until okra is tender, about 10 minutes. Season to taste with salt and pepper.

BUTTER BEANS, MOSTACCIOLI, AND HAM STEW

45 *This dish has a subtle anchovy flavor—the anchovies can be deleted, if you prefer.*

4 entrée servings

1½ cups frozen small butter beans

2 cans (14½ ounces each) reduced-sodium fat-free chicken broth

4 ounces each: uncooked mostaccioli, diced, reduced-sodium baked ham

½ can (2-ounce size) anchovies, rinsed, drained, mashed

2 teaspoons minced garlic

1 small mild chili, chopped

½ cup sliced scallions

¼ cup (1 ounce) grated Romano cheese

Salt and pepper, to taste

Per Serving:
Calories: 289
% calories from fat: 16
Protein (g): 23.5
Carbohydrate (g): 36
Fat (g): 4.9
Saturated fat (g): 2
Cholesterol (mg): 28.4
Sodium (mg): 783

Exchanges:
Milk: 0.0
Vegetable: 0.0
Fruit: 0.0
Bread: 2.5
Meat: 2.0
Fat: 0.0

1. Heat all ingredients, except Romano cheese, salt, and pepper to boiling in large saucepan; reduce heat and simmer, covered, until pasta is tender, about 10 minutes. Stir in cheese; season to taste with salt and pepper.

HAM AND PEPPER STEW WITH POLENTA

45 *The microwave method for cooking polenta eliminates lumps and the constant stirring necessary when polenta is made on the stovetop.*

4 entrée servings

1 each: chopped medium onion, minced garlic clove

2 teaspoons olive oil

1 can (14½ ounces) reduced-sodium diced tomatoes, undrained

1 can (15 ounces) tomato sauce

8 ounces reduced-sodium ham steak, cubed

1½ cups chopped mixed green, red, and yellow bell peppers

1 bay leaf

1½ teaspoons dried Italian seasoning

Salt and pepper, to taste

Microwave Polenta (see p. 530)

2 tablespoons grated Parmesan cheese

1. Sauté onion and garlic in oil in large saucepan until onion is tender, about 5 minutes. Add remaining ingredients, except salt, pepper, Microwave Polenta, and Parmesan cheese; heat to boiling. Reduce heat and simmer, covered, until vegetables are tender, about 15 minutes. Discard bay leaf; season to taste with salt and pepper. Serve over Microwave Polenta; sprinkle with cheese.

Per Serving:
Calories: 394
% calories from fat: 21
Protein (g): 21
Carbohydrate (g): 57.8
Fat (g): 9.2
Saturated fat (g): 2.7
Cholesterol (mg): 36.5
Sodium (mg): 687

Exchanges:
Milk: 0.0
Vegetable: 0.0
Fruit: 0.0
Bread: 4.0
Meat: 2.0
Fat: 0.0

COUNTRY BEEF STEW

This long-simmered stew is delicious served over noodles or rice.

4 entrée servings

2 pounds lean beef stew meat, cubed

1 cup each: chopped onion, celery

3 cloves garlic, minced

2½ cups reduced-sodium beef broth

½ cup dry red wine or beef broth

2 tablespoons tomato paste

½ teaspoon each: dried thyme and rosemary leaves

1 large bay leaf

2 cups each: cubed unpeeled potato, thickly sliced carrots

1 cup cubed parsnip or turnip

½ cup frozen peas

¼ cup all-purpose flour

½ cup cold water

Salt and pepper, to taste

Per Serving:
Calories: 326
% calories from fat: 16
Protein (g): 33.5
Carbohydrate (g): 29.6
Fat (g): 5.8
Saturated fat (g): 2
Cholesterol (mg): 70.9
Sodium (mg): 171

Exchanges:
Milk: 0.0
Vegetable: 2.0
Fruit: 0.0
Bread: 1.5
Meat: 3.0
Fat: 0.0

1. Cook beef in lightly greased large saucepan over medium heat until browned, 5 to 8 minutes. Add onion, celery, and garlic; cook until tender, about 5 minutes. Add broth, wine, tomato paste, and herbs; heat to boiling. Reduce heat and simmer, covered, until beef is tender, 1 to 1½ hours, adding parsnips and peas during last 20 minutes. Heat stew to boiling; stir in combined flour and water, stirring until thickened, about 1 minute. Discard bay leaf; season to taste with salt and pepper.

TRADITIONAL BEEF STEW

Here's a simplified version of an old family favorite.

4 entrée servings

1 pound beef round steak, cut into thin strips

2 small onions, cut into wedges

1 teaspoon olive oil

1½ cups fat-free beef broth

½ cup dry red wine or beef broth

1 tablespoon cocoa

2 medium potatoes, cubed

3 carrots, thickly sliced

2 cups cut wax beans

Salt and pepper, to taste

Per Serving:
Calories: 292
% calories from fat: 16
Protein (g): 26
Carbohydrate (g): 29.7
Fat (g): 5.1
Saturated fat (g): 1.5
Cholesterol (mg): 55
Sodium (mg): 140

Exchanges:
Milk: 0.0
Vegetable: 0.0
Fruit: 0.0
Bread: 2.0
Meat: 3.0
Fat: 0.0

1. Cook beef and onions in oil in Dutch oven over medium heat until beef is browned, 8 to 10 minutes. Add broth, wine, and cocoa; heat to boiling. Reduce heat and simmer, covered, until beef is tender, about 1 hour, adding vegetables during last 20 minutes. Season to taste with salt and pepper.

BEEF AND VEGETABLE STEW

This beef stew boasts an ample assortment of vegetables to make a well-rounded meal.

6 entrée servings

1½ pounds lean beef round steak, cubed (1-inch)

1½ cups beef broth

½ cup red wine or water

1 teaspoon Worcestershire sauce

2 bay leaves

1 clove garlic, minced

6 medium carrots, quartered

4 each: quartered small potatoes and onions

2 small zucchini, sliced

1 cup small mushrooms

1 tablespoon cornstarch

¼ cup cold water

Salt and pepper, to taste

Per Serving:
Calories: 289
% calories from fat: 13
Protein (g): 24.5
Carbohydrate (g): 35.9
Fat (g): 4.1
Saturated fat (g): 1.4
Cholesterol (mg): 55
Sodium (mg): 96

Exchanges:
Milk: 0.0
Vegetable: 1 0
Fruit: 0.0
Bread: 1.5
Meat: 3.0
Fat: 0.0

1. Cook beef in lightly greased Dutch oven over medium heat until browned, about 10 minutes. Add broth, wine, Worcestershire sauce, bay leaves, and garlic; heat to boiling. Reduce heat and simmer, covered, until beef is tender, about 1 hour, adding vegetables during last 30 minutes. Heat stew to boiling; stir in combined cornstarch and water, stirring, until stew is thickened, about 1 minute. Discard bay leaves; season to taste with salt and pepper.

SIMPLE BEEF STEW

*Serve this Italian-seasoned beef stew over noodles, rice, or Microwave
Polenta (see p. 530).*

6 entrée servings

2 pounds lean beef for stew, cubed (1-inch)
2 each: chopped medium onions, minced cloves garlic
½ cup each: reduced-sodium beef broth, dry red wine
    or beef broth
2 teaspoons dried Italian seasoning
1 can (14½ ounces) Italian plum tomatoes,
    undrained, chopped
Salt and pepper, to taste

Per Serving:
Calories: 290
% calories from fat: 34
Protein (g): 35.4
Carbohydrate (g): 8.6
Fat (g): 10.7
Saturated fat (g): 3.8
Cholesterol (mg): 103
Sodium (mg): 246

Exchanges:
Milk: 0.0
Vegetable: 1.5
Fruit: 0.0
Bread: 0.0
Meat: 5.0
Fat: 0.0

1. Cook beef in lightly greased Dutch oven over medium heat until
browned, 10 to 12 minutes. Add onions and garlic, and cook until
lightly browned, 3 to 4 minutes. Add broth, wine, Italian seasoning
and tomatoes with liquid; heat to boiling. Reduce heat and simmer,
covered, until beef is tender, 1 to 1½ hours. Season to taste with
salt and pepper.

FAMILY FAVORITE BEEF STEW

*Add your family's favorite vegetables to this stew. A great recipe for using
leftover vegetables too!*

8 entrée servings

1½ cups chopped onions
4 cloves garlic, minced
½–¾ teaspoon each: dried marjoram and thyme leaves
1 bay leaf
1–2 tablespoons canola oil
2 pounds lean beef stew meat, cubed (1-inch)
3 tablespoons flour
1 can (14½ ounces) each: undrained reduced-sodium
    diced tomatoes, reduced-sodium fat-free beef broth
2 cups each: cubed unpeeled medium potatoes,
    rutabaga or turnips

Per Serving:
Calories: 314
% calories from fat: 22
Protein (g): 32.8
Carbohydrate (g): 28.5
Fat (g): 7.5
Saturated fat (g): 2.3
Cholesterol (mg): 70.9
Sodium (mg): 134

Exchanges:
Milk: 0.0
Vegetable: 0.0
Fruit: 0.0
Bread: 2.0
Meat: 3.0
Fat: 0.0

1 cup thickly sliced carrots

2 large ribs celery, sliced

2–3 teaspoons low-sodium Worcestershire sauce

Salt and pepper, to taste

1. Sauté onions, garlic, and herbs in oil in large saucepan 5 minutes; add beef and cook until browned, about 5 minutes. Stir in flour; cook 1 minute. Add tomatoes with liquid and broth; heat to boiling. Reduce heat and simmer, covered, until beef is tender, about 1 hour, adding vegetables during last 20 minutes. Discard bay leaf; season to taste with Worcestershire sauce, salt, and pepper.

BEEF RAGOUT

Serve this stew over rice, noodles, or a cooked grain, such as barley or oat groats.

8 entrée servings

2 pounds lean beef stew meat, cubed (1-inch)

3 cups reduced-sodium beef broth

1 clove garlic, chopped

1 teaspoon each: dried oregano and thyme leaves

2 cups each: sliced carrots, celery

8 ounces small white onions

Salt and pepper, to taste

Per Serving:
Calories: 215
% calories from fat: 35
Protein (g): 27.1
Carbohydrate (g): 7.2
Fat (g): 8.4
Saturated fat (g): 2.9
Cholesterol (mg): 77.2
Sodium (mg): 386

Exchanges:
Milk: 0.0
Vegetable: 1.0
Fruit: 0.0
Bread: 0.0
Meat: 3.5
Fat: 0.0

1. Cook beef in lightly greased Dutch oven over medium heat until browned, 10 to 12 minutes. Add broth, garlic, and herbs and heat to boiling; reduce heat and simmer, covered, until beef is tender, about 1 hour, adding carrots, celery and onions during last 30 minutes. Season to taste with salt and pepper.

SLOW-COOKER BEEF AND CABBAGE STEW

A robust beef stew that includes both potatoes and rice. The potatoes add chunky texture and the rice helps thicken the flavorful sauce.

4 entrée servings

1 each: large finely chopped onion, sliced carrot

2 garlic cloves, minced

1 pound each: cubed unpeeled potatoes, cubed lean beef round steak

1½ cups each: coarsely shredded cabbage, fat-free beef broth

¼ cup uncooked long-grain rice

½ cup dry red wine or beef broth

¼ cup catsup

2 teaspoons brown sugar

1½ teaspoons each: cider vinegar, dried thyme leaves

½ teaspoon dry mustard

Salt and pepper, to taste

Per Serving:
Calories: 450
% calories from fat: 27
Protein (g): 28.5
Carbohydrate (g): 45.9
Fat (g): 13.4
Saturated fat (g): 5.0
Cholesterol (mg): 67.8
Sodium (mg): 397

Exchanges:
Milk: 0.0
Vegetable: 0.0
Fruit: 0.0
Bread: 3.0
Meat: 3.0
Fat: 1.0

1. Combine all ingredients, except salt and pepper, in slow cooker and stir well. Cover and cook on High 1 hour. Reduce heat to Low and cook until meat is tender, 7 to 8 hours. Season to taste with salt and pepper.

HARVEST STEW

Summer's harvest yields sun-ripened tomatoes and squash for this sumptuous stew, served over creamy polenta.

8 entrée servings

2 pounds lean beef stew meat, cubed (1-inch)

1–2 tablespoons canola oil

½ cup chopped onion

2 tablespoons flour

1 cup reduced-sodium fat-free beef broth

4 medium tomatoes, chopped

¾ teaspoon each: dried marjoram and savory leaves

3 cups cubed butternut or Hubbard squash

3 medium zucchini, cubed

Salt and pepper, to taste

6 cups Polenta (double recipe) (see p. 661)

(see p. 661)

Per Serving:
Calories: 284
% calories from fat: 20
Protein (g): 25.2
Carbohydrate (g): 32.4
Fat (g): 6.6
Saturated fat (g): 1.7
Cholesterol (mg): 55
Sodium (mg): 84

Exchanges:
Milk: 0.0
Vegetable: 1.0
Fruit: 0.0
Bread: 1.5
Meat: 3.0
Fat: 0.0

1. Cook beef in oil in Dutch oven over medium heat until browned, about 5 minutes; add onion and cook until tender, about 5 minutes. Add flour and cook 1 minute. Add broth, tomatoes, and herbs; heat to boiling. Reduce heat and simmer, covered, until beef is tender, about 1 hour, adding squash and zucchini during last 15 minutes. Season to taste with salt and pepper. Serve over Polenta.

ORANGE-SCENTED BEEF STEW

Orange and tomato juices combine to give this stew a unique flavor accent.

6 entrée servings

1½ pounds lean beef stew meat, cubed

1½ tablespoons canola oil

¾ cup reduced-sodium fat-free beef broth, divided

1 cup each: reduced-sodium tomato juice, orange juice

Grated zest of 1 orange

2 teaspoons cornstarch

Salt and pepper, to taste

6 ounces spinach noodles, cooked, warm

Per Serving:
Calories: 338
% calories from fat: 30
Protein (g): 30.2
Carbohydrate (g): 27.8
Fat (g): 11.2
Saturated fat (g): 2.7
Cholesterol (mg): 80.6
Sodium (mg): 132

Exchanges:
Milk: 0.0
Vegetable: 0.0
Fruit: 0.0
Bread: 2.0
Meat: 3.0
Fat: 0.0

1. Cook beef in oil in Dutch oven over medium heat until browned, about 10 minutes. Add ½ cup beef broth, tomato juice, orange juice, and zest; heat to boiling. Reduce heat and simmer, covered, until beef is tender, about 1 hour. Heat stew to boiling; stir in combined cornstarch and remaining ¼ cup beef broth, stirring until thickened, about 1 minute. Season to taste with salt and pepper. Serve over spinach noodles.

BEEF BURGUNDY

Serve this delicious stew over noodles or rice, with a crisp green salad on the side.

6 entrée servings

1½ pounds lean beef eye of round, cubed (1½-inch)

1 tablespoon olive oil

¼ cup all purpose flour

1 cup each: reduced-sodium beef broth, Burgundy
   wine or water

1 teaspoon each: dried marjoram and thyme leaves

2 bay leaves

1½ cups chopped onions

3 cups sliced carrots

8 ounces small whole mushrooms

Salt and pepper, to taste

12 ounces egg noodles, cooked, warm

Per Serving:
Calories: 522
% calories from fat: 25
Protein (g): 35.3
Carbohydrate (g): 55
Fat (g): 14.3
Saturated fat (g): 4.6
Cholesterol (mg): 96.5
Sodium (mg): 309

Exchanges:
Milk: 0.0
Vegetable: 1.0
Fruit: 0.0
Bread: 3.0
Meat: 4.0
Fat: 1.0

1. Cook beef in oil in Dutch oven over medium heat until browned, about 10 minutes; stir in flour and cook 1 minute. Add broth, wine, and herbs; heat to boiling. Transfer to oven and bake, covered, at 350 degrees until beef is tender, 1 to 1½ hours, adding vegetables during last 30 minutes. Discard bay leaves; season to taste with salt and pepper. Serve over noodles.

BOEUF À LA BOURGUIGNON

This French-inspired stew is perfect for special occasions, when ordinary beef stew is not quite elegant enough!

8 entrée servings

2 pounds lean beef stew meat

1½ cups each: peeled pearl onions, chopped onions, sliced mushrooms

3 tablespoons flour

1 cup each: Burgundy or other red wine, fat-free beef broth

1 tablespoon tomato paste

Herb bouquet (1 teaspoon each: thyme, rosemary, and tarragon tied in a cheesecloth bag)

½ cup chopped parsley

Salt and pepper, to taste

Per Serving:
Calories: 230
% calories from fat: 23
Protein (g): 30.4
Carbohydrate (g): 7.4
Fat (g): 5.6
Saturated fat (g): 2
Cholesterol (mg): 70.9
Sodium (mg): 98

Exchanges:
Milk: 0.0
Vegetable: 1.0
Fruit: 0.0
Bread: 0.0
Meat: 4.0
Fat: 0.0

1. Cook beef in lightly greased Dutch oven over medium heat until browned, 8 to 10 minutes. Remove and reserve. Add onions and mushrooms to Dutch oven and sauté until mushrooms are tender, about 5 minutes. Sprinkle with flour and cook 2 minutes. Stir in reserved beef, wine, broth, tomato paste, and herb bouquet; heat to boiling. Reduce heat and simmer, covered, until beef is tender, about 1 hour. Discard herb bouquet; stir in parsley and season to taste with salt and pepper.

WINE-BRAISED BEEF STEW

The slow simmering gives this dish a rich flavor. A good-quality Chianti works well in this stew.

6 entrée servings

1½ pounds boneless beef round steak, cubed

2 tablespoons flour

1–2 tablespoons olive oil

1 teaspoon minced garlic

2 cups sliced mushrooms

1 cup each: chopped onion, reduced-sodium fat-free beef broth, dry red wine or beef broth

1 can (15 ounces) tomato sauce

1 teaspoon dried thyme leaves

2 each: large bay leaves, sliced ribs celery

12 baby carrots

6 small potatoes, halved

Salt and pepper, to taste

Per Serving:
Calories: 366
% calories from fat: 18
Protein (g): 31.2
Carbohydrate (g): 36.9
Fat (g): 7.4
Saturated fat (g): 2.2
Cholesterol (mg): 55.9
Sodium (mg): 115

Exchanges:
Milk: 0.0
Vegetable: 2.0
Fruit: 0.0
Bread: 2.0
Meat: 3.0
Fat: 0.0

1. Toss beef with flour; cook in oil in Dutch oven over medium heat until browned, 8 to 10 minutes. Add garlic, mushrooms, and onion; cook until onion is tender, about 5 minutes. Add broth, wine, tomato sauce, and herbs and heat to boiling; transfer Dutch oven to oven and bake at 350 degrees, covered, until beef is tender, 1 to 1½ hours, adding celery, carrots, and potatoes during last 30 minutes. Discard bay leaves; season to taste with salt and pepper.

BEEF STEW DA VINCI

A bounty of Italian flavors, served over linguine!

4 entrée servings

1¼ pounds lean beef round steak, cubed (1-inch)
1 cup each: chopped onion, green bell peppers
1 clove garlic, minced
¼ cup dried shallots
1 can (14½ ounces) diced tomatoes, undrained
1 teaspoon each: beef bouillon crystals, dried basil leaves, garlic powder
1 cup sliced mushrooms
Salt and pepper, to taste
6 ounces linguine, cooked, warm
¼ cup each: chopped parsley, grated Parmesan cheese (1 ounce)

Per Serving:
Calories: 425
% calories from fat: 17
Protein (g): 41.3
Carbohydrate (g): 44.8
Fat (g): 7.9
Saturated fat (g): 3.0
Cholesterol (mg): 66.5
Sodium (mg): 479

Exchanges:
Milk: 0.0
Vegetable: 0.0
Fruit: 0.0
Bread: 3.0
Meat: 4.0
Fat: 0.0

1. Cook beef, onion, bell peppers, garlic, and shallots in lightly greased large saucepan over medium heat until meat is browned, about 10 minutes, Add tomatoes with liquid, bouillon crystals, basil, garlic powder, and mushrooms; heat to boiling; reduce heat and simmer, covered, until meat is tender, about 1 hour. Simmer, uncovered, 15 minutes longer, if thicker consistency is desired. Season to taste with salt and pepper. Serve over linguine; sprinkle with parsley and Parmesan cheese.

HOME-STYLE STEAK STEW

Enjoy this simple beef and tomato-based stew over pasta, polenta, or rice.

4 entrée servings

1 pound lean beef round steak, cut into thin strips
2 teaspoons olive oil
1 large onion, chopped
2 garlic cloves, minced
1 tablespoon flour
1 can (14½ ounces) reduced-sodium diced
   tomatoes, undrained
1 can (8 ounces) tomato sauce
½ cup reduced-sodium fat-free beef broth or water
1 teaspoon dried Italian seasoning
¾ cup frozen peas
8 ounces spaghetti, cooked, warm
Salt and pepper, to taste

Per Serving:
Calories: 446
% calories from fat: 18
Protein (g): 34.9
Carbohydrate (g): 55.5
Fat (g): 8.6
Saturated fat (g): 2.2
Cholesterol (mg): 53.9
Sodium (mg): 104

Exchanges:
Milk: 0.0
Vegetable: 2.0
Fruit: 0.0
Bread: 3.0
Meat: 3.0
Fat: 0.0

1. Cook beef in lightly greased large skillet until browned, about 8 minutes; add onion and garlic and cook until onion is tender, about 5 minutes. Stir in flour and cook 1 minute. Add remaining ingredients, except peas, spaghetti, salt, and pepper; heat to boiling. Reduce heat and simmer, covered, until meat is tender, 45 to 60 minutes. Simmer, uncovered, 10 to 15 minutes, if thicker consistency is desired. Season to taste with salt and pepper. Serve over spaghetti.

ROSEMARY BEEF STEW

6 entrée servings

1 cup finely chopped onion

1 large garlic clove, minced

2 teaspoons olive oil

1½ pounds lean beef stew meat, cubed

1½ tablespoons flour

2 cups fat-free beef broth

2 tablespoons dry sherry (optional)

1 can (15 ounces) tomato sauce

1 teaspoon dried rosemary leaves

1 bay leaf

½ cup each: sliced carrots, celery

3 cups cut green beans

Salt and pepper, to taste

4 cups cooked rice, warm

Per Serving:
Calories: 404
% calories from fat: 23
Protein (g): 30.9
Carbohydrate (g): 46.7
Fat (g): 10.1
Saturated fat (g): 3.4
Cholesterol (mg): 60.6
Sodium (mg): 596

Exchanges:
Milk: 0.0
Vegetable: 0.0
Fruit: 0.0
Bread: 3.0
Meat: 3.0
Fat: 0.0

1. Sauté onion and garlic in oil in Dutch oven until onion is tender, about 5 minutes; add meat and cook until browned, about 5 minutes. Sprinkle with flour and cook 2 minutes. Add broth, sherry, tomato sauce, and herbs; heat to boiling. Reduce heat and simmer, covered, until meat is tender, about 1 hour, adding vegetables during last 20 minutes. Simmer, uncovered, 15 minutes, if thicker consistency is desired. Discard bay leaf; season to taste with salt and pepper; serve over rice.

STEAK AND SWEET POTATO STEW

Apples give this autumn stew a touch of sweetness.

4 entrée servings

1 pound lean beef round steak, cubed (¾-inch)

¼ cup all-purpose flour

2 medium onions, cut into thin wedges

1 teaspoon olive oil

2 cups reduced-sodium fat-free beef broth

1 pound sweet potatoes, peeled, cubed

1 teaspoon dried savory leaves

2 medium McIntosh apples, unpeeled, thickly sliced

½ cup frozen peas

Salt and pepper, to taste

Per Serving:
Calories: 442
% calories from fat: 13
Protein (g): 34.2
Carbohydrate (g): 62.3
Fat (g): 6.7
Saturated fat (g): 2.1
Cholesterol (mg): 55.9
Sodium (mg): 197

Exchanges:
Milk: 0.0
Vegetable: 0.0
Fruit: 1.0
Bread: 3.0
Meat: 3.0
Fat: 0.0

1. Toss beef with flour; cook beef and onions in oil in large saucepan over medium heat until browned, 5 to 8 minutes. Add broth and heat to boiling; reduce heat and simmer, covered, until beef is tender, 45 to 60 minutes, adding sweet potatoes and savory the last 10 minutes. Add apples and peas; simmer until apples are tender, about 5 minutes. Season to taste with salt and pepper.

BEEF STROGANOFF

A favorite for buffet entertaining, this dish enjoys well-deserved popularity.

4 entrée servings

1 pound lean beef eye of round or sirloin steak, cut into thin strips

1 tablespoon margarine or butter

3 cups sliced mushrooms

½ cup sliced onion

2 cloves garlic, minced

2 tablespoons flour

1½ cups reduced-sodium beef broth

1 teaspoon Dijon mustard

½ teaspoon dried thyme leaves

½ cup fat-free sour cream

Salt and pepper, to taste

3 cups cooked noodles, warm

Per Serving:
Calories: 423
% calories from fat: 21
Protein (g): 39
Carbohydrate (g): 45.1
Fat (g): 10
Saturated fat (g): 2.2
Cholesterol (mg): 64
Sodium (mg): 167

Exchanges:
Milk: 0.0
Vegetable: 1.0
Fruit: 0.0
Bread: 2.5
Meat: 4.0
Fat: 0.0

1. Cook beef in margarine in large saucepan over medium heat until browned, about 5 minutes; remove meat and reserve. Add mushrooms, onion, and garlic to saucepan; sauté until tender,

5 to 8 minutes; stir in flour and cook 1 minute. Add beef, beef broth, mustard, and thyme and heat to boiling; reduce heat and simmer, covered, until beef is tender, 45 to 60 minutes. Reduce heat to low; stir in sour cream and cook until hot, 2 to 3 minutes. Season to taste with salt and pepper; serve over noodles.

CREAMY BEEF STROGANOFF WITH RICE

Horseradish adds a pleasant sharpness of flavor; increase the amount if you like.

4 entrée servings

1 cup onion, chopped

2 large cloves garlic, minced

2 teaspoons margarine or butter

1 pound lean beef top round steak, cubed (2-inch)

1 tablespoon flour

8 ounces fresh mushrooms, sliced

2 cups fat-free beef broth

¼ cup red Burgundy wine (optional)

3 tablespoons tomato paste

1 teaspoon each: prepared horseradish, dried
    thyme leaves

1 bay leaf

¾ cup fat-free sour cream

Salt and pepper, to taste

1 cup rice, cooked, warm

Per Serving:
Calories: 438
% calories from fat: 15
Protein (g): 36.1
Carbohydrate (g): 55.8
Fat (g): 6.9
Saturated fat (g): 2
Cholesterol (mg): 72.3
Sodium (mg): 412

Exchanges:
Milk: 0.0
Vegetable: 2.0
Fruit: 0.0
Bread: 3.0
Meat: 3.0
Fat: 0.0

1. Sauté onion and garlic in margarine in large saucepan until tender, about 10 minutes; add meat and cook until browned, about 10 minutes. Add flour and cook 1 minute. Add remaining ingredients, except sour cream, salt, pepper, and rice; heat to boiling. Reduce heat and simmer, covered, until meat is tender, 45 to 60 minutes; stir in sour cream and cook until hot, 3 to 4 minutes. Discard bay leaf; season to taste with salt and pepper. Serve over rice.

HUNGARIAN-STYLE BEEF STEW

Serve this rich-tasting stew with warm crusty bread to soak up the delicious sauce.

6 entrée servings

1 pound lean beef round steak, cut into thin strips
1 cup finely chopped onion
1 large garlic clove, minced
1½ cups reduced-sodium fat-free beef broth
½ cup dry red wine or reduced-sodium fat-free
   beef broth
1 can (15 ounces) tomato sauce
1 teaspoon each: dried thyme leaves, paprika
1 bay leaf
¼ teaspoon dry mustard
2 each: sliced large carrots, ribs celery
1 pound peeled potatoes, cubed
½ cup fat-free sour cream
Salt and pepper, to taste

Per Serving:
Calories: 441
% calories from fat: 27
Protein (g): 30.6
Carbohydrate (g): 44.8
Fat (g): 13.2
Saturated fat (g): 4.9
Cholesterol (mg): 72.8
Sodium (mg): 724

Exchanges:
Milk: 0.0
Vegetable: 0.0
Fruit: 0.0
Bread: 3.0
Meat: 3.0
Fat: 1.0

1. Cook beef, onion, and garlic in lightly greased Dutch oven over medium heat until beef is browned, about 10 minutes. Stir in broth, wine, tomato sauce, herbs, and dry mustard and heat to boiling; reduce heat and simmer, covered, until meat is tender, 45 to 60 minutes, adding vegetables during last 20 minutes. Stir in sour cream and cook until hot, 3 to 4 minutes. Discard bay leaf; season to taste with salt and pepper.

HUNGARIAN GOULASH

Hungarian goulash is oven-baked to tender goodness.

6 entrée servings

2 pounds lean beef round steak, cubed
1 medium onion, finely chopped
1 teaspoon minced garlic
2 tablespoons flour
1½ teaspoons paprika
1 bay leaf
1 can (14½ ounces) diced tomatoes, undrained
1 cup fat-free sour cream
Salt and pepper, to taste
12 ounces egg noodles, cooked, warm

Per Serving:
Calories: 471
% calories from fat: 17
Protein (g): 44.6
Carbohydrate (g): 50.5
Fat (g): 8.7
Saturated fat (g): 2.9
Cholesterol (mg): 123.5
Sodium (mg): 367

Exchanges:
Milk: 0.0
Vegetable: 1.0
Fruit: 0.0
Bread: 3.0
Meat: 4.0
Fat: 0.0

1. Cook beef, onion, and garlic in lightly greased Dutch oven over medium heat until beef is browned, about 10 minutes; sprinkle with flour and paprika and cook 1 minute. Stir in bay leaf and tomatoes with liquid; transfer to oven and bake, covered, at 325 degrees, until beef is tender, 1 to 1½ hours, stirring in sour cream during last 10 minutes. Season to taste with salt and pepper. Serve over noodles.

MIDDLE EASTERN BEEF AND BEAN HOT POT

Sweet spices give Middle Eastern flavor accents to this stew.

8 entrée servings

1 cup dried Great Northern beans
1 pound lean beef stew meat, cubed
2 cups chopped onions
2 large garlic cloves, minced
2 teaspoons olive oil
1¼ quarts fat-free beef broth
1 teaspoon dried thyme leaves
½ teaspoon ground cinnamon
⅛ teaspoon ground cloves

Per Serving:
Calories: 427
% calories from fat: 17
Protein (g): 35
Carbohydrate (g): 52
Fat (g): 8.1
Saturated fat (g): 4.4
Cholesterol (mg): 71
Sodium (mg): 595

Exchanges:
Milk: 0.0
Vegetable: 2.0
Fruit: 0.0
Bread: 3.0
Meat: 3.0
Fat: 0.0

1¼ cup rice, cooked
1½ cups diced tomatoes
Salt and pepper, to taste

1. Cover beans with 2 inches water in Dutch oven and heat to boiling. Boil 2 minutes; remove from heat and let stand, covered, 1 hour. Drain.

2. Cook beef, onions, and garlic in oil in Dutch oven over medium heat until beef is browned, about 10 minutes; add beans and remaining ingredients, except rice, tomatoes, salt, and pepper; heat to boiling. Reduce heat and simmer, covered, until beans and meat are tender, 1 to 1½ hours, adding tomatoes during last 15 minutes. Discard bay leaves; season to taste with salt and pepper.

CURRIED BEEF STEW WITH CHIVE DUMPLINGS

Part of the beef in this aromatic stew is coarsely chopped, giving the stew an extra-rich texture.

8 entrée servings

2 pounds lean beef stew meat
1–2 tablespoons canola oil
1½ cups chopped onions
3 tablespoons flour
1½ teaspoons curry powder
2 cups reduced-sodium beef broth
1 large tomato, coarsely chopped
2 bay leaves
1 package (10 ounces) frozen peas
Salt and pepper, to taste
Chive Dumplings (recipe follows)

Per Serving:
Calories: 297
% calories from fat: 22
Protein (g): 27.1
Carbohydrate (g): 29.4
Fat (g): 7.3
Saturated fat (g): 1.9
Cholesterol (mg): 55.3
Sodium (mg): 416

Exchanges:
Milk: 0.0
Vegetable: 0.0
Fruit: 0.0
Bread: 2.0
Meat: 3.0
Fat: 0.0

1. Cut 1 pound beef into scant 1-inch cubes; coarsely chop remaining 1 pound beef. Cook beef in oil in Dutch oven over medium heat until browned, about 5 minutes; add onions and cook until tender, 5 to 8 minutes. Stir in flour and curry powder and cook 1 minute. Add beef broth, tomato, and bay leaf and heat to boiling; reduce heat and simmer, covered, until beef is tender, about 1 hour, adding peas during last 10 minutes. Discard bay leaf, season to taste with salt and pepper.

2. Heat stew to boiling; spoon Chive Dumplings dough into 8 mounds on top of stew. Reduce heat and simmer, uncovered, 10 minutes; simmer, covered, until dumplings are dry on top, about 10 minutes.

Chive Dumplings

1⅔ cups reduced-fat all-purpose baking mix
2 tablespoons finely chopped chives
¼–½ teaspoon curry powder
⅔ cup fat-free milk

1. Combine baking mix, chives, and curry powder in medium bowl; mix in milk, forming a soft dough.

BEEF AND ANCHO CHILI STEW

Complement this delicious stew with sour cream; serve with warm tortillas.

8 entrée servings

3 cups boiling water
4–6 ancho chilies, stems, seeds, and veins discarded
4 medium tomatoes, cut into wedges
2 pounds lean beef eye of round steak, cubed (¾-inch)
1 large onion, chopped
2 cloves garlic, minced
1 teaspoon each: minced jalapeño chili, dried oregano leaves, crushed cumin seeds
2 tablespoons flour
Salt and pepper, to taste
Red Pepper Rice (see p. 571)

Per Serving:
Calories: 393
% calories from fat: 31
Protein (g): 29.7
Carbohydrate (g): 38.5
Fat (g): 13.8
Saturated fat (g): 5.0
Cholesterol (mg): 67.8
Sodium (mg): 406

Exchanges:
Milk: 0.0
Vegetable: 2.0
Fruit: 0.0
Bread: 2.0
Meat: 3.0
Fat: 1.0

1. Pour boiling water over chilies in bowl; let stand until softened, about 10 minutes. Process chilies, water, and tomatoes in food processor or blender until smooth.

2. Cook beef in lightly greased Dutch oven over medium heat until browned, about 8 minutes. Add onion, garlic, jalapeño chili, and herbs; cook until onion is tender, about 5 minutes. Stir in flour; cook 1 minute. Add ancho chili mixture; heat to boiling. Reduce heat and simmer, covered, until beef is tender, 45 to 60 minutes. Season to taste with salt and pepper; serve over Red Pepper Rice.

SLOW-COOKER BARBECUED BEEF AND BEAN STEW

This spicy barbecued beef and bean dinner is sure to please!

6 entrée servings

1½ cups finely chopped onions

1 can (8 ounces) tomato sauce

½ cup mild or medium salsa

2 tablespoons cider vinegar

1½ tablespoons brown sugar

1 tablespoon chili powder

2 teaspoons Worcestershire sauce

1 pound lean beef round steak, cut into narrow strips

2 garlic cloves, minced

6 cups cooked dried or 4 cans (15 ounces each) rinsed, drained kidney beans

Salt and pepper, to taste

Per Serving:
Calories: 363
% calories from fat: 14
Protein (g): 35
Carbohydrate (g): 44
Fat (g): 5.8
Saturated fat (g): 1.8
Cholesterol (mg): 63
Sodium (mg): 398

Exchanges:
Milk: 0.0
Vegetable: 1.0
Fruit: 0.0
Bread: 2.5
Meat: 3.0
Fat: 0.0

1. Combine all ingredients, except salt and pepper, in slow cooker; cover, and cook on High 1 hour. Reduce heat to Low and cook until beef is tender, 5 to 6 hours. Season to taste with salt and pepper.

FIVE-SPICE BEEF STEW

A simple-to-make stew with lots of Asian flavor, thanks to five-spice powder and Chinese chili sauces.

4 entrée servings

1 pound lean beef round steak, cubed (1-inch)

1 cup each: orange juice, reduced-sodium fat-free beef broth

1 tablespoon low-sodium teriyaki sauce

1¼ teaspoons five-spice powder

1 medium onion, cut into thin wedges

1 red bell pepper, thinly sliced

2 cups coarsely sliced Napa cabbage

1 teaspoon Chinese chili sauce with garlic

4 ounces bean thread noodles

Salt and pepper, to taste

Per Serving:
Calories: 321
% calories from fat: 14
Protein (g): 28.8
Carbohydrate (g): 39.3
Fat (g): 5
Saturated fat (g): 1.8
Cholesterol (mg): 55.9
Sodium (mg): 208

Exchanges:
Milk: 0.0
Vegetable: 1.0
Fruit: 0.0
Bread: 2.0
Meat: 3.0
Fat: 0.0

1. Heat beef, orange juice, broth, teriyaki sauce, five-spice powder, and onion to boiling in large saucepan. Reduce heat and simmer, covered, until beef is tender, 45 to 60 minutes, adding vegetables and chili sauce during last 15 minutes.

2. While stew is cooking, soak bean threads in hot water to cover in large bowl for 15 minutes; drain and stir into stew. Season to taste with salt and pepper.

ASIAN BEEF STEW WITH SESAME NOODLES

This ginger-spiked stew can be prepared in a large, covered wok, if you prefer.

8 entrée servings

2 pounds lean beef stew meat, cubed (1-inch)

1–2 tablespoons canola oil

1½ cups water

2 each: thin slices gingerroot, halved cloves garlic, sliced green onions

2–4 tablespoons reduced-sodium soy sauce

1 tablespoon each: sugar, cornstarch

2 tablespoons dry sherry or water

Salt and pepper, to taste

Sesame Noodles (recipe follows)

1 tablespoon sesame seeds, toasted

Finely chopped cilantro, as garnish

Per Serving:
Calories: 295
% calories from fat: 23
Protein (g): 26.8
Carbohydrate (g): 27.6
Fat (g): 7.3
Saturated fat (g): 1.7
Cholesterol (mg): 57.1
Sodium (mg): 518

Exchanges:
Milk: 0.0
Vegetable: 0.0
Fruit: 0.0
Bread: 2.0
Meat: 3.0
Fat: 0.0

1. Cook beef in oil in large saucepan over medium heat until browned, about 10 minutes. Add water, gingerroot, garlic, green onions, soy sauce, and sugar; heat to boiling. Reduce heat and simmer, covered, until beef is tender, 45 to 60 minutes. Heat stew to boiling; stir in combined cornstarch and sherry, stirring, until thickened, about 1 minute. Season to taste with salt and pepper. Serve over Sesame Noodles; sprinkle with sesame seeds and cilantro.

Sesame Noodles

Makes 8 servings

1 package (12 ounces) Asian or any thin noodles, cooked, warm

2–4 teaspoons reduced-sodium soy sauce

2 teaspoons Asian sesame oil

2 green onions, thinly sliced

1. Toss warm noodles with remaining ingredients.

CHUCK WAGON STEW WITH DILL DUMPLINGS

One of the heartiest stews you can rustle up!

6 entrée servings

1½ pounds lean beef round steak, cubed (¾-inch)

Flour

½ cup chopped onion

1 tablespoon canola oil

1 can (14½ ounces) reduced-sodium diced
tomatoes, undrained

¾ cup reduced-sodium fat-free beef broth

3 each: cubed small unpeeled potatoes, large
sliced carrots

1 can (15 ounces) red kidney beans, rinsed, drained

¼ cup all-purpose flour

½ cup cold water

2–3 teaspoons low-sodium Worcestershire sauce

Salt and pepper, to taste

Dill Dumplings (recipe follows)

Per Serving:
Calories: 437
% calories from fat: 17
Protein (g): 30.8
Carbohydrate (g): 59
Fat (g): 8.4
Saturated fat (g): 2.1
Cholesterol (mg): 55.3
Sodium (mg): 693

Exchanges:
Milk: 0.0
Vegetable: 2.0
Fruit: 0.0
Bread: 3.0
Meat: 3.0
Fat: 0.0

1. Coat beef lightly with flour. Cook beef and onion in oil in large saucepan over medium until beef is browned, 5 to 8 minutes. Add tomatoes with liquid and broth; heat to boiling. Reduce heat and simmer, covered, until beef is tender, 45 to 60 minutes, adding potatoes, carrots, and beans during last 15 minutes. Heat stew to boiling; stir in combined ¼ cup flour and water, stirring until thickened, about 1 minute. Season to taste with Worcestershire sauce, salt, and pepper.

2. Heat stew to boiling; spoon Dill Dumplings dough into 6 mounds on top of stew. Reduce heat and simmer, uncovered, 10 minutes; simmer, covered, until dumplings are dry on top, about 10 minutes.

Dill Dumplings

1½ cups reduced-fat all-purpose baking mix

2 teaspoons dried dill weed

½ cup fat-free milk

1. Mix baking mix, dill weed, and milk in bowl to make a soft dough.

MEATBALL AND PASTA STEW

Onion-and-cheese-seasoned meatballs combine with vegetables and tricolor pasta for a delectable stew.

4 entrée servings

8 ounces ground beef eye of round

1 egg white, lightly beaten

½ cup quick oats

3 tablespoons dried minced onions, divided

2 teaspoons dried Italian seasoning, divided

½ cup (2 ounces) grated Romano cheese

1 can (14½ ounces) plum tomatoes, undrained, chopped

3 cans (14 ounces each) fat-free beef broth

4 ounces tri-color corkscrew pasta

2 cups small broccoli florets

Salt and pepper, to taste

Per Serving:
Calories: 335
% calories from fat: 19
Protein (g): 29.9
Carbohydrate (g): 39.1
Fat (g). 7.1
Saturated fat (g): 3.3
Cholesterol (mg): 42.2
Sodium (mg): 577

Exchanges:
Milk: 0.0
Vegetable: 2.0
Fruit: 0.0
Bread: 2.0
Meat: 3.0
Fat: 0.0

1. Combine beef, egg white, oats, 1 tablespoon dried onions, ½ teaspoon Italian seasoning, and Romano cheese in a bowl. Shape mixture into 16 meatballs. Cook meatballs in lightly greased Dutch oven on medium heat until browned, about 10 minutes. Stir in tomatoes with liquid, broth, and remaining 2 tablespoons dried onions and 1½ teaspoons Italian seasoning; heat to boiling. Add pasta and broccoli; reduce heat and simmer, uncovered, 10 minutes or until pasta is al dente. Season to taste with salt and pepper.

HEARTY MEATBALL 'N VEGGIE STEW

For flavor variation in the Hearty Meatballs, substitute 8 ounces low-fat Italian-style turkey sausage for 8 ounces of the ground beef.

6 entrée servings

Hearty Meatballs (recipe follows)
1½ cups reduced-sodium beef broth
1 can (28 ounces) reduced-sodium diced
    tomatoes, undrained
1 teaspoon dried Italian seasoning
3 each: medium cubed zucchini, thickly sliced carrots
½ cup frozen peas
2 tablespoons cornstarch
¼ cup cold water
Salt and pepper, to taste
12 ounces noodles or fettuccine, cooked, warm

Per Serving:
Calories: 554
% calories from fat: 26
Protein (g): 35.8
Carbohydrate (g): 65.3
Fat (g): 16
Saturated fat (g): 5.8
Cholesterol (mg): 105.8
Sodium (mg): 536

Exchanges:
Milk: 0.0
Vegetable: 2.0
Fruit: 0.0
Bread: 4.0
Meat: 3.0
Fat: 1.0

1. Cook Hearty Meatballs in lightly greased Dutch oven over medium heat until browned, 5 to 8 minutes. Add broth, tomatoes with liquid, and Italian seasoning; heat to boiling. Reduce heat and simmer, covered, 30 minutes, adding vegetables during last 15 minutes of cooking time. Heat stew to boiling; stir in combined cornstarch and water, stirring, until stew is thickened, about 1 minute. Season to taste with salt and pepper. Serve stew over noodles.

Hearty Meatballs
Makes 18 meatballs

1½ pounds lean ground beef
⅓ cup finely chopped onion
1 egg
½ cup unseasoned dry bread crumbs
2 cloves garlic, minced
1–2 teaspoons beef-flavor bouillon crystals
½ teaspoon salt
¼ teaspoon pepper

1. Mix all ingredients in bowl; shape mixture into 18 meatballs.

PORK TENDERLOIN STEW WITH GREMOLATA

45 *Gremolata, a refreshing blend of garlic, lemon peel, and parsley, is often used to flavor stews and soups.*

4 entrée servings

1 pound pork tenderloin, cubed (1-inch)
4 shallots, thinly sliced
1 teaspoon olive oil
1 cup reduced-sodium fat-free beef broth
2 medium potatoes, cubed
1 can (14½ ounces) diced tomatoes, undrained
Salt and pepper, to taste
Gremolata (recipe follows)

Per Serving:
Calories: 289
% calories from fat: 17
Protein (g): 28.6
Carbohydrate (g): 31.2
Fat (g): 5.5
Saturated fat (g): 1.6
Cholesterol (mg): 65.7
Sodium (mg): 523

Exchanges:
Milk: 0.0
Vegetable: 0.0
Fruit: 0.0
Bread: 2.0
Meat: 3.0
Fat: 0.0

1. Cook pork and shallots in oil in large saucepan over medium heat until lightly browned, about 8 minutes. Stir in broth, potatoes and tomatoes with liquid; heat to boiling. Reduce heat and simmer, covered, until potatoes are tender, about 15 minutes. Season to taste with salt and pepper. Pass Gremolata to stir into stew.

Gremolata

Makes about ½ cup

1 cup packed parsley sprigs
1–2 tablespoons grated lemon zest
4 large cloves garlic, minced

1. Process all ingredients in food processor until finely minced.

CANTONESE PORK STEW

45 *Lean beef or boneless, skinless chicken breast can be substituted for the pork in this sweet-sour stew.*

6 entrée servings

1½ pounds lean pork steak, cut into thin strips

2 tablespoons canola oil

1 cup each: sliced onion, red bell pepper, mushrooms

1 can (8 ounces) tomato sauce

3 tablespoons brown sugar

1½ tablespoons cider vinegar

2 teaspoons Worcestershire sauce

1 tablespoon dry sherry (optional)

Salt and pepper, to taste

3 cups cooked rice, warm

Per Serving:
Calories: 384
% calories from fat: 29
Protein (g): 30.9
Carbohydrate (g): 36
Fat (g): 12.1
Saturated fat (g): 3.1
Cholesterol (mg): 64.4
Sodium (mg): 321

Exchanges:
Milk: 0.0
Vegetable: 1.0
Fruit: 0.0
Bread: 2.0
Meat: 4.0
Fat: 0.0

1. Cook pork in oil in large skillet over medium heat until browned, 5 to 8 minutes; stir in onion, bell pepper, and mushrooms and cook 5 minutes. Add remaining ingredients, except salt, pepper, and rice, and heat to boiling; reduce heat and simmer, covered, until pork is tender, about 20 minutes. Season to taste with salt and pepper; serve over rice.

PORK AND PEPPER STEW

45 *For convenience, 1 package (16 ounces) frozen stir-fry blend can be substituted for the onion and bell peppers in this recipe.*

4 entrée servings

1 pound pork tenderloin, cut into thin strips

1 tablespoon olive oil

1 can (15 ounces) tomato sauce

1½ cups each: sliced onions, red and green bell peppers

2 tablespoons dry sherry (optional)

1 teaspoon each: minced garlic, dried basil and thyme leaves

Salt and pepper, to taste

8 ounces fusilli, cooked, warm

Per Serving:
Calories: 464
% calories from fat: 17
Protein (g): 33.9
Carbohydrate (g): 58.6
Fat (g): 8.4
Saturated fat (g): 2
Cholesterol (mg): 65.7
Sodium (mg): 99

Exchanges:
Milk: 0.0
Vegetable: 3.0
Fruit: 0.0
Bread: 3.0
Meat: 3.0
Fat: 0.0

1. Cook pork in olive oil in large skillet over medium heat until browned, 5 to 8 minutes; add tomato sauce, vegetables, sherry, garlic, and herbs. Heat to boiling; reduce heat and simmer, covered, until pork is tender, about 15 minutes. Simmer, uncovered, until thickened to desired consistency, about 5 minutes. Season to taste with salt and pepper. Serve over fusilli.

MEDITERRANEAN CURRIED STEW

45 *Brightly colored Turmeric Rice completes this dish perfectly.*

6 entrée servings

1 pound pork tenderloin or boneless, skinless chicken breast, cubed (¾-inch)

2 tablespoons olive oil

1 small eggplant, unpeeled, cubed (1-inch)

½ cup each: sliced onion, chopped green bell pepper, celery

2 cloves garlic, minced

1 tablespoon flour

½ teaspoon each: ground cinnamon, nutmeg, curry powder, cumin

⅛ teaspoon cayenne pepper

2 cans (14½ ounces, each) reduced-sodium diced tomatoes, undrained

½ cup reduced-sodium vegetable broth

1 cup each: cubed zucchini, butternut squash

1 can (15 ounces) garbanzo beans, rinsed, drained

Salt and pepper, to taste

Turmeric Rice (see p. 475)

3 tablespoons each: raisins, toasted slivered almonds

Per Serving:
Calories: 446
% calories from fat: 22
Protein (g): 25.3
Carbohydrate (g): 61.3
Fat (g): 11.1
Saturated fat (g): 2
Cholesterol (mg): 43.8
Sodium (mg): 427

Exchanges:
Milk: 0.0
Vegetable: 3.0
Fruit: 0.0
Bread: 3.0
Meat: 2.0
Fat: 1.0

1. Cook pork in oil in large saucepan over medium heat until browned, about 5 minutes. Add eggplant, onion, bell pepper, celery, and garlic and cook until eggplant is beginning to brown, about 5 minutes. Stir in flour, spices, and cayenne pepper; cook 1 minute. Add tomatoes with liquid, broth, squash, and beans; heat to boiling. Reduce heat and simmer, covered, until pork and vegetables are tender, about 15 minutes. Season to taste with salt and pepper. Serve over Turmeric Rice and sprinkle with raisins and almonds.

CARIBBEAN GINGER, BEAN, AND PORK STEW

45 *Fresh gingerroot accents the flavor contrasts in this colorful stew.*

6 entrée servings

12–16 ounces lean pork loin, cubed

1 tablespoon olive oil, chopped gingerroot

1 cup each: chopped onion, red bell pepper

2 teaspoons each: minced garlic, jalapeño chili

1 can (15 ounces) each: black beans, black-eyed peas, rinsed, drained

¾ cup fresh or frozen cut okra

⅓ cup each: orange juice, jalapeño chili jelly or orange marmalade

½ teaspoon dried thyme leaves

1 can (11 ounces) Mandarin orange segments, drained

Salt and pepper, to taste

3 cups cooked brown or white rice

Per Serving:
Calories: 369
% calories from fat: 15
Protein (g): 18.9
Carbohydrate (g): 66.3
Fat (g): 6.8
Saturated fat (g): 1.6
Cholesterol (mg): 24.6
Sodium (mg): 704

Exchanges:
Milk: 0.0
Vegetable: 0.0
Fruit: 1.0
Bread: 3.0
Meat: 2.0
Fat: 0.0

1. Cook pork in oil in large skillet over medium heat until browned, 5 to 8 minutes. Add gingerroot, onion, bell pepper, garlic, and jalapeño chili and cook until tender, about 5 minutes. Add black beans, black-eyed peas, okra, orange juice, jelly, and thyme; heat to boiling. Reduce heat and simmer, covered, until okra is tender, about 10 minutes. Add orange segments; cook 1 to 2 minutes. Season to taste with salt and pepper; serve over rice.

SAVORY STEWED PORK AND CHORIZO

This versatile stewed dish can also be served rolled in a tortilla or used as a topping for tostadas.

6 entrée servings

12 ounces pork tenderloin, cubed (1-inch)

Chorizo (see p. 131)

1 small onion, sliced

1 clove garlic, minced

2 large tomatoes, chopped

¼ teaspoon each: dried oregano and thyme leaves

1 bay leaf

2–3 pickled jalapeño chilies, finely chopped

1 tablespoon pickled jalapeño chili juice

Salt and pepper, to taste

4 cups cooked rice, warm

Per Serving:
Calories: 298
% calories from fat: 15
Protein (g): 27.2
Carbohydrate (g): 35
Fat (g): 4.7
Saturated fat (g): 1.5
Cholesterol (mg): 65.7
Sodium (mg): 313

Exchanges:
Milk: 0.0
Vegetable: 0.0
Fruit: 0.0
Bread: 2.0
Meat: 3.0
Fat: 0.0

1. Simmer pork in 2 inches water in medium saucepan, covered, until tender, 20 to 30 minutes. Cool; drain, reserving 1 ½ cups broth. Finely shred pork.

2. Make Chorizo, but do not make patties. Cook Chorizo, onion, and garlic in lightly greased large skillet over medium heat until Chorizo is browned, crumbling with a fork. Add pork, reserved broth, tomatoes, herbs, jalapeño chilies and juice and heat to boiling; reduce heat and simmer, covered, 10 minutes. Simmer, uncovered, about 10 minutes (mixture should be moist). Discard bay leaf; season to taste with salt and pepper. Serve over rice.

TOMATILLO PORK STEW

Tomatillos add a special flavor to this South-of-the-Border version of pork stew.

8 entrée servings

1½ cups chopped onions

1 small poblano chili or green bell pepper, chopped

4 cloves garlic, minced

1 tablespoon canola oil

2 pounds boneless lean pork loin, cubed (¾-inch)

2 tablespoons flour

¾ teaspoon dried oregano leaves

½ teaspoon ground cumin

½ cup reduced-sodium fat-free chicken broth

2 large tomatoes, chopped

12 ounces tomatillos, husked, chopped

1 can (4 ounces) mild or hot chopped green chilies

1–2 teaspoons lime juice

Salt and pepper, to taste

5 cups cooked rice

Minced cilantro and pine nuts, as garnish

Per Serving:
Calories: 374
% calories from fat: 24
Protein (g): 32.1
Carbohydrate (g): 37.6
Fat (g): 99
Saturated fat (g): 2.9
Cholesterol (mg): 64.4
Sodium (mg): 118

Exchanges:
Milk: 0.0
Vegetable: 2.0
Fruit: 0.0
Bread: 2.0
Meat: 3.0
Fat: 0.0

1. Sauté onions, poblano chili, and garlic in oil in large saucepan 2 to 3 minutes; add pork and cook until browned, about 5 minutes. Stir in flour and herbs and cook 2 minutes. Add broth, tomatoes, tomatillos, and green chilies and heat to boiling; reduce heat and simmer, covered, until pork is tender, 40 to 50 minutes. Season to taste with lime juice, salt, and pepper. Serve over rice; sprinkle with cilantro and pine nuts.

PORK, POTATO, AND CABBAGE STEW

45 *Shredded potatoes thicken the sauce in this robust pork stew.*

4 entrée servings

1 pound each: cubed boneless lean pork loin, finely shredded peeled red potatoes

1 can (14½ ounces) reduced-sodium stewed tomatoes

1 can (15 ounces) tomato sauce

3 cups thinly sliced cabbage

1 large onion, finely chopped

2 garlic cloves, minced

1 tablespoon brown sugar

2 teaspoons each: balsamic vinegar, dried thyme leaves

1 bay leaf

Salt and pepper, to taste

Per Serving:
Calories: 328
% calories from fat: 18
Protein (g): 23.4
Carbohydrate (g): 45.4
Fat (g): 6.8
Saturated fat (g): 2.2
Cholesterol (mg): 49.3
Sodium (mg): 101

Exchanges:
Milk: 0.0
Vegetable: 3.0
Fruit: 0.0
Bread: 2.0
Meat: 2.0
Fat: 0.0

1. Heat all ingredients, except salt and pepper, to boiling in large saucepan; reduce heat and simmer, covered, until pork is tender, 30 to 40 minutes. Discard bay leaf; season to taste with salt and pepper.

PORK AND SAUERKRAUT STEW

Serve this delicious stew in shallow bowls with crusty rye rolls.

4 entrée servings

1 pound boneless lean pork loin, cubed (¾-inch)

2 teaspoons olive oil

1 large onion, finely chopped

1 can (14½ ounces) reduced-sodium diced tomatoes, undrained

1 teaspoon caraway seeds

1 package (16 ounces) fresh sauerkraut, drained

12 ounces red potatoes, thinly sliced

¼–½ cup fat-free sour cream

Salt and pepper, to taste

Per Serving:
Calories: 245
% calories from fat: 25
Protein (g): 18.2
Carbohydrate (g): 28.5
Fat (g): 7
Saturated fat (g): 2
Cholesterol (mg): 39.7
Sodium (mg): 650

Exchanges:
Milk: 0.0
Vegetable: 2.0
Fruit: 0.0
Bread: 1.0
Meat: 2.0
Fat: 0.0

1. Cook pork in oil in large skillet over medium heat until browned, 5 to 8 minutes. Add remaining ingredients, except potatoes, sour cream, salt, and pepper; heat to boiling. Reduce heat and simmer, covered, until pork is tender, about 45 minutes, adding potatoes during last 20 minutes. Stir in sour cream; season to taste with salt and pepper.

FINNISH PORK STEW WITH BEETS AND NOODLES

This Scandinavian dish is tasty and colorful.

4 entrée servings

1 pound boneless lean pork loin, cubed (2-inch)
1 cup chopped onion
1 can (16 ounces) julienned beets, undrained
3 tablespoons cider vinegar
½ cup fat-free beef broth
1½ teaspoons prepared horseradish
½ teaspoon dried thyme leaves
2 teaspoons cornstarch
¼ cup cold water
Salt and pepper, to taste
8 ounces egg noodles, cooked, warm

Per Serving:
Calories: 291
% calories from fat: 21
Protein (g): 20
Carbohydrate (g): 38
Fat (g). 6.9
Saturated fat (g): 2.2
Cholesterol (mg): 78
Sodium (mg): 345

Exchanges:
Milk: 0.0
Vegetable: 1.5
Fruit: 0.0
Bread: 2.0
Meat: 2.0
Fat: 0.0

1. Cook pork and onion in lightly greased large skillet over medium heat until pork is browned, about 8 minutes. Drain beets; stir ½ cup beet juice into skillet with vinegar, broth, horseradish, and thyme. Heat to boiling; reduce heat and simmer, covered, until pork is tender, about 30 to 45 minutes. Heat stew to boiling; stir in combined cornstarch and water, stirring, until thickened, about 1 minute. Add beets and simmer, covered until hot, about 5 minutes. Season to taste with salt and pepper. Serve over noodles.

IRISH LAMB STEW

An Irish comfort food, this simply seasoned stew is always welcome on cold winter evenings.

6 entrée servings

1½ pounds boneless lean leg of lamb, cubed (¾-inch)
2 medium onions, sliced
1–2 tablespoons canola oil
3 tablespoons flour
2 cups reduced-sodium fat-free chicken broth
½ teaspoon dried thyme leaves
1 bay leaf
6 each: quartered medium potatoes, thickly sliced
    medium carrots
1–1½ teaspoons low-sodium Worcestershire sauce
Salt and pepper, to taste

Per Serving:
Calories: 312
% calories from fat: 20
Protein (g): 21.4
Carbohydrate (g): 41
Fat (g): 6.9
Saturated fat (g): 1.9
Cholesterol (mg): 48.5
Sodium (mg): 130

Exchanges:
Milk: 0.0
Vegetable: 2.0
Fruit: 0.0
Bread: 2.0
Meat: 2.0
Fat: 0.0

1. Cook lamb and onions in oil in Dutch oven over medium heat until lamb is browned, about 8 minutes; sprinkle with flour and cook 1 minute. Add chicken broth and herbs and heat to boiling. Reduce heat and simmer, covered, until lamb is tender, 45 to 60 minutes, adding potatoes and carrots during last 20 minutes. Discard bay leaf; season to taste with Worcestershire sauce, salt, and pepper.

VARIATIONS

Irish Lamb Stew with Parsley Dumplings — Make lamb stew as above. Make Dill Dumplings (see p. 454), substituting 2 tablespoons finely chopped parsley for the dill weed; spoon dumpling mixture onto boiling stew. Reduce heat and simmer, uncovered, 10 minutes; simmer, covered, 10 minutes or until dumplings are dry on top.

Easy Shepherd's Pie — Make stew as above, substituting 3 to 4 medium parsnips for the potatoes; pour into 1½-quart casserole. Mash 1 pound peeled, cooked, Idaho potatoes; mix in ¼ cup fat-free sour cream, 2 to 3 tablespoons fat-free milk, and 1 tablespoon margarine or butter; season to taste with salt and pepper. Spoon potatoes over top of stew. Bake at 400 degrees until potatoes are browned, about 10 minutes.

HEARTY ROSEMARY LAMB STEW WITH SWEET POTATOES

The pairing of rosemary and lamb is classic, distinctive, and delightful.

4 entrée servings

1 pound boneless lamb shoulder, fat trimmed, cubed (¾-inch)

1 teaspoon olive oil

1 large onion, cut into thin wedges

2 tablespoons chopped fresh or 1 teaspoon dried rosemary leaves

3 cups reduced-sodium fat-free beef broth

2 bay leaves

1 pound sweet potatoes, peeled, cubed (¾-inch)

1½ cups cut green beans

Salt and pepper, to taste

Per Serving:
Calories: 285
% calories from fat: 23
Protein (g): 20.6
Carbohydrate (g): 34.7
Fat (g): 7.4
Saturated fat (g): 2.5
Cholesterol (mg): 47.2
Sodium (mg): 171

Exchanges:
Milk: 0.0
Vegetable: 1.0
Fruit: 0.0
Bread: 2.0
Meat: 2.0
Fat: 0.0

1. Cook lamb in oil in large saucepan over medium heat until browned, about 8 minutes. Add onion and rosemary and cook 5 minutes. Add broth and bay leaves and heat to boiling; reduce heat and simmer, covered, until lamb is tender, 1 to 1½ hours, adding sweet potatoes and green beans during last 15 minutes. Discard bay leaves; season to taste with salt and pepper.

LAMB RATATOUILLE

In this version of ratatouille, the vegetables are roasted and combined with stewed lamb.

8 entrée servings

Savory Tomato Sauce (recipe follows)

2 pounds boneless lean lamb shoulder, cubed (1-inch)

¼ cup dry vermouth or chicken broth

2 tablespoons lemon juice

Salt and pepper, to taste

1 medium eggplant, unpeeled, cubed (1-inch)

2 each: thickly sliced large zucchini and onions,
cubed green bell peppers

Vegetable cooking spray

¾ teaspoon dried rosemary leaves

½ teaspoon dried thyme leaves

1–2 tablespoons olive oil

Rosemary or parsley sprigs, as garnish

Per Serving:
Calories: 193
% calories from fat: 30
Protein (g): 18
Carbohydrate (g): 15.4
Fat (g): 6.6
Saturated fat (g): 1.8
Cholesterol (mg): 48.5
Sodium (mg): 60

Exchanges:
Milk: 0.0
Vegetable: 3.0
Fruit: 0.0
Bread: 0.0
Meat: 2.0
Fat: 0.0

1. Combine Savory Tomato Sauce, lamb, vermouth, and lemon juice in large Dutch oven; heat to boiling. Reduce heat and simmer, covered, until lamb is very tender, about 1 hour. Season to taste with salt and pepper.

2. Arrange vegetables in single layer on greased aluminum-foil jelly roll pan; spray with cooking spray and sprinkle with herbs. Roast at 425 degrees until lightly browned and tender, 30 to 40 minutes. Drizzle vegetables with oil and sprinkle lightly with salt and pepper. Spoon lamb and tomato mixture over vegetables on large serving platter; garnish with rosemary sprigs.

Savory Tomato Sauce

Makes about 1 quart

5 large tomatoes, peeled, coarsely chopped

⅔ cup each: finely chopped celery, green bell pepper, sliced green onions

¾ cup reduced-sodium tomato juice

½ teaspoon each: ground cumin, garlic powder

⅛ teaspoon ground cloves

Salt and pepper, to taste

1. Heat all ingredients, except salt and pepper, to boiling in large saucepan. Reduce heat and simmer, covered 15 minutes; simmer, uncovered, until a medium sauce consistency, 10 to 15 minutes. Season to taste with salt and pepper.

SLOW-COOKER IRISH STEW

For a no-fuss dinner, try this lamb stew.

6 entrée servings

1½ pounds boneless lamb shoulder, fat trimmed, cubed (1-inch)
6 each: sliced medium potatoes, carrots
3 small onions, quartered
2 teaspoons dried rosemary leaves
½ teaspoon dried thyme leaves
1 bay leaf
2 cups water
Salt and pepper, to taste

Per Serving:
Calories: 320
% calories from fat: 17
Protein (g): 18.5
Carbohydrate (g): 48.5
Fat (g): 6.5
Saturated fat (g): 2.3
Cholesterol (mg): 47.2
Sodium (mg): 74

Exchanges:
Milk: 0.0
Vegetable: 3.0
Fruit: 0.0
Bread: 2.0
Meat: 2.0
Fat: 0.0

1. Combine all ingredients, except salt and pepper, in slow cooker and cook, covered, on High 1 hour. Reduce heat to Low and cook until lamb and vegetables are very tender, 10 to 12 hours. Discard bay leaf; season to taste with salt and pepper.

SAVORY LAMB STEW

Enjoy this rich and flavorful combination of lamb shanks, lentils, vegetables, and spices.

6 entrée servings

2 pounds lamb shanks, fat trimmed
1 tablespoon flour
2 teaspoons olive oil
2 cups chopped onions
2 garlic cloves, minced
2 cups fat-free chicken broth
1 can (14½ ounces) diced tomatoes, undrained
½ cup each: brown lentils, sliced carrots, chopped green bell pepper
2 bay leaves
2 teaspoons dried thyme leaves
¼ teaspoon each: ground cinnamon and cloves

Per Serving:
Calories: 325
% calories from fat: 26
Protein (g): 25
Carbohydrate (g): 40
Fat (g): 7.8
Saturated fat (g): 2.2
Cholesterol (mg): 56
Sodium (mg): 246

Exchanges:
Milk: 0.0
Vegetable: 1.5
Fruit: 0.0
Bread: 2.0
Meat: 2.0
Fat: 0.0

Salt and pepper, to taste

1¼ cups brown rice, cooked, warm

1. Coat lamb shanks with flour; cook in oil in Dutch oven over medium heat until browned, about 10 minutes. Add onions and garlic and cook until tender, about 5 minutes. Stir in remaining ingredients, except salt, pepper, and rice; heat to boiling. Reduce heat and simmer, covered, 1 to 1½ hours or until lamb shanks are tender. Discard bay leaves. Remove lamb shanks; remove lean meat and cut into bite-sized pieces. Return meat to stew; season to taste with salt and pepper. Serve over rice.

LAMB STEW WITH CHILIES

For a variation on this stew, beef eye of round steak and beef broth can be substituted for the lamb and chicken broth.

4 entrée servings

1 pound boneless lamb shoulder, fat trimmed, cubed (¾-inch)

1 each: sliced large onion, minced small jalapeño chili

4 cloves garlic, minced

1½ teaspoons dried Italian seasoning

2 tablespoons flour

1 cup reduced-sodium fat-free chicken broth

2 cans (14½ ounces each) reduced-sodium diced tomatoes, undrained

2–3 cans (4 ounces each) chopped mild green chilies

1 cup each: cubed potatoes, yellow summer squash

½ cup whole kernel corn

Salt and pepper, to taste

Per Serving:
Calories: 293
% calories from fat: 15
Protein (g): 22.8
Carbohydrate (g): 41.6
Fat (g): 5.3
Saturated fat (g): 1.7
Cholesterol (mg): 48.5
Sodium (mg): 270

Exchanges:
Milk: 0.0
Vegetable: 2.0
Fruit: 0.0
Bread: 2.0
Meat: 2.0
Fat: 0.0

1. Cook lamb, onion, jalapeño chili, and garlic in lightly greased large saucepan over medium heat until browned, about 8 minutes; stir in Italian seasoning and flour and cook 1 minute. Add chicken broth, tomatoes with liquid, and green chilies and heat to boiling; reduce heat and simmer, covered, until lamb is tender, 1 to 1½ hours, adding potatoes, squash, and corn during the last 10 minutes. Season to taste with salt and pepper.

LAMB AND TURNIP STEW WITH CILANTRO

This homestyle lamb dish has been updated with fresh sage and cilantro.

4 entrée servings

1 pound boneless lamb shoulder, fat trimmed,
   cubed (1-inch)

1 medium onion, chopped

1 tablespoon minced garlic

1 teaspoon olive oil

¼ cup all-purpose flour

2½ cups reduced-sodium tomato juice

½ cup dry red wine or tomato juice

1 tablespoon fresh or 1 teaspoon dried sage leaves

2 cups each: cubed potatoes, turnips

Salt and pepper, to taste

½ cup chopped cilantro

Per Serving:
Calories: 269
% calories from fat: 24
Protein (g): 17.4
Carbohydrate (g): 30
Fat (g): 7.3
Saturated fat (g): 2.4
Cholesterol (mg): 47.2
Sodium (mg): 81

Exchanges:
Milk: 0.0
Vegetable: 0.0
Fruit: 0.0
Bread: 2.0
Meat: 2.0
Fat: 0.0

1. Cook lamb, onion, and garlic in oil in large saucepan until browned, about 8 minutes; stir in flour and cook 1 minute. Add tomato juice, wine, and sage and heat to boiling; reduce heat and simmer, covered, until lamb is tender, 1 to 1½ hours, adding vegetables during last 20 minutes. Season to taste with salt and pepper; stir in cilantro.

MOROCCAN LAMB STEW

Sweet spices season this stew and raisins, almonds, and hard-cooked eggs provide colorful garnish.

8 entrée servings

2 pounds boneless lean leg of lamb, cubed (¾-inch)

1½ cups chopped onions

2 large cloves garlic, minced

2 teaspoons minced gingerroot

1½ cups reduced-sodium fat-free chicken broth

1 cup reduced-sodium tomato purée

½ teaspoon ground cinnamon

¼ teaspoon ground turmeric

1 bay leaf

Salt and pepper, to taste

⅓ cup raisins

¼ cup whole almonds, toasted

2 hard-cooked eggs, chopped

Chopped cilantro, as garnish

5 cups cooked couscous or rice, warm

Per Serving:
Calories: 308
% calories from fat: 20
Protein (g): 23.8
Carbohydrate (g): 37.4
Fat (g): 6.6
Saturated fat (g): 2
Cholesterol (mg): 101.5
Sodium (mg): 103

Exchanges:
Milk: 0.0
Vegetable: 1.0
Fruit: 0.0
Bread: 2.0
Meat: 2.5
Fat: 0.0

1. Cook lamb in lightly greased Dutch oven over medium heat until browned, 5 to 8 minutes; remove from pan. Add onions, garlic, and gingerroot to Dutch oven; sauté until onions are tender, about 5 minutes. Add lamb, chicken broth, tomato purée, and spices; heat to boiling. Reduce heat and simmer, covered, until lamb is tender, 45 to 60 minutes. Simmer, uncovered, until thickened to desired consistency, about 10 minutes longer. Discard bay leaf, season to taste with salt and pepper. Stir in raisins. Spoon stew onto rimmed serving platter; sprinkle with almonds, eggs, and cilantro. Serve over couscous.

LAMB AND VEGETABLE TAJINE

A staple of Moroccan cuisine, tajines are traditionally cooked in earthen-ware pots. Serve with Pita Bread (see p. 639).

6 entrée servings

½ cup each: chopped onion, sliced celery

1–2 teaspoons each: minced gingerroot, garlic

1 cinnamon stick

2 teaspoons each: paprika, ground cumin, coriander

12–16 ounces cooked lean lamb or beef, cubed

2 cans (14½ ounces each) reduced-sodium diced
  tomatoes, undrained

½ cup reduced-sodium vegetable broth

1 can (15 ounces) garbanzo beans, rinsed, drained

1 cup each: chopped butternut squash, turnip

1 large carrot, sliced

1½ cups halved green beans

1 cup pitted prunes

¼ cup pitted small black olives

Salt and pepper, to taste

4½ cups cooked couscous, warm

Per Serving:
Calories: 466
% calories from fat: 15
Protein (g): 24.8
Carbohydrate (g): 76.9
Fat (g): 8.4
Saturated fat (g): 2
Cholesterol (mg): 38.9
Sodium (mg): 580

Exchanges:
Milk: 0.0
Vegetable: 3.0
Fruit: 0.0
Bread: 4.0
Meat: 2.0
Fat: 0.0

1. Sauté onion, celery, gingerroot, garlic in lightly greased Dutch oven until onion is tender, about 5 minutes. Stir in spices; cook 1 minute. Add remaining ingredients, except salt, pepper, and couscous; heat to boiling. Reduce heat and simmer, covered, until vegetables are tender, about 20 minutes. Season to taste with salt and pepper; serve over couscous.

MARRAKECH LAMB STEW

For a simplified version of this flavorful stew, substitute 3 cans (15 ounces each) navy or Great Northern beans for the dry beans. Add canned beans to stew during last 30 minutes of cooking time.

8 entrée servings

8 ounces dried navy or Great Northern beans

2 pounds boneless lean leg of lamb, cubed (1-inch)

1–2 tablespoons olive oil

4 ounces portobello or cremini mushrooms, coarsely chopped

½ cup each: sliced carrots, onion

3 large cloves garlic, minced

¼ cup all-purpose flour

1 teaspoon ground cumin

½ teaspoon each: dried thyme and savory leaves

2 bay leaves

1 quart reduced-sodium fat-free chicken broth

½ cup dry white wine or chicken broth

1–2 tablespoons tomato paste

¾ cup sliced roasted red peppers

3 cups sliced spinach

Salt and pepper, to taste

5 cups cooked couscous or rice, warm

Per Serving:
Calories: 409
% calories from fat: 15
Protein (g): 31.2
Carbohydrate (g): 52.6
Fat (g): 6.8
Saturated fat (g): 1.9
Cholesterol (mg): 48.5
Sodium (mg): 164

Exchanges:
Milk: 0.0
Vegetable: 1.0
Fruit: 0.0
Bread: 3.0
Meat: 3.0
Fat: 0.0

1. Cover beans with water in large saucepan; heat to boiling. Boil 2 minutes, remove from heat and let stand, covered, 1 hour. Drain.

2. Cook lamb in oil in Dutch oven over medium heat until browned, about 5 minutes; add mushrooms, carrots, and onion and cook until onion is tender, about 5 minutes. Add flour and herbs; cook 1 minute. Add broth, wine, and beans; heat to boiling. Reduce heat and simmer, covered, until lamb and beans are tender, 45 to 60 minutes, adding tomato paste, roasted red peppers, and spinach during last 10 minutes. Discard bay leaves; season to taste with salt and pepper. Serve over couscous.

CURRIED LAMB STEW

Known in India as Rogan Josh, this flavorful stew is best prepared 1 to 2 days in advance for flavors to meld. Serve with a variety of condiments for flavor and color contrast.

12 entrée servings

3 pounds boneless lean leg of lamb, cubed (1-inch)

1¼ cups low-fat plain yogurt

¼ teaspoon crushed red pepper

2 cups chopped onions

1 tablespoon minced gingerroot

2 cloves garlic, minced

2 teaspoons coriander seeds, lightly crushed

1 teaspoon each: lightly crushed cumin seeds,
    ground turmeric

½ teaspoon each: lightly crushed cardamom seeds,
    ground cinnamon

1–2 tablespoons margarine or butter

1 cup reduced-sodium fat-free chicken broth

Salt and pepper, to taste

Turmeric Rice (recipe follows)

Condiments: raisins, toasted slivered almonds, chopped onion and
    cucumber, finely chopped cilantro or parsley

Per Serving:
Calories: 257
% calories from fat: 21
Protein (g): 19.8
Carbohydrate (g): 29.4
Fat (g): 5.9
Saturated fat (g): 2
Cholesterol (mg): 49.9
Sodium (mg): 82

Exchanges:
Milk: 0.0
Vegetable: 0.0
Fruit: 0.0
Bread: 2.0
Meat: 2.0
Fat: 0.0

1. Combine lamb, yogurt, and red pepper in bowl; refrigerate, covered, several hours or overnight, stirring occasionally.

2. Sauté onions, gingerroot, garlic, and spices in margarine in Dutch oven until onions are tender, 5 to 8 minutes. Stir in lamb mixture and chicken broth; heat to boiling. Reduce heat and simmer, covered, until lamb is tender, 50 to 60 minutes. Season to taste with salt and pepper. Serve over Turmeric Rice; pass condiments (not included in nutritional data).

Turmeric Rice
Makes 12 servings (about ⅔ cup each)

4½ cups water
2 cups uncooked long-grain rice
¾ teaspoon turmeric
¼ teaspoon salt

1. Heat water to boiling in large saucepan; stir in rice, turmeric and salt; reduce heat and simmer, covered, until rice is tender, 20 to 25 minutes.

LAMB BIRIANI

Biriani is a traditional Indian meat-and-rice dish that can be made with lamb, chicken, or beef. Although the meat can be served over any white rice, it's best with an aromatic rice, such as basmati or jasmine.

4 entrée servings

1 pound boneless lean leg of lamb, cubed (¾-inch)
2 cups chopped onions
1 garlic clove, minced
2 teaspoons canola oil
1 cup fat-free chicken broth
1 teaspoon each: ground coriander, ginger
½ teaspoon chili powder
¼ teaspoon each: ground cinnamon, cloves
¾ cup fat-free plain yogurt
Salt and pepper, to taste
Basmati Rice Pilaf (recipe follows)

Per Serving:
Calories: 280
% calories from fat: 26
Protein (g): 22
Carbohydrate (g): 30
Fat (g): 82
Saturated fat (g): 2.1
Cholesterol (mg): 46
Sodium (mg): 332

Exchanges:
Milk: 0.0
Vegetable: 1.5
Fruit: 0.0
Bread: 1.5
Meat: 2.0
Fat: 0.5

1. Cook lamb in lightly greased Dutch oven over medium heat until browned, about 10 minutes; Add onions and garlic and cook in oil until tender, about 5 minutes. Add broth and spices and heat to boiling. Reduce heat and simmer, covered, until meat is tender, 30 to 45 minutes. Stir in yogurt; season to taste with salt and pepper. Serve over rice.

Basmati Rice Pilaf
Makes about 3 cups

1 cup chopped onion
2 teaspoons canola oil
1 cup uncooked basmati rice
2¼ cups fat-free chicken broth
Pinch saffron (optional)
¼ teaspoon white pepper
1 medium carrot, finely shredded

1. Sauté onion in oil in large saucepan until tender, about 5 minutes; stir in rice and cook until lightly browned, about 3 minutes. Add remaining ingredients and heat to boiling. Reduce heat and simmer, covered, 20 minutes or until rice is tender.

SAVORY VEAL STEW

Caraway and anise seeds provide an unexpected flavor nuance in this stew.

8 entrée servings

2 pounds lean veal leg, cubed (¾-inch)
3 cloves garlic, minced
1 teaspoon caraway seeds, crushed
¾ teaspoon anise seeds, crushed
2 bay leaves
1 cup reduced-sodium fat-free chicken broth
½ cup dry white wine or chicken broth
1 small head cabbage, cut into 8 wedges
3 leeks (white parts only) thickly sliced
2 cups sliced mushrooms, sliced
1 tablespoon cornstarch
3 tablespoons water
½ cup reduced-fat sour cream
Salt and pepper, to taste

Per Serving:
Calories: 284
% calories from fat: 28
Protein (g): 32.4
Carbohydrate (g): 16.5
Fat (g): 8.8
Saturated fat (g): 2.9
Cholesterol (mg): 104.5
Sodium (mg): 161

Exchanges:
Milk: 0.0
Vegetable: 3.0
Fruit: 0.0
Bread: 0.0
Meat: 4.0
Fat: 0.0

1. Heat veal, garlic, herbs, broth, and wine to boiling in large Dutch oven; reduce heat and simmer, covered, until veal is tender, about 1 hour, adding cabbage, leeks, and mushrooms during last

20 minutes. Heat stew to boiling; stir in combined cornstarch and water, stirring until thickened, about 1 minute. Reduce heat to low; discard bay leaf. Stir in sour cream; season to taste with salt and pepper.

VEAL STEW SAUVIGNON

45 *This fragrant stew is also delicious served over an aromatic rice, such as basmati or jasmine.*

4 entrée servings

1 pound boneless veal cutlets, cut into thin strips
2 teaspoons olive oil
1 medium onion, halved, thinly sliced
1 teaspoon minced garlic
1 cup fat-free chicken broth
½ cup sauvignon blanc or other dry white wine
1 tablespoon tomato paste
1 teaspoon dried marjoram leaves
2 cups small cauliflower florets, torn Swiss chard or spinach
Salt and pepper, to taste
8 ounces fettuccine, cooked, warm

Per Serving:
Calories: 427
% calories from fat: 15
Protein (g): 33.4
Carbohydrate (g): 51
Fat (g): 6.9
Saturated fat (g): 1.6
Cholesterol (mg): 90.5
Sodium (mg): 318

Exchanges:
Milk: 0.0
Vegetable: 1.0
Fruit: 0.0
Bread: 3.0
Meat: 3.0
Fat: 0.0

1. Cook veal in oil in large saucepan over medium heat until browned, about 5 minutes; add onion and garlic and sauté 2 to 3 minutes. Add broth, wine, tomato paste, cauliflower, and marjoram and heat to boiling; reduce heat and simmer, covered, until veal and cauliflower are tender, about 15 minutes. Stir in Swiss chard; cook until wilted, 1 to 2 minutes. Season to taste with salt and pepper. Serve over fettuccine.

MEDITERRANEAN VEAL STEW

Beef or pork can be substituted for the veal in this delicious recipe.

6 entrée servings

1½ pounds lean veal leg, cubed

2 tablespoons olive oil

2 cloves garlic, minced

2 tablespoons flour

2 cups fat-free chicken broth

½ cup each: coarsely chopped onion, carrots

¾ teaspoon each: dried thyme and basil leaves

1 bay leaf

1 can (14½ ounces) petite diced tomatoes, undrained

2 tablespoons tomato paste

⅓ cup pitted olives

2 tablespoons drained capers

Salt and pepper, to taste

6 cups cooked linguine, warm

Per Serving:
Calories. 458
% calories from fat: 28
Protein (g): 39
Carbohydrate (g): 43.2
Fat (g) 14.3
Saturated fat (g): 2.6
Cholesterol (mg): 114.4
Sodium (mg): 651

Exchanges:
Milk: 0.0
Vegetable: 2.0
Fruit: 0.0
Bread: 2.0
Meat: 4.0
Fat: 0.0

1. Cook veal in oil in Dutch oven over medium heat until browned, about 10 minutes; add garlic and flour and cook 1 minute. Add chicken broth, onion, carrots, and herbs, and heat to boiling; reduce heat and simmer, covered, until veal is tender, about 30 minutes. Add tomatoes with liquid, tomato paste, olives, and capers; heat to boiling. Reduce heat and simmer, uncovered, until thickened to desired consistency, about 10 minutes. Discard bay leaf; season to taste with salt and pepper. Serve over pasta.

OSSO BUCCO

Gremolata, a pungent mixture of finely chopped parsley, lemon zest, and garlic, is traditionally added to this classic northern Italian stew.

6 entrée servings

6 medium veal shanks (about 4 pounds), fat trimmed
Flour
1–2 tablespoons olive oil
2 ribs celery, thinly sliced
1 medium onion, chopped
3 each: finely chopped medium carrots, minced cloves garlic
2 cans (14½ ounces each) reduced-sodium diced tomatoes, undrained
½ cup dry white wine or water
¾ teaspoon each: dried basil and thyme leaves
2 bay leaves
Gremolata (see p. 457), divided
Salt and pepper, to taste
4 cups cooked rice, warm

Per Serving:
Calories: 364
% calories from fat: 15
Protein (g): 28.8
Carbohydrate (g): 44.5
Fat (g): 6.2
Saturated fat (g): 1.7
Cholesterol (mg): 85.8
Sodium (mg): 91

Exchanges:
Milk: 0.0
Vegetable: 2.0
Fruit: 0.0
Bread: 2.0
Meat: 3.0
Fat: 0.0

1. Coat veal shanks lightly with flour; cook in oil in Dutch oven over medium heat until browned, about 10 minutes. Add celery, onion, carrots, and garlic and cook until tender, 3 to 5 minutes. Add tomatoes with liquid, wine, and herbs; heat to boiling. Reduce heat and simmer, covered, until veal is tender, about 1½ hours. Discard bay leaves; stir in ¼ cup Gremolata and season to taste with salt and pepper. Serve over rice; pass remaining Gremolata.

TWO-MEAT GOULASH

Caraway and fennel seeds add new flavor interest to this distinctive goulash.

8 entrée servings

1 pound each: cubed (¾-inch) lean beef eye of round
  steak, lean pork loin

1–2 tablespoons canola oil

1½ cups chopped onions

2 cloves garlic, minced

2 tablespoons each: paprika, flour

½ teaspoon each: crushed caraway and fennel seeds

2 bay leaves

1 cup reduced-sodium fat-free beef broth

1 can (14½ ounces) reduced-sodium diced tomatoes,
  undrained

2 tablespoons reduced-sodium tomato paste

4 ounces small mushrooms, halved

½ cup fat-free or reduced-fat sour cream

Salt and pepper, to taste

1 pound noodles, cooked, warm

Per Serving:
Calories: 443
% calories from fat: 16
Protein (g): 36.7
Carbohydrate (g): 53.9
Fat (g): 8.1
Saturated fat (g): 2.2
Cholesterol (mg): 59.7
Sodium (mg): 333

Exchanges:
Milk: 0.0
Vegetable: 1.0
Fruit: 0.0
Bread: 3.0
Meat: 4.0
Fat: 0.0

1. Cook beef and pork in oil in Dutch oven over medium heat until browned, 5 to 8 minutes; add onions and garlic and sauté until onions are tender, about 5 minutes. Stir in paprika, flour, and herbs and cook 1 minute. Add broth, tomatoes with liquid, and tomato paste; heat to boiling. Reduce heat and simmer, covered, until meats are tender, about 45 minutes, adding mushrooms during last 10 minutes. Stir in sour cream and simmer 2 to 3 minutes; discard bay leaves and season to taste with salt and pepper. Serve over noodles.

LAMB AND BEEF STEW WITH COGNAC

The flavors of two meats, wine, and cognac blend uniquely in this elegant oven stew.

6 entrée servings

¾ cup dry white wine or apple juice

3 tablespoons cognac or apple juice

½ teaspoon ground cinnamon

¼ teaspoon ground mace

1 pound each: cubed (¾-inch) lean beef eye of round steak and leg of lamb

1–2 tablespoons canola oil

2 tablespoons flour

½ cup each: finely chopped celery, carrots, onion

Salt and pepper, to taste

2 cups each: baby carrots, small broccoli florets, tiny white onions, cooked crisp-tender, warm

Per Serving:
Calories: 314
% calories from fat: 25
Protein (g): 30.7
Carbohydrate (g): 19
Fat (g): 8.6
Saturated fat (g): 2.5
Cholesterol (mg): 74
Sodium (mg): 123

Exchanges:
Milk. 0.0
Vegetable: 4.0
Fruit 0.0
Bread: 0.0
Meat: 3.0
Fat: 0.0

1. Pour combined wine, cognac, cinnamon, and mace over meats in glass bowl; refrigerate, covered, 6 hours or overnight, stirring occasionally. Drain, reserving marinade.

2. Cook meats in oil in Dutch oven over medium heat until browned, about 8 minutes; sprinkle with flour and cook 1 to 2 minutes. Add chopped vegetables and reserved marinade to Dutch oven; heat to boiling. Transfer Dutch oven to oven and bake, covered, at 350 degrees until meats are tender, about 45 minutes; season to taste with salt and pepper. Spoon stew into shallow serving platter; arrange carrots, broccoli, and onions around meat.

TWO-MEAT, TWO-MUSHROOM STEW

Substitute any favorite dried and fresh mushrooms for the shiitake mushrooms in this richly flavored stew.

6 entrée servings

½ cup boiling water

3 medium dried shiitake mushrooms

1 cup chopped onion

½ teaspoon fennel seeds, lightly crushed

1 tablespoon olive oil

12 ounces each: boneless cubed (¾-inch) pork
    loin, veal leg

2 tablespoons flour

½ cup each: dry white wine, reduced-sodium
    chicken broth

4 ounces small cremini or white button
    mushrooms, halved

Salt and pepper, to taste

4 cups cooked brown or white, rice

Per Serving:
Calories: 384
% calories from fat: 22
Protein (g): 33.9
Carbohydrate (g): 36.8
Fat (g): 9
Saturated fat (g): 2.7
Cholesterol (mg): 89.4
Sodium (mg): 221

Exchanges:
Milk: 0.0
Vegetable: 1.0
Fruit: 0.0
Bread: 2.0
Meat: 4.0
Fat: 0.0

1. Pour boiling water over dried mushrooms in small bowl; let stand until mushrooms are softened, 5 to 10 minutes. Drain, reserving liquid; strain liquid. Slice mushrooms into thin strips, discarding hard centers.

2. Sauté onion and fennel seeds in oil in large saucepan 2 to 3 minutes; add meats and cook over medium heat until lightly browned, 5 to 8 minutes. Sprinkle with flour and cook 1 minute. Add wine, broth, and reserved mushroom liquid; heat to boiling. Reduce heat and simmer, covered, until meats are tender, about 1 hour, adding mushrooms during last 10 minutes. Season to taste with salt and pepper. Serve over rice.

KARELIAN RAGOUT

Allspice gently seasons beef, pork, and lamb in this Finnish stew. Serve over cooked rice or noodles, if you wish, with warm bread or rolls.

12 entrée servings

1 pound each: cubed (1-inch) boneless lean beef
  eye-of-round steak, leg of lamb, pork loin

Flour

1 teaspoon ground allspice

Salt and pepper, to taste

4 medium onions, thinly sliced

1 quart reduced-sodium fat-free beef broth

6 whole allspice berries

4 whole peppercorns

2 bay leaves

¼ cup finely chopped parsley

Per Serving:
Calories: 163
% calories from fat: 29
Protein (g): 23.5
Carbohydrate (g): 4.6
Fat (g): 5.1
Saturated fat (g): 1.8
Cholesterol (mg): 55.9
Sodium (mg): 107

Exchanges:
Milk: 0.0
Vegetable: 0.0
Fruit: 0.0
Bread: 0.0
Meat: 3.0
Fat: 0.0

1. Coat meats lightly with flour; sprinkle with ground allspice; sprinkle lightly with salt and pepper. Layer meats and onions in Dutch oven; add remaining ingredients, except parsley, and heat to boiling. Reduce heat and simmer, covered, until meats are tender, about 1 hour. Discard bay leaves; season to taste with salt and pepper. Stir in parsley.

STEW WITH THREE MEATS

The combined flavors of beef, veal, and pork make this stew especially good.

6 entrée servings

1 large onion, finely chopped
8 ounces each: cubed (1-inch) boneless lean beef
    round, pork loin, veal leg
1 cup each: water, reduced-sodium fat-free beef broth
1 teaspoon paprika
1 can (14½ ounces) Italian plum tomatoes,
    undrained, chopped
Salt and pepper, to taste

Per Serving:
Calories: 225
% calories from fat: 26
Protein (g): 34.7
Carbohydrate (g): 4.8
Fat (g): 6.4
Saturated fat (g): 2.2
Cholesterol (mg): 96.2
Sodium (mg): 172

Exchanges:
Milk: 0.0
Vegetable: 0.0
Fruit: 0.0
Bread: 0.0
Meat: 4.0
Fat: 0.0

1. Cook onion, beef, pork, and veal in lightly greased Dutch oven until browned, about 10 minutes. Add remaining ingredients, except salt and pepper, and heat to boiling; reduce heat and simmer, covered, until meats are tender, about 1 hour. Season to taste with salt and pepper.

THREE-MEAT GOULASH

The mingled juices of three kinds of meat yield unsurpassed flavor.

12 entrée servings

8 ounces mushrooms, sliced
1 cup chopped onion
½ cup thinly sliced green onions
1–2 tablespoons canola oil
1 tablespoon paprika
1 teaspoon caraway seeds, crushed
½ teaspoon dried dill weed
1 pound each: cubed (¾-inch) boneless beef eye of
    round steak, lean pork loin, lean veal leg
2 cups reduced-sodium fat-free beef broth
4 large tomatoes, coarsely chopped
4–6 tablespoons reduced-sodium tomato paste

Per Serving:
Calories: 446
% calories from fat: 18
Protein (g): 40.3
Carbohydrate (g): 49.5
Fat (g): 8.6
Saturated fat (g): 3.1
Cholesterol (mg): 85.4
Sodium (mg): 125

Exchanges:
Milk: 0.0
Vegetable: 1.0
Fruit: 0.0
Bread: 3.0
Meat: 4.0
Fat: 0.0

¾ cup reduced-fat sour cream

3 tablespoons flour

Salt and pepper, to taste

1½ pounds noodles, cooked, warm

1. Sauté mushrooms, onion, and green onions in oil in large Dutch oven 5 minutes; stir in paprika, caraway seeds, and dill weed and cook 1 minute. Remove and reserve. Add meats to Dutch oven; cook over medium heat until browned, 8 to 10 minutes. Return vegetables to Dutch oven; add beef broth, tomatoes, and tomato paste and heat to boiling. Reduce heat and simmer, covered, until meats are tender, about 45 minutes. Stir in combined sour cream and flour and cook until thickened, 2 to 3 minutes. Season to taste with salt and pepper. Serve over noodles.

SAUSAGE AND BEAN STEW

Serve this hearty winter stew over Polenta (see p. 661) with warm Garlic Bread (see p. 645).

8 entrée servings

1½ cups chopped onions

½ cup chopped green bell pepper

2 cloves garlic, minced

1–2 tablespoons olive oil

1 pound reduced-fat smoked turkey sausage, sliced

½ teaspoon each: dried thyme and savory leaves

1 bay leaf

2 tablespoons flour

1 quart water

2 cans (14½ ounces each) reduced-sodium diced tomatoes, undrained

2 cans (15½ ounces each) light red kidney beans, rinsed, drained

1 can (15½ ounces) Great Northern beans, rinsed, drained

Salt and pepper, to taste

Per Serving:
Calories: 255
% calories from fat: 15
Protein (g): 19.2
Carbohydrate (g): 39.4
Fat (g): 4.6
Saturated fat (g): 1.1
Cholesterol (mg): 26.5
Sodium (mg): 791

Exchanges:
Milk: 0.0
Vegetable: 1.0
Fruit: 0.0
Bread: 2.0
Meat: 2.0
Fat: 0.0

1. Sauté onions, bell pepper, and garlic in olive oil in large saucepan 3 to 4 minutes; add sausage and herbs and sauté until sausage is browned, about 5 minutes. Stir in flour and cook 1 minute. Add remaining ingredients, except salt and pepper, and heat to boiling. Reduce heat and simmer, covered, 30 minutes. Discard bay leaf; season to taste with salt and pepper.

ACORN SQUASH STEW WITH SMOKED SAUSAGE

45 *Smoked sausage adds great flavor to this chunky, vegetable-rich stew.*

4 entrée servings

8 ounces reduced-sodium smoked turkey sausage, halved lengthwise, sliced

1 teaspoon olive oil

2 teaspoons flour

1 can (14 ounces) fat-free beef broth

2 pounds acorn squash, peeled, seeded, cubed (1-inch)

1 medium onion, cut into thin wedges

1 can (14½ ounces) stewed tomatoes

1 cup frozen peas

Salt and pepper, to taste

Per Serving:
Calories: 298
% calories from fat: 11
Protein (g): 17.2
Carbohydrate (g): 54.9
Fat (g): 4
Saturated fat (g): 1
Cholesterol (mg): 26.5
Sodium (mg): 709

Exchanges:
Milk: 0.0
Vegetable: 0.0
Fruit: 0.0
Bread: 3.0
Meat: 2.0
Fat: 0.0

1. Cook sausage in oil in Dutch oven over medium heat until lightly browned, about 5 minutes; sprinkle with flour and cook 1 minute. Add broth, squash, onion, and tomatoes and heat to boiling; reduce heat and simmer, covered, until squash is tender, about 10 minutes. Add peas and simmer until hot, about 3 minutes. Season to taste with salt and pepper.

TEN

Poultry Stews

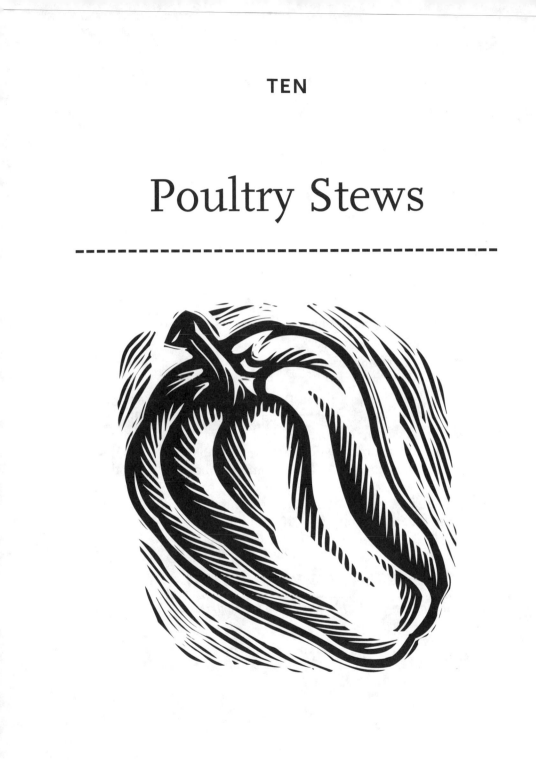

CHICKEN STEW AND DUMPLINGS

45 *This stew can be made quickly using convenient canned and frozen ingredients.*

4 entrée servings

1 pound boneless, skinless chicken breasts, cubed
2 tablespoons margarine or butter
1 cup water
1 cup sliced onion
1 can (10¾ ounces) reduced-sodium, reduced-fat
   condensed cream of chicken soup
1¼ plus ⅓ cup fat-free milk, divided
1 package (10 ounces) frozen mixed vegetables
¼ teaspoon each: salt and pepper
1 cup reduced-fat baking mix

Per Serving:
Calories: 453
% calories from fat: 30
Protein (g): 33.2
Carbohydrate (g): 46.1
Fat (g): 15
Saturated fat (g). 3 9
Cholesterol· (mg): 83.5
Sodium (mg): 853

Exchanges:
Milk: 0.0
Vegetable: 0.0
Fruit: 0.0
Bread: 3.0
Meat: 4.0
Fat: 0.5

1. Cook chicken in margarine in Dutch oven until browned on all sides, about 10 minutes. Add water and onion; heat to boiling. Reduce heat and simmer, covered, until chicken is cooked, about 20 minutes. Stir in soup, 1¼ cups milk, vegetables, salt, and pepper. Heat stew to boiling; spoon combined baking mix and remaining ⅓ cup milk into 4 mounds on top of stew. Reduce heat and simmer, uncovered, 10 minutes; simmer, covered, until dumplings are dry on top, about 10 minutes.

SPEEDY CHICKEN AND RAVIOLI STEW

45 *Use any favorite flavor of refrigerated fresh ravioli in this quick and nutritious bean stew.*

4 entrée servings

1 pound chicken tenders, cubed
¾ cup chopped onion
4 teaspoons minced garlic
2 cans (15 ounces each) kidney beans, rinsed, drained
1 can (14½ ounces) reduced-sodium diced tomatoes, undrained
½ teaspoon dried thyme leaves

1 package (9 ounces) fresh sun-dried tomato ravioli, cooked, warm

Salt and pepper, to taste

Per Serving:
Calories: 410
% calories from fat: 12
Protein (g): 39.1
Carbohydrate (g): 53.3
Fat (g): 5.7
Saturated fat (g): 2.4
Cholesterol (mg): 63.5
Sodium (mg): 984

Exchanges:
Milk: 0.0
Vegetable: 1.0
Fruit: 0.0
Bread: 3.0
Meat: 3.0
Fat: 0.0

1. Cook chicken, onion, and garlic in lightly greased large skillet over medium heat until browned, 5 to 8 minutes. Stir in beans, tomatoes with liquid, and thyme; heat to boiling. Reduce heat and simmer, covered, until chicken is cooked, about 5 minutes. Stir in ravioli and cook until hot, 2 to 3 minutes. Season to taste with salt and pepper.

ALFREDO CHICKEN STEW

45 *A creamy, low-fat alfredo sauce makes this stew especially good.*

4 entrée servings

1 pound boneless, skinless chicken breast, cubed
3 tablespoons margarine or butter
¼ cup sliced green onions
1 teaspoon minced garlic
¼ cup each: sliced green onion, all-purpose flour
1 teaspoon dried basil leaves
2½ cups fat-free milk
4 ounces cut asparagus (1½-inch)
½ cup frozen tiny peas
½ cup (2 ounces) shredded Parmesan cheese
Salt and pepper, to taste
8 ounces fettuccine, cooked, warm

Per Serving:
Calories: 507
% calories from fat: 29
Protein (g): 42
Carbohydrate (g): 47.7
Fat (g): 16
Saturated fat (g): 4
Cholesterol (mg): 87
Sodium (mg): 394

Exchanges:
Milk: 0.5
Vegetable: 2.0
Fruit: 0.0
Bread: 2.0
Meat: 4.0
Fat: 0.5

1. Sauté chicken in margarine in large saucepan until lightly browned, about 5 minutes; add green onions and garlic and sauté 3 minutes longer. Stir in flour and basil and cook 1 minute; stir in milk and heat to boiling, stirring until thickened, about 1 minute. Reduce heat and simmer, covered, until chicken is cooked, about 20 minutes, adding asparagus and peas during last 5 minutes. Stir in cheese; season to taste with salt and pepper. Serve over fettuccine.

QUICK CHICKEN AND VEGETABLE STEW

45 *Puréed beans provide a perfect thickening for the stew and canned vegetables speed preparation.*

6 entrée servings

1 pound chicken tenders

¾ cup each: sliced carrots, chopped onion

2 teaspoons minced garlic

1 can (15 ounces) navy beans, rinsed, drained

2 cups reduced-sodium fat-free chicken broth, divided

1 can (16 ounces) Italian-style zucchini with
   mushrooms in tomato sauce

1 can (15 ounces) black beans, rinsed, drained

1 cup frozen peas

1½ teaspoons dried Italian seasoning

Salt and pepper, to taste

8 ounces egg noodles, cooked, warm

Per Serving:
Calories: 434
% calories from fat: 9
Protein (g): 35.5
Carbohydrate (g): 63.3
Fat (g) 4.5
Saturated fat (g): 1
Cholesterol (mg): 78.6
Sodium (mg): 809

Exchanges:
Milk: 0.0
Vegetable: 1 0
Fruit 0.0
Bread: 4.0
Meat: 2.0
Fat: 0.0

1. Cook chicken, carrots, onion, and garlic in lightly greased large saucepan over medium heat until chicken is browned, about 8 minutes. Purée navy beans with half the broth in blender; add to saucepan with remaining broth, zucchini, black beans, peas, and Italian seasoning. Heat to boiling. Reduce heat and simmer, covered, 10 minutes. Season to taste with salt and pepper. Serve over noodles.

CHICKEN STEW PAPRIKASH

45 *Serve this stew with thick slices of warm Peasant Bread (see p. 650).*

4 entrée servings

1 pound chicken tenders, halved crosswise

2 each: finely chopped medium onions, minced cloves garlic

1 tablespoon canola oil

1 medium green bell pepper, chopped

1 cup sliced mushrooms

1 can (14½ ounces) stewed tomatoes

2½–3 teaspoons paprika

1 teaspoon poppy seeds

¼–½ cup reduced-fat sour cream

Salt and pepper, to taste

4 cups cooked noodles, warm

Per Serving:
Calories: 468
% calories from fat: 17
Protein (g): 38
Carbohydrate (g): 58.1
Fat (g): 8.9
Saturated fat (g): 2.2
Cholesterol (mg): 74
Sodium (mg): 331

Exchanges:
Milk: 0.0
Vegetable: 3.0
Fruit: 0.0
Bread: 3.0
Meat: 3.0
Fat: 0.0

1. Cook chicken, onions, and garlic in oil in large saucepan over medium heat until chicken is browned, about 5 minutes. Add bell pepper and mushrooms and cook 5 minutes. Add tomatoes with liquid, paprika, and poppy seeds and heat to boiling; reduce heat and simmer, covered, until chicken is tender, about 15 minutes. Stir in sour cream and simmer 1 to 2 minutes. Season to taste with salt and pepper; serve over noodles.

KASHMIR CHICKEN STEW

45 *This hearty stew is flavored with sweet Middle Eastern spices and raisins.*

6 entrée servings

1½ cups chopped onions

¾ cup chopped red bell pepper

2 teaspoons minced garlic

⅛–¼ teaspoon crushed red pepper

2 tablespoons olive oil

12 ounces boneless, skinless chicken breast, cubed (1-inch)

1 teaspoon each: ground cumin, cinnamon

2 cans (15 ounces each) navy beans, rinsed, drained

1 can (14½ ounces) Italian-style stewed tomatoes

⅓ cup raisins

Salt and pepper, to taste

4 cups cooked couscous, warm

Per Serving:
Calories: 470
% calories from fat: 13
Protein (g): 29.3
Carbohydrate (g): 72.9
Fat (g): 7
Saturated fat (g): 1.2
Cholesterol (mg): 34.5
Sodium (mg): 614

Exchanges:
Milk: 0.0
Vegetable: 2.0
Fruit: 0.0
Bread: 4.0
Meat: 2.0
Fat: 0.0

1. Sauté onions, bell pepper, garlic, and red pepper in oil in large saucepan 2 to 3 minutes. Add chicken, cumin, and cinnamon; cook over medium heat until chicken is lightly browned, about 5 minutes. Add remaining ingredients, except salt, pepper, and couscous; heat to boiling. Reduce heat and simmer, covered, 10 minutes. Season to taste with salt and pepper; serve over couscous.

CREAMY CHICKEN CURRY STEW

45 *Apple and raisins flavor this delicious curry.*

4 entrée servings

1 small tart apple, unpeeled, cubed
½ cup chopped onion
1 clove garlic, minced
1 teaspoon curry powder
¼ teaspoon ground ginger
2 teaspoons vegetable oil
3 tablespoons flour
1 cup reduced-sodium fat-free chicken broth
¾ cup fat-free half-and-half or fat-free milk
1½ cups cubed cooked chicken breast
¼ cup raisins
Salt and pepper, to taste
3 cups cooked rice, warm

Per Serving:
Calories: 419
% calories from fat: 20
Protein (g): 23.5
Carbohydrate (g): 58.1
Fat (g): 9.2
Saturated fat (g): 2.1
Cholesterol (mg) 43.5
Sodium (mg): 132

Exchanges:
Milk: 0.0
Vegetable: 0.0
Fruit: 1.0
Bread: 3.0
Meat: 2.0
Fat: 0.5

1. Sauté apple, onion, garlic, curry powder, and ginger in oil in large skillet until tender, about 5 minutes. Stir in flour; cook 1 to 2 minutes. Stir in broth and half-and-half; heat to boiling, stirring until thickened, about 1 minute. Stir in chicken and raisins; cook until hot, 2 to 3 minutes. Season to taste with salt and pepper; serve over rice.

CRANBERRY CHICKEN STEW

45 *Apples, cranberry sauce, raisins, and vinegar blend to make a sweet and tangy stew.*

4 entrée servings

1 cup each: chopped onion, jellied cranberry sauce
½ cup dark raisins
1 tablespoon each: apple cider vinegar, brown sugar
1 pound boneless, skinless chicken breast, cubed
1 teaspoon dried thyme leaves
2 tart apples, thinly sliced
Salt and pepper, to taste
8 ounces egg noodles, cooked, warm

Per Serving:
Calories: 571
% calories from fat: 4
Protein (g): 35.6
Carbohydrate (g): 102
Fat (g): 2.4
Saturated fat (g): 0.5
Cholesterol (mg): 65.8
Sodium (mg): 129

Exchanges:
Milk: 0.0
Vegetable: 0.0
Fruit: 2.0
Bread: 4.0
Meat: 3.0
Fat: 0.0

1. Sauté onion in lightly greased large saucepan 5 minutes; stir in remaining ingredients, except apples, salt, pepper, and noodles. Heat to boiling; reduce heat and simmer, covered, until chicken is cooked, about 15 minutes, adding apples during last 5 minutes. Season to taste with salt and pepper; serve over noodles.

CHICKEN STEW PROVENÇAL

45 *Bursting with garlic and herb flavors, this stew is reminiscent of dishes from the Provence region of France.*

4 entrée servings

1 pound boneless, skinless chicken breast, cubed (¾-inch)
4 teaspoons minced garlic
2 teaspoons olive oil
1 can (28 ounces) diced tomatoes, undrained
4 medium potatoes, peeled, thinly sliced
½ cup each: dry white wine, chicken broth
1½ teaspoons herbs de Provence or bouquet garni
Salt and pepper, to taste
Finely chopped basil, as garnish

Per Serving:
Calories: 352
% calories from fat: 14
Protein (g): 29.6
Carbohydrate (g): 37.2
Fat (g): 5.6
Saturated fat (g): 1.2
Cholesterol (mg): 69
Sodium (mg): 364

Exchanges:
Milk: 0.0
Vegetable: 2.0
Fruit: 1.0
Bread: 2.0
Meat: 3.0
Fat: 0.0

1. Cook chicken and garlic in oil in large saucepan over medium heat until chicken is browned, about 5 minutes. Add remaining ingredients, except salt, pepper, and basil; heat to boiling. Reduce heat and simmer, covered, 20 minutes or until chicken is cooked and potatoes are tender. Season to taste with salt and pepper; sprinkle each serving generously with basil.

SWEET POTATO CHICKEN STEW

45

The stew is also delicious made with russet potatoes, or a combination of russet and sweet potatoes.

4 entrée servings

1 pound boneless, skinless chicken breast, cubed (1-inch)

¼ cup all purpose flour

2–3 teaspoons chili powder

½ teaspoon garlic powder

2 tablespoons margarine or butter

1½ cups reduced-sodium fat-free chicken broth

1 large green bell pepper, thinly sliced

1 can (17 ounces) sweet potatoes, drained, cubed (1-inch)

Salt and pepper, to taste

Per Serving:
Calories: 342
% calories from fat: 24
Protein (g): 30.7
Carbohydrate (g): 33.3
Fat (g): 9
Saturated fat (g): 2
Cholesterol (mg): 69
Sodium (mg): 261

Exchanges:
Milk: 0.0
Vegetable: 0.0
Fruit: 0.0
Bread: 2.0
Meat: 3.0
Fat: 0.5

1. Coat chicken with combined flour, chili powder, and garlic powder; cook in margarine in large skillet over medium heat until browned, about 5 minutes. Stir in broth and bell pepper; heat to boiling. Reduce heat and simmer, covered, until chicken is cooked, about 15 minutes, adding sweet potatoes during last 5 minutes. Season to taste with salt and pepper.

CHICKEN GUMBO

45 *A quick gumbo that can't be beat!*

4 entrée servings

1 pound chicken breast, cooked, cubed
2½ cups reduced-sodium fat-free chicken broth
1 cup onion, chopped
2 cloves garlic, minced
1 can (14½ ounces) stewed tomatoes, undrained
8 ounces small okra, tops trimmed
¼ cup red or green bell pepper, chopped
1 teaspoon each: dried basil and thyme leaves
⅛–¼ teaspoon crushed red pepper
Salt and pepper, to taste
3 cups cooked rice, warm

Per Serving:
Calories: 424
% calories from fat: 11
Protein (g): 42.5
Carbohydrate (g): 49.8
Fat (g): 5.2
Saturated fat (g): 1.4
Cholesterol (mg): 87.5
Sodium (mg): 413

Exchanges:
Milk: 0.0
Vegetable: 1.0
Fruit: 0.0
Bread: 3.0
Meat: 3.0
Fat: 0.0

1. Heat all ingredients, except salt, pepper, and rice, to boiling in large saucepan; reduce heat and simmer, covered, until okra is tender, about 15 minutes. Season to taste with salt and pepper; serve over rice.

LEMON CHICKEN STEW

45 *Fresh lemon juice and jalapeño chili boost the flavor in this very quick stew.*

6 entrée servings

1 pound boneless, skinless chicken breast, cubed
1 jalapeño chili, minced
2 cloves garlic, minced
2 teaspoons olive oil
2 cans (14½ ounces each) diced tomatoes, undrained
2 cups fresh or frozen broccoli florets
¼–⅓ cup lemon juice
1 teaspoon instant chicken bouillon crystals
¼ cup finely chopped fresh or 2 teaspoons dried
   basil leaves
Salt and pepper, to taste
12 ounces angel hair pasta, cooked, warm
Shredded Parmesan cheese, as garnish

Per Serving:
Calories: 310
% calories from fat: 17
Protein (g): 26.2
Carbohydrate (g): 38.2
Fat (g): 5.8
Saturated fat (g): 1.5
Cholesterol (mg): 109.8
Sodium (mg): 783

Exchanges:
Milk: 0.0
Vegetable: 2.0
Fruit: 0.0
Bread: 2.0
Meat: 2.0
Fat: 0.0

1. Cook chicken, jalapeño chili, and garlic in oil in large saucepan over medium heat until lightly browned, about 5 minutes. Stir in tomatoes with liquid, broccoli, lemon juice, bouillon crystals, and basil; heat to boiling. Reduce heat and simmer, uncovered, until chicken and broccoli are cooked, about 10 minutes. Season to taste with salt and pepper. Serve over pasta; sprinkle with Parmesan cheese.

EL PASO CHICKEN STEW

45 *Serve this stew over rice, sprinkled with tortilla chips and cheese, or with Green Chili Cornbread (see p. 654).*

4 entrée servings

1 pound boneless, skinless chicken breast, cubed
½ package (1.25-ounce size) reduced-sodium taco-seasoning mix, divided
1 tablespoon peanut or canola oil
2 cans (14½ ounces each) Mexican-style stewed tomatoes, undrained
1 can (15 ounces) pinto beans, rinsed, drained

2 cups each: cut green beans whole kernel corn

Salt and pepper, to taste

Per Serving:
Calories: 407
% calories from fat: 16
Protein (g): 34.9
Carbohydrate (g): 51.1
Fat (g): 7.6
Saturated fat (g): 1.5
Cholesterol (mg): 69
Sodium (mg): 862

Exchanges:
Milk: 0.0
Vegetable: 1.0
Fruit: 0.0
Bread: 3.0
Meat: 3.0
Fat: 0.0

1. Coat chicken with half the taco seasoning mix. Cook chicken in oil in large skillet until lightly browned, about 5 minutes. Stir in remaining taco-seasoning mix and remaining ingredients, except salt and pepper; heat to boiling. Reduce heat and simmer, uncovered, until chicken is cooked and vegetables are tender, about 10 minutes. Season to taste with salt and pepper.

PICNIC CHICKEN STEW

45 *Canned garbanzo and baked beans combine with chicken in a chili powder-spiked stew.*

8 entrée servings

Per Serving:
Calories: 251
% calories from fat: 14
Protein (g): 18.1
Carbohydrate (g): 39.1
Fat (g): 4.1
Saturated fat (g): 0.8
Cholesterol (mg): 25.9
Sodium (mg): 616

Exchanges:
Milk: 0.0
Vegetable: 2.0
Fruit: 0.0
Bread: 2.0
Meat: 1.0
Fat: 0.0

12 ounces boneless, skinless chicken breast, cubed

1 each: chopped large onion, red bell pepper

2 cloves garlic, minced

1 tablespoon peanut or canola oil

2 cans (15 ounces each) baked beans or pork
   and beans

1 can (15 ounces) garbanzo beans, rinsed, drained

1 can (14½ ounces) reduced-sodium diced
   tomatoes, undrained

2–3 teaspoons chili powder

¾ teaspoon dried thyme leaves

Salt and pepper, to taste

1. Cook chicken, onion, bell pepper, and garlic in oil in large saucepan until lightly browned, about 8 minutes. Stir in remaining ingredients, except salt and pepper; heat to boiling. Reduce heat and simmer, uncovered, until thickened to desired consistency, about 8 minutes.

SWEET-AND-SOUR ISLAND STEW

45 *Sweet-and-sour flavors team with chicken, pineapple, and beans for this island-inspired dish—delicious with jasmine rice or couscous.*

6 entrée servings

1½ pounds chicken tenders, halved

1 tablespoon vegetable oil

1 cup each: sliced onion, green and red bell peppers

2 teaspoons each: minced garlic, gingerroot, jalapeño chili

3 cups reduced-sodium fat-free chicken broth

1 can (20 ounces) unsweetened pineapple chunks, drained, juice reserved

1 can (15 ounces) black beans, rinsed, drained

2 tablespoons each: light brown sugar, apple cider vinegar

2–3 teaspoons curry powder

2 tablespoons cornstarch

Salt and pepper, to taste

Per Serving:
Calories: 288
% calories from fat: 12
Protein (g): 29.7
Carbohydrate (g): 34.7
Fat (g): 3.9
Saturated fat (g): 0.3
Cholesterol (mg): 48.2
Sodium (mg): 537

Exchanges:
Milk: 0.0
Vegetable: 1.0
Fruit: 0.5
Bread: 1.0
Meat: 3.0
Fat: 0.0

1. Cook chicken in oil in large skillet over medium heat until browned, about 8 minutes; remove from skillet. Add onion, bell peppers, garlic, gingerroot, and jalapeño chili to skillet; sauté until tender, about 5 minutes. Stir in chicken and remaining ingredients, except reserved pineapple juice and cornstarch; heat to boiling. Stir in combined cornstarch and reserved pineapple juice, stirring until thickened, about 1 minute. Season to taste with salt and pepper.

COCONUT CHICKEN STEW

45 *This spicy Indonesian-influenced stew is enhanced with the unique flavor of coconut milk.*

6 entrée servings

1½ pounds boneless, skinless chicken breast, cubed

¼ cup sliced green onions

1 clove garlic, minced

2 teaspoons each: minced gingerroot, canola oil

⅔ cup each: sliced onion, green and red bell pepper

1 can (15 ounces) red beans, rinsed, drained

1 cup each: light unsweetened coconut milk, reduced-sodium fat-free chicken broth

1 tablespoon cornstarch

2 tablespoons lime juice

Salt and cayenne pepper, to taste

4 cups cooked rice, warm

Finely chopped cilantro, as garnish

Per Serving:
Calories: 404
% calories from fat: 15
Protein (g): 35.1
Carbohydrate (g): 48
Fat (g): 7
Saturated fat (g): 1.1
Cholesterol (mg): 69
Sodium (mg): 333

Exchanges:
Milk: 0.0
Vegetable: 1.0
Fruit: 0.0
Bread: 3.0
Meat: 3.0
Fat: 0.0

1. Cook chicken, green onions, garlic, and gingerroot in oil in large skillet over medium heat until lightly browned, about 5 minutes. Stir in onion, bell peppers, beans, coconut milk, and broth; heat to boiling. Reduce heat and simmer, uncovered, until chicken is cooked and vegetables are tender, about 10 minutes. Heat stew to boiling; stir in combined cornstarch and lime juice, stirring until thickened, about 1 minute. Season to taste with salt and cayenne pepper. Serve over rice; sprinkle generously with cilantro.

LUAU CHICKEN STEW

45 *Pineapple juice gives this stew its delicious sweet-sour flavor.*

6 entrée servings

1½ pounds boneless, skinless chicken breast, cubed

¼ cup all-purpose flour

1 tablespoon peanut or canola oil

8 ounces mushrooms, sliced

2 medium carrots, diagonally sliced

1 each: thinly sliced small red onion, minced
  clove garlic

1 cup reduced-sodium fat-free chicken broth

½ cup unsweetened pineapple juice

2–3 tablespoons each: rice or cider vinegar,
  reduced-sodium soy sauce

2 small tomatoes, cut into thin wedges

1 cup frozen peas

Salt and pepper, to taste

4 cups cooked rice, warm

Per Serving:
Calories: 381
% calories from fat: 14
Protein (g): 32.9
Carbohydrate (g): 47.1
Fat (g): 5.9
Saturated fat (g): 1.3
Cholesterol (mg): 69
Sodium (mg): 301

Exchanges:
Milk: 0.0
Vegetable: 0.0
Fruit: 0.0
Bread: 3.0
Meat: 3.0
Fat: 0.0

1. Coat chicken with flour; cook in oil in large skillet over medium heat until browned, about 8 minutes. Add mushrooms, carrots, onion, and garlic and cook until tender, about 5 minutes. Stir in broth, pineapple juice, vinegar, and soy sauce; heat to boiling. Reduce heat and simmer, uncovered, until chicken is cooked and sauce has thickened, about 10 minutes. Stir in tomatoes and peas; simmer, covered, until hot, 3 to 4 minutes. Season to taste with salt and pepper; serve over rice.

ISLAND CHICKEN STEW

45 *The combination of sauce ingredients gives this chicken dish a wonderful flavor.*

6 entrée servings

1 each: finely chopped large onion, green bell pepper

1½ pounds boneless, skinless chicken breast, cubed

1 can (8 ounces) crushed pineapple, undrained

¾ cup fat-free beef broth

2 tablespoons reduced-sodium soy sauce

1 tablespoon brown sugar

2 teaspoons rice vinegar

½ teaspoon ground ginger

¼ cup dry sherry or fat-free beef broth

1 tablespoon flour

Salt and pepper, to taste

4 cups cooked rice, warm

Per Serving:
Calories: 330
% calories from fat: 5
Protein (g): 30.4
Carbohydrate (g): 43.3
Fat (g): 1.7
Saturated fat (g): 0.5
Cholesterol (mg): 65.7
Sodium (mg): 280

Exchanges:
Milk: 0.0
Vegetable: 0.0
Fruit: 0.0
Bread: 3.0
Meat: 3.0
Fat: 0.0

1. Sauté onion and bell pepper in lightly greased large saucepan until tender, about 5 minutes; stir in remaining ingredients, except dry sherry, flour, salt, pepper, and rice; heat to boiling. Reduce heat and simmer, covered, until chicken is cooked, about 15 minutes. Heat stew to boiling; stir in combined sherry and flour, stirring, until thickened, about 1 minute. Season to taste with salt and pepper. Serve over rice.

HOME-STYLE TURKEY STEW

45 *A great family meal that's very fast to prepare!*

4 entrée servings

12 ounces boneless, skinless turkey breast,
   cubed (¾-inch)
2 medium onions, cut into thin wedges
4 ounces mushrooms, halved
2 teaspoons olive oil
1 cup each: sliced carrots, cubed unpeeled potatoes
1 can (14½ ounces) reduced-sodium fat-free
   chicken broth
1 teaspoon each: dried thyme leaves, celery seeds
1 cup frozen peas
Salt and pepper, to taste

Per Serving:
Calories: 158
% calories from fat: 26
Protein (g): 21.1
Carbohydrate (g): 7
Fat (g): 4.5
Saturated fat (g): 1
Cholesterol (mg): 44.7
Sodium (mg): 63

Exchanges:
Milk: 0.0
Vegetable: 0.0˜
Fruit: 0.0
Bread: 0.5
Meat: 3.0
Fat: 0.0

1. Cook turkey, onions, and mushrooms in oil in large saucepan over medium heat until lightly browned, about 8 minutes. Add remaining ingredients, except peas, salt, and pepper; heat to boiling. Reduce heat and simmer, covered, until turkey is cooked and vegetables are tender, about 20 minutes, adding peas during last 5 minutes. Season to taste with salt and pepper.

TURKEY STEW CACCIATORE

45 *Turkey cutlets are cut into bite-sized pieces to make a quick cooking cacciatore-style skillet meal.*

4 entrée servings

¾ cup each: sliced mushrooms, cubed zucchini
2 tablespoons olive oil
1 pound turkey breast cutlets, sliced (2-inch)
2 tablespoons flour
¾ teaspoon dried oregano leaves
1 can (14½ ounces) stewed tomatoes
⅓ cup water
Salt and pepper, to taste
4 cups cooked pasta or rice, warm

1. Sauté mushrooms and zucchini in oil in large skillet until lightly browned, about 5 minutes. Coat turkey pieces with combined flour and oregano; add to skillet with any remaining flour mixture. Cook over medium heat until turkey begins to brown, about 5 minutes. Stir in tomatoes and water; heat to boiling. Reduce heat and simmer, covered, until turkey is cooked and mixture is slightly thickened, about 10 minutes. Season to taste with salt and pepper; serve over pasta.

Per Serving:
Calories: 579
% calories from fat: 16
Protein (g): 32.4
Carbohydrate (g): 87.7
Fat (g): 10.6
Saturated fat (g): 1.8
Cholesterol (mg): 44.7
Sodium (mg): 265

Exchanges:
Milk: 0.0
Vegetable: 3.0
Fruit: 0.0
Bread: 4.0
Meat: 3.0
Fat: 1.0

SWEET-SOUR TURKEY STEW

45 *This colorful dish is a perfect way to use leftover turkey, pork, or chicken.*

4 entrée servings

½ cup each: sliced onion, red and green bell peppers
1–2 teaspoons Asian sesame oil
1 can (8 ounces) pineapple tidbits, packed in juice, undrained
⅓ cup each: packed light brown sugar, cider vinegar
2 tablespoons cornstarch
1 cup cut green beans
1½ cups cubed cooked turkey
1 cup cubed tomato
1–2 tablespoons reduced-sodium soy sauce
Salt and pepper, to taste
2 cups cooked rice, warm

Per Serving:
Calories: 359
% calories from fat: 8
Protein (g): 20.5
Carbohydrate (g): 63
Fat (g): 3.4
Saturated fat (g): 0.8
Cholesterol (mg): 36.2
Sodium (mg): 192

Exchanges:
Milk: 0.0
Vegetable: 2.0
Fruit: 1.0
Bread: 2.0
Meat: 2.0
Fat: 0.0

1. Sauté onion and bell peppers in oil in large skillet until tender, about 5 minutes. Drain pineapple, reserving ⅓ cup juice. Stir combined juice, brown sugar, vinegar, and cornstarch into skillet and heat to boiling, stirring until thickened, about 1 minute. Add beans; reduce heat and simmer, covered, until beans are tender, about 10 minutes. Stir in pineapple, turkey, tomato, and soy sauce; simmer until hot, 2 to 3 minutes. Season to taste with salt and pepper; serve over rice.

ITALIAN SAUSAGE STEW WITH HOT PEPPERS

45 *This stew will remind you of a sassy Italian hot sausage and pepper sandwich!*

4 entrée servings

12–16 ounces Italian-style turkey sausage, sliced (1-inch)

2 small onions, cut into thin wedges

1 tablespoon chopped garlic

½–1 small jalapeño chili, thinly sliced

2 cups reduced-sodium fat-free chicken broth

1 can (14½ ounces) reduced-sodium diced tomatoes, undrained

1 zucchini, halved lengthwise, thickly sliced

4 ounces rigatoni

1½ teaspoons dried Italian seasoning

⅛–¼ teaspoon crushed red pepper

Salt and pepper, to taste

¼ cup (1 ounce) shredded Parmesan cheese

Per Serving:
Calories: 317
% calories from fat: 16
Protein (g): 24.8
Carbohydrate (g): 43.1
Fat (g): 5.8
Saturated fat (g): 2.2
Cholesterol (mg): 43.6
Sodium (mg): 738

Exchanges:
Milk: 0.0
Vegetable: 2.0
Fruit: 0.0
Bread: 2.0
Meat: 2.0
Fat: 0.0

1. Cook sausage, onions, garlic, and jalapeño chili in lightly greased large saucepan over medium heat until sausage is lightly browned, about 5 minutes. Add remaining ingredients, except salt, pepper, and Parmesan cheese, and heat to boiling. Reduce heat and simmer, covered, until pasta is al dente, about 10 minutes. Season to taste with salt and pepper; sprinkle each serving with 1 tablespoon cheese.

ITALIAN-STYLE BEAN AND VEGETABLE STEW WITH POLENTA

45 *This colorful mélange can also be served over pasta, rice, or squares of warm cornbread.*

6 entrée servings

12 ounces Italian-style turkey sausage, casings removed

1½ cups each: chopped onions, portobello mushrooms

4 cloves garlic, minced

2 tablespoons olive oil

2 cups broccoli florets and sliced stems

1 cup sliced yellow summer squash

1 can (15 ounces) each: rinsed drained garbanzo
and red kidney beans

1 can (14½ ounces) reduced-sodium diced
tomatoes, undrained

1½ teaspoons dried Italian seasoning

⅛–¼ teaspoon crushed red pepper

Salt and pepper, to taste

1 package (16 ounces) prepared Italian herb
polenta, warm

Per Serving:
Calories: 380
% calories from fat: 27
Protein (g): 21.7
Carbohydrate (g): 49.6
Fat (g): 11.9
Saturated fat (g): 2.5
Cholesterol (mg): 30.4
Sodium (mg): 833

Exchanges:
Milk: 0.0
Vegetable: 3.0
Fruit: 0.0
Bread: 3.0
Meat: 1.0
Fat: 1.0

1. Cook sausage, onions, mushrooms, and garlic in oil in large saucepan over medium heat until onions are tender and sausage browned, 8 to 10 minutes. Add remaining ingredients, except salt, pepper, and polenta; heat to boiling; reduce heat and simmer, covered, until broccoli is tender, 5 to 8 minutes. Season to taste with salt and pepper. Serve over polenta.

CREOLE SAUSAGE AND CORN STEW

45 *Use any reduced-fat sausage you like in this stew—vegetarian sausage links are delicious too.*

4 entrée servings

12–16 ounces reduced-fat smoked or spicy sausage
links, sliced (1-inch)

1 cup chopped onion

½ cup chopped green bell pepper

2 tablespoons flour

2 cups whole kernel corn

1 can (28 ounces) reduced-sodium diced tomatoes
with roasted garlic, undrained

½ teaspoon dried thyme leaves

Salt and pepper, to taste

Per Serving:
Calories: 254
% calories from fat: 14
Protein (g): 18.8
Carbohydrate (g): 41
Fat (g): 4.2
Saturated fat (g): 1.3
Cholesterol (mg): 39.7
Sodium (mg): 570

Exchanges:
Milk: 0.0
Vegetable: 0.0
Fruit: 0.0
Bread: 2.0
Meat: 2.0
Fat: 0.0

1. Cook sausage, onion, and bell pepper in large skillet over medium heat until sausage is well browned, about 5 minutes; stir in flour and cook 1 to 2 minutes. Stir in corn, tomatoes with liquid, and thyme; heat to boiling. Reduce heat and simmer, covered, 10 minutes. Simmer uncovered until thickened to desired consistency, 5 to 10 minutes. Season to taste with salt and pepper.

BLACK BEAN AND OKRA GUMBO

45

The gumbo is delicious served over warm Green Chili Cornbread (see p. 654).

8 entrée servings

8–12 ounces smoked turkey sausage, sliced
2 cups small mushrooms
1 cup each: chopped onion, sliced carrots
¾ cup each: chopped red and green bell peppers
1 tablespoon olive oil
2 cups vegetable broth
1 can (14½ ounces) stewed tomatoes with chilies
2 cans (15 ounces each) black beans, rinsed, drained
2 cups cut okra
1 tablespoon chili powder
1 teaspoon gumbo file
Salt and pepper, to taste

Per Serving:
Calories: 376
% calories from fat: 8
Protein (g): 16.7
Carbohydrate (g): 18.3
Fat (g): 2.9
Saturated fat (g): 0.7
Cholesterol (mg): 18.3
Sodium (mg): 832

Exchanges:
Milk: 0.0
Vegetable: 2.0
Fruit: 0.0
Bread: 4.0
Meat: 1.0
Fat: 0.0

1. Cook sausage, mushrooms, onion, carrots, and bell peppers in oil in Dutch oven over medium heat until sausage is lightly browned, 5 to 8 minutes. Add remaining ingredients, except salt and pepper; heat to boiling. Reduce heat and simmer, covered, until vegetables are tender, about 10 minutes. Simmer, uncovered, until thickened to desired consistency, 5 to 10 minutes. Season to taste with salt and pepper.

SAUSAGE, POTATO, AND BELL PEPPER STEW

45 *An attractive skillet stew with the vibrant colors of bell peppers.*

4 entrée servings

3 cups thinly sliced mixed red, green, and yellow
 bell peppers

1 cup thinly sliced onion

8 ounces smoked turkey sausage, thinly sliced

1 tablespoon flour

5 cups thinly sliced red potatoes

½ cup quartered sun-dried tomatoes (not in oil),
 softened

¾ cup reduced-sodium fat-free chicken broth

1 teaspoon each: dried thyme and marjoram leaves

Salt and pepper, to taste

Per Serving:
Calories: 258
% calories from fat: 19
Protein (g): 13.7
Carbohydrate (g): 42.8
Fat (g): 5.7
Saturated fat (g): 1.4
Cholesterol (mg): 28.2
Sodium (mg): 736

Exchanges:
Milk: 0.0
Vegetable: 3.0
Fruit: 0.0
Bread: 3.0
Meat: 1.0
Fat: 0.0

1. Cook bell peppers, onion, and sausage in lightly greased large skillet over medium heat until sausage is browned, about 8 minutes; sprinkle with flour and cook 1 minute. Add remaining ingredients, except salt and pepper, and heat to boiling; reduce heat and simmer, covered, until vegetables are tender, about 15 minutes. Season to taste with salt and pepper.

SMOKY GARBANZO BEAN STEW

45 *Smoked turkey sausage gives this stew lots of flavor; the beans and vegetables make it extra-nutritious.*

6 entrée servings

8–12 ounces smoked turkey sausage, sliced

1 tablespoon olive oil

1 each: chopped large onion, green bell pepper

2 each: sliced medium zucchini, minced cloves garlic

1 can (28 ounces) reduced-sodium diced
   tomatoes, undrained

2 cans (15 ounces each) garbanzo beans,
   rinsed, drained

1½ cups cut green beans

2 teaspoons dried oregano leaves

Salt and pepper, to taste

Per Serving:
Calories 298
% calories from fat: 17
Protein (g): 15.9
Carbohydrate (g): 48.9
Fat (g): 5.8
Saturated fat (g): 1.1
Cholesterol (mg): 17.6
Sodium (mg): 556

Exchanges:
Milk: 0.0
Vegetable: 1.0
Fruit: 0.0
Bread: 2 0
Meat: 1.0
Fat: 0.5

1. Cook sausage in oil in large saucepan over medium heat until browned, about 5 minutes. Add onion, bell pepper, zucchini, and garlic; cook until vegetables are tender, about 5 minutes. Add remaining ingredients, except salt and pepper; heat to boiling. Reduce heat and simmer, uncovered, until vegetables are tender, about 15 minutes. Season to taste with salt and pepper.

CHICKEN STEW WITH PARSLEY DUMPLINGS

For a meal another time, omit the dumplings and serve this savory stew over noodles or Real Mashed Potatoes (see p. 595).

6 entrée servings

1 cup chopped onion

3 carrots, thickly sliced

½ cup sliced celery

3 cups reduced-sodium chicken broth, divided

1½ cups cubed boneless, skinless chicken breast

¾ teaspoon dried sage leaves

½ cup frozen peas

¼ cup all-purpose flour

Salt and pepper, to taste

Parsley Dumplings (recipe follows)

Per Serving:
Calories: 233
% calories from fat: 20
Protein (g): 19.2
Carbohydrate (g): 26.7
Fat (g): 5.1
Saturated fat (g): 1.4
Cholesterol (mg): 35.5
Sodium (mg): 383

Exchanges:
Milk: 0.0
Vegetable: 2.0
Fruit: 0.0
Bread: 1.0
Meat: 1.5
Fat: 0.5

1. Sauté onion, carrots, and celery in lightly greased large saucepan until tender, about 5 minutes. Add 2½ cups chicken broth, chicken, and sage; heat to boiling. Reduce heat and simmer, covered, until chicken is cooked and vegetables are tender, about 15 minutes; stir in peas. Heat to boiling; stir in combined flour and remaining ½ cup chicken broth, stirring until thickened, about 1 minute. Season to taste with salt and pepper.

2. Heat stew to boiling; spoon Parsley Dumplings dough into 6 mounds on top of stew. Reduce heat and simmer, uncovered, 10 minutes; simmer, covered, until dumplings are dry on top, about 10 minutes.

Parsley Dumplings
Makes 6 dumplings

¾ cup all-purpose flour

1 teaspoon baking powder

¼ teaspoon salt

1½ tablespoons vegetable shortening

2 tablespoons finely chopped parsley

⅓ cup 2% reduced-fat milk

1. Combine flour, baking powder, and salt in small bowl. Cut in shortening with pastry blender until mixture resembles coarse crumbs. Stir in parsley and milk to make a soft dough.

CHICKEN FRICASSEE

Cloves and bay leaf add a flavor update to this dish; the traditional herbs, rosemary and thyme can be substituted.

6 entrée servings

6 skinless chicken breast halves (6 ounces each)

1 cup each: onion wedges, sliced carrots, celery

2 cloves garlic, minced

3 tablespoons flour

2 cans (14½ ounces each) reduced-sodium fat-free chicken broth

16 whole cloves, tied in a cheesecloth bag

2 bay leaves

1 teaspoon lemon juice

Salt and pepper, to taste

12 ounces fettuccine, cooked, warm

Per Serving:
Calories: 361
% calories from fat: 13
Protein (g): 35.9
Carbohydrate (g): 41.5
Fat (g): 5.1
Saturated fat (g): 0.9
Cholesterol (mg): 78.6
Sodium (mg): 401

Exchanges:
Milk: 0.0
Vegetable: 2.0
Fruit: 0.0
Bread: 2.0
Meat: 3.0
Fat: 0.0

1. Cook chicken in lightly greased large skillet over medium heat until browned, about 8 minutes. Remove from skillet. Add vegetables and garlic to skillet and sauté 5 minutes; stir in flour and cook 1 minute. Return chicken to skillet; add remaining ingredients, except salt, pepper, and pasta and heat to boiling. Reduce heat and simmer, covered, until chicken is cooked, about 20 minutes; simmer, uncovered, until stew is thickened to desired consistency, about 10 minutes. Discard cloves and bay leaves; season to taste with salt and pepper. Serve over fettuccine.

CHICKEN STEW WITH SUNFLOWER SEED DUMPLINGS

A recipe from the heartland with old-fashioned flavor and unique dumplings.

8 entrée servings

1 large onion, thinly sliced

2 ribs celery, sliced

3 pounds skinless chicken breasts and thighs

¾ cup reduced-sodium fat-free chicken broth

½ cup dry vermouth or chicken broth
1 teaspoon minced garlic
½ teaspoon dried thyme leaves
4 each: cubed (½-inch) new potatoes, thickly
   sliced carrots
Salt and pepper, to taste
Sunflower Seed Dumplings (recipe follows)

Per Serving:
Calories: 397
% calories from fat: 19
Protein (g); 42.7
Carbohydrate (g): 32.7
Fat (g): 8.1
Saturated fat (g): 1.9
Cholesterol (mg): 103.8
Sodium (mg): 368

Exchanges:
Milk: 0.0
Vegetable: 0.0
Fruit: 0.0
Bread: 2.0
Meat: 5.0
Fat: 0.0

1. Sauté onion and celery in lightly greased Dutch oven until onion is tender, about 5 minutes. Add chicken, broth, vermouth, garlic, and thyme; heat to boiling. Reduce heat and simmer, covered, until chicken is tender, 30 to 40 minutes, adding potatoes and carrots last 15 minutes. Season to taste with salt and pepper.

2. Heat stew to boiling; spoon Sunflower Seed Dumplings dough into 8 mounds on top of stew. Reduce heat and simmer, uncovered, 10 minutes; simmer, covered, until dumplings are dry on top, about 10 minutes.

Sunflower Seed Dumplings
Makes 8 dumplings

1 cup unbleached flour
2 teaspoons baking powder
¼ teaspoon salt
2 tablespoons margarine or butter
1 tablespoon toasted sunflower seeds
½ cup fat-free milk

1. Combine flour, baking powder, and salt in medium bowl. Cut in margarine with pastry blender until mixture resembles coarse crumbs; Mix in sunflower seeds and milk to form a soft dough.

BRUNSWICK STEW

Serve with warm Vinegar Biscuits (see p. 660) for real down-home taste.

4 entrée servings

1 pound boneless, skinless chicken breast, cubed (1-inch)

½ cup each: chopped onion, green bell pepper

⅛–¼ teaspoon crushed red pepper

2 tablespoons canola oil

3 tablespoons flour

2 cups reduced-sodium fat-free chicken broth

1 can (15 ounces) butter beans, rinsed, drained

1 can (14½ ounces) diced tomatoes, undrained

1 cup whole kernel corn

½ cup sliced fresh or frozen okra

Salt and pepper, to taste

Per Serving:
Calories: 348
% calories from fat: 27
Protein (g): 30.6
Carbohydrate (g): 37.5
Fat (g): 11.3
Saturated fat (g): 2.6
Cholesterol (mg): 51.7
Sodium (mg): 630

Exchanges:
Milk: 0.0
Vegetable: 1.0
Fruit: 0.0
Bread: 2.0
Meat: 3.0
Fat: 0.5

1. Cook chicken, onion, bell pepper, and crushed red pepper in oil in large saucepan until lightly browned, about 10 minutes. Sprinkle with flour and cook 2 minutes. Stir in remaining ingredients, except salt and pepper; heat to boiling. Reduce heat and simmer, covered, until chicken is cooked and okra is tender, about 20 minutes. Season to taste with salt and pepper.

CHICKEN AND MASHED POTATO STEW

Mounds of cheesy mashed potatoes top this hearty stew.

4 entrée servings

1 pound boneless, skinless chicken breast,
  cubed (1-inch)

Flour

1 tablespoon canola oil

½ cup each: chopped onion, carrot, celery, frozen
  peas

1½ cups reduced-sodium fat-free chicken broth

½ teaspoon each: dried rosemary and thyme leaves

Salt and pepper, to taste

2 cups (½ recipe) Real Mashed Potatoes (see p. 595)

1 egg yolk

½ cup (2 ounces) shredded reduced-fat Cheddar cheese

1-2 tablespoons melted margarine or butter

Per Serving:
Calories: 378
% calories from fat: 26
Protein (g): 29.9
Carbohydrate (g): 35.1
Fat (g): 10.7
Saturated fat (g): 2.1
Cholesterol (mg): 122.4
Sodium (mg): 420

Exchanges:
Milk: 0.0
Vegetable: 1.0
Fruit: 0.0
Bread: 2.0
Meat: 3.0
Fat: 1.0

1. Coat chicken with flour; cook in oil in large saucepan over medium heat until browned, about 8 minutes. Add vegetables, broth, and herbs and heat to boiling; reduce heat and simmer, covered, until vegetables are tender and chicken is cooked, about 15 minutes. Season to taste with salt and pepper.

2. Make Real Mashed Potatoes, mixing in egg yolk and cheese. Spoon potato mixture into 4 mounds on greased cookie sheet and refrigerate until chilled, about 30 minutes. Drizzle potatoes with margarine; bake at 425 degrees until browned, about 15 minutes. Top bowls of stew with potatoes.

APRICOT CHICKEN STEW

Apricot jam and Dijon mustard flavor the wine sauce for this stew.

6 entrée servings

6 boneless, skinless chicken breast halves
  (4 ounces each), quartered

⅓ cup all-purpose flour

1 teaspoon paprika

⅓ cup each: finely chopped carrots, ribs celery,
  sliced green onions

2 tablespoons margarine or butter

½ cup each: reduced-fat fat-free chicken broth, dry
  white wine or chicken broth, apricot jam

2 tablespoons Dijon mustard

1 teaspoon dried rosemary leaves, crushed

½ cup petite peas

Salt and pepper, to taste

4 cups cooked rice, warm

Per Serving:
Calories: 433
% calories from fat: 12
Protein (g): 31
Carbohydrate (g): 57
Fat (g): 5.7
Saturated fat (g): 1.2
Cholesterol (mg): 65.7
Sodium (mg): 299

Exchanges:
Milk: 0.0
Vegetable: 0.0
Fruit: 0.0
Bread: 4.0
Meat: 3.0
Fat: 0.0

1. Coat chicken with combined flour and paprika. Cook chicken, carrots, celery, and green onions in margarine in large skillet until chicken is browned, 5 to 8 minutes. Stir in combined broth, wine, jam, mustard, and rosemary; heat to boiling. Reduce heat and simmer, covered, until chicken is cooked, about 20 minutes, adding peas during last 5 minutes. Season to taste with salt and pepper; serve over rice.

CHICKEN STEW PAPRIKASH

Lean veal can be substituted for the chicken in this recipe.

4 entrée servings

1 pound boneless, skinless chicken breast, cubed (¾-inch)

1 tablespoon margarine or butter

1 cup each: chopped onion, mushrooms

4 cloves garlic, minced

2 tablespoons flour

¾ cup reduced-sodium chicken broth

¼ cup dry white wine or chicken broth

1 cup chopped tomato

1 teaspoon paprika

½ cup fat-free sour cream

Salt and white pepper, to taste

3 cups cooked noodles, warm

Per Serving:
Calories: 416
% calories from fat: 18
Protein (g): 35.9
Carbohydrate (g): 47.9
Fat (g): 8.4
Saturated fat (g): 1.4
Cholesterol (mg): 69
Sodium (mg): 139

Exchanges:
Milk: 0.0
Vegetable: 1.0
Fruit: 0.0
Bread: 3.0
Meat: 3.0
Fat: 0.0

1. Cook chicken in margarine in large saucepan until browned, 8 to 10 minutes; add onion, mushrooms, and garlic and cook 5 minutes. Stir in flour and cook 1 minute. Add broth, wine, tomato, and paprika and heat to boiling; reduce heat and simmer, covered, until chicken is tender, 15 to 20 minutes. Stir in sour cream and cook until hot, 2 to 3 minutes. Season to taste with salt and white pepper; serve over noodles.

CHICKEN VERONIQUE

Red and green seedless grapes add flavor and color to the company fare.

4 entrée servings

1 pound chicken tenders, halved

⅓ cup thinly sliced leek (white part only) or green onions

2 cloves garlic, minced

1 tablespoon canola oil

2 tablespoons flour

2 cups reduced-sodium fat-free chicken broth

¼ cup dry white wine (optional)

½ teaspoon dried tarragon leaves

½ cup each: halved red and green seedless grapes

Salt and pepper, to taste

Per Serving:
Calories: 340
% calories from fat: 15
Protein (g): 28.5
Carbohydrate (g): 17.9
Fat (g): 4.9
Saturated fat (g): 0.6
Cholesterol (mg): 65.7
Sodium (mg): 274

Exchanges:
Milk: 0.0
Vegetable: 0.0
Fruit: 0.0
Bread: 1.0
Meat: 3.0
Fat: 2.0

1. Cook chicken, garlic, and green onions in oil in large skillet over medium heat until chicken is browned, about 5 minutes; sprinkle with flour and cook 1 minute. Add broth, wine, and tarragon and heat to boiling; reduce heat and simmer, covered, until chicken is tender, about 15 minutes, adding grapes during last 5 minutes. Season to taste with salt and pepper.

SLOW-COOKER COUNTRY CHICKEN STEW

This stew is also delicious served on squares of cornbread (see Index).

6 entrée servings

1 cup fat-free chicken broth
1 can (6 ounces) tomato paste
1 cup each: chopped onion, green bell pepper
2 cups coarsely chopped cabbage
2 large garlic cloves, minced
1 bay leaf
1 tablespoon each: lemon juice, Worcestershire
   sauce, sugar
2 teaspoons each: dried basil leaves, Dijon mustard
3–4 drops hot pepper sauce
1½ pounds boneless, skinless chicken breasts,
   cubed (2-inch)
Salt and pepper, to taste
1 cup rice, cooked, warm

Per Serving:
Calories: 217
% calories from fat: 7
Protein (g): 29.5
Carbohydrate (g): 20.5
Fat (g): 1.7
Saturated fat (g): 0.4
Cholesterol (mg): 65.7
Sodium (mg): 430

Exchanges:
Milk: 0.0
Vegetable: 1.0
Fruit: 0.0
Bread: 1.0
Meat: 3.0
Fat: 0.0

1. Combine chicken broth and tomato paste in slow cooker; stir in remaining ingredients, except salt, pepper, and rice; cover and cook on High 1 hour. Change setting to low and cook 5 to 6 hours. Discard bay leaf; season to taste with salt and pepper. Serve over rice.

SLOW-COOKER BURGUNDY CHICKEN STEW

Serve with a green salad and warm bread to complete the meal.

6 entrée servings

1 chicken (about 2½ pounds), cut up

⅔ cup sliced green onions

18 pearl onions, peeled

8 ounces whole medium mushrooms

1 clove garlic, crushed

½ teaspoon dried thyme leaves

6 small new potatoes, unpeeled, scrubbed

1 cup each: reduced-sodium fat-free chicken broth, Burgundy wine or reduced-sodium fat-free chicken broth

Salt and pepper, to taste

Per Serving:
Calories: 292
% calories from fat: 16
Protein (g): 24.2
Carbohydrate (g): 30.5
Fat (g): 5.2
Saturated fat (g): 1.4
Cholesterol (mg): 60.2
Sodium (mg): 91

Exchanges:
Milk: 0.0
Vegetable: 0.0
Fruit: 0.0
Bread: 2.0
Meat: 3.0
Fat: 0.0

1. Cook chicken and green onions in large skillet over medium heat until chicken is browned, about 10 minutes. Place in slow cooker with remaining ingredients, except wine, salt and pepper. Cover and cook on Low 8 to 10 hours, adding wine during last hour. Season to taste with salt and pepper.

SLOW-COOKER CHICKEN AND MUSHROOM STEW

One nice feature of the slow cooker is that mushrooms develop a rich, hearty flavor without sautéing. Be sure to use large, bone-in chicken breasts, as small ones will cook too quickly.

4 entrée servings

1¼ cups reduced-sodium fat-free chicken broth

1 can (6 ounces) tomato paste

1 tablespoon Worcestershire sauce

1 large onion, chopped

2 each: minced garlic cloves, coarsely shredded
    large carrots

8 ounces mushrooms, sliced

1 bay leaf

4 large skinless chicken breast halves, fat trimmed

2 teaspoons dried Italian seasoning

¼ teaspoon dry mustard

Salt and pepper, to taste

8 ounces spaghetti, cooked, warm

Per Serving:
Calories: 338
% calories from fat: 6
Protein (g): 29.5
Carbohydrate (g): 41.4
Fat (g): 2.1
Saturated fat (g): 0.5
Cholesterol (mg): 54.3
Sodium (mg): 300

Exchanges:
Milk: 0.0
Vegetable: 0.0
Fruit: 0.0
Bread: 3.0
Meat: 3.0
Fat: 0.0

1. Combine broth, tomato paste, and Worcestershire sauce in slow cooker; stir in remaining ingredients, except salt, pepper, and spaghetti. Cover and cook on High 1 hour. Change setting to Low and cook 5 to 6 hours. Remove chicken and cut into bite-size pieces, discarding bones; stir back into slow cooker. Discard bay leaf; season to taste with salt. Serve over spaghetti.

COQ AU VIN

This easy version of the French classic can be assembled in advance and refrigerated if you like; increase baking time by 15 minutes.

6 entrée servings

6 boneless, skinless chicken breast halves (4 ounces each), cut into halves

4 slices reduced-sodium bacon, diced

3 green onions, sliced

12 pearl onions, peeled, halved

8 ounces whole small mushrooms

6 small new potatoes, halved

1 teaspoon minced garlic

½ teaspoon each: dried thyme leaves, salt

¼ teaspoon pepper

½ cup each: chicken broth, Burgundy wine or chicken broth

Per Serving:
Calories: 343
% calories from fat: 13
Protein (g): 31.2
Carbohydrate (g): 39.3
Fat (g): 4.9
Saturated fat (g): 1.5
Cholesterol (mg): 73.2
Sodium (mg): 357

Exchanges:
Milk: 0.0
Vegetable: 1.0
Fruit: 0.0
Bread: 2.0
Meat: 3.0
Fat: 0.0

1. Place chicken and bacon in 2½-quart casserole. Add remaining ingredients, except broth and wine; pour broth and wine over. Bake, covered, at 325 degrees until chicken and potatoes are tender, 1 to 1½ hours.

CHICKEN STEW VERONIQUE

45 *No one will guess this elegant dish is so easy to prepare!*

4 entrée servings

1 cup sliced mushrooms

2 tablespoons each: sliced green onions, vegetable oil

1 pound boneless, skinless chicken breast, cubed

1 tablespoon flour

¼ cup dry white wine or chicken broth

1 cup each: reduced-sodium fat-free chicken broth, halved seedless green grapes

1 tablespoon drained capers

Salt and pepper, to taste

2 cups cooked rice, warm

Per Serving:
Calories: 341
% calories from fat: 27
Protein (g): 29.6
Carbohydrate (g): 28.8
Fat (g): 10.1
Saturated fat (g): 1.8
Cholesterol (mg): 69
Sodium (mg): 184

Exchanges:
Milk: 0.0
Vegetable: 0.0
Fruit: 0.5
Bread: 1.5
Meat: 3.0
Fat: 0.5

1. Sauté mushrooms and green onions in oil in large skillet until tender, about 5 minutes; add chicken and cook until browned, about 5 minutes. Sprinkle with flour and cook 1 minute. Stir in wine and broth; heat to boiling. Reduce heat and simmer, covered, until chicken is cooked, about 20 minutes, adding grapes and capers during last 5 minutes; season to taste with salt and pepper. Serve over rice.

45-MINUTE PREPARATION TIP: Begin cooking rice before preparing the rest of the recipe.

TARRAGON-MUSTARD CHICKEN STEW

Tarragon and mustard team up to give this chicken its tangy flavor.

4 entrée servings

1 pound boneless, skinless chicken breast, cubed

1 cup chopped onion

2 large ribs celery, chopped

2 teaspoons olive oil

1½ cups fat-free chicken broth

2 tablespoons Dijon mustard

2 teaspoons brown sugar

1 teaspoon lemon juice

2½ teaspoons dried tarragon leaves

2 teaspoons cornstarch

¼ cup water

Salt and pepper, to taste

1 cup rice, cooked, warm

Per Serving:
Calories: 252
% calories from fat: 17
Protein (g): 29.6
Carbohydrate (g): 19.7
Fat (g): 4.3
Saturated fat (g): 0.9
Cholesterol (mg): 75.1
Sodium (mg): 396

Exchanges:
Milk: 0.0
Vegetable: 0.0
Fruit: 0.0
Bread: 1.0
Meat: 3.0
Fat: 0.0

1. Sauté chicken, onion, and celery in oil in large saucepan until lightly browned, about 10 minutes. Add broth, mustard, sugar, lemon juice, and tarragon; heat to boiling. Reduce heat and simmer, covered, until chicken is cooked, about 20 minutes. Heat to boiling; stir in combined cornstarch and water, stirring, until thickened, 1 to 2 minutes. Season to taste with salt and pepper; serve over rice.

HONEY-MUSTARD CHICKEN STEW

The honey-mustard flavor of this delicious chicken recipe is enhanced by the addition of curry powder.

4 entrée servings

1 pound boneless, skinless chicken breast, cubed

1 cup chopped onion

2 teaspoons olive oil

1¾ cups reduced-sodium fat-free chicken broth

2 tablespoons honey

1 tablespoon Dijon mustard

1–2 teaspoons curry powder

2 cups small cauliflower florets

1 large carrot, thinly sliced

Salt and pepper, to taste

1 cups rice, cooked, warm

Per Serving:
Calories: 276
% calories from fat: 13
Protein (g): 30.3
Carbohydrate (g): 28.6
Fat (g): 4.0
Saturated fat (g): 0.8
Cholesterol (mg): 65.8
Sodium (mg): 430

1. Cook chicken and onion in oil in large saucepan over medium heat until chicken is lightly browned, about 8 minutes. Add remaining ingredients, except salt, pepper, and rice, and heat to boiling. Reduce heat and simmer, covered, until chicken is tender, 15 to 20 minutes. Simmer, uncovered, until stew has thickened to desired consistency, 5 to 10 minutes. Season to taste with salt and pepper; serve over rice.

Exchanges:
Milk: 0.0
Vegetable: 0.0
Fruit: 0.0
Bread: 2.0
Meat: 3.0
Fat: 0.0

ORANGE CHICKEN AND VEGETABLE STEW

Both orange juice and zest are used to accent this flavorful stew.

6 entrée servings

6 boneless, skinless chicken breast halves
  (4 ounces each)

1 large onion, sliced

2 cloves garlic, chopped

1 tablespoon flour

3 medium tomatoes, chopped

½ teaspoon each: dried marjoram and thyme leaves

1 piece cinnamon stick (1-inch)

1½ cups orange juice

2 teaspoons grated orange zest

2 large carrots, thickly sliced

3 medium potatoes, unpeeled, cubed

Salt and pepper, to taste

Per Serving:
Calories: 318
% calories from fat: 10
Protein (g): 29.4
Carbohydrate (g): 42.4
Fat (g): 3.5
Saturated fat (g): 0.9
Cholesterol (mg): 69
Sodium (mg): 87

Exchanges:
Milk: 0.0
Vegetable: 2.0
Fruit: 0.5
Bread: 1.5
Meat: 2.5
Fat: 0.0

1. Cook chicken in lightly greased Dutch oven over medium heat until browned, about 5 minutes on each side. Remove chicken from Dutch oven. Add onion and garlic to Dutch oven and sauté until tender, 5 to 8 minutes. Stir in flour and cook 1 to 2 minutes. Add chicken and remaining ingredients, except salt and pepper; heat to boiling. Reduce heat and simmer, covered, until chicken is cooked and vegetables are tender, about 20 minutes. Season to taste with salt and pepper.

CHICKEN AND PASTA STEW MARENGO

The orange-scented tomato sauce, lightly seasoned with herbs and wine, benefits from day-ahead preparation, giving flavors an opportunity to meld.

6 entrée servings

6 small boneless, skinless chicken breast halves
  (4 ounces each), quartered
Flour
1 tablespoon olive oil
1 small onion, chopped
3 cloves garlic, minced
1 can (14½ ounces) reduced-sodium chicken broth
½ cup dry white wine or chicken broth
2 cups sliced mushrooms
3 tablespoons tomato paste
2 tablespoons grated orange zest
1 teaspoon each: dried tarragon and thyme leaves
Salt and pepper, to taste
12 ounces pappardelle or other wide flat pasta, cooked, warm

Per Serving:
Calories: 343
% calories from fat: 16
Protein (g): 25 4
Carbohydrate (g): 42.7
Fat (g): 6.1
Saturated fat (g): 1.1
Cholesterol (mg): 43.5
Sodium (mg): 133

Exchanges:
Milk: 0.0
Vegetable: 1.0
Fruit: 0.0
Bread: 2.5
Meat: 2.5
Fat: 0.0

1. Coat chicken lightly with flour. Cook in oil in Dutch oven over medium heat until browned, about 5 minutes; add onion and garlic and cook until tender, 3 to 4 minutes. Add chicken broth, wine, mushrooms, tomato paste, orange zest, and herbs; heat to boiling. Reduce heat and simmer, covered, until chicken is cooked, about 20 minutes. Cook uncovered until thickened to desired consistency, about 10 minutes. Season to taste with salt and pepper; serve over pasta.

CHICKEN STEW WITH SPINACH RICE

Spinach Rice is a flavorful accompaniment to this French-style stew.

6 entrée servings

1 chicken (about 2 pounds), cut up

½–1 tablespoon olive oil

1 each: chopped medium onion, clove garlic

1 tablespoon flour

1 cup each: reduced-sodium fat-free chicken broth,
   sliced mushrooms

¼ cup pitted black olives

8 medium tomatoes, seeded, coarsely chopped

1 can (6 ounces) reduced-sodium tomato paste

½ teaspoon each: dried basil, tarragon, and
   oregano leaves

Generous pinch ground nutmeg

2 medium zucchini, sliced

1 medium red bell pepper, sliced

Salt and pepper, to taste

Spinach Rice (recipe follows)

Per Serving:
Calories: 491
% calories from fat: 29
Protein (g): 33.3
Carbohydrate (g): 54.7
Fat (g): 16.4
Saturated fat (g): 3.6
Cholesterol (mg): 67.5
Sodium (mg): 417

Exchanges:
Milk: 0.0
Vegetable: 2.0
Fruit: 0.0
Bread: 2.5
Meat: 4.0
Fat: 1.0

1. Cook chicken in oil in large skillet over medium heat until browned on all sides, about 10 minutes. Add onion and garlic and cook 3 minutes; stir in flour and cook 1 minute. Stir in broth, mushrooms, olives, tomatoes, tomato paste, and herbs; heat to boiling. Reduce heat and simmer, covered, until chicken is cooked, 30 to 40 minutes, adding zucchini and bell pepper during last 10 minutes. Season to taste with salt and pepper. Serve over Spinach Rice.

Spinach Rice

Makes 4 cups

¼ cup chopped onion

1¼ cups uncooked rice

2½ cups reduced-sodium fat-free chicken broth

2 cups packed spinach leaves, sliced

1. Sauté onion lightly greased medium saucepan until tender, 2 to 3 minutes; stir in rice and broth and heat to boiling. Reduce heat and simmer, covered, until rice is tender, about 25 minutes, stirring in spinach during last 10 minutes.

MEDITERRANEAN CHICKEN STEW

Wine, balsamic vinegar, black olives, and rosemary blend to create a Mediterranean flavor.

6 entrée servings

6 skinless chicken breast halves (6 ounces each)
1½ cups reduced-sodium fat-free chicken broth
½ cup dry white wine or chicken broth
¼ cup balsamic vinegar
8 ounces small mushrooms
6 plum tomatoes, seeded, chopped
¼ cup halved black or Greek olives
3 cloves garlic, minced
1½ teaspoons each: dried rosemary and thyme leaves
Salt and pepper, to taste

Per Serving:
Calories: 201
% calories from fat: 11
Protein (g): 29.5
Carbohydrate (g): 11.2
Fat (g): 2.4
Saturated fat (g): 0.6
Cholesterol (mg): 65.7
Sodium (mg): 258

Exchanges:
Milk: 0.0
Vegetable: 0.0
Fruit: 0.0
Bread: 1.0
Meat: 3.0
Fat: 0.0

1. Cook chicken breasts in lightly greased Dutch oven until browned on all sides, about 10 minutes. Add remaining ingredients, except salt and pepper; heat to boiling. Reduce heat and simmer, covered, until chicken is cooked, 30 to 40 minutes. Simmer, uncovered, if thicker consistency is desired, about 10 minutes. Season to taste with salt and pepper.

HUNTER'S STEW

Any game brought back from the hunt was used in this stew of Italian origin; serve over pasta or rice.

4 entrée servings

1 pound boneless, skinless chicken breast, cubed (1-inch)
¼ cup all-purpose flour
1½ tablespoons olive oil
2 medium onions, chopped
1 medium carrot, coarsely diced
1 cup each: diced red and green bell pepper
2 large garlic cloves, minced

1 can (14½ ounces) reduced-sodium Italian-style diced tomatoes, undrained

1½–2 cups reduced-sodium fat-free chicken broth

¼ cup each: tomato paste, water

¾ teaspoon each: dried thyme and marjoram leaves

Salt and pepper, to taste

Per Serving:
Calories: 291
% calories from fat: 24
Protein (g): 32.1
Carbohydrate (g): 23.8
Fat (g): 7.9
Saturated fat (g): 1.5
Cholesterol (mg): 73.6
Sodium (mg): 393

Exchanges:
Milk: 0.0
Vegetable: 3.0
Fruit: 0.0
Bread: 0.5
Meat: 3.5
Fat: 0.0

1. Coat chicken with flour; sauté in oil in Dutch oven until browned, about 8 minutes. Stir in onions, carrot, bell peppers, and garlic; sauté until vegetables are tender, about 5 minutes. Add remaining ingredients, except salt and pepper; heat to boiling. Reduce heat and simmer, covered, until chicken is tender, about 25 minutes. Season to taste with salt and pepper.

TUSCAN CHICKEN STEW

Serve this hearty Tuscan stew over rice or pasta.

6 entrée servings

1 cup boiling fat-free chicken broth

1 ounce dried porcini or shiitake mushrooms

1½ pounds boneless, skinless chicken breast halves, cubed (1-inch)

¾ cup chopped onion

3 cloves garlic, minced

2 tablespoons each: olive oil, flour

½ cup dry white wine or reduced-sodium fat-free chicken broth

1 can (14 ounces) Italian-seasoned diced tomatoes, undrained

1 can (15 ounces) cannellini or other white beans, rinsed, drained

Salt and pepper, to taste

Per Serving:
Calories: 233
% calories from fat: 29
Protein (g): 28.3
Carbohydrate (g): 9.2
Fat (g): 7.5
Saturated fat (g): 1.4
Cholesterol (mg): 69
Sodium (mg): 439

Exchanges:
Milk: 0.0
Vegetable: 2.0
Fruit: 0.0
Bread: 0.0
Meat: 3.0
Fat: 0.0

1. Pour broth over mushrooms in small bowl; let stand until softened, about 10 minutes. Drain mushrooms; strain and reserved broth. Slice mushrooms, discarding any tough pieces.

2. Cook chicken in oil in large skillet over medium heat until browned, about 5 minutes; sprinkle with flour and cook 1 minute. Stir in wine, tomatoes with liquid, beans, reserved broth, and mushrooms; heat to boiling. Reduce heat and simmer, covered, until chicken is cooked, about 20 minutes. Cook, uncovered, if thicker consistency is desired, 5 to 10 minutes; season to taste with salt and pepper.

CHICKEN STEW PEPERONATA

Serve this very simple but delicious Tuscan stew over rice or your favorite pasta.

4 entrée servings

1 pound boneless, skinless chicken breast, cubed (1-inch)
½ teaspoon minced garlic
1 tablespoon olive oil
1 cup each: sliced onion, red and green bell pepper
1 can (14½ ounces) chunky Italian-seasoned crushed tomatoes
Salt and pepper, to taste
2 tablespoons grated Parmesan cheese

Per Serving:
Calories: 215
% calories from fat: 29
Protein (g): 28.5
Carbohydrate (g): 9.7
Fat (g): 7
Saturated fat (g): 1.8
Cholesterol (mg): 71
Sodium (mg): 674

Exchanges:
Milk: 0.0
Vegetable: 2.0
Fruit: 0.0
Bread: 0.0
Meat: 3.0
Fat: 0.0

1. Cook chicken and garlic in oil in large skillet over medium heat until lightly browned; remove from skillet. Add onion and bell peppers to skillet and sauté until softened, 3 to 4 minutes; reduce heat to medium-low and cook until very soft, 10 to 15 minutes. Stir in chicken and tomatoes and heat to boiling; reduce heat and simmer, covered, until chicken is cooked, about 10 minutes. Season to taste with salt and pepper; sprinkle with Parmesan cheese.

CHICKEN AND PASTA SKILLET STEW

Sun-dried tomatoes and black olives lend an earthy flavor to this colorful stew.

4 entrée servings

½ cup each: chopped onion, green bell pepper

1 tablespoon olive oil

1 pound boneless, skinless chicken breast, cubed (1-inch)

2 tablespoons flour

4 ounces rigatoni, cooked

1 can (14½ ounces) Italian-seasoned diced tomatoes, undrained

¾ cup chicken broth

1 teaspoon dried marjoram leaves

3 tablespoons chopped sun-dried tomatoes (not in oil)

¼ cup chopped, pitted Greek olives, halved

1 large zucchini, cubed

Salt and pepper, to taste

Per Serving:
Calories: 330
% calories from fat: 25
Protein (g): 30.9
Carbohydrate (g): 30.7
Fat (g): 9.1
Saturated fat (g): 1.6
Cholesterol (mg): 69
Sodium (mg): 761

Exchanges:
Milk: 0.0
Vegetable: 1.0
Fruit: 0.0
Bread: 2.0
Meat: 3.0
Fat: 0.0

1. Sauté onion and bell pepper in olive oil in large skillet until tender, about 5 minutes; add chicken and cook, until browned, about 5 minutes. Stir in flour; cook 1 to 2 minutes. Stir in remaining ingredients, except zucchini, salt, and pepper. Heat to boiling; reduce heat and simmer, covered, until chicken is cooked, about 20 minutes, adding zucchini during last 10 minutes. Season to taste with salt and pepper.

TOMATO-CHICKEN STEW

This recipe is great served over rice or Herbed Polenta (see p. 661).

6 entrée servings

1½ pounds boneless, skinless chicken breast, cubed
1 cup sliced onion
2 cloves garlic, minced
1 tablespoon canola oil
1 can (14½ ounces) diced tomatoes, undrained
1½ cups reduced-sodium fat-free chicken broth
¼ cup low-sodium tomato paste
½ cup dry white wine or chicken broth
2 teaspoons lemon juice
1 bay leaf
½ teaspoon dried oregano leaves
¼ teaspoon dried thyme leaves
2 cups sliced mushrooms
1 can (15 ounces) Great Northern beans, rinsed, drained
Salt and pepper, to taste

Per Serving:
Calories: 253
% calories from fat: 19
Protein (g): 32
Carbohydrate (g): 18.1
Fat (g): 5.5
Saturated fat (g): 1
Cholesterol (mg): 69
Sodium (mg): 659

Exchanges:
Milk: 0.0
Vegetable: 1.0
Fruit: 0.0
Bread: 1.0
Meat: 3.0
Fat: 0.0

1. Cook chicken, onion, and garlic in oil in Dutch oven over medium heat until chicken is browned, about 10 minutes. Add remaining ingredients, except salt and pepper; heat to boiling. Reduce heat and simmer, covered, until chicken is cooked, about 20 minutes. Simmer, uncovered, if thicker consistency is desired, about 10 minutes. Discard bay leaf; season to taste with salt and pepper.

STEWED CHICKEN MARINARA

Team this stew with Focaccia (see p. 641) and a salad for an easy Italian meal.

4 entrée servings

1½ cups chopped onions
½ cup each: finely chopped celery, carrot
2 cloves garlic, minced
1 pound boneless, skinless chicken breast, cubed

1 teaspoon dried Italian seasoning

1 can (14½ ounces) crushed tomatoes

1 cup each: chopped zucchini, quartered mushrooms

Salt and pepper, to taste

8 ounces ziti, cooked, warm

Per Serving:
Calories: 356
% calories from fat: 16
Protein (g): 28.1
Carbohydrate (g): 48.6
Fat (g): 6.8
Saturated fat (g): 1.5
Cholesterol (mg): 51.7
Sodium (mg): 544

Exchanges:
Milk: 0.0
Vegetable: 2 0
Fruit: 0.0
Bread: 2.0
Meat: 3.0
Fat: 0.0

1. Cook onions, celery, carrot, garlic, and chicken in lightly greased large saucepan over medium heat until vegetables are tender, about 8 minutes. Add Italian seasoning, tomatoes, zucchini, and mushrooms; heat to boiling. Reduce heat and simmer, covered, until chicken is cooked, about 20 minutes. Simmer, uncovered, if thicker consistency is desired, about 10 minutes. Season to taste with salt and pepper; serve over ziti.

CHICKEN, MUSHROOM, AND TOMATO STEW WITH POLENTA

To simplify preparation, 1 pound boneless, skinless chicken breast can be used; cut into 1-inch pieces. Cooking time will be about 20 minutes.

4 entrée servings

1 medium onion, chopped

2 garlic cloves, minced

2 teaspoons olive oil

8 ounces mushrooms, sliced

1 large carrot, thinly sliced

2 cans (14½ ounces each) Italian plum tomatoes, undrained, coarsely chopped

1 can (8 ounces) tomato sauce

2 tablespoons tomato paste

1 teaspoon each: sugar, dried basil and thyme leaves

2¼ pounds skinless chicken breast, fat trimmed

Salt and pepper, to taste

Microwave Polenta (see p. 530)

Per Serving:
Calories: 403
% calories from fat: 17
Protein (g): 38
Carbohydrate (g): 46
Fat (g) 7.8
Saturated fat (g): 1.9
Cholesterol (mg): 85
Sodium (mg): 691

Exchanges:
Milk: 0.0
Vegetable: 3.0
Fruit: 0.0
Bread: 1.5
Meat: 4.0
Fat: 0.0

1. Sauté onion and garlic in oil in Dutch oven until onion is tender, about 5 minutes. Add remaining ingredients, except salt, pepper, and Microwave Polenta; heat to boiling. Reduce heat and simmer, covered, until chicken is cooked, 35 to 45 minutes. Remove chicken and cut meat into ½-inch pieces, discarding bones. Return chicken to Dutch oven; season to taste with salt and pepper. Serve over Microwave Polenta.

Microwave Polenta

Makes about 3 cups

1⅓ cups yellow cornmeal

½ teaspoon salt

3 cups water

1 cup 1% low-fat milk

1 medium onion, diced

1. Combine all ingredients in 2½-quart glass casserole. Cook, uncovered, on High power 8 to 9 minutes, whisking halfway through cooking time. Whisk until smooth, cover, and cook on High 6 to 7 minutes. Remove from microwave, whisk, and let stand, covered, 3 to 4 minutes.

CHICKEN CACCIATORE

This stew was made from any game brought back from the day's hunting and would vary slightly from kitchen to kitchen.

4 entrée servings

8 ounces each: boneless, skinless chicken
  breast, thighs

2 teaspoons dried oregano leaves

½ teaspoon garlic powder

3 cups quartered mushrooms

1 cup each: chopped onion, green bell pepper

6 cloves garlic, minced

2 cans (14½ ounces each) reduced-sodium diced
  tomatoes, undrained

½ cup dry red wine or water

1 bay leaf

4 teaspoons cornstarch

Per Serving:
Calories: 411
% calories from fat: 15
Protein (g): 30.9
Carbohydrate (g): 53.7
Fat (g): 7.2
Saturated fat (g): 1.7
Cholesterol (mg): 65.5
Sodium (mg): 199

Exchanges:
Milk: 0.0
Vegetable: 4.0
Fruit: 0.0
Bread: 2.0
Meat: 3.0
Fat: 0.0

¼ cup water

Salt and pepper, to taste

3 cups cooked noodles, warm

1. Cut chicken into large pieces; sprinkle chicken with combined oregano and garlic powder and cook in lightly greased large Dutch oven over medium heat until browned, 5 to 8 minutes. Remove from pan. Add mushrooms, onion, bell pepper, and garlic to Dutch oven; sauté until mushrooms are softened, 3 to 4 minutes. Add chicken, tomatoes with liquid, wine, and bay leaf; heat to boiling. Reduce heat and simmer, covered, until chicken is cooked, about 30 minutes. Heat to boiling; stir in combined cornstarch and water, stirring until thickened, about 1 minute. Discard bay leaf; season to taste with salt and pepper and serve over noodles.

CHICKEN STEW WITH WHITE WINE

Serve this stew with rice and Italian bread to soak up the delicious broth.

4 entrée servings

4 boneless, skinless chicken breast halves

2 teaspoons olive oil

1 medium onion, chopped

2 large garlic cloves, minced

2 tablespoons flour

¾ cup each: reduced-sodium fat-free chicken broth, dry white wine or chicken broth

1 cup each: small broccoli florets, cubed yellow summer squash

1 bay leaf

1 teaspoon each: dried oregano and thyme leaves

Salt and pepper, to taste

Per Serving:
Calories: 224
% calories from fat: 16
Protein (g): 29.1
Carbohydrate (g): 8.3
Fat (g): 3.8
Saturated fat (g): 0.7
Cholesterol (mg): 68.5
Sodium (mg): 194

Exchanges:
Milk: 0.0
Vegetable: 1.0
Fruit: 0.0
Bread: 0.0
Meat: 3.0
Fat: 0.0

1. Cook chicken in oil in large skillet over medium heat until browned on both sides, about 8 minutes. Move chicken to side of skillet; add onion and garlic and sauté until tender, 3 to 4 minutes. Sprinkle with flour and cook 1 to 2 minutes. Add remaining ingredients, except salt and pepper; heat to boiling. Reduce heat and simmer, covered, until chicken is cooked and vegetables are tender, 15 to 20 minutes; simmer, uncovered, if thicker consistency is desired, 5 to 10 minutes. Discard bay leaf; season to taste with salt and pepper.

CHICKEN STEW, ROMAN-STYLE

Serve this delicious stew with Easy Herb Lavosh (see p. 644).

6 entrée servings

1 chicken (3 ½ pounds), cut into pieces
1 cup each: thinly sliced red and yellow bell pepper
3 cloves garlic, minced
1 tablespoon flour
¼ cup dry white wine or water
2 cans (28 ounces each) Italian plum tomatoes, undrained, chopped
2 tablespoons fresh or 1 tablespoon dried oregano leaves
Salt and pepper, to taste

Per Serving:
Calories: 208
% calories from fat: 33
Protein (g): 20.4
Carbohydrate (g): 13.6
Fat (g): 7.8
Saturated fat (g): 2.1
Cholesterol (mg): 52.3
Sodium (mg): 462

Exchanges:
Milk: 0.0
Vegetable: 2.5
Fruit: 0.0
Bread: 0.0
Meat: 2.5
Fat: 0.0

1. Cook chicken in lightly greased Dutch oven over medium heat until browned, about 10 minutes; remove from pan. Add bell peppers and garlic to Dutch oven and sauté until tender, about 8 minutes; sprinkle with flour and cook 1 minute. Add chicken, wine, tomatoes with liquid, and oregano; heat to boiling. Reduce heat and simmer, covered, until chicken is cooked, 35 to 45 minutes. Season to taste with salt and pepper.

MED-RIM CHICKEN STEW

Serve this excellent Mediterranean-style stew over Polenta (see p. 661).

4 entrée servings

1 pound boneless, skinless chicken breasts, cubed
(1½-inch)

½ cup chopped onion

1 cup sliced mushrooms

1 clove garlic, minced

1–2 tablespoons olive oil

2 tablespoons flour

1 cup reduced-sodium fat-free chicken broth

½ cup dry white wine or chicken broth

4 medium tomatoes, quartered

1 teaspoon each: dried thyme, rosemary, and
tarragon leaves

¼ cup sliced black or Greek olives

Salt and pepper, to taste

Per Serving:
Calories: 32.8
% calories from fat 27
Protein (g): 29
Carbohydrate (g): 20.9
Fat (g): 10
Saturated fat (g): 1.7
Cholesterol (mg): 69
Sodium (mg): 376

Exchanges:
Milk: 0.0
Vegetable: 2.0
Fruit: 0.0
Bread: 0.5
Meat: 3.0
Fat: 1.5

1. Cook chicken, onion, mushrooms, and garlic in oil in large skillet until chicken is browned, about 8 minutes; stir in flour and cook 1 to 2 minutes. Add remaining ingredients, except salt and pepper; heat to boiling. Reduce heat and simmer, covered, until chicken is cooked, about 20 minutes. Season to taste with salt and pepper.

CHICKEN VEGETABLE STEW WITH LENTILS

This healthy stew combines chicken and lentils with a medley of vegetables.

6 entrée servings

1 chicken (about 3 pounds), cut up

1 tablespoon canola oil

½ cup each: thickly sliced celery, carrots, broccoli stalks, chopped onion

2 cloves garlic, minced

2 cups fat-free chicken broth

1 can (14½ ounces) diced tomatoes, undrained

1 cup dried lentils

½ teaspoon dried marjoram leaves

3 slices bacon, cooked crisp, crumbled

Salt and pepper, to taste

Per Serving:
Calories: 344
% calories from fat: 18
Protein (g): 41.3
Carbohydrate (g): 24.6
Fat (g): 6.4
Saturated fat (g): 1.7
Cholesterol (mg): 104.5
Sodium (mg): 437

Exchanges:
Milk: 0.0
Vegetable: 0.0
Fruit: 0.0
Bread: 1.5
Meat: 4.0
Fat: 0.0

1. Sauté chicken in oil in Dutch oven until browned on all sides, about 10 minutes; remove. Add vegetables and garlic to Dutch oven and sauté until tender, about 5 minutes. Return chicken to pan and add broth, tomatoes with liquid, lentils, and marjoram; heat to boiling. Reduce heat and simmer, covered, until chicken and lentils are cooked, about 30 to 40 minutes. Stir in bacon; season to taste with salt and pepper.

MEXICAN CHICKEN, PORK, AND PINEAPPLE STEW

Enjoy flavor accents of tropical fruit, sweet cinnamon, and piquant ancho chili in this stew; serve over rice or couscous.

6 entrée servings

2 tablespoons slivered almonds

1 tablespoon sesame seeds

1 (1-inch) piece cinnamon stick

3 ancho chilies, seeds, and veins discarded, coarsely chopped

2 medium tomatoes, coarsely chopped

1 can (14½ ounces) reduced-sodium fat-free chicken broth, divided

12 ounces each: pork tenderloin and boneless skinless chicken breast, cubed (1½-inch)

1 cup each: fresh or canned pineapple chunks, sliced ripe plantain, cubed peeled jicama

Salt and pepper, to taste

Per Serving:
Calories: 239
% calories from fat: 22
Protein (g): 28.1
Carbohydrate (g): 19.6
Fat (g): 5.9
Saturated fat (g): 1.4
Cholesterol (mg): 67.2
Sodium (mg): 81

Exchanges:
Milk: 0.0
Vegetable: 1.0
Fruit: 1.0
Bread: 0.0
Meat: 3.0
Fat: 0.0

1. Cook almonds, sesame seeds, and cinnamon in lightly greased medium skillet over medium heat until browned, 3 to 4 minutes; remove from skillet. Add chilies and tomatoes to skillet and cook over medium heat until chilies are soft, 3 to 4 minutes. Process almond and chili mixtures and 1 cup broth in food processor or blender until smooth.

2. Sauté pork and chicken in lightly greased large saucepan until browned, about 5 minutes. Add chili mixture and remaining broth and heat to boiling. Reduce heat and simmer, covered, until meats are tender, about 30 minutes, adding fruit and jicama during last 10 minutes. Season to taste with salt and pepper.

GREEN SALSA CHICKEN STEW

The homemade Refried Black Beans are especially good, but canned can be substituted for convenience.

6 entrée servings

6 boneless, skinless chicken breast halves

1 tablespoon canola oil

⅓ cup chopped onion

1 clove garlic, chopped

2 cups mild or hot green salsa

3 cups packed sliced romaine lettuce leaves

1–1½ cups reduced-sodium fat-free chicken broth

¼ cup fat-free sour cream

1 tablespoon flour

¼ cup chopped cilantro

Salt and pepper, to taste

Refried Black Beans (recipe follows)

3 cups cooked rice, warm

Per Serving:
Calories: 459
% calories from fat: 13
Protein (g): 39.5
Carbohydrate (g): 57.9
Fat (g): 6.2
Saturated fat (g): 1.4
Cholesterol (mg): 73
Sodium (mg): 386

Exchanges:
Milk: 0.0
Vegetable: 0.0
Fruit: 0.0
Bread: 4.0
Meat: 3.0
Fat: 0.0

1. Cook chicken in oil in large skillet over medium heat until browned on both sides, about 8 minutes. Stir in onion and garlic; cook 2 minutes. Process salsa, lettuce, and 1 cup broth in food processor or blender until almost smooth. Add to skillet; heat to boiling. Reduce heat and simmer, covered, until chicken is cooked, about 30 minutes, adding remaining ½ cup broth if needed for desired consistency. Stir in combined sour cream and flour, stirring until thickened, about 1 minute. Stir in cilantro; season to taste with salt and pepper. Serve over Refried Black Beans and rice.

Refried Black Beans
Makes about 3 cups

1¼ cups dried black beans
½ cup chopped onion
Salt and pepper, to taste

1. Cover beans with 2 inches water in large saucepan; heat to boiling and boil, uncovered, 2 minutes. Let stand, covered, 1 hour. Drain beans; cover with 2 inches water and heat to boiling; reduce heat and simmer until tender, about 1 hour. Drain, reserving 2 cups liquid.

2. Sauté onion in lightly greased large skillet until tender, about 5 minutes. Add 1 cup beans and 1 cup reserved liquid to skillet. Cook over high heat, mashing beans until almost smooth with potato masher or meat mallet. Add half the remaining beans and liquid; continue cooking and mashing beans. Repeat with remaining beans and liquid. Season to taste with salt and pepper.

ISLAND CHICKEN STEW

This curried chicken stew is uniquely garnished with sliced plantain and cashews.

6 entrée servings

1½ pounds boneless, skinless chicken breast, cubed

¼ cup sliced green onions

2 tablespoons margarine or butter, divided

1½ cups reduced-sodium fat-free chicken broth

½ cup each: dried apples, apricots, raisins

2–3 teaspoons curry powder

⅛–¼ teaspoon crushed red pepper

2–3 teaspoons lime juice

Salt and pepper, to taste

1 ripe plantain or banana, sliced

4 cups cooked rice, warm

¼ cup chopped cashews

Per Serving:
Calories: 485
% calories from fat: 23
Protein (g): 26.2
Carbohydrate (g): 68.7
Fat (g): 12.6
Saturated fat (g): 28
Cholesterol (mg): 51.7
Sodium (mg): 147

Exchanges:
Milk: 0.0
Vegetable: 0.0
Fruit: 2.0
Bread: 2.5
Meat: 3.0
Fat: 0.5

1. Sauté chicken and green onions in 1 tablespoon margarine in large saucepan until chicken is browned, about 8 minutes. Add broth, dried fruit, curry powder, and red pepper; heat to boiling. Reduce heat and simmer, covered, until chicken is tender, about 20 minutes. Season to taste with lime juice, salt, and pepper. Sauté plantain in small skillet in remaining 1 tablespoon margarine. Serve stew over rice; top with sautéed plantain and cashews.

CARIBBEAN STEWED CHICKEN WITH BLACK BEANS

The flavors of the islands come alive in this chicken-and-black bean skillet dinner.

4 entrée servings

1 pound boneless, skinless chicken breast, cut into thin strips
1 medium onion, chopped
2 garlic cloves, minced
2 teaspoons olive oil
1 cup fat-free chicken broth
1 can (8 ounces) tomato sauce
2–4 tablespoons light rum (optional)
1 green bell pepper, diced
½ teaspoon ground cinnamon
¼ teaspoon ground cloves
1 can (16 ounces) black beans, rinsed, drained
Salt and cayenne pepper; to taste
1¼ cups rice, cooked, warm

Per Serving:
Calories 336
% calories from fat: 9
Protein (g): 20
Carbohydrate (g): 50
Fat (g): 3.4
Saturated fat (g): 1.0
Cholesterol (mg): 32
Sodium (mg): 390

Exchanges:
Milk: 0.0
Vegetable: 0.5
Fruit: 0.0
Bread: 3.0
Meat: 2.0
Fat: 0.0

1. Sauté chicken, onion, and garlic in oil in large skillet until browned, about 10 minutes. Add remaining ingredients, except black beans, salt, cayenne pepper, and rice, and heat to boiling. Reduce heat and simmer until chicken is tender, about 20 minutes. Add beans and simmer until hot, 2 to 3 minutes. Season to taste with salt and cayenne pepper; serve over rice.

CHICKEN STEW WITH ARTICHOKES

45

Serve Red Pepper Rice (see p. 571) as a flavorful complement to this chicken stew.

4 entrée servings

1 pound boneless, skinless chicken breast, cubed (1-inch)
⅓ cup each: chopped onion, thinly sliced celery
⅓ teaspoon dried oregano leaves

1 tablespoon olive oil

1 can (14½ ounces) petite diced tomatoes, undrained

½ can (15 ounces) quartered canned artichoke hearts

½ cup halved ripe olives

Salt and pepper, to taste

Per Serving:
Calories: 228
% calories from fat: 27
Protein (g): 29.3
Carbohydrate (g): 11.3
Fat (g): 6.8
Saturated fat (g): 1.1
Cholesterol (mg): 73
Sodium (mg): 223

1. Cook chicken, vegetables, and oregano in oil in large saucepan over medium heat until chicken is lightly browned, about 10 minutes. Add tomatoes with liquid, artichoke hearts, and olives and heat to boiling; reduce heat and simmer, covered, until chicken is cooked, about 20 minutes. Season to taste with salt and pepper.

Exchanges:
Milk: 0.0
Vegetable: 2.0
Fruit: 0.0
Bread: 0.0
Meat: 3.0
Fat: 0.0

SPANISH CHICKEN AND RICE STEW

The Spanish name of this dish, arroz con pollo, translates as "rice with chicken."

6 entrée servings

1 pound boneless, skinless chicken breast, cubed (1½-inch)

2 teaspoons olive oil

1 large onion, chopped

2 garlic cloves, minced

3 cups fat-free chicken broth

1 to 2 tablespoons dry sherry (optional)

1 each: diced large green and red bell pepper

¼ teaspoon crushed saffron threads (optional)

1¼ cups uncooked rice

1 cup frozen green peas

Salt and cayenne pepper, to taste

Per Serving:
Calories: 246
% calories from fat: 12
Protein (g): 15
Carbohydrate (g): 35
Fat (g): 3.1
Saturated fat (g): 1.0
Cholesterol (mg): 30
Sodium (mg): 255

Exchanges:
Milk: 0.0
Vegetable: 1.0
Fruit: 0.0
Bread: 2.0
Meat: 1.5
Fat: 0.0

1. Cook chicken in oil in Dutch oven over medium heat until lightly browned, 8 to 10 minutes. Add onion and garlic and cook until onion is tender, about 5 minutes. Add remaining ingredients, except peas, salt, and pepper and heat to boiling. Reduce heat and simmer, covered, until rice is tender, about 25 minutes, stirring in peas during last 5 minutes. Season to taste with salt and cayenne pepper.

PAELLA

Paella, a staple of Spanish cookery, was traditionally prepared with whatever the cook had on hand, so it can be made with a variety of ingredients.

4 entrée servings

8 ounces chicken tenders, halved

3 ounces Canadian bacon, cut into thin strips

1 large onion, chopped

2 garlic cloves, minced

2 teaspoons olive oil

2¾ cups reduced-sodium fat-free chicken broth

¼ teaspoon crushed saffron threads (optional)

1 can (14½ ounces) Italian-style diced
   tomatoes, undrained

1 can (14¾ ounces) artichoke hearts, drained, halved

1 each: diced large red and green bell pepper, diced

¾ teaspoon each: dried thyme and basil leaves

¼ teaspoon cayenne pepper

1¼ cups uncooked rice

8 ounces peeled, deveined medium shrimp

Salt and pepper, to taste

Per Serving:
Calories: 371
% calories from fat: 11
Protein (g): 28
Carbohydrate (g): 56
Fat (g): 4.6
Saturated fat (g): 1.2
Cholesterol (mg): 101
Sodium (mg): 678

Exchanges:
Milk: 0.0
Vegetable: 2.0
Fruit: 0.0
Bread: 3.0
Meat: 2.0
Fat: 0.0

1. Cook chicken, Canadian bacon, onion, and garlic in oil in Dutch oven over medium heat until lightly browned, about 10 minutes. Add remaining ingredients, except shrimp, salt, and pepper; heat to boiling. Reduce heat and simmer, covered, until rice is tender, about 25 minutes. Add shrimp and simmer until shrimp are cooked, about 5 minutes. Season to taste with salt and pepper.

CHICKEN STEW, CATALAN-STYLE

Lightly sautéed eggplant, zucchini, and bell peppers are added to this stew near the end of cooking time.

4 entrée servings

1 chicken (about 3 pounds), cut up

2 tomatoes, chopped

½ cup reduced-sodium fat-free chicken broth

½ cup dry white wine or chicken broth

½ cup tomato sauce

1 teaspoon dried basil leaves

1 cup finely chopped onion

1 small eggplant, cubed

1 cup each: sliced zucchini, chopped green or
red bell peppers

1 clove garlic, minced

¼ cup chopped cilantro

Salt and pepper, to taste

Per Serving:
Calories: 357
% calories from fat: 24
Protein (g): 39.8
Carbohydrate (g): 24.2
Fat (g): 9.6
Saturated fat (g): 2.6
Cholesterol (mg): 108.4
Sodium (mg): 294

Exchanges:
Milk: 0.0
Vegetable: 5.0
Fruit: 0.0
Bread: 0.0
Meat: 4.0
Fat: 0.0

1. Cook chicken in lightly greased Dutch oven over medium heat until browned on all sides, about 10 minutes; add tomatoes, broth, wine, tomato sauce, and basil. Heat to boiling; reduce heat and simmer, covered, until chicken is cooked, about 45 minutes.

2. Sauté vegetables and garlic in lightly greased large skillet until lightly browned, 10 to 12 minutes; add to Dutch oven during last 20 minutes that chicken is cooking. Stir in cilantro; season to taste with salt and pepper.

CHICKEN STEW ATHENOS

45 *Cinnamon, lemon, and feta cheese give this tomato-based stew the signature flavors of Greece.*

4 entrée servings

1 pound boneless, skinless chicken breast, cubed
(¾-inch)

1 teaspoon olive oil

1 can (14½ ounces) reduced-sodium stewed
tomatoes, undrained

1 tablespoon lemon juice

2 teaspoons minced garlic

1 each: cinnamon stick, bay leaf

½ cup chicken broth

1–2 tablespoons dry sherry (optional)

Salt and pepper, to taste

8 ounces egg noodles, cooked, warm

¼ cup (1 ounce) crumbled feta cheese

Per Serving:
Calories: 412
% calories from fat: 17
Protein (g): 34.4
Carbohydrate (g): 46
Fat (g): 7.9
Saturated fat (g): 2.5
Cholesterol (mg): 124.2
Sodium (mg): 370

Exchanges:
Milk: 0.0
Vegetable: 2.0
Fruit: 0.0
Bread: 2.0
Meat: 4.0
Fat: 0.0

1. Cook chicken in oil in large saucepan over medium heat until lightly browned, about 8 minutes. Add tomatoes with liquid, lemon juice, garlic, cinnamon stick, bay leaf, and sherry. Heat to boiling; reduce heat and simmer, covered, until chicken is cooked, about 15 minutes. Season to taste with salt and pepper; discard bay leaf and cinnamon stick. Serve over noodles; sprinkle with cheese.

MIDDLE EASTERN-STYLE CHICKEN STEW

Couscous cooks quickly and lends a uniquely pleasing texture to this stew.

4 entrée servings

1 pound boneless, skinless chicken breast, cubed
   (1-inch)
¾ cup each: chopped onion, green bell pepper
2 garlic cloves, minced
2 teaspoons olive oil
1¾ cups fat-free chicken broth
2 cups chopped tomato
1 can (15 ounces) garbanzo beans, rinsed, drained
¼ cup raisins
1 bay leaf
1½ teaspoons dried thyme leaves
1 teaspoon ground cumin
¼ teaspoon ground allspice
1 cup couscous
Salt and pepper, to taste

Per Serving:
Calories: 389
% calories from fat: 12
Protein (g): 24
Carbohydrate (g): 63
Fat (g): 5.4
Saturated fat (g): 1
Cholesterol (mg): 34
Sodium (mg): 235

Exchanges:
Milk: 0.0
Vegetable: 1.0
Fruit: 1.0
Bread: 3.0
Meat: 1.5
Fat: 0.0

1. Cook chicken, onion, bell pepper, and garlic in oil in Dutch oven over medium heat until lightly browned, about 10 minutes. Add remaining ingredients, except couscous, salt, and pepper; heat to boiling. Reduce heat and simmer, covered, until chicken is cooked, 20 to 25 minutes; discard bay leaf. Add couscous and heat to boiling; remove from heat and let stand, covered, 5 to 10 minutes. Season to taste with salt and pepper.

MOROCCAN CHICKEN STEW WITH COUSCOUS

Tantalize your taste buds with this extra-easy version of a Middle Eastern stew.

4 entrée servings

1 pound boneless, skinless chicken breast, cubed (¾-inch)

½ teaspoon each: ground cinnamon, coriander

1 teaspoon olive oil

⅛–¼ teaspoon crushed red pepper

2 cans (14½ ounces each) stewed tomatoes

½ cup each: quartered dried apricots, currants

2 teaspoons minced garlic

½ teaspoon cumin seeds

Salt and pepper, to taste

1 cup couscous, cooked, warm

Per Serving:
Calories: 499
% calories from fat: 8
Protein (g): 34.5
Carbohydrate (g): 80.1
Fat (g): 4.8
Saturated fat (g): 1.1
Cholesterol (mg): 69
Sodium (mg): 498

Exchanges:
Milk: 0.0
Vegetable: 2.0
Fruit: 0.0
Bread: 2.5
Meat: 3.0
Fat: 0.0

1. Sprinkle chicken with combined cinnamon and coriander. Cook chicken in oil in Dutch oven over medium heat until lightly browned, about 10 minutes. Add remaining ingredients, except salt, pepper, and couscous, and heat to boiling. Reduce heat and simmer, covered, until chicken is cooked, 15 to 20 minutes. Serve over couscous.

MOROCCAN CHICKEN AND CHICKPEA STEW

This dish is great for entertaining because it serves eight and can be doubled easily.

8 entrée servings

8 skinless chicken breast halves (6 ounces each)

4 cloves garlic, crushed

3 tablespoons lemon juice

2 teaspoons ground ginger

½ teaspoon black pepper

¾ cup each: chopped and sliced onion

1 tablespoon flour

1 teaspoon ground turmeric

1 cinnamon stick

1 can (14½ ounces) reduced-sodium fat-free chicken broth

1 can (15 ounces) chickpeas, rinsed, drained

½ cup raisins

Salt, to taste

Per Serving:
Calories: 357
% calories from fat: 23
Protein (g): 42.9
Carbohydrate (g): 24.3
Fat (g): 9
Saturated fat (g): 2.4
Cholesterol (mg): 115.7
Sodium (mg): 254

Exchanges:
Milk: 0.0
Vegetable: 0.0
Fruit: 0.0
Bread: 2.0
Meat: 4.0
Fat: 0.0

1. Brush chicken breasts with combined garlic and lemon juice; sprinkle with combined ginger and pepper. Refrigerate, covered, 1 hour.

2. Sauté chopped and sliced onion in lightly greased large saucepan until tender, about 6 minutes; stir in flour and turmeric and cook 1 minute. Add chicken and remaining ingredients, except salt, and heat to boiling; reduce heat and simmer until chicken is cooked, about 20 minutes. Discard cinnamon stick; season to taste with salt.

GARDEN STEW WITH CHICKEN AND COUSCOUS

Take advantage of your garden's bounty with this quick and easy stew, substituting vegetables you have in abundance.

6 entrée servings

6 boneless, skinless chicken breast halves
(4 ounces each)

2 medium onions, thickly sliced

8 ounces shiitake or white mushrooms, sliced,
tough stems discarded

1 small jalapeño chili, finely chopped

1 tablespoon flour

2 cups reduced-sodium fat-free chicken broth

2 medium zucchini, sliced

1 medium turnip, cubed

8 ounces baby carrots, halved

4 medium tomatoes, coarsely chopped

½ cup loosely packed cilantro leaves

Salt and pepper, to taste

2 packages (5.9 ounces each) couscous, spice packets
discarded, cooked, warm

Per Serving:
Calories: 397
% calories from fat: 6
Protein (g): 29
Carbohydrate (g): 63
Fat (g): 2.7
Saturated fat (g): 0.7
Cholesterol (mg): 46
Sodium (mg): 141

Exchanges:
Milk: 0.0
Vegetable: 3.0
Fruit: 0.0
Bread: 3.0
Meat: 2.0
Fat: 0.0

1. Cook chicken in lightly greased large Dutch oven over medium heat until browned on both sides, about 10 minutes. Season to taste with salt and pepper. Remove from pan. Add onions, mushrooms, and jalapeño chili to Dutch oven; sauté until tender, about 8 minutes. Stir in flour; cook 1 minute. Add broth, zucchini, turnip, and carrots; heat to boiling. Reduce heat and simmer, covered, until vegetables are tender and chicken is cooked, about 20 minutes, adding tomatoes and cilantro during last 5 minutes. Season to taste with salt and pepper. Serve over couscous.

GINGER-ORANGE CHICKEN AND SQUASH STEW

Any winter squash, such as acorn, butternut, or Hubbard, is appropriate for this orange and ginger accented stew; sweet potatoes can be used too.

6 entrée servings

1½ pounds boneless, skinless chicken breast, cubed

1 cup each: coarsely chopped onions, green
   bell peppers

2 cloves garlic, minced

1 tablespoon olive oil

3 cups cubed, peeled winter yellow squash

2 medium Idaho potatoes, peeled, cubed

1 can (14½ ounces) reduced-sodium diced
   tomatoes, undrained

2 cups reduced-sodium fat-free chicken broth

½ cup orange juice

1 tablespoon grated orange zest

½ teaspoon ground ginger

½ cup fat-free sour cream

Salt and pepper, to taste

4 cups cooked noodles or brown basmati rice, warm

Per Serving:
Calories: 482
% calories from fat: 12
Protein (g): 38.7
Carbohydrate (g): 67.0
Fat (g): 6.6
Saturated fat (g): 1.4
Cholesterol (mg): 111.6
Sodium (mg): 264.5

Exchanges:
Milk: 0.0
Vegetable: 0.0
Fruit: 0.0
Bread: 4.0
Meat: 3.0
Fat: 0.0

1. Cook chicken, onions, bell peppers, and garlic in oil in large saucepan over medium heat until chicken is browned and vegetables are tender, 8 to 10 minutes. Add squash, potatoes, tomatoes with liquid, broth, orange juice and zest, and ginger; heat to boiling. Reduce heat and simmer, uncovered, until chicken is cooked and vegetables are tender, about 20 minutes. Reduce heat to low and stir in sour cream; season to taste with salt and pepper. Serve over noodles.

CHICKEN STEW WITH DRIED FRUIT

Dried fruits make a flavorful sweet broth for chicken.

4 entrée servings

1 pound boneless, skinless chicken breast, cubed (1½-inch)

1 each: chopped large onion, minced garlic clove

2 teaspoons olive oil

1¼ cups fat-free chicken broth

2 to 4 tablespoons light rum (optional)

1½ cups mixed raisins, coarsely chopped pitted prunes and dried apricots

½ red bell pepper, diced

½ teaspoon ground ginger

1 bay leaf

Salt and pepper, to taste

1 cup rice, cooked, warm

Per Serving:
Calories: 406
% calories from fat: 9
Protein (g): 19
Carbohydrate (g): 68
Fat (g): 4.2
Saturated fat (g): 0.8
Cholesterol (mg): 36
Sodium (mg): 105

Exchanges:
Milk: 0.0
Vegetable: 1.0
Fruit: 2.0
Bread: 2.5
Meat: 1.5
Fat: 0.0

1. Cook chicken, onion, and garlic in oil in large saucepan until chicken is browned, about 8 minutes. Add remaining ingredients, except salt, pepper, and rice; heat to boiling. Reduce heat and simmer, covered, until chicken is cooked, about 20 minutes. Simmer, uncovered, if thicker consistency is desired, 5 to 10 minutes. Discard bay leaf and season to taste with salt and pepper; serve over rice.

CURRY-GINGER CHICKEN STEW

This stew is seasoned with a unique Ginger Spice Blend.

10 entrée servings

2 cups chopped onions
2 cloves garlic, finely chopped
2 tablespoons each: canola oil, flour
Curry-Ginger Spice Blend (recipe follows)
2 cut up chickens (about 2½ pounds each)
1½ cups reduced-sodium fat-free chicken broth
1 cup chopped, peeled, seeded tomatoes
1½ cups frozen peas
½ cup low-fat plain yogurt
¼ cup chopped cilantro
Salt and pepper, to taste
5 cups cooked rice, warm

Per Serving:
Calories: 334
% calories from fat: 27
Protein (g): 28.8
Carbohydrate (g): 31.3
Fat (g): 9.8
Saturated fat (g): 2.2
Cholesterol (mg): 73
Sodium (mg): 328

Exchanges:
Milk: 0.0
Vegetable: 0.0
Fruit: 0.0
Bread: 2.0
Meat: 3.0
Fat: 0.5

1. Sauté onions and garlic in oil in Dutch oven until tender, about 8 minutes; stir in flour and Curry-Ginger Spice Blend and cook 2 minutes. Stir in chicken and cook over medium heat 5 minutes. Stir in broth and tomatoes; heat to boiling. Reduce heat and simmer, covered, until chicken is cooked, 30 to 45 minutes, adding peas and yogurt during last 5 minutes. Stir in cilantro and season to taste with salt and pepper. Serve over rice.

Curry-Ginger Spice Blend

Makes about ¼ cup

2 tablespoons finely chopped gingerroot
1 tablespoon sesame seeds
2 teaspoons coriander seeds
1 teaspoon each: cumin seeds, ground turmeric, salt
¼ teaspoon peppercorns, fennel seeds
⅛–¼ teaspoon crushed red pepper

1. Process all ingredients in blender until finely ground.

CURRIED CHICKEN AND APPLE STEW

The flavors of apple and ginger make this stew a special treat. Serve with Basmati Rice Pilaf (see p. 476).

6 entrée servings

1½ pounds boneless, skinless chicken breast halves

2 tablespoons margarine or butter

1 cup each: chopped onion, peeled cooking apples, sliced carrots

1 teaspoon minced garlic

1½ tablespoons curry powder

1 teaspoon ground ginger

2 tablespoons flour

2 cups reduced-sodium fat-free chicken broth

Salt and pepper, to taste

1 cup fat-free plain yogurt

Per Serving:
Calories: 232
% calories from fat: 22
Protein (g): 30.7
Carbohydrate (g): 13.9
Fat (g): 5.6
Saturated fat (g): 1.2
Cholesterol (mg): 66.5
Sodium (mg): 336

Exchanges:
Milk: 0.0
Vegetable: 0.0
Fruit: 1.0
Bread. 0.0
Meat: 3.0
Fat: 0.0

1. Cook chicken in margarine in Dutch oven over medium heat until browned on all sides, about 10 minutes. Remove chicken and reserve. Add onion, apples, carrots, and garlic to Dutch oven and sauté 5 minutes; stir in curry powder, ginger, and flour and cook 2 minutes. Stir in broth and reserved chicken; heat to boiling. Reduce heat and simmer, covered, until chicken is cooked, about 20 minutes. Season to taste with salt and pepper; stir in yogurt.

INDIAN CURRY CHICKEN AND VEGETABLE STEW

The mixture of spices in the Curry Seasoning gives this stew a unique flavor; however, 3 tablespoons of curry powder can be substituted.

4 entrée servings

1 large onion, finely chopped

1 cup light coconut milk or fat-free milk

2 tablespoons white wine vinegar

1 can (14½ ounces) crushed tomatoes

1 can (6 ounces) tomato paste

2 tablespoons brown sugar

1 can (14½ ounces) reduced-sodium vegetable broth

1–2 tablespoons Curry Seasoning (recipe follows)

1 pound chicken tenders, halved

8 ounces mushrooms, coarsely chopped

1 cup each: diced potato, carrots, sliced okra, small
   cauliflower florets, cut green beans

3 cups cooked brown rice, warm

Per Serving:
Calories: 509
% calories from fat: 12
Protein (g): 38.7
Carbohydrate (g): 76.7
Fat (g): 6.8
Saturated fat (g): 2.8
Cholesterol (mg): 65.7
Sodium (mg): 861

Exchanges:
Milk: 0.0
Vegetable: 0.0
Fruit: 0.0
Bread: 5.0
Meat: 3.0
Fat: 0.0

1. Heat onion, coconut milk, vinegar, tomatoes, tomato paste, brown sugar, broth, and Curry Seasoning to boiling in large saucepan; reduce heat and simmer, covered, 5 minutes. Stir in remaining ingredients, except brown rice; heat to boiling. Reduce heat and simmer, covered, until chicken is cooked, about 25 minutes. Simmer, uncovered, if thicker consistency is desired, 5 to 10 mintues. Serve over brown rice.

Curry Seasoning
Makes about 2 tablespoons

2 teaspoons ground coriander

1 teaspoon ground turmeric, chili powder

½ teaspoon each: ground cumin, dry mustard,
   ground ginger, black pepper

1. Combine all ingredients.

CURRIED CHICKEN AND VEGETABLE STEW

A variety of spices and herbs are combined to make the fragrant curry that seasons this dish.

4 entrée servings

12–16 ounces boneless, skinless chicken breast, cubed

½ cup chopped onion

2 cloves garlic

1 tablespoon flour

½ small head cauliflower, cut into florets

2 each: cubed medium potatoes, thickly sliced carrots

1 large tomato, chopped

1½ cups reduced-sodium fat-free chicken broth

¾ teaspoon ground turmeric

½ teaspoon each: dry mustard, ground cumin and coriander

1–2 tablespoons lemon juice

Salt and cayenne pepper, to taste

Per Serving:
Calories: 250
% calories from fat: 11
Protein (g): 28.4
Carbohydrate (g): 29
Fat (g): 3.1
Saturated fat (g): 0.7
Cholesterol (mg): 51.7
Sodium (mg): 203

Exchanges:
Milk: 0.0
Vegetable: 2.0
Fruit: 0.0
Bread: 1.0
Meat: 2.0
Fat: 0.0

1. Sauté chicken, onion, and garlic in lightly greased large saucepan until chicken is browned, 5 to 6 minutes. Stir in flour and cook 1 minute. Add vegetables, broth, spices, and herbs to saucepan; heat to boiling. Reduce heat and simmer, covered, until chicken is cooked and vegetables are tender, about 20 minutes. Season to taste with lemon juice, salt, and cayenne pepper.

THAI-SPICED CHICKEN AND CARROT STEW

Peanut sauce, gingerroot, and sesame oil add plenty of Asian-style flavor to this dish! 1 tablespoon peanut butter and ¼–½ teaspoon crushed red pepper can be substituted for the Thai peanut sauce.

4 entrée servings

1 pound boneless, skinless chicken breast, cubed

4 carrots, diagonally sliced

1 tablespoon each: minced gingerroot and garlic

1 can (14½ ounces) reduced-sodium fat-free chicken broth

1 tablespoon each: reduced-sodium soy sauce, Thai peanut sauce

¾ cup sliced scallions

1 teaspoon sugar

½ teaspoon Asian sesame oil

3 cups cooked rice, warm

Per Serving:
Calories: 358
% calories from fat: 11
Protein (g): 32.8
Carbohydrate (g): 44.4
Fat (g): 4.3
Saturated fat (g): 1.3
Cholesterol (mg): 69
Sodium (mg): 371

Exchanges:
Milk: 0.0
Vegetable: 2.0
Fruit: 0.0
Bread: 2.0
Meat: 3.0
Fat: 0.0

1. Heat chicken, carrots, gingerroot, garlic, broth, and soy sauce to boiling in large saucepan; reduce heat and simmer, covered, until chicken is cooked and carrots are tender, about 15 minutes. Add peanut sauce, scallions, sugar, and Asian sesame oil; simmer, covered, 5 minutes longer. Serve over rice.

SHERRIED CHICKEN STEW

Chicken is simmered in a delicious ginger, sherry, and soy accented broth.

4 entrée servings

1 pound boneless, skinless chicken breast, cubed

1 teaspoon Asian sesame oil

1 cup each: chopped onion, sliced snow peas

½ cup chopped red bell pepper

1 teaspoon each: minced garlic, gingerroot

1 cup reduced-sodium fat-free chicken broth

2 to 4 tablespoons dry sherry (optional)

1½ tablespoons cornstarch

3–4 tablespoons low-sodium soy sauce

12 ounces Chinese egg noodles or vermicelli, cooked, warm

¼ cup sliced green onions

1. Cook chicken in oil in large skillet over medium heat until browned, about 5 minutes; stir in onion, snow peas, bell pepper, garlic, and gingerroot. Sauté 5 minutes; stir in broth and sherry and heat to boiling. Reduce heat and simmer, covered, until chicken is cooked, about 20 minutes. Heat stew to boiling; stir in combined cornstarch and soy sauce, stirring until thickened, about 1 minute. Serve over noodles; sprinkle with green onions.

Per Serving:
Calories: 366
% calories from fat: 8
Protein (g): 35.1
Carbohydrate (g): 44.2
Fat (g): 3.0
Saturated fat (g): 0.5
Cholesterol (mg): 65.7
Sodium (mg): 871

Exchanges:
Milk: 0.0
Vegetable: 0.0
Fruit: 0.0
Bread: 3.0
Meat: 3.0
Fat: 0.0

SWEET-SOUR CHICKEN AND VEGETABLE STEW

Chicken and vegetables are simmered in cider and seasoned with honey and vinegar for a refreshing sweet-sour flavor.

6 entrée servings

1 pound boneless, skinless chicken breast, cubed

½ cup each: chopped shallots, red bell pepper

2 cloves garlic, minced

1 can (14½ ounces) reduced-sodium diced tomatoes, undrained

1 cup apple cider or apple juice

1½ tablespoons each: honey, cider vinegar

1 bay leaf

¼ teaspoon ground nutmeg

2 cups cubed peeled butternut or acorn yellow squash

1 cup each: cubed peeled Idaho and sweet potatoes, peeled tart apples, and whole kernel corn

Salt and pepper, to taste

4 cups cooked basmati rice, warm

Per Serving:
Calories: 373
% calories from fat: 4
Protein (g): 23.3
Carbohydrate (g): 64.1
Fat (g): 1.8
Saturated fat (g): 0.3
Cholesterol (mg): 43.8
Sodium (mg): 85

Exchanges:
Milk: 0.0
Vegetable: 0.0
Fruit: 0.0
Bread: 4.0
Meat: 2.0
Fat: 0.0

1. Cook chicken, shallots, bell pepper, and garlic in lightly greased large saucepan over medium heat until chicken is browned, about

8 minutes. Add remaining ingredients, except corn, salt, pepper, and rice; heat to boiling. Reduce heat and simmer, covered, until vegetables are tender and chicken is cooked, about 15 minutes, adding apples and corn during last 5 minutes. Discard bay leaf; season to taste with salt and pepper. Serve over rice.

TURKEY RAGOUT WITH WHITE WINE

Turkey simmers with white wine and herbs to make a flavorful stew; delicious over rice or Polenta (see p. 661).

6 entrée servings

1½ pounds skinless turkey breast, cubed (1-inch)
Flour
2 tablespoons olive oil
2 each: minced large garlic cloves, coarsely chopped carrots
1 each: chopped large onion, sliced rib celery
2½ cups sliced mushrooms
1 can (14½ ounces) Italian plum tomatoes, undrained, chopped
½ cup dry white wine or chicken broth
¼ cup reduced-sodium fat-free chicken broth
½ teaspoon each: dried rosemary and sage leaves
Salt and pepper, to taste

Per Serving:
Calories: 226
% calories from fat: 24
Protein (g): 30
Carbohydrate (g): 8.1
Fat (g): 5.8
Saturated fat (g): 1.0
Cholesterol (mg): 71.3
Sodium (mg): 97

Exchanges:
Milk: 0.0
Vegetable: 0.0
Fruit: 0.0
Bread: 0.5
Meat: 3.0
Fat: 0.0

1. Coat turkey with flour; cook in oil in large skillet over medium heat until turkey is browned, 8 to 10 minutes. Add vegetables and sauté until they begin to brown, about 5 minutes. Stir in remaining ingredients, except salt and pepper; heat to boiling. Reduce heat and simmer, covered, until turkey is cooked, about 20 minutes. Season to taste with salt and pepper.

TURKEY-WILD RICE STEW

Turkey, vegetables, and wild rice combine to create a delicious supper stew.

4 entrée servings

1 pound boneless, skinless turkey breast, cubed

½ cup chopped onion

1 teaspoon olive oil

3 cups reduced-sodium fat-free chicken broth

½ cup wild rice

1½ cups each: small broccoli florets, sliced carrots

1 tablespoon chopped fresh or 1 teaspoon dried
   sage leaves

Salt and pepper, to taste

Per Serving:
Calories: 250
% calories from fat: 13
Protein (g): 29
Carbohydrate (g): 24.6
Fat (g): 3.8
Saturated fat (g): 0.9
Cholesterol (mg): 44.7
Sodium (mg): 196

Exchanges:
Milk: 0.0
Vegetable: 1.0
Fruit: 0.0
Bread: 1.0
Meat: 3.0
Fat: 0.0

1. Cook turkey and onion in oil in large saucepan over medium heat until lightly browned, about 5 minutes. Add broth and wild rice; heat to boiling. Reduce heat and simmer, covered, until rice is tender, about 50 minutes, adding broccoli, carrots, and sage during last 10 minutes. Season to taste with salt and pepper.

TURKEY STEW, MILAN-STYLE

This recipe recalls the tangy flavor of osso bucco, the Italian classic dish featuring veal shanks braised in wine.

6 entrée servings

1½ pounds skinless turkey breast, cubed (1-inch)
3 tablespoons flour
2 teaspoons olive oil
1 large onion, chopped
2 garlic cloves, minced
½ cup dry white wine or beef broth
1¾ cups reduced-sodium fat-free beef broth
1 can (8 ounces) reduced-sodium tomato paste
8 baby carrots, halved
2 ribs celery, thinly sliced
1½ dried thyme leaves
2 bay leaves
3 strips lemon zest (2-inch)
Salt and pepper, to taste
1½ cups rice, cooked

Per Serving:
Calories: 300
% calories from fat: 9
Protein (g): 32.4
Carbohydrate (g): 26.8
Fat (g): 2.9
Saturated fat (g): 0.6
Cholesterol (mg): 74.4
Sodium (mg): 170.1

Exchanges:
Milk: 0.0
Vegetable: 0.0
Fruit: 0.0
Bread: 2.0
Meat: 3.0
Fat: 0.0

1. Coat turkey with flour; cook in oil in Dutch oven over medium heat until browned, about 8 minutes. Stir in onion and garlic; cook until tender, about 5 minutes. Stir in remaining ingredients, except salt, pepper, and rice, and heat to boiling. Reduce heat and simmer, covered, until turkey is cooked, about 20 minutes. Discard bay leaves; season to taste with salt and pepper. Serve over rice.

TURKEY SANCOCHE

45 *Sancoche is a hearty stew of meats, fish, vegetables, and seasonings that hails from Latin America.*

4 entrée servings

1 pound boneless, skinless turkey breast, cubed (¾-inch)
2 cups cubed, peeled butternut squash
1 cup each: cubed peeled sweet and white potato, chopped onion

1 can (15 ounces) black beans, rinsed, drained

1 can (14½ ounces) reduced-sodium fat-free chicken broth

1 jalapeño chili, minced

1 teaspoon toasted cumin seeds

Salt and pepper, to taste

¼ cup coarsely chopped cashews

Per Serving:
Calories: 324
% calories from fat: 18
Protein (g): 29.6
Carbohydrate (g): 43.7
Fat (g): 7.2
Saturated fat (g): 1.5
Cholesterol (mg): 44.7
Sodium (mg): 652

Exchanges:
Milk: 0.0
Vegetable: 0.0
Fruit: 0.0
Bread: 2.5
Meat: 2.0
Fat: 0.0

1. Heat all ingredients, except salt, pepper, and cashews, to boiling in large saucepan. Reduce heat and simmer, covered, until turkey is cooked and vegetables are tender, about 20 minutes. Season to taste with salt and pepper. Sprinkle each bowl of stew with cashews.

SOUTHWEST TURKEY STEW WITH CHILI-CHEESE DUMPLINGS

Turkey stew with Southwest seasonings, topped with savory Chili-Cheese Dumplings, make an outstanding meal.

6 entrée servings

1½ pounds turkey breast, cubed (1-inch)

1 tablespoon peanut or canola oil

1 each: chopped green and red bell pepper, medium onion, minced jalapeño chili

2 cloves garlic, minced

1 tablespoon chili powder

1 teaspoon ground cumin

1 can (15 ounces) chili beans in spicy sauce, undrained

1 can (14½ ounces) reduced-sodium stewed tomatoes

1 cup reduced-sodium fat-free chicken broth

Salt and pepper to taste

Chili-Cheese Dumplings (see pg. 592)

Per Serving:
Calories: 352
% calories from fat: 25
Protein (g): 30
Carbohydrate (g): 37.7
Fat (g): 10.2
Saturated fat (g): 2.7
Cholesterol (mg): 48.5
Sodium (mg): 786

Exchanges:
Milk: 0.0
Vegetable: 2.0
Fruit: 0.0
Bread: 2.0
Meat: 3.0
Fat: 0.0

1. Cook turkey in oil in large saucepan over medium heat until browned, about 10 minutes; stir in bell peppers, onion, jalapeño chili, garlic, chili powder, and cumin. Cook until onion is tender, about 5 minutes. Stir in beans and liquid, tomatoes, and broth. Heat to boiling; reduce heat and simmer, covered, 10 minutes. Season to taste with salt and pepper.

2. Heat stew to boiling; spoon Chili-Cheese Dumplings dough into 6 mounds on stew. Reduce heat and simmer, covered, until dumplings are dry on top, about 10 minutes.

TURKEY STEW WITH APRICOTS AND CHILIES

This quick and easy recipe proves that leftover turkey doesn't have to be boring. The tangy combination of chilies and apricots is reminiscent of Indian flavors.

4 entrée servings

1 cup chopped onion

2 garlic cloves, minced

2 teaspoons canola oil

1¼ cups fat-free chicken broth

1 teaspoon ground cumin

½ teaspoon each: ground allspice

10 dried apricots, quartered

2 to 3 tablespoons chopped canned green chilies

1 cup chopped fresh tomato

1 pound cooked turkey breast, cubed (1-inch)

¼ cup chopped cilantro

Salt and pepper, to taste

1 cup rice, cooked, warm

Per Serving:
Calories: 319
% calories from fat: 7
Protein (g): 27
Carbohydrate (g): 46
Fat (g): 2.6
Saturated fat (g): 0.7
Cholesterol (mg): 65
Sodium (mg): 260

Exchanges:
Milk: 0.0
Vegetable: 0.0
Fruit: 0.5
Bread: 2.0
Meat: 3.0
Fat: 0.0

1. Sauté onion and garlic in oil in large saucepan until onion is tender, about 5 minutes. Add remaining ingredients, except cilantro, salt, pepper, and rice; heat to boiling. Reduce heat and simmer, covered, until turkey is tender, about 20 minutes. Stir in cilantro and season to taste with salt and pepper; serve over rice.

ITALIAN-STYLE TURKEY SAUSAGE AND FENNEL STEW

Use your preference of sweet or hot Italian-style turkey sausage in this harvest garden stew.

4 entrée servings

12 ounces Italian-style turkey sausage, sliced
1 medium onion, cut into thin wedges
1 can (14½ ounces) reduced-sodium diced tomatoes, undrained
1 cup reduced-sodium fat-free chicken broth
1 pound butternut squash, peeled, cubed
8 Brussels sprouts, halved
2 parsnips, sliced
1 small fennel bulb, sliced
Pinch crushed red pepper (optional)
1 teaspoon dried Italian seasoning
Salt and pepper, to taste

Per Serving:
Calories: 310
% calories from fat: 26
Protein (g): 21.8
Carbohydrate (g): 39.4
Fat (g): 9.7
Saturated fat (g): 2.6
Cholesterol (mg): 45.6
Sodium (mg): 780

Exchanges:
Milk: 0.0
Vegetable: 2.0
Fruit: 0.0
Bread: 2.0
Meat: 2.0
Fat: 0.0

1. Cook sausage and onion in lightly greased large saucepan over medium heat until sausage is browned, about 10 minutes; add remaining ingredients, except salt and pepper, and heat to boiling. Reduce heat and simmer, covered, until vegetables are tender, about 20 minutes. Season to taste with salt and pepper.

ELEVEN

Seafood Stews

CREOLE FISH STEW

45 *Rich flavors, quick and easy preparation—who could ask for more?*

4 entrée servings

2 cups chopped onions

1 cup each: chopped green bell pepper, celery

½ teaspoon dried thyme leaves

⅛–¼ teaspoon crushed red pepper

2 teaspoons each: minced garlic, olive oil

1 can (28 ounces) reduced-sodium diced
  tomatoes, undrained

¼ cup dry white wine or water

1 pound cod fillets, cubed

2 tablespoons reduced-sodium soy sauce

1 tablespoon paprika

2 bay leaves

Salt and pepper, to taste

3 cups cooked rice, warm

Per Serving:
Calories: 378
% calories from fat: 10
Protein (g): 28
Carbohydrate (g): 56.1
Fat (g): 4.1
Saturated fat (g): 0.7
Cholesterol (mg): 48.6
Sodium (mg): 385

Exchanges:
Milk: 0.0
Vegetable: 1.0
Fruit: 0.0
Bread: 3.0
Meat: 3.0
Fat: 0.0

1. Sauté onions, bell pepper, celery, thyme, red pepper, and garlic in oil in large saucepan until tender and lightly browned, about 10 minutes. Stir in remaining ingredients, except salt, pepper, and rice; heat to boiling. Reduce heat and simmer, covered, until fish is tender and flakes with a fork, about 10 minutes. Discard bay leaves; season to taste with salt and pepper; serve over rice.

CAJUN SHRIMP, CORN, AND BEAN STEW

45 *A milk-based shrimp stew with a spicy tang! Serve this stew with crusty bread or over rice.*

4 entrée servings

1 each: chopped medium onion, minced jalapeño chili

2 cloves garlic, minced

1 teaspoon dried thyme leaves

½ teaspoon dried oregano leaves

1 tablespoon margarine or butter

2 tablespoons flour

2 cups fat-free milk

1 cup each: broccoli florets, cream-style corn

1 can (15 ounces) red beans, rinsed, drained

12–16 ounces shrimp, peeled, deveined

Salt, to taste

Hot pepper sauce, to taste

Per Serving:
Calories: 311
% calories from fat: 14
Protein (g): 26.4
Carbohydrate (g): 42.3
Fat (g): 4.8
Saturated fat (g): 1
Cholesterol (mg): 132.2
Sodium (mg): 677

Exchanges:
Milk: 0.0
Vegetable: 2.0
Fruit: 0.0
Bread: 2.0
Meat: 2.0
Fat: 0.0

1. Sauté onion, jalapeño chili, garlic, and herbs in margarine in large saucepan until tender, about 5 minutes. Stir in flour; cook 1 minute. Stir in milk and heat to boiling, stirring until thickened, about 1 minute. Stir in vegetables and heat to boiling; reduce heat and simmer until vegetables are tender, about 10 minutes. Add shrimp and simmer until shrimp are cooked, 2 to 3 minutes. Season to taste with salt and hot pepper sauce.

SHRIMP AND VEGETABLE STEW

45 *The sausage adds a good smoky flavor to this easy stew.*

4 entrée servings

1 cup each: halved baby carrots and small Brussels sprouts, whole kernel corn

1 medium onion, cut into thin wedges

1 can (14½ ounces) stewed tomatoes

4 ounces smoked turkey sausage, thickly sliced

1 teaspoon chili powder

12–16 ounces peeled, deveined medium shrimp

Salt and pepper, to taste

3 cups cooked rice, warm

Per Serving:
Calories: 361
% calories from fat: 7
Protein (g): 25.6
Carbohydrate (g): 59.6
Fat (g): 2.8
Saturated fat (g): 0.8
Cholesterol (mg): 143.2
Sodium (mg): 594

Exchanges:
Milk: 0.0
Vegetable: 3.0
Fruit: 0.0
Bread: 3.0
Meat: 1.0
Fat: 0.0

1. Heat all ingredients, except shrimp, salt, pepper, and rice to boiling in large saucepan; reduce heat and simmer, covered, until vegetables are tender, about 15 minutes, adding shrimp during last 5 minutes. Season to taste with salt and pepper; serve over rice.

THAI-STYLE SHRIMP STEW

45 *This lovely dish gets its fabulous flavor from shrimp, bok choy, scallions, and Chinese chili sauce. The Chinese chili sauce is HOT, so use cautiously!*

4 entrée servings

4 ounces bean threads or cellophane noodles,
   cut (2-inch)

2 cups each: reduced-sodium fat-free chicken broth,
   chopped bok choy

¼ cup rice wine vinegar

1–2 teaspoons Chinese chili sauce with garlic

1 pound peeled, deveined medium shrimp

1 cup each: sliced red bell pepper, sliced scallions,
   fresh or canned rinsed drained bean sprouts

Reduced-sodium soy sauce, to taste

Salt and pepper, to taste

Per Serving:
Calories: 236
% calories from fat: 5
Protein (g): 23.7
Carbohydrate (g): 31.2
Fat (g): 1.2
Saturated fat (g): 0.3
Cholesterol (mg): 173.3
Sodium (mg): 395

Exchanges:
Milk: 0.0
Vegetable: 3.0
Fruit: 0.0
Bread: 1.0
Meat: 1.5
Fat: 0.0

1. Pour hot water over bean threads to cover; let stand until softened, about 10 minutes. Drain and reserve.

2. Heat remaining ingredients except bean threads, bean sprouts, soy sauce, salt, and pepper to boiling in large saucepan. Reduce heat and simmer, covered, until shrimp are cooked, about 5 minutes. Stir in reserved bean threads and bean sprouts; simmer, until hot, 2 minutes longer. Season to taste with soy sauce, salt, and pepper.

SAVORY FISH STEW

45 *Serve with generous squares of warm Roasted Chili Cornbread (see p. 655).*

8 entrée servings

1 cup chopped onion

4 cloves garlic, minced

2 tablespoons olive oil

1½ teaspoons each: dried basil and oregano leaves

½ teaspoon ground turmeric

2 bay leaves

1 can (28 ounces) stewed tomatoes

2 cups clam juice or water

¾ cup dry white wine or water

1 pound cod or other whitefish fillets, sliced (1-inch)

8 ounces each: peeled deveined shrimp, bay scallops

Salt and pepper, to taste

Per Serving:
Calories: 175
% calories from fat: 20
Protein (g): 21.5
Carbohydrate (g): 10.2
Fat (g): 4
Saturated fat (g): 0.7
Cholesterol (mg): 79.7
Sodium (mg): 539

Exchanges:
Milk: 0.0
Vegetable: 2.0
Fruit: 0.0
Bread: 0.0
Meat: 2.0
Fat: 0.0

1. Sauté onion and garlic in oil in large saucepan until tender, about 5 minutes. Stir in basil, oregano, turmeric, and bay leaves; cook 1 to 2 minutes. Add tomatoes, clam juice, and wine; heat to boiling. Reduce heat and simmer, covered, 20 minutes. Add seafood and simmer, covered, until cod is tender and flakes with a fork, 5 to 8 minutes. Discard bay leaves; season to taste with salt and pepper.

VARIATION

Creamy Scallop Stew — Make recipe, omitting oregano, tomatoes, white wine, cod, and shrimp. Heat stew to boiling; stir in combined ¼ cup all-purpose flour and 1 cup fat-free half-and-half or fat-free milk. Boil, stirring, until thickened, about 1 minute. Add 2 pounds bay scallops; reduce heat and simmer, covered, until scallops are cooked, 5 to 8 minutes. Season to taste with salt and pepper.

FRUITS OF THE SEA STEW

Fennel seed, orange zest, and white wine add subtle flavor to this aromatic stew.

8 entrée servings

3 carrots, chopped

1 large onion, thinly sliced

3 cloves garlic, minced

1–2 tablespoons margarine or butter

1 tablespoon each: flour, minced orange zest

1 teaspoon fennel seeds, lightly crushed

1 quart Fish Stock (see p. 8) or clam juice

½ cup dry white wine or water

5 medium tomatoes, peeled, chopped

2 pounds firm fish fillets (cod, red snapper, salmon, orange roughy halibut, etc.), cut into pieces (1½-inch)

¼ cup chopped parsley

Salt and pepper, to taste

Per Serving:
Calories: 174
% calories from fat: 14
Protein (g): 22.8
Carbohydrate (g): 10.1
Fat (g): 2.6
Saturated fat (g): 0.5
Cholesterol (mg): 51.9
Sodium (mg): 110

Exchanges:
Milk: 0.0
Vegetable: 2.0
Fruit: 0.0
Bread: 0.0
Meat: 2.0
Fat: 0.0

1. Sauté carrots, onion, and garlic in margarine in large saucepan until onion is tender, about 8 minutes; add flour, orange zest, and fennel seeds and cook 1 to 2 minutes. Add stock, wine, and tomatoes; heat to boiling. Reduce heat and simmer, covered, 30 minutes. Add fish and simmer, covered, until fish is tender and flakes with a fork, about 10 minutes. Stir in parsley; season to taste with salt and pepper.

VARIATION

Fish Stew Salsa Verde — Make recipe as above, sautéing 1 chopped small jalapeño chili with the carrots, onion, and garlic. Decrease tomatoes to 3 and add 1 pound chopped, husked tomatillos, ½ teaspoon crushed cumin seeds, and ½ teaspoon dried oregano leaves; omit fennel seeds and orange zest. Sprinkle each serving generously with finely chopped cilantro.

FISH STEW WITH VEGETABLES AND GARLIC

45 *This dish is a garlic lover's dream. Serve with crusty bread and salad for a wonderful meal.*

6 entrée servings

1 large red onion, sliced

4–6 large garlic cloves, finely chopped

2 tablespoons olive oil

2–3 pounds small red potatoes, sliced

2 each: thickly sliced large carrots, ribs celery

2 cups clam juice or water

1 teaspoon dried basil leaves

2½ pounds whitefish fillets, cubed (2-inch)

1–2 tablespoons lemon juice

Salt and pepper, to taste

Per Serving:
Calories: 358
% calories from fat: 17
Protein (g): 38.8
Carbohydrate (g): 34.2
Fat (g): 7
Saturated fat (g): 1.2
Cholesterol (mg): 100.2
Sodium (mg): 177
Milk: 00
Vegetable: 1.0
Fruit: 0.0
Bread: 2 0
Meat: 4.0
Fat: 0.0

1. Sauté onion and garlic in oil in Dutch oven until tender, about 5 minutes. Add potatoes, carrots, celery, clam juice, and basil and heat to boiling; reduce heat and simmer 15 minutes. Add fish and simmer, covered, until fish is tender and flakes with a fork, about 10 minutes. Season to taste with lemon juice, salt, and pepper.

CIOPPINO WITH PASTA

A California favorite! Feel free to substitute other kinds of fresh fish, according to season, availability, and price.

6 entrée servings

1 cup each: chopped green bell pepper, onion,
    sliced mushrooms
4 cloves garlic, minced
1 tablespoon each: olive oil, flour
3 cups chopped tomatoes
½ cup each: clam juice, dry white wine or clam juice
1 tablespoon tomato paste
2 teaspoons each: dried oregano and basil leaves
1 teaspoon ground turmeric
8 ounces each: sea scallops, sliced crabmeat (½-inch)
4 ounces halibut or haddock steak, cubed, (1-inch)
12 mussels, scrubbed
Salt and pepper, to taste
12 ounces fettuccine, cooked, warm

Per Serving:
Calories: 516
% calories from fat: 24
Protein (g): 32.6
Carbohydrate (g): 63
Fat (g): 13.6
Saturated fat (g): 2.8
Cholesterol (mg): 107.8
Sodium (mg): 685

Exchanges:
Milk: 0.0
Vegetable: 3.0
Fruit: 0.0
Bread: 3 0
Meat: 3 0
Fat: 1.0

1. Sauté bell pepper, onion, mushrooms, and garlic in oil in large saucepan until onion is tender, about 5 minutes; stir in flour and cook 1 minute Stir in tomatoes, clam juice, wine, tomato paste, and herbs; heat to boiling. Reduce heat and simmer, covered, 10 minutes. Simmer, uncovered, until thickened to desired consistency, about 10 minutes. Add seafood; simmer, covered, until halibut is tender and flakes with a fork, about 10 minutes. Discard any mussels that have not opened; season to taste with salt and pepper. Serve over fettuccine.

GEORGIA FISH AND VEGETABLE STEW

45

Serve with Herbed-Garlic Breadsticks (see p. 638).

6 entrée servings

2 cups chopped onions
1 large garlic clove, minced
2 teaspoons margarine or butter

1½ cups each: fat-free chicken broth, clam juice

3½ cups cubed, peeled potatoes (¾-inch)

2 cups coarsely chopped cauliflower

1–2 tablespoons dry sherry (optional)

1 bay leaf

1 teaspoon each: dried thyme and basil leaves

¼ teaspoon dry mustard

¾ cup 1% reduced-fat milk

8 ounces each: cubed (1½-inch) lean whitefish
   (flounder, turbot, or haddock), medium peeled
   deveined shrimp, bay scallops

2 to 3 teaspoons lemon juice

Salt and white pepper, to taste

Per Serving:
Calories: 288
% calories from fat: 13
Protein (g): 31.5
Carbohydrate (g): 29.4
Fat (g): 4.4
Saturated fat (g): 0.9
Cholesterol (mg): 101
Sodium (mg): 793

Exchanges:
Milk: 0.0
Vegetable: 0.0
Fruit: 0.0
Bread: 2.0
Meat: 3.0
Fat: 0.0

1. Sauté onions and garlic in margarine in Dutch oven until onion is tender, about 5 minutes. Add broth, clam juice, vegetables, sherry, herbs, and dry mustard; heat to boiling. Reduce heat and simmer, covered, until vegetables are tender, about 15 minutes; discard bay leaf. Process 3 cups stew in food processor or blender until smooth. Return to Dutch oven and stir in milk. Add seafood and simmer, covered, until fish is tender and flakes with a fork, 5 to 8 minutes. Season to taste with lemon juice, salt, and white pepper.

BAYOU SNAPPER STEW

45 *Serve this Southern-style favorite with Green Chili Cornbread (see p. 654). Flounder, sole, or whitefish fillets can be substituted for the red snapper.*

4 entrée servings

1 each: chopped medium onion, green bell
   pepper, carrot

2 cloves garlic, minced

1–2 tablespoons olive oil

1 can (14½ ounces) reduced-sodium stewed tomatoes

½ cup each: frozen cut okra, clam juice or water

1 pound red snapper fillets, cut into pieces (1-inch)

2–3 teaspoons Worcestershire sauce

Salt and cayenne pepper, to taste

4–6 cups cooked rice, warm

Hot pepper sauce

Per Serving:
Calories: 414
% calories from fat: 13
Protein (g): 29.8
Carbohydrate (g): 59.2
Fat (g): 5.9
Saturated fat (g): 0.9
Cholesterol (mg): 41.6
Sodium (mg): 184

Exchanges:
Milk: 0.0
Vegetable: 2.0
Fruit: 0.0
Bread: 3.0
Meat: 3.0
Fat: 0.0

1. Sauté onion, bell pepper, carrot, and garlic in oil in large saucepan until onion is tender, about 5 minutes. Add tomatoes, okra, and clam juice; heat to boiling. Reduce heat and simmer, covered, 10 minutes. Add fish and Worcestershire sauce; simmer, covered, until fish is tender and flakes with a fork, about 10 minutes. Season to taste with salt and cayenne pepper. Serve over rice in bowls. Serve with hot pepper sauce.

GULF COAST SNAPPER STEW

This Gulf Coast favorite has a robust sauce with just a hint of cayenne heat. The red snapper is marinated, then cooked and added to the Creole sauce. Red Pepper Rice is the perfect accompaniment.

6 entrée servings

1½ pounds red snapper fillets

4 cloves garlic, minced

½ teaspoon paprika

¼ teaspoon cayenne pepper

1 each: chopped medium onion, green bell pepper, thinly sliced rib celery

4 green onions, sliced

1–2 tablespoons canola oil

1 can (14½ ounces) reduced-sodium diced tomatoes, undrained

½ cup clam juice or water

2–3 tablespoons tomato paste

¾ teaspoon dried oregano leaves

1 bay leaf

Salt and red pepper sauce, to taste

Red Pepper Rice (recipe follows)

Per Serving:
Calories: 445
% calories from fat: 18
Protein (g): 21.4
Carbohydrate (g): 70.4
Fat (g): 9.1
Saturated fat (g): 2.5
Cholesterol (mg): 25.2
Sodium (mg): 303

Exchanges:
Milk: 0.0
Vegetable: 2.0
Fruit: 0.0
Bread: 4 0
Meat: 2.0
Fat: 0.0

1. Rub fish fillets with combined garlic, paprika, and cayenne pepper; refrigerate, covered, 1 hour; cut fillets into 1-inch pieces. Sauté onion, bell pepper, celery, and green onions in oil in large saucepan until tender, about 5 minutes. Add tomatoes with liquid, clam juice, tomato paste, oregano, and bay leaf and heat to boiling; reduce heat and simmer, covered, 10 minutes. Add fish; simmer, uncovered, until fish is tender and flakes with a fork, about

8 minutes. Discard bay leaf; season to taste with salt and hot pepper sauce. Serve over Red Pepper Rice.

Red Pepper Rice
Makes 6 servings

1½ cups uncooked long-grain rice
¼ teaspoon ground turmeric
½ teaspoon paprika
1 roasted red pepper, coarsely chopped

1. Cook rice according to package directions, stirring turmeric into cooking water. Stir paprika and roasted red pepper into cooked rice.

VARIATION

Catfish Creole — Make recipe as above, substituting catfish fillets for the red snapper, and ½ teaspoon each dried marjoram and thyme leaves, celery seeds, and ground cumin for the oregano and bay leaf. Serve over cooked rice.

CARIBBEAN SWEET-SOUR SALMON STEW

45 *Sweet and sour flavors team with salmon, pineapple, and beans in this island-inspired stew.*

6 entrée servings

1 cup each: coarsely chopped onion, sliced red and
green bell peppers

4 cloves garlic, minced

2 teaspoons minced gingerroot

1 jalapeño chili, finely chopped

1 can (20 ounces) pineapple chunks in juice,
undrained

2–3 tablespoons each: light brown sugar, cider vinegar

2–3 teaspoons curry powder

1½ tablespoons cornstarch

¼ cup cold water

1–1½ pounds salmon steaks, cubed (1½-inch)

1 can (15 ounces) black beans, rinsed, drained

Salt and pepper, to taste

4 cups cooked rice, warm

Per Serving:
Calories: 350
% calories from fat: 6
Protein (g): 17.9
Carbohydrate (g): 67.1
Fat (g): 2.5
Saturated fat (g): 0.4
Cholesterol (mg): 28.6
Sodium (mg): 334

Exchanges:
Milk: 0.0
Vegetable: 0.0
Fruit: 1.0
Bread: 3.0
Meat: 1.5
Fat: 0.0

1. Sauté onion, bell peppers, garlic, gingerroot, and jalapeño
chili in lightly greased large skillet until onion is tender, about
5 minutes. Drain pineapple, adding enough water to juice to make
1½ cups. Add pineapple and juice, brown sugar, vinegar, and curry
powder to skillet; heat to boiling. Stir in combined cornstarch and
water, stirring until thickened, about 1 minute. Stir in salmon and
beans; simmer, covered, until salmon is tender and flakes with a
fork, about 5 minutes. Season to taste with salt and pepper. Serve
over rice.

SEAFOOD STEW WITH RISOTTO, MILANESE STYLE

45 *A combination of microwave and range-top cooking simplifies preparation of this unique stew.*

4 entrée servings

1 medium onion, chopped

1 garlic clove, minced

¼ teaspoon crushed saffron threads (optional)

2 teaspoons olive oil

1–1½ cups reduced-sodium fat-free chicken broth, divided

1 can (14½ ounces) reduced-sodium diced tomatoes, undrained

1 cup diced zucchini

8 ounces each: bay scallops, peeled deveined medium shrimp

Microwave Risotto (recipe follows)

¼ cup (1 ounce) grated Parmesan cheese

Salt and pepper, to taste

Per Serving:
Calories: 353
% calories from fat: 17
Protein (g): 31.8
Carbohydrate (g): 39.7
Fat (g): 6.9
Saturated fat (g): 1.9
Cholesterol (mg): 114.7
Sodium (mg): 527

Exchanges:
Milk: 0.0
Vegetable: 2.0
Fruit: 0.0
Bread: 2.0
Meat: 3.0
Fat: 0.0

1. Sauté onion, garlic, and saffron in oil in large saucepan until onion is tender, about 5 minutes. Add 1 cup broth, tomatoes with liquid, and zucchini; heat to boiling. Reduce heat and simmer, covered, 5 minutes. Stir in scallops and shrimp and simmer, uncovered, until shrimp and scallops are cooked, about 5 minutes. Stir in Microwave Risotto and Parmesan cheese; simmer until hot, about 5 minutes, adding remaining ½ cup broth, if desired. Season to taste with salt and pepper.

Microwave Risotto

Makes 4 servings

¾ cup uncooked arborio rice

2 teaspoons olive oil

2⅔ cups reduced-sodium fat-free chicken broth

½ teaspoon dried thyme leaves

Salt and white pepper

1. Combine rice and oil in 2½-quart microwave-safe casserole; microwave, uncovered, on High power 1 minute. Stir in remaining ingredients, except salt and white pepper; microwave, covered, on High, 7 to 8 minutes, turning casserole ½ turn after 4 minutes. Stir well and microwave, uncovered, on High, 11 to 13 minutes longer or until broth is absorbed. Let stand, covered, 2 to 3 minutes. Season to taste with salt and pepper.

FISH AND SUN-DRIED TOMATO STEW

45 *The combination of tomato sauce and sun-dried tomatoes lends rich tomato flavor. Red snapper or other firm-fleshed whitefish can be substituted for the halibut.*

4 entrée servings

1 large onion, chopped
1 teaspoon minced garlic
1 tablespoon olive oil
1 cup clam juice or reduced-fat chicken broth
1 can (8 ounces) tomato sauce
3 tablespoons chopped, softened sun-dried tomatoes (not in oil)
1 teaspoon dried marjoram leaves
½ teaspoon dried oregano leaves
1 pound halibut steaks, sliced (1-inch)
Salt and pepper, to taste

Per Serving:
Calories: 204
% calories from fat: 30
Protein (g): 25.4
Carbohydrate (g): 9.6
Fat (g): 6.8
Saturated fat (g): 0.9
Cholesterol (mg): 36.1
Sodium (mg): 232

Exchanges:
Milk: 0.0
Vegetable: 2.0
Fruit: 0.0
Bread: 0.0
Meat: 3.0
Fat: 0.0

1. Sauté onion and garlic in oil in large skillet until tender and browned, about 8 minutes. Stir in clam juice, tomato sauce, sun-dried tomatoes, and herbs; heat to boiling. Reduce heat and simmer, covered, 5 minutes. Add fish; simmer, covered, until fish is tender and flakes with a fork, about 5 minutes. Season to taste with salt and pepper.

FISH STEW MARSALA

45 *Marsala wine adds a distinctive, appealing note to this simple Italian fish stew. Substitute any lean white fish you prefer.*

4 entrée servings

1 cup each: chopped onion, red and green
   bell peppers
½ cup chopped celery
1 teaspoon minced garlic
1½ tablespoons olive oil
2½ cups reduced-sodium fat-free chicken broth
⅓ cup dry Marsala wine or chicken broth
1 teaspoon dried thyme leaves
¼ cup reduced-sodium tomato paste
1 pound haddock steaks, cubed (2-inch)
2–3 tablespoons lemon juice
2 cups medium pasta shells, cooked, warm
Salt and pepper, to taste

Per Serving:
Calories: 409
% calories from fat: 15
Protein (g): 33
Carbohydrate (g): 49
Fat (g): 7
Saturated fat (g): 1
Cholesterol (mg): 65.2
Sodium (mg): 206

Exchanges:
Milk: 0.0
Vegetable: 1.0
Fruit: 0.0
Bread: 3.0
Meat: 3.0
Fat: 0.0

1. Sauté onion, bell peppers, celery, and garlic in oil in large skillet until tender and lightly browned, about 5 minutes. Add broth, wine, and thyme; heat to boiling. Reduce heat and simmer, uncovered, 10 minutes. Stir in tomato paste and haddock; simmer, covered, until fish is tender and flakes with a fork, about 5 minutes. Season to taste with lemon juice. Stir in pasta; season to taste with salt and pepper.

45-MINUTE PREPARATION TIP: Begin cooking pasta before preparing the rest of the recipe.

EASY BOUILLABAISSE

45 *This easy version of a bouillabaisse can be made in less than 30 minutes!*

8 entrée servings

1 cup chopped onion

½ cup chopped celery

1 clove garlic, minced

1–2 tablespoons olive oil

1 cup each: water, dry white wine or clam juice

2 cans (14½ ounces each) reduced-sodium diced
  tomatoes, undrained

3 leeks (white parts only) thinly sliced

1 bay leaf

1 teaspoon each: dried thyme leaves, grated
  orange zest

1½ pounds salmon steaks, cubed (1½-inch)

8 ounces each: crabmeat, bay scallops

12 mussels, scrubbed

¼ cup chopped parsley

Salt and pepper, to taste

Per Serving:
Calories: 307
% calories from fat: 37
Protein (g): 32.6
Carbohydrate (g): 10.1
Fat (g): 12.4
Saturated fat (g): 2.3
Cholesterol (mg): 82.6
Sodium (mg): 439

Exchanges:
Milk: 0.0
Vegetable: 2.0
Fruit: 0.0
Bread: 0.0
Meat: 4.0
Fat: 0.0

1. Sauté onion, celery, and garlic in oil in Dutch oven until onion is tender, about 5 minutes. Add remaining ingredients, except seafood, parsley, salt, and pepper; heat to boiling. Reduce heat and simmer, covered, 10 minutes. Add seafood and simmer, covered, until salmon is tender and flakes with a fork, about 10 minutes. Discard any unopened mussels. Stir in parsley; season to taste with salt and pepper.

BOUILLABAISSE ST. TROPEZ

The love for bouillabaisse is universal; aioli sauce adds the finishing touch.

8 entrée servings

8 ounces each: haddock or halibut fillets, cod, sole,
   or flounder fillets, cubed crabmeat, cubed lobster
   meat, shucked oysters

1 quart water

½ cup chopped onion

2 cloves garlic, minced

1–2 tablespoons olive oil

1 can (14½ ounces) reduced-sodium diced
   tomatoes, undrained

⅛ teaspoon each: crushed saffron threads
   (optional), fennel seeds

1 bay leaf

½ teaspoon each: dried basil and thyme leaves

⅛–¼ teaspoon crushed red pepper

¼ cup all-purpose flour

½ cup water

Salt and pepper, to taste

8 slices each: lemon, French bread

Aioli (recipe follows)

Per Serving:
Calories: 290
% calories from fat: 18
Protein (g): 30.2
Carbohydrate (g): 27.7
Fat (g): 5.7
Saturated fat (g): 1.2
Cholesterol (mg): 116.3
Sodium (mg): 701

Exchanges:
Milk: 0.0
Vegetable: 1.0
Fruit: 0.0
Bread: 1.5
Meat: 3.0
Fat: 0.0

1. Arrange all seafood in large Dutch oven; add water and heat just
to boiling; reduce heat and simmer, covered, until haddock and cod
are tender and flake with a fork, 5 to 8 minutes. Remove seafood
and arrange on serving platter; keep warm. Measure cooking liquid,
adding enough water to make 5 cups; reserve.

2. Sauté onion and garlic in oil in large Dutch oven until tender,
about 5 minutes. Add reserved cooking liquid, tomatoes with liquid,
saffron, herbs, and crushed red pepper; heat to boiling. Reduce
heat and simmer, covered, 15 minutes. Heat stew to boiling; stir in
combined flour and ½ cup water, stirring until thickened, about 1
minute. Discard bay leaf; season to taste with salt and pepper. Stir
in lemon slices.

3. Spread bread slices with Aioli and place in bottoms of soup
bowls; ladle stew over bread. Let each person add desired seafood
to stew. Serve with remaining Aioli.

Aioli

Makes about ¾ cup

¾ cup fat-free mayonnaise
1 teaspoon each: tarragon vinegar, lemon juice
½–1 teaspoon Dijon mustard
3 cloves garlic, minced
Salt and white pepper, to taste

1. Mix all ingredients, except salt and white pepper; season to taste with salt and white pepper.

MEDITERRANEAN FISHERMEN'S STEW

Bottled clam juice makes a quick and easy alternative to homemade fish stock in this recipe.

4 entrée servings

1 large onion, chopped
4 teaspoons minced garlic
1 teaspoon olive oil
1 can (28 ounces) Italian plum tomatoes, undrained, chopped
2 each: sliced medium zucchini, carrots
1¼ cups clam juice
½–1 teaspoon lemon pepper
1 pound cod, cubed (1-inch)
1 tablespoon finely chopped fresh or 1 teaspoon dried basil leaves
½ cup chopped parsley
Salt and pepper, to taste

Per Serving:
Calories: 192
% calories from fat: 12
Protein (g): 23.9
Carbohydrate (g): 19.9
Fat (g): 2.9
Saturated fat (g): 0.4
Cholesterol (mg): 48.6
Sodium (mg): 282

Exchanges:
Milk: 0.0
Vegetable: 2.0
Fruit: 0.0
Bread: 0.0
Meat: 3.0
Fat: 0.0

1. Sauté onion and garlic in oil in Dutch oven until tender, about 5 minutes. Add tomatoes with liquid, zucchini, carrots, clam juice, and lemon pepper; heat to boiling. Reduce heat and simmer, covered, 20 to 25 minutes. Add cod and basil; simmer, uncovered, until cod is tender and flakes with a fork, 5 to 10 minutes. Stir in parsley; season to taste with salt and pepper.

SCALLOP STEW, ITALIAN-STYLE

45 *Scallops make a quick and easy skillet stew, which is also healthy and low in fat.*

4 entrée servings

1 each: chopped medium onion, chopped medium green bell pepper, minced garlic clove

2 teaspoons olive oil

1 can (14½ ounces) Italian-style plum tomatoes, undrained, chopped

1 cup fat-free chicken broth

2–4 tablespoons cup dry sherry (optional)

1 bay leaf

1 teaspoon dried basil leaves

2 cups small broccoli florets

2 teaspoons cornstarch

¼ cup cold water

12 –16 ounces bay or sea scallops

Salt and pepper, to taste

1 cups long-grain white rice, cooked, warm

Per Serving:
Calories: 339
% calories from fat: 9
Protein (g): 22
Carbohydrate (g): 50
Fat (g): 3.5
Saturated fat (g): 0.4
Cholesterol (mg): 37
Sodium (mg): 352

Exchanges:
Milk: 0.0
Vegetable: 2.0
Fruit: 0.0
Bread: 2.5
Meat: 2.0
Fat: 0.0

1. Sauté onion, green pepper, and garlic in oil in large skillet until onion is tender, about 5 minutes. Add tomatoes with liquid, broth, sherry, bay leaf, basil, and broccoli; heat to boiling. Reduce heat and simmer, covered, until broccoli is crisp-tender, about 5 minutes. Heat stew to boiling; add combined cornstarch and water, stirring until thickened, about 1 minute. Add scallops, reduce heat, and simmer, covered, until cooked and opaque, about 5 minutes. Season to taste with salt and pepper. Serve over rice.

SCALLOP, SHRIMP, AND PEPPER STEW WITH PASTA

45 *A light, colorful medley that's simple to make.*

4 entrée servings

2 cups diced mixed red, yellow, and green bell peppers (1-inch)

1 large onion, coarsely chopped

2 large garlic cloves, minced

2 tablespoons olive oil

1½ cups clam juice or reduced-sodium fat-free chicken broth

⅓ cup chopped fresh parsley

1½ tablespoons lemon juice

1 teaspoon grated lemon zest

½ teaspoon dried thyme leaves

Pinch crushed red pepper

1 large ripe tomato, peeled, coarsely chopped

8 ounces each: peeled deveined medium shrimp, bay scallops

Salt and pepper, to taste

8 ounces uncooked vermicelli, cooked, warm

Per Serving:
Calories: 434
% calories from fat: 20
Protein (g): 39.2
Carbohydrate (g): 52.0
Fat (g): 9.8
Saturated fat (g): 1.3
Cholesterol (mg): 116.2
Sodium (mg): 987

Exchanges:
Milk: 0.0
Vegetable: 1.0
Fruit: 0.0
Bread: 3.0
Meat: 3.0
Fat: 0.0

1. Sauté bell peppers, onion, and garlic in oil in large saucepan until onion begins to brown, 8 to 10 minutes. Add remaining ingredients, except shrimp, scallops, salt, pepper, and pasta; heat to boiling. Reduce heat and simmer, covered, 10 minutes. Add shrimp and scallops; simmer, covered, until shrimp and scallops are cooked, about 5 minutes. Season to taste with salt and pepper. Serve over vermicelli.

SHRIMP AND SAUSAGE GUMBO

45 *Okra thickens the gumbo while giving it a characteristic Creole flavor.*

4 entrée servings

4 ounces smoked turkey sausage, halved, thinly sliced

1 red bell pepper, chopped

1 clove garlic, minced

1 teaspoon margarine or butter

2 cans (14 ounces each) reduced-sodium
  stewed tomatoes

8 ounces each: fresh or frozen sliced okra, peeled
  deveined shrimp

⅛–¼ teaspoon crushed red pepper

Salt, to taste

3 cups cooked rice, warm

Per Serving:
Calories: 316
% calories from fat: 14
Protein (g): 19.9
Carbohydrate (g): 48.9
Fat (g): 5
Saturated fat (g): 1.2
Cholesterol (mg): 104.4
Sodium (mg): 395

Exchanges:
Milk: 0.0
Vegetable: 3.0
Fruit: 0.0
Bread: 2.0
Meat: 2.0
Fat: 0.0

1. Sauté sausage, bell pepper, and garlic in margarine in large saucepan until browned, about 5 minutes. Stir in tomatoes and okra; heat to boiling. Reduce heat and simmer, covered, 10 minutes. Add shrimp and crushed red pepper and simmer, covered, until shrimp are cooked, about 5 minutes. Season to taste with salt. Serve over rice.

SHRIMP, ARTICHOKE, AND PEPPER STEW

45 | *This skillet stew is quick, easy, and brimming with flavor.*

4 entrée servings

⅔ cup each: sliced onion, red and green bell pepper

1 teaspoon minced garlic

1 tablespoon olive oil

1 can (14½ ounces) reduced-sodium chunky
  tomato sauce

1 can (14 ounces) artichoke hearts, drained, quartered

¾ cup chicken or vegetable broth

1–2 tablespoons dry sherry (optional)

2 teaspoons dried Italian seasoning

12 ounces peeled deveined medium shrimp

Salt and pepper, to taste

8 ounces penne, cooked, warm

Per Serving:
Calories: 415
% calories from fat: 11
Protein (g): 26.1
Carbohydrate (g): 60.8
Fat (g): 5.1
Saturated fat (g): 0.8
Cholesterol (mg): 130
Sodium (mg): 438

Exchanges:
Milk: 0.0
Vegetable: 3.0
Fruit: 0.0
Bread: 3.0
Meat: 2.0
Fat: 0.0

1. Sauté onion, bell pepper, and garlic in oil in large skillet until tender, about 5 minutes; add tomato sauce, artichoke hearts, broth, and sherry. Heat to boiling; reduce heat and simmer, covered, 5 minutes. Stir in Italian seasoning and shrimp and simmer, covered, until shrimp are cooked, about 5 minutes. Season to taste with salt and pepper. Serve over penne.

VARIATIONS

Shrimp and Okra Stew — Make recipe as above, omitting bell peppers, dry sherry, and penne and substituting 2 cups fresh or frozen cut okra for the artichoke hearts. Serve over Polenta (see p. 661) and sprinkle with parsley.

Shrimp and Artichoke Stew au Vin — Make recipe as above, substituting ¼–½ cup dry white wine for the sherry; omit penne. Stir ½ to 1 cup fat-free half-and-half or fat-free milk into stew and simmer until hot, about 5 minutes. Stir in 2 to 4 tablespoons grated Parmesan cheese; serve in shallow bowls with Garlic Bread (see p. 645).

ITALIAN-STYLE FISH STEW

45 *Enjoy the flavors of Italy in this well-seasoned fish stew.*

4 entrée servings

3 large garlic cloves, minced

1 tablespoon olive oil

1½ pounds tomatoes, peeled, chopped

1 tablespoon dried Italian seasoning

½ cup chopped parsley

⅛–¼ teaspoon crushed red pepper

1 cup chicken broth or clam juice

½ cup each: dry white wine or chicken broth,
   sliced mushrooms

1 pound grouper or other firm-fleshed fish steaks,
   thinly sliced

Salt and pepper, to taste

Per Serving:
Calories: 201
% calories from fat: 23
Protein (g): 24.1
Carbohydrate (g): 10.5
Fat (g): 5.3
Saturated fat (g): 0.9
Cholesterol (mg): 41.6
Sodium (mg): 67

Exchanges:
Milk: 0.0
Vegetable: 2.0
Fruit: 0.0
Bread: 0.0
Meat: 3.0
Fat: 0.0

1. Sauté garlic in oil in Dutch oven until golden, 1 to 2 minutes. Add remaining ingredients, except fish, salt, and pepper; heat to boiling. Reduce heat and simmer, covered, 10 minutes. Add fish and simmer, covered, until fish is tender and flakes with a fork, about 10 minutes. Season to taste with salt and pepper.

HERBED SHRIMP STEW WITH RICE

45 *Enjoy an easy-to-make, herb-seasoned stew with a bounty of perfectly cooked shrimp.*

4 entrée servings

1 each: chopped medium onion, diced rib celery

2 garlic cloves, minced

1 tablespoon each: olive oil, flour

1 can (14½ ounces) diced tomatoes with garlic, undrained

1 cup clam juice or vegetable broth

½ cup chopped parsley

1 teaspoon each: dried thyme and basil leaves

1 pound medium shrimp, peeled, deveined

3 cups cooked rice, warm

Salt and pepper, to taste

Per Serving:
Calories: 367
% calories from fat: 14
Protein (g): 32.1
Carbohydrate (g): 47.7
Fat (g): 5.9
Saturated fat (g): 1.0
Cholesterol (mg): 172.4
Sodium (mg): 618

Exchanges:
Milk: 0.0
Vegetable: 0.0
Fruit: 0.0
Bread: 3.0
Meat: 3.0
Fat: 0.0

1. Sauté onion, celery, and garlic in oil in large saucepan until tender, about 5 minutes; stir in flour and cook 1 to 2 minutes. Add remaining ingredients, except shrimp, rice, salt, and pepper, and heat to boiling. Reduce heat and simmer, covered, 5 minutes. Add shrimp and rice and simmer, covered, until shrimp are cooked, about 5 minutes. Season to taste with salt and pepper.

VARIATION

Shrimp and Garlic Stew — Make Caramelized Garlic: Cook 25 peeled cloves garlic in 2 to 4 tablespoons olive oil in small skillet over medium to medium-low heat until garlic is golden, 20 to 25 minutes. Coarsely mash garlic with 1 to 2 tablespoons dry white wine. Make recipe as above, omitting garlic and rice. Pass Caramelized Garlic to stir into stew.

SPICY SHRIMP AND RICE STEW

This full-bodied shrimp and rice stew is seasoned with a creative combination of spices.

6 entrée servings

1 each: chopped large onion, carrot, rib celery, medium green bell pepper

2 large garlic cloves, minced

2 teaspoons olive oil

3 cups reduced-sodium fat-free chicken broth

1 can (14½ ounces) reduced-sodium diced tomatoes, undrained

1 bay leaf

1½ teaspoons dried thyme leaves

¾ teaspoon paprika

1 cup uncooked rice

1 pound peeled, deveined medium shrimp

Salt, cayenne, and black pepper, to taste

Per Serving:
Calories: 217
% calories from fat: 9
Protein (g): 14.2
Carbohydrate (g): 34.6
Fat (g): 2.1
Saturated fat (g): 0.4
Cholesterol (mg): 87.5
Sodium (mg): 217

Exchanges:
Milk: 0.0
Vegetable: 1.0
Fruit: 0.0
Bread: 2.0
Meat: 1.0
Fat: 0.0

1. Sauté vegetables and garlic in oil in large saucepan until onion is tender, about 5 minutes. Add remaining ingredients, except shrimp, salt, cayenne, and black pepper, and heat to boiling. Reduce heat and simmer, covered, until rice is tender, about 20 minutes. Add shrimp; simmer, covered, until shrimp are cooked, about 5 minutes. Discard bay leaf; season to taste with salt, cayenne, and black pepper.

CREOLE STEW WITH SHRIMP AND HAM

Crisply cooked strips of ham and dry sherry add complementary flavors to this stew.

6 entrée servings

4 ounces lean ham, cut into thin strips

1–2 tablespoons canola oil

½ cup each: chopped onion, celery, red or green bell pepper

3 cloves garlic, minced

1 can (28 ounces) stewed tomatoes

2–3 tablespoons tomato paste

½ cup clam juice or water

2–4 tablespoons dry sherry (optional)

¼–½ teaspoon hot pepper sauce

1–1½ pounds peeled, deveined shrimp

Salt and pepper, to taste

4 cups cooked rice, warm

Per Serving:
Calories: 301
% calories from fat: 14
Protein (g): 22
Carbohydrate (g): 43
Fat (g): 4.5
Saturated fat (g): 0.9
Cholesterol (mg): 126
Sodium (mg): 778

Exchanges:
Milk: 0.0
Vegetable: 2.0
Fruit: 0.0
Bread: 2.0
Meat: 2.0
Fat: 0.0

1. Cook ham in oil in large saucepan over medium-high heat until browned and crisp, 3 to 4 minutes; remove and reserve. Add onion, celery, bell pepper, and garlic to saucepan and sauté until vegetables are tender, 5 to 8 minutes. Add tomatoes, tomato paste, clam juice, sherry, and hot pepper sauce; heat to boiling. Reduce heat and simmer, covered, 30 minutes. Add reserved ham and shrimp and simmer, covered, until shrimp are cooked, about 5 minutes. Season to taste with salt and pepper; serve over rice.

LOBSTER AND SHRIMP STEW

45 *This luxurious stew can, of course, be made entirely with lobster or with shrimp.*

6 entrée servings

1 each: chopped medium onion, leek (white part only)

2 cloves garlic, minced

1–2 tablespoons margarine

½ teaspoon each: dried oregano, thyme and marjoram leaves, lightly crushed fennel seeds, ground turmeric

1 cup clam juice

3 large tomatoes, chopped

12 ounces each: peeled deveined shrimp, sliced (¾-inch) shelled lobster tail

Salt and pepper, to taste

Turmeric Rice (see p. 475)

Per Serving:
Calories: 375
% calories from fat: 8
Protein (g): 25.7
Carbohydrate (g): 58.3
Fat (g): 3.5
Saturated fat (g): 0.7
Cholesterol (mg): 124.5
Sodium (mg): 429

Exchanges:
Milk: 0.0
Vegetable: 2.0
Fruit: 0.0
Bread: 3.0
Meat: 2.0
Fat: 0.0

1. Sauté onion, leek, and garlic in margarine in large saucepan until tender, 5 to 8 minutes; stir in herbs and cook 1 to 2 minutes. Add clam juice and tomatoes; heat to boiling. Reduce heat and simmer, covered, 15 minutes. Add shrimp and lobster; simmer, covered, until shrimp and lobster are cooked, about 5 minutes, Season to taste with salt and pepper. Serve over Turmeric Rice.

VARIATIONS

Shrimp, Chicken, and Sausage Stew — Make recipe as above, substituting fat-free chicken broth for the clam juice, and cubed chicken breast for the lobster. Sauté 4 ounces sliced reduced-sodium, reduced-fat turkey sausage with the onion, leek, and garlic. Season to taste with hot pepper sauce.

Lobster Stew Cantonese — Make recipe as above, substituting 6 green onions for the leek, pineapple juice for the clam juice, and lobster for the shrimp; omit herbs. Add 1 cup pineapple chunks and 2 ounces trimmed snow peas to stew with the lobster, simmering until lobster is cooked and snow peas are crisp-tender, about 5 minutes Season to taste with 1 to 2 teaspoons each cider vinegar and soy sauce.

TWELVE

Vegetarian Stews

CHILI-BEAN AND CORN CHILI

V

This quick chili is a great start for any meal.

45

4 entrée servings

1 can (14 ounces) chili beans, undrained
1 cup reduced-sodium vegetable broth
1 can (14½ ounces) Italian plum tomatoes, drained, chopped
2 green bell peppers, chopped
1 cup whole kernel corn
1 medium onion, chopped
2 teaspoons minced garlic
2–3 teaspoons chili powder
Salt and pepper, to taste

Per Serving:
Calories: 150
% calories from fat: 7
Protein (g): 8.8
Carbohydrate (g): 31.5
Fat (g): 1.3
Saturated fat (g): 0.1
Cholesterol (mg): 0
Sodium (mg): 524

Exchanges:
Milk: 0.0
Vegetable: 0.0
Fruit: 0.0
Bread: 2.0
Meat: 0.0
Fat: 0.0

1. Heat all ingredients, except salt and pepper, to boiling in large saucepan; reduce heat and simmer, covered, 15 to 20 minutes. Season to taste with salt and pepper.

CURRIED COCONUT STEW

V

Cooked angel hair pasta can be substituted for the rice stick noodles.

6 entrée servings

1 cup each: chopped onion, red bell peppers
2 tablespoons minced gingerroot
1 tablespoon minced garlic
3–4 tablespoons curry powder
3 cups each: vegetable broth, coconut milk
1 cup each: broccoli florets, cubed, peeled, seeded butternut squash
1 tablespoon each: grated lime zest, Oriental chili paste
½ package (8-ounce size) rice stick noodles
¼ cup each: all-purpose flour, cold water, lime juice
Salt and pepper, to taste
Chopped cilantro, as garnish

Per Serving:
Calories: 218
% calories from fat: 28
Protein (g): 4.1
Carbohydrate (g): 37.1
Fat (g): 7.2
Saturated fat (g): 0.1
Cholesterol (mg): 0
Sodium (mg): 627

Exchanges:
Milk: 0.0
Vegetable: 1.0
Fruit: 0.0
Bread: 2.0
Meat: 0.0
Fat: 1.0

1. Sauté onion, bell peppers, gingerroot, and garlic in lightly greased large skillet until tender, about 5 minutes. Stir in curry powder; cook 1 minute. Add broth, coconut milk, vegetables, lime zest, and chili paste; heat to boiling. Reduce heat and simmer, covered, until vegetables are tender, about 15 minutes.

2. While stew is cooking, pour cold water over noodles in large bowl; let stand until noodles are separate and soft, about 5 minutes. Stir noodles into 4 quarts boiling water in large saucepan; reduce heat and simmer, uncovered, until tender, about 5 minutes. Drain. Heat stew to boiling; stir in combined flour, cold water, and lime juice until thickened, about 1 minute. Season to taste with salt and pepper. Serve over noodles; sprinkle generously with cilantro.

VEGETABLE STEW WITH CHEESE TORTELLINI

LO

Serve this simple vegetable stew over your favorite kind of tortellini.

45

4 entrée servings

4 small green or yellow zucchini, cubed

1 green bell pepper, chopped

1 cup sliced mushrooms

½ cup finely chopped onion

1 can (14½ ounces) stewed tomatoes

1 can (14½ ounces) reduced-sodium vegetable broth

¼ teaspoon allspice

½ teaspoon each: dried chervil and basil leaves

Salt and pepper, to taste

1 package (9 ounces) fresh cheese tortellini, cooked, warm

Per Serving:
Calories: 276
% calories from fat: 15
Protein (g): 13.4
Carbohydrate (g): 47.3
Fat (g): 5
Saturated fat (g): 2
Cholesterol (mg): 33.9
Sodium (mg): 511

Exchanges:
Milk: 0.0
Vegetable: 3.0
Fruit: 0.0
Bread: 2.0
Meat: 0.0
Fat: 1.0

1. Heat all ingredients, except salt, pepper, and tortellini, to boiling in large saucepan; reduce heat and simmer, covered, 15 minutes. Season to taste with salt and pepper; serve over tortellini.

VEGGIE STEW WITH CHILI-CHEESE DUMPLINGS

L

One green bell pepper and one small jalapeño chili can be substituted for the poblano chili.

6 entrée servings

2 cups chopped onions

1 cup each: coarsely chopped poblano chili, red and yellow bell peppers

3 cloves garlic, minced

2–3 tablespoons chili powder

1½–2 teaspoons ground cumin

¾ teaspoon each: dried oregano and marjoram leaves

2 tablespoons olive oil

2 cans (14½ ounces each) reduced-sodium diced tomatoes, undrained

1 can (15 ounces) each: black-eyed peas and red beans, rinsed, drained

1½ cups cubed, peeled butternut or acorn squash

1 cup fresh or frozen thawed, okra

Salt and pepper, to taste

Chili-Cheese Dumplings (recipe follows)

Per Serving:
Calories: 433
% calories from fat: 29
Protein (g): 17.4
Carbohydrate (g): 65.9
Fat (g): 14.9
Saturated fat (g): 2.7
Cholesterol (mg): 3.7
Sodium (mg): 713

Exchanges:
Milk: 0.0
Vegetable: 3.0
Fruit: 0.0
Bread: 3.0
Meat: 1.0
Fat: 2.0

1. Sauté onions, poblano chili, bell peppers, garlic, and herbs in oil in large saucepan until onion is tender, about 10 minutes. Stir in remaining ingredients, except salt and pepper and Chili-Cheese Dumplings; heat to boiling. Reduce heat and simmer, covered, until okra and squash are tender, 8 to 10 minutes. Season to taste with salt and pepper.

2. Heat stew to boiling; spoon Chil-Cheese Dumplings dough into 6 mounds on top of stew. Reduce heat and simmer, uncovered, 10 minutes; simmer, covered, until dumplings are dry on top, about 10 minutes.

Chili-Cheese Dumplings

Makes 6 dumplings

⅔ cup all-purpose flour

⅓ cup yellow cornmeal

1½ teaspoons baking powder

1 teaspoon chili powder

½ teaspoon salt
2 tablespoons vegetable shortening
¼ cup (1 ounce) shredded reduced-fat Monterey Jack cheese
½ cup fat-free milk

1. Combine flour, cornmeal, baking powder, chili powder, and salt in medium bowl; cut in shortening with pastry blender until mixture resembles coarse crumbs. Mix in cheese and milk to form a soft dough.

VEGGIE STEW WITH BULGUR

V *Nutritious bulgur helps thicken this stew. Serve with warm, crusty Italian bread.*

4 entrée servings

¾ cup boiling water
½ cup bulgur
2 medium onions, coarsely chopped
2 cups thickly sliced carrots
1 cup diced unpeeled Idaho potatoes
1 each: thickly sliced red and green bell pepper
2 medium zucchini, cubed
1 medium yellow summer squash, cubed
2 cups halved cremini or white mushrooms
2–3 cloves garlic, minced
1 can (14½ ounces) reduced-sodium diced tomatoes, undrained
1–2 cups spicy tomato juice
1 teaspoon each: dried thyme and oregano leaves
Salt and pepper, to taste

Per Serving:
Calories: 259
% calories from fat: 5
Protein (g): 9.9
Carbohydrate (g): 57.4
Fat (g): 1.4
Saturated fat (g): 0.2
Cholesterol (mg): 0
Sodium (mg): 694

Exchanges:
Milk: 0.0
Vegetable: 5.0
Fruit: 0.0
Bread: 2.0
Meat: 0.0
Fat: 0.0

1. Stir boiling water into bulgur in bowl; let stand until bulgur is softened, about 20 minutes.

2. Sauté vegetables and garlic in lightly greased large saucepan until onions are tender, 8 to 10 minutes. Add bulgur and remaining ingredients, except salt and pepper; heat to boiling. Reduce heat and simmer, covered, until vegetables are tender and stew is thickened, 15 to 20 minutes. Season to taste with salt and pepper.

CABBAGE RAGOUT WITH REAL MASHED POTATOES

L

Fresh fennel, gingerroot, and apple lend aromatic highlights to this cabbage stew. If fresh fennel is not available, substitute celery and increase the amount of fennel seeds to 1½ teaspoons.

6 entrée servings

1 medium eggplant (about 1¼ pounds), unpeeled, thickly sliced

Vegetable cooking spray

1 cup chopped onion

½ cup thinly sliced fennel bulb

1 tablespoon each: minced garlic, gingerroot

1 teaspoon fennel seeds, crushed

8 cups thinly sliced cabbage

2 cups reduced-sodium vegetable broth

2 medium apples, peeled, coarsely chopped

1 cup fat-free sour cream

Salt and pepper, to taste

Real Mashed Potatoes (recipe follows)

Per Serving:
Calories: 249
% calories from fat: 10
Protein (g): 8.5
Carbohydrate (g): 50
Fat (g): 3
Saturated fat (g): 0.5
Cholesterol (mg): 8.8
Sodium (mg): 255

Exchanges:
Milk: 0.0
Vegetable: 0.0
Fruit: 0.0
Bread: 3.0
Meat: 0.0
Fat: 0.5

1. Cook 5 or 6 eggplant slices over medium heat in lightly greased large skillet until browned on the bottom, 3 to 5 minutes. Spray tops of slices with cooking spray and turn; cook until browned, 3 to 5 minutes. Repeat with remaining eggplant. Cut eggplant into 1-inch cubes and reserve.

2. Sauté onion, fennel, garlic, gingerroot, and fennel seeds in lightly greased large saucepan until onion is tender, 3 to 5 minutes. Add cabbage and broth and heat to boiling; reduce heat and simmer, covered, until cabbage is wilted, about 5 minutes. Stir in apples and cook, covered, until apples are tender, about 5 minutes. Stir in reserved eggplant and sour cream; cook, covered, over medium heat until hot, 3 to 4 minutes. Season to taste with salt and pepper; serve over potatoes.

Real Mashed Potatoes

Makes about 4 cups

2 pounds Idaho potatoes, unpeeled, quartered, cooked
½ cup fat-free sour cream
¼ cup fat-free milk, hot
2 tablespoons margarine or butter
Salt and pepper, to taste

1. Mash potatoes, or beat until smooth, in medium bowl, adding sour cream, milk, and margarine. Season to taste with salt and pepper.

HASTY STEW

V

45

This stew is easily made in less than 45 minutes and boasts fresh flavors and textures.

4 entrée servings

2 medium onions, cut into wedges
8 ounces mushrooms, sliced
2 cloves garlic, minced
1 teaspoon dried savory leaves
1 bay leaf
2 medium zucchini, sliced
12 ounces potatoes, unpeeled, cubed
8 ounces cauliflower florets
2 cans (14½ ounces each) vegetable broth
1 large tomato, cut into wedges
Salt and pepper, to taste
3 cups cooked millet or couscous, warm

Per Serving:
Calories: 404
% calories from fat: 6
Protein (g): 13.4
Carbohydrate (g): 84.6
Fat (g): 2.6
Saturated fat (g): 0.4
Cholesterol (mg): 0
Sodium (mg): 116

Exchanges:
Milk: 0.0
Vegetable: 3.0
Fruit: 0.0
Bread: 4.5
Meat: 0.0
Fat: 0.0

1. Sauté onions, mushrooms, garlic, and herbs in lightly greased large saucepan until onions are tender, about 5 minutes. Add zucchini, potatoes, cauliflower, and broth to saucepan; heat to boiling. Reduce heat and simmer, covered, until vegetables are tender, about 15 minutes, adding tomato during last 5 minutes. Season to taste with salt and pepper; discard bay leaf. Serve over millet.

RAGOUT OF WINTER VEGETABLES

V *On a chilly day, there's something soul-warming about a flavorful one-dish meal like this.*

4 entrée servings

8 ounces mushrooms, quartered

1 large onion, chopped

3 cloves garlic, minced

2 teaspoons olive oil

2 cans (14½ ounces each) reduced-sodium vegetable broth

½ cup uncooked mixed wild and white rice

3 small sweet potatoes, peeled, cubed

2 carrots, sliced

1 teaspoon dried thyme leaves

Salt and pepper, to taste

Per Serving:
Calories: 270
% calories from fat: 11
Protein (g): 6.9
Carbohydrate (g): 55.4
Fat (g): 3.6
Saturated fat (g): 0.4
Cholesterol (mg): 0
Sodium (mg): 408

Exchanges:
Milk: 0.0
Vegetable: 1.0
Fruit: 0.0
Bread: 3.0
Meat: 0.0
Fat: 0.5

1. Sauté mushrooms, onion, and garlic in oil in large saucepan until lightly browned, about 8 minutes. Add broth and rice and heat to boiling; reduce heat and simmer, covered, 15 minutes. Add sweet potatoes, carrots, and thyme; simmer, covered, until vegetables are tender and rice is cooked, about 15 minutes. Season to taste with salt and pepper.

SQUASH AND POTATO GOULASH

LO *This goulash would also be delicious with Herb Dumplings (see p. 602).*

6 entrée servings

1 clove garlic, minced

2 medium onions, coarsely chopped

1½ cups each: diced red and green bell pepper

2 tablespoons canola or canola oil

3 cups each: cubed peeled butternut squash, Idaho potatoes

1 can (14½ ounces) diced tomatoes, undrained

½ cup dry white wine or vegetable broth

2 cups vegetable broth

3 tablespoons paprika

1 cup fat-free sour cream

Salt and pepper, to taste

4 cups cooked wide noodles, warm

Chopped parsley, as garnish

Caraway seeds, as garnish

Per Serving:
Calories: 491
% calories from fat: 9
Protein (g): 15.3
Carbohydrate (g): 95.8
Fat (g): 5
Saturated fat (g): 0.9
Cholesterol (mg): 39.8
Sodium (mg): 533

Exchanges:
Milk: 0.0
Vegetable: 3.0
Fruit: 0.0
Bread: 5.0
Meat: 0.0
Fat: 1.0

1. Sauté garlic, onions, and bell peppers in oil in large saucepan until tender, about 8 minutes. Add remaining vegetables, wine, and broth; heat to boiling. Reduce heat and simmer, covered, until vegetables are tender, about 20 minutes; simmer, uncovered, if thicker consistency is desired, 5 to 10 minutes. Stir in paprika and sour cream; season to taste with salt and pepper. Serve over noodles; sprinkle with parsley and caraway seeds.

SWEET-SOUR SQUASH AND POTATO STEW

V

45

The vegetables are simmered in cider and seasoned with honey and vinegar for a refreshing sweet-sour flavor.

6 entrée servings

½ cup each: chopped shallots, red bell pepper

2 cloves garlic, minced

1 can (14½ ounces) reduced-sodium diced tomatoes, undrained

1 cup apple cider or apple juice

1½ tablespoons each: honey, cider vinegar

1 bay leaf

¼ teaspoon ground nutmeg

3 cups each: cubed peeled butternut or acorn squash, Idaho potatoes

2 cups each: cubed peeled sweet potatoes, sliced unpeeled tart green apples

1½ cups whole kernel corn

Salt and pepper, to taste

4 cups cooked basmati or jasmine rice, warm

Per Serving:
Calories: 411
% calories from fat: 4
Protein (g): 9.7
Carbohydrate (g): 95.9
Fat (g): 1.8
Saturated fat (g): 0.2
Cholesterol (mg): 0
Sodium (mg): 52

Exchanges:
Milk: 0.0
Vegetable: 3.0
Fruit: 1.0
Bread: 3.5
Meat: 0.0
Fat: 0.0

1. Sauté shallots, bell pepper, and garlic in lightly greased large saucepan until softened, about 4 minutes. Add tomatoes with liquid, cider, honey, vinegar, bay leaf, nutmeg, squash, Idaho and sweet potatoes to saucepan. Heat to boiling, reduce heat and simmer, covered, until potatoes are tender, about 15 minutes. Add apples and corn and simmer until apples are tender, about 5 minutes. Discard bay leaf; season stew to taste with salt and pepper. Serve over rice.

WINTER STEW STROGANOFF

LO

45

A warming stew for cold winter evenings. Substitute turnips, parsnips, or rutabagas for one of the potatoes, if you like.

6 entrée servings

3 medium onions, thinly sliced

8 ounces mushrooms, halved

3 tablespoons margarine

1 pound each: cubed peeled Idaho and sweet potatoes

1 cup frozen peas

1½ cups vegetable broth

1 tablespoon each: dry mustard, sugar

1 cup fat-free sour cream

Salt and pepper, to taste

4 cups cooked wide noodles, warm

Per Serving:
Calories: 414
% calories from fat: 13
Protein (g): 14.4
Carbohydrate (g): 78.9
Fat (g): 6.1
Saturated fat (g): 1
Cholesterol (mg): 39.8
Sodium (mg): 653

Exchanges:
Milk: 0.0
Vegetable: 2.0
Fruit: 0.0
Bread: 4.5
Meat: 0.0
Fat: 1.0

1. Sauté onions and mushrooms in margarine in large saucepan until onions are tender, about 8 minutes. Stir in Idaho and sweet potatoes, peas, broth, dry mustard, and sugar; heat to boiling. Reduce heat and simmer, covered, until potatoes are tender, about 15 minutes. Stir in sour cream; simmer until hot, 2 to 3 minutes. Season to taste with salt and pepper; serve over noodles.

FIRESIDE STEW

L

45

Chock-full of vegetables and pasta and melty with cheese, this stew is sure to please!

8 entrée servings

1 can (15 ounces) each: rinsed drained navy and red kidney beans

1 can (14½ ounces) each: undrained, diced tomatoes with roasted garlic, reduced-sodium vegetable broth

1 cup each: sliced carrots, cubed zucchini

½ cup chopped onion

2 cloves garlic, minced

1 teaspoon dried Italian seasoning

6 ounces small shell pasta

Salt and pepper, to taste

1 cup (4 ounces) shredded reduced-fat Monterey Jack cheese

Per Serving:
Calories: 263
% calories from fat: 11
Protein (g): 15.4
Carbohydrate (g): 43.6
Fat (g): 3.4
Saturated fat (g): 1.9
Cholesterol (mg): 10.1
Sodium (mg): 665

Exchanges:
Milk: 0.0
Vegetable: 2.0
Fruit: 0.0
Bread: 2.0
Meat: 1.0
Fat: 0.0

1. Heat all ingredients, except pasta, salt, pepper, and cheese to boiling in large saucepan; stir in pasta, reduce heat and simmer, covered, until vegetables are tender and pasta is *al dente*, about 10 to 12 minutes; season to taste with salt and pepper. Serve with cheese to stir into soup.

WILD MUSHROOM STEW

V

45

This stew includes three flavorful varieties of fresh mushrooms. Dried mushrooms, softened in hot water, can be substituted for some of the fresh mushrooms for an even richer taste.

6 entrée servings

2 cups each: chopped portobello mushrooms, sliced shiitake, cremini, or white mushrooms

1 cup each: sliced leeks (white parts only), chopped red bell pepper

½ cup chopped onion

1 tablespoon minced garlic

⅛–¼ teaspoon crushed red pepper

2 tablespoons olive oil

3 tablespoons flour

1½ cups reduced-sodium vegetable broth

½ cup dry white wine or vegetable broth

3 cans (15 ounces each) Great Northern beans, rinsed, drained

4 cups sliced Swiss chard or spinach

½ teaspoon each: dried rosemary and thyme leaves

Salt and pepper, to taste

Blue Cheese Polenta (see p. 661)

Per Serving:
Calories: 341
% calories from fat: 13
Protein (g): 16.3
Carbohydrate (g): 63
Fat (g): 5.5
Saturated fat (g): 0.8
Cholesterol (mg): 0
Sodium (mg): 758

Exchanges:
Milk: 0.0
Vegetable: 3.0
Fruit: 0.0
Bread: 3.0
Meat: 1.0
Fat: 1.0

1. Sauté mushrooms, leeks, bell pepper, onion, garlic, and red pepper in oil in large saucepan until tender, about 10 minutes. Stir in flour; cook 1 to 2 minutes. Stir in remaining ingredients, except salt, pepper, and polenta; heat to boiling. Reduce heat and simmer, covered, 10 minutes. Season to taste with salt and pepper; serve over Blue Cheese Polenta.

WINTER BEAN AND VEGETABLE STEW

V

Serve this satisfying stew with Multigrain Batter Bread (see p. 650).

45

6 entrée servings

1 cup each: chopped onion, cubed peeled Idaho and
  sweet potato
½ cup each: sliced carrot, parsnip, chopped green
  bell pepper
2 cloves garlic, minced
2 tablespoons olive oil
1 tablespoon flour
1½ cups reduced-sodium vegetable broth
1 can (15 ounces) black beans, rinsed, drained
1 can (13¼ ounces) baby lima beans, rinsed, drained
1 large tomato, cut into wedges
¾ teaspoon dried sage leaves
Salt and pepper, to taste

Per Serving:
Calories: 238
% calories from fat: 20
Protein (g): 10.8
Carbohydrate (g): 42.4
Fat (g): 5.7
Saturated fat (g): 0.7
Cholesterol (mg): 0
Sodium (mg): 399

Exchanges:
Milk: 0.0
Vegetable: 2.0
Fruit: 0.0
Bread: 2.0
Meat: 0.0
Fat: 1.0

1. Sauté vegetables and garlic in oil in large saucepan 5 minutes;
stir in flour and cook 1 minute. Add remaining ingredients, except
salt and pepper, and heat to boiling. Reduce heat and simmer,
covered, until vegetables are tender, 15 to 20 minutes; season to
taste with salt and pepper.

WHEAT BERRY AND LENTIL STEW WITH DUMPLINGS

L *Use vegetable shortening that is trans-fat free for the dumplings.*

8 entrée servings

1 cup wheat berries

2 medium onions, chopped

½ cup each: chopped celery, sliced carrots

4 cloves garlic, minced

1 teaspoon dried savory leaves

3 cups reduced-sodium vegetable broth

2 pounds russet potatoes, unpeeled, cubed

1½ cups cooked lentils

Salt and pepper, to taste

Herb Dumplings (recipe follows)

Per Serving:
Calories: 414
% calories from fat: 10
Protein (g): 16.8
Carbohydrate (g): 78.6
Fat (g): 4.7
Saturated fat (g): 0.6
Cholesterol (mg): 0.3
Sodium (mg): 259

Exchanges:
Milk: 0.0
Vegetable: 1.0
Fruit: 0.0
Bread: 5.0
Meat: 0.0
Fat: 0.5

1. Soak wheat berries overnight in 2 to 3 inches water in saucepan. Heat to boiling; reduce heat and simmer, covered, until wheat berries are tender, 45 to 55 minutes. Drain.

2. Sauté onions, celery, carrots, garlic, and savory in lightly greased large saucepan until onions are tender, about 5 minutes. Add broth and potatoes and heat to boiling; reduce heat and simmer, covered, until vegetables are tender, 10 to 15 minutes. Stir in wheat berries and lentils; simmer, covered, until hot, about 5 minutes. Season to taste with salt and pepper.

3. Heat stew to boiling; spoon Herb Dumplings dough in 8 mounds on top of stew. Reduce heat and simmer, uncovered, 10 minutes; simmer, covered, until dumplings are dry on top, about 10 minutes.

Herb Dumplings

Makes 8 dumplings

½ cup each: all-purpose flour, yellow cornmeal

1½ teaspoons baking powder

½ teaspoon each: dried sage and thyme leaves, salt

2 tablespoons vegetable shortening

½ cup fat-free milk

1. Combine flour, cornmeal, baking powder, herbs, and salt in small bowl. Cut in shortening with pastry blender until mixture resembles coarse crumbs. Stir in milk to make a soft dough.

LENTIL AND VEGETABLE STEW

L *This lentil stew is flavored with chili peppers, ginger, and lots of garlic. It's very spicy; adjust the seasoning according to your taste, but remember that the flavors will mellow as the stew simmers.*

8 entrée servings

3 large onions, sliced

2 cups frozen peas

8 ounces each: chopped carrots, green beans

3 large tomatoes, chopped

2–4 hot chili peppers, mashed into a paste, or
   1–2 teaspoons cayenne pepper

1 tablespoon minced gingerroot

1 stick cinnamon

10 cloves garlic

6 each: whole cloves, crushed cardamom pods

1 teaspoon ground turmeric

½ teaspoon dried mint leaves, crushed

6 medium potatoes, cubed

½ cup dried lentils

2 cups couscous, cooked, warm

Low-fat plain yogurt, as garnish

Per Serving:
Calories: 380
% calories from fat: 2
Protein (g): 14.4
Carbohydrate (g): 79.7
Fat (g): 1
Saturated fat (g): 0.2
Cholesterol (mg): 0
Sodium (mg): 55

Exchanges:
Milk: 0.0
Vegetable: 4.0
Fruit: 0.0
Bread: 4.0
Meat: 0.0
Fat: 0.0

1. Sauté onions in lightly greased large saucepan 5 minutes; reduce heat to medium-low and cook until golden brown, about 10 minutes. Remove ½ cup onions and reserve for garnish. Add remaining ingredients, except couscous and yogurt; heat to boiling. Reduce heat and simmer, covered, until vegetables and lentils are tender, about 20 minutes. Serve over couscous; garnish with reserved onions and dollops of yogurt.

BEAN-THICKENED VEGETABLE STEW

o   *Puréed beans provide the perfect thickening for this stew.*

6 entrée servings

½ cup each: sliced carrots, chopped onion

3 cloves garlic, minced

1¾ cups Basic Vegetable Stock (see p. 9)

2 cups chopped tomatoes

1½ cups sliced mushrooms

1 yellow summer squash, sliced

1 can (15 ounces) each: rinsed, drained black and
  puréed navy beans

1 cup frozen peas

¾ teaspoon each: dried thyme and oregano leaves

2 bay leaves

Salt and pepper, to taste

4 cups cooked noodles, warm

Per Serving:
Calories: 348
% calories from fat: 5
Protein (g): 18.3
Carbohydrate (g): 71.8
Fat (g): 1.9
Saturated fat (g): 0.2
Cholesterol (mg): 0
Sodium (mg): 589

Exchanges:
Milk: 0.0
Vegetable: 2.0
Fruit: 0.0
Bread: 4.0
Meat: 0.0
Fat: 0.0

1. Sauté carrots, onion, and garlic in lightly greased large saucepan until tender, about 5 minutes. Stir in remaining ingredients, except salt, pepper, and noodles; heat to boiling. Reduce heat and simmer, covered, until vegetables are tender, about 15 minutes. Discard bay leaves; season to taste with salt and pepper. Serve over noodles.

BEAN AND SQUASH STEW

V

Stews don't have to be long-cooked to be good—this delicious stew is simmered to savory goodness in less than 45 minutes. Serve with Peasant Bread (see p. 650).

45

6 entrée servings

1½ cups each: chopped onions, green bell peppers

2 teaspoons minced roasted garlic

1 tablespoon flour

2 cups cubed, peeled butternut or acorn squash

2 cans (14½ ounces each) reduced-sodium diced tomatoes, undrained

1 can (15 ounces) red kidney beans, rinsed, drained

1 can (13¼ ounces) baby lima beans, rinsed, drained

½–¾ teaspoon dried Italian seasoning

Salt and pepper, to taste

Per Serving:
Calories: 239
% calories from fat: 5
Protein (g): 14
Carbohydrate (g): 50.5
Fat (g): 1.4
Saturated fat (g): 0.2
Cholesterol (mg): 0
Sodium (mg): 160

Exchanges:
Milk: 0.0
Vegetable: 3 0
Fruit: 0.0
Bread: 2.0
Meat: 0.5
Fat: 0.0

1. Sauté onions, bell peppers, and garlic in lightly greased large saucepan until tender, about 8 minutes. Stir in flour; cook 1 minute. Add remaining ingredients, except salt and pepper; heat to boiling. Reduce heat and simmer until squash is tender, 10 to 15 minutes. Season to taste with salt and pepper.

LENTIL STEW WITH SPICED COUSCOUS

V *Double or triple the recipe, as this stew freezes well.*

6 entrée servings

1 cup each: chopped onion, red or green bell pepper, celery, carrots

1 teaspoon minced garlic

1 tablespoon olive oil

2 cups each: dried lentils, reduced-sodium vegetable broth

1 can (14½ ounces) diced tomatoes, undrained

1½ cups water

1 teaspoon dried oregano leaves

½ teaspoon ground turmeric

Salt and pepper, to taste

Spiced Couscous (recipe follows)

Per Serving:
Calories: 420
% calories from fat: 9
Protein (g): 24
Carbohydrate (g): 71
Fat (g): 4.1
Saturated fat (g): 0.6
Cholesterol (mg): 0
Sodium (mg): 355

Exchanges:
Milk: 0.0
Vegetable: 3.0
Fruit: 0.0
Bread: 4.0
Meat: 0.0
Fat: 1.0

1. Sauté onion, bell pepper, celery, carrots, and garlic in oil in large saucepan until tender, about 10 minutes. Add remaining ingredients, except salt, pepper, and Spiced Couscous; heat to boiling. Reduce heat and simmer, covered, until lentils are tender, about 30 minutes. Season to taste with salt and pepper; serve over Spiced Couscous.

Spiced Couscous
Makes about 3 cups

⅓ cup sliced green onions
1 clove garlic, minced
⅛–¼ teaspoon crushed red pepper
½ teaspoon ground turmeric
1 teaspoon olive oil
1⅔ cups reduced-sodium vegetable broth
1 cup couscous

1. Sauté green onions, garlic, red pepper, and turmeric in oil in medium saucepan until onions are tender, about 3 minutes. Stir in broth; heat to boiling. Stir in couscous; remove from heat and let stand, covered, 5 minutes or until broth is absorbed.

HEARTY BEAN STEW WITH GREENS

V

45

Focaccia (see p. 641) and fresh fruit would be perfect accompaniments to this stew.

6 entrée servings

½ cup each: dried garbanzo and kidney beans
2 quarts reduced-sodium vegetable broth
1 medium onion, sliced
2 cloves garlic, minced
1 cup each: cubed potatoes, zucchini
½ cup each: thinly sliced carrots, uncooked elbow macaroni
¼ cup quick-cooking oats
2 cups sliced spinach or watercress
2–4 tablespoons lemon juice
Salt and pepper, to taste

Per Serving:
Calories: 230
% calories from fat: 7
Protein (g): 10 6
Carbohydrate (g): 44.6
Fat (g): 1.7
Saturated fat (g): 0.2
Cholesterol (mg): 0
Sodium (mg): 279

Exchanges:
Milk: 0.0
Vegetable: 3.0
Fruit: 0.0
Bread: 2.0
Meat: 0.0
Fat: 0.0

1. Cover beans with 2 inches water in Dutch oven; heat to boiling. Boil 2 minutes. Remove from heat and let stand, covered, about 1 hour; drain.

2. Return beans to Dutch oven. Add broth, onion, and garlic; heat to boiling. Reduce heat and simmer, covered, until beans are tender, about 1 hour, adding potatoes, zucchini, carrots, macaroni, and oats during last 15 minutes. Add spinach and simmer until wilted, about 1 minute. Season to taste with lemon juice, salt, and pepper.

SWEET BEAN STEW WITH DUMPLINGS

L *This vegetable stew is a sweet, chili-flavored treat, delicious with or without the Spicy Cheddar Dumplings.*

8 entrée servings

2 cups diced red or green bell peppers

2 teaspoons minced garlic

1½ cups each: chopped onions, cubed, peeled sweet potatoes, zucchini, apple cider or apple juice

3 cans (15 ounces each) pinto beans, rinsed, drained

2 cans (14½ ounces each) chili-seasoned diced tomatoes, undrained

½ cup raisins

2 teaspoons chili powder

1 teaspoon cumin seeds, lightly crushed

½ teaspoon ground cinnamon

Salt and pepper, to taste

Spicy Cheddar Dumplings (recipe follows)

Per Serving:
Calories: 371
% calories from fat: 15
Protein (g): 13.6
Carbohydrate (g): 69.8
Fat (g): 6.1
Saturated fat (g): 1.7
Cholesterol (mg): 4
Sodium (mg): 717

Exchanges:
Milk: 0.0
Vegetable: 2.0
Fruit: 0.0
Bread: 4.0
Meat: 0.0
Fat: 1.0

1. Sauté bell peppers, garlic, and onions in lightly greased large saucepan until tender, about 8 minutes. Stir in remaining ingredients, except salt, pepper, and Spicy Cheddar Dumplings; heat to boiling. Reduce heat and simmer, covered, until potatoes are almost tender, about 10 minutes. Season to taste with salt and pepper.

2. Heat stew to boiling; spoon Spicy Cheddar Dumplings dough into 8 mounds on top of stew. Reduce heat and simmer, uncovered, 10 minutes; simmer, covered, until dumplings are dry on top, about 10 minutes.

Spicy Cheddar Dumplings
Makes 8 dumplings

½ cup each: yellow cornmeal, all-purpose flour
1 teaspoon baking powder
¼–½ teaspoon crushed red pepper
2 tablespoons each: margarine, whole kernel corn
¼ cup (1 ounce) shredded sharp Cheddar cheese
½ cup fat-free milk

1. Combine cornmeal, flour, baking powder, and red pepper in medium bowl. Cut in margarine with pastry blender until mixture resembles coarse crumbs. Stir in corn and cheese; stir in milk to make a soft dough.

BLACK BEAN AND SPINACH STEW

V

45

The amount of chilies and gingerroot in this heartily spiced dish can be decreased if less hotness is desired.

8 entrée servings

1 cup each: chopped onion, red bell pepper, cubed zucchini
2 jalapeño chilies, finely chopped
2 teaspoons minced garlic
1 tablespoon each: chopped gingerroot, olive oil
2–3 teaspoons chili powder
1 teaspoon ground cumin
½ teaspoon cayenne pepper
3 cans (15 ounces each) black beans, rinsed, drained
1 can (14½ ounces) diced tomatoes, undrained
3 cups sliced spinach
Salt, to taste
4 cups cooked rice, warm

Per Serving:
Calories: 237
% calories from fat: 11
Protein (g): 10.2
Carbohydrate (g): 53.8
Fat (g): 3.6
Saturated fat (g): 0.3
Cholesterol (mg): 0
Sodium (mg): 789

Exchanges:
Milk: 0.0
Vegetable: 1.0
Fruit: 0.0
Bread: 3.0
Meat: 0.0
Fat: 0.0

1. Sauté onion, bell pepper, zucchini, jalapeño chilies, garlic, and gingerroot in oil in large saucepan until tender, about 8 minutes. Stir in chili powder, cumin, and cayenne pepper; cook 1 to 2 minutes. Stir in beans and tomatoes with liquid; heat to boiling.

Reduce heat and simmer, covered, until zucchini is tender, about 10 minutes; uncover and cook until stew is desired thickness, about 5 minutes. Stir in spinach; cook until wilted, about 1 minute. Season to taste with salt; serve over rice.

EASY CREOLE SKILLET STEW

V

45

Easy to make, and fast too—dinner can be on the table in less than 45 minutes! Serve over rice, if desired.

4 entrée servings

1 package (8 ounces) vegetarian sausage links, halved
1 cup chopped onion
2 cloves garlic, minced
2 cups whole kernel corn
1 medium zucchini, sliced
2 cans (14½ ounces each) reduced-sodium stewed
   tomatoes
2 tablespoons flour
¼ cup water
Salt and pepper, to taste

Per Serving:
Calories: 245
% calories from fat: 19
Protein (g): 14.9
Carbohydrate (g): 38.7
Fat (g): 5.7
Saturated fat (g): 0.9
Cholesterol (mg): 0
Sodium (mg): 392

Exchanges:
Milk: 0.0
Vegetable: 2.5
Fruit: 0.0
Bread: 1.0
Meat: 2.0
Fat: 0.0

1. Cook vegetarian sausage in lightly greased large skillet over medium heat until browned, about 8 minutes; add onion and garlic and sauté until tender, about 5 minutes. Stir in corn, zucchini, and tomatoes; heat to boiling. Reduce heat and simmer, uncovered, 10 minutes. Heat mixture to boiling; stir in combined flour and water, stirring until thickened, about 1 minute. Season to taste with salt and pepper.

SOUTHERN STEW WITH DUMPLINGS

L   *Corn, okra, and lima beans simmer in this home-style stew.*

45   **6 entrée servings**

1½ cups each: sliced carrots, celery

2 cups reduced-sodium vegetable broth

2 teaspoons low-sodium Worcestershire sauce

½ teaspoon each: dried oregano and thyme leaves

1 package (10 ounces) each: frozen lima beans, whole kernel corn, sliced okra

Salt and pepper, to taste

Herb Dumplings (see p. 602)

Per Serving:
Calories: 254
% calories from fat: 18
Protein (g): 8.1
Carbohydrate (g): 45.5
Fat (g): 5.2
Saturated fat (g): 1.2
Cholesterol (mg): 0.4
Sodium (mg): 435

Exchanges:
Milk: 0.0
Vegetable: 3.0
Fruit: 0.0
Bread: 2.0
Meat: 0.0
Fat: 1.0

1. Heat all ingredients, except salt, pepper, and Herb Dumplings to boiling in large saucepan; reduce heat and simmer, covered, until carrots and celery are almost tender, about 10 minutes. Season to taste with salt and pepper.

2. Heat stew to boiling; spoon Herb Dumplings dough into 6 mounds on top of stew. Reduce heat and simmer, uncovered, 10 minutes; simmer, covered, until dumplings are dry on top, about 10 minutes.

SOUTHERN VEGETABLE STEW

V   *Team this Southern favorite with Green Chili Cornbread (see p. 654).*

45   **4 entrée servings**

1 thickly sliced, peeled small eggplant

1 medium zucchini, thickly sliced

¼ cup sliced green onions

¾ cup each: coarsely chopped green and red bell pepper

4 cloves garlic, minced

2 cups reduced-sodium vegetable broth

1 can (14½ ounces) reduced-sodium diced tomatoes, undrained

Per Serving:
Calories: 170
% calories from fat: 8
Protein (g): 5.7
Carbohydrate (g): 34.4
Fat (g): 1.6
Saturated fat (g): 0.2
Cholesterol (mg): 0
Sodium (mg): 94

Exchanges:
Milk: 0.0
Vegetable: 6.0
Fruit: 0.0
Bread: 0.0
Meat: 0.0
Fat: 0.0

8 ounces pearl onions, peeled

2 teaspoons paprika

1 cup coarsely shredded or sliced carrots

4 ounces fresh or frozen thawed sliced okra

1–1½ teaspoons coarse-grain mustard

Hot pepper sauce, to taste

Salt and pepper, to taste

1. Sauté eggplant, zucchini, green onions, bell peppers, and garlic in lightly greased large saucepan until tender, softened, 8 to 10 minutes. Add broth, tomatoes with liquid, pearl onions, and paprika; heat to boiling. Reduce heat and simmer until vegetables are tender, about 15 minutes. Season to taste with mustard, hot pepper sauce, salt, and pepper.

HOT 'N SPICY BEAN AND VEGETABLE STEW

V *Make this stew as fiery as you like with serrano or other hot chilies!*

6 entrée servings

1½ cups chopped onions

2–3 teaspoons each: minced serrano chilies, garlic

1 tablespoon flour

1½ teaspoons dried oregano leaves

¾ teaspoon ground cinnamon

½ teaspoon ground cloves

1 bay leaf

2 cans (14½ ounces each) reduced-sodium diced tomatoes, undrained

1½ cups Basic Vegetable Stock (see p. 9)

1 tablespoon red wine vinegar

4 each: sliced carrots, cubed, unpeeled red potatoes

1 can (15 ounces) each: rinsed drained black and pinto beans

Salt and pepper, to taste

Per Serving:
Calories: 284
% calories from fat: 5
Protein (g): 15.4
Carbohydrate (g): 60.8
Fat (g): 2
Saturated fat (g): 0.1
Cholesterol (mg): 0
Sodium (mg): 527

Exchanges:
Milk: 0.0
Vegetable: 3.0
Fruit: 0.0
Bread: 3.0
Meat: 0.0
Fat: 0.0

1. Sauté onions, chilies, and garlic in lightly greased large saucepan until tender, about 5 minutes; stir in flour and seasonings and cook 1 to 2 minutes. Add remaining ingredients, except salt and pepper;

heat to boiling. Reduce heat and simmer, covered, until vegetables are tender, 15 to 20 minutes. Discard bay leaf; season to taste with salt and pepper.

TOFU AND VEGETABLE STEW

V *As with most stews, vegetables in this dish can vary according to season and availability.*

4 entrée servings

½ cup each: sliced onion, celery

3 cloves garlic, minced

4 cups Rich Mushroom Stock (see p. 13)

2 cups sliced, peeled red potatoes

6 medium carrots, sliced

1 bay leaf

1 teaspoon ground cumin

½ teaspoon dried thyme leaves

1 package (10 ounces) frozen chopped
  spinach, thawed

1 package (10½ ounces) firm light tofu or tempeh,
  cubed (½-inch)

¼ cup minced parsley

Salt and pepper, to taste

Per Serving:
Calories: 239
% calories from fat: 8
Protein (g): 11.1
Carbohydrate (g): 43.8
Fat (g): 2.3
Saturated fat (g): 0.2
Cholesterol (mg): 0
Sodium (mg): 182

Exchanges:
Milk: 0.0
Vegetable: 4.0
Fruit: 0.0
Bread: 1.5
Meat: 0.5
Fat: 0.0

1. Sauté onion, celery, and garlic in lightly greased large saucepan until tender, about 4 minutes. Add stock, potatoes, carrots, and herbs to saucepan; heat to boiling. Reduce heat and simmer, covered, until vegetables are tender, about 15 minutes. Add spinach and simmer 2 to 3 minutes; add tofu and parsley and cook until hot, 2 to 3 minutes. Discard bay leaf; season to taste with salt and pepper.

TEX-MEX VEGETABLE STEW

V

Poblano chilies range from mild to very hot in flavor, so taste a tiny bit before using. If the chili is very hot, you may want to substitute some sweet green bell pepper.

6 entrée servings

½ cup each: chopped red onion, seeded poblano chili

3 cloves garlic, minced

2 cans (14½ ounces each) tomatoes with chilies, undrained

1 can (15 ounces) black beans, rinsed, drained

1 cup reduced-sodium vegetable broth

12 small new potatoes, halved

4 medium carrots, thickly sliced

3 ears corn, cut into pieces (2-inch)

2 tablespoons balsamic vinegar

1 tablespoon chili powder

2 teaspoons ground cumin

½ teaspoon dried oregano leaves

2 cups frozen peas, thawed

½ cup finely chopped cilantro

Salt and pepper, to taste

Per Serving:
Calories: 423
% calories from fat: 5
Protein (g): 16.7
Carbohydrate (g): 92.5
Fat (g): 2.4
Saturated fat (g): 0.2
Cholesterol (mg): 0
Sodium (mg): 793

Exchanges:
Milk: 0.0
Vegetable: 3.0
Fruit: 0.0
Bread: 5.0
Meat: 0.0
Fat: 0.0

1. Sauté onion, poblano chili, and garlic in lightly greased large saucepan until tender, 4 minutes. Add remaining ingredients, except peas, cilantro, salt, and pepper; heat to boiling. Reduce heat and simmer, covered, until vegetables are tender, about 20 minutes, stirring in peas and cilantro during the last 5 minutes. Season to taste with salt and pepper.

MEXI-BEANS 'N GREENS STEW

V *Four cans (15 ounces each) pinto beans, rinsed and drained, can be substituted for the dried beans; add to stew with the tomatoes.*

8 entrée servings

2 cups dried pinto beans

½ cup each: coarsely chopped onion, poblano chili, red bell pepper

4 cloves garlic, minced

1 tablespoon each: finely chopped gingerroot, serrano chilies

2 tablespoons olive oil

2 teaspoons each: chili powder, dried oregano leaves

1 teaspoon ground cumin

3 cups water

1 can (14½ ounces) diced tomatoes, undrained

2 cups coarsely chopped turnip or mustard greens

Salt and cayenne pepper, to taste

Per Serving:
Calories: 228
% calories from fat: 16
Protein (g): 11 7
Carbohydrate (g): 37.9
Fat (g): 4.4
Saturated fat (g): 0.6
Cholesterol (mg): 0
Sodium (mg): 233

Exchanges:
Milk: 0.0
Vegetable: 2 0
Fruit: 1.0
Bread: 2.0
Meat: 0.0
Fat: 1.0

1. Cover beans with 2 inches water in large saucepan; heat to boiling and boil, uncovered, 2 minutes. Remove from heat and let stand, covered, 1 hour; drain.

2. Sauté onion, poblano chili, bell pepper, garlic, gingerroot, and serrano chilies in oil in large saucepan until tender, 8 to 10 minutes. Stir in chili powder and herbs; cook 1 to 2 minutes. Add 3 cups water and beans; heat to boiling. Reduce heat and simmer, covered, until beans are tender, about 1 hour, adding more water if necessary. Stir in tomatoes with liquid and turnip greens; simmer, covered, 10 minutes; simmer, uncovered, until thickened to desired consistency, about 15 minutes. Season to taste with salt and cayenne pepper.

MEXICAN ANCHO CHILI STEW

V *This stew has lots of delicious sauce, so serve with crusty warm rolls or warm tortillas. Vary the amount of ancho chilies to taste.*

4 entrée servings

4–6 ancho chilies, stems, seeds, and veins discarded

2 cups boiling water

4 medium tomatoes, cut into wedges

6–8 Mexican-style vegetarian burgers, crumbled

1 large onion, chopped

2 cloves garlic, minced

1 teaspoon each: minced serrano or jalapeño chili, dried oregano leaves, crushed cumin seeds

2 tablespoons flour

Salt and pepper, to taste

Per Serving:
Calories: 275
% calories from fat: 13
Protein (g): 11.9
Carbohydrate (g): 50.9
Fat (g): 4.3
Saturated fat (g): 0.1
Cholesterol (mg): 0
Sodium (mg): 735

Exchanges:
Milk: 0.0
Vegetable: 2.0
Fruit: 0.0
Bread: 2.5
Meat: 0.5
Fat: 0.5

1. Place ancho chilies in bowl; pour boiling water over. Let stand until chilies are softened, about 10 minutes. Process chilies, with water and tomatoes, in food processor or blender until smooth. Cook crumbled vegetarian burgers, onion, garlic, serrano chili, and herbs in lightly greased large saucepan until onion is tender, about 5 minutes. Stir in flour; cook 1 to 2 minutes. Add chili and tomato mixture; heat to boiling. Reduce heat and simmer, covered, 15 to 20 minutes. Season to taste with salt and pepper.

MEXICAN-STYLE VEGETABLE STEW

V *A winter vegetable offering with a Mexican flair, spooned over strands of spaghetti squash. Serve with warm squares of Green Chili Cornbread (see p. 654).*

4 entrée servings

1 medium spaghetti squash, halved, seeded

½ cup each: chopped onion, green pepper

1 carrot, thickly sliced

2 cloves garlic, minced

1 tablespoon flour

2 medium unpeeled russet potatoes, thickly sliced

1 cup cubed rutabaga (1-inch)

1½ cups Basic Vegetable Stock (see p. 9)

1 can (14½ ounces) diced tomatoes and
 chilies, undrained

Salt and pepper, to taste

Chopped cilantro, as garnish

Per Serving:
Calories: 166
% calories from fat: 6
Protein (g): 5.3
Carbohydrate (g): 37.3
Fat (g): 1.1
Saturated fat (g): 0.2
Cholesterol (mg): 0
Sodium (mg): 437

Exchanges:
Milk: 0.0
Vegetable: 2.5
Fruit: 0.0
Bread: 1.5
Meat: 0.0
Fat: 0.0

1. Place squash halves, cut sides down, in baking pan; add ½ inch water. Bake, covered, at 350 degrees until tender, 30 to 40 minutes. Using fork, scrape squash to separate into strands; scoop into bowl and keep warm.

2. Sauté onion, green pepper, carrot, and garlic in lightly greased large saucepan until tender, 8 to 10 minutes. Stir in flour; cook 1 minute. Add potatoes, rutabaga, stock, and tomatoes with liquid; heat to boiling. Reduce heat and simmer, covered, until vegetables are tender, about 15 minutes. Season to taste with salt and pepper. Serve stew over spaghetti squash; sprinkle with cilantro.

COLOMBIAN-STYLE VEGETABLE STEW

v *This delicious stew is a comfort food. Be sure to add the cilantro; it's an important flavor element.*

6 entrée servings

4 garlic cloves, minced

1¼ cups chopped onions

2 tablespoons canola oil

2 cans (14½ ounces each) reduced-sodium diced tomatoes, undrained

6 each: cubed peeled small potatoes, thickly sliced carrots, ribs celery

6 ears corn, cut into pieces (1½-inch)

2 ½ cups reduced-sodium vegetable broth

½ cup dry white wine or vegetable broth

2 bay leaves

1½ tablespoons white wine vinegar

1 teaspoon dried cumin

¾ teaspoon dried oregano leaves

1 can (15 ounces) chickpeas, rinsed, drained

2 cups frozen peas

¾ cup chopped cilantro

Salt and pepper, to taste

Per Serving:
Calories: 503
% calories from fat: 14
Protein (g): 15.8
Carbohydrate (g): 93
Fat (g): 8.1
Saturated fat (g): 0.8
Cholesterol (mg): 0
Sodium (mg): 757

Exchanges:
Milk: 0.0
Vegetable: 4.0
Fruit: 0.0
Bread: 4.5
Meat: 0.0
Fat: 1.5

1. Sauté garlic and onions in oil in large saucepan until tender, about 5 minutes. Add remaining ingredients, except chickpeas, peas, cilantro, salt, and pepper; heat to boiling. Reduce heat and simmer, covered, until vegetables are tender and sauce is thickened, about 20 minutes, adding chickpeas and peas during last 5 minutes. Simmer, uncovered, until thickened to desired consistency, 10 to 15 minutes. Stir in cilantro; discard bay leaves. Season to taste with salt and pepper.

ARGENTINEAN STEW IN A PUMPKIN SHELL

L

This stew is traditionally served in a pumpkin shell. This meatless version is delicious and beautiful.

12 entrée servings

5 garlic cloves, minced

2 cups coarsely chopped red onions

1 large green bell pepper, chopped

3 tablespoons canola oil

1¼ quarts reduced-sodium vegetable broth

½–1 cup dry white wine or vegetable broth

2 cans (14½ ounces each) diced tomatoes, undrained, coarsely chopped

2 tablespoons each: brown sugar, white wine vinegar

2 bay leaves

1 teaspoon dried oregano leaves

5 cups each: cubed peeled potatoes, sweet potatoes, butternut squash

8 ears corn, cut into pieces (1½-inches)

1 pound zucchini, thickly sliced

10 peaches, peeled, halved

Salt and pepper, to taste

Pumpkin Shell (recipe follows)

Per Serving:
Calories: 420
% calories from fat: 16
Protein (g): 8
Carbohydrate (g): 82
Fat (g): 7.5
Saturated fat (g): 0.7
Cholesterol (mg): 0
Sodium (mg): 769

Exchanges:
Milk: 0.0
Vegetable: 2.0
Fruit: 0.5
Bread: 4.0
Meat: 0.0
Fat: 1.5

1. Sauté garlic, onions, and bell pepper in oil in Dutch oven until onion is tender, about 8 minutes. Add remaining ingredients, except corn, zucchini, peaches, salt, pepper, and Pumpkin Shell; heat to boiling. Reduce heat and simmer, covered, 30 minutes, adding corn, zucchini, and peaches during last 10 minutes. Discard bay leaves; season to taste with salt and pepper.

2. Spoon stew into Pumpkin Shell in baking pan; bake, covered with pumpkin lid, at 375 degrees, 10 minutes.

Pumpkin Shell

Makes 1 large shell

1 firm pumpkin, 10–12 pounds, scrubbed

¼ cup margarine or butter, melted

⅓ cup sugar

1. Cut a 7-inch-diameter circle in top of pumpkin; remove fiber and seeds. Brush margarine inside shell and lid; sprinkle with sugar. Place pumpkin and lid on greased cookie sheet; bake at 375 degrees until pumpkin is almost tender but still holds it shape, 30 to 45 minutes. Invert pumpkin to drain liquid.

ROMANIAN STEW WITH RED WINE AND GRAPES

v *Make this stew, known as Ghiveciu, with the same good red wine you serve with it.*

6 entrée servings

4 cups each: cubed, peeled potatoes, eggplant

2 cups small cauliflower florets

2½ cups each: coarsely chopped cabbage, cubed peeled celery root

1½ cups each: cut green beans, halved baby carrots

1 tablespoon minced garlic

2 each: coarsely chopped large red onions, red bell peppers

¼ cup each: margarine (divided), chopped parsley

¾ teaspoon each: dried thyme and marjoram leaves

Salt and pepper, to taste

1½ cups reduced-sodium vegetable broth

½–1 cup dry red wine or vegetable broth

¼ cup tomato paste

2 tablespoons molasses

1 bay leaf

2 large tomatoes, coarsely chopped

1 cup seedless green grapes

½ cup frozen peas

Per Serving:
Calories: 339
% calories from fat: 12
Protein (g): 8.2
Carbohydrate (g): 64.8
Fat (g): 4.9
Saturated fat (g): 0.9
Cholesterol (mg): 0
Sodium (mg): 657

Exchanges:
Milk: 0.0
Vegetable: 4.0
Fruit: 0.5
Bread: 2.5
Meat: 0.0
Fat: 1.0

1. Steam potatoes, eggplant, cauliflower, cabbage, celery root, green beans, and carrots, or cook in 2 inches simmering water, until crisp-tender. Sauté garlic, onions, and bell peppers in 2 tablespoons margarine in saucepan until tender, 8–10 minutes. Add parsley, thyme, and marjoram. Arrange vegetables in 3 ½-quart casserole, alternating layers of steamed and sautéed vegetables, ending with sautéed vegetables, and sprinkling layers lightly with salt and pepper. Heat broth, wine, tomato paste, molasses, bay leaf, and remaining 2 tablespoons margarine to boiling in small saucepan; pour over vegetables. Bake, covered, at 350 degrees 45 minutes, adding tomatoes, grapes, and peas during last 20 minutes. Discard bay leaf.

RAVIOLI AND VEGETABLE STEW WITH BASIL

L

45

Love ravioli? In the mood for a stew? This dish offers both, and it's packed with fresh vegetables—squash, tomatoes, carrots, and escarole, too.

4 entrée servings

2 cans (14 ounces each) reduced-sodium
   vegetable broth
2 carrots, sliced
1¼ cups chopped yellow summer squash
3 plum tomatoes, coarsely chopped
1 package (20 ounces) frozen small cheese ravioli
⅛–¼ teaspoon crushed red pepper
2 cups torn escarole or kale
½ cup chopped fresh or 1½ tablespoons dried
   basil leaves
Salt and pepper, to taste

Per Serving:
Calories: 331
% calories from fat: 19
Protein (g): 16.5
Carbohydrate (g): 51.8
Fat (g): 7.2
Saturated fat (g): 3.9
Cholesterol (mg): 38.6
Sodium (mg): 416

Exchanges:
Milk: 0.0
Vegetable: 4.0
Fruit: 0.0
Bread: 2.0
Meat: 0.0
Fat: 1.5

1. Heat broth and vegetables to boiling in large saucepan; reduce heat and simmer, covered, until vegetables are crisp-tender, 8 to 10 minutes. Add ravioli and crushed red pepper; simmer, uncovered, until ravioli are al dente, about 10 minutes, adding escarole and basil during last 2 to 3 minutes. Season to taste with salt and pepper.

ITALIN BEAN AND PASTA STEW

L *This traditional dish is a cross between a soup and a stew—thick, rich, and flavorful.*

6 entrée servings

1 each: large chopped onion, carrot, rib celery
  minced garlic clove
2 teaspoons olive oil
3½ cups reduced-sodium vegetable broth
1 can (14½ ounces) Italian plum tomatoes,
  undrained, chopped
2½ cups cooked cannellini or 1 can (19 ounces) cannellini or Great Northern beans, drained
½ teaspoon each: dried oregano and basil leaves
3 ounces elbow macaroni, cooked
Salt and pepper, to taste
Grated Parmesan cheese

Per Serving:
Calories: 212
% calories from fat: 9
Protein (g): 10.6
Carbohydrate (g): 37.8
Fat (g): 2.0
Saturated fat (g): 0.3
Cholesterol (mg): 0
Sodium (mg): 356

Exchanges:
Milk: 0.0
Vegetable: 1.0
Fruit: 0.0
Bread: 2.0
Meat: 1.0
Fat: 0.0

1. Sauté onion, carrot, celery, and garlic in oil in large saucepan until tender, about 5 minutes. Add remaining ingredients, except macaroni, salt, pepper, and Parmesan cheese. Heat to boiling; reduce heat and simmer, covered, until vegetables are tender, about 20 minutes, adding macaroni during last 5 minutes. Season to taste with salt and pepper. Pass Parmesan cheese to sprinkle on stew.

ITALIAN BEAN STEW

V

45

Cannellini beans are a favorite Italian bean, but almost any dried bean can be used in this easy recipe. Four cans (15 ounces each) cannellini or other white beans can be substituted.

8 entrée servings

1 medium onion, chopped

1½ cups diced zucchini

½ cup finely chopped, softened sun-dried tomatoes (not in oil)

1 garlic clove, minced

1 tablespoon olive oil

1¾ cups dried white cannellini or Great Northern beans, cooked

1 can (14½ ounces) reduced-sodium stewed tomatoes, undrained

1 can (8 ounces) tomato sauce

1½ teaspoons dried basil leaves

1 teaspoon dried oregano leaves

Salt and pepper, to taste

Per Serving:
Calories: 143
% calories from fat: 14
Protein (g): 8.2
Carbohydrate (g): 24.1
Fat (g): 2.4
Saturated fat (g): 0.4
Cholesterol (mg): 0
Sodium (mg): 84

Exchanges:
Milk: 0.0
Vegetable: 2.0
Fruit: 0.0
Bread: 1.0
Meat: 0.0
Fat: 0.5

1. Sauté onion, zucchini, sun-dried tomatoes, and garlic in oil in large saucepan until onion is tender, about 5 minutes; add remaining ingredients, except salt and pepper. Heat to boiling; reduce heat and simmer, covered, until vegetables are tender, about 8 minutes. Season to taste with salt and pepper.

CHICKPEA AND ROASTED PEPPER STEW WITH CREAMY POLENTA

L

Polenta is a nice change from pasta or rice; this version is especially easy because it's made in the microwave.

4 entrée servings

1 medium onion, chopped

1 garlic clove, minced

2 teaspoons olive oil

1 can (15 ounces) each: rinsed drained chickpeas,
   tomato sauce
1 can (14½ ounces) reduced-sodium stewed tomatoes
1 jar (7 ounces) roasted red peppers, drained,
   chopped
1 medium zucchini, chopped
1 teaspoon dried Italian seasoning
Salt and pepper, to taste
¼ cup (1 ounce) grated Parmesan cheese
Microwave Polenta (see p. 530)

Per Serving:
Calories: 471
% calories from fat: 14
Protein (g): 16.3
Carbohydrate (g): 88.9
Fat (g): 7.3
Saturated fat (g): 1.9
Cholesterol (mg): 7.5
Sodium (mg): 601

Exchanges:
Milk: 0.0
Vegetable: 2.0
Fruit: 0.0
Bread: 5.0
Meat: 0.0
Fat: 1.0

1. Sauté onion and garlic in oil in large saucepan until tender, about 5 minutes. Add remaining ingredients, except salt, pepper, and Parmesan cheese; heat to boiling. Reduce heat and simmer, covered, until vegetables are tender, about 15 minutes. Season to taste with salt and pepper. Stir Parmesan cheese into Microwave Polenta; serve stew over polenta.

THREE-BEAN STEW WITH POLENTA

L *Use any kind of canned or cooked dried beans; one 15-ounce can of drained beans yields 1½ cups.*

4 entrée servings

1 cup chopped onion
½ cup chopped red bell pepper
1 teaspoon minced roasted garlic
1 tablespoon flour
1 can (15 ounces) each: black-eyed peas, black beans,
   and red beans, rinsed, drained
1 can (14½ ounces) reduced-sodium diced
   tomatoes, undrained
1½ teaspoons dried Italian seasoning
¾ cup reduced-sodium vegetable broth
Salt and pepper, to taste
Polenta (see p. 661)

Per Serving:
Calories: 299
% calories from fat: 14
Protein (g): 17.5
Carbohydrate (g): 56
Fat (g): 5.3
Saturated fat (g): 0.6
Cholesterol (mg): 0
Sodium (mg): 587

Exchanges:
Milk: 0.0
Vegetable: 2.0
Fruit: 0.0
Bread: 3.0
Meat: 0.5
Fat: 0.0

1. Sauté onion, bell pepper, and roasted garlic in lightly greased large saucepan until tender, about 5 minutes; stir in flour and cook 1 minute. Add remaining ingredients, except salt, pepper and Polenta; heat to boiling. Reduce heat and simmer, covered, 10 minutes. Season to taste with salt and pepper. Serve stew over Polenta.

RATATOUILLE WITH FETA AIOLI

L *Greek feta cheese imparts a welcome tang to this Mediterranean stew.*

4 entrée servings

2 medium onions, sliced

1 medium eggplant, peeled, cubed

2 teaspoons olive oil

1 can (28 ounces) petite-diced tomatoes, undrained

2 small zucchini, halved, thinly sliced

1 yellow bell pepper, thinly sliced

3 teaspoons minced garlic

2 teaspoons dried Italian seasoning

Salt and pepper, to taste

Feta Aioli (recipe follows)

Per Serving:
Calories: 164
% calories from fat: 15
Protein (g): 6.7
Carbohydrate (g): 31.7
Fat (g): 3.1
Saturated fat (g): 0.5
Cholesterol (mg): 0
Sodium (mg): 522

Exchanges:
Milk: 0.0
Vegetable: 3.0
Fruit: 0.0
Bread: 1.0
Meat: 0.0
Fat: 0.5

1. Sauté onions and eggplant in oil in Dutch oven until onions are tender, about 8 minutes. Add remaining ingredients, except salt, pepper, and Feta Aioli, and heat to boiling. Reduce heat and simmer, covered, until vegetables are tender, about 20 minutes. Season to taste with salt and pepper; serve with Feta Aioli.

Feta Aioli
Makes about ½ cup

¼ cup each: crumbled fat-free feta cheese (1 ounce), fat-free mayonnaise
2–3 cloves garlic, minced

1. Process all ingredients in food processor until smooth.

CURRIED MEDITERRANEAN STEW WITH COUSCOUS

L

45

Serve this stew with a selection of condiments, as it can be enjoyed with a variety of flavor accents.

4 entrée servings

8 ounces fresh or frozen thawed whole okra

1 cup chopped onion

1 teaspoon minced garlic

2 tablespoons olive oil

1 cup each: whole kernel corn, sliced mushrooms

2 medium carrots, sliced

1½ teaspoons curry powder

1 cup reduced-sodium vegetable broth

⅔ cup couscous

1 medium tomato, chopped

Salt and pepper, to taste

Condiments: reduced-fat plain yogurt, chopped
   cucumber, chopped peanuts, raisins

Per Serving:
Calories: 280
% calories from fat: 24
Protein (g): 7.9
Carbohydrate (g): 47.8
Fat (g): 7.7
Saturated fat (g): 1
Cholesterol (mg): 0
Sodium (mg): 46

Exchanges:
Milk: 0.0
Vegetable: 3.0
Fruit: 0.0
Bread: 2.0
Meat: 0.0
Fat: 1.5

1. Sauté okra, onion, and garlic in oil in large saucepan 5 minutes. Stir in corn, mushrooms, carrots, and curry powder; cook 2 minutes. Add broth and heat to boiling; reduce heat and simmer, covered, until vegetables are tender, 8 to 10 minutes. Stir in couscous and tomato; remove from heat and let stand, covered, until couscous is tender and broth absorbed, about 5 minutes. Season to taste with salt and pepper. Serve stew with condiments (not included in nutritional data).

EGGPLANT AND BEAN CURRY STEW

V *The flavorful curry seasoning is created by making a simple paste of onion, garlic, and herbs.*

4 entrée servings

2 medium red potatoes, peeled, cubed (¾-inch)

1 tablespoon olive oil

1 small eggplant, unpeeled, cubed (¾-inch)

¼ cup onion, chopped

1 teaspoon minced garlic

½ teaspoon each: ground coriander, cumin, turmeric

⅛–¼ teaspoon crushed red pepper

½ cup plus 2 tablespoons water, divided

1 can (14½ ounces) reduced-sodium diced tomatoes, undrained

1 can (15 ounces) garbanzo beans, rinsed, drained

Salt and pepper, to taste

¼ cup finely chopped cilantro

Per Serving:
Calories: 242
% calories from fat: 21
Protein (g): 8.2
Carbohydrate (g): 41.8
Fat (g): 6
Saturated fat (g): 0.8
Cholesterol (mg): 0
Sodium (mg): 446

Exchanges:
Milk: 0.0
Vegetable: 2.0
Fruit: 0.0
Bread: 2.0
Meat: 0.0
Fat: 1.0

1. Sauté potatoes in oil in large saucepan until browned, about 5 minutes; remove and reserve. Add eggplant to saucepan; cook over medium to medium-low heat until lightly browned, stirring frequently. Remove eggplant and reserve. Process onion, garlic, herbs, crushed red pepper, and 2 tablespoons water in food processor until a smooth paste. Add to saucepan and cook over medium-low heat 1 to 2 minutes, stirring to prevent burning. Add reserved potatoes and eggplant, remaining ½ cup water, tomatoes with liquid, and beans; heat to boiling. Reduce heat and simmer, covered, until potatoes and eggplant are tender, about 20 minutes. Season to taste with salt and pepper; stir in cilantro.

CURRIED SOYBEAN AND POTATO STEW

V *The curry seasoning in this recipe is a combination of four aromatic spices. Any white beans, such as garbanzo, navy, Great Northern, or cannellini, can be substituted for the soybeans.*

4 entrée servings

1 cup chopped onion
1 medium red bell pepper, chopped
2 teaspoons minced garlic
1 jalapeño chili, finely chopped
2 teaspoons ground turmeric
1 teaspoon ground cumin
½ teaspoon ground coriander
¼ teaspoon ground ginger
4 medium russet potatoes, peeled, cubed
2½ cups cooked dried or rinsed, drained canned soybeans
1 medium cooking apple, peeled, cubed
1–1½ cups vegetable broth
2 teaspoons lemon juice
2 tablespoons chopped cilantro
Salt and pepper, to taste

Per Serving:
Calories: 368
% calories from fat: 24
Protein (g): 22
Carbohydrate (g): 52.7
Fat (g): 10.4
Saturated fat (g): 1.5
Cholesterol (mg): 0
Sodium (mg): 28

Exchanges:
Milk: 0.0
Vegetable: 2.0
Fruit: 0.0
Bread: 2.5
Meat: 1.5
Fat: 1.0

1. Sauté onion, bell pepper, garlic, and jalapeño chili in lightly greased large saucepan until tender, about 5 minutes. Stir in spices; cook 1 minute. Add potatoes, soybeans, apple, and water; heat to boiling. Reduce heat and simmer, covered, until vegetables are tender, about 20 minutes. Stir in lemon juice and cilantro; season to taste with salt and pepper.

CURRIED VEGETABLE STEW

V

45

A variety of spices and herbs are combined to make the fragrant curry that seasons this dish.

4 entrée servings

½ cup chopped onion

2 cloves garlic

1 small head cauliflower, cut into florets

2 each: peeled, cubed medium potatoes, sliced carrots

1½ cups reduced-sodium vegetable broth

¾ teaspoon ground turmeric

¼ teaspoon each: dry mustard, ground cumin and
    coriander

1 tablespoon flour

2 tablespoons cold water

1 large tomato, chopped

¼ cup chopped parsley

1–2 tablespoons lemon juice

Salt, cayenne, and black pepper, to taste

Per Serving:
Calories: 81
% calories from fat: 6
Protein (g): 3.7
Carbohydrate (g): 15.8
Fat (g): 0.6
Saturated fat (g): 0
Cholesterol (mg): 0
Sodium (mg): 57.2

Exchanges:
Milk: 0.0
Vegetable: 2 0
Fruit: 0.0
Bread: 1.0
Meat: 0.0
Fat: 0.0

1. Sauté onion and garlic in lightly greased large saucepan until tender, about 5 minutes. Add cauliflower, potatoes, carrots, broth, and herbs; heat to boiling. Reduce heat and simmer, covered, until vegetables are tender, 10 to 15 minutes. Heat stew to boiling; stir in combined flour and water, stirring until thickened, about 1 minute. Stir in tomato, parsley, and lemon juice; simmer, uncovered, 5 minutes. Season to taste with salt, cayenne, and black pepper.

VEGETABLE TAJINE

V

From the Moroccan cuisine, tajines are traditionally cooked in earthenware pots. Serve with couscous and Pita Bread (see p. 639).

6 entrée servings

½ cup each: chopped onion, sliced carrot, celery

1–2 teaspoons minced gingerroot

1 teaspoon minced garlic

1 cinnamon stick

2 teaspoons each: paprika, ground cumin and coriander

2 cans (14½ ounces each) reduced-sodium diced tomatoes, undrained

1 can (15 ounces) garbanzo beans, rinsed, drained

1 cup each: chopped butternut or acorn squash, turnip or rutabaga, pitted prunes

1½ cups cut green beans

¼ cup pitted small black olives

1 cup vegetable broth or orange juice

Salt and pepper, to taste

4 cups cooked couscous, warm

Per Serving:
Calories: 386
% calories from fat: 10
Protein (g): 12.5
Carbohydrate (g): 78.7
Fat (g): 4.6
Saturated fat (g): 0.6
Cholesterol (mg): 0
Sodium (mg): 540

Exchanges:
Milk: 0.0
Vegetable: 3.0
Fruit: 1.0
Bread: 3 0
Meat: 0.0
Fat: 1.0

1. Sauté onion, carrot, celery, gingerroot, and garlic in lightly greased Dutch oven until tender, about 8 minutes. Stir in spices; cook 1 minute. Add remaining ingredients, except salt, pepper, and couscous; heat to boiling. transfer to oven and bake, covered, at 350 degrees until vegetables are tender, 20 to 30 minutes. Season to taste with salt and pepper. Serve over couscous.

VEGETABLE STEW MARENGO

V

A delicious dish that picks up the colors and flavors of the Mediterranean.

45   **4 entrée servings**

1 package (10½ ounces) firm light tofu, cubed (1-inch)

2 tablespoons olive oil

1 cup each: chopped onion, diced zucchini, whole small mushrooms

1 teaspoon minced garlic

1 tablespoon flour

1 can (14½ ounces) diced tomatoes, undrained

¾ cup vegetable broth

1 strip orange zest (3 x 1 inch)

½ teaspoon each: dried thyme and oregano leaves

Salt and pepper, to taste

3 cups cooked couscous, or rice, warm

Per Serving:
Calories: 349
% calories from fat: 27
Protein (g): 16.7
Carbohydrate (g): 48.4
Fat (g): 10.8
Saturated fat (g): 1
Cholesterol (mg): 0
Sodium (mg): 608

Exchanges:
Milk: 0.0
Vegetable: 3.0
Fruit: 0.0
Bread: 2.0
Meat: 1.0
Fat: 1.5

1. Cook tofu in oil in large saucepan over medium heat until browned on all sides, about 5 minutes. Remove from pan. Add onion, zucchini, mushrooms, and garlic to saucepan; sauté until tender, about 5 minutes. Stir in flour and cook 1 to 2 minutes. Add tomatoes with liquid, broth, orange zest, herbs, and tofu; heat to boiling. Reduce heat and simmer, covered, until vegetables are tender, about 15 minutes. Season to taste with salt and pepper. Serve over couscous.

SEVEN-VEGETABLE STEW WITH COUSCOUS

V *A Moroccan favorite that will please family or guests.*

12 entrée servings

1½ cups chopped onions

3 garlic cloves, minced

2 teaspoons ground cinnamon

1 teaspoon paprika

½ teaspoon each: ground ginger and turmeric

3–4 cups reduced-sodium vegetable broth

3 cans (15 ounces each) garbanzo beans, rinsed, drained

1 small cabbage, cut into 12 wedges

1 large eggplant, cubed

8 ounces each: sliced carrots, cubed small potatoes, turnips, cut green beans, cubed, peeled pumpkin or Hubbard squash

4 medium tomatoes, quartered

1 package (10 ounces) frozen artichoke hearts, quartered

½ cup each: raisins, chopped parsley

Salt and cayenne pepper, to taste

8 cups cooked couscous, warm

Per Serving:
Calories: 495
% calories from fat: 11
Protein (g): 17.6
Carbohydrate (g): 97.5
Fat (g): 64
Saturated fat (g): 1.7
Cholesterol (mg): 0
Sodium (mg): 295

Exchanges:
Milk: 0.0
Vegetable: 6.0
Fruit: 0.0
Bread: 5.0
Meat: 0.0
Fat: 1.0

1. Sauté onions, and garlic in lightly greased large Dutch oven until tender, about 8 minutes; add spices and cook 1 to 2 minutes. Add remaining ingredients, except salt, cayenne pepper, and couscous and heat to boiling. Reduce heat and simmer, covered, until vegetables are tender, about 20 minutes. Season to taste with salt and cayenne pepper. Serve over couscous.

AFRICAN SWEET POTATO STEW

V

45

A spicy garlic paste seasons this delicious stew. Serve with Turmeric Rice (see p. 475), if you like.

6 entrée servings

1 cup sliced onion
Garlic Seasoning Paste (recipe follows)
1½ pounds sweet potatoes, peeled, cubed
2 cans (15 ounces each) chickpeas, rinsed, drained
1½ cups fresh or frozen sliced okra
1 can (28 ounces) diced tomatoes, undrained
1½ cups reduced-sodium vegetable broth
Salt and pepper, to taste
Hot pepper sauce, to taste
3 cups cooked couscous, warm

Per Serving:
Calories: 517
% calories from fat: 8
Protein (g): 15.7
Carbohydrate (g): 104.8
Fat (g): 4.9
Saturated fat (g): 0.6
Cholesterol (mg): 0
Sodium (mg): 544

Exchanges:
Milk: 0.0
Vegetable: 0.0
Fruit: 0.0
Bread: 7.0
Meat: 0.0
Fat: 0.5

1. Sauté onion in lightly greased large saucepan until tender, about 5 minutes; stir in Garlic Seasoning Paste and cook, stirring, 1 minute. Add remaining ingredients, except salt, pepper, hot pepper sauce, and couscous; heat to boiling. Reduce heat and simmer, covered, until vegetables are tender, about 15 minutes. Simmer, uncovered, until stew has thickened to desired consistency, 5 to 10 minutes. Season to taste with salt, pepper, and hot pepper sauce. Serve over couscous.

Garlic Seasoning Paste

6 cloves garlic
2 slices gingerroot (¼-inch)
2 teaspoons each: paprika, cumin seeds
½ teaspoon ground cinnamon
1–2 tablespoons olive oil

1. Process all ingredients in food processor or blender until smooth.

INDIAN BEAN AND VEGETABLE STEW

V

45

This stew is an easy version of the classic khichuri, an Indian bean and grain dish.

4 entrée servings

1 can (13 ounces) adzuki or red beans, rinsed, drained

½ cup uncooked basmati rice

2 cans (14½ ounces each) reduced-sodium vegetable broth

1 teaspoon each: ground cumin, minced gingerroot

¼ teaspoon ground turmeric

1 small jalapeño chili, minced

3 carrots, thinly sliced

2 cups cut wax beans

4 plum tomatoes, chopped

Salt and pepper, to taste

¼ cup toasted sunflower seeds

Per Serving:
Calories: 496
% calories from fat: 9
Protein (g): 10.9
Carbohydrate (g): 101.1
Fat (g): 5.1
Saturated fat (g): 0.6
Cholesterol (mg): 0
Sodium (mg): 276

Exchanges:
Milk: 0.0
Vegetable: 1.0
Fruit: 0.0
Bread: 6.0
Meat: 0.0
Fat: 1.0

1. Heat all ingredients, except tomatoes, salt, pepper, and sunflower seeds, to boiling in large saucepan. heat to boiling. Reduce heat and simmer, covered, until vegetables and rice are tender, about 20 minutes, adding tomatoes the last 5 minutes. Season to taste with salt and pepper. Sprinkle with sunflower seeds.

COCONUT-SQUASH STEW

V *Unsweetened coconut milk gives this Asian-inspired stew its subtle coconut flavor.*

8 entrée servings

1½ cups each: chopped onions, sliced carrots

1 cup chopped celery

1–2 serrano or jalapeño chilies, chopped

1 tablespoon each: minced garlic, gingerroot, canola oil

6 cups cubed, peeled butternut or acorn squash

2 cans (15 ounces each) chickpeas, rinsed, drained

1 can (14½ ounces) diced tomatoes, undrained

1 can (14 ounces) light coconut milk

3–4 tablespoons each: reduced-sodium soy sauce, lime juice, chopped cilantro

Salt, to taste

4–6 cups cooked rice, warm

Per Serving:
Calories: 344
% calories from fat: 15
Protein (g): 10.2
Carbohydrate (g): 64.5
Fat (g): 5.8
Saturated fat (g): 0.4
Cholesterol (mg): 0
Sodium (mg): 647

Exchanges:
Milk: 0.0
Vegetable: 1.0
Fruit: 0.0
Bread: 4.0
Meat: 0.0
Fat: 1.0

1. Sauté onions, carrots, celery, serrano chili, garlic, and gingerroot in oil in large saucepan until lightly browned, about 10 minutes. Add remaining ingredients, except cilantro, salt, and rice; heat to boiling. Reduce heat and simmer, covered, until squash is tender, about 15 minutes. Season to taste with salt; stir in cilantro. Serve over rice.

FRESH VEGETABLE STEW

V

Use any vegetables on hand for this quick veggie stew.

45   **4 entrée servings**

4 green onions, sliced

2 medium tomatoes, chopped

2 each: sliced small carrots, turnips

8 ounces green beans, halved

8 each: frozen or canned artichoke hearts,
    small new potatoes

2 cups reduced-sodium vegetable broth, divided

½ teaspoon dried marjoram leaves

¼ teaspoon dried thyme leaves

4 slices vegetarian bacon, fried crisp, crumbled

1 cup frozen peas

8 asparagus spears, cut (2-inch)

1½ tablespoons flour

Salt and pepper, to taste

3 cups cooked rice, warm

Per Serving:
Calories: 431
% calories from fat: 7
Protein (g): 13.9
Carbohydrate (g): 89.5
Fat (g): 3.3
Saturated fat (g): 0.5
Cholesterol (mg): 0.0
Sodium (mg): 391

Exchanges:
Milk: 0.0
Vegetable: 0.0
Fruit: 0.0
Bread: 6.0
Meat: 0.0
Fat: 0.0

1. Heat green onions, tomatoes, carrots, turnips, green beans, artichoke hearts, potatoes, broth, and herbs to boiling in large saucepan; reduce heat and simmer, covered, until vegetables are tender, about 15 minutes, adding vegetarian bacon, peas, and asparagus during last 5 minutes. Heat stew to boiling, stir in combined remaining ½ cup broth and flour, stirring until thickened, about 1 minutes. Season to taste with salt and pepper; serve over rice.

THIRTEEN

Breads

and

Accompaniments

CROUTONS

Croutons can brighten a soup, add crunch to a salad, and provide a flavor accent for many dishes.

12 servings

3 cups cubed firm or day-old French or Italian
   bread (½–¾–inch)
Vegetable cooking spray

Per Serving:
Calories: 20
% calories from fat: 13
Protein (g): 0.6
Carbohydrate (g): 3.7
Fat (g): 0.3
Saturated fat (g): 0.1
Cholesterol (mg): 0
Sodium (mg): 39

Exchanges:
Milk: 0.0
Vegetable: 0.0
Fruit: 0.0
Bread: 0.0
Meat: 0.0
Fat: 0.0

1. Spray bread cubes with cooking spray; arrange in single layer on jelly roll pan. Bake at 375 degrees until browned, 8 to 10 minutes, stirring occasionally. Cool; store in airtight container up to 2 weeks.

VARIATIONS

Italian-Style Croutons — Spray Italian bread cubes with vegetable cooking spray; sprinkle with combined 1 teaspoon garlic powder and 1 teaspoon dried Italian seasoning and toss. Bake as above.

Sourdough Croutons — Spray sourdough bread cubes with vegetable cooking spray; sprinkle with 2 teaspoons bouquet garni and toss. Bake as above.

Parmesan Croutons — Spray Italian bread cubes with vegetable cooking spray; sprinkle with 1 to 2 tablespoons grated Parmesan cheese and toss. Bake as above.

Rye Caraway Croutons — Spray rye bread cubes with vegetable cooking spray; sprinkle with 2 teaspoons crushed caraway seeds and toss. Bake as above.

Sesame Croutons — Spray bread cubes with vegetable cooking spray; sprinkle with 3 to 4 teaspoons sesame seeds and toss. Bake as above.

Herb Croutons — Spray multigrain or whole wheat bread cubes with vegetable cooking spray; sprinkle with 2 teaspoons dried herbs or herb combinations, and toss. Bake as above.

Garlic Croutons — Spray whole wheat or white bread with olive oil cooking spray and sprinkle generously with garlic powder. Bake as above.

Chili Croutons — Spray bread cubes with cooking spray and sprinkle lightly with chili powder and ground cumin. Bake as above.

BRUSCHETTA

45

These simple-to-make Italian garlic toasts are a base for many toppings, and can compliment any soup or stew.

12 servings (2 each)

1 loaf unsliced French bread (8 ounces) (about 15 inches long)
Olive oil cooking spray
2 cloves garlic, halved

Per Serving:
Calories: 53
% calories from fat: 10
Protein (g): 1.7
Carbohydrate (g): 10
Fat (g): 0.6
Saturated fat (g): 0.1
Cholesterol (mg): 0.0
Sodium (mg): 115

Exchanges:
Milk: 0.0
Vegetable: 0.0
Fruit: 0.0
Bread: 0.5
Meat: 0.0
Fat: 0.0

1. Cut bread into 24 slices; spray both sides of bread lightly with cooking spray. Broil on cookie sheet 4 inches from heat source until browned, 2 to 3 minutes on each side. Rub top sides of bread slices with cut sides of garlic.

VARIATIONS

Herb Bruschetta — Make recipe as above, sprinkling one side of bread with desired dried herb leaves, such as basil, oregano, or dried Italian seasoning before broiling.

Parmesan Bruschetta — Make recipe as above, sprinkling one side of bread with 1 teaspoon grated Parmesan cheese before broiling; watch carefully so cheese does not burn.

Tomato-Basil Bruschetta — Make recipe as above, except spread bread with combined 2 tablespoons olive oil, and 2 teaspoons each minced garlic and dried basil leaves. Top each bread slice with a tomato slice and sprinkle lightly with salt and pepper; garnish with basil sprigs.

SESAME BREAD STICKS

Made easily with a food processor, these breadsticks are the perfect accompaniment to a meal.

12 servings

2⅓–2¾ cups all-purpose white flour, divided
1 package rapid-rising dry yeast
1 cup water
1½ tablespoons olive oil, divided
¾ teaspoon salt
3 tablespoons sesame seeds
Sea salt (optional)

Per Serving:
Calories: 117
% calories from fat: 23
Protein (g): 3.3
Carbohydrate (g): 19
Fat (g): 3
Saturated fat (g): 0.4
Cholesterol (mg): 0
Sodium (mg): 135

Exchanges:
Milk: 0.0
Vegetable: 0.0
Fruit: 0.0
Bread: 1.0
Meat: 0.0
Fat: 1.0

1. Process 1⅓ cups white flour and yeast in food processor until mixed. Heat water, 1 tablespoon oil, and salt to boiling in small saucepan; add to running food processor. Add 1 cup flour and process until dough forms a firm ball, adding more flour if necessary. Transfer dough to greased bowl. Lightly brush top of dough with ½ the remaining olive oil. Let rise, covered, in warm place until doubled in size, about 45 minutes. Punch down dough.

2. Shape dough into twelve 10-inch breadsticks and arrange on greased cookie sheets; brush with remaining oil and sprinkle with sesame seeds and sea salt. Bake at 425 degrees until browned, about 15 minutes.

HERBED-GARLIC BREADSTICKS

These breadsticks are easily made with purchased frozen roll dough!

8 servings

1 tablespoon yellow cornmeal
8 frozen yeast dough rolls, thawed
Olive oil cooking spray
½ teaspoon each: garlic powder, dried marjoram leaves

1. Sprinkle lightly greased cookie sheet evenly with cornmeal. Stretch and roll each dough ball into a 12-inch stick; place on baking sheet and press ends to the baking sheet. Spray with cooking spray; sprinkle with garlic and marjoram. Let stand, loosely covered, in warm place until doubled in size, about 30 minutes. Bake at 425 degrees until golden, about 10 minutes.

Per Serving:
Calories: 80
% calories from fat: 17
Protein (g): 2.2
Carbohydrate (g): 14.3
Fat (g): 1.5
Saturated fat (g): 0.3
Cholesterol (mg): 1.4
Sodium (mg): 137

Exchanges:
Milk: 0.0
Vegetable: 0.0
Fruit: 0.0
Bread: 1.0
Meat: 0.0
Fat: 0.0

PITA BREADS

Also called Syrian bread or pocket breads. If desired, the pitas can be split and filled for sandwiches.

12 servings

1 package active dry yeast
1⅓ cups warm water (110–115 degrees)
¼ teaspoon sugar
1½ tablespoons olive oil
3–4 cups all-purpose flour, divided
1 teaspoon salt

Per Serving:
Calories: 131
% calories from fat: 14
Protein (g): 3.5
Carbohydrate (g): 24.2
Fat (g): 2
Saturated fat (g): 0.3
Cholesterol (mg): 0
Sodium (mg): 178

Exchanges:
Milk: 0.0
Vegetable: 0.0
Fruit: 0.0
Bread: 2.0
Meat: 0.0
Fat: 0.0

1. Combine yeast, warm water, and sugar in large bowl; let stand 5 minutes. Add oil, 3 cups flour, and salt, mixing until smooth. Mix in enough remaining 1 cup flour to make smooth dough. Knead dough on floured surface until smooth and elastic, about 5 minutes. Place in greased bowl; let stand, covered, in warm place until double in size, about 1 hour. Punch dough down.

2. Shape dough into 12 balls; let stand, covered, 30 minutes (dough will not double in size). Roll balls of dough on floured surface into rounds 5 to 6 inches in diameter; place 2 to 3 inches apart on greased cookie sheets; let stand 30 minutes. Bake, 1 pan at a time, at 500 degrees until pitas are puffed and brown, 3 to 5 minutes. Remove to wire racks and cool.

SPINACH-MUSHROOM FLATBREAD

L

This attractive bread is made in a freeform shape and topped with spinach and Parmesan cheese. The bread can be made in advance and reheated at 300 degrees, loosely wrapped in foil, for 15 to 20 minutes.

1 loaf (12–16 servings)

2½–3½ cups all-purpose flour, divided

1½ cups whole wheat flour

2 tablespoons sugar

1½ teaspoons dried rosemary leaves, crushed

½ teaspoon each: dried thyme leaves, salt

1 package fast-rising yeast

2 cups very hot water (125–130 degrees)

¼ cup sliced onion

3 cloves garlic, minced

2 cups torn spinach leaves

1 cup sliced cremini or white mushrooms

¼ cup (2 ounces) shredded reduced-fat mozzarella cheese

2–3 tablespoons grated fat-free Parmesan cheese

Per Serving:
Calories: 190
% calories from fat: 5
Protein (g): 7
Carbohydrate (g): 38.8
Fat (g): 1
Saturated fat (g): 0.4
Cholesterol (mg): 1.3
Sodium (mg): 123

Exchanges:
Milk: 0.0
Vegetable: 0.0
Fruit: 0.0
Bread: 2.5
Meat: 0.0
Fat: 0.0

1. Combine 2½ cups all-purpose flour, whole wheat flour, sugar, herbs, salt, and yeast in large bowl; add water, mixing until smooth. Mix in enough remaining 1 cup all-purpose flour to make soft dough. Knead dough on floured surface until smooth and elastic, about 5 minutes. Place in greased bowl; let rise, loosely covered, in warm place until double in size, 30 to 45 minutes. Punch dough down.

2. Pat dough into a round on floured surface. Pull the edges of the dough into a freeform shape, about 10 x 14 inches. Transfer dough to greased cookie sheet and let stand 20 minutes (dough will rise, but will not double in size). Bake at 350 degrees until golden, about 20 minutes.

3. While bread is baking, sauté onion and garlic in lightly greased skillet until tender, 3 to 4 minutes. Add spinach and mushrooms; cook, covered, over medium until spinach is wilted, about 5 minutes. Cook, uncovered, until mushrooms are tender, about 5 minutes. Remove from heat. Arrange spinach mixture over top of baked bread; sprinkle with cheeses. Return to oven until cheese is melted, 5 to 10 minutes. Transfer to wire rack and cool.

FOCACCIA

L *Focaccia can be frozen, so bake extra to have on hand.*

2 focaccia (10 servings each)

4–5½ cups bread or all-purpose flour, divided
1 package (¼ ounce) fast-rising yeast
1 teaspoon each: sugar, salt
1¾ cups very hot water (125–130 degrees)
Olive oil cooking spray
¼ cup (1 ounce) grated Parmesan cheese

Per Serving:
Calories: 139
% calories from fat: 5
Protein (g): 5.2
Carbohydrate (g): 28.2
Fat (g): 0.8
Saturated fat (g): 0.2
Cholesterol (mg): 1
Sodium (mg): 131

Exchanges:
Milk: 0.0
Vegetable: 0.0
Fruit: 0.0
Bread: 2.0
Meat: 0.0
Fat: 0.0

1. Combine 4 cups flour, yeast, sugar, and salt in large mixing bowl. Add water, mixing until smooth. Mix in enough remaining 1½ cups flour to make soft dough. Knead dough on floured surface until dough is smooth and elastic, about 5 minutes. Place in greased bowl; turn greased side up and let rise, covered, in warm place until double in size, about 1 hour. Punch dough down.

2. Divide dough into halves. Roll 1 piece dough on floured surface to fit jelly roll pan, 15 x 10 inches; ease dough into greased pan. Repeat with remaining dough. Let dough rise until double in size, 45 to 60 minutes. Make ¼-inch-deep indentations with fingers to "dimple" the dough; spray lightly with cooking spray and sprinkle with Parmesan cheese. Bake at 425 degrees until browned, about 30 minutes. Cool in pans on wire racks.

VARIATION

Leek and Onion Focaccia — Make bread as above, except do not sprinkle with cheese. Combine ½ cup each thinly sliced leek (white part only), sliced yellow onion, sliced red onion, and 1 tablespoon olive oil, spread over dough and sprinkle with cheese. Bake as above.

TOMATO-BASIL FOCACCIA

Win rave reviews when you serve this flavorful bread. Refrigerated pizza dough cuts prep time to practically nothing.

8 servings

Olive oil cooking spray
1 tablespoon yellow cornmeal
1 package (10 ounces) refrigerated pizza dough
2 plum tomatoes, thinly sliced
2 teaspoons minced garlic
10 basil leaves, minced

Per Serving:
Calories: 90
% calories from fat: 12
Protein (g): 3
Carbohydrate (g): 16.8
Fat (g): 1.2
Saturated fat (g): 0.2
Cholesterol (mg): 0
Sodium (mg): 176

Exchanges:
Milk: 0.0
Vegetable: 0.0
Fruit: 0.0
Bread: 1.0
Meat: 0.0
Fat: 0.0

1. Spray a perforated pizza pan with cooking spray; sprinkle with cornmeal. Gently stretch dough into 12-inch circle on pan. Spray top of dough lightly with cooking spray. Arrange tomatoes on dough; sprinkle with garlic and basil. Let rise, loosely covered, in warm place until doubled in size, about 30 minutes. Bake at 425 degrees until golden brown, 10 to 12 minutes.

INDIVIDUAL OLIVE FOCACCIAS

Thinly sliced stuffed olives and caramelized onion rings top personal-sized focaccias—perfect to serve with soup!

8 servings

Vegetable cooking spray
1 tablespoon yellow cornmeal
8 frozen yeast dough rolls, thawed
1 large onion, thinly sliced
1 teaspoon each: olive oil, sugar
8 pimiento-stuffed green olives, thinly sliced
½ teaspoon poppy seeds

Per Serving:
Calories: 99
% calories from fat: 24
Protein (g): 2.5
Carbohydrate (g): 16.4
Fat (g): 2.6
Saturated fat (g): 0.5
Cholesterol (mg): 1.4
Sodium (mg): 216

Exchanges:
Milk: 0.0
Vegetable: 0.0
Fruit: 0.0
Bread: 1.0
Meat: 0.0
Fat: 0.5

1. Spray a large cookie sheet with cooking spray; sprinkle with cornmeal. Gently stretch each roll into a 4-inch circle on pan; spray lightly with cooking spray.

2. Sauté onion in oil in large skillet 2 to 3 minutes; sprinkle with sugar and sauté until onions are golden, 8 to 10 minutes. Arrange onions and olives on bread rounds; sprinkle with poppy seeds. Let rise, loosely covered, in warm place until doubled in size, about 30 minutes. Bake at 425 degrees until golden brown, 9 to 11 minutes.

OLIVE FLATBREAD CRISPS

Served warm from the oven, these food processor-fast flatbread wedges are wonderful with soups.

24 servings

2¼–2½ cups all-purpose flour, divided

1 package (¼ ounce) fast-rising dry yeast

¾ cup water

1½ tablespoons olive oil, divided

¾ teaspoon salt

½ cup pitted, chopped green olives

1 tablespoon grated Parmesan cheese

Per Serving:
Calories: 56
% calories from fat: 23
Protein (g): 1.5
Carbohydrate (g): 9.1
Fat (g): 1.4
Saturated fat (g): 0.2
Cholesterol (mg): 0.2
Sodium (mg): 145

Exchanges:
Milk: 0.0
Vegetable: 0.0
Fruit: 0.0
Bread: 0.5
Meat: 0.0
Fat: 0.5

1. Process 1¼ cups flour and yeast in food processor fitted with steel blade until mixed well. Heat water, 1 tablespoon oil, and salt to boiling in small saucepan; add to food processor with machine running. Add 1 cup flour and process until dough form a ball, adding more flour, if necessary. Transfer dough to greased bowl. Lightly brush top of dough with half the remaining olive oil. Let rise, covered, in warm place until doubled in size, about 25 minutes. Punch down dough.

2. Knead olives into dough; roll into a round on lightly floured work surface and brush with remaining olive oil. Bake on greased baking sheet at 450 degrees until bread is browned, about 15 minutes; sprinkling with Parmesan cheese during the last 2 to 3 minutes. Cut into 24 wedges.

EASY HERB LAVOSH

Quick, easy, delicious, and versatile!

6 servings

1 large lavosh (16-inch)
Vegetable or olive oil cooking spray
½–¾ teaspoon caraway seeds or other desired herbs

1. Spray top of lavosh lightly with cooking spray and sprinkle with herbs. Bake on a cookie sheet at 350 degrees until browned, 4 to 6 minutes (watch carefully, as lavosh can burn easily).

Per Serving:
Calories: 132
% calories from fat: 3
Protein (g): 5
Carbohydrate (g): 29.9
Fat (g): 0.6
Saturated fat (g): 0.1
Cholesterol (mg): 0
Sodium (mg): 1

Exchanges:
Milk: 0.0
Vegetable: 0.0
Fruit: 0.0
Bread: 2.0
Meat: 0.0
Fat: 0.0

VARIATION

Parmesan-Thyme Lavosh — Make recipe as above, substituting dried thyme leaves for the caraway seeds and sprinkling with ¼ cup (1 ounce) grated Parmesan cheese.

WHOLE WHEAT LAVOSH

A flat cracker bread that is perfect to serve with soups, or with appetizer dips and spreads.

8 lavosh

½ cup fat-free milk, warm (110–115 degrees)
1 package active dry yeast
2⅓ cups whole wheat flour
½–1 cup all-purpose flour, divided
½ teaspoon salt
1 egg white, lightly beaten
1 tablespoon water

Per Serving:
Calories: 186
% calories from fat: 4
Protein (g): 7.7
Carbohydrate (g): 38.5
Fat (g): 0.8
Saturated fat (g): 0.2
Cholesterol (mg): 0.3
Sodium (mg): 150

Exchanges:
Milk: 0.0
Vegetable: 0.0
Fruit: 0.0
Bread: 2.5
Meat: 0.0
Fat: 0.0

1. Mix milk and yeast in large bowl; let stand 5 minutes. Mix in whole wheat flour, ½ cup all-purpose flour, and salt; mix in enough remaining ½ cup all-purpose flour to make a smooth dough. Let stand, covered, 15 to 20 minutes.

2. Divide dough into 8 equal pieces. Roll each on lightly floured surface into a 3-inch round; place on greased cookie sheet. Brush combined egg white and water over top of dough. Bake at 425 degrees until crisp and browned, 5 to 8 minutes, turning over halfway through baking time. (Lavosh will become crisper upon cooling, so do not overbake.) Cool on wire rack.

GARLIC BREAD

45

Select a good quality French or Italian loaf for this aromatic bread, or use sourdough bread for a flavorful variation.

4 servings

4 thick slices French or Italian bread
Olive oil cooking spray
2 cloves garlic, halved

Per Serving:
Calories: 71
% calories from fat: 10
Protein (g): 2.3
Carbohydrate (g): 13.5
Fat (g): 0.8
Saturated fat (g): 0.2
Cholesterol (mg): 0
Sodium (mg): 152

1. Spray both sides of bread generously with cooking spray. Broil on cookie sheet 4 inches from heat source until browned, about 1 minute on each side. Rub both sides of hot toast with cut sides of garlic.

Exchanges:
Milk: 0.0
Vegetable: 0.0
Fruit: 0.0
Bread: 1.0
Meat: 0.0
Fat: 0.0

VARIATION

Parmesan Garlic Bread — Combine 2 tablespoons grated Parmesan cheese and 4 teaspoons minced garlic. Spray bread with cooking spray as above and spread top of each slice with cheese mixture. Broil as above, or wrap loosely in foil and bake at 350 degrees until warm, about 10 minutes.

HEARTY VEGETABLE-RYE BREAD

Cauliflower adds moistness and subtle flavor to this aromatic rye loaf.

1 loaf (10–12 servings)

1 package active dry yeast

⅓ cup warm water (110–115 degrees)

1 teaspoon sugar

1 cup pureed cooked cauliflower

1 tablespoon each: melted margarine or butter, light
    molasses, spicy brown mustard

2–3 cups all-purpose flour, divided

1 cup rye flour

½ teaspoon salt

1½ teaspoons each: caraway and fennel seeds,
    crushed, divided

1 teaspoon dried dill weed

Melted margarine or butter

Per Serving:
Calories: 177
% calories from fat: 9
Protein (g): 5.3
Carbohydrate (g): 34.8
Fat (g): 1.9
Saturated fat (g): 0.3
Cholesterol (mg): 0
Sodium (mg): 149

Exchanges:
Milk: 0.0
Vegetable: 0.0
Fruit: 0.0
Bread: 2.0
Meat: 0.0
Fat: 0.5

1. Mix yeast, warm water, and sugar in large bowl; let stand 5
minutes. Mix in cauliflower, 1 tablespoon margarine, molasses,
and mustard until blended. Mix in 2 cups all-purpose flour, rye
flour, salt, 1 teaspoon each caraway and fennel seeds, and dill weed.
Mix in enough remaining 1 cup all-purpose flour to make smooth
dough. Knead dough on floured surface until smooth and elastic,
about 5 minutes. Place in greased bowl; let stand, covered, in warm
place until double in size, about 1 hour. Punch dough down.

2. Shape dough into long or round loaf on greased cookie sheet.
Let rise, loosely covered, until double in size, 45 to 60 minutes.
Make 3 or 4 slits in top of loaf with sharp knife; brush with melted
margarine and sprinkle with remaining ½ teaspoon each caraway
and fennel seeds. Bake at 350 degrees until bread is golden and
sounds hollow when tapped, 40 to 50 minutes. Transfer to wire
rack and cool.

ROASTED RED PEPPER BREAD

Bake this bread in a freeform long or round shape, or in a loaf pan. For convenience, use jarred roasted red pepper.

1 loaf (16 servings)

2¼–2¾ cups all-purpose flour, divided

¾ cup whole wheat flour

¼ cup (1 ounce) grated fat-free Parmesan cheese

1½ teaspoons dried Italian seasoning, divided

½ teaspoon salt

1 package fast-rising active dry yeast

1¼ cups very hot water (125–130 degrees)

1 tablespoon olive oil

4 ounces reduced-fat mozzarella cheese, cubed (½-inch)

½ cup coarsely chopped roasted red pepper

1 egg white, beaten

Per Serving:
Calories: 119
% calories from fat: 16
Protein (g): 5.6
Carbohydrate (g): 19
Fat (g): 2.2
Saturated fat (g): 0.9
Cholesterol (mg): 3.8
Sodium (mg): 133

Exchanges:
Milk: 0.0
Vegetable: 0.0
Fruit: 0.0
Bread: 1.5
Meat: 0.0
Fat: 0.5

1. Combine 2¼ cups all-purpose flour, whole wheat flour, Parmesan cheese, 1 teaspoon Italian seasoning, salt, and yeast in large bowl; add hot water and oil, mixing until blended. Mix in mozzarella cheese, red pepper, and enough remaining ½ cup all-purpose flour to make smooth dough. Knead dough on floured surface until smooth and elastic, about 5 minutes. Place in greased bowl; let rise, covered, in warm place until double in size, about 30 minutes. Punch dough down.

2. Shape dough into loaf and place in greased 9 x 5-inch loaf pan. Let stand, covered, until double in size, about 30 minutes. Make 3 or 4 slits in top of loaf with sharp knife. Brush egg white over dough and sprinkle with remaining Italian seasoning. Bake at 375 degrees until loaf is golden and sounds hollow when tapped, 35 to 40 minutes. Remove from pan and cool on wire rack.

LIMA BEAN WHEAT BREAD

Any kind of puréed bean can be used in this moist, dense bread.

3 loaves (10–12 servings each)

2 packages active dry yeast

¼ cup warm water (110–115 degrees)

1 cup each: rinsed drained canned lima beans,
   cold water

2 cups fat-free milk

4–6 tablespoons melted margarine or butter

⅓ cup sugar

4½–5½ cups all-purpose flour, divided

1½ cups whole wheat flour

1½ teaspoons salt

Fat-free milk, for glaze

Per Serving:
Calories: 125
% calories from fat: 13
Protein (g): 4
Carbohydrate (g): 23.2
Fat (g): 1.9
Saturated fat (g): 0.4
Cholesterol (mg): 0.3
Sodium (mg): 133

Exchanges:
Milk: 0.0
Vegetable: 0.0
Fruit: 0.0
Bread: 1.5
Meat: 0.0
Fat: 0.5

1. Mix yeast and warm water in small bowl; let stand 5 minutes.
Process beans and 1 cup cold water in food processor or blender
until smooth. Mix bean purée, 2 cups fat-free milk, margarine, and
sugar in large bowl. Mix in yeast mixture, 4½ cups all-purpose
flour, whole wheat flour, and salt. Mix in enough remaining 1 cup
all-purpose flour to make soft dough. Knead dough on floured
surface until smooth and elastic, about 5 minutes. Place in greased
bowl and let rise, covered, in warm place until double in size, about
1 hour. Punch dough down.

2. Divide dough into 3 equal pieces. Shape each into oval loaf on
greased cookie sheet. Let rise, loosely covered, until double in size,
about 45 minutes; brush with milk. Bake at 375 degrees until
loaves are golden and sound hollow when tapped, about 1 hour.
Transfer to wire racks and cool.

VARIATION

White Bean Rye Bread — Make recipe as above, substituting
Great Northern or navy beans for the lima beans, and rye flour for
the whole wheat flour. Add 1½ teaspoons lightly crushed caraway
seeds to the dough; sprinkle loaves lightly with additional seeds
before baking.

SWEET POTATO BRAIDS

Canned pumpkin can be substituted for the sweet potatoes, if desired.

2 loaves (12 servings each)

2 packages active dry yeast
¼ cup warm fat-free milk (110–115 degrees)
1 cup mashed cooked sweet potatoes
1¾ cups fat-free milk
¼ cup canola oil
1 egg
3–4 cups all-purpose flour, divided
2 cups whole wheat flour
1 teaspoon salt

Per Serving:
Calories: 156
% calories from fat: 17
Protein (g): 4.9
Carbohydrate (g): 27.7
Fat (g): 2.9
Saturated fat (g): 0.5
Cholesterol (mg): 9.2
Sodium (mg): 105

Exchanges:
Milk: 0.0
Vegetable: 0.0
Fruit: 0.0
Bread: 2.0
Meat: 0.0
Fat: 0.5

1. Mix yeast and warm milk in large bowl; let stand 5 minutes. Mix in sweet potatoes, 1¾ cups milk, oil, and egg until blended; mix in 3 cups all-purpose flour, whole wheat flour, and salt. Mix in enough remaining 1 cup all-purpose flour to make smooth dough. Knead dough on floured surface until smooth and elastic, about 5 minutes. Place in greased bowl; let rise, covered, in warm place until double in size, about 1 hour. Punch dough down.

2. Divide dough into halves; divide each half into thirds. Roll pieces of dough into strips, 12 inches long. Braid 3 strips; fold ends under and place on greased cookie sheet. Repeat with remaining dough. Let rise, loosely covered, until double in size, 30 to 45 minutes. Bake at 375 degrees until breads are golden and sound hollow when tapped, 45 to 55 minutes. Transfer to wire racks and cool.

MULTIGRAIN BATTER BREAD

Batter bread preparation is quick and easy, requiring no kneading and only one rise.

2 loaves (16 servings each)

3¼ cups all-purpose flour

1 cup whole wheat flour

¼ cup soy flour or quick-cooking oats

¾ cup quick-cooking oats

¼ cup sugar

½ teaspoon salt

2 packages fast-rising yeast

1 cup cooked brown rice

2¼ cups fat-free milk, hot (125–130 degrees)

2 tablespoons vegetable oil

Per Serving:
Calories: 97
% calories from fat: 13
Protein (g): 3.5
Carbohydrate (g): 17.9
Fat (g): 1.4
Saturated fat (g): 0.2
Cholesterol (mg): 0.3
Sodium (mg): 43

Exchanges:
Milk: 0.0
Vegetable: 0.0
Fruit: 0.0
Bread: 1.0
Meat: 0.0
Fat: 0.5

1. Combine flours, oats, sugar, salt, and yeast in large bowl; add rice, milk, and oil, mixing until smooth. Spoon into 2 greased 8 x 4-inch bread pans; let stand, covered, until double in size, about 30 minutes. Bake at 375 degrees until loaves are browned and sound hollow when tapped, 35 to 40 minutes. Remove from pans and cool on wire racks.

PEASANT BREAD

Five grains and ground pecans combine in this hearty dense-textured country-style bread. Wonderful toasted, this bread is also delicious with honey.

2 small loaves (8–10 servings each)

2 packages active dry yeast

½ cup warm water (110–115 degrees)

1¼ cups whole wheat flour

½ cup each: millet, cracked wheat, yellow cornmeal, bulgur wheat, quick cooking oats, ground pecans

1 teaspoon salt

1¼ cups lukewarm water

¼ cup honey

2 tablespoons canola oil

1–2 cups unbleached all-purpose flour

Per Serving:
Calories: 197
% calories from fat: 22
Protein (g): 5.4
Carbohydrate (g): 34.2
Fat (g): 5
Saturated fat (g): 0.6
Cholesterol (mg): 0
Sodium (mg): 137

Exchanges:
Milk: 0.0
Vegetable: 0.0
Fruit: 0.0
Bread: 2.0
Meat: 0.0
Fat: 1.0

1. Mix yeast and ½ cup warm water in large bowl; let stand 5 minutes. Mix in remaining ingredients, except all-purpose flour; mix in enough all-purpose flour to make smooth dough. Knead dough on floured surface until smooth and elastic, about 5 minutes (dough will be heavy and difficult to maneuver). Place in greased bowl; let rise, covered, in warm place until double in size, about 1½ hours. Punch dough down.

2. Divide dough into halves; shape into round loaves on greased baking sheet. Let stand, loosely covered, until double in size, about 1½ hours. Bake at 350 degrees until loaves are deep golden brown and sound hollow when tapped, about 40 minutes. Transfer to wire racks to cool.

POTATO BREAD

Breads made with mashed potatoes are very moist and retain their freshness well. This dough can be made in advance and refrigerated up to 5 days.

2 loaves (16 servings each)

1 package active dry yeast

1½ cups warm water (110–115 degrees)

2 tablespoons sugar

3 tablespoons margarine or butter, room temperature

2 eggs

1 cup mashed potatoes, lukewarm

5½–6½ cups all-purpose flour, divided

1 cup whole wheat flour

1 teaspoon salt

Fat-free milk

Per Serving:
Calories: 121
% calories from fat: 13
Protein (g): 3.6
Carbohydrate (g): 22.7
Fat (g): 1.7
Saturated fat (g): 0.4
Cholesterol (mg): 13.4
Sodium (mg): 103

Exchanges:
Milk: 0.0
Vegetable: 0.0
Fruit: 0.0
Bread: 1.5
Meat: 0.0
Fat: 0.5

1. Mix yeast and warm water in large bowl; let stand 5 minutes. Mix in sugar, margarine or butter, eggs, and mashed potatoes until blended; mix in 5½ cups all-purpose flour, whole wheat flour, and salt. Mix in enough remaining 1 cup all-purpose flour to make smooth dough. Knead dough on floured surface until smooth and elastic, about 5 minutes. Place in greased bowl; let rise, covered, in warm place until double in size, 1 to 1½ hours. Punch dough down.

2. Divide dough into halves; shape into loaves and place in greased 9 x 5-inch loaf pans. Let stand, loosely covered, until double in size, about 45 minutes. Brush tops of loaves with milk. Bake at 375 degrees until loaves are golden and sound hollow when tapped, about 45 minutes. Remove from pans; cool on wire racks.

THREE-GRAIN MOLASSES BREAD

Molasses and brown sugar give this hearty quick bread a special flavor.

1 loaf (16 servings)

1 cup each: all-purpose flour, whole wheat flour, yellow cornmeal
1 teaspoon baking soda
½ teaspoon salt
1¼ cups water
½ cup each: light molasses, packed light brown sugar
3 tablespoons vegetable oil

Per Serving:
Calories: 155
% calories from fat: 17
Protein (g): 2.5
Carbohydrate (g): 30.5
Fat (g): 3
Saturated fat (g): 0.4
Cholesterol (mg): 0
Sodium (mg): 153

Exchanges:
Milk: 0.0
Vegetable: 0.0
Fruit: 0.0
Bread: 2.0
Meat: 0.0
Fat: 0.5

1. Mix all ingredients in bowl; pour into greased 9 x 5-inch loaf pan. Bake at 350 degrees until wooden pick comes out clean, about 1 hour. Remove bread from pan and cool on wire rack.

BREAD MACHINE CORNBREAD

Here's an easy machine bread that's a perfect go-with for chilies, chowders, or stews. To add a little nip in each bite, add ½ teaspoon crushed red pepper along with the salt and sugar.

1 loaf (12 servings)

1 cup water
1 tablespoon canola oil
½ teaspoon salt
1 tablespoon sugar
2½ cups bread flour
½ cup yellow cornmeal
1 package active dry yeast

Per Serving:
Calories: 136
% calories from fat: 11
Protein (g): 4.2
Carbohydrate (g): 26.4
Fat (g): 1.6
Saturated fat (g): 0.1
Cholesterol (mg): 0.1
Sodium (mg): 102

Exchanges:
Milk: 0.0
Vegetable: 0.0
Fruit: 0.0
Bread: 2.0
Meat: 0.0
Fat: 0.0

1. Place ingredients in bread machine pan in order given in ingredient list. Program machine for basic white bread; press start. When bread has finished baking, remove it from pan. Cool on wire rack.

GREEN CHILI CORNBREAD

45
Cornbread, Southwest-style! If using mild canned chilies, consider adding a teaspoon or two of minced jalapeño chili for a piquant accent.

9 servings

¼ cup chopped red bell pepper

2 cloves garlic, minced

½ teaspoon cumin seeds, crushed

1¼ cups yellow cornmeal

¾ cup all-purpose flour

2 teaspoons baking powder

1 teaspoon sugar

½ teaspoon each: baking soda, salt

1¼ cups buttermilk

½ cup canned cream-style corn

1 can (4 ounces) chopped hot or mild green chilies, well drained

2 eggs

3½ tablespoons margarine or butter, melted

Per Serving:
Calories: 184
% calories from fat: 29
Protein (g): 5.6
Carbohydrate (g): 27.6
Fat (g): 6.1
Saturated fat (g): 1.3
Cholesterol (mg): 24.9
Sodium (mg): 563

Exchanges:
Milk: 0.0
Vegetable: 0.0
Fruit: 0.0
Bread: 2.0
Meat: 0.0
Fat: 1.0

1. Sauté bell pepper, garlic, and cumin seeds in lightly greased small skillet until bell pepper is tender, 2 to 3 minutes. Combine cornmeal, flour, baking powder, sugar, baking soda, and salt in large bowl. Mix in bell pepper mixture, buttermilk, and remaining ingredients; spread in greased 8-inch-square baking pan. Bake at 425 degrees until golden, about 30 minutes. Cool in pan on wire rack; serve warm.

ROASTED CHILI CORNBREAD

45 *Roasted chilies and corn cut from the cob make this a bread to remember!*

9 servings (1 piece each)

2 ears corn, in the husks

1 each: halved small red bell pepper, poblano and jalapeño chili

3 green onions, white parts only

Vegetable cooking spray

½ teaspoon each: ground cumin, dried oregano leaves

1½ cups all-purpose flour

½ cup yellow cornmeal

3 tablespoons light brown sugar

2¾ teaspoons baking powder

½–¾ teaspoon salt

2 eggs, lightly beaten

1 cup buttermilk

3 tablespoons minced cilantro

Per Serving:
Calories: 176
% calories from fat: 8
Protein (g): 6.3
Carbohydrate (g): 35
Fat (g): 1.6
Saturated fat (g): 0.4
Cholesterol (mg): 24.7
Sodium (mg): 283

Exchanges:
Milk: 0.0
Vegetable: 1.0
Fruit: 0.0
Bread: 2.0
Meat: 0.0
Fat: 0.0

1. Soak corn in water to cover for 30 minutes; drain. Arrange corn and vegetables in single layer on greased foil-lined jelly roll pan. Spray with cooking spray; sprinkle vegetables, except corn, with cumin and oregano. Roast at 425 degrees until browned and tender, about 40 minutes. Let corn stand until cool enough to handle; remove and discard husks and cut corn kernels off cobs. Chop remaining vegetables into ¼-inch pieces.

2. Combine flour, cornmeal, brown sugar, baking powder, and salt in medium bowl; add combined eggs and buttermilk, mixing just until combined. Stir in vegetables and cilantro. Pour batter into greased and floured 8-inch baking pan. Bake at 350 degrees until corn bread is browned and toothpick comes out clean, 35 to 40 minutes. Cool in pan on wire rack; serve warm.

JALAPEÑO CORNBREAD

The secret to the moistness in this spicy cornbread is puréed white beans.

9 servings

¼ cup chopped green bell pepper

1–2 teaspoons minced jalapeño chili

2 cloves garlic, minced

¾ teaspoon dried oregano leaves

½ teaspoon ground cumin

¼–½ teaspoon crushed red pepper

¼ cup margarine or butter

1⅓ cups all-purpose flour

⅔ cup yellow cornmeal

1 tablespoon sugar

2 teaspoons baking powder

½ teaspoon each: baking soda, salt

1 cup each: canned rinsed drained Great Northern
    beans, divided, buttermilk

2 eggs

¼ cup canned cream-style corn

Per Serving:
Calories: 202
% calories from fat: 30
Protein (g): 6.6
Carbohydrate (g): 29.8
Fat (g): 7
Saturated fat (g): 1.6
Cholesterol (mg): 48.1
Sodium (mg): 508

Exchanges:
Milk: 0.0
Vegetable: 0.0
Fruit: 0.0
Bread: 2.0
Meat: 0.0
Fat: 1.5

1. Sauté bell pepper, jalapeño chili, garlic, oregano, cumin, and crushed red pepper in margarine or butter in small skillet until bell pepper is tender, about 5 minutes; cool.

2. Combine flour, cornmeal, sugar, baking powder, baking soda, and salt in large bowl. Process ⅔ cup beans in food processor until smooth; add buttermilk, eggs, and corn and process, until smooth. Add to flour mixture, mixing just until ingredients are blended; fold in remaining ⅓ cup beans and pepper mixture. Pour batter into greased 8- or 9-inch-square pan. Bake at 425 degrees until cornbread is browned and toothpick inserted in center comes out clean, about 40 minutes. Cool in pan on wire rack; serve warm.

DILL-CREAM CHEESE BISCUITS

Fresh dill adds pizzazz to these tender biscuits. And because they're a drop rather than a rolled biscuit, they're fast to make.

12 servings

2 cups unbleached all-purpose flour

3 teaspoons baking powder

¼ teaspoon salt

2½ tablespoons each: cold margarine or butter cut into pieces, fat-free cream cheese

2 tablespoons finely chopped fresh or 2 teaspoons dried dill weed

¾ cup fat-free milk

Per Serving:
Calories: 106
% calories from fat: 22
Protein (g): 3.2
Carbohydrate (g): 17.1
Fat (g): 2.6
Saturated fat (g): 0.5
Cholesterol (mg): 0.5
Sodium (mg): 224

Exchanges:
Milk: 0.0
Vegetable: 0.0
Fruit: 0.0
Bread: 1.0
Meat: 0.0
Fat: 0.5

1. Combine flour, baking powder, and salt in medium bowl. Cut in margarine and cream cheese until mixture resembles coarse crumbs. Mix in dill; mix in milk with fork until ingredients are just combined. Drop dough by tablespoons onto greased cookie sheet, making 12 biscuits. Bake at 450 degrees until lightly browned, 10 to 12 minutes. Serve warm.

WHEAT BISCUITS WITH POPPY SEEDS

These slightly nutty-tasting biscuits are delicious!

12 servings

1½ cups unbleached all-purpose flour

½ cup whole wheat flour

3 teaspoons baking powder

¼ teaspoon salt

1 tablespoon poppy seeds

3 tablespoons cold margarine or butter, cut into pieces

¾ cup fat-free milk

Per Serving:
Calories: 109
% calories from fat: 28
Protein (g): 3
Carbohydrate (g): 16.8
Fat (g): 3.4
Saturated fat (g): 0.7
Cholesterol (mg): 0.3
Sodium (mg): 212

Exchanges:
Milk: 0.0
Vegetable: 0.0
Fruit: 0.0
Bread: 1.0
Meat: 0.0
Fat: 0.5

1. Combine flours, baking powder, salt, and poppy seeds in medium bowl. Cut in margarine until flour mixture resembles coarse crumbs. Mix in milk with fork until ingredients are just combined. Drop dough by tablespoons onto greased cookie sheet, making 12 biscuits. Bake at 450 degrees until lightly browned, 10 to 12 minutes. Serve warm.

QUICK SELF-RISING BISCUITS

45

Two cups all-purpose flour, combined with 1 tablespoon baking powder and ½ teaspoon salt, can be substituted for the self-rising flour.

18 servings

1 tablespoon vegetable shortening
2 cups self-rising flour
¾–1 cup fat-free milk
1 tablespoon margarine or butter, melted

Per Serving:
Calories: 65
% calories from fat: 21
Protein (g): 1.7
Carbohydrate (g): 10.8
Fat (g): 1.4
Saturated fat (g): 0.3
Cholesterol (mg): 0.2
Sodium (mg): 189

Exchanges:
Milk: 0.0
Vegetable: 0.0
Fruit: 0.0
Bread: 1.0
Meat: 0.0
Fat: 0.0

1. Cut shortening into flour in medium bowl until mixture resembles coarse crumbs. Stir in enough milk to make a soft dough. Roll dough on floured surface to ½–inch thickness; cut into 18 biscuits with 2-inch cutter. Place in greased 13 x 9-inch baking pan; brush with melted margarine. Bake at 425 degrees until golden, about 15 minutes. Serve warm.

VARIATIONS

Chive Biscuits — Make biscuits as above, mixing 3 tablespoons snipped fresh or dried chives into the dough.

Parmesan Biscuits — Make biscuits as above; sprinkle with 2 tablespoons grated fat-free Parmesan cheese before baking.

SWEET POTATO BISCUITS

45

Sweet potatoes offer moistness and a delicate sweetness to these biscuits. For a nonsweet biscuit, white potatoes can be substituted.

18 biscuits

¾ cup mashed, cooked sweet potatoes

3–4 tablespoons margarine or butter, melted

⅔ cup fat-free milk

2 cups all-purpose flour, divided

4 teaspoons baking powder

1 tablespoon brown sugar

½ teaspoon salt

Fat-free milk

Ground nutmeg

Per Serving:
Calories: 82
% calories from fat: 23
Protein (g): 1.8
Carbohydrate (g): 14
Fat (g): 2.1
Saturated fat (g): 0.4
Cholesterol (mg): 0.1
Sodium (mg): 161

Exchanges:
Milk: 0.0
Vegetable: 0.0
Fruit: 0.0
Bread: 1.0
Meat: 0.0
Fat: 0.5

1. Mix sweet potatoes and margarine in medium bowl; stir in ⅔ cup milk. Mix in 1¾ cups flour, baking powder, brown sugar, and salt. Mix in remaining ¼ cup flour if dough is too sticky to handle easily. Knead dough on floured surface 5 to 6 times. Roll on floured surface to ½–inch thickness; cut into 18 biscuits with 2-inch round cutter and place close together on greased baking sheet. Brush biscuits lightly with milk and sprinkle with nutmeg. Bake at 425 degrees until golden, 12 to 15 minutes. Serve warm.

VARIATION

Herbed Mashed Potato Biscuits — Make recipe as above, omitting sugar and substituting mashed Idaho potatoes for the sweet potatoes; add 1 teaspoon bouquet garni or dried Italian seasoning to the dough. Bake as above.

VINEGAR BISCUITS

45

Vegetable shortening contributes to the fine texture of these biscuits. Vegetable shortening with no trans-fats is now available.

12 biscuits

¾ cup fat-free milk

¼ cup cider vinegar

3 tablespoons vegetable shortening, melted

2 cups all-purpose flour

1½ teaspoons baking soda

1 teaspoon cream of tartar

½ teaspoon salt

Per Serving:
Calories: 109
% calories from fat: 27
Protein (g): 2.7
Carbohydrate (g): 17.1
Fat (g): 3.2
Saturated fat (g): 0.8
Cholesterol (mg): 0.3
Sodium (mg): 255

Exchanges:
Milk: 0.0
Vegetable: 0.0
Fruit: 0.0
Bread: 1.0
Meat: 0.0
Fat: 0.5

1. Mix milk, vinegar, and shortening; mix into combined flour, baking soda, cream of tartar, and salt in medium bowl. Knead dough on generously floured surface 1 to 2 minutes. Pat dough into ½–inch thickness; cut into 12 biscuits with 3-inch round cutter. Bake on greased cookie sheet at 425 degrees until golden, 10 to 12 minutes. Serve warm.

WILD RICE MUFFINS

Wild rice adds crunchy texture and a nutritional boost to these muffins.

12 muffins (1 each)

1 cup fat-free milk

4 tablespoons margarine or butter, melted

1 egg

½ cup wild rice, cooked, cooled

1 cup all-purpose flour

½ cup whole wheat flour

3 tablespoons baking powder

1 tablespoon sugar

½ teaspoon salt

Per Serving:
Calories: 136
% calories from fat: 30
Protein (g): 4.6
Carbohydrate (g): 19.4
Fat (g): 4.5
Saturated fat (g): 0.9
Cholesterol (mg): 18.1
Sodium (mg): 494

Exchanges:
Milk: 0.0
Vegetable: 0.0
Fruit: 0.0
Bread: 1.5
Meat: 0.0
Fat: 0.5

1. Mix milk, margarine, egg, and rice in large bowl. Add combined flours, baking powder, sugar, and salt, mixing just until dry ingredients are moistened. Spoon batter into 12 greased muffin cups. Bake at 400 degrees until browned, 20 to 25 minutes. Remove from pans and cool on wire racks.

POLENTA

45 *This basic recipe can be modified to your taste—note the variations below.*

6 side-dish servings

3 cups water
¾ cup yellow cornmeal
Salt and pepper, to taste

1. Heat water to boiling in large saucepan; gradually stir in cornmeal. Cook over medium to medium-low heat, stirring until polenta thickens enough to hold its shape but is still soft, 5 to 8 minutes.

Per Serving:
Calories: 63
% calories from fat: 4
Protein (g): 1.5
Carbohydrate (g): 13
Fat (g): 0.3
Saturated fat (g): 0.0
Cholesterol (mg): 0.0
Sodium (mg): 0.5

Exchanges:
Milk: 0.0;
Vegetable: 0.0
Fruit: 0.0
Bread: 1.0
Meat: 0.0
Fat: 0.0

VARIATIONS

Blue Cheese Polenta — Make recipe as above, stirring ½ cup (2 ounces) crumbled blue cheese, or other blue veined cheese, into the cooked polenta.

Goat Cheese Polenta — Make recipe as above, stirring ¼ to ½ cup (1 to 2 ounces) crumbled goat cheese into the cooked polenta.

Garlic Polenta — Sauté ¼ cup finely chopped onion and 4 to 6 cloves minced garlic in 1 tablespoon olive oil in large saucepan until tender, 2 to 3 minutes; add water, as above, and complete recipe.

Roasted Pepper-Goat Cheese Polenta — Make recipe as above, gently stirring ¼ to ½ cup crumbled goat cheese and ⅓ cup coarsely chopped roasted red pepper into the cooked polenta.

Basil Polenta — Sauté 3 sliced green onions, 2 cloves garlic, and 1 teaspoon dried basil leaves in 2 teaspoons olive oil in large saucepan until tender, about 2 minutes; add water, as above, and complete recipe.

SPINACH PESTO

45 *Spoon into a soup or stew for extra flavor. It's delicious to serve with any favorite pasta, or as a topping for sliced tomato or vegetable salads.*

4 servings (about 2 tablespoons each)

1 cup loosely packed spinach
¼ cup loosely packed basil leaves
1–2 cloves garlic
1 tablespoon grated fat-free Parmesan cheese
2 tablespoons olive oil
1–2 teaspoons lemon juice
Salt and pepper, to taste

Per Serving:
Calories: 68
% calories from fat: 86
(16% with 2 oz. pasta)
Protein (g): 1
Carbohydrate (g): 1.4
Fat (g): 6.8
Saturated fat (g): 0.9
Cholesterol (mg): 0
Sodium (mg): 22

Exchanges:
Milk: 0.0
Vegetable: 0.0
Fruit: 0.0
Bread: 0.0
Meat: 0.0
Fat: 1.5

1. Process all ingredients, except lemon juice, salt, and pepper, in food processor or blender until almost smooth. Season to taste with lemon juice, salt, and pepper. Serve at room temperature.

VARIATIONS

Spinach-Cilantro Pesto — Make recipe as above, adding ¼ cup packed cilantro leaves, 2 cloves garlic, and ¼ to ½ teaspoon ground cumin; substitute lime juice for the lemon juice.

Cilantro Pesto — Make recipe as above, using ½ cup spinach and 1½ cups packed cilantro and adding 3 tablespoons pine nuts or walnuts; omit basil.

SUN-DRIED TOMATO PESTO

45 *Serve this pesto to stir into a soup or stew for flavor accent.*

4 servings (about 2 tablespoons each)

½ cup each: softened sun-dried tomatoes (not in oil), packed basil leaves
2 cloves garlic
3 tablespoons olive oil
2 tablespoons grated fat-free Parmesan cheese
Salt and pepper, to taste
¼-½ cup water

1. Process sun-dried tomatoes, basil, garlic, oil, and cheese in food processor or blender, adding enough water to make a smooth, spoonable mixture. Season to taste with salt and pepper. Serve at room temperature.

Per Serving:
Calories: 90
% calories from fat: 68
(26% with 2 oz. of pasta)
Protein (g): 2
Carbohydrate (g): 6
Fat (g): 7
Saturated fat (g): 1
Cholesterol (mg): 0.5
Sodium (mg): 171

Exchanges:
Milk: 0.0
Vegetable: 1.0
Fruit: 0.0
Bread: 0.0
Meat: 0.0
Fat: 1.5

FENNEL PESTO

45

Perfect with soups, stews, pasta, or sliced tomatoes. Or stir into fat-free sour cream for a marvelous veggie dip.

4 servings (about 2 tablespoons each)

½ tablespoon fennel seeds

½ cup chopped fennel bulb or celery

¼ cup loosely packed parsley

1 clove garlic

1–2 tablespoons water

½–1 tablespoon olive oil

2 tablespoons each: grated fat-free Parmesan cheese, walnuts

Salt and pepper, to taste

Per Serving:
Calories: 35
% of calories from fat: 61
(17% with 2 oz. pasta)
Protein (g): 1.3
Carbohydrate (g): 2.3
Fat (g): 2.5
Saturated fat (g): 0.3
Cholesterol (mg): 0
Sodium (mg): 21

Exchanges:
Milk: 0.0
Vegetable: 0.5
Fruit: 0.0
Bread: 0.0
Meat: 0.0
Fat: 0.5

1. Soak fennel seeds in hot water in small bowl; let stand 10 minutes; drain. Process fennel seeds and remaining ingredients, except salt and pepper, in food processor or blender until almost smooth. Season to taste with salt and pepper. Serve at room temperature.

RED PEPPER PESTO

45 *Make this pesto with jarred roasted peppers, or roast your own, following directions in the recipe for Roasted Red Pepper Sauce (see p. 164).*

4 servings (about 2 tablespoons each)

1 cup each: roasted red peppers, packed basil leaves
2 cloves garlic
¼ cup (1 ounce) grated fat-free Parmesan cheese
1 teaspoon each: sugar, balsamic vinegar
3 tablespoons olive oil
Salt and pepper, to taste

1. Process all ingredients, except salt and pepper, in food processor or blender until smooth. Season to taste with salt and pepper. Serve at room temperature.

Per Serving:
Calories: 124
% of calories from fat: 71 (30% with 2 oz. pasta)
Protein (g): 2.7
Carbohydrate (g): 6.8
Fat (g): 10.3
Saturated fat (g): 1.4
Cholesterol (mg): 0
Sodium (mg): 46

Exchanges:
Milk: 0.0
Vegetable: 1.0
Fruit: 0.0
Bread: 0.0
Meat: 0.0
Fat: 2.0

ROASTED SWEET PEPPER RELISH

45 *Stir this intensely flavored relish into any soup or stew to enhance flavors.*

8 servings (about 3 tablespoons each)

4 large red bell peppers, cut into halves
2 teaspoons sugar

1. Place peppers, skin sides up, on a broiler pan. Broil 4 to 6 inches from heat source until skins are blistered and blackened. Place peppers in plastic bag for 5 minutes; remove skins. Finely chop peppers; stir in sugar. Refrigerate until ready to use.

Per Serving:
Calories: 14
% calories from fat: 4
Protein (g): 0.3
Carbohydrate (g): 3.4
Fat (g): 0.1
Saturated fat (g): 0
Cholesterol (mg): 0
Sodium (mg): 1

Exchanges:
Milk: 0.0
Vegetable: 0.0
Fruit: 0.0
Bread: 0.0
Meat: 0.0
Fat: 0.0

SQUASH DINNER ROLLS

Use pumpkin, Hubbard, or acorn squash for these rolls; mashed sweet potatoes can be used also. If a loaf is preferred, bake in a greased 8 x 4-inch loaf pan until loaf is browned and sounds hollow when tapped, about 40 minutes.

24 servings

1½–2½ cups all-purpose flour, divided

1 cup whole wheat flour

2 packages fast-rising yeast

1–2 teaspoons salt

½ cup fat-free milk

¼ cup honey

1–2 tablespoons margarine or butter

¾ cup mashed cooked winter squash

1 egg

Per Serving:
Calories: 70
% calories from fat: 11
Protein (g): 2.2
Carbohydrate (g): 13.5
Fat (g): 0.9
Saturated fat (g): 0.2
Cholesterol (mg): 9
Sodium (mg): 100

Exchanges:
Milk: 0.0
Vegetable: 0.0
Fruit: 0.0
Bread: 1.0
Meat: 0.0
Fat: 0.0

1. Combine 1½ cups all-purpose flour, whole wheat flour, yeast, and salt in large bowl. Heat milk, honey, and margarine or butter in small saucepan to 125–130 degrees; add to flour mixture, mixing until smooth. Mix in squash, egg, and enough remaining 1 cup all-purpose flour to make smooth dough. Knead dough on floured surface until smooth and elastic, about 5 minutes. Place in greased bowl; let stand, covered, in warm place until double in size, 30 to 45 minutes. Punch dough down. Divide dough into 24 pieces; shape into round rolls and place in greased muffin cups. Bake at 375 degrees until browned, 20 to 25 minutes. Remove from pans and cool on wire racks.

VARIATION

Raisin-Walnut Pumpkin Bread — Make recipe as above, substituting mashed cooked or canned pumpkin for the squash and adding ½ cup each raisins and chopped walnuts. Shape into loaf in 9 x 5-inch loaf pan and let rise; bake at 375 degrees until loaf is browned and sounds hollow when tapped, about 40 minutes. Remove from pan; cool on wire rack.

PITA CHIPS

45

Perfect to serve as a crunchy accompaniment to many soups, the chips are also great with appetizer dips.

6 servings (8 each)

3 whole wheat pocket breads
Butter-flavored cooking spray
3–4 teaspoons dried Italian seasoning or other
  desired herbs

1. Open breads and separate each into 2 halves;
cut each half into 8 wedges. Arrange wedges,
soft sides up, in single layer on jelly roll pan.
Spray with cooking spray and sprinkle with
dried Italian seasoning. Bake at 425 degrees
until browned and crisp, 5 to 10 minutes.

Per Serving:
Calories: 86
% calories from fat: 8
Protein (g): 3.2
Carbohydrate (g): 17.7
Fat (g): 0.9
Saturated fat (g): 0.1
Cholesterol (mg): 0
Sodium (mg): 171

Exchanges:
Milk: 0.0
Vegetable: 0.0
Fruit: 0.0
Bread: 1.0
Meat: 0.0
Fat: 0.0

VARIATIONS

Seasoned Pita Chips — Make recipe above, substituting 1 to 2
teaspoons chili powder, ground cumin or garlic powder for the
dried Italian seasoning.

Parmesan Pita Chips — Make recipe above, substituting 2 to 3
tablespoons grated Parmesan cheese for the dried Italian seasoning.

ENGLISH MUFFIN BREAD

*This quick and easy single-rise bread has a coarse texture similar to English
muffins. The Cinnamon-Raisin Bread variation is delicious with fruit soups.*

1 loaf (16 servings)

1½–2½ cups all-purpose flour, divided
½ cup quick-cooking oats
1 package active dry yeast
¼ teaspoon baking soda
1 teaspoon salt
1¼ cups warm fat-free milk (110–115 degrees)

1 tablespoon honey

Cornmeal

1. Combine 1½ cups flour, oats, yeast, baking soda, and salt in large bowl. Add milk and honey, mixing until smooth. Stir in enough remaining 1 cup flour to make a thick batter. Pour into greased, cornmeal-coated 8 x 4-inch loaf pan. Let rise, covered, in warm place until double in size, 45 to 60 minutes. Bake at 400 degrees until bread is golden and sounds hollow when tapped, 25 to 30 minutes. Remove from pan and cool on wire rack.

Per Serving:
Calories: 79
% calories from fat: 4
Protein (g): 2.9
Carbohydrate (g): 15.9
Fat (g): 0.4
Saturated fat (g): 0.1
Cholesterol (mg): 0.3
Sodium (mg): 163

Exchanges:
Milk: 0.0
Vegetable: 0.0
Fruit: 0.0
Bread: 1.0
Meat: 0.0
Fat: 0.0

VARIATION

Cinnamon-Raisin Bread — Make recipe as above, adding 1 teaspoon ground cinnamon and ½ cup raisins to the batter; do not coat loaf pan with cornmeal.

SOFT PRETZELS

To achieve their typical dense, chewy texture, pretzels are cooked in boiling water before baking. A great, and different, accompaniment for many soups and stews.

12 pretzels

1 package active dry yeast
½ cup warm water (110–115 degrees)
1 tablespoon sugar
1 cup fat-free milk, heated to simmering, cooled
2–4 cups all-purpose flour, divided
1 teaspoon salt
2 quarts water
1 tablespoon baking soda
1 egg, beaten
1 tablespoon cold water
Toppings: poppy seeds, sesame seeds, coarse salt, herbs, dried onion flakes

Per Serving:
Calories: 152
% calories from fat: 5
Protein (g): 5.2
Carbohydrate (g): 30.2
Fat (g): 0.8
Saturated fat (g): 0.2
Cholesterol (mg): 18.1
Sodium (mg): 509

Exchanges:
Milk: 0.0
Vegetable: 0.0
Fruit: 0.0
Bread: 2.0
Meat: 0.0
Fat: 0.0

1. Mix yeast, warm water, and sugar in large bowl; let stand 5 minutes. Add fat-free milk, 2 cups flour, and salt, beating until smooth. Mix in enough remaining 2 cups flour to make smooth dough. Knead dough on floured surface until smooth and elastic, about 5 minutes. Place in greased bowl; let rise, covered, in warm place until double in size, 45 to 60 minutes. Punch dough down.

2. Roll dough on floured surface to rectangle 16 x 12 inches. Cut dough lengthwise into 12 strips, 1 inch wide. Roll one strip dough with palms of hands until rounded and 18 to 20 inches long. Form loop, holding ends of strip and twisting strip 2 times. Bring ends of strip down and fasten at opposite sides of loop to form pretzel shape. Repeat with remaining dough, transferring pretzels to floured surface. Let pretzels stand, lightly covered, 30 minutes (they may not double in size).

3. Heat 2 quarts water to boiling in large saucepan; stir in baking soda. Transfer pretzels, a few at a time, into boiling water; boil until dough feels firm, about 1 minute. Remove pretzels from boiling water with slotted spoon, draining well. Place on generously greased foil-lined cookie sheets. Brush pretzels with combined egg and cold water; sprinkle with desired toppings (not included in nutritional data). Bake at 400 degrees until golden, 18 to 20 minutes. Remove to wire racks and cool.

GRANOLA BREAD

This healthy whole wheat bread is made with an electric mixer and has only 1 rise.

2 loaves (16 servings each)

2 packages active dry yeast
¾ cup warm water (110–115 degrees)
2 tablespoons light brown sugar
1¼ cups buttermilk
3 cups all-purpose flour
¾–1½ cups whole wheat flour, divided
2 teaspoons baking powder
1 teaspoon salt

Per Serving:
Calories: 200
% calories from fat: 17
Protein (g): 3.1
Carbohydrate (g): 38.9
Fat (g): 3.8
Saturated fat (g): 0.6
Cholesterol (mg): 9
Sodium (mg): 131

Exchanges:
Milk: 0.0
Vegetable: 0.0
Fruit: 0.0
Bread: 2.5
Meat: 0.0
Fat: 0.5

2–3 tablespoons margarine or butter, room temperature
1½ cups low-fat granola
Buttermilk

1. Mix yeast, warm water, and brown sugar in large mixer bowl; let stand 5 minutes. Mix in buttermilk, all-purpose flour, ¾ cup whole wheat flour, baking powder, salt, and margarine on low speed until smooth. Mix in granola and enough remaining ¾ cup whole wheat flour to make a smooth dough (dough will be slightly sticky.) Knead dough on floured surface until smooth and elastic, about 5 minutes.

2. Divide dough into halves. Roll each into a rectangle 18 x 10 inches. Roll up, beginning at short ends; press ends to seal. Place loaves, seam sides down, in greased 9 x 5-inch loaf pans. Let rise, covered, in warm place until double in size, about 1 hour; brush with buttermilk. Bake at 375 degrees until loaves are golden and sound hollow when tapped, 40 to 45 minutes. Remove from pans and cool on wire racks.

CRANBERRY-NUT WHEAT LOAF

The flavors of dried cranberries and walnuts complement sweet fruit soups.

1 loaf (16 servings)

1 package active dry yeast
¾ cup warm water (110–115 degrees)
3 tablespoons honey
2–3 tablespoons margarine or butter,
   room temperature
1 egg
1–2 cups all-purpose flour, divided
1 cup whole wheat flour
1 teaspoon salt
1 cup dried cranberries
⅔ cup coarsely chopped walnuts
Fat-free milk, for glaze

Per Serving:
Calories: 153
% calories from fat: 27
Protein (g): 4.1
Carbohydrate (g): 24.6
Fat (g): 4.7
Saturated fat (g): 0.6
Cholesterol (mg): 0
Sodium (mg): 141

Exchanges:
Milk: 0.0
Vegetable: 0.0
Fruit: 0.5
Bread: 1.0
Meat: 0.0
Fat: 1.0

1. Mix yeast, warm water, and honey in large bowl; let stand 5 minutes. Add margarine, egg, 1 cup all-purpose flour, whole wheat flour, and salt, mixing until blended. Mix in cranberries, walnuts, and enough remaining 1 cup all-purpose flour to make smooth dough. Knead dough on floured surface until smooth and elastic, about 5 minutes. Place in greased bowl; let rise, covered, in warm place until double in size, 1 to 1½ hours. Punch dough down. Shape dough into a loaf and place in greased 9 x 5-inch loaf pan. Let stand, covered, until double in size, about 45 minutes. Brush top of loaf with fat-free milk. Bake at 375 degrees until loaf is golden and sounds hollow when tapped, 35 to 40 minutes. Remove from pan and cool on wire rack.

BUBBLE LOAF

Also called Bath Buns and Monkey Bread, this pull-apart loaf is easy to make, fun to eat, and perfect for potluck offerings and parties. The recipe can be halved and baked in a 6-cup fluted cake pan.

1 loaf (16 servings)

2 packages active dry yeast
1 cup fat-free milk, warm (110–115 degrees)
6 tablespoons margarine or butter, room temperature
¼ cup sugar
3 eggs
4 cups all-purpose flour
½ teaspoon salt

Per Serving:
Calories: 186
% calories from fat: 27
Protein (g): 5.3
Carbohydrate (g): 28.3
Fat (g): 5.5
Saturated fat (g): 1.2
Cholesterol (mg): 40.2
Sodium (mg): 137

Exchanges:
Milk: 0.0
Vegetable: 0.0
Fruit: 0.0
Bread: 2.0
Meat: 0.0
Fat: 1.0

1. Stir yeast into milk in bowl; let stand 2 to 3 minutes. Beat margarine or butter and sugar until fluffy in large bowl; beat in eggs, 1 at a time. Mix in combined flour and salt alternately with milk mixture, beginning and ending with dry ingredients and beating well after each addition. Let stand, covered, in warm place until dough doubles in size, about 1 hour. Punch dough down.

2. Drop dough by large spoonfuls into greased 10-inch tube pan. Let rise, covered, until dough is double in size, about 30 minutes. Bake at 350 degrees until browned, 25 to 30 minutes. Cool in pan on wire rack 10 minutes; remove from pan. Serve warm.

FRUITED BRAN BREAD

Use any combination of dried fruit you want in this quick, healthy, no-rise batter bread.

1 loaf (16 servings)

1¼ cups all-purpose flour

½ cup whole wheat flour

2 teaspoons baking powder

½ teaspoon each: baking soda, salt

1½ cups whole bran cereal

1⅓ cups buttermilk

¾ cup packed light brown sugar

3 tablespoons margarine or butter, melted

1 egg

1 cup coarsely chopped mixed dried fruit

¼–½ cup chopped walnuts

Per Serving:
Calories: 169
% calories from fat: 20
Protein (g): 4.1
Carbohydrate (g): 33.1
Fat (g): 4.2
Saturated fat (g): 0.8
Cholesterol (mg): 14.1
Sodium (mg): 261

Exchanges:
Milk: 0.0
Vegetable: 0.0
Fruit: 0.0
Bread: 2.0
Meat: 0.0
Fat: 0.5

1. Combine flours, baking powder, baking soda, salt, and bran cereal in medium bowl. Add buttermilk, brown sugar, margarine, and egg, mixing just until dry ingredients are moistened. Gently fold in dried fruit and walnuts. Pour into greased and floured 9 x 5-inch loaf pan. Bake at 350 degrees until wooden pick inserted in center comes out clean, about 1 hour. Remove from pan; cool on wire rack before slicing.

BANANA BREAD

Brown sugar gives this banana bread a caramel flavor; the applesauce adds moistness.

1 loaf (16 servings)

4 tablespoons margarine or butter, room temperature
¼ cup applesauce
2 eggs
2 tablespoons fat-free milk or water
¾ cup packed light brown sugar
1 cup mashed bananas (2–3 medium bananas)
1¾ cups all-purpose flour
2 teaspoons baking powder
½ teaspoon baking soda
¼ teaspoon salt
¼ cup coarsely chopped walnuts or pecans

Per Serving:
Calories: 151
% calories from fat: 28
Protein (g): 2.9
Carbohydrate (g): 24.9
Fat (g): 4.8
Saturated fat (g): 0.9
Cholesterol (mg): 26.7
Sodium (mg): 160

Exchanges:
Milk: 0.0
Vegetable: 0.0
Fruit: 0.5
Bread: 1.0
Meat: 0.0
Fat: 1.0

1. Beat margarine, applesauce, eggs, milk, and brown sugar in large mixer bowl until smooth. Add banana and mix at low speed; beat at high speed 1 to 2 minutes. Mix in combined flour, baking powder, baking soda, and salt; mix in walnuts. Pour into greased 8 x 4-inch loaf pan. Bake at 350 degrees until bread is golden and toothpick inserted in center comes out clean, 55 to 60 minutes. Cool in pan 10 minutes; remove from pan and cool on wire rack.

CARDAMOM-PEAR MUFFINS

Any dried fruit can be substituted for the pears, and cinnamon can be substituted for the cardamom.

12 muffins

1 cup fat-free milk

4 tablespoons margarine or butter, melted

1 egg

2 cups all-purpose flour

⅓ cup plus 2 tablespoons sugar, divided

3 teaspoons baking powder

½ teaspoon salt

1 cup chopped dried pears

1 teaspoon grated orange or lemon zest

½ teaspoon ground cardamom

Per Serving:
Calories: 193
% calories from fat: 21
Protein (g): 3.7
Carbohydrate (g): 35.4
Fat (g): 4.5
Saturated fat (g): 1
Cholesterol (mg): 18.1
Sodium (mg): 232

Exchanges:
Milk: 0.0
Vegetable: 0.0
Fruit: 0.0
Bread: 2.0
Meat: 0.0
Fat: 1.0

1. Mix milk, margarine, and egg in medium bowl. Add combined flour, ⅓ cup sugar, baking powder, and salt, mixing just until dry ingredients are moistened. Gently mix in pears and orange zest. Spoon batter into 12 greased muffin cups; sprinkle with remaining 2 tablespoons sugar and cardamom. Bake at 400 degrees until muffins are browned and toothpick inserted in centers of muffins comes out clean, 20 to 25 minutes. Remove from pans and cool on wire racks.

FOURTEEN

Memorable Menus

Enjoy these menus for fabulous family meals, easy entertaining, and festive celebrations too! The 10 menus in this chapter have been designed to take the guesswork out of meal planning. Preparation tips let you know exactly when each recipe can be prepared and guide you through each meal.

Recipes for some menu items, such as braised cabbage or tossed green salad, are not given because these are items you already know how to make.

Feel free to substitute a favorite recipe in any menu, or look through this book for other ideas.

Nutritional analyses are given for each recipe as well as for the entire menu. For menu items without recipes, nutritional analyses are based on a per person serving of ½ cup of a side dish, 1 cup of salad greens with 2 tablespoons of fat-free salad dressing, and 1 teaspoon of margarine or butter with each serving of bread or biscuits.

DOWN EAST DINNER

New England Clam Chowder (see p. 103)

Tangy Coleslaw*

Vinegar Biscuits (see p. 660)

Boston Cream Cake*

* Recipes follow

PREPARATION TIPS

Day Before: Make cake layers and Vanilla Cream Filling for Boston Cream Cake; do not assemble.

Early in the Day: Make Tangy Coleslaw. Make Vinegar Biscuits.

1 Hour Before Serving: Make New England Clam Chowder. Make Chocolate Glaze; assemble and glaze Boston Cream Cake. Reheat Vinegar Biscuits.

Per 1 Serving of Entire Menu:
Calories: 710
% calories from fat: 24
Protein (g): 22.9
Carbohydrate (g): 112.6
Fat (g): 19.1
Saturated fat (g): 4.2
Cholesterol (mg): 113.5
Sodium (mg): 1538

Exchanges:
Milk: 0.0
Vegetable: 1.0
Fruit: 0.0
Bread: 6.5
Meat: 2.0
Fat: 2.0

TANGY COLESLAW

45 *Dijon mustard adds the special tang to this crisp slaw.*

6 side-dish servings

⅓ cup fat-free mayonnaise

1–2 tablespoons Dijon mustard

2 teaspoons sugar

1 teaspoon fresh lemon juice

1 medium cabbage, shredded

Salt and pepper, to taste

Per Serving:
Calories: 34
% calories from fat: 18
Protein (g): 1.2
Carbohydrate (g): 6.4
Fat (g): 0.7
Saturated fat (g): 0.1
Cholesterol (mg): 0
Sodium (mg): 624

Exchanges:
Milk: 0.0
Vegetable: 1.5
Fruit: 0.0
Bread: 0.0
Meat: 0.0
Fat: 0.0

1. Mix combined mayonnaise, mustard, sugar, and lemon juice into cabbage; season to taste with salt and pepper.

BOSTON CREAM CAKE

A comfort food, with chocolatey glaze and a luxurious cream filling. Although sometimes called a "pie," it is, indeed, a cake.

12 servings

8 tablespoons margarine or butter, room temperature

1¼ cups sugar

2 eggs

1 teaspoon vanilla

2⅔ cups all-purpose flour

3 teaspoons baking powder

½ teaspoon salt

1⅔ cups fat-free milk

Vanilla Cream Filling (recipe follows)

Chocolate Glaze (recipe follows)

Per Serving:
Calories: 353
% calories from fat: 23
Protein (g): 6.6
Carbohydrate (g): 61.3
Fat (g): 9.3
Saturated fat (g): 2
Cholesterol (mg): 54.2
Sodium (mg): 305

Exchanges:
Milk: 0.0
Vegetable: 0.0
Fruit: 0.0
Bread: 4.0
Meat: 0.0
Fat: 1.5

1. Beat margarine, sugar, eggs, and vanilla until smooth in medium bowl. Mix in combined flour, baking powder, and salt alternately with milk, beginning and ending with dry ingredients. Pour into 2 greased and floured 8- or 9-inch-round cake pans.

2. Bake at 350 degrees until cakes spring back when touched, about 40 minutes. Cool in pans on wire rack 10 minutes; remove from pans and cool. Place 1 cake layer on serving plate; spread with Vanilla Cream Filling. Top with second cake layer and spoon Chocolate Glaze over.

Vanilla Cream Filling
Makes about 1¼ cups

¼ cup sugar
2 tablespoons cornstarch
1 cup fat-free milk
1 egg, beaten
½ teaspoon vanilla

1. Mix sugar and cornstarch in small saucepan; whisk in milk and heat to boiling. Boil, whisking, until thickened, about 1 minute. Whisk about ½ the milk mixture into beaten egg in small bowl; whisk back into saucepan. Whisk over low heat 30 to 60 seconds. Stir in vanilla and cool.

Chocolate Glaze
Makes about ½ cup

1 cup powdered sugar
2 tablespoons unsweetened cocoa
½ teaspoon vanilla
1–2 tablespoons fat-free milk

1. Mix all ingredients, using enough milk to make glaze consistency.

TUSCAN REPAST

Tuscan Bean Soup (see p. 397)

Spinach Pesto (see p. 662)

Savory Parmesan Toast*

Mixed Fruit Tortoni*

* Recipes follow

PREPARATION TIPS

1–2 Days in Advance: Make Tuscan Bean Soup. Make Spinach Pesto. Make Mixed Fruit Tortoni.

30 Minutes Before Serving: Reheat Tuscan Bean Soup. Spoon Spinach Pesto into serving bowl for each person to add to soup. Make Savory Parmesan Toast.

Per 1 Serving of Entire Menu:
Calories: 640
% calories from fat: 31
Protein (g): 32.6
Carbohydrate (g): 79.1
Fat (g): 22.4
Saturated fat (g): 5.1
Cholesterol (mg): 123
Sodium (mg): 1096

Exchanges:
Milk: 0.0
Vegetable: 2.0
Fruit: 1.0
Bread: 4.0
Meat: 3.0
Fat: 2.0

SAVORY PARMESAN TOAST

45 *Also delicious served with salads, pasta, or grilled meats.*

6 servings (2 slices each)

4 eggs

¼ cup fat-free milk

¼ teaspoon each: salt, pepper

2 cloves garlic, halved

12 slices Italian bread

1–2 tablespoons fennel seeds, lightly crushed

¼ cup (1 ounce) grated Parmesan cheese

Per Serving:
Calories: 236
% calories from fat: 26
Protein (g): 11.4
Carbohydrate (g): 32
Fat (g): 6.6
Saturated fat (g): 2.2
Cholesterol (mg): 144.5
Sodium (mg): 558

Exchanges:
Milk: 0.0
Vegetable: 0.0
Bread: 2.0
Meat: 1.0
Fruit: 0.0
Fat: 1.0

1. Whisk eggs, milk, salt, and pepper together in large pie plate. Rub garlic cloves gently on both sides of bread slices. Dip bread into egg mixture to coat both sides generously; sprinkle both sides of bread slices with fennel seeds. Cook bread in lightly greased griddle or large skillet over medium heat until browned on the bottom, 2 to 3 minutes. Sprinkle top of each slice with about 1 teaspoon Parmesan cheese; turn and cook until browned, 2 to 3 minutes.

MIXED FRUIT TORTONI

45

Traditionally made with heavy cream and candied fruits, our version of this Italian favorite uses fresh seasonal fruits and low-fat topping.

12 servings

1½ cups fresh or frozen thawed raspberries

½ cup pitted, halved sweet cherries, divided

⅓ cup each: cubed peeled apricots, pineapple

¼ cup sugar

3 envelopes (1.3 ounces each) low-fat whipped topping mix

1½ cups 2% milk

¼ cup chopped pistachio nuts or slivered almonds, divided

Per Serving:
Calories: 126
% calories from fat: 28
Protein (g): 2.1
Carbohydrate (g): 18.2
Fat (g): 3.5
Saturated fat (g): 0.7
Cholesterol (mg): 2
Sodium (mg): 32

Exchanges:
Milk: 0.0
Vegetable: 0.0
Fruit: 1.5
Bread: 0.0
Meat: 0.0
Fat: 0.5

1. Process raspberries in food processor or blender until smooth; strain and discard seeds. Reserve 12 cherry halves. Toss remaining cherries, apricots, pineapple and sugar in small bowl. Beat whipped topping and milk in large bowl at high speed until topping forms soft peaks, about 4 minutes; fold in raspberry purée, sugared fruits, and 2 tablespoons nuts. Spoon into 12 paper-lined muffin cups; garnish tops of each with reserved cherry halves and remaining nuts. Freeze until firm, 6 hours or overnight.

NOTE: If desired, 1 tablespoon sherry or ½ teaspoon sherry extract can be folded into the whipped topping mixture.

SUPER BOWL SUPPER

Toasted Onion Dip*

Cincinnati Chili (see p. 115)

Garlic Bread (see p. 645)

Tossed Green Salad

Touchdown Bars*

* Recipes follow

PREPARATION TIPS

1–2 Days in Advance: Make Toasted Onion Dip. Make
Cincinnati Chili; do not cook spaghetti or prepare garnishes.
Make Touchdown Bars.

1 Hour Before Serving: Cook spaghetti and prepare garnishes
for Cincinnati Chili. Reheat Cincinnati Chili. Make tossed green
salad. Make Garlic Bread.

Per 1 Serving of Entire Menu:
Calories: 650
% calories from fat: 16
Protein (g): 31.2
Carbohydrate (g): 106.9
Fat (g): 11.2
Saturated fat (g): 3.7
Cholesterol (mg): 34.6
Sodium (mg): 1351

Exchanges:
Milk: 0.0
Vegetable: 2.0
Fruit: 0.0
Bread: 6.0
Meat: 3.0
Fat: 0.0

TOASTED ONION DIP

45 *This dip brings back memories of the popular dip made with onion soup mix! Toasting the dried onion flakes is the flavor secret.*

12 servings (about 2 tablespoons each)

3–4 tablespoons dried onion flakes

8 ounces fat-free cream cheese, room temperature

⅓ cup each: reduced-fat plain yogurt,
   fat-free mayonnaise

2 small green onions, chopped

2 cloves garlic, minced

¼ teaspoon crushed beef bouillon cube

2–3 tablespoons fat-free milk

½–1 teaspoon lemon juice

2–3 drops hot pepper sauce

Salt and white pepper, to taste

Dippers: assorted vegetable relishes and bread sticks

Per Serving:
Calories: 32
% calories from fat: 4
Protein (g): 3.3
Carbohydrate (g): 3.9
Fat (g): 0.1
Saturated fat (g): 0.1
Cholesterol (mg): 0.4
Sodium (mg): 223

Exchanges:
Milk: 0.0
Vegetable: 0.0
Fruit: 0.0
Bread: 0.0
Meat: 0.5
Fat: 0.0

1. Cook onion flakes in small skillet over medium to medium-low heat until toasted, 3 to 4 minutes, stirring frequently; remove from heat. Mix cream cheese, yogurt, mayonnaise, green onions, garlic, and bouillon in medium bowl until smooth, adding enough milk to make desired dipping consistency. Stir in onions; season to taste with lemon juice, pepper sauce, salt, and white pepper. Serve with dippers (not included in nutritional data).

TOUCHDOWN BARS

Save these flavorful cookies for the last touchdown!

30 cookies (1 per serving)

2¼ cups graham cracker crumbs
1 can (14 ounces) fat-free sweetened condensed milk
½ cup reduced-fat semisweet chocolate morsels
½ can (3½-ounce size) flaked coconut
⅓ cup chopped walnuts
2 teaspoons vanilla
¼ teaspoon salt

Per Serving:
Calories: 125
% calories from fat: 27
Protein (g): 2.5
Carbohydrate (g): 20.9
Fat (g): 4
Saturated fat (g): 1.8
Cholesterol (mg): 0
Sodium (mg): 75

Exchanges:
Milk: 0.0
Vegetable: 0.0
Fruit: 0.0
Bread: 1.5
Meat: 0.0
Fat: 0.5

1. Mix all ingredients in bowl; press evenly into greased 11 x 7 inch baking pan. Bake at 350 degrees until set and browned, 20 to 30 minutes. Cool on wire rack.

FIESTA OLÉ!

Sombrero Dip*

Tortilla Soup (see p. 289)

Tossed Green Salad

Green Chili Cornbread (see p. 654)

Caramel Flan*

* Recipes follow

PREPARATION TIPS

1–2 Days in Advance: Make tortilla strips for Tortilla Soup. Make Green Chili Cornbread. Make Caramel Flan; do not unmold.

Early in the Day: Assemble ingredients for Sombrero Dip. Make Tortilla Soup.

45 Minutes Before Serving: Make Sombrero Dip. Make tossed green salad. Unmold Caramel Flan. Reheat Tortilla Soup. Reheat Green Chili Cornbread.

Per 1 Serving of Entire Menu:
Calories: 724
% calories from fat: 19
Protein (g): 44.5
Carbohydrate (g): 105.7
Fat (g): 15.6
Saturated fat (g): 3.5
Cholesterol (mg): 229
Sodium (mg): 1914

Exchanges:
Milk: 0.0
Vegetable: 1.0
Fruit: 0.0
Bread: 6.0
Meat: 4.0
Fat: 1.0

SOMBRERO DIP

45 *Use Florida avocados for the Guacamole, as they're lower in fat than the California variety.*

6 servings

¼ cup each: chopped poblano chili, onion
½ cup (¼ recipe) cooked, crumbled Chorizo (see p. 131)
4–5 leaves romaine lettuce
1 can (15 ounces) refried beans
½ cup each: prepared medium or hot salsa, chopped romaine lettuce, tomato
Speedy Guacamole (recipe follows)
¼ cup (1 ounce) shredded fat-free Cheddar cheese
½ cup fat-free sour cream
1 green onion, thinly sliced
Baked tortilla chips

Per Serving:
Calories: 175
% calories from fat: 16
Protein (g): 13.3
Carbohydrate (g): 25
Fat (g): 3.2
Saturated fat (g): 0.7
Cholesterol (mg): 23.7
Sodium (mg): 214

Exchanges:
Milk: 0.0
Vegetable: 2.0
Fruit: 0.0
Bread: 1.0
Meat: 1.0
Fat: 0.0

1. Sauté poblano chili and onion until tender in lightly greased skillet, 3 to 5 minutes; stir in Chorizo. Line a dinner plate with lettuce; cover with refried beans to within 2 inches of edge of lettuce. Spoon salsa over beans, leaving edge of bean layer showing. Spoon Chorizo mixture over salsa; sprinkle with chopped lettuce and tomato, leaving edge of Chorizo showing. Spoon Speedy Guacamole over lettuce and tomato and sprinkle with Cheddar cheese. Spoon sour cream in large dollop on top; sprinkle with green onion. Serve with tortilla chips (not included in nutritional data).

Speedy Guacamole
Makes about ⅔ cup

1 medium avocado
½ small onion, finely chopped
1–2 tablespoons finely chopped jalapeño chili, cilantro
Salt and white pepper, to taste

1. Coarsely mash avocado in small bowl; mix in onion, jalapeño chili, and cilantro. Season to taste with salt and pepper.

CARAMEL FLAN

45

❄

◊

Unbelievably delicate and fine in texture, this flan is one you'll serve over and over again.

8 servings

½ cup sugar, divided

4 cups fat-free milk

5 eggs, lightly beaten

2 teaspoons vanilla

Per Serving:
Calories: 140
% calories from fat: 14
Protein (g): 8.3
Carbohydrate (g): 21.3
Fat (g): 2.1
Saturated fat (g): 0.7
Cholesterol (mg): 81.9
Sodium (mg): 114

Exchanges:
Milk: 0.5
Vegetable: 0.0
Fruit: 0.0
Bread: 1.0
Meat: 0.0
Fat: 0.5

1. Heat ¼ cup sugar in small skillet over medium high heat until sugar melts and turns golden, stirring occasionally (watch carefully as the sugar can burn easily!). Quickly pour caramel into bottom of 2-quart soufflé dish, tilting to spread caramel over bottom. Cool.

2. Mix milk and remaining ¼ cup sugar in medium saucepan; heat until beginning to bubble at the edges. Whisk milk mixture gradually into eggs in bowl; stir in vanilla. Pour mixture through strainer into soufflé dish. Place soufflé dish in roasting pan on middle oven rack; cover with lid or foil. Pour 2 inches hot water into roasting pan. Bake at 350 degrees until sharp knife inserted halfway between center and edge of custard comes out clean, about 1 hour. Remove soufflé dish and cool on wire rack. Refrigerate 8 hours or overnight. To unmold, loosen edge of custard with sharp knife. Place rimmed serving dish over soufflé dish and invert.

VARIATION

Orange Flan — Make recipe above, substituting ¼ cup orange juice concentrate for ¼ cup of the milk, and adding 1 egg and 1 teaspoon orange extract.

COMFORT FOOD FAVORITES

Chicken Noodle Soup (see p. 196)

Multigrain Batter Bread (see p. 650)

Waldorf Salad*

Hot Fudge Pudding Cake*

* Recipes follow

PREPARATION TIPS

1–2 Days in Advance: Make Chicken-Noodle Soup. Make 1 loaf of Multi-Grain Batter Bread (½ recipe).

1 Hour Before Serving: Make Hot Fudge Pudding Cake. Make Waldorf Salad. Reheat Chicken-Noodle Soup. Reheat Multi-Grain Batter Bread.

Per 1 Serving of Entire Menu:
Calories: 971
% calories from fat: 21
Protein (g): 29
Carbohydrate (g): 161.7
Fat (g): 22.8
Saturated fat (g): 2.9
Cholesterol (mg): 33.8
Sodium (mg): 1079

Exchanges:
Milk: 0.0
Vegetable: 0.0
Fruit: 1.5
Bread: 8.0
Meat: 3.0
Fat: 3.0

WALDORF SALAD

45 *This colorful version of Waldorf salad uses both red and green apples. Add miniature marshmallows, if your family insists!*

4 side-dish servings

2 cups unpeeled, cubed red and green apples

1 cup sliced celery

¼ cup each: chopped, toasted walnuts, raisins, fat-free mayonnaise, sour cream

2–3 teaspoons lemon juice

1–2 tablespoons honey

Per Serving:
Calories: 149
% calories from fat: 26
Protein (g): 3.5
Carbohydrate (g): 26.5
Fat (g): 4.7
Saturated fat (g): 0.3
Cholesterol (mg): 0
Sodium (mg): 227

Exchanges:
Milk: 0.0
Vegetable: 0.5
Fruit: 1.5
Bread: 0.0
Meat: 0.0
Fat: 1.0

1. Combine apples, celery, walnuts, and raisins in bowl. Mix in combined remaining ingredients.

HOT FUDGE PUDDING CAKE

45
◊ *For the ultimate treat serve warm, topped with scoops of sugar-free ice cream or frozen yogurt.*

6 servings

1 cup all-purpose flour

½ cup packed light brown sugar

6 tablespoons Dutch process cocoa, divided

1½ teaspoons baking powder

¼ teaspoon salt

½ cup fat-free milk

2 tablespoons vegetable oil

1 teaspoon vanilla

⅓ cup granulated sugar

1½ cups boiling water

Per Serving:
Calories: 259
% calories from fat: 18
Protein (g): 4.1
Carbohydrate (g): 49.1
Fat (g): 5.2
Saturated fat (g): 0.9
Cholesterol (mg): 0.4
Sodium (mg): 240

Exchanges:
Milk: 0.0
Vegetable: 0.0
Fruit: 0.0
Bread: 3.0
Meat: 0.0
Fat: 1.0

1. Combine flour, brown sugar, 3 tablespoons cocoa, baking powder, and salt in medium bowl. Add combined milk, oil, and vanilla to flour mixture, mixing well. Spoon batter into greased 8- or 9-inch square baking pan; sprinkle with combined remaining 3 tablespoons cocoa and granulated sugar. Pour boiling water over batter; do not stir. Bake at 350 degrees until cake springs back when touched, about 30 minutes. Cool on wire rack 5 to 10 minutes; serve warm.

VARIATION

Mocha Latte Pudding Cake — Make cake as above, substituting granulated sugar for the brown sugar and adding 1 tablespoon instant espresso coffee powder and ½ teaspoon ground cinnamon to flour mixture. Serve warm pudding cake with a scoop of sugar-free vanilla or chocolate ice cream and light whipped topping.

IT'S THE LUCK O' THE IRISH!

Irish Lamb Stew (see p. 465)

Braised Cabbage

Cheese-Caraway Scones*

Oatmeal Cake*

* Recipes follow

PREPARATION TIPS

1–2 Days in Advance: Make Irish Lamb Stew. Make Cheese-Caraway Scones. Make Oatmeal Cake; do not make Broiled Pecan Frosting.

1 Hour Before Serving: Make braised cabbage. Reheat Irish Lamb Stew. Reheat Cheese-Caraway Scones. Make Broiled Pecan Frosting and complete Oatmeal Cake.

Per 1 Serving of Entire Menu:
Calories: 832
% calories from fat: 33
Protein (g): 30.6
Carbohydrate (g): 117.7
Fat (g): 30.4
Saturated fat (g): 6.2
Cholesterol (mg): 82.3
Sodium (mg): 750

Exchanges:
Milk: 0.0
Vegetable: 3.0
Fruit: 0.0
Bread: 7.0
Meat: 3.0
Fat: 3.0

CHEESE-CARAWAY SCONES

The mix of grains yields hearty-textured scones.

6 servings

½ cup all-purpose flour

¼ cup each: whole wheat flour, yellow cornmeal

1½ teaspoons baking powder

¼ teaspoon salt

1 tablespoon each: softened margarine, canola oil

¼ cup (1 ounce) shredded Cheddar cheese

1 egg

⅓ cup fat-free milk

2 teaspoons caraway seeds

Paprika

Per Serving:
Calories: 142
% calories from fat: 39
Protein (g): 5.1
Carbohydrate (g): 17
Fat (g): 6.2
Saturated fat (g): 1.6
Cholesterol (mg): 5.2
Sodium (mg): 298

Exchanges:
Milk: 0.0
Vegetable: 0.0
Fruit: 0.0
Bread: 1.0
Meat: 0.0
Fat: 1.0

1. Combine flours, cornmeal, baking powder, and salt in large bowl; stir in margarine, oil, and cheese, mixing until mixture is crumbly. Stir in combined egg, milk, and caraway seeds, mixing until blended. Knead dough into ball on floured board. Roll into 7-inch circle and cut into 6 even wedges. Dust tops of each wedge with a little paprika. Arrange wedges in greased 9-inch pie pan. Bake at 375 degrees until scones are browned, 15 to 20 minutes.

OATMEAL CAKE

Make frosting just before serving for a warm treat.

15 servings

1 cup quick-cooking oats

1¼ cups boiling water

6 tablespoons margarine or butter

1 cup each: granulated and packed light brown sugar

2 eggs

1⅓ cups cake flour

1 teaspoon each: baking soda, ground cinnamon

½ teaspoon salt

Per Serving:
Calories: 327
% calories from fat: 28
Protein (g): 3.3
Carbohydrate (g): 56.4
Fat (g): 10.6
Saturated fat (g): 2
Cholesterol (mg): 28.6
Sodium (mg): 273

Exchanges:
Milk: 0.0
Vegetable: 0.0
Fruit: 0.0
Bread: 4.0
Meat: 0.0
Fat: 1.5

¼ teaspoon ground nutmeg
Generous pinch ground cloves
Boiled Pecan Frosting (recipe follows)

1. Mix oats, boiling water, and margarine in large bowl, stirring until margarine is melted; let stand 15 to 20 minutes. Mix in sugars and eggs. Mix in combined remaining ingredients, except Boiled Pecan Frosting. Pour batter into greased 13 x 9-inch baking pan. Bake at 350 degrees until toothpick inserted in center comes out clean, about 35 minutes. Cool on wire rack 10 to 15 minutes.

2. Spread Boiled Pecan Frosting evenly on cake. Broil 4 inches from heat source until mixture is bubbly and pecans browned, about 1 minute.

Boiled Pecan Frosting

½ cup packed light brown sugar
3 tablespoons each: flour, margarine or butter
½ teaspoon ground cinnamon
2 tablespoons fat-free milk
⅓ cup coarsely chopped pecans

1. Heat all ingredients, except pecans, to boiling in small saucepan, stirring frequently; cook, stirring, over medium heat 2 minutes. Remove from heat; stir in pecans.

CARIBBEAN CAPER

Caribbean Chicken Stew (see p. 537)

Spinach and Melon Salad*

Herbed-Garlic Breadsticks (see p. 638)

Baked Key Lime Pie*

* Recipes follow

PREPARATION TIPS

1 Day in Advance: Make Caribbean Chicken Stew; do not cook rice.

Early in the Day: Make Baked Key Lime Pie. Make Herbed-Garlic Breadsticks.

1 Hour Before Serving: Cook rice and chop peanuts for Caribbean Chicken Stew. Reheat Caribbean Chicken Stew. Make Spinach and Melon Salad. Reheat Herbed Breadsticks.

Per 1 Serving of Entire Menu:
Calories: 975
% calories from fat: 20
Protein (g): 39.8
Carbohydrate (g): 157.3
Fat (g): 21.8
Saturated fat (g): 4.5
Cholesterol (mg): 141.1
Sodium (mg): 519

Exchanges:
Milk: 0.5
Vegetable: 0.5
Fruit: 2.0
Bread: 7.0
Meat: 3.0
Fat: 3.0

SPINACH AND MELON SALAD

45 *A colorful salad, accented with sweet Honey Dressing.*

8 side-dish servings

8 cups torn spinach
1½ cups each: watermelon, honeydew, and
   cantaloupe balls
⅓ cup each: thinly sliced cucumber, red onion
Honey Dressing (recipe follows)

1. Combine all ingredients in salad bowl
and toss.

Honey Dressing

Makes about ½ cup

2–3 tablespoons honey
1–2 tablespoons each: red wine vinegar, olive oil
2–3 tablespoons each: orange and lime juice
1 teaspoon dried tarragon leaves
⅛ teaspoon salt

1. Mix all ingredients.

Per Serving:
Calories: 85
% calories from fat: 36
Protein (g): 1.7
Carbohydrate (g): 13.2
Fat (g): 3.6
Saturated fat (g): 0.5
Cholesterol (mg): 0
Sodium (mg): 50

Exchanges:
Milk: 0.0
Vegetable: 0.0
Fruit: 1.0
Bread: 0.0
Meat: 0.0
Fat: 0.5

BAKED KEY LIME PIE

The traditional pie, but baked with a mile-high meringue.

8 servings

1 can (14 ounces) fat-free sweetened condensed milk

½ cup key or Persian lime juice

⅓ cup water

3 egg yolks, lightly beaten

1 tablespoon finely grated lime zest

8-inch reduced-fat graham cracker crust

4 egg whites

¼ teaspoon cream of tartar

½ cup sugar

Per Serving:
Calories: 370
% calories from fat: 13
Protein (g): 10.4
Carbohydrate (g): 70
Fat (g): 5.4
Saturated fat (g): 1.1
Cholesterol (mg): 88.4
Sodium (mg): 206

Exchanges:
Milk: 0.0
Vegetable: 0.0
Fruit: 0.0
Bread: 4.5
Meat: 0.0
Fat: 1.0

1. Mix sweetened condensed milk, lime juice, water, egg yolks, and lime zest in large bowl until smooth; pour into crust. Bake at 350 degrees for 30 minutes; remove to wire rack.

2. During last 5 minutes of baking time, using clean bowl and beaters, beat egg whites and cream of tartar to soft peaks in large bowl. Beat to stiff peaks, adding sugar gradually. Spread meringue over hot filling, sealing to edge of crust. Increase oven temperature to 400 degrees. Bake until meringue is browned, about 5 minutes. Cool on wire rack; refrigerate at least 1 hour.

MARDI GRAS MAGIC

Shrimp and Sausage Gumbo (see p. 581)

Lemon-Spiked Garlic Greens*

Sweet Potato Biscuits (see p. 659)

Bananas Foster*

* Recipes follow

PREPARATION TIPS

1 Day in Advance: Make Shrimp and Sausage Gumbo. Make Sweet Potato Biscuits.

1 Hour Before Serving: Make Lemon-Spiked Garlic Greens. Reheat Shrimp and Sausage Gumbo. Reheat Sweet Potato Biscuits. Assemble ingredients for Bananas Foster.

15 Minutes Before Dessert: Make Bananas Foster.

Per 1 Serving of Entire Menu:
Calories: 726
% calories from fat: 22
Protein (g): 31
Carbohydrate (g): 112.9
Fat (g): 18.1
Saturated fat (g): 3.2
Cholesterol (mg): 157.8
Sodium (mg): 648

Exchanges:
Milk: 0.0
Vegetable: 5.0
Fruit: 2.0
Bread: 4.0
Meat: 2.0
Fat: 2.0

LEMON-SPIKED GARLIC GREENS

45 *Kale, collard, turnip, or beet greens make excellent choices for this quick and easy healthful dish.*

4 side-dish servings

¼ cup each: finely chopped onion, red bell pepper

4 cloves garlic, minced

1½ pounds greens, coarsely chopped

½ cup water

1–2 tablespoons lemon juice

Salt and pepper, to taste

1 hard-cooked egg, chopped

Per Serving:
Calories: 58
% calories from fat: 23
Protein (g): 5.9
Carbohydrate (g): 7
Fat (g): 1.7
Saturated fat (g): 0.4
Cholesterol (mg): 53.3
Sodium (mg): 43

Exchanges:
Milk: 0.0
Vegetable: 2.0
Fruit: 0.0
Bread: 0.0
Meat: 0.0
Fat: 0.0

1. Sauté onion, bell pepper, and garlic in lightly greased large saucepan until tender, 3 to 4 minutes. Add greens and water; heat to boiling. Reduce heat and simmer, covered, until greens are wilted, 4 to 5 minutes; drain. Season to taste with lemon juice, salt, and pepper; sprinkle with egg.

BANANAS FOSTER

45 *A real taste of New Orleans!*

4 servings

¼ cup packed light brown sugar

1½ teaspoons cornstarch

½ cup water

1 tablespoon rum or ½ teaspoon rum extract

1 teaspoon vanilla

2 medium bananas, sliced

¼ cup toasted pecan halves

1⅓ cups frozen low-fat vanilla yogurt

Per Serving:
Calories: 236
% calories from fat: 20
Protein (g): 3.4
Carbohydrate (g): 43
Fat (g): 5.5
Saturated fat (g): 0.5
Cholesterol (mg): 0
Sodium (mg): 5

Exchanges:
Milk: 0.0
Vegetable: 0.0
Fruit: 2.0
Bread: 1.0
Meat: 0.0
Fat: 1.0

1. Mix brown sugar and cornstarch in small saucepan; stir in water and heat to boiling. Boil, stirring, until thickened, about 1 minute. Stir in rum and vanilla; add bananas and simmer until warm, 1 to 2 minutes. Stir in pecans; serve warm over frozen yogurt.

ITALIAN HOLIDAY

Three-Bean Stew with Polenta (see pp. 623, 661)

Broccoli Parmesan*

Individual Olive Focaccias (see p. 642)

Tiramisu*

* Recipes follow

PREPARATION TIPS

1 Day in Advance: Make Mock Mascarpone for Tiramisu. Make Three-Bean Stew; do not make Polenta.

Early in the Day: Make Individual Olive Focaccias. Make Tiramisu. Assemble ingredients for Broccoli Parmesan.

45 Minutes Before Serving: Make Polenta. Make Broccoli Parmesan. Reheat Three-Bean Stew with Polenta. Reheat Olive Focaccias.

Per 1 Serving of Entire Menu:
Calories: 833
% calories from fat: 21
Protein (g): 37.9
Carbohydrate (g): 131.1
Fat (g): 19.7
Saturated fat (g): 5.7
Cholesterol (mg): 176.2
Sodium (mg): 1439

Exchanges:
Milk: 0.0
Vegetable: 3.0
Fruit: 0.0
Bread: 8.0
Meat: 2.0
Fat: 1.5

BROCCOLI PARMESAN

45 *Broccoli rabe can be substituted for the broccoli.*

6 servings

⅓ cup chopped shallots or green onions

2 cloves garlic, chopped

1½ pounds broccoli florets and sliced stems, cooked crisp-tender

1 tablespoon balsamic vinegar or lemon juice

4–6 (1–1½ ounces) tablespoons shredded Parmesan cheese

1½–2 tablespoons chopped toasted pine nuts

1. Sauté shallots and garlic in lightly greased large skillet until tender, about 2 minutes. Stir in broccoli and sauté until warm, about 3 minutes. Stir in vinegar and cheese; sprinkle with pine nuts.

Per Serving:
Calories: 69
% calories from fat: 28
Protein (g): 4.8
Carbohydrate (g): 7.4
Fat (g): 2.1
Saturated fat (g): 0.8
Cholesterol (mg): 2.6
Sodium (mg): 91

Exchanges:
Milk: 0.0
Vegetable: 2.0
Fruit: 0.0
Bread: 0.0
Meat: 0.0
Fat: 0.5

TIRAMISU

You'll never believe this luscious Italian favorite is low fat!

9 servings

Mock Mascarpone (recipe follows)
½ cup sugar
2 tablespoons dark rum or 1 teaspoon rum extract
8 ounces ladyfingers (36)
1 cup cold espresso or strong coffee
Chocolate shavings, as garnish

Per Serving:
Calories: 309
% calories from fat: 19
Protein (g): 16.9
Carbohydrate (g): 43.4
Fat (g): 6.5
Saturated fat (g): 3
Cholesterol (mg): 172.2
Sodium (mg): 493

Exchanges:
Milk: 0.0
Vegetable: 0.0
Fruit: 0.0
Bread: 3.0
Meat: 2.0
Fat: 0.0

1. Mix Mock Mascarpone, sugar, and rum. Split ladyfingers in half lengthwise. Quickly dip cut sides of 18 ladyfinger halves into espresso and arrange, cut sides up, in bottom of 9-inch square glass baking dish; spread with half the mascarpone mixture. Repeat with remaining ladyfinger halves, espresso, and mascarpone mixture. Sprinkle with chocolate shavings. Refrigerate, loosely covered, until chilled, 3 to 4 hours. Cut into squares to serve.

Mock Mascarpone
Makes about 1¼ cups

8 ounces fat-free cream cheese, room temperature
3 tablespoons reduced-fat sour cream
2–3 tablespoons 2% reduced-fat milk

1. Beat cream cheese until fluffy; mix in sour cream and milk. Refrigerate several hours or up to several days.

HARVEST DINNER

Country Beef Stew (see p. 433)

Baked Acorn Squash*

Lettuce Wedges with Ranch Dressing

Mile-High Apple Pie*

* Recipes follow

PREPARATION TIPS

1–2 Days in Advance: Make Country Beef Stew.

Early in the Day: Make Mile-High Apple Pie.

1 Hour Before Serving: Make Baked Acorn Squash. Reheat Country Beef Stew. Make lettuce wedges.

Per 1 Serving of Entire Menu:
Calories: 840
% calories from fat: 21
Protein (g): 38.3
Carbohydrate (g): 131.6
Fat (g): 20
Saturated fat (g): 6
Cholesterol (mg): 178.3
Sodium (mg): 1433

Exchanges:
Milk: 0.0
Vegetable: 2.0
Fruit: 2.0
Bread: 7.0
Meat: 3.0
Fat: 1.0

BAKED ACORN SQUASH

Squash baked to tender goodness with honey and sweet spices.

4 first-course servings

2 small acorn or Hubbard squash, halved, seeded
1 cup orange juice
2 tablespoons honey
1 teaspoon each: ground cinnamon and nutmeg

1. Place squash in baking dish; fill centers
with combined remaining ingredients. Bake,
loosely covered, at 350 degrees until tender,
45 to 60 minutes.

Per Serving:
Calories: 120
% calories from fat: 4
Protein (g): 2.1
Carbohydrate (g): 29.1
Fat (g): 0.6
Saturated fat (g): 0.2
Cholesterol (mg): 0
Sodium (mg): 6

Exchanges:
Milk: 0.0
Vegetable: 0.0
Fruit: 1.0
Bread: 1.0
Meat: 0.0
Fat: 0.0

MILE-HIGH APPLE PIE

*Nothing is more American than real homemade apple pie. Enjoy it warm,
with a generous scoop of fat-free frozen yogurt.*

10 servings

Double Pie Crust (recipe follows)
8 cups peeled, cored, sliced tart baking apples
1 cup sugar
4–5 tablespoons all-purpose flour
¾ teaspoon ground cinnamon
¼ teaspoon ground nutmeg
⅛ teaspoon each: ground cloves, salt
2 tablespoons margarine or butter, cut into
    pieces (optional)

Per Serving:
Calories: 309
% calories from fat: 24
Protein (g): 3
Carbohydrate (g): 57
Fat (g): 8.5
Saturated fat (g): 1.7
Cholesterol (mg): 0
Sodium (mg): 240

Exchanges:
Milk: 0.0
Vegetable: 0.0
Fruit: 0.0
Bread: 3.5
Meat: 0.0
Fat: 1.0

1. Roll ⅔ of the Double Pie Crust on floured surface to form circle
2 inches larger than inverted 9-inch pie pan; ease pastry into pan.
Toss apples with combined sugar, flour, spices, and salt in large
bowl; arrange apples in pastry and dot with margarine.

2. Roll remaining Double Pie Crust on floured surface to fit top
of pie and place over apples. Trim edges of pastry to within ½ inch

of pan; fold top pastry over bottom pastry and flute. Cut vents in top crust. Bake pie at 425 degrees until apples are fork-tender and pastry browned, 40 to 50 minutes. Cover pastry with aluminum foil if becoming too brown. Cool on wire rack 15 to 20 minutes before cutting.

Double Pie Crust

Makes 8- or 9-inch double pie crust

1¾ cups all-purpose flour
3 tablespoons sugar
½ teaspoon salt
5–6 tablespoons cold margarine or butter, cut into pieces
5–7 tablespoons ice water

1. Combine flour, sugar, and salt in medium bowl; cut in margarine with pastry blender until mixture resembles coarse crumbs. Add water, a tablespoon at a time, mixing with fork, until dough forms.

INDEX

ABOUT THE EDITORS

Sue Spitler enjoys cooking soups and stews for her friends in Long Beach, Indiana. She has gained a national reputation as the editor of Surrey's *1,001 Recipes* series, among many other cookbooks.

Linda R. Yoakam, M.S., R.D., is a dietitian and nutritional expert with an extensive practice in the Chicago area.

METRIC GUIDELINES

With the tables below and a little common sense, you'll have no trouble making these recipes using metric measurements. We have rounded off the liters, milliliters, centimeters and kilos to make conversion as simple as possible.

SOME BENCHMARKS—ALL YOU REALLY NEED TO KNOW

Water boils at 212°F

Water freezes at 32°F

325°F is the oven temperature for roasting

A 250 mL measure replaces one 8 oz cup

A 15 mL measure replaces one tablespoon

A 5 mL measure replaces one teaspoon

A 20 cm x 20 cm baking pan replaces a U.S. 8" x 8" baking pan

A 22.5 x 22.5 cm baking pan replaces a U.S. 9" x 9" baking pan

A 30 cm x 20 cm baking pan replaces a U.S. 12" x 8" baking pan

A 22.5 cm pie pan replaces a 9" pie pan

A 21.25 cm x 11.25 cm loaf pan replaces an 8" x 4" loaf pan

A 1.5 liter casserole, sauce pan or soufflé dish replaces a 1 1/2 qt dish

A 3 liter casserole, sauce pan or soufflé dish replaces a 3 qt dish

5 cm is about 2 inches

1 pound is a little less than 500 gm

2 pounds is a little less than 1 kg

OVEN TEMPERATURES

175°F	80°C	350°F	180°C
200°F	100°C	375°F	190°C
225°F	110°C	400°F	200°C
250°F	120°C	425°F	220°C
275°F	140°C	450°F	240°C
300°F	150°C	500°F	260°C

FAHRENHEIT TO U.K. GAS STOVE MARKS

275°F	mark 1	400°F	mark 6
300°F	mark 2	425°F	mark 7
325°F	mark 3	450°F	mark 8
350°F	mark 4	475°F	mark 9
375°F	mark 5		

VOLUME

1/4 cup	50 mL	4 cups (1 quart)	0.95 L
1/2 cup	125 mL	1.06 quarts	1 L
1/3 cup	75 mL	4 quarts (1 gallon)	3.8 L
3/4 cup	175 mL		
1 cup	250 mL	1 teaspoon	5 mL
1 1/4 cups	300 mL	1/2 teaspoon	2 mL
1 1/2 cups	375 mL	1/4 teaspoon	1 mL
2 cups	500 mL	1 tablespoon	15 mL
2 1/2 cups	625 mL	2 tablespoons	25 mL
3 cups	750 mL	3 tablespoons	50 mL

WEIGHT

1 oz	25 gm
2 oz	50 gm
1/4 pound	125 gm (4 oz.)
1 pound	500 grams
2 pounds	1 kg
5 pounds	2 1/2 kg

LENGTH

1/2 inch	1 cm
1 inch	2.5 cm
4 inches	10 cm

This material was prepared with the assistance of the Canadian Home Economics Association and the American Association of Family and Consumer Services